PEACE, PROGRESS *and the* PROFESSOR

"C. Henry Smith fearlessly welcomed questions: What does it mean for Mennonite identity and engagement that many of the deepest held values of the early Anabaptists have been enshrined in most Western democracies? How are Mennonite believers to be held accountable and responsible for the civic, cultural, and religious public square of which they can no longer claim substantial marginal status? Bush's life of C. Henry Smith offers a wonderful role model for navigating these and other questions for twenty-first-century Mennonite educators and others willing to engage the world in new ways."
—*James E. Brenneman, president of Goshen College*

"Meticulously researched, carefully contextualized, and beautifully written, *Peace, Progress, and the Professor* is a riveting read. Perry Bush captures the unlikely, ironic, and embattled life of C. Henry Smith, the pioneering historian who, in the early twentieth century, helped American Mennonites discover a usable past."
—*Richard T. Hughes, distinguished professor emeritus, Messiah College*

"Bush's biography of C. Henry Smith is a critical, accessible and nuanced examination of the first 'dean of Mennonite history in North America.' An astute biographer, Bush makes Smith's legacy relevant for his day and ours. The advice C. Henry Smith gave his students eighty years ago is as fresh and needed today in the Mennonite church: 'Read widely. Don't believe it all. Make up your own mind. Be willing to cooperate. Keep your head.'"
—*Susan Schultz Huxman, president and professor, Conrad Grebel University College*

"Perry Bush has given us the lively and fascinating story of an educator, banker, and public intellectual who sought to shape a Mennonite identity that was both in harmony with the past and in tune with the times. C. Henry Smith still has something to say to us in the twenty-first century, and Perry Bush has skillfully brought Smith's message into our contemporary conversations."
—*Steven M. Nolt, professor of history, Goshen College*

"C. Henry Smith was, for me, a boyhood hero. He helped thousands of us appreciate and embrace our Anabaptist heritage and invited us to see our Mennonite faith as relevant to living in an expanding global world. This absorbing biography draws us into the engaging Mennonite story of the twentieth century."
—*Robert S. Kreider, historian and retired college administrator*

PEACE, PROGRESS and the PROFESSOR

THE MENNONITE HISTORY OF C. HENRY SMITH

PERRY BUSH

Herald Press
Harrisonburg, Virginia
Kitchener, Ontario

Library of Congress Cataloging-in-Publication Data
Bush, Perry.
  Peace, progress, and the professor : the Mennonite history of C. Henry Smith / Perry Bush.
    pages cm. -- (Studies in Anabaptist and Mennonite history series ; 49)
  Includes bibliographical references.
  ISBN 978-0-8361-9986-4 (hardcover : alk. paper) 1. Smith, C. Henry, 1875-1948. 2. Church historians--United States--Biography. 3. Mennonites--History. 4. Mennonite Church--History. I. Title.
  BR139.S6B87 2015
  289.7092--dc23
  [B]
                                         2014048951

PEACE, PROGRESS, AND THE PROFESSOR
© 2015 by Herald Press, Harrisonburg, Virginia 22802
    Released simultaneously in Canada by Herald Press,
    Kitchener, Ontario N2G 3R1. All rights reserved.
Library of Congress Control Number: 2014048951
International Standard Book Number: 978-0-8361-9986-4 (hardcover)
International Standard Book Number: 978-0-8361-9962-8 (paperback)
Printed in United States of America
Cover design by Reuben Graham, design by Reuben Graham
Cover photo from Mennonite Historical Library, Bluffton University
Author photo by Kerry Bush
Photos and illustrations used in this book are used by permission, and their sources are given with each caption.

All rights reserved. This publication may not be reproduced, stored in a retrieval system, or transmitted in whole or in part, in any form, by any means, electronic, mechanical, photocopying, recording, or otherwise without prior permission of the copyright owners.

To order or request information, please call 1-800-245-7894.
Or visit www.heraldpress.com.

19 18 17 16 15   10 9 8 7 6 5 4 3 2 1

*To Preston F. Bush and Piper Bush Cartland,
my teachers in the ways of faith*

Contents

Foreword 9
Preface and Acknowledgments 13

1: Geography of a Prairie Childhood 23
2: Becoming C. 49
3: The Democracy of Learning 77
4: In the Service of a Usable Past 101
5: How to Write the Mennonite Story 131
6: The Way of Exile 155
7: The "Most Liberal Wing" 187
8: Forays down a Winding Road 225
9: Diverging Readings of Anabaptist History 245
10: The Mennonite Intellectual in a Time of Crisis 273
11: The Final Mennonite History 309
12: Epilogue 351

Notes 363
Selected Bibliography 419
Index 435
Studies in Anabaptist and Mennonite History Series 453
The Author 457

Foreword

The Mennonite history that C. Henry Smith taught and wrote was a big and beautiful story with a dramatic beginning, a twisting and conflict-driven plot, and an open-ended conclusion that highlighted his people's prospects and challenges. But the story Smith told also had a specific goal: advancing the peace witness of the Mennonite church as well as the hope for human peace in the modern world.

At the end of the first edition of his now classic *The Story of the Mennonites*, published as World War II raged, Smith reviewed the actions taken by Mennonite churches in the aftermath of World War I to nurture the way of peace through committees, institutes, and literature. Such educational activities had strengthened the peace convictions of the Mennonites, Smith believed, and "given them a new realization of the soundness of their faith for the troubles of a warring world." Consequently, while no one could say "how the Mennonites, and especially the conscientious objector will fare in future wars," Smith was confident that Mennonites were "much better prepared to defend their faith than they were in the last war."

These remarks highlight two aspects of the Mennonite story that were crucial for C. Henry Smith's life and work: peace and education. Smith was deeply committed to the costly peace witness of his Mennonite people, and he believed that education was the most important way to strengthen that witness. Such education for peace would include knowledge about the particular history of the Mennonite peace church tradition, a history that Smith devoted much of his professional life to teaching, researching, and writing. But such peace education would also address the broader political context, in which peace was repeatedly disrupted by bloody and brutal warfare.

As Perry Bush ably explains in this attractively written and deeply informed biography, the projects of peace and education often failed to deliver the outcomes that Smith expected. Smith lived through two disastrous global wars that challenged easy optimism about human abilities to resolve conflict through peaceful means. But he also carried out his teaching and research in Mennonite college settings that were hindered from their educational missions by church conflicts, academic rivalries, the personal failings of faculty colleagues, and the challenges of the Depression era.

In Bush's telling, C. Henry Smith—the Amish Mennonite farm boy turned cosmopolitan academic—navigated the promising and perilous landscape of early twentieth-century modernity with remarkable skill and wisdom. Leaving behind the fields and livestock of central Illinois while retrieving anew the historical and spiritual materials of the Mennonite past, Smith crafted a thoroughly modern yet deeply faithful life of scholarship and enterprise. While fully invested in the common good, he was unflinchingly loyal to his particular heritage. Never one to hide from the facts, Smith was capable of revising his perspectives as new experiences challenged his habits of thinking. The horrible futility of World War I called into question his confident progressive politics. The shocking race-based violence of Nazi Germany led to his rejection of the white supremacy he had been tempted by in his earlier years. Smith's thinking about such political and moral issues was a matter of consequence since he was a public intellectual, not merely a professional scholar. He spoke about these matters in churches as well as at the Rotary Club. He shared his views in the classroom, but also on the airwaves.

Smith's public persona was anchored in the deep attachments of his personal life—to the Mennonite people that he wrote so affectionately about, but also to the love of his life, whom he courted and married and cared for until death did them part. In fact, C. Henry Smith's romance with Laura Ioder, charmingly narrated with delightful detail by Bush, can be seen as a metaphor for the ways Smith served all the loves of his life—his people's history, their stubborn commitment to peace, the glittering potential of the modern world, the great progressive causes of the early twentieth century, the church colleges that employed him, and the midwestern American communities whose peace and wellbeing he sought.

My friend and colleague Perry Bush is well suited to tell the story of C. Henry Smith's life in part because Bush has been seduced by the same romances that overtook Smith: the romance of the life of the mind and of belonging to a peculiar people, and the romance of difficult causes. For what cause could be more difficult than seeking peace on earth and justice for all through faithfulness to the way of Jesus Christ? As a public intellectual himself, who not only teaches and preaches but also appears regularly on radio and television broadcasts, Bush writes books about a usable past and advocates in the public square for a fairer future. In many ways, Perry Bush embodies in the opening decades of the twenty-first century the Anabaptist peace convictions that C. Henry Smith projected in the first half of the twentieth.

Indeed, the Mennonite history of C. Henry Smith that Bush describes in this book and exemplifies in his life is far from over. This history is a big and beautiful story whose end must finally be entrusted to Jesus Christ, the author and finisher of our faith. Thanks be to God.

Gerald J. Mast, Series Editor
Studies in Anabaptist and Mennonite History

Preface and Acknowledgments

Nearly all religious bodies wrestle with the ancient question of how much to accommodate to outside society while not surrendering basic group beliefs: how, in Christian parlance, to "be in the world but not of the world." Mennonite-related groups seem to have struggled with this problem more intensely than most. Memories of Anabaptist ancestors put to death in large numbers by the reigning church-states of their day strengthened a subsequent Mennonite determination to keep their distance from society. Throughout most of their history in North America, they constructed socioeconomic walls that reinforced their physical and cultural separation and further reinforced these walls with a theology that branded outside cultural intrusions as "worldly" and sinful.

Beginning in the second half of the nineteenth century, however, such cultural walls began to crumble. Through a fulcrum of irresistible forces—changing technologies in transportation, communications, and agriculture; the crusades of the national warfare state; and the blandishments of a burgeoning and increasingly attractive outside culture—Mennonites and Amish struggled with how to manage the delicate process of acculturation. Their responses differed widely. Many individuals succumbed completely to these forces, left their church communities, and fully assimilated into mainstream American and Canadian societies. Other Anabaptist groups, particularly the Amish and other Old Orders, reinforced their traditional religious and cultural walls with stricter church discipline while simultaneously brokering these pressures in ways that preserved their Old Order identities.[1]

A middle path between these two polar responses was carved out by some of today's larger extant Mennonite denominations: the Mennonite Brethren Church, and the progenitor bodies of today's Mennonite Church USA—the "Old," or Mennonite, Church (hereafter abbreviated MC) and and the General Conference (GC) Mennonite Church. In the past century and a half, these Mennonites have tried to navigate the tensions of an oncoming modernity in a manner that preserved their basic ethnoreligious identities, but without the hierarchical discipline of their Old Order cousins. The matter seemed especially critical in the latter nineteenth century and through the middle part of the twentieth, when the assimilating pressures struck the churches with particular force. In a process shot through with irony, Mennonites from both the MC and GC groups tried to preserve the bonds that had held them together through organizational and ideational structures they had borrowed from outside society. Some attempted to resist the enticements of American society by adopting a cultural and theological import called Protestant fundamentalism. Others advocated a renewed dedication to basic Mennonite values through a creative engagement with mainstream American progressive reform. Ecclesiastical sparks soon flew from these divergent responses, and the resulting conflict would shape the tone and content of the American Mennonite story for at least a hundred years.

This second response—advocating a selective acceptance of outside culture—was principally fashioned by a set of Mennonite educators. Geographically it emanated from Mennonite college towns like Goshen, Indiana; North Newton, Kansas; and Bluffton, Ohio. Some of its key disciples, Mennonite college presidents like Lloyd Ramseyer and Edmund G. Kaufman, would carry the vision forward at least into the 1960s. Yet its heyday was in the first half of the twentieth century. Throughout much of that time, one of its most influential and persuasive advocates was a Mennonite college professor named C. Henry Smith.

Depending on the lens through which Mennonites of his day viewed him, Smith would probably have been either the most sophisticated or the worldliest Mennonite they had ever met. In an era when Mennonite ethnicity and tradition reigned supreme, no one could question his credentials. He was, as he underscored publicly on more than one occasion, "an all-round Mennonite," a point he was sometimes not above employing on behalf of his larger intellectual agenda. "The fact that I began my religious career in Illinois as an Amishman, then in Indiana joined the 'Old' Mennonites, to transfer later to the Central Conference, and in recent years to unite with the General Conference," he proclaimed in 1943, "ought to qualify me as a fairly cosmopolitan Mennonite in my outlook and sympathy." In his professional career and persona, Smith redefined Mennonite behavior in a manner that some from his church would have found exciting and others unsettling. He sported a Phi Beta Kappa key on his everyday attire, a handsome suit. In younger days he cultivated a taste for opera and the theater. He traveled to Mexico and across the Pacific, and he strode confidently through the streets of principal European cities. He sat in seminars with major world leaders and could comment knowledgeably on international political and economic affairs. Back home he found himself increasingly called upon to share his insights with audiences ranging from Mennonite churches to civic groups to high school graduation exercises. For a few short years he even developed a following on regional radio. His financial acumen facilitated his founding of not one but two banks and a small personal fortune. In the process he became such a pillar of Main Street in his home village that upon his death in 1948, the attendant physician noted the occupation of the deceased on his death certificate simply as "bank president."[2]

Relative to the rural, plain-dressing Mennonites of his day, Smith was urbane, polished, and wealthy, but above all else he was a historian. To many of them he simply defined the role. In an era when his people had just begun to send their offspring to high schools, Smith pursued advanced degrees. He lived in a time when his church had no archives and few records besides cemetery ledgers and church membership rolls. Yet he managed to produce a string of books on Mennonite history that came to serve as the basic vehicles through which generations of his people came to understand their shared past. All his life he remained intensely curious about Mennonites and their stories. New acquaintances could scarcely go more than a few minutes into a conversation with him, someone who knew him recalled, without his persistent, gentle inquiries into their genealogies. Students often encountered this as a conversation starter on the first day of class. Who are your parents, Smith wanted to know; your grandparents, your community, your home congregation? He took what he learned—the "bare facts" that he imagined he had bagged with the tenacity of a big-game hunter—and simmered them into exciting, engaging narratives that for decades inspired and held the Mennonite historical imagination.[3]

It was primarily through Smith's work as a historian that he expressed his vision for his church. Because of their history, he argued, Mennonites seemed uniquely positioned to offer valuable contributions to a society that no longer remained beyond the boundaries of their isolated rural communities. It seemed clear to him that the Mennonite tradition had left them with a rich inheritance they should rightly now share with others, including signal contributions like their basic democratic individualism and their heritage of religious toleration and church-state separation. The way that Smith reframed Mennonite history—and envisioned the proper Mennonite posture in his day—ushered them from the margins to the mainstream of North American societies. To him and his fellows, a selective and carefully navigated Mennonite acculturation into mainstream society was not a process to be feared. Instead, they welcomed it. This is not to say that the vision remained static. Smith first emerged as one of his church's foremost intellectuals in his early thirties, and remained so until his death four decades later. Over such a span of time, of course his worldview evolved. The searing, traumatic Mennonite experience in the Great War would do much to puncture Smith's progressive optimism, and he would begin to regard outside society with a sharper, much more critical eye. Even so, to the end of his life he continued to take his intellectual cues from larger liberal Protestantism and remained convinced of the potential of the Mennonite contribution to American society, especially in the area of peacemaking.

Such an agenda met with deep-seated and impassioned resistance. While Smith's training as an empirical, "objective" historian kept him from fully realizing it, of course he was borrowing extensively from the outside. Other Mennonites borrowed from different sources, which would put them on a direct collision course with Smith and his progressive colleagues. The ensuing contest took shape in a number of different venues, but to a fair degree—for peculiarly Mennonite reasons—it unfolded in the field of history. Deep-seated Mennonite separatist tendencies had become expressed physically in a devotion to rural isolation, and ideologically in a suspicion of education. As a result, the historian C. Norman Kraus has argued, Mennonites had scant theological training or resources when they encountered problems with deep theological overtones, such as the inroads of an increasingly attractive national society and culture. Instead they took their theology from others, and in the first part of the twentieth century, many turned to Protestant fundamentalism. "The threat inherent in the growing social change produced a mood among Mennonite leaders," Kraus writes, "which made them highly susceptible to the fundamentalist anxiety that swept the country from about 1908–25." The conflict that then erupted between Mennonite fundamentalists and their progressive opponents (whom they styled "modernists") could not help but spill over into the related discipline of history. By the 1920s, with the contest at fever pitch, young new scholar-activists like Harold Bender discovered that history was a safer field in which to work out critical theological problems, but only to a degree. When Smith pioneered modern Mennonite historical writing, he thus did so in increasingly contested historical terrain.[4]

Fundamentally, Smith, his colleagues, and combatants all set out to answer a basic and critical theological question for their church: What does it mean to be a Mennonite in the modern world? The answers they produced are central to understanding the Mennonite experience in twentieth-century North America. They can be seen in the Mennonite history of C. Henry Smith.

Exploring the life and times of C. Henry Smith has been an immensely rich and rewarding experience for the past five or so years. In the process, I have incurred a great many debts, intellectual and otherwise, to all sorts of fine people. The least I can do is publicly to thank them here.

This book would not have been possible without the financial support of the C. Henry Smith Trust. In addition to funding matters like student assistant help and travel to archives, their generous financial support secured for me nearly a full year away from teaching responsibilities in 2009–10, during which time I completed most of the research for this narrative and began the writing. The trust's directors—John Smith and James Hisstand of Goshen College, and James Harder of Bluffton University—are all dedicated and committed academics. Hence their eagerness to see that a completed biography of the trust's founder never interfered in any way with their commitment to my interpretive freedom as an author. I am deeply grateful to them for putting the project in my lap, for the resources and freedom they provided, and for their confidence that I would see it through.

In May 2010, John Smith accompanied me on a research trip to C. Henry Smith's boyhood home in west-central Illinois. The experience still stands out in my mind as one of the highlights of the entire project. Not only was John was an amiable and enjoyable traveling companion, but along the way he introduced me to other like-minded people, all of whom furthered this project in various and engaging ways. I need to extend my heartfelt appreciation to Bill and Lydia Hohulin of Goodfield, Illinois, for hosting me while there. Not only did they welcome me to one of the most amazing homes in the Midwest, but in their warmth and good humor provided a rich introduction to the Apostolic Christian Church. Ardys Serpette, Julie Hendricks, and the staff of the Illinois Mennonite Heritage Center in Metamora, Illinois, put documents in front of me that helped open up the Smiths' Amish Mennonite world in the Gilded Age. Bob Scherts and Bill Crist of Metamora did the same in an experiential manner. Late one memorable afternoon, they drove me in an old pickup truck through the high water of a flooding Partridge Creek to the remains of the old Christian Smith homestead, there in the timber west of Metamora. As a keepsake, they handed me a brick from the old farmstead, which I readily understood was, literally and figuratively, a bit of the foundation of the Smith family story in America. As I promised, I deposited it with the Smith materials at Bluffton University. Finally, on that trip I will never forget the nearly accidental connection we made with Dudley Bowers and Elaine Burress Bowers of Princeton, in Bureau County, Illinois, not far from the Ioder family homestead near Tiskilwa. There Elaine graciously shared her memories of her aunt Laura Ioder Smith. Moreover, sitting there at her kitchen table, she reached into an old metal picnic box and pulled out a whole cache of Smith materials I had thought long lost, including C. Henry's letters to Laura from their earliest days together. She insisted I take all these papers with me back to Bluffton. The entire contents of the box now rest with the Smith collection at the Bluffton University archives, furnishing, together with Laura's extant letters, perhaps as complete a record of a Mennonite courtship that we have anywhere in North America.

I enjoyed similarly fruitful and productive research trips elsewhere. I need to express my appreciation to John Thiessen and staffers of the Mennonite Library and Archives at Bethel College in North Newton, Kansas, for their patient and helpful assistance. Likewise, in several trips to Goshen College I benefited from the time and energies of Joe Springer of the Mennonite Historical Library, and of Rich Preheim and Colleen McFarland of the Archives of the Mennonite Church. While in Goshen I was comfortably hosted by J. R. and Susan Burkholder, and then by John and Joan Smith. While researching at Bethel College, I enjoyed the warm hospitality of Bob and Lois Kreider, who are always fascinating to spend time with. Dinnertime conversations about what I found in the archives that day quickly gave way to their unlocking their storehouse of memories of Smith and his world. In this they, like other people I interviewed, ushered me into a deeper grasp of someone whose presence I could otherwise only know through books and papers.

The bulk of my research focused on Smith's papers, which are housed at the Bluffton University Archives and Special Collections. I am deeply indebted to the staff there. Library director Mary Jean Johnson furnished me a private study room and eagerly cooperated with the enterprise in every way. Interlibrary loan specialist Audra Oglesbee was her usual efficient and friendly self, and Paul Weaver and Kathleen Aufderhaar provided expert reference help, as always. I need to single out Bluffton's superb archivist, Carrie Phillips, for particular thanks. Carrie worked with me all through this project, from systematically pulling out the Smith papers, box by box, at its beginning, to helping identify and scan photos at its end. She boosted the project in a great number of ways and, like the rest of her library colleagues, is a delight to work with.

In a similar manner, Smith's story would not have emerged here without the active cooperation of the wider Bluffton University community. A half century ago in the 1960s, Sally Weaver Sommer was one of those little neighborhood kids who would sometimes visit an old widow named Mrs. Smith at her home on the south edge of campus and make her laugh. Now she is my academic dean, and in this role found a number of ways to facilitate the completion of this project. Willis Sommer, Bluffton's provost at the time, was also helpful as he and Sally worked out the particulars of my leave from teaching. I also benefited from a 2010–11 research grant from the Bluffton University Research Center. Through the project I appreciated the academic companionship of Randy Keeler, Martina Cucchiara, Troy Osborne, Jeff Gundy, Lamar Nisly, and other Bluffton faculty colleagues. Over the past years they periodically asked questions about the project and listened patiently to more stories about Smith than they probably wanted to hear. Pete Suter helped me make sense of Smith's banking and financial papers, and Steve Rodabaugh assisted with computer matters. Linda Suter translated some letters from Smith correspondents who wrote in German. Bluffton students have been involved, too. I have harnessed the energies of five years of history department student assistants, who have spent hours photocopying, note-taking, and double-checking citations. I want again to thank Hillary Crawford, Brendan Haggerty, Katy Hamann, Brent Householder, Tyler Johnson, Dylan Mann, Natalie Nikitas, Megan Patton, Nikolas Peckinpaugh, Marisa Rose, Nadin-Sarah Salkic, and Ben Wesseler. Special thanks must go to Joel Wildermuth, whom the Smith Trust assigned to this project in its genesis and who labored away in the archives with me with such diligence and good humor. My faculty colleague Gerald Mast has been a coconspirator in this project from the very start, and here at the end is serving as an editor of it. Throughout the process, he spent hours reading and critiquing chapters, suggesting new research angles and ideas, and never lagging in his infectious, all-consuming enthusiasm for all matters Mennonite. He has been a true intellectual companion along the way, and this book is much richer for it.

As chapter drafts emerged, they received careful readings and thoughtful critiques from Robert Kreider and Justin King. Janis Thiessen of the University of Winnipeg provided some useful insights into Smith's exchange with Bender and Friedmann. It was a pleasure to work with the fine folks at Herald Press, particularly with editorial director Amy Gingerich and managing editor Valerie Weaver-Zercher. In addition, this manuscript was greatly strengthened by two conscientious and dedicated reviewers from Herald Press, who clearly invested a number of hours in their assignment. They uncovered a number of factual mistakes, poor word choices, and other writing infelicities, and raised some larger interpretive issues that gave me a good deal of food for thought.

Finally, I need to thank Kerry, Jackson, and Cassidy Bush, who five years ago generously welcomed Dr. Smith as a regular presence in our household. Despite the many demands he was making on their father's time and attention, they would often inquire how he was getting along and tolerate my extensive replies in good humor. Amidst the many pressures of her life, Elysia Caldwell Bush paid some attention to Dr. Smith, but much more to me. I am more grateful for her than I can say.

1
Geography of a Prairie Childhood

"I am a thoroughbred Mennonite," C. Henry Smith declared shortly after his fiftieth birthday, an age when the passage of time had afforded him such a moment of clarity. Shortly before or after that day, in June of 1925, he sat down at his desk and in his scrawling, nearly indecipherable handwriting, penned a lengthy memoir of his childhood and education. Then he let it sit for nearly two decades until 1943, when he typed it up, mimeographed fifty copies, and distributed them to family and close friends. In 1962, fifteen years after Smith's death, his widow, Laura, worked closely with Faith & Life Press in Newton, Kansas, to publish the memoir in its entirety. Smith's fellow General Conference Mennonite historian Cornelius Krahn, in his glowing preface, left no doubt as to what the publisher hoped to accomplish in the book. In *Mennonite Country Boy: The Education of C. Henry Smith*, they held up Smith as an exemplary model: the young Amish Mennonite boy whose thirst for education would lead him to untold heights of academic accomplishment while never losing touch with his humble heritage. Yet such purposes were far from Smith's original intentions. As he related on page one, he merely wanted to "commit to paper some of the pleasant memories of boyhood days" for the enjoyment of loved ones. That Smith himself found the task immensely enjoyable is evident in his crackling and witty prose. The many enthusiastic letters he received from his audience assured him that the project had been a success.[1]

Because Smith never intended his memoir to be published, it is much more trustworthy as a historical document than it otherwise might have been. Not only is it an immensely revealing window into his reading of the Mennonite social and religious landscape of the 1920s, but it shines historical light on aspects of his and others' experiences that otherwise would have been lost. From Smith's story, for example, one can extrapolate a lot about the founding generation of Mennonite educators and the shared ambitions and hopes that had produced them. Better yet, Smith's memoir fleshes out, with no need of extrapolation, the world of Amish Mennonites on the Illinois prairies in the latter part of the nineteenth century. Out of this richly hybridized "Dutch" American environment would emerge an eager young scholar thoroughly primed to make his own way as an educational pioneer in the exciting intellectual milieu of progressivism.[2]

"A Nose for Good Land"

"[P]hysically and spiritually," Smith declared as he began explaining his ancestry, "I claim to be a full-blooded Mennonite. . . . I doubt whether a single non-Mennonite could be found among all my forebears during the past four hundred years." These are key lines for him. Certainly he was capable of describing Anabaptist-Mennonite belief systems at some length. He did so in all his major books. He was certainly aware that Anabaptists began as a body knitted together only because of common beliefs, and that outsiders sometimes came to join them because of the attractiveness of those beliefs. Indeed, near the end of his life, as the crises of World War II inescapably demonstrated the degree to which the acids of modernity had eaten away at the holding power of Mennonite blood ties, he would come to rest his hopes for the Mennonite future on the foundation of shared convictions. At the same time, even in the midst of that war, he would resist entreaties by other Mennonite scholars and church leaders—Harold Bender, for example—to engage in more theologically tinged writing. No—for most of his life, Smith understood Mennonites as a "faith and race," a "distinct human type," like Jews. For this reason, he paid careful attention to Mennonite ancestry and remained the court of ultimate recourse for many early Mennonite genealogists. His files of correspondence bulge with letters of inquiry from people across the Mennonite landscape wanting Smith's help in tracking down this or that branch of Yoders or Millers. In order to begin to understand Smith as a person, it is thus necessary to pay close attention to things that mattered deeply to him: blood ties and Smith genealogy.[3]

In the early nineteenth century, a new wave of Amish and Mennonite immigrants boarded wooden sailing vessels and made the transatlantic crossing from Switzerland, Germany, and the German-French borderlands. Like so many other millions of American immigrants, they were driven by a common mixture of "push" and "pull" factors. A host of reasons induced them to leave Europe: crop failures, heavy taxes, land shortages, the threat of a military draft, and the residue of social chaos in the wake of the Napoleonic wars. They were pulled across the ocean by the lure of religious freedom and the prospect of cheap land. Tens of thousands of Amish and Mennonites came for such reasons, most arriving first in Pennsylvania, many making their way further: some south into the Shenandoah Valley of Virginia, some north into Ontario, and others pushing westward into the new prairie states of Indiana, Illinois, and Iowa.[4]

Between 1815 and 1860, about three thousand Amish and Mennonites departed the German regions of Bavaria and Hesse and the German-French borderlands of Alsace-Lorraine for the American Midwest. They had recently been subjected to a variety of influences. Many had been drawn to pietistic expressions of Christianity, a more emotionally charged worship of Jesus as a personal savior. This had dulled the edge separating them from outside society, while at the same time increased repression and the threat of military conscription may have intensified it. Many of these immigrants made the journey quite poor and were forced to stop for some years in older Mennonite settlements in Pennsylvania before proceeding farther west in search of cheaper land. One person setting up a homestead attracted others, a process that begat Amish and Mennonite congregations and other elements of growing communities. In 1836, for example, a Mennonite family named Albrecht led an exodus from Bavaria and the Palatinate in Germany to north-central Illinois, stopping first in Chicago and then to the west side of the Illinois River in search of better farmland. Within a decade, more migrants, with names like Burkey and Ioder, followed, carving out farms in the timber around a small hamlet named Tiskilwa, a dozen miles from the seat of Bureau County in Princeton. By 1873 they would form their own congregation, Willow Springs Mennonite Church, named after a small spring in the heart of the settlement. Similarly, in the early 1850s another group of Mennonites, with names like Kreider, Rupp, and Ebersole, began to furrow their ploughs into the rich farmland near the small city of Sterling in northern Illinois. Descendants of eighteenth-century immigrants to Pennsylvania, soon they established a congregation called Science Ridge, which would grow at such a rate it would shortly become the largest Mennonite church in the state.[5]

In 1830 a few Amish families began make their way up the Illinois River in central Illinois to carve out farms east of the river. On the west side of the river was a small hamlet that had formed around the site of the old Fort Peoria. The tide of Amish immigration increased markedly two years later with the short, inglorious campaign called Black Hawk's War and its culminating massacre of the Sauk Tribe. With hundreds of thousands of acres suddenly open to white settlement, fair numbers of Amish immigrants from Alsace-Lorraine arrived in the area. Disembarking first at Wesley City on the east side of the Illinois River across from Peoria, Amish pioneers proceeded eastward up the feeder streams flowing into the river, principally along Black Partridge and Dillon Creeks, and a subsidiary river called the Mackinaw. (These were families with names like Sommer, Imhoff, Camp, Leman, and Schertz. Two generations later, young Henry Smith would find his main playmates among cousins bearing all those names.) In the later 1830s, these Amish families and their "English" pioneer neighbors established a small village, finally called Metamora, on the high ground east of Partridge Creek.[6]

In 1833 a thirty-one-year-old Amish immigrant named Christian Schmidt and his sister Marie homesteaded near their fellow Amish along Partridge Creek, putting up a log cabin and constructing the necessary furniture from the woods. In 1836 he and an associate bought eighty acres of land at $1.25 per acre. Schmidt had arrived in Lancaster County, Pennsylvania, in 1829 from Lorraine, France, and had worked for four years to save money for a land purchase farther west. During these Lancaster years, shortly after he arrived, he changed his last name to the common American name of Smith. (From the beginning, it would seem, the Smiths were open to a process that social historians would later call *acculturation*.) In 1838 he married another Lorraine immigrant living nearby, Catherine Bechler. It remains a minor irony that Henry Smith, for whom ancestral matters were so

Christian Smith's homestead along Partridge Creek, near Metamora, Illinois, circa 1910. BUASC.

important, never could trace his family roots back any further than his paternal grandfather. He searched diligently for records across Alsace-Lorraine but never found them, while the certainty that escaped him existed not in Europe but in a box of Smith family records then in possession of his first cousin Elizabeth Sommer Massanari, not far away in Fisher, Illinois. None of the family knew such records existed. Had Henry found them, they would have unlocked all sorts of family mysteries: the names of Christian Smith's parents (Barbara Gingrich and Christian Schmidt), their home village, their occupations (millers), and other priceless genealogical data on his family's roots in the Lorraine he thought long lost.[7]

All of Henry Smith's grandparents, paternal and maternal, had died before or shortly after his birth, so he never knew any of them. Yet the words he used to describe Christian Smith were part of family lore and might have been used to describe himself. His grandfather, Henry wrote in 1925, "was said to be short of stature, of sturdy build, even-tempered, and possessed of more than an ordinary sense of humor." He was an enterprising sort, with the skills one needed to prosper in what his grandson later called the "howling wilderness" of the Illinois frontier. Fellow Amish pioneered the first wagons suitable for hauling grain along the rough-hewn roads of central Illinois. Christian Smith carried his produce to the market center in Pekin by means of a crude wagon he himself had invented by taking a broad log and jerry-rigging a rod through the center of it to work as an axle. Once, when returning to Partridge Creek with two swine he had been unable to sell, he encountered a man who wanted the pigs and had a stove to trade. Smith eagerly made the swap, and for days afterward his wife, Catherine, entertained neighbors who had come from miles away to see a true marvel in that rough pioneer community: a stove.[8]

Mennonites, Goshen historian Willard Smith remembered his uncle Henry often saying, "had a nose for good land." Certainly, compared with the life they had known in Europe, Illinois seemed a rich and promising land indeed, with enough hard work. Game abounded in the woods, and the soil was fertile and heavily timbered. Once cleared away with axes, it could provide the needed comforts of life and certain luxuries—all the coffee one could drink and "meat everyday"—that had been unimaginable back in Alsace-Lorraine. Good land or not, however, frontier life was hard and uncertain. While the midwestern states reverberated to the free-labor ideology and the myth of the "self-made man," actual economic realities had begun to change. By 1850 acquiring an adequate farm required upward of $1,500, a small fortune beyond the reach of many; in 1860 a quarter of all Illinois farmers were farm laborers. The task of clearing wooded lands required a lifetime of backbreaking labor, most done in numbing isolation. Nearby neighbors could not protect each other from the common ravages of epidemic disease. Typhoid, tuberculosis, pneumonia, and especially the dreaded Asiatic cholera could wipe out whole families, and someone convulsing to the "shakes" of malaria was an everyday sight in frontier communities. Death rates remained high, by contemporary standards, through the nineteenth century. In later letters to Henry Smith from his siblings at the turn of the century, it is hard to find a letter that does not report the death of one or another member of the community. Many of them were elderly, but others not. In 1899 such letters told of the death of Henry's eighteen-year-old sister Martha, who succumbed to an unnamed stomach ailment after writhing for days in much pain. "She bore it all patiently and with Christian fortitude," Henry wrote in her obituary, recording that she murmured, as she lay dying, "I am coming, yes I am coming."[9]

As Martha Smith's last words suggest, a world like this one, in which death was a common visitor, reinforced a popular religiosity. Amish pioneers were first of all Amish, and their church came with them as they traveled up the rivers and creeks of Illinois. By the time that first, founding generation had passed, in 1878, the entire area of McLean, Tazewell, and Woodford Counties was so laced with Amish farmers that they had established thirteen separate congregations. The first one, formed in 1833 along Partridge Creek, was the first German-speaking congregation of any kind in the state. As the volume of Amish immigration increased, other congregations formed from this nucleus, selecting their preachers by lot and meeting in homes or barns in accordance with Amish custom. In 1854, however, the Partridge congregation broke with practice and built their first meetinghouse near the creek timberlands a few miles west of Metamora. This was the congregation in which Christian and Catherine Smith raised their growing family. Their sense of God's presence and something of their Amish theology was reflected in the words they penned in the family Bible in 1839 upon the arrival of their firstborn child, Magdalena. "Lord!" they beseeched, "Constantly teach her through your goodwill that she never willfully falls into a single sin. Lead her that in happiness she can better fear You and keep Your command."[10]

All of these elements—the creek and timberlands, the demands of farm labor, the physical and spiritual centrality of the church—would have set the parameters for the life of Henry's father, John. He was born in 1843 to Christian and Catherine Smith in the farmstead along Partridge Creek, their only son amid five daughters. He learned to read and write during episodic wintertime visits to the district schoolhouse, but like other young men in the community, his real training took place in the fields and the woods. The skills he developed there served him well his whole life. He became known as a marksman, craftsman, and horseman of some repute, and also a healer of horses. He likewise shared the wry Smith sense of humor. In just one of the tales that became part of family lore, he once observed children splashing about in a mud puddle. "Watch out, boys," he cautioned them, "you'll get your

Sunday pants dirty." When the Civil War draft of 1864 threatened to pull him into the army, he dutifully followed church teaching and, with supporting testimony from his pastor at the Partridge church as to his nonresistant principles, was given permission to pay the commutation fee instead. The war's end found Smith occupied with other concerns. In 1865 he married a local Amish woman, Magdalena Schertz (whose ancestry their son Henry would also trace back to France) in something of a precedent-breaking move. Normally Amish weddings took place in the home, but this couple decided to be married in the Partridge meetinghouse. Other innovations would follow.[11]

More immediately the young couple engaged in the shared tasks of raising corn and children. These processes would ensue in a world that was very much in flux. The coming of the locomotive had begun dramatically to affect the midwestern countryside long before the Civil War, and wartime developments accelerated the pace of change. Within a few short years, the railroad would help to transform Chicago into the region's great metropolis, keep Illinois fastened to the Union during the war, and bring immediate and dramatic change to the lives of anyone connected to the farm. More of the technological developments enjoyed by city folk, such as the phonograph and the sewing machine, were available to rural midwesterners along with a host of factory-made goods that railroad boxcars brought to their doorsteps. The volume of immigrants drawn to cheap farmland within reach of the market increased to a flood tide. By 1860, nearly half of the Illinois countryside had been carved into working farms. Fifteen years later, estimates one historian, more than three-quarters of Illinois farms were within five miles of a railroad. Land prices shot skyward, along with a corresponding increase both in landless farmers and rural economic inequality. By 1890, one historian has concluded, across rural Illinois, economic mobility had largely become "frozen." Meanwhile, farmers who had bought land early and retained it enjoyed a steady increase in farm prices from 1897 on.[12]

To some degree, even with the fluctuations of an uncontrolled industrial economy, the Smiths and other Amish Mennonite pioneer families were lucky. They had arrived early enough to buy still relatively affordable land and then benefit from the growth in land and crop prices that followed. Some, like John Smith, or a Mennonite farmer and stock-raiser in Bureau County named William Ioder, found themselves with excess income to invest in other enterprises. Their interest, naturally, ran toward land. Before the end of his life, Smith owned some chunks of farmland in Illinois and other states as far away, perhaps, as New Mexico. More immediately, by about the Civil War Amish and Mennonite farmers began to realize that the most fertile land lay not along Illinois waterways but out on the flatlands. Even before the war, heavier ploughs, which could break the tough grasslands sod, had been developed. Not long afterward in central Illinois, a second generation of Amish farmers came up out of the creek bottoms and headed eastward onto the prairie. Their churches, of course, came with them. The better to serve a more dispersed membership, in 1889 the Partridge congregation erected a frame structure a mile east of Metamora. Meanwhile, in a move that appears to have been entirely harmonious, another segment of the old Partridge congregation put up another white frame building a few miles further east called the Roanoke Church. The Smiths were among them, and members alternated services between the two buildings.[13]

In 1870 John and Magdalena Smith bought a fine farmstead three miles east of Metamora and built an addition on the home for John's father. Before the decade was out, the value of their land and that of their neighbors would escalate further to then-unimaginable heights, upward of sixty dollars per acre. Already by 1878, they owned 240 acres worth $14,400. Meanwhile they obeyed the biblical injunction to be fruitful and multiply. Their firstborn, a son named Joseph, had arrived in 1868, followed by seven more children, first boys and then girls, all born two to three years apart in the farmhouse on the Metamora stage road: Samuel in 1873, John in 1877, Catherine in 1879, Martha in 1881, Emma in 1883, and Ellen in 1886. A son they named Henry was born about halfway down that lineup, between Samuel and John, on an early summer's day in June 1875.[14]

Mennonite Country Boy

Smith wrote his memoir early in the twentieth century, long before Amish farm neighborhoods had metamorphosed into tourist attractions. Prodded by Smith and other early scholars of their tradition, Mennonites were just beginning to realize that their normal ways of conducting life amounted to something that anthropologists would grandly label a "folk culture." So it is fascinating to turn the pages of Smith's memoir and watch the impressions unroll from his Amish Mennonite childhood on the Illinois prairie, images so immersed in that culture they could have been written in *fraktur*. One of Smith's first memories is of himself at age four or five, sitting with his mother and other women as they chatted gaily around a quilting frame while his father, in the background, directs a group of men at a traditional Amish barn raising. The narrow geographic limits of his childhood world were defined by the farms of relatives all around; the farthest boundaries lay in the villages of Roanoke six miles to the east and Metamora half that distance westward along the stage road. Beyond the western edge was the old Smith homestead along Partridge Creek. Periodic visits there "possessed all the thrills of a great adventure": the family's six-seater open buggy filled with Smith children, the passage from the flatlands down into the timber, expertly navigated by his father's skill with horses, and then the fording of the creek and the romping with the cousins that followed. Holding all the images together is the larger setting that Smith's skilled writing constantly evokes: the rich fabric of Amish Mennonite family and community, which enveloped his childhood like a blanket.[15]

Amid all the Currier-and-Ives depictions of the farmstead, however—the lyrical evocations of the glories of nature and the quoting of Wordsworth—lay the tough realities of farm labor, which Smith did not attempt to hide. While they faced better economic prospects than their poorer neighbors, the Smith kids still had to work. About 1885, soon after his tenth birthday, young Henry joined his older brothers as a farmhand. As late as 1920, relates one historian, farm families in northern states still worked eleven hours a day. Younger children came to this standard gradually, but their list of chores steadily lengthened, especially on "red-letter days in the small boy's calendar" like threshing time (in "Dutch" parlance, *thrashing*).[16] On the Smiths' farm and on those of their neighbors in the 1880s and 1890s, thrashing was done to oats. Smith devoted fair portions of a detailed chapter to thrashing day. Given the fact that he seemed to be working primarily from memory, it is remarkable how closely his account parallels the work of at least one later historian of farm technology—from the size of the threshing crew

Henry Smith's boyhood home: John and Magdalena Smith's homestead, taken from the back pasture, east of Metamora, Illinois. BUASC.

they hired, the description of threshing machine, the reciprocal threshing relations between neighbors, even to the cultural expectations surrounding the big meal that farm women spread out at noonday for the crew. (Magdalena Smith got it right and saved herself social disgrace: her table featured the special delicacy of beef.) Afterward Henry joined his family and the crew in the stupor of exhaustion, but the next day the chores still beckoned and the cycle of farm work continued.[17]

At about Smith's twelfth birthday, in June 1887, after the big "Last Day" on the school calendar, he started his "apprenticeship as a full farm hand in corn-planting time." He went at it so hard that first day, he remembered, that he worked one of the horses to death. He occasionally mentioned such harder realities: the constant danger of biting flies and bees that could panic the horses, the relentless beating of the summer sun, and the boring desolation of fall plowing. Yet the balm of nostalgia seems to have softened his memories of that summer and others, coloring his recollections of something like haymaking time so much that one could believe he lived in a world without such things as heat and sweat. At the same time, he certainly would have been aware of other, more attractive ways of life. Popular writers of the day like Hamlin Garland won fame and small fortune by their ability to capture in fiction the kinds of relative deprivations felt especially by farm youth. By the late 1880s, rural America was increasingly being penetrated by the enticements of city culture, which the ready availability of mail-order catalogues brought into farm parlors. For a bright young man looking forward to nothing better every day than following the sway of a horse rump back and forth across a field for twelve hours at a stretch, such baubles would have glittered brightly. Yet this was Smith's world, six days a week. On the seventh day there was church.[18]

Child of a Changing Church

In his recent reflections on the life of C. Henry Smith, Mennonite intellectual Robert Kreider admitted he was "puzzled" as to why Smith waited until halfway through his memoir to include any discussion of the significance of church in his life. Why did matters of faith seem to be so "low-key" for him? Kreider knew Smith's world well; his own parents and grandparents had been cut from the same fabric of Amish Mennonite community on the Illinois prairie. So he raised a good question. The only answer, perhaps, could lie in the possibility that the young Henry Smith grew up so immersed in the world of Amish Mennonite faith that neglecting to make overt mention of it was like failing to comment on the air he breathed.[19]

Smith had likely internalized the unconscious habits and folkways of Amish Mennonite life and worship early on in his boyhood. He did not, for example, notice the absence of the crescendo of an organ chord accompanying a hymn; since his people did not permit any musical instrument bigger than a "French harp" (a harmonica), an organ would have struck him as a bizarre sound. He took it for granted that men of age wore long beards but always shaved their upper lips. With no watch to guide him, he knew how long he could slip away to check on the horses, thereby escaping a long sermon, and still make it back inside the meetinghouse for the closing prayer. Indeed, like the other men and boys gathered in the churchyard, young Henry could perfectly time his return based on the homiletic predilections of the particular preacher. This would have been a dicey thing, because he also knew how important it was not to offend the pastor.[20]

For the people in the pews, Smith children included, the Amish Mennonite preacher loomed large: as a spiritual leader and figure of power and importance in the community. Not that these were necessarily men of deep spiritual insight. In line with their prevailing custom, most preachers were ordinary men of the community whom chance or the Holy Spirit had selected for the position by means of the lot. They had little formal education and even less training, and deliberately so. For centuries both Amish and Mennonites, observed the scholar Norman Kraus, had relied on a "pre-theological Biblicism" to guide their lives, "a kind of artless freedom under the guidance of the Spirit to use Scriptures for admonishing the brotherhood." Preachers were to depend on the Spirit for their congregational messages, not, says Susan Fisher Miller, on "previous study or a sheaf of notes." Instead of a crafted, formal sermon, the result was a "sing-song, chanting style of rote delivery," a product which certainly maintained the bonds of tradition but which may also may explain the attraction, for many Amish and Mennonites, of the emotional revival services of their non-Mennonite Protestant neighbors.[21]

In his memoir, Smith did not overlook the limitations of Amish Mennonite preachers; by 1925 he had fair reason to regard the power of church hierarchs with some unhappiness. But as he cast his mind backward, what mostly came back to him were memories of his childhood preachers as men of high integrity and faithful servants of their people. They had received no training for their job and received no remuneration. And for a model of the self-sacrificing preacher, Henry needed to look no further than his own household. The Roanoke congregation ordained John Smith as a minister in 1887, when Henry was in his early teens, and then made him bishop a few years later. Henry thus saw his father late on a Saturday night after a full day of work in the fields, struggling to stay awake as he put a sermon together with his limited education while the rest of the family trundled off to bed. Henry was there at the Smith home one cold January day when his father pulled up into the driveway, having married a young couple and then driven for miles in an open buggy in biting wind, pounding his hands against his knees to keep them warm. The temperature was at twenty below zero, and he came in the house with his ears frozen. Bishop Smith had received from the couple, for his trouble, the grand sum of a "ten-cent handkerchief." Raised in such a context, Henry's decision for church membership at age fifteen was "no mere matter of form," but neither was it predicated by a deeply felt emotional call. In a letter to Harold Bender forty years later, he summarized the matter in something akin to shorthand: "Baptized 1890 Metamora church by Bishop Joseph Bachman."[22]

Put simply, Henry Smith was a child of the church. Yet his was a church and a people in the throes of deep and far-reaching transformation. Certainly, the Amish had never been immune to change, in the old world or the new. Their ways were governed by an adherence to basic cultural precepts, like an unspoken body of rules called the *Ordnung* and the ancient devotion to humility, manifested in plain dress and strong patterns of separation from the world. Clothing was, of course, a prevailing symbol of humility. Individual Amish members who chose to violate church standards—by wearing jewelry or a mustache, for example, or amusing themselves at fairs or shows, or cutting their hair, or forgetting their bonnet—faced at first a public reprimand, and then, for repeat offenders, placement under the ban. But these rules were never uniform. Partly this was because of the wide variation in their origins in different parts of Europe and different migration patterns. Partly it was due to strong Amish patterns of congregational polity. But part of it had to do with the comparative abundance of their new American homeland. As the nineteenth century wore on, individual Amish people in various locales had begun to acquire a bit more excess income. They were tempted to spend it on personal adornment, more comfortable homes, and other matters that tougher ministers and fellow Amish regarded as worldly and impermissible. The natural Amish response was to expand the boundary markers with the world: an unwritten, oral tradition called *Ordnungen*. These began as early as 1809. But new rules could only stem, not stop, the tide of change, which flowed even more strongly after the Civil War. By 1870, notes the Amish historian Paton Yoder, buttons were widely used in Amish congregations in Illinois, and the existence of numerous photos (objects ostensibly prohibited) of families and groups of young Amish men and women testify to the growing acceptance of other cultural styles. Those styles clearly permeated the Amish Mennonite community of Metamora/Roanoke. While Magdalena Smith was once "severely reprimanded" by an older woman of the congregation for daring to sew a bit of lace on her bonnet, her son Henry recalled that younger boys in particular were awarded wide latitude as to dress; indeed, he said, we were "slaves to passing fads." Boys could get away with such things, but the adults were faced with decisions about matters that the traditional mindset of *Ordnung* had not foreseen. What about the use of lightning rods—was this a frivolous adornment or a necessity? What about crop or life insurance? Moreover, what to do when some Amish authorities prohibited such things and others permitted them?[23]

In the short run, the confusion gave birth to a series of Amish ministers' meetings called the *Dienerversammlung*, which met annually from 1862 to 1878 to sort out these and many other related questions. The first four meetings, Yoder summarizes, succeeded in polarizing the Amish into two different camps based on their responses and "crystallized the schism" between them. In the long run, the confusion would lead to the fragmentation of the Amish world in nineteenth-century North America. After 1865, unhappy with the way matters were trending, the traditionalists ceased coming to the *Dienerversammlung* meetings. This, Amish historians argue, is a good point to mark the beginning of today's Old Order Amish. The remaining leaders, says Yoder, "fumbled, regrouped and then began to devise an organizational structure." They set up boundaries to mark off those who had gone too far, but that "would include the middle-of-the-road Amish Mennonites." A slow process of group formation ensued in a series of ad hoc ministers' meetings, which lasted into the 1890s. By then this loose coalition of Amish leaders had formed a clear new group with an agreed-upon name—the Amish Mennonites—and three district conferences: Eastern, Indiana-Michigan, and Western District. This latter conference, consisting of Amish Mennonites in Iowa and principally Illinois, officially formed in 1890 with a series of charter understandings that reaffirmed commitment to basic Anabaptist precepts like nonresistance. They were more open to outside society than the traditionalists, but still demanded a tough discipline from their members. They stipulated plain and modest dress and condemned jewelry, participation in secret societies (i.e., the lodge and populist groups), and attendance at things like parties (including birthday parties), fairs, ball games, shows, horse races, and political gatherings.[24]

Hence, the Amish Mennonites emerged as a kind of middle group with many similarities to their MC Mennonite neighbors. (This common ground eventually grew to the point that, in 1920, the two groups formally merged.) Their process of group identity was both eased and sharpened by the simultaneous emergence of another Amish Mennonite group that became particularly significant in Illinois. These were the followers of a craggy and powerful Amish bishop in central Illinois named Joseph Stuckey. The breaking point with Stuckey seems to have been his refusal to excommunicate one of his followers, Joseph Joder, for the latter's theological universalism. But Stuckey had begun to signal his differing views from other Amish and Amish Mennonites on a variety of issues, including more openness to outside innovations like Sunday schools and musical instruments, more flexibility on the plain dress, and his disinterest in the use of the ban. Traveling incessantly from his base in his home congregation of North Danvers, Illinois, he would work hard to knit his followers together into a coherent group called the Central Conference. Its foundation would rest in a firm coalition of allied Amish Mennonite congregations in central Illinois—North Danvers, Congerville, East Washington—many of them not far from Metamora/Roanoke.[25]

This sequence of events powerfully affected the Partridge Creek Amish. The last of the big *Dienerversammlung* meetings was held at the Roanoke meetinghouse in 1878, and members of that congregation were key participants in those deliberations. The heart of the new Western District Amish Mennonite Conference was central Illinois. The Roanoke church hosted its annual gatherings three times and was one of its key founding congregations. John Smith played an increasingly significant role in many of these developments. Long known for his informal abilities in conflict resolution, he was ordained bishop in the early 1890s by the new Western District Conference, which assigned him to increasingly significant leadership roles. He attended fourteen of its first sixteen annual gatherings, served as moderator, assistant moderator, or secretary nine times, and was increasingly given special assignments. For example, in 1898 he was appointed to work with two Mennonite leaders to explore possibilities of military exemption for their young men during the Spanish-American War. A special interest of Smith's seems to have been cooperative work with the MC Mennonites, hopes he affirmed in 1893 when he appeared as a featured speaker at the Illinois Mennonite Conference meeting. (On the other hand, although a sort of rapprochement had occurred between the Amish Mennonites and Stuckey Amish elsewhere in Illinois as late as 1900—over three decades after the split occurred—the Amish Mennonites of central Illinois still voiced Stuckey's name with opprobrium.)[26]

Certainly Henry Smith and his siblings would have been front-and-center witnesses to many of these developments. There was, for one, the language transition from German to English, which was well underway among the Amish Mennonites in the later nineteenth century. The Smith children were apparently so comfortable in English that the linguistic difficulties of their parents' generation could become a source of mirth. One spring evening in 1899, for example, Martha wrote to Henry that she could hardly concentrate on her work, so distracted was she by the way one of her father's visitors mangled English. "You are a pretty large family that goes to the dish," he had said, when what he really meant was when the family went to the table. Moreover, she reported, the laughter nearly audible in her handwriting, he "always talks about my *frau* [italics in the original]." Shifts were underway in other areas, as well. Central Illinois was known as "liberal Amish territory" across the church, and not only because of Stuckey's influence there. His own father, Henry remarked later, "was rather liberal for his day in respect to the old customs," though he obeyed church restrictions, which increased in the Smith home after their father's ordination. The Smith siblings subtly pushed their father in more tolerant directions, or else acted on their own without him. When Henry's older brother Joseph went up for baptism in 1884, he removed the buttons from his coat beforehand and quietly sewed them back on afterward. Perhaps influenced by his daughters, John Smith asked the Western District Conference delegates in 1899 if women would be allowed to wear hats. "I hope the answer will be that we can wear them," Martha wrote to Henry.[27]

John Smith took the lead in other innovations that the freer climate in the Amish Mennonite context allowed and encouraged. One of these was Sunday schools, which began in some locales before the Civil War and rapidly grew afterward. By the 1880s, with some fits and starts, the innovation had taken hold in the Metamora/Roanoke congregation with Smith's active involvement. In 1889 he became its first Sunday school superintendent. Certainly the older generation was concerned about their children's faith development, but part of their enthusiasm was also to help their children learn or remember their German, since the lessons were all taught in the ancestral tongue. Half a century later, Henry Smith could still recall key details of the experience: the little colored slips of paper he received for memorizing Bible verses, the German language primer they read from, and the "tickling sensation of Uncle Chris's beard on the back of my neck as he leaned down over my shoulder to trace the letters across the pages of my yellow binder."[28]

At about the same time, the Partridge church eagerly adopted another import from the outside: singing schools. Like Sunday schools, these appeared in Amish Mennonite and Mennonite settings in the antebellum years, and then flourished afterward. In them, participants learned such skills as vocal harmony and how to read music by shaped notes. The schools clearly had both a spiritual and social function; no doubt part of their lure was the opportunity for young men and women to be together. John Smith helped in establishing one such school in the Partridge congregation in 1887, where participants learned not German-language hymns but American gospel songs at the hands of a singing master named Simon Hertzler. From age fifteen on, Henry attended it for several summers and remembered it decades later as "one of the bright spots in our young lives each Saturday evening."[29]

In sum, in all these different contexts—work, church, and the fabric of the Amish Mennonite community—Henry Smith and his siblings learn to walk a line that grew finer with every new attraction presented by American society. This was, of course, a society no longer entirely outside the boundaries of their Amish world. Their church had begun a series of adjustments, but Amish Mennonite young people faced a particularly delicate balancing act that would increase in intensity with each step they took in school.

A Solitary Intellectual Life

For a man who would spend most of his life in the classroom, Smith admitted in 1925 that when he was a boy he had "hated school and everything connected with it." Still immersed in a boy's enchantment with the world of nature, young Henry felt the four square walls of the country schoolhouse to be a prison. Illinois had not enhanced the educational experience by rejecting proposed school reforms. Most rural children attended school only slightly more than eighty days a year. There they tended to be taught by poorly trained teenagers who, according to Smith, subjected their charges to boring exercises in rote memorization. (The ordeal brightened only briefly during recess, where the "Dutch" and "Yankee" children seemed to have created something like a hybridized, Amish-American play space. When the grass was green, they played "Dutchball," a version of baseball with modified rules; in winter, they engaged in vast snowball wars as "Old Settlers" vs. "Indians.") Nor did the Smith children receive much intellectual stimulation at home. Evenings there tended to be "cheerless," Smith recalled, especially in the summertime after a twelve- to fourteen-hour workday on the farm. Sometimes the family had the energy to play some dominoes or sing hymns together, but they enjoyed no radio, telephone, gramophone, or mail delivery. His father's library offered few books beyond a Bible, a concordance, and a volume on horse diseases, though at some point the Smith family began to receive the *Herold der Wahrheit*, the German-language edition of the Mennonite weekly *Herald of Truth*.[30]

One of the nearly inexplicable wonders in explaining not only the life of Henry Smith but also other budding young Mennonite intellectuals—many of whom were passing their days as midwestern farm boys at about the same time—is how they became intellectuals at all. For Smith it began with a visit to a set of "more genteel" and "literarily inclined" cousins near the village of Washington, a half dozen miles away, who subscribed to a weekly magazine for children called the *Youth's Companion* and who actually had a copy of *Swiss Family Robinson* they agreed to loan him. But Smith's academic fire seemed to have been really lit by an exciting new teacher named Willie Whitmire. He took over the country schoolhouse on the Metamora road in Smith's early adolescence. Young and personable, with "the gift of vitalizing every subject he touched," Whitmire made learning exciting. He passed out poems by Longfellow and Whittier. He taught elementary geography by means of a clay volcano he constructed. Best of all, for young Henry Smith, Whitmire opened his mind to the world of books.[31]

One cold December afternoon not long after Smith started back to school (John Smith did not permit his children to return until after the harvest), Henry arrived back home with a volume of Tennyson Whitmire had loaned him. He sat down and devoured the story, a romantic melodrama called *Enoch Arden*, in one evening. He gradually built his own private library of cheap paperback classics he acquired through the mail. Smith also acquired a consciousness about books and learning to the point that, shortly before his eighteenth birthday some years later, he sat down one evening and made a cumulative list of the books he had read, year by year. First, clearly inspired by Whitmire, he stuck to classics: *Robinson Crusoe*, the writings of Washington, *The Raven and Other Stories* by Edgar Allen Poe, and *The Legend of Sleepy Hollow* by Washington Irving ("who became my favorite boyhood author"). He pored over texts on natural history and heroic biographies of Caesar, Cromwell, and Patrick Henry. These latter works, he noted in his journal, he consumed "mostly in the corn field," as he went up and down the rows on spring days. At age fifteen, he confessed, he read "a good deal of trash," but the next year he turned his attention once again to finer stuff: a book on astronomy; *Julius Caesar*, *Othello*, and *Hamlet* by Shakespeare; Franklin's *Autobiography*; and the romantic tales of King Arthur and his knights as penned by Sir Walter Scott in *Ivanhoe*. Passersby along the Metamora road would have seen an Amish Mennonite lad, perched on top of a corn planter, absorbed in a book. In his mind, if not yet in body, young Henry Smith was beginning to part ways with the Amish farm. He knew, moreover, whom to credit. In 1895, before the two lost contact, he sent his old teacher a letter to thank him for his role in opening up a wider world to his awareness. "I cannot recall ever receiving a letter that gave me more pleasure," Whitmire responded, encouraging Smith to keep at education and, perhaps, to join him someday in his practice as a medical doctor.[32]

Whitmire only taught in the little schoolhouse along the Metamora road for two years, but the intellectual seed he had planted had taken root. The county superintendent was so impressed with Smith's academic record that he suggested to Smith he consider applying for an appointment to the U.S. military academy at West Point, New York. Clearly the superintendent knew nothing of the Amish, to whom such an idea was unthinkable. Shortly afterward, however, Smith approached his parents with an idea almost as bizarre. With Whitmire's model clearly in mind, he had decided, Henry told them, to become a schoolteacher. One can only imagine the hesitation with which his parents would have greeted the idea. For Amish Mennonite young men, the ideal occupation was farming. In fact, Henry said later, many people in his childhood community "believed it would be impossible to be a good Mennonite except on the farm." Certainly, Smith's parents had begun to consider other options for their third son. He had been unusually sickly as a child, and such a "delicate constitution" made other occupations more suitable: storekeeper, harness-maker, or craftsman of some sort. School teaching was only an acceptable vocation for Yankees, and even among them, for schoolgirls or "old maids." It came as a surprise, then, that John and Magdalena Smith gave their son the go-ahead. Shortly before his sixteenth birthday, Smith went down to the county seat in Eureka and successfully passed the county examination for high school admission. It set him on a life course, he wrote later, "from which I have not wavered one moment since."[33]

Smith began his pursuit of higher education at a propitious moment in American educational history. So undefined was the American high school that before 1890—about the time Smith started—U.S. educational officials did not even include high schools as a separate category in educational statistics. Beginning in that year, however, the category exploded, especially because of a 167 percent rise in the number of public high schools. This revolution was not yet discernible in the small village of Metamora, population six hundred. Very few country teenagers from his world attended high school, Smith remembered later, "and Mennonite boys never." His parents would not allow their third son to start school before corn husking was done, however. It was two months into the academic year when Henry appeared in the halls of the single building housing the Metamora schools and attempted to catch up with his classmates. This delayed start did not appear to hold him back, for his intellectual life shot off in a variety of directions. Within two months he was receiving the highest grades in the class. Instead of the watch that Smith boys normally received from their parents on their sixteenth birthday, Henry suggested to his parents that he would prefer a telescope. John Smith consented and further fed his son's enthusiasm by building him a tripod and a platform on the farm windmill for better viewing. Before long Henry could make out four of the moons of

Jupiter. He jumped on a suggestion that Whitmire had made, and talked his father into subscribing to a weekly Chicago newspaper called the *Inter-Ocean*, a Republican paper that matched John Smith's political proclivities. Through reading this publication, Henry further encountered a world far beyond that of farm and church. He followed each new development in the trials of the Haymarket bombers with breathless anticipation, and thrilled to the twists and turns of the Cleveland-Harrison presidential race of 1888. As soon as election results were confirmed, the *Inter-Ocean* rushed bundles of newspapers onto a train and sent it south from Chicago into the Illinois countryside, spreading the news of Harrison's victory as it traveled. It is not hard to imagine young Henry in such a crowd at the Metamora depot, eavesdropping on the political talk and excitedly awaiting the coming of the "Election Special" train.[34]

Smith was one of the first Amish Mennonite teenagers in town memory to attempt high school, and he soon caught the eye of some of the old-stock Yankees in town, who began feeding him books and engaging him in conversation. The Metamora newspaper editor showed him his private collection of geological specimens, and also a letter he had once received from Abraham Lincoln. A Metamora merchant likewise shared Lincoln lore. This would have been a popular topic of conversation, for the town was saturated with it. Metamora was an important spot on the Illinois Eighth Circuit Court in the years before the war. As an important Springfield lawyer, Lincoln had often stayed there for days practicing law, pitching horseshoes, and swapping stories with townsfolk. As a boy in the 1850s, John Smith himself had sometimes encountered Lincoln on the streets, and a Smith aunt had waited on him in a local tavern when he and his political opponent, Stephen Douglas, spoke in Metamora while traveling through the area during their famous senatorial debates of 1858. Not surprisingly, at Metamora High School, Henry Smith gravitated toward history and geography. In his high school journal he once transcribed his talking points from a classroom debate where his side argued the affirmative on the question of whether or not reading fiction was harmful. Even the best writers, Smith maintained, were often immoral, and young people would be better off if they stayed away from such stuff. The other side argued that one could learn history from fiction, but Smith argued no. A dozen years later at the University of Chicago, he would learn to express such concepts with greater academic polish, but one of his basic intellectual approaches already seemed set. "So we see that while we are hunting a few historical facts," Smith's talking points read, "we are often compelled to read a great deal of rubbish in order to get a few facts." (His notes also record that the affirmative case won the debate).[35]

John Smith permitted his bright son to attend school only during the winter months. Hence, in two years Henry's high school experience only totaled, he remembered later, "two short winter terms of three months each." Through extra study at home, he had managed to keep up with his class. If Smith could remain in school through that final spring term, his principal informed him, he would graduate with his classmates. Smith knew it was impossible; his parents needed his labor on the farm. Besides, at that time the state of Illinois did not require a high school diploma for a teacher's certificate. So one Saturday in late May 1893, he and his cousin Ben Schertz hitched up a "two-wheeled sulky" to one of the farm mares for the dozen-mile round trip to Eureka. There they sat for the county teacher's examination, and then celebrated their passing scores on the way home by secretly smoking cigars (which promptly made them sick). In September Henry was already busy teaching in a country school nearby, doing his best to keep his pupils—"lusty, untutored young savages"—focused on their studies. Much of the time he exchanged chalk for the birch rod, which he did not hesitate to apply. Even so, he discovered he enjoyed teaching.[36]

Something else more important than smoking cigars happened to Smith on that trip to Eureka with his cousin Ben. In 1925 Smith recognized it as "a turning point in my life . . . the termination of my days on the farm." With his teaching certificate he would go out and make forty dollars a month, a comparatively small sum in his later life, but "princely wages" for a young man fresh off the farm. Most of that he would turn over to his parents, but he still kept enough in his pockets to allow himself an increasing series of extravagances: regular haircuts by the barber in town, a tailor-made suit, linen collars that had to be sent to Peoria to be washed, kid gloves, patent-leather shoes, and a snappy fedora hat. Like his life of reading, his progress in high school and now his life as a young teacher were taking him further away from his childhood community of farm and church. He seemed

Henry Smith at about age eighteen, 1893. BUASC.

eager to leave it behind. Smith knew that townsfolk regarded his people as queer and peculiar. Amish traits that he might have looked past as a child—the "unusual dress regulations imposed upon the girls," or the way that grown, big-bearded Amish men publicly greeted each other on the streets of the village with a holy kiss—left him keenly embarrassed as an Amish-American teenager. "I developed an inferiority complex as a result of these boyhood impressions," he wrote, "from which I have never recovered."[37]

One wonders if Smith's reticence was as pronounced as he remembered it later. The same shy Amish Mennonite boy who appeared at the Metamora school supposedly lacking social graces was capable, shortly thereafter, of disappearing down one of the "lovers' lanes" in the woods about town and carving his name, next to that of a girl named Alice, into the bark of a tree. His memoir does seem perfectly accurate, however, when he described the two different worlds he inhabited, and the increasing difficulty he experienced in trying to keep them in balance. From Monday through Friday of each week, his mind thrilled to matters like the poetry of Tennyson and Shakespeare and accounts of Caesar's victories against the Gauls. "On Sunday I sat for several hours on a hard straight-backed bench in a plain little meetinghouse, listening to a farmer-preacher discoursing in German on the sins of wearing a gold watch-chain or attending the county fair." Smith could manage for a time by compartmentalizing the two spheres of his life and not giving his family many hints about what was happening to him on winter mornings when he left the farm and headed into town. As a result, "my intellectual life was a solitary one." It was clear that his family did not and could not understand.[38]

Smith's parents assumed a public grace about their son's apparent oddities. He once overheard his mother simply explain to an aunt that "Henry always has his nose in a book." All the signs, though, pointed to a less happy ending and one that at least some of the Amish Mennonites at the Partridge meetinghouse would have been able to foresee. They knew the story too well: bright young people leave the community and never come back. This certainly seemed to be Henry's path forward unless his church could find a way to adjust. So far the prospects did not seem good. In 1895 the Western District Amish Mennonite Conference considered and rejected a proposal to build their own high schools. The questions thus remained with a quiet but heightened urgency. Would the Amish and Mennonite congregations create an institutional means by which their bright young people could pursue education but still feel comfortable in the church? As the century drew to an end, the answer remained elusive for the Amish Mennonite churches. But the direction was clear for Henry Smith. Just outside his church lay an American society with unimaginable delights, and the doorway into it, he realized, was higher education. He wanted in.[39]

2
Becoming C.

At the turn of the twentieth century, the nation's political and cultural leaders began addressing a series of neglected economic and social problems, and a soaring, crusading progressivism took hold of American national life. It was during this era of political and cultural ferment that both Henry Smith and his church began to pursue higher education. The Amish Mennonite and Mennonite churches would emerge from the era with an aggressive new leadership and a remarkable series of new institutions and ecclesiastical structures. Smith would mark the era with a new series of letters behind his name and a new one in front of it.

The Doorway of Prohibition

As did many other rural Americans, Smith and many in his church entered into progressive reform through the beckoning doorway of the Prohibition movement. "For most people today," writes one of its principal historians, "it is difficult to imagine the aura of debauchery and degradation which for a century Americans associated with the old-time saloon." And with good reason. While Americans' levels of alcohol consumption had declined from the horrific and destructive levels common in the early nineteenth century, through the Gilded Age it remained an unmistakable and chronic problem. After the Civil War, concurrent with the rapid growth of a massive brewing industry, Americans shifted their drinking from hard liquor to beer, and in the twenty years from 1880 to 1900, the number of the nation's saloons doubled. Correspondingly, by 1890 agitation against the saloon had burned across the American landscape for more than half a century. The image of the habitual drunk—the wife abuser, the lecherous seducer of young women, the brute whose children cried with hunger while he drank away the family grocery money—had been, Norman Clark observes, "seared across the American conscience for generations." Throughout that time the war against alcohol was for millions of Americans the major reform in American life. By century's end, prohibitionist fervor had further intensified because the war was not going well. The liquor lobby—"the most fiendish, corrupt and hell-soaked institution that ever crawled out of the slime of the eternal pit," screamed the moderator of the Presbyterian General Assembly—had succeeded in repealing Prohibition laws in all but three states, and per-capita levels of alcohol consumption were once again shooting upward.[1]

As Amish Mennonites began to lower slightly the walls they had erected between themselves and outside society, Prohibition would be one of the first cultural-political imports they would admit. Reflecting European culture, the traditional Amish rulebook had not drawn a firm line against alcohol. Alsatian Amish immigrants, including their ministers, routinely passed the whiskey jug to guests and fermented their own wine. With the onset of the *Dienerversammlung* meetings in the 1860s, however, this began to change, especially among the groups more open to outside currents. The Mennonite Church organ *Herald of Truth*, read by many Amish Mennonites, swung firmly to the temperance position by the 1880s, reprinting many articles from the Protestant press. The Stuckey Amish began to preach total abstinence from alcohol, a position that many Amish Mennonites gradually embraced. In this new cause they were led by some of the younger leaders more open to change, including Bishop John Smith. Rejecting advice from fellow ministers to preach the gospel and leave such matters to people's consciences, Smith increasingly raised his voice against the evils of alcohol and tobacco. Meanwhile the Western District Conference began to denounce alcohol with harder words and to exert tougher church discipline against members who frequented the saloon.[2]

The problem that such Amish Mennonite activists would discover was that embracing causes like Prohibition inexorably led to more complicated political choices. By the 1890s the power of the liquor lobby had grown to the point where the national "Prohibition Party" was moribund and an embrace of temperance by either major political party led directly to sure and certain losses in state and national elections. It was time for temperance advocates to refine their tactics, which they did with a device called the "local option." Simply put, this gave local people instead of state governments the power to restrict or outlaw alcohol consumption in their communities. It began to be championed in 1895 by a particularly effective new political pressure group, the Anti-Saloon League (ASL). By 1900, thirty-seven states had passed such laws, usually in conjunction with other reform measures like direct primary laws so that prohibitionists could run dry candidates in party primaries. The new tactic reinvigorated the prohibitionist crusade across the country and certainly so in Illinois, where advocates discovered the local option a great tool, in the words of one scholar, for "attacking the saloon wherever it was vulnerable." There the ASL, armed with its new device, "transformed the Illinois temperance movement from a blundering nativist crusade into an efficient political machine." In 1898 it began to work especially closely with its natural allies in rural Protestant churches.[3]

As a politically minded young man coming of age in rural Illinois, Henry Smith may well have attended to such developments even without his father's activism on the issue. In their push for the local option, prohibitionists began to focus special attention on what they grandly labeled "the World's Whisky Center": the city of Peoria. There distilleries were so huge that, as Henry's grandnephew John J. Smith later recalled, if the wind was right, as late the 1950s you could smell them all the way to Eureka. Sometimes to the Smith siblings the evil of alcohol seemed as close as the Metamora road. "To-night there is a dance in town there are so many people going down," Henry's sister Ella wrote him in 1899. "Some yell terrible ugly. I bet tonight when they go home their be [sic] lots of them drunk." In the pages of his high school journal, Henry demonstrated his firm engagement with the intricacies of prohibitionist politics of the moment. "Twenty five snakes running through the streets—that's free whiskey," he reasoned. "Twenty five snakes gathering into a box in which 25 holes are made, by authority of the court—that is low license. Ten of the holes are closed and the snakes get out through the other fifteen, that is high license. Drive all the snakes over to the next village—that is local option. Kill all the snakes, that is prohibition."[4]

The Illinois ASL was finally able to get a local option bill through the state legislative process, and by 1907 most of the state was dry. While the wisdom of particular temperance tactics apparently escaped Smith, he certainly would have been influenced by them in many ways. There was, for example, the reformers' ready adoption of the methods of enlightened social sciences. The ASL attacked the liquor industry by compiling massive statistics about its impact on social ills like crime rates and poverty. Smith would have also been influenced by the manner in which temperance reformers refused to compartmentalize their consciences to a single issue. In her position as leader of the Women's Christian Temperance Union, for example, Frances Willard also joined the Knights of Labor, endorsed the Populist crusade, and campaigned for women's suffrage. Equally important, Willard and other temperance reformers also paved the way for other reforms by hitching their cause to an enhanced role for the state. In demanding that government, in Clark's words, "exert an authoritarian, pervasive and confident moral stewardship," they envisioned it as a lever for protecting the "essentially pietist character of their way of life."[5]

In this drive for greater state power, people like Willard (who began her public life on the staff of evangelical revivalist Dwight Moody) also illustrated the growing power of a politicized evangelicalism, something that would also touch not only Smith but his larger church. A number of historians argue that the evangelical establishment of rural America in the Gilded Age fueled Prohibition and other interlinked causes. Denominational distinctions aside, these crusading evangelicals shared a deep devotion to certain core precepts like democracy, the power and dignity of the common person, and America's divine mission to the world. Moreover, as the nineteenth century drew to a close, Mennonite and Amish Mennonite leaders would have a harder time distancing themselves from these fellow Christians. Nor would they have wanted to. For by the turn of the century, the Amish and Mennonite world itself had begun to perceive and respond to a whole host of new passions and concerns.[6]

The "Social Question"

Not long after the Civil War, new winds began to blow across Amish and Mennonite communities that inexorably drew them closer to the patterns and concerns of their evangelical neighbors. "By opening themselves to American Protestantism," argues the historian Theron Schlabach, "Mennonites and Amish Mennonites found a religiously-approved way to become more American." Since the changes devolved most notably from Mennonite revival meetings, older scholars described them with terms like *revival* or a Mennonite *awakening*. But recent historians have rejected such terminology because of the implication that an older generation had been asleep. Nor do words like *acculturation* quite fit (though such a process was certainly underway, most notably in the concurrent shift, conflicted in some quarters, from German to English). Schlabach makes a good case that a better word for this revitalization process was a Mennonite and Amish Mennonite *quickening*.[7]

The quickening would be led by emerging new leaders who were themselves agents of change. One of them was an ambitious Mennonite publisher, entrepreneur, and pastor named John Funk. Raised in eastern Pennsylvania and converted in a Presbyterian revival, Funk had come to Chicago to work in the lumber business before the Civil War. There he met and befriended the evangelist Dwight Moody, who drew him into Sunday school organizing and missions work. In a fateful decision for his church, in 1867 Funk moved to the small city of Elkhart in northern Indiana and began publishing Sunday school tracts—and, most importantly, the *Herald of Truth*, which soon emerged as the central church organ for the Amish Mennonites and the MC Mennonites. For the rest of the century, Funk's paper resolutely pushed a quickened Mennonite agenda. Propelled by a steady stream of articles about Anabaptist-Mennonite history, the publication called readers to activism on a variety of issues, ranging from Sunday schools to mission work, plain living, progressive politics, and higher education.[8]

Funk made his mark on Mennonite history both because of such accomplishments and also for the band of followers he drew to Elkhart to work in his publishing house. Several of these developed into major leaders who would have significant impact not only on Smith but also on an entire emerging cohort of Mennonite educators. Chief among them was John S. Coffman. A Virginia farmer and teacher who had taken refuge in Pennsylvania from Confederate draft officers during the Civil War, Coffman was ordained as a minister in 1875 and began submitting articles to the *Herald of Truth*. Shortly afterward Funk invited him to Elkhart to work as an assistant editor. But it was on an 1881 preaching trip to a small Mennonite congregation in Michigan where Coffman found his real calling. In a series of "protracted meetings" there over four days, nine new converts stepped forward for baptism. This launched him into a successful eighteen-year career as the premier Mennonite evangelist of his generation.[9]

The church, Coffman discovered, seemed ripe for revival. So poor was the overall quality of Mennonite and Amish Mennonite preaching—at the hands of untrained farmer-preachers selected by the lot—that many good church members were drifting over to revival services in nearby Baptist or Methodist churches. Coffman's genius lay in his ability to deliver the revival message in chords and rhythms that were recognizably Mennonite. In scholar Susan Fisher Miller's words, he put together "the apparent, and necessary, oxymoron of Mennonite revivalism." Physically striking and possessed with a remarkable personal magnetism and charisma, Coffman managed to strike a moderate tone between the staid formalism of traditional Mennonite preaching and the intense emotionalism of contemporary Protestant evangelists. One convert recalled that while preaching "he didn't move around much and seldom moved his hands"; it was his effervescent preaching style, permeated by a gentle, loving presence, that brought people toward the altar. Coffman did his homework carefully beforehand, gearing his message to the perceived needs of the community, and relied on word of mouth to bring in local people. Commonly the churches were half-full when he began a series of meetings and overflowing by the time he left. Moreover, he moved easily between different groups, thereby establishing patterns of Mennonite ecumenicity, visiting and revisiting Mennonite and Amish Mennonite congregations from Ontario to Iowa. He worked incessantly; in 1891 alone he preached 331 sermons in a hundred or more meetinghouses. Of course he met with resistance, and so did Funk. Coffman's message and mechanics may have been soothingly Mennonite but they were also jarringly new, and seemed to some to fly in the face of beloved tradition. In 1892, for example, an Amish bishop in Lancaster, Pennsylvania, denounced "the J. S. Coffman faction," which was "putting in their best licks getting all the revivals they can." In central Ohio, congregations that embraced Funk's program were referred to locally as "the Funks," and by their opponents as the "sinful Funks." But Coffman and his allies could reply with some justification that adapting some techniques from the outside, like nighttime revivals and hymn sings, was the only way to keep young Mennonites interested in their church. Moreover, he combined his revival call with a reinforcement of distinctive Mennonite practices like nonresistance and plain dress.[10]

Increasingly Coffman was joined by an aggressive younger colleague from Allen County, Ohio, named Menno Simons Steiner. He was born in 1866, the son of a farmer-pastor and grandson of the founder of the important MC Zion congregation three miles west of Bluffton. In 1889 Funk lured him away from an early career as an Ohio schoolteacher and put him to work in his publishing company in Elkhart. But it was Coffman who really seemed to light Steiner's fire. At a Coffman revival near Bluffton in 1885, Steiner, says his biographer, "finally yielded his life to Christ." Thereafter he followed Jesus in a general way but took his specific marching orders from Coffman. Steiner rapidly moved into increasing positions of leadership in a series of initiatives that he and more senior "quickened" leaders spawned: the Mennonite Board of Charitable Homes, key churchwide Sunday school conferences, and promoter of the Mennonite Old People's Home near Rittman, Ohio. A generation younger and with less tact and more force than Coffman, whom he idolized, Steiner sometimes chafed against the caution of the church's old guard. "The Lord made some people a smoothing plane," Steiner remarked on more than one occasion, "but He created me a ripsaw."[11]

As they moved relentlessly across the Mennonite and Amish Mennonite landscape, Coffman and Steiner in turn excited the passions and commitments of a younger generation of Mennonite young people, some of them teenagers, who would go on to perform critical roles in their church. In 1891, for instance, Coffman appeared for a series of nighttime meetings at Science Ridge Mennonite Church near Sterling, Illinois. Initially it had not been clear if he would be allowed to come there at all, given the deep opposition he inspired among some of the church's dominant families. Evening meetings of any kind had never before been held at the church, and the congregation provided no lamps. With participants reading hymns by candlelight, the revival proceeded. Coffman downplayed emotional appeals but after a powerful altar call, forty people stepped forward to signal their conversion. Among them was a local farm boy then enrolled in high school named Noah Byers. Before long he began to think more seriously about devoting his life to church service, for which he would need, he reasoned, higher education. Similarly, at Bethel Mennonite Church outside of Garden City, Missouri, in 1894, a fourteen-year-old Missouri farm boy named John E. Hartzler sat listening to Coffman's message. Though the services were cut short soon afterward because congregational leaders locked Coffman out of the church, Hartzler realized later that it was while listening to Coffman's cadences that he felt the call to preach.[12]

In 1890 Coffman journeyed to Morgan County, Missouri, for a series of meetings, especially seeking out a prominent local Mennonite named Daniel Kauffman. Respected widely enough in the community to have been just nominated by his party to run for circuit clerk and county recorder, Kauffman dutifully attended Coffman's revival and resisted his appeals until the last possible minute. "While the last verse of the last hymn was being sung," he remembered later, "I came forward and gave my hand to the evangelist and my heart to the Lord." Shortly afterward he wrote to Funk's publishing house in Elkhart for books on Mennonite doctrine.[13]

On many occasions, Coffman and later Steiner preached their way across Illinois. March 13, 1889, found Coffman in Woodford County, where, he noted in his diary, he took dinner with a collection of local ministers, including "Smith of the Metamora church. . . . They seem clever, earnest men." The next day he conducted services "at the new church near Metamora. They have *quite* a nice congregation here." Four years later, in February 1893, Coffman was back in the community, visiting the sick, networking with pastors, and traversing with ease the invisible boundaries between Amish Mennonite, Stuckey Amish, MC Mennonite, and General Conference Mennonite churches. On the weekend of February 18–19, his diary notes, he preached to a packed house at the "Metamora Amish church." "Nearly everyone turned out in their sleds & sleighs" to hear him preach: from the parable of the laborers in Matthew 20 that evening, then from Hebrews 11 at the Sunday school the next morning ("sub[ject]: choosing to do right, in contrast with force. A historical discourse"). That evening he preached from John 4:4 on "the humiliation of Christ; the cost of the soul." Coffman seemed to gain energy from the size of the crowd, but still had some concerns about the receptiveness to his message at Metamora. "They have a large [Sunday] school but lack some in active work and life," he recorded in his diary. While he had a "rather pleasant visit" at Metamora and "was sure our meetings did good there," he wrote Steiner later that week, he felt he "could not ask for direct results" (i.e., conversions) "at that place."[14]

Still, he could have harbored no reservations about the enthusiasm for his visit from his hosts. On that revival weekend "I staid at Bro John Smith" and the following Monday at the home of his eldest son, Joseph Smith. Coffman "had a pleasant visit with this family" before John Smith took him visiting around the Metamora community. It would certainly have been this 1893 visit (as well as, perhaps, the 1889 one) where Coffman so profoundly affected Henry Smith. Smith remembered the visit with clarity thirty years later, specifically Coffman's sermon, preached in English, in which "he showed himself thoroughly at home in the fields of literature and history and other subjects which I had been studying in school." The evangelist "seemed a kindred spirit, so different than our own uneducated preachers." Equally illuminating was the conversation Smith enjoyed with Coffman in the buggy ride back to the Smith farmstead afterward, when "he told me a number of interesting things about the stars which I had just been reading about." If his congregation had had a pastor like Coffman, Smith remembered his teenaged self thinking, "how much more interesting church going would be!"[15]

There were a number of reasons why the brightening new lights of Mennonite education—Smith, Byers, Kauffman, and Hartzler prominent among them—soon gravitated to Coffman's magnetic pull and orbited around him until his death. While such evangelists stressed Mennonite distinctives such as plain living and nonresistance, they and other quickened leaders rapidly achieved institutional power and influence in part because they more fully embraced the process of selective borrowing already underway. It happened through a variety of avenues. Take, for example, the important realm of gender roles. The scholar Brenda Martin Hurst argues that in their speaking, bearing, and physical presence, evangelists like Steiner and especially Coffman created a positive way for Coffman's disciples to understand themselves as Mennonite men in an era when gender roles were changing quickly. The borrowing intensified also because of the changing sociological and spatial dynamics of the Amish Mennonite world in the later nineteenth century. Some Amish Mennonites and MC Mennonites had begun to leave their rural isolation and move into town, taking up occupations and urban lifestyles. Congregations of teachers and merchants ordained people like Funk, Schlabach points out, because they wanted preachers who would deliver the gospel in English and in more educated tones.[16]

The selective borrowing of this Amish and Mennonite quickening came mostly from evangelical Protestant neighbors. It was intentional enough that, Schlabach argues, "what emerged was not pure revival or pure acculturation but a new synthesis." Some of the borrowing seemed healthy and functional. The entire Sunday school movement was, of course, an outside import, as were patterns in Coffman's revivals, the new hymnody (Amish Mennonites like the Smith children sang the hymns popularized by Moody's song leader, Ira Sankey), the new Mennonite missions enthusiasm, and the new denominational structures and educational institutions that the quickened leaders developed. As with other evangelical Protestants, it was easy for them to blur the lines between the various causes. In 1893, for example, sponsored by a new organization called the Mennonite Sunday School Conference, Steiner and his associates selected a site on West Eighteenth Street in Chicago for the first Mennonite urban mission, and Steiner himself moved there to head up the work. Certainly it would have delighted Steiner, in his gung ho temperance enthusiasm, that the building they had rented for the mission was a converted saloon.[17]

Yet the freedom and at times undiscriminating nature of the borrowing also admitted other, more troubling elements into the Amish and Mennonite world, as well. Part of this was simply a language shift that suggested a blurring of the old boundaries of Amish and Mennonite separation from the world. The young activists liked the militant language of crusading evangelicalism; "terms like 'active' and 'aggressive,'" Schlabach notes, "became code words for the quickened." Daniel Kauffman preferred a new term, *aggresso-conservatism*, and his contemporaries took evident pride in their activism and their immersion in steady, energetic, "progressive work." In opening themselves up to the culture and causes of their evangelical Protestant neighbors, Mennonites and Amish Mennonites also adopted other aspects that lay further outside of their traditional framework. From Mennonite missions modeled on those of their Protestant neighbors, for example, came a subtle Mennonite adoption of the troubling evangelical elevation of Christian doctrine over Christian ethics. Also imported were strains of American nationalism, racism, and the ethnocentric missionary paternalism that propelled the new crusading cause of imperialism into vicious and colonialist encounters like the American war of conquest in the Philippines.[18]

In this latter kind of borrowing, Amish and Mennonites who reverberated to the quickening also appropriated liberally from a source that was both religious and secular, and that was emerging into a dominant political and cultural current in American society by the turn of the century. Put more simply, many of them became progressives. In 1885 an evangelical church leader named Josiah Strong published *Our Country*, a widely read book that was at once a passionate declaration for Christian activism on behalf of the poor and an overtly racist tract laying out God's special ordination of white America as God's civilizing agent to the benighted, savage races of the world. The General Conference Mennonite publishing house in Berne, Indiana, thought enough of Strong's treatise in 1892 that they published a German-language edition for Mennonite audiences. Meanwhile other young activists, Steiner among them, published their own analyses of American civil religion in a Mennonite vein. Many of them began to appear in a special paper Steiner created in 1894 to reach a new generation of Mennonite youth, the *Young People's Paper*. "That young people have been left to grope their way in the dark on many questions—the social question in particular—is admitted on every side," he proclaimed in the opening issue. In subsequent issues and particularly in an 1899 book, *Pitfalls and Safeguards*, Steiner developed at length the call of "the social question" on the Mennonite conscience. Though saturated in Victorian-era piety, his analyses are still remarkable for their detailed description of systemic injustice and for their clarity on the extent of Christian responsibility for the poor. He described, for example, the terrible burdens borne by black sharecroppers in the South, condemned economic inequality as anti-Christian and, citing people like Strong and the Social Gospel leader Washington Gladden, excoriated the "starvation wages" leveled out to the poor. While Steiner also rebuked poor people for wasting their wages in evils like drink and the theater, through his writings he began nudging his church, and especially Mennonite youth, toward an embrace of progressive reform. Likewise, amid his revivals Coffman had pushed his listeners toward missions activism and lectured them on Christian responsibility for the poor.[19]

There seems little doubt that such analyses permeated many Mennonite and Amish Mennonite communities. Certainly they penetrated central Illinois. The Metamora church donated money to Steiner's Chicago mission from its beginning, and in 1892 the Western District Amish Mennonite Conference adopted a profoundly declaratory resolution in embrace of Christ's commandment to preach the gospel to all nations. Through the first decade of the new century, Henry Smith's stepsister, Agnes Albrecht, carefully noted Steiner's preaching visits and stays at the Smith home, as well as those by his associates like Daniel Kauffman, Daniel D. Oyer, John E. Hartzler, and others. The Smith family spent the Christmas holiday of 1906 working at the Chicago mission. Steiner's new paper for Mennonite youth was barely a year old when he received a letter, apparently unsolicited, from a "Henry Smith of Metamora, Illinois," offering both advice and praise. "I think that articles written by Mennonites are more interesting to our people than some other authors long dead might be," nineteen-year-old Smith suggested, though quickly adding, "I like the paper very much as it is. It ought to be in the hands of every young man and woman in America who is interested in the welfare of the human race." Even with this enthusiasm for Steiner and Coffman, however, the budding intellectual in his late teens also displayed a determined capacity to think for himself. "A wave of puritanical censorship, first sponsored by certain Indiana Michigan evangelists, was spreading through Illinois congregations at this time," he noted in 1925, "radically transforming the recreational life of the young people." The innocuous old parlor games—"Skip to m' Lou" and others that he so cherished as a boy—were suddenly deemed worldly and replaced by more sedate affairs and hymn sings. Thoroughly disgusted, Smith and a few friends "stole away occasionally to Flanagan or Hopedale, where Indiana puritanism had not yet cast its gloom."[20]

Finally, the writings and preaching of people like Funk, Coffman, Steiner, and others resonated deeply among this emerging new generation of young Mennonite intellectuals for another critical reason. Coffman had struck a deep and responsive chord in young Henry Smith at the Metamora church that cold February evening in 1893 because he had begun to model to his listeners that faith and reason were fully compatible, not contradictory. Previously, Amish and MC Mennonites who had hungered for more education had left the church. It was presumably partly to help stop this exodus in 1894 that Steiner began pushing the (MC) Mennonite Illinois Conference to create a Mennonite Bible institute along the line of Moody's. He and Coffman were disappointed when the conference rejected the idea, but, as it turned out, they would only need to wait. By the next year, developments were underway in the Amish and MC Mennonite world in the American Midwest to further Steiner's vision in a more productive direction. In the young disciples they had cultivated, Coffman and Steiner would discover they already had the perfect people at hand to lead the way. They just needed a little more education.[21]

Hungry for Knowledge

It was ironic, then, that the original initiative for what became Elkhart Institute came not from the progressive Christian idealism of activists like Coffman and Steiner but from the profit-minded pragmatism of a Mennonite homeopathic doctor named Henry A. Mumaw. Throughout the 1880s Mumaw had founded two other such schools in little midwestern towns to meet a need he perceived for professional training among farm boys who had tired of the plough. He was also interested in making a little money for himself. Ever attuned to similar possibilities, Funk attended the first organizational meeting for such a new school with Mumaw and other interested men from his Prairie Street Mennonite Church in Elkhart. Steiner came over from Chicago that fall to address the first student body, while he and Coffman privately brainstormed ways to bring the school under the sponsorship of the Mennonite Church. Still, nobody from the church offered Mumaw much more than encouragement from afar, leaving the doctor free to improvise with an eye firmly fixed on the financial bottom line. Beginning in September 1894, he hired several associates to teach subjects about which they knew little to four students in a hall rented from the Elkhart chapter of the Grand Army of the Republic, the post–Civil War Union veteran's group.[22]

Smith arrived in Elkhart the following May, eager to begin summer classes and having convinced his father that he needed more education to continue to function as a schoolteacher. Neither father nor son knew much more about the Elkhart Institute than what they had read in some circulars that had arrived at the Smith home in the mail. They knew it had been founded by a Mennonite and that it was near Coffman's home in Elkhart, which was enough. One lesson that Henry might have taken from his first encounter with postsecondary education was to be more discerning with what he read, and to pay attention to the inclusion of words like *accreditation* in school promotion materials. For mostly what he initially encountered in Elkhart was a disappointment. Not that he had a bad summer. Far from it: after an initial bout with homesickness, he found at the Elkhart Institute a set of comrades his own age who liked to have fun, and "a string of lakes nearby where fishing was good." There were band concerts in the park, a few interesting lectures, the fun social interaction of the literary societies, and a local river, "the romantic St. Joe inviting numerous boat rides and picnic parties." But he did not learn much from the classes. These, he discovered, mostly repeated what he had learned in high school, and some of them were taught by his fellow students. The final straw came a few weeks after he arrived, when Mumaw approached him and asked if he wanted to teach a course in geography. "Realizing I could learn very little here," Smith remembered later, he packed his bags and headed home to Illinois before the summer term had ended, feeling thoroughly unfulfilled.[23]

By his late teens Smith had become a serious student, and the Elkhart Institute had not spoken to that. Nor would several more years of rural school teaching. Nowhere was his early infatuation with education better displayed than in his first published articles, which appeared that spring of 1895 as he approached his twentieth birthday. Smith had written Steiner the previous winter, not only to thank him for his new paper but to offer some of his writing, which Steiner promptly accepted. In "Reading and Home Education," a rambling paean to the value of education, Smith conceded the value of a college education, especially to the poor. Yet he elaborated on the driving need for people to educate themselves with or without it, which could happen through careful and selective reading on their own, and especially through studying the stars and the ways of nature. "With all these advantages," he concluded, "there is no reason and no excuse for any young man or woman of even ordinary abilities and a sound physique to remain uneducated." The next month he lectured the readers of the *Young People's Paper* on "the true aim of education." This would not be found, he declared, in "simply knowing facts abstractly," for "the mind stuffed full of facts (puffed up with knowledge) is not necessarily an educated mind." Much of the article consisted of a thorough condemnation of the numbing exercises in rote memorization he was then subjecting children to as a country school teacher. "What moral lesson do I learn from memorizing the spelling book?" he asked. "A hearty disgust for everything artificial." Education was not about abstract concepts but demanded personal "physical, moral and mental" development.[24]

In his explication of such concepts, like moral development at the heart of education, Smith was undoubtedly reflecting concepts that came to him through two popular new books on pedagogy he had picked up to help him as a teacher. They were written by Dr. Charles McMurry, a professor at the state teaching institute not far away from Metamora in the (aptly named) town of Normal. By the fall of 1896, Smith had decided to attend there. Illinois State Normal University (ISNU) seemed an established school, and he was clearly finished with his career as a country schoolteacher. In retrospect, he realized, "I made my choice blindly. I was not particularly concerned about perfecting myself in the art of teaching. I was merely hungry for knowledge."[25]

At first glance, Smith's experience at Normal appeared to replicate on a larger, more extended scale the same kinds of intellectual frustration that he had met with at Elkhart. Socially he bore no signs of a supposedly insecure Amish Mennonite lad. In fact, he seemed to flourish. By October, he wrote home, he was settled with his roommate, his cousin John Camp, in a boarding house in the nearby village of Normal, managed by a kindly woman who rekindled the fire in their fireplace while they were in class. He busied himself with his studies but also with sports, playing tennis with his roommates and winning

Henry Smith with the ISNU track team, circa 1896–98. Smith is seated front left, next to bicycle. BUASC.

the 220-yard dash at the campus field day. He took singing lessons, improving his tenor to a point of joining a male quartet so musically accomplished they found themselves in demand at faculty functions. He was elected vice president of the Philadelphia Literary Society and anchored their debate team. Off campus he sang in the choir at the Methodist church, and that fall joined an "immense throng" flocking to a speech by the Democratic presidential candidate William Jennings Bryan at a public park in nearby Bloomington. Smith managed to hear little of what Bryan said, but did recall, thirty years later, his smile and "the charm of his personality" as he worked the crowd. That was not enough for Smith: that November, having turned twenty-one the previous June, he followed family training and dutifully marked his first ballot for the Republican William McKinley.[26]

Academically, however, as with Elkhart, Smith remembered ISNU as mediocre at best, just "a big elementary training school." Since as far as he could tell it offered no degrees, it did not deserve the name of a university or even a college. Not long after Smith arrived, he discovered he would have no choice in his curriculum but just the same classes in reading, writing, and arithmetic he had endured back in country school. The text for his history class was, in fact, Barnes's *Brief History*, the exact same book he had been handed at Metamora High School. Worse yet was the level of classroom instruction, where he and his fellow students, then men and women in their twenties, were assigned seats, reprimanded if they whispered to their neighbors, and in other ways subjected to the same severe classroom discipline they had endured as children. The only difference was that ISNU professors substituted severe and nasty sarcasm in place of the birch rod.[27]

To augment the dismal nature of the experience further, through the fall of Smith's second year there, he began receiving news from home about his mother's failing health. Early the previous summer, Magdalena Smith had taken to her bed. Thirty years later he recalled his mother as a prematurely aged woman with gnarled and calloused hands, supposedly in the prime of life at age fifty-four, but worn down by a life of hard farm labor and the routine self-denial exacted upon Amish women. Now she lay dying of "consumption" (tuberculosis), the common disease of the poor, undoubtedly coughing up blood and growing gradually weaker. What made it maddening was that "we were not poor; father was considered well-to-do by his neighbors." In January 1898, Henry received a telegram from his brother Joe, saying "Mother very low, come home." Henry made it home a few days before the end.[28]

It is not surprising that he did not finish the three-year course at ISNU; perhaps it is surprising he lasted as long as he did. In the spring of his second year, he journeyed to Iowa to speak at a Mennonite Sunday school convention, and three of his professors, refusing to allow him to make up work he missed, failed him in their courses. By the spring of 1898, Smith was finished with Illinois Normal and later wrote off his two years there as a waste. Yet the momentum from his experience would propel him forward in at least one key way. For it was at ISNU where he began a long involvement with the premier student Christian movement of his day, the Young Men's Christian Association (YMCA).[29]

"I am superintendent of the Young Men's Christian Association here and they want me to go to a meeting of all the associations in the

United States at Lake Geneva," Smith complained to his sister Martha from Normal on a hot day in June 1897. "I didn't much like to go because I wanted to be home pretty soon but I almost had to go." It was a good thing he did. Three decades later he recalled camping in "the open tents under the big trees," the water "clear as crystal" in Wisconsin's "beautiful blue lake," and an introduction to water sports so complete he needed to buy his first swimming suit. He did not think then to mention any of the religious purposes for which the ISNU campus Y chapter had ostensibly sent him there, except for a hymn he found himself humming afterward and his discovery that "religion need not be divorced from brains, physical prowess or social prestige." But he came back to campus so totally devoted to the Y cause that, a year later, the school yearbook noted his "unflagging zeal" and "fidelity to duty" as campus chapter president.[30]

By the late 1890s, the YMCA had long ago developed enough institutional strength to influence its young devotees a great deal. Created in London in the early 1840s, it migrated across the Atlantic a short time later, thoroughly immersed in evangelical subculture and specifically in a great revival in American urban centers on the eve of the Civil War. It took firm root there as a moral hedge for Christians against a perceived urban corruption, and also, for the same reason, in college towns. Campus chapters sprang up in places like Cornell, Grinnell, and the University of Mississippi as early as the war years and then multiplied rapidly afterward, concurrent with an ongoing postwar boom in American higher education. Like the Ys in general, these campus groups devoted themselves to personal evangelism and Bible studies, with revivals a major focus and a growing emphasis on world evangelism and overseas missions. The evangelist Moody played an early central role, especially at summer Y conferences, where young leaders would gather for an exciting combination of prayer, hymn sings, Bible studies, and sports. Lake Geneva was such a gathering, but the first one began in 1886 in Moody's hometown of Northfield, Massachusetts. Soon the Ys began to develop their own leaders. In 1889, for example, a Yale student named Sherwood Eddy began a lifetime of Y-related missions work by coming forward at a Moody altar call at a summer conference in Northfield. By then the Ys had developed a rich evangelical subculture all their own, formed of equal parts youthful exuberance, missions commitment, and Christian devotion. At century's end, in line with the politicized, progressive evangelicalism that had begun to sweep the country, the YMCA and YWCA (Young Women's Christian Association) had begun to step gingerly into service work in urban ghettoes, jail outreach, and other initial forays into social justice activity. No wonder some of Coffman's Mennonite converts were drawn to it.[31]

Lake Geneva became a signal moment for Smith, not only because it attached him to Y work but also because of whom he met there. It was on the train heading north from Chicago toward Lake Geneva in that early summer of 1897 where Smith enjoyed the antics of "a group of Northwestern students wearing little purple caps and diminutive purple ties" sitting in the corner of his Pullman car, "entertaining the rest of us with their college songs and yells." One of the purple-clad shouters and singers was Noah Byers. When someone at the conference later told Smith that Byers was a fellow Mennonite, Smith sought him out, and the two began a deep friendship and an academic alliance that would last the rest of Smith's life. Of course they hit it off, given the almost eerily similar parallels in their lives. Byers was two years older than Smith and raised in similar circumstances on a Mennonite farm near Sterling, Illinois, a hundred or so miles upstate from Metamora. His father had died before his first birthday, leaving his widowed mother no choice but to assign her two sons to farm labor even more rigorously than had the Smith parents. Even so, she also pushed Byers upward in country school and then in high school in Sterling. The only Mennonite there, he attended part time and delayed his graduation because of his farm duties. Nonetheless, he developed a fascination with the world of ideas. After a year as a country schoolteacher, Byers entered Northwestern hoping to become a medical doctor, but his personal conversion at a Coffman revival at the Science Ridge church had fastened him more directly to the church. His uncle had worked with Steiner to found the Chicago Mennonite Mission, and while a student Byers taught Sunday school there. Yet it was the Northwestern Y chapter that really seemed to capture his interest, enlisting him as an executive officer and sending him to conferences like the one at Lake Geneva. He was considering overseas mission work upon his graduation in 1898 when Coffman intervened with another plan in mind. This plan would change both Smith's life and Byers's life, and also the course of Mennonite higher education.[32]

"Not for Mere Selfish Ends"

In the two years during which Smith was enduring the boring classes at Illinois Normal and Byers was completing his zoology major at Northwestern, Coffman had been busy cementing church control over Mumaw's little institute in Elkhart and getting himself put in charge of it. Mumaw first opened the door to this development early in 1895, when he suggested forming a corporation to own and manage his school. Coffman and an ally named J. S. Hartzler jumped to the task, selling stock in a company called the Elkhart Institute Association. From the beginning it was understood that the money would be used for an endowment, a new building, and a school with avowedly Christian purposes. The list of stockholders soon grew to more than two hundred, many of them from places like Ontario and eastern Pennsylvania, where Coffman had labored intensively with his revival campaigns. That summer, construction began on a school building on a lot situated diagonally across the street from the Prairie Street church, where Coffman was ordained as minister. In the spring of 1896, a coalition of Elkhart Institute stockholders, Steiner prominent among them, maneuvered to elect Coffman president of the school's board of directors, Hartzler vice president, and Mumaw secretary. Unhappy at his loss of control, Mumaw resigned within two months to start a rival institution, leaving two Mennonite schools under the direct purview of the Prairie Street church. Like several other of Mumaw's educational projects, this "Elkhart Normal School and Business College" would die on the vine shortly thereafter, but not without first intensifying factional discord in the congregation.[33]

In a somewhat ominous harbinger for the future, then, early efforts by Amish Mennonites and MC Mennonites to found an institution of higher education would serve as a source of ongoing church conflict. In the summer of 1898, these and a host of other problems would be dumped in the lap of the Elkhart Institute's new principal. This figure, Coffman quickly determined, would be Byers. Instead of going into the mission field yourself, Coffman suggested to Byers persuasively, perhaps the church is calling you to be a teacher of missionaries. For a twenty-five-year-old recent college graduate and newlywed—that summer he had married a fellow Mennonite from Sterling and Elkhart Institute grad named Emma LeFevre—it would have been a heady assignment. Yet Byers also knew well that the list of candidates for the position was very short. He himself was the only Mennonite in his denomination he could think of who was both a college graduate and who had had any teaching experience.[34]

Byers did not realize then that some of his new professors' job qualifications were even more meager. Coffman was doing the faculty hiring that summer, and he already had his eye on another budding young Amish Mennonite intellectual whom he knew from one of his revival tours in Illinois five years before. Smith had always treated his studies as all-important, but he blithely dismissed the failing grades he received from three ISNU professors because he already had a job offer in his pocket from Coffman. "None of us," Byers remembered later, "knew how little academic work Mr. Smith had to his credit." Coffman and Hartzler sensed it but merely cautioned Smith to pursue further training in any academic field that interested him. In actuality there were few other available candidates. Coffman was more concerned that Smith might balk at the salary they were offering him—about forty dollars a month, less than they had paid his predecessor and no more than he had earned teaching country school. But the work itself—teaching older students at a church institution—promised immeasurable intellectual compensation. Smith jumped at the opportunity, though he was careful to sound out his father about it first. John Smith gave his blessing, along with twenty dollars, "hoping you will not forget to do your duty in your Christian work as well as in your school work."[35]

In mid-September 1898, Smith left Metamora for Elkhart, two hundred or so miles away, on his bicycle. He was twenty-three years old. He carried no road map but generally followed rail lines toward the northeast. Arriving at Coffman's front door three days later, weary, mud-spattered, and sporting three days' growth of beard, he had dodged dogs and thundershowers and made part of the trip by train. The Coffman family, he was relieved to discover, seemed willing to look past his initial appearance. He proceeded to board with them for the next two years, struck by their "fine spirit of Christian devotion, as well as the high tone of refinement and culture" in their home. As he remembered it in 1925, his first two years in Elkhart were "perhaps the most pleasant of my entire educational career," and nothing in any documents from the time undermines that impression. Within two months he was already writing home his firm intention to stay there at least an additional year, and with good reason. There was, for example, the transformation that had come over the Elkhart Institute. No longer was it a "private venture run for profit" in a shabby rented hall. Now housed in a handsome new three-story building, it had become a church institution controlled by a body of forward-thinking Mennonites who had sensed the desperate need in their church for a college to train their young people. There was the institute's mission, which Smith would have embraced wholeheartedly: to "furnish the best possible opportunities to young men and women to prepare themselves for the various duties of life, not for mere selfish ends, but to become of the greatest possible use to others." There were the students, Smith remembered, many of whom "were about my own age, serious minded, and devoted to their studies, thus making the classroom contacts a source of real pleasure and not an arduous grind." He would have been entranced by the city of Elkhart itself, a bustling burg of fourteen thousand people served by four different rail lines and five different newspapers, two of them dailies. Beyond it was the charming Indiana countryside, "with its woods and lakes, and the romantic St. Joe" River. Though he did not mention it thirty years later, Smith's experience in Elkhart, in that autumn of 1898, was also clearly romantic for reasons besides the river. "Guess the next thing we will hear you'll be married next summer," his sister Katie wrote him in mid-December. "We would have been pleased to see you home Christmas but I suppose somebody will be pleased in our place."[36]

Katie Smith had been misinformed; her brother had no wedding plans. He was too busy with his new duties, teaching English and Latin to Elkhart students. Smith found himself assigned to the Bible department, along with Byers, Coffman, a historian named Norman Gingrich, and Daniel Kauffman, who taught church doctrine. Of course Smith had had no more specific training for teaching literature than any other subject, but what he lacked in terms of preparation, Byers said, he made up for with enthusiasm, hard work, and pep. To help him teach American literature, Smith recalled, he came across a book called

Smith, a new instructor at Elkhart Institute, at the home of John S. Coffman, 1898. BUASC.

Philosophy of Literature by an Indiana educator named Thompson, just as he was "floundering about in my English teaching, trying to find some tangible and objective objectives of study in my class work." In the very least, Thompson's book helped him to appreciate the aesthetic element in literature, especially when he carried William Cullen Bryant's poetry to read beside the St. Joseph River on an October afternoon. Within a year, Smith felt comfortable enough in teaching English to write authoritatively about it in the institute's newsletter. Reflecting something of the new infatuation with scientific methodologies he had picked up along the way in academia, he stated that educators beyond the sciences had also recently grasped that the student learned best "by his own observations rather than through the observations of others." This was why they taught rhetoric at Elkhart by having students not only study masterpieces by Wordsworth and Shakespeare, but also write for themselves. Smith, as always, refused to confine his intellectual curiosity only to subjects at hand. He corresponded, for instance, with Coffman's brother-in-law Lewis Heatwole, a Virginia Mennonite preacher who had studied at the University of Virginia and operated a weather station. As a fair amateur astronomer, Heatwole was able to answer some of Smith's many questions about the stars.[37]

Smith was most proud, thirty years later, of the institute's "all-Mennonite faculty," and it was in these years that he and Byers developed a cohort of young Mennonite intellectuals who would become fast friends and academic allies in the coming years. Nearly all of them—Mennonite or Amish Mennonite farm boys who had become excited by ideas—shared similar life stories. By the late 1890s, for example, arriving to study at the Elkhart Institute was John E. Hartzler, an Amish Mennonite farm boy who had been saved in a revival, called into the pastorate by a Coffman sermon, and now so full of Christian passion he would sneak away from campus to preach on Elkhart street corners. Not long after the turn of the new century, Henry's brother Joe wrote from back home, saying he was at a Sunday school conference in the Illinois town of Gridley, where "I met a fellow there by the name of Boyd Smucker. He enquired about you [and] said he met you at Elkhart already." An Elkhart Institute grad, Smucker hailed from the important MC Mennonite Oak Grove congregation in Wayne County, Ohio, and already aspired to be an orator. Within a decade, as a teacher of that subject, he would be a fellow faculty member of both Smith and Byers, and would remain so the rest of his life. For an even more exact typecast of this emerging Mennonite academic model, take the twenty-four-year-old new student that Byers welcomed to campus in the fall of 1900, an eastern Ohio farm lad named Paul Whitmer. He had begun absorbing books at a young age, starting with McGuffey Readers and children's versions of Shakespeare's plays, and then moving on to Hawthorne and Irving. Like Smith and Byers, Whitmer passed the county teachers' examination and worked for some years as a rural schoolteacher before making a belated entrance to college. While at Elkhart he managed to spend time volunteering at the Mennonite mission in Chicago and to take extra classes at Moody Bible Institute. Hence, when Byers suggested he complete college and some seminary, with an eye to teaching Bible at his alma mater someday, Whitmer was more than receptive.[38]

Both inside and outside of class, these students would have been inculcated in the same rich brew of heady intellectualism and progressive Christian activism into which their young professors had been steeped in their own recent student days. Given the size of the early student bodies with which they worked, Byers and Smith could only try to replicate their academic milieu in the tiniest of microcosms. In that fall of 1898, for example, they taught a grand total of twenty-four students, each of whom paid a tuition of twenty-four dollars if they studied all four terms. But the small student body did not deter them from laying the foundation of a rich extracurricular life: the Vesperian and Avon Literary societies for women students, and the Coming Men of America Debating Club and the Aurora Society for men. The incipient elements of a sports tradition began in 1897 at the hands of a new instructor recruited to Elkhart by Coffman and hired to teach what was then called "physical culture." This was a former Amishman from Pennsylvania named Joseph W. Yoder. As a young man, he had broken with his heritage because of his hunger for higher education and a desire to attend Juniata College. He would become another Smith kindred spirit and lifelong correspondent, especially in his later emergence as a novelist of the Amish. More immediately, Yoder and a fellow instructor named Leila Munsell would organize the Elkhart Institute Tennis Association.[39]

Byers and Smith saw to it that the major extracurricular student organization on campus was the Young People's Christian Association (YPCA), their own coed version of the Ys. To help kindle Y and missions enthusiasm, in November 1898 Byers brought back his old college roommate, then a traveling secretary with the national Student Volunteer Movement for Foreign Missions, for four days of speeches. By the following summer, the student Y group had dispatched a student named Irvin Detweiler (who would also one day emerge as an important academic partner to both Smith and Byers) to Lake Geneva. As an Elkhart student, Hartzler would also make a trip to Lake Geneva as YPCA president. Altogether the YPCA soon had the campus so humming with missions fervor that in just two years, between 1898 and 1900, the Elkhart Institute would send the first five Mennonite missionaries to India. The energetic young professors placed the Y activity at the front and center of campus life, but by the turn of the century the formal and informal mentoring of students took place in and well beyond it. By the fall of 1898, under the auspices of the newly formed YPCA, Byers began inviting students to an all-school social, usually held at his house. At one such event in March 1899, for example, toastmaster Byers called upon board president Coffman to deliver remarks on "Prospects of the Institute." This was followed by a speech by Smith

Faculty and students of Elkhart Institute, 1899. Smith is seated in the second row, second from right. Byers is seated in the second row, fifth from right. BUASC.

on "School Spirit." In the wintertime faculty-student activities included bobsledding together; when the weather warmed, they would head to the "St. Joe" for boating.[40]

It was altogether a rich, exciting time there at Elkhart Institute, those early days of what Smith called "Mennonite educational pioneering." He encapsulated its spirit perfectly in a chapel address he delivered in his second year there. "We are all slaves more or less," he began. "None of us are entirely free. . . . The entire struggle for existence," he bluntly told students, "in fact, is simply a struggle of freedom from slavery" to various forms of bondage: to narrow thinking, to one's habits and biases, to the force of one's environment and training, and to the "slavery of that deluding monster called Public Opinion." Very few people "ever make much progress in this struggle for freedom of thought. Consequently, few of us ever become great, for a great man is one who is original and free." Those who were truly free from such bondage—Socrates, Luther, Jesus—could expect only persecution and martyrdom. Clearly Smith had entirely rejected an older Amish worldview that taught its adherents to follow without question the traditions of the ancestors. It is hard to understand how, with such opinions, he could ever fit comfortably again into an Amish or MC Mennonite context that restricted or filtered the adoption of ideas. The important task of the moment, he proclaimed, was to break free of any kind of intellectual or personal bondage: "The whole object of education is to break up old habits of thought. The ruts into which we have fallen must be destroyed," he announced, "not because old habits of thinking are always wrong (although many times they are) but because without this freedom growth is impossible."[41]

To pursue this freedom fully and to legitimate the influence he hoped to hold, in that spring of 1899 Smith decided he needed more education, as represented in the form of academic degrees. To help remedy his academic deficiencies, he had spent some weeks in Ann Arbor, Michigan, the previous summer, enrolled in summer school at the University of Michigan. But Smith knew he needed full-time study and, despite the scanty salaries at Elkhart Institute, had even saved up enough money to begin to pay for it. Somehow he managed to parlay the University of Michigan classes and several entrance examinations into a letter of acceptance to the University of Illinois. Though Smith resigned his position at Elkhart, Byers clearly understood then that he would be back.[42]

Some years before this decision, however, Smith had already marked his intellectual transformation by adding an initial, "C.," to the front of his name. His parents, his story went, had simply forgotten to give him a middle name, and he never found out why. Adding initials was apparently something of a fad among the teenagers of his day—sort of a Gilded Age tattoo—though for few of them was the addition as permanent as it came to be for Smith. He began signing his name with a "C." added in front on school applications and then on his early publications; soon he found it stuck. At the time, no doubt, the change appealed immensely to his adolescent vanities. "Henry Smith" was plain as beans, "commonplace and unattractive," while "C. Henry Smith" seemed, to that Amish Mennonite teenager, "rather pleasing and distinguished," and even, in nuances of late Victorian culture long lost today, with an air of professorial erudition. In his adult encounters with various bureaucracies, Smith had many occasions to regret the addition. Officials of various sorts, he discovered, would not accept a mere initial. If he would not provide them his full first name, they would assign him one. Registrars at the University of Illinois, for instance, would christen him "Charles." When traveling in Europe thirty years later, U.S. State Department officials would name him "Cecil" in his passport, thus forcing him to undergo the inane little ritual of signing his name as such whenever travel officials called for his full signature. Late in his teens and for some years after, however, for Henry Smith the "C." was perfect. As the old century came to a close, it would symbolize the transformation of a hayseed Amish boy into a serious young man of culture and learning, poised to walk boldly into the halls of academia and then with equal purpose into the new era that beckoned.[43]

3
The Democracy of Learning

On a cold winter evening in mid-February 1896, John Coffman mounted the podium and looked out at a sea of eight hundred upturned faces jammed into the main assembly room at the brand-new Elkhart Institute building on Prairie Street. They had come to dedicate the building, and it had fallen to Coffman to deliver the main address. Surprisingly, for a preacher of a thousand sermons, he seemed to be nervous. A few days beforehand, he had even bought a bottle of prescription medicine to help calm his stomach, along with a new suit of clothes for the event. He knew it was a momentous occasion, and that he would have critics. He certainly was aware that the title of his address by itself—"The Spirit of Progress"—would have set off alarm bells for many Mennonites who remained faithfully wedded to the ways of the ancestors.[1]

As Coffman proceeded, the concerns of some and the elation of others would have deepened. For the spirit of progress that he portrayed was mostly a positive one. To be sure, traditionalists would have taken heart in his lengthy elaboration of the seeming immorality of the age. Coffman was, first of all, an evangelist, and his address followed the classic (albeit slightly modified) revival pattern. He proceeded from a portrayal of the glitter of human potential—now displayed so abundantly in the great technological and scientific achievements of the day—to the inescapable degradation of that potential by human sin. Of course they could not hope to escape the bonds of history. The great civilizations of Egypt, Greece, and Renaissance Italy, with all their astonishing art and intellect, nevertheless succumbed to the corrosive forces of debauched human nature, the age-old seductions of selfishness, sloth, sexual immorality, and idolatry. The signs of such corruption were discernible, he pointed out, were all around them. At that point in the address, for the traditionalists assembled there, the obvious and age-old Amish and Mennonite rhetorical rejoinder would have been merely to repeat the treasured biblical phrasing in 2 Corinthians: "Wherefore come out from among them, and be ye separate, saith the Lord."[2]

That evening, however, it was not cultural separation that Coffman came to preach, but engagement. Like any good evangelist, he did not leave his congregation lost in the hopelessness of sin but resolutely built them up for the altar call. To get there he proceeded mainly from history, presenting a narrative of the past thoroughly in line with the established Mennonite historical consensus of the day. Since the days of the apostles, this teaching ran, key kernels of original gospel truth had rested with a small band of dissenters from state churches. In medieval times, in Coffman's words, these "little bands of despised and persecuted Christians," groups like Albigensians, Henricans, and Waterlandians, hid away in the mountains of Europe, carefully safeguarding "the spirit of progress like the dormant fires of an inactive volcano, ready to burst forth at any unsuspected moment." An especially important figure in this historical development was a Frenchman in Lyon named Peter Waldo, whose followers called themselves the "Waldenses." For three centuries, Coffman taught, the Waldenses kept the spirit of progress alive before it burst forth in the Protestant Reformation at the hands of the radical Anabaptists. Compared with what would be acceptable to key Mennonite historians a decade or two later, Coffman's list of Anabaptist heroes was a relatively large and inclusive one. It encompassed not only the Zurich radicals of 1523–25, such as Conrad Grebel, Felix Manz, and George Blaurock, but also reformers from nearby German provinces like Hans Denck and Balthasar Hubmaier. All, Coffman said, "taught the same doctrine" they had inherited from the Waldenses. It was Menno Simons who shaped the doctrine into a coherent body of thought and mentored a group of disciples to pass it on.[3]

Now, almost four centuries later, Coffman declared, we stand as the inheritors of that truth, and of ancestors who had so carefully maintained "the spirit of progress in the line of education." Unfortunately, Mennonites had been slow to warm to the possibilities that education offered. One could scarcely blame "some of our most noble-hearted people" for their opposition, Coffman admitted. They had seen how young people who had been educated in English "were almost always lost to the church." Even so, the church had paid a great price: a loss of its ancient intellectual vitality and an intellectual stagnation that had lasted for centuries. Instead of thousands of congregations, Mennonites only had a few hundred, due to this intellectual hibernation and also to "the want of intelligent, educated teaching in the English language." They met that evening in a central instrument by which that deficiency might be corrected. While the Elkhart Institute was no more than a small "speck on the great educational field of this broad land," for Mennonites, Coffman asserted, it symbolized "a welling up of a pent-up stream that could no longer be suppressed." Indeed, they stood at "a transition point in our beloved brotherhood . . . the final crossing over of a large body of our people . . . from the German language into the language of the country." Would they now shrink back from the task at hand, as dangerous and seductive as the world might be? They dare not, Coffman told his audience, because the world needed their message. A quick glance at current events—the "World's Peace Congresses," the "Venezuelan question," "bleeding Armenia"—revealed that many outsiders were increasingly receptive to what Mennonites had to say. In response to that beckoning invitation, Coffman built to his crescendo, let the Elkhart Institute "be like a light upon a stately tower, casting luster far among the shadows." And let it do all this, he concluded with a flourish, in "the name of *Jesus*, JESUS, JESUS."[4]

Coffman's address amounted to nothing less than a ringing manifesto for Mennonite higher education. He delivered it in the Mennonite expression of one of the central organizing vehicles of American progressivism: an institution of higher education, or what a leading progressive educator would call the "democracy of learning." Set in such a context, Coffman's vision so thoroughly captivated a generation of Mennonite educators that, as late as thirty years hence, rival progressive and conservative groups would still be trying to establish themselves as the true inheritors of Coffman's legacy. He himself had little to say about the matter; less than four years after his Elkhart address, he died of stomach cancer at age fifty-one. His closest companion, Menno

Steiner, increasingly consumed by his own health problems, took up farming back home near Bluffton, Ohio.[5]

Hence, Coffman's immediate mantle would thus fall upon a set of younger disciples. His educational vision would be carried forth by Noah Byers and the emerging cohort of young Mennonite educators whom Coffman had tapped to work with Byers at Elkhart. The historical tradition that Coffman had sketched out in 1896 would primarily come to rest, considerably reshaped, in the capable hands of C. Henry Smith. In the fall of 1900, Smith began his serious pursuit of academic credentials as a student of English at the University of Illinois, emerging from the process a half dozen years later as the premier Mennonite historian of his generation. As such, he would devote himself to producing for his acculturating people one of the key ideational structures they needed in order to find an acceptable place in Progressive Era North America. He would provide them a usable past.[6]

The Social Gospel Solution for Social Ills

By the turn of the century, Mennonites certainly needed scholars of their past to help them navigate their way into the confusing present. Like all Americans, they lived in an era of sweeping social, technological, and economic change. Persons born before the Civil War who lived a decade or two into the new century would watch their society be transformed by a series of previously unimaginable developments. Slavery had come to an end. Millions of immigrants, speaking dozens of different languages, poured into huge metropolitan centers from a wide array of countries. New urban ghettoes stretched for miles. The American economy shifted quickly from light to heavy industry, principally railroads, oil, machinery, and steel. The size and scope of the emerging manufacturing enterprises facilitated the development of large corporations. These were governed by a tiny new economic elite, the celebrated "titans of industry," like steel master Andrew Carnegie, railroad baron Jay Gould, oil tycoon John D. Rockefeller, and financier J. P. Morgan. For people of means, which included a burgeoning new middle class, the wealth and entrepreneurial energy of the age made available technological wonders powered by the sudden marvel of electricity: electric stoves, vacuum cleaners, sewing machines, and phonographs. The increasing availability of telephones rendered communication nearly instantaneous. Electric railway cars revolutionized urban transportation and gave birth to growing "streetcar suburbs" around industrial urban cores. Urban folk benefited first from such developments, but it did not take long for some to penetrate the countryside. In a letter to her brother Henry in April 1901, for example, Ella Smith mentioned that their new telephone had begun to function after its installation the day before.[7]

Certainly a great many of these changes exerted a positive effect on people's lives, but as in other eras of massive wealth creation, the new money and the comforts it brought were not equally shared. Already by 1890, the poorest half of the country owned less than 5 percent of its wealth, while the richest 1 percent owned over half. The growing wealth inequalities exacerbated the tensions and national sense of dislocation. The changes had been too jarring and had come too fast. Individual reforms had percolated throughout the era: civil service and municipal reform, Prohibition, and the rural economic and political revolt of populism. It took the national economic panic of 1893, two historians argue, to knit them all together into the national reform crusade of progressivism.[8]

Like the movement itself, the historiography of progressivism is complex and varied, but a couple of generalities seem safe. It emerged as a response to the multifaceted social problems engendered by the rise of industrial capitalism. As part of this national movement, Americans from across the political spectrum pursued dozens of different major reforms, but the reform crusade seemed especially to draw the energies of the new middle class, many of whom joined because of a sense of religious devotion, encapsulated in shorthand as the "Social Gospel." Drawing on the new methodologies of an enlightened social science, many of the ensuing reforms seemed jointly to express a simultaneous drive for social justice and also social control. (Prohibition, immigration reform, and early settlement house and social work are all good examples.) Finally, regardless of their individual focus or class basis, for a great many progressives, the problems that had energized them could be solved, at least in part, by using the tools and power of a beneficent state.[9]

Besides their middle-class origins, progressive activists, and especially intellectuals, seemed to share several other common characteristics. A fairly high number of them, argues the historian Jean Quandt, emerged from rural areas and small towns, origins that would have made their reaction to urbanizing and industrializing America particularly acute. Many also had been born and raised in the politicized evangelicalism of antebellum and Gilded Age America, where a pietistic acceptance of Christian responsibility for social ills—again, Prohibition is a good example—reverberated down to them from Methodist or Presbyterian pulpits. It is almost uncanny how many were nurtured in a childhood reverence for Lincoln and a devotion to his party. Indeed, Lincoln worship was so pronounced across the Gilded Age North that both advocates and opponents of Prohibition efforts commonly enlisted him as the unanswerable moral champion of their opposing causes. The Anti-Saloon League even produced a youth arm called the "Lincoln Leagues." Also central to the shared intellectual heritage of many progressive activists were the currents of thought they absorbed in university educations. These included a rejection of social Darwinism and other legitimating props for the unjust social order then under construction by the titans of industry and their apologists.[10]

Clearly, many in the emerging first generation of Mennonite educators came to embrace progressive reform out of similar trajectories. Smith is, of course, the premier example here, with a father who cherished his childhood encounters with Lincoln, modeled temperance activism, and welcomed quickened Mennonite leaders like Steiner and Coffman into their home. In 1907 Henry Smith wrote home to townsfolk in Metamora with an endorsement of a proposed "Lincoln Douglas Day." He retained a lifelong devotion to the rail-splitter despite his changing political party loyalties. Even in his old age, Willard Smith remembered, his uncle Henry was "much interested in Lincoln." Not just in their childhoods in the politicized evangelicalism of rural America, but also in many other ways, the emerging Mennonite educators of Smith's generation shared such similar backgrounds and commitments it is easy to understand why they so easily formed such bonds of solidarity. For instance, while Byers befriended Steiner, plunged into Y work, and worked at the Chicago mission in his college days, his first embrace of progressivism began earlier, in high school, when he read the utopian novel *Looking Backward* by the socialist Edward Bellamy. "I think it influenced me for the rest of my life," he recalled later, "to be more critical of the present order and more sympathetic to progressive ideas." In his explication of the joys of oratory and embrace of "physical culture" as a means of character development, Boyd Smucker had clearly been influenced by Progressive Era thinking on the professionalization of recreation. Paul Whitmer shared his father's Republican Party loyalties and his lively interest in current events, but his intellectual and political development was especially sparked when, as a farm boy, he came across a serialized biography of Lincoln in the local newspaper. It so captivated him he proceeded to read all the Lincoln biographies he could find in the various public and college libraries he encountered in the coming years. In Menno Steiner's hometown of Bluffton in 1900, the new Central Mennonite College welcomed an aggressive young intellectual named Noah Hirschy as its first president. A Mennonite pastor who had been raised on an Indiana farm and studied theology at Oberlin College, Hirschy had, within three years of his arrival, ringingly endorsed both women's suffrage and government ownership of utilities and plunged into the local option campaign, which, to his delight, successfully banished saloons from the village.[11]

The economic and social climate of the day plainly shaped the intellectual and personal commitments of these future educators; as with so many other Americans at the time, it also helped to propel them into education in the first place. Not long after the Civil War, the particular needs of a rapidly growing industrial economy clearly sparked a massive growth in secondary and especially postsecondary education. The rates of college attendance of young people aged eighteen to twenty-one began an unchecked rise. In 1880 less than 2 percent of such young people went to college. In 1900 the figure stood at 4 percent, and by 1920, it had doubled to 8 percent. An urbanizing, industrializing country needed fewer farmhands and more people with specialized training. It especially needed more professionals: bookkeepers, clerks, doctors, lawyers, architects, and engineers of all stripes. The numbers of such professionals quadrupled from 1870 to 1910, and an in-group orientation, memberships in new professional organizations, and a specialized vocabulary obtained in the mastery of a small field of expertise—in short, a professional culture—began to function at the heart of the new, Progressive Era middle class. American colleges and universities boomed. Major new universities like Stanford, Cornell, and Johns Hopkins arose from nothing in a few short years, while the Morrill Act of 1862 facilitated the birth of a major new feature of the American educational landscape: the land-grant college. Three decades later, undergraduates at huge new state-supported universities in the Midwest and West—the University of California, the University of Illinois, Ohio State University—began to supplant Ivy Leaguers as the typical American college students.[12]

The small minority of American young people fortunate enough to attend college began to pioneer the normative features of undergraduate life. These included phenomena like the fraternities and sororities, religious groups like the Ys, and the new frenzy over intercollegiate sports. Somehow, in the midst of it all, students supposedly pursued academic grades. The new American universities, like older ones, reflected the racism and ethnocentrism of their society. They were almost entirely white and restricted the participation of groups like Jews. But within these limitations, the new universities also reflected the inherent promise of American life. With less than 5 percent of similarly aged young people in college in 1900, for instance, graduates could expect to receive professional positions of remarkable expertise and responsibility.[13]

Byers and Smith are good examples from the Mennonite world at the time. So is the educational and professional journey of another of their future colleagues, a Swiss Mennonite immigrant named Jacob Thierstein. A baker's son in love with books, Thierstein immigrated with his family to Kansas from Switzerland at age sixteen. Seven years later, in 1890, he entered the General Conference Mennonite seminary in Halstead, Kansas, and then the University of Kansas, where in 1896 he graduated with an AB degree (the abbreviated Latin name for a BA, *artium baccalaureus*). In 1904 the mere professional qualifications of a bachelor's degree and some intervening years as a high school principal were enough to win Thierstein an appointment as the new president of Freeman Junior College in South Dakota. With such examples multiplied by the hundreds of thousands across the country in these years, it is little wonder why so many Americans thrilled to the promise of higher education. As an example, regard the hopes of Andrew Draper, president of the University of Illinois, who in 1904 tried to encapsulate what his university stood for. "Its high mission," Draper proclaimed, "is to bind men together in a democracy of learning, and to extend the noblest fraternity in all the wide world."[14]

In the fall of 1900, Smith entered Draper's democracy of learning, where he worked hard, did his best, and tried to get out as fast as he possibly could. He took the maximum number of classes allowed, pursued extra credits through special exams, crammed in extra classes over vacations, and in all other ways tried to shorten his stay. "I hope the time will go around fast for the next couple of years," he wrote home soon after he arrived. "I don't want to stay here any longer than I have to." The University of Illinois at the turn of the century would have been an interesting place to be. It had 2,300 students, new football bleachers, and in 1901 became connected to the town of Champaign by a trolley line. But Smith showed little interest in any of it: none in the sports scene, none in the fraternities, and absolutely none in the undergrad drinking parties, which were many. When famous speakers came to campus, like former Civil War generals Oliver Otis Howard and John B. Gordon, there is no record he went to hear them. He wanted to get through. At age twenty-five, he was older than most of his peers. Besides, he was presumably eager to resume teaching back in Elkhart with a proper academic degree or two attached to his name.[15]

By September Smith had secured lodging in a comfortable (but, at $3.75 per week, "awfully high"-priced) boardinghouse and plunged into academic life. This he found invigorating, especially when compared with his experience at Normal. There the student was "a schoolboy," while in Champaign he "was regarded as a man." Smith studied hard and so immersed himself in books that by his first Thanksgiving in Champaign he wondered in a letter home, "Did pap make a book case for me?" Even a brush with academic authorities turned out well. Specifically this meant President Draper and Major Fechet, the commanding officer of compulsory student military training. Smith was a dutiful student, but an even more dedicated Mennonite. Within his first weeks at Illinois, in obedience to this higher obligation, he met with these men personally and petitioned to be excused from military drill. Draper and Fechet, to his surprise, immediately recognized his freedom of conscience.[16]

With the benefit of hindsight, Smith later realized that his all-consuming drive to rush through college as fast as possible "was all a big

Leadership cabinet of the University of Illinois YMCA, 1902. Smith standing front left. BUASC.

mistake." He missed many opportunities to obtain "the general culture and training which is essential to a well-rounded education"; specifically he regretted not accepting an invitation extended to him to join a major campus fraternity. Yet two opportunities for social engagement he did not pass up. He sang with the campus glee club, and, more importantly, he joined the Y. By the end of his first year, he was on his way to Lake Geneva again. In the intervening months he had been so involved in Y activities he found himself elected chair of the Bible study committee and vice president of the entire YMCA. Neither of these were inconsequential positions. The Illinois Y's membership grew almost 400 percent, from three hundred members in 1900 to eight hundred five years later, making it one of the fastest-growing Y campus chapters in the country. Moreover, in Y leadership and especially in Bible study work, Smith would be strategically positioned to watch—and also probably be influenced by—a significant series of shifts, not just in the history of the YMCA but also in that of American religion.[17]

In the latter half of the nineteenth century, scholars argue, a disestablishment of American religion rapidly accelerated on American college and university campuses. Originally even the big state universities were understood to be culturally and generically Christian. Chapel was required of students at nearly all American higher educational institutions; most of their presidents were overtly Christian and demanded such commitments from their professors. As early as the 1890s, however, these dynamics had begun to change. Even and perhaps especially at the land-grant universities, a "broad, non-sectarian evangelicalism" had given way to official religious disestablishment and an unofficial but growing enthusiasm for the Social Gospel. Such shifts certainly were apparent at the University of Illinois. After the administration reinforced compulsory chapel in a major legal fight in the mid-1880s, it was quietly abolished in 1894. Before Draper began his tenure in 1894, Social Gospel minister Washington Gladden was a leading candidate for the university's presidency. The official movement of Y activities from campus buildings to official buildings off campus in the later 1890s probably did not reflect the religious disestablishment so much as an intensification of Y activities. When Smith arrived in 1900, with membership limited to "members of good standing in an evangelical church," the University of Illinois Ys still enlisted about a third of all male students and (in 1904) over 63 percent of all women undergrads. Officially opened in 1899, the new Y house was soon bustling with activity: prayer meetings, Bible studies (with annual Bible lectures and visits by leading theologians and revivalists), a "White Cross Army" to push purity, and various social events and receptions for new students. In 1901 the YMCA brought the organization's national secretary J. R. Mott to campus, and seven hundred men, Smith probably included, crammed into the chapel to hear him.[18]

It is possible to overstate the radical nature of many of the changes. In Smith's student years, progressivism was just beginning to ferment in the Ys nationally and also at the University of Illinois. Nationally the organization reflected, argues YMCA historian David Setran, "a conservative social gospel theological stance," which attributed social problems to "individual moral failings" as opposed to "structural issues." At Illinois much of the Y's focus remained on individual salvation. The key shift occurred in Smith's particular assignment, the realm of Bible study. In his years there, these sessions shifted from faculty- to student-led and followed inductive Bible study texts created specifically for campus chapters. "In each association Bible study holds an important place," read the small "Students' Hand-Book," which the Illinois Ys passed out free to all students in these years. Groups of six to ten men and women met separately, it explained, to follow different courses of study laid out for them by the national YMCA. In 1901–2 these courses included studies of the Old Testament, Paul's epistles, and the life of Christ. While the Old Testament course was written by a Moody Bible Institute professor, the general program seemed to follow the theological prescriptions of Mott's good friend, William Rainey Harper, president of the new University of Chicago (where Smith would soon study). Long ago he had begun to argue that students should study the Bible as scientifically and objectively as scholars in other disciplines, all of which were shaking, at the time, to the new epistemological landslides that followed in the wake of the Darwinian revolution. Harper himself was a great fan of historical and cultural approaches to Bible study. By 1894 he was leading the way in jettisoning an older, factually inerrant view of the Bible as intellectually unacceptable "bibliolatry." It may have been through the safely evangelical devotion to Bible study, then, that fifty thousand students in YMCA campus chapters across the country, Smith among them, received their first introduction to what became called, for lack of a better term, "liberal theology."[19]

The intellectual challenges that scientific discoveries apparently posed to traditional Christian precepts had begun to heat up decades before Darwin began publishing his ideas, but the publication of Darwin's writings superheated the ensuing debate. From an acceptance of evolutionary frameworks and scientific methodologies as the *sine qua non* means of acquiring knowledge, it was an easy step for many Christian thinkers, Chicago's Harper prominent among them, to embrace such approaches in scholarly Bible study. Heavily shaped by historicist thinking imported from Germany, Harper and others put forth groundbreaking ideas such as the notion that the Holy Scriptures were documents rooted in history and that the Bible was a collection of history, prophecy, poetry, and folklore put together over a thousand years by human beings. Theology itself could be read and interpreted as *historical theology*, an evolving of theological positions resonant with their historical context. A complex range of intellectual positions emerged, grouped together under the unwieldy rubric of theological *liberalism* (or, in a later, more highly charged phrase, *modernism*). The leading proponents of such ideas ranged from Social Gospel apostles like Walter Rauschenbusch, for whom Christ's persona and divinity remained central, to "scientific modernists" (the historian Winthrop Hudson's phrase) like Shailer Matthews of the University of Chicago divinity school, who put their faith in science as the ultimate validation of religion. Indeed, asserted Matthews, "scientists know more about nature and man than did the theologians who drew up the creeds and confessions."[20]

Despite the wide variation in positions, most liberal Christian thinkers of the day shared some basic assumptions. Human beings were not damned sinners at heart, but free moral agents inclined to be good. Certainly at times they made bad moral choices (*sin* became an uncomfortable term for many) but could be educated away from these unfortunate habits. God had designed evolution ultimately to benefit human beings, and hence the story of humanity was one of inexorable progress. In this manner, many came to conclude that the kingdom of God was achievable within history through human action. The scientific and social breakthroughs of the day—the new wealth, the peace congresses, the revolutions in transportation and communication—were unmistakable signs that it was on its way. Soon after the turn of the century, Harper installed a number of key liberal theologians at the divinity school of his new University of Chicago, including Matthews, and did his best to accentuate their public prominence, such as setting up a special lecture series for them in 1903. People like Matthews did not need anyone to prod them into the academic limelight, however. Their extensive writings and ecumenical activism—Matthews would serve as president of the Federal Council of Churches from 1912 to 1916—would soon make Chicago synonymous with theological liberalism.[21]

It seems evident that by the turn of the century the YMCA-YWCA movement was heavily shaped by such ideas, signaling a key turn in the organization's history, Setran argues, away from its conservative evangelicalism foundation. The trend was especially pronounced, he says, in "the trajectory of YMCA Bible study curricula in these years." In a 1909 address to an assembly of college Y general secretaries, a leading YMCA official declared that it was high time to dispense with the outmoded idea that the Bible was "an infallible instrument of divine revelation, to be accepted literally and obeyed implicitly." The larger changes in theological thinking had also permeated popular culture to such an extent that they would be picked up by aspiring young intellectuals in the Midwest. Smith began to write on such ideas even before he arrived in Champaign. In April 1900, as he worked at admission to the University of Illinois, he informed readers of the Elkhart *Institute Monthly* that "the literature of the Bible was inspired. It contains a divine message, but that message was delivered through human agencies." The Bible was written before the printing press, he pointed out, its chapters and verses assigned by Jewish rabbis. Hence it appears in "no logical order of any kind. Poetry is written like prose." Because it is so hard to decipher, "it won't do to translate the Bible too literally." Doing so produces "narrow-minded religious fanatics," while reading it too figuratively "makes free thinkers and agnostics. In fact," Smith concluded, "it doesn't matter so much whether all the Biblical narratives were actual occurrences or not, just so we learn and apply their truths."[22]

Two years later, as Smith finished up at Illinois, he returned to Elkhart to speak in chapel and share with students, in an address on "The Meaning of Education," something of what he had been learning. It seemed abundantly apparent to him by then that "the human race has been making steady progress in every line of effort and field of observation," a trend that had been especially clear over the past quarter century. Ranging over a wide number of different fields—theology, geology, astronomy, and history—and building from a clear acceptance of theistic evolution, the young intellectual praised "scientific knowledge" as something that "means more than an accumulation of facts. It influences both our happiness and destiny in life." Through it, he said, we can see the work of God. Only by developing both their mental and spiritual capacities, Smith told Elkhart students, would they find "true education." This would not be rewarded in monetary gain, but "in those things which make us free from the bondage of ignorance and superstition, and in everything that goes to make life worth living."[23]

By the end of Smith's second year at Illinois, he realized that by scraping together his accumulated credits from Normal and Ann Arbor and working every angle at Champaign, including a few more hours of summer school, he would have enough academic credit for a bachelor's degree. The university would not officially award him the degree, however, until the end of the following academic year. Years later university officials informed him that they had established a Phi Beta Kappa chapter and had selected him as a charter member, one of seven students so honored from the several hundred graduates of the class of 1903. Smith retained enough of his Amish sensibilities to write the chapter secretary to say they must have meant some other Smith. But he did not hesitate to attend the initiation ceremony, and he wore his Phi Beta Kappa key pinned to his suit jacket the rest of his life. These would have been trying moments for Smith's Amish humility. Plainly he had begun to make a name for himself in the Mennonite world. While Smith family devotion to this tradition might have made them reluctant to admit it, there was no doubt they were proud, as well. "Pa heard something about you way out in Ohio, something he never heard before, it pleased him so," his sister Emma wrote him in 1901. "He said people think so much of you there, those that know you."[24]

Smith's humility received more challenges in the years to come. As he finished up in Champaign in that spring of 1902, he made two more fateful choices. First, he decided that, eager as he had been to get through with his education, he was not done with it yet. He had determined to apply to the graduate school at the University of Chicago. There, he decided, he would study history. In the context of the times, Chicago made sense. No doubt there were news stories circulating across Illinois about the magnificent new university that Harper was constructing in Chicago with liberal infusions of Mr. Rockefeller's money. The decision for history appears in Smith's autobiography almost like an afterthought. He stated it directly and with no explanation why. It would have profound reverberations for decades afterwards, however—not only for Smith, but for the larger body of his Amish and Mennonite people and how they understood their past.[25]

Progressive Promises of the University of Chicago

As a young intellectual with progressive inclinations, Smith found his way to Chicago. In the first years of the new century, the university pulled in such people like a magnet, and the city beyond it drew in everybody else. On the verge of becoming the nation's second-biggest metropolitan area, Chicago had been shuddering to explosive levels of growth, which simultaneously demonstrated both its lovely and sordid effects. On the plus side were its soaring skyscrapers, the fancy hotels and glittering department stores in "the Loop" downtown, the elegant mansions of its captains of industry, and the tree-shaded neighborhoods where it housed its growing middle class. In 1892–93 Chicago had demonstrated its promise for the entire world in the fabulous "White City" of the Columbian Exposition, which the city erected on ten thousand acres it had emptied on the edge of the South Side neighborhood of Hyde Park. The downside of Chicago's growth was manifested in the people who did the bulk of its work. On the eve of the Civil War, the city's population had reached 300,000 people. Three decades later it had more than tripled, to 1.1 million. Migrants had flooded to Chicago from every corner of the world to work in its stockyards, steel mills, and seemingly endless train yards. Most could expect to receive for their labors only the foul reward of poverty. Off work, they headed home to crowded tenement neighborhoods that stretched for miles and furnished repeated outbreaks of typhoid and cholera. Arriving to start summer school in the late spring of 1902, Smith would have stepped off the train into noisy, confusing streets clogged with horses and people, enveloped in a perpetual haze of coal smoke. It was a strange new environment indeed for a Mennonite country boy.[26]

In this frantic metropolitan setting between 1890 and 1892, a persuasive crew of Baptist educators induced a dedicated Baptist lay leader named Rockefeller to forget about a possible site in Washington, D.C., and build a top-tier Baptist university in the West. Energized by Harper and powered by Rockefeller's millions, in a few short years they had secured huge sections of prime Chicago real estate near the old Columbian exposition site and began the construction of mammoth buildings. It did not matter if things were raw and unfinished or that one did not have an ancient tradition to build upon. In America, with enough money, writes the historian George Marsden, one could buy gothic buildings and hallowed halls and all "the appearance of tradition" one could afford. One could even obtain a top-rate faculty. Harper quickly launched what one historian called "the greatest mass raid on American college faculties in history." When classes commenced in October 1892, he had secured 120 new professors to teach them, including five former professors from Yale, fifteen from Clark, and eight former college or seminary presidents. In the professorial ranks was row after row of bona fide academic stars. The history department could boast of Harry Pratt Judson, who proved such a capable administrator he would succeed Harper as Chicago's president after the latter's sudden death in 1906. It soon included the noted legal scholar Andrew C. McLaughlin, who would write some of the foundational texts in American constitutional history. The real star of the department was its chair, the eminent professor J. Franklin Jameson, who had helped found the prestigious *American Historical Review* and then succeeded McLaughlin as its editor. Jameson would hold this position for twenty-five years, and wielded a baron-like power across the entire American historical profession.[27]

Little of the power and eminence of a great university was visible at the University of Chicago as it began. When Judson first visited in 1892, all he could see was "wilderness," and when Smith arrived ten years later, he saw that the university "was still pretty much in the pioneer stage." Harper had so carefully planned for future expansion that in 1902 large, open lots yawned across major sections of the campus and numerous "unfinished brick walls" marked the sites of future buildings. "Nearby," Smith remembered, "was a low, one-story, ramshackle brick structure with a flat roof which they said was the library." He found a room in a private home a block from the open expanse of campus. A cow barn and chicken house stood near it, and the barnyard noises made the transplanted farm boy feel more at home. Even Smith's fine grades from Illinois could not entirely outweigh his hurry-up academic record, and he was probably lucky to have been admitted to Chicago at all. He was luckier still when the university registrar inexplicably awarded him thirty-two academic credits for his previous work instead of Chicago's original offer of eighteen. Once Smith finished up his Illinois degree with classes at Chicago that summer, and squeezed in a few more hours early in the fall, it was just enough to get in. He was officially admitted to the graduate program as of October 1, 1902, and plunged into a hodgepodge of classes. In that first year alone, as he worked on his master's degree, they ranged from medieval and modern history (in the same semester) to "Land Policy in America" to "The Pre-Raphaelite Movement." The following summer he nourished his Mennonite ties by singing in the choir in the Mennonite Mission on West Eighteenth Street.[28]

Smith would spend a total of four years studying at the University of Chicago and, apart from his specific training as a historian, was no doubt was deeply influenced by several of the dominant intellectual trends there. A major current, of course, was progressivism. There were a number of reasons why the national reform movement forged such ready ties with academia in general and with Chicago in particular. Many of the solutions to the festering problems that progressive reformers addressed were found in the ministrations of enlightened social science. Where else would such expertise be developed except in the nation's research universities? Given the extent of the Darwinian revolution and the clamor for scientific approaches as the most trustworthy expressions of knowledge, these universities developed new fields that could then be applied to the nation's social problems. With the deep progressive faith in the curative powers of democracy, university experts began to produce treatises on the "science" of governing. Related disciplines also took on an applied, this-world orientation, especially connecting history with fields like social policy and politics. Out of this background, Smith would spend much of his academic career with the official title of professor of history and government, and may never have questioned why the two fields were linked.[29]

All these conceptions would have reverberated with particular power in Chicago. From bases at the University of Chicago in the South Side to the squalid ghetto west of the Loop, where Christian reformer Jane Addams and her settlement house coworkers pioneered the field of social work at Hull House, in many ways the city functioned as the heart of Christian progressivism for the entire Midwest. The key to national survival was the individual conscience, lectured the university's president, Judson, in 1913, and "the most effective motive of the individual conscience [is] found in religion." In 1903 Harper assumed control of a fading monthly publication, renamed it *The World Today*, and installed Matthews as its editor. Soon it became a beacon for Social Gospel progressivism across the Midwest. One of Judson's first academic recruits for his department was a promising young political scientist named Charles E. Merriam, who turned out to be as much a progressive activist as a scholar. Ever since his student days at Columbia, where he had volunteered for the mayoral campaign of the Tammany Hall foe Seth Low, Merriam had been operating under the belief that the only sound basis for the study of politics was participation in it. Smith took several classes from Merriam, including "Party Government" and "Municipal Problems." Though he had left Chicago when Merriam made his boldest political moves—terms as city alderman and then unsuccessful campaigns in 1911 and 1915 as a reform candidate for mayor of Chicago—his subsequent career suggests he clearly absorbed a good deal of Merriam's teaching. Among the relevant lessons was the call to root one's political positions in solid social science research, on the one hand, and on the other, to manifest them somehow in concrete action in the world.[30]

Smith's other intellectual inheritance from Chicago was something of its underlying cultic faith in the national enterprise, a devotion that later scholars would later identify with terms like *civil religion*. Everywhere "across the nation at the turn of the century," Marsden writes, "one could find academic leaders, both conservatives and progressives, who would not have been ashamed to view themselves as missionaries for the higher cultures based on science and the unifying ethical ideals of Jesus. Nowhere was the equivalent task being carried on more explicitly than at Chicago." Harper in particular repeatedly articulated a deep faith in America as God's chosen nation and the regular recipient of divine favor. In such conceptions, he and his fellow Chicago academicians found themselves perfectly in tune with the larger religious expressions of the Progressive Era. They were common chords in the Social Gospel.[31]

In the spring of 1903, Smith had absorbed and reflected back enough of this package of teaching to be awarded his master's degree in history. A few weeks later, his bachelor's degree from Illinois arrived in the mail. Just as important as the degrees, however, was a small incident that had happened during that academic year, followed by two key decisions he made because of it. One day he sat in the divinity school library, abstractly leafing through the pages of a book on Baptist history, when a name he recognized jumped out at him from lines of print. It was Menno Simons. As Smith turned the pages more carefully, he quickly realized that the book's author identified Menno as "one of the founders of the Baptist faith." Reading further, he discovered that this was a common claim among Baptist historians and also those from the Congregational church. Altogether the notion floored the young scholar. "I had always thought of Mennonites as an obscure, peculiar people, with strange, unpopular practices" and "little influence in the world," he wrote in 1925. To realize suddenly that others might regard them as founding practitioners of critical aspects of Western religious thought like freedom of conscience and Christian peacemaking "was a revelation to me . . . I no longer needed to apologize for my humble faith." As he recalled the moment two decades later, it was then that he decided to spread that discovery in the public sphere. The foundational contributions of his Mennonite people deserved "wider publicity." So, "before I left the university I had decided to make a thorough investigation of their history and, if possible, to write a comprehensive treatise on the subject for publication."[32]

He also determined, moreover, that he would make a living as a college professor. He hardly knew what else to do with his life; in fact, "I drifted into it." He had no burning desire "to do anything great," to become rich or in other ways "make myself useful in the world." What he did want was "to know life, to acquire knowledge, to travel, to explore, to acquire experience, to develop an enriched personality." Teaching seemed an apt means of doing all this; indeed, "graduate study in history hardly fitted one for anything else." Having decided on the two great purposes of his life, even then, in that spring of 1903, Smith seemed to have an inkling that he could somehow harness them to the unmet social and intellectual needs of his ethnoreligious people. Through academia he had begun to taste the fruits of Progressive Era American culture and found them good. Perhaps he could share such bounties with his church while at the same time communicating Mennonite contributions to society. The initial meeting ground for this process of productive cross-fertilization would be the small but potent field of Mennonite higher education.[33]

The New Professoriate of Young Goshen College

In the fall of 1903, Smith headed back to north-central Indiana, where the Elkhart Institute had metamorphosed into Goshen College. In the three years he had been gone, the institute had been so engulfed in conflict that a new location seemed wise. Certainly there were other factors, as well. The building had become too small to accommodate its growing student body, and the limited size and swampy location of its lot—the building and its furnace flooded regularly—precluded further expansion there. But the main trouble came from the persisting strife in the Prairie Street congregation across the street. Mumaw's second little institute had died, but factional conflict sparked by the two rival schools had not. In 1900, led by Mennonite doctrine instructor Daniel Kauffman, students and faculty broke away to form their own, separate congregation, meeting in Elkhart stores and then in the institute chapel, while Mumaw allied himself with the increasingly strict and hierarchical authority of the reigning Mennonite bishop, sixty-five-year-old John Funk. A special investigating committee appointed by the larger church officially healed the schism in 1902, but it was plain to nearly everybody that the institute would have to move.[34]

For several years it had been less than clear that the school would move to nearby Goshen. Not that the little town was somehow unattractive. Located a dozen or so miles southeast of Elkhart, Goshen had about eight thousand residents and was well served by trains and an electric interurban line. Moreover, it had gained local fame as the "Maple City" because of the trees shading its long, wide streets. But as the factional crisis deepened at the Elkhart Institute, its leaders had begun to consider a variety of locations, all with an eye to transforming it into a four-year college. In 1899 Byers and Steiner talked of moving it to West Liberty, Ohio. Two years later, having considered and then rejected relocating to the site of a failed General Conference Mennonite school in Wadsworth, Ohio, Byers thought a new location near Lancaster, Pennsylvania, had real possibilities. Mennonites in the East, Steiner reported, were especially anxious for a school closer to them. Byers admitted in early 1903 that he was "not at all tied to Elkhart or the west" as much as he was committed "to the best educational interests of the church as a whole." He knew that Goshen was working on raising a $50,000 inducement, but doubted they would get it. Within a few months, however, the town had come up with a fifth of that amount, which the institute's trustees decided was enough.[35]

In early June 1903, 150 Elkhart students, faculty, and friends boarded interurban streetcars to a wheat field on the south side of Goshen, where they joined a crowd of equal size officially to break ground for the first building at Goshen College. Since Byers was off at Harvard that year (finishing his master of philosophy under such luminaries as William James and George Santayana), Smith represented the school at the ceremony. He mounted a wooden platform to provide a few brief remarks, reported the *Goshen Democrat*, "on the character of the college." By the time seventy-seven students arrived for opening classes late the following September, the first building, a dormitory named East Hall, had gone up just in time, with Byers and other administrative staff carrying away boards and sweeping up wood shavings the day before. The completion of the administration building in January 1904 furnished a more suitable place for academic instruction, and professors plunged into the work with a gusto that Smith recalled with crystal clarity decades later. They had a faculty back then of ten members, he noted, nine of them under the age of thirty and "inspiring teachers" all. They had "no superannuated ministers nor outworn church workers" in the bunch, only young professors who were "still eager students themselves" who had "not yet outgrown their youthful enthusiasms." Byers took equal pride in the faculty, trumpeting the graduate degrees they held and reporting to Steiner that if he did not think "that this is the best school for Mennonites in the U.S. to get the grade of work that we offer . . . I would resign at once." Students seemed to agree, for they poured into the new school for college-prep and then actual junior college classes. By its fourth year, the mostly Mennonite student body reached 138 students, a jump of 50 percent from the previous fall. Their academic leaders plunged them into the same alluring mix of energized teaching and exciting extracurricular activity, especially Y work, which had so shaped preceding student generations at Elkhart. The YPCA quickly organized a Sunday school on the east side of Goshen, Steiner came in from Ohio for a short Bible course, and J. E. Hartzler and Irvin Detweiler lectured on evangelism and missions work. "We were all pioneers," Whitmer remembered as an old man, "and had a deep interest in our new college."[36]

Smith was integrally involved in nearly all of it: teaching history, editing the new college newspaper, *The College Record*, and overseeing the library, which was in particularly sad shape. When he arrived back in Goshen, it consisted of one row of books on a bare shelf in the back of a classroom in East Hall. Plainly this would not do, and Smith pushed to expand such academic resources, critical for any self-respecting college. He also had ready channels for influencing larger academic policies due to the fact that, still a bachelor, he boarded with the Byers family and regularly discussed administrative and other matters with the college president over the breakfast table.[37]

One fruit of such conversations was a plan the two hatched to get Mennonite students talking more about peace. At their pushing, the Goshen faculty issued a call to other peace church colleges, particularly those associated with the Friends, Brethren, and Mennonites, to send representatives to Goshen to strengthen their joint convictions. The first in what would soon emerge as an annual gathering occurred at Goshen in June 1905 to discuss the theme "Education for Peace." The seven initial participating colleges created the rudiments of what would be an ongoing relationship in a new organization they called the "Intercollegiate Peace Association," and also began an annual peace oratorical contest as a regular feature of it. (More than a century later, thanks to permanent funding established in Smith's will, this competition still lives on as the "C. Henry Smith Peace Oratorical Contest.")[38]

At one point in their daily breakfast conversations, the two young academic leaders would have put down their coffee cups, realizing they had reached a divergence of opinion about church-college relations. While the disagreement did not seem seriously to mar their friendship, it did highlight the significantly different ideas the two then had about the proper degree of power the church should exercise over academic life. For some years Byers had been advocating to replace the college board of trustees, most of whom were elected from around Elkhart, with a wider board made up of representatives from district conferences across the church. "The institution necessarily started as a local affair," he explained to Steiner in 1901, "but I think the time has now come when our people as a whole should take a more active part in the management so that the growing educational interests should be provided for and kept unified." With wider church ownership would come more control, Goshen's president knew, but also, he hoped, more financial and other support. The move was partially made in 1901, and then reinforced in 1905 at Byers's urging. "This plan, of course," Byers admitted later, "put the college under the control of a more conservative board." Smith thought it a manifestly bad idea, and "later when difficulties arose," Byers said, "he occasionally reminded me of it." Byers insisted into his elderly years that the move was "the right thing to do." An early Goshen historian has suspected, however, that he may have had second thoughts later on, for difficulties with church conservatives certainly arose.[39]

More immediately, both Smiths, father and son, found it politic to steer clear of the fight at the Prairie Street congregation and wider conflicts that reverberated outward from it. As an Elkhart Institute and Goshen College trustee, and a Mennonite leader with reputed financial means, John Smith was a wished-for ally on all sides. Yet in 1901 he resisted entreaties from Funk to buy $10,000 worth of stock in his publishing company, though this certainly would have helped the bishop in his ultimately unsuccessful struggle with Kauffman over which of them would control it. At the same time, the elder Smith refused to buy stock in the Elkhart Institute because of his apparent resentment over the poor salary they had paid his son. Thus it may well have been John Smith's factional independence, as well as his son's absence from Prairie Street when the conflict was at its apex, that facilitated Henry's access to Funk's personal library in Elkhart and its remarkable collection of Mennonite-related materials.[40]

In the summer of 1904, after his first year at Goshen, Smith allowed himself his first extensive tourist trip, boarding a train for Denver and taking in thrilling sights of the Rocky Mountains and the old West. Afterward he came back to Indiana and buried himself in Funk's library, which the embattled old bishop "very kindly placed at my disposal." He clearly meant to begin delivering on his vow of a year before to use his abilities as a scholar to bring his Mennonite people that "wider publicity" he thought they deserved. Results were forthcoming almost immediately. In September Smith informed students in the *Goshen College Record* of the immense scholarly and churchly riches of the *Martyrs Mirror*, the great record book of the Anabaptist martyrs, especially highlighting the 1887 edition that Funk's publishing house had produced. Four months later he educated students and the wider church in a published article on the importance of Mennonite history. The fascinating history of these great pioneers of Western religious thought, he pointed out, had been "written mostly by their enemies" and ignored by most historians. It was high time, he implied, for that neglect to end. He had work to do.[41]

4
In the Service of a Usable Past

In 1903, now having received his bachelor's and his master's degrees, Smith was already one of the most highly educated persons in his church and seemed totally committed to the cause of Mennonite higher education as manifested at Goshen. By his second year there, however, he made the momentous decision to return to Chicago for his doctorate. Like other critical choices in his early years, he never entirely explained it. He only noted in his autobiography that over the two years at Goshen he had nearly managed to free himself from debt and that his father, who had accepted his academic aspirations and had "implicit faith in my judgment as to what was best for me," agreed to bankroll further study. Nonetheless, he quickly made plans to head back to Chicago and place himself in the hands of the eminent historians there. From them, he knew, he would receive the thorough, up-to-date training in the writing of scientific history. Other developments would occur in his final years at Chicago that he could not have anticipated. The lofty achievement of a PhD, however, was a goal he could measure. It would be the final step, he thought, to becoming a totally objective historian on behalf of his Mennonite people and in the service of a usable past.[1]

The Great Dream of Objectivity

Smith had scarcely been back at Goshen for a year when, in October 1904, he began writing his old professor Jameson, then still at Chicago, angling for a fellowship in the doctoral program. Without one, he told Jameson, he could not hope to come back to school, at least for several more years. He spelled out his intentions plainly: "The field I wish to work up for my thesis is Mennonite history," with a particular focus on Anabaptist origins in Europe. He would arrive at Chicago thoroughly prepared to do serious work, he persuaded Jameson. He laid out his preliminary research in Funk's library and his plans for future research in Pennsylvania, promising to send along a list of all of Funk's books in case Jameson might find some "in which you might personally be interested." In the meantime, he told Jameson, he had enclosed in the letter various articles on both Mennonite history and himself that he had clipped out from Mennonite periodicals. He hoped these would demonstrate the interest the wider church had in his research and also support his contention that the field was "profitable" and "in many respects a new one." Furthermore, he had the necessary languages: "I have a fair command of German and am getting the Dutch." Finally, Smith seemed to be in his usual hurry with regard to the normal academic expectations. In a certain chutzpah that displayed few traces of an Amish-derived inferiority complex, he proposed to Jameson that he would simply skip most of the university's standard requirements and head straight to Amsterdam for research, though pledging to come back to Chicago for niceties like classes "later on."[2]

While it may have taken Jameson a few moments to recover from the last part of Smith's proposal, he moved almost immediately to lower his student's horizons a bit. Within a week Smith was responding to a reply from his professor with the hasty admission that "I should be glad to spend a year at Chicago first before going to Europe." Jameson also seemed to have redirected Smith's initial research gaze from Anabaptist origins in Europe to the history of Mennonites in Indiana. Yet Smith's subsequent letters suggest that other aspects had struck a favorable nerve with his old professor. At this point in his academic career, coincidentally, Jameson had begun to evince a new interest in American religious history. In 1905 he would push the Carnegie Institute to fund the research of a Wisconsin professor in the Vatican archives. His presidential address before the American Historical Association in 1907 dealt in part with the impact of religious figures on the national character. A decade later, though not a Catholic, he would be instrumental in helping to found the *Catholic Historical Review*. Smith's proposal to develop the new scholarly subfield of Mennonite history may have appealed to him. Moreover, Smith had been careful to speak the new language of scientific history in direct and alluring ways. Both at Chicago and at the University of Illinois, he claimed, he had "had good training in historical research . . . to get at the facts and present them in an unprejudiced manner." Altogether, writes the historian Keith Sprunger, Smith had "already imagined himself writing the University-of-Chicago version of Mennonite history. It would be progressive, open-minded, libertarian and intellectual."[3]

At any rate, Smith moved Jameson enough to win his acceptance as one of his doctoral students. Within a few weeks after he arrived on campus that fall, he had so thoroughly impressed listeners at a meeting of the history club with a paper he presented from his initial research at Funk's library that he was promptly elected president of the organization. Better yet, the following April, upon the recommendation of the history department and signed by President Judson, he received official notification that the university was granting him a fellowship for the munificent sum (for 1906) of $320.[4]

By September 1905, Smith had moved back from Goshen to Chicago, settling into Snell Hall, which since 1902 had served as the unofficial home for the campus YMCA. Already marked as one of the leading comers in the new crop of history grad students and now thirty years old, Smith seems to have ignored most of the hall's social activities: the first-year initiations on Halloween, the water fights, and the late-night bull sessions (though he did serve on the house "standing committee for auditing" in 1905–6, took part in the hall's annual tennis contest, and successfully auditioned for a spot in the university's choir). Mostly he focused on his classes and the demands of his fellowship with his usual scholarly energy.[5]

Through Smith's courses and his hours with his professors, he likewise absorbed the cutting-edge methodological approach then permeating the nation's history departments. At Chicago Smith was thoroughly inculcated in what the historian Peter Novick has notably called the "noble dream" of objectivity. Like nearly all other academic disciplines, history had been deeply reshaped by the intellectual triumph of the scientific revolution. As scientific approaches gained near-universal acceptance as the ultimate method of establishing the validity of knowledge, the new discipline of history established its validity by incorporating them, especially as pioneered by the historicist school of thinking coming across the Atlantic from Germany with the historian Leopold von Ranke and his disciples. Their eager acceptance of scientific history meant that, as summarized by two scholars, historians believed "in using a rigorously empirical method of investigation and in attempting to discern the chains of cause and effect in accounting for specific historical events." This could only occur, the thinking went, by scholars thoroughly emptying their heads of prior biases and achieving total objectivity. Thus prepared, they were ready to commence the arranging and rearranging of the facts they had uncovered through their painstaking research into the primary documents of the past. Only through such methods could they truly understand, in Ranke's magical phrase, "how things really happened." The esteemed Herbert Baxter Adams was so enamored of the scientific method that he moved his graduate history seminars at Johns Hopkins into an old biology lab, where his grad students—including at one point Jameson and a fellow classmate, an erudite and promising southern chap named Woodrow Wilson—examined old government documents on converted dissection tables.[6]

Beginning in the later nineteenth century and well into the new one, the same passion for scientific objectivity thoroughly captivated the history department at the University of Chicago. Department chair Jameson was one of its leading exponents in the country. After his departure in 1905, the direction of Smith's thesis and the rest of his graduate program passed into the hands of the legal scholar McLaughlin, who, upon his arrival in 1906, seems to have inherited many of Jameson's grad students. This was, for Smith, probably a fortunate development. So popular was McLaughlin among his students that they privately endowed him with the affectionate nickname of "Andy Mac"; Smith remembered him decades later as "extremely democratic and approachable, always willing to help. Most of my work was under his sympathetic direction." Smith graded undergraduate papers for McLaughlin and soaked in his teaching on topics ranging from the early colonies to the American Revolution, along with a heavy dose of McLaughlin's specialty, U.S. constitutional history, which displayed a deep commitment to the party of Lincoln and the political stances of liberal republicanism. Through such vehicles Smith clearly absorbed a great deal of his mentor's worldview and methodology. McLaughlin was absolutely devoted to scientific objectivity. "History is not written or taught for the purpose of inculcating any particular moral or immoral lesson," he would write in 1916. "Careful, accurate, truthful examination of historical facts and evidences is a virtue in itself."[7]

The intellectual historian Eileen Ka-May Cheng has recently offered a thoughtful rebuttal to prevailing accounts of the supposedly pure-and-simple objectivity of this founding generation of American historians. Scholars like Jameson and his colleagues, she argues, may have displayed a greater subtlety in their thought than people like Novick have accorded them. For instance, the summary report of a special "Committee of Seven" (one of which was McLaughlin) to the American Historical Association in 1897 did stress the importance of empirical objectivity. But it also included the use of political problems, current events, moral values, and other humanistic approaches to history as integral to any high school curriculum. On the other hand, McLaughlin seems to have never fully addressed the intellectual contradiction between his devotion to objectivity, on the one hand, and his political commitments, on the other. James Buchanan's biographer, Philip Klein, who studied under McLaughlin at Chicago in the later 1920s, found him so favorably inclined toward partisan republicanism in his teaching that "one could think he was a politician rather than a historian." He'd take a controversial subject, Klein remembered later, "talk a bit and say, 'Who is to judge? Who is to judge?' Well, the answer was, *he* was to judge [italics in the original]." McLaughlin never tried to be fair to historical figures like antebellum democrats and slaveholders, Klein remembered, or attempted to understand them in their historic context. The major thing Klein recalled McLaughlin teaching him was that "it's possible for a very famous man to be so biased it's hard to call him a historian." One wonders if all of McLaughlin's grad students were as discerning as Klein. Willard Smith took summer classes at the University of Chicago in the early 1930s, including particular classes in historiography and methodology under professor Marcus Jernegan. Professor Jernegan, Willard Smith discovered, had likewise done his doctorate at Chicago in the first years of the twentieth century and remembered his uncle Henry well from their years together as grad students. Jernegan, Willard recalled, taught them a consummate dedication to the pursuit of objective truth. While Jernegan recognized that human limitations rendered them unable ever fully to grasp the ideal, objectivity remained the goal supreme. "You can't believe anything strongly," he catechized, "and be a good historian."[8]

There seems little doubt that C. Henry Smith grasped the basic lesson well, but maybe not its internal tensions. He began his doctoral studies already committed to objectivity, and all that happened to him at Chicago seems to have reinforced it. He would do a capable job writing Mennonite history, he told Jameson, because "I am not prejudiced either way." In his treatment of the American Mennonite story, he wrote in 1909 in the introduction to his first book, "I have tried to be impartial to the various branches of the church." By 1925 he was expressing the concept more poetically, comparing the "process of chasing down isolated facts" to something akin to a scholarly hunting expedition. "To me the pleasure of running down an elusive fact," he rhapsodized, "was as great as capturing of big game to the hunter." As late as the eve of World War II, as he gently tried to dissuade two elderly Mennonite missionaries from their devotion to the Waldensian origins of Anabaptism, he recognized the importance of tradition but built his case from evidence. In the end, it was Smith's immersion in the great dream of objectivity, with all its capacity to both inspire historians and beguile them, which marked his scholarly career, for good and for ill. He had perhaps learned more from McLaughlin than he knew.[9]

Chicago historians also schooled Smith in several other aspects of the dominant intellectual currents of their discipline, themes that registered a similarly enduring impact on his thought. Darwinian notions were accepted as a matter of course, as were the exciting new ideas put forth in 1893 by the Wisconsin historian Frederick Jackson Turner on the significance of the frontier on American history. Smith proved an ardent student. "In the extension of the frontier of the country, history has been constantly repeating itself," he informed the Elkhart County Historical Society sometime in his Goshen years. Turner and other Progressive Era "New Historians" readily pled guilty to a contemporaneous orientation, openly dedicating themselves to provide for reformers a politically serviceable and usable past. Smith would devote his career to a like project for Mennonites. Reflecting the strong currents of American nationalism sweeping through the nation's intellectual life at the turn of the century, American history had become the central focus of the emerging American historical profession. Jameson's immediate redirection of the main focus of Smith's scholarship from European to American Mennonitism is a perfect example of this academic predilection. In like manner, in line with the intellectual needs and bearing of the Progressive Era, Jameson and the other leaders of the profession were glad to harness their discipline to the civic needs of the country, not so much in the inculcation of mindless patriotism (at least, before World War I) but in teaching students how history could help solve social problems. Smith's popular writings would be similarly full of practical moral lessons, and he would devote much energy toward preparing his Mennonite students for the civic duties required to function as fully as American citizens as their Mennonite commitments would allow. Finally, scholars like McLaughlin helped to socialize their graduate students into the workaday behavior expected in the discipline, not only in prosaic matters like the long hours of on-the-job training grading papers but also in modeling appropriate conduct for the emerging new profession of history. Smith, for instance, worked to rearrange his Christmas plans of 1907 around the annual meeting of the American Historical Association, then gathering in Madison, Wisconsin.[10]

In these and so many other ways, both Smith's understanding of how to function as a historian and his larger worldview were deeply shaped by his academic training at Chicago. What did not change was his all-consuming haste to jump ahead. Even before he finished his doctorate, he had begun to apply much of what he had learned to his writing of Mennonite history. The ensuing lessons would soon reverberate across the church.

Mennonites as Pioneers in the "Onward Rush of Civilization"

When Smith began writing North American Mennonite history as a grad student at Chicago, his scholarly trail had already been paved by many predecessors. Despite their general distrust of education, through the past two centuries various Mennonites, mostly preachers, had been writing about their shared past, some with more ability than others. An early bishop named Jacob Gottschalk had penned a preliminary sketch of the history of Pennsylvania Mennonites as early as 1712. The pace of Mennonite history writing accelerated in the years after the Civil War. In 1888 a self-taught deacon at the historic Germantown congregation named Daniel Cassel published the first major work on the subject, his

History of the Mennonites. While uneven in its content and riddled with errors, Cassel's work was at least an advance over existing works, most of which served as apologetics in service to one party or another in various church schisms. By Cassel's time German Mennonite scholars were heavily interested in Anabaptist history, and some of this work had begun to include short surveys of the experience of the Anabaptist descendants in North America. Henry P. Krehbiel produced the *History of the General Conference of Mennonites of North America* in 1898, but the most notable work along this line was the extensive and polished Mennonite historical writing of Cornelius H. Wedel, a major leader of Kansas Mennonites at the turn of the century and a longtime president of Bethel College. Well trained in the writing of scientific history from his postgraduate education in a Presbyterian seminary, Wedel was a capable scholar. In his four-volume history of the Mennonites from early Anabaptism to the present day, his commitment to objectivity led him to be quite critical at times of his Mennonite people for their spiritual lethargy and excessive legalism. At the same time, however, like most other extant books in Mennonite history by the turn of the century, Wedel's work shared two characteristics that curtailed its utility to an acculturating people interested in a usable past. First, the great portion of his interest focused on European developments. Only eighty pages of his four volumes concerned the Mennonite experience in North America. Second, as with most of these other books, Wedel wrote only in German, which diminished the accessibility of his work to the large number of Mennonites east of the Mississippi who had largely shifted to English.[11]

Thus, the body of extant historical work was plainly inadequate for the church of Smith's day. Smith was quite aware of the limitations of the available corpus of published work on Mennonite history, and in a scarcely masked advertisement for himself, he announced his ability to address them. "What we need is some one [sic] with proper training in history," he told the church in 1905, "a mind unprejudiced either for or against, plenty of time, a command of the necessary foreign languages, and a sufficient interest and faith in his work to gather all this information and present it in a connected story to the public." This bold deviation from the humility ethic was likely prompted by the recent appearance of a general history of the church that eastern

Mennonites read in large numbers. Bible expositor Kauffman and Goshen College secretary and part-time instructor J. S. Hartzler had put together their *Mennonite Church History* and published it with Kauffman's Mennonite publishing house in Scottdale, Pennsylvania. The significance of such competitor books was apparent even in parlor conversation back home in Illinois. "I was glad when I read in Ella's letter that perhaps you would not go to Holland," his sister Emma wrote him. "Pa would feel a whole lot better. It has worried him a great deal. . . . He said if you would only give it up so you had better give it up." Undoubtedly such lines worried Henry Smith. Both he and Emma were well aware of the source of financial power in the family. "You know plenty without going out there [to Holland]," Emma pointed out, "and Pa said you would not make so much money on that book because there are so many different ones out already."[12]

But Smith had no intention of giving up; instead he threw himself into his research with intensity. Even as he met the demands of his classes, he worked steadily at it. He learned what he could of the larger sociohistorical background inhabited by colonial Mennonites by poring over books in the university libraries. He gathered more data through a steady stream of correspondence from informants across the Mennonite landscape. From such people came not only the elusive facts he so diligently hunted but also the faint outlines of larger conceptual schemes that would later appear, in more polished form, in his writing. In 1904, for example, an elderly correspondent named Simon Baechler wrote him to relay what he remembered of the origins of the Flanagan and Meadows congregations in central Illinois. Describing himself as "the only surviving preacher that helped to organize those churches," Baechler remembered the years shortly after the end of the Civil War, when "there was a spirit of division in the Mennonite Church." He classified the emerging camps as "the *old school* or *conservatifs* and the *liberals* or *Progressifs* [italics in the original]." Joseph Stuckey came around to help organize the liberals, he summarized, and eventually these two Central Conference congregations emerged. "God moves in a mistarious way his wonders to perform," Baechler told Smith. From a woman in West Liberty, Ohio, Smith learned of the beginnings of a congregation in Moultrie County, Illinois. Her parents came there to rent land in 1883, Amanda Troyer recalled in 1907. Mennonite preachers periodically visited to hold communion services and perform baptisms. Gradually a congregation grew, and had just organized its first Sunday school by the previous spring. There was another reason for the new congregation, Troyer admitted. Her family wanted "more spiritual freedom and liberty as the old order people are very formal, strict in their teaching, and have some very queer ideas." Smith diligently filed such notes away for later consultation.[13]

In the summer of 1906, Smith managed to get away for his first extensive research trip, sifting through Mennonite records in the Shenandoah Valley of Virginia and the densely populated Mennonite and Amish settlement in Lancaster County, Pennsylvania. Funk had done his best to pave his entrée into such places, furnishing a letter that endorsed his research and that Smith undoubtedly carried with him. Even so, Smith quickly discovered he would not find abundant information. Because of deep patterns of separation and a suspicion of outside society inherited from the persecution of Anabaptist ancestors centuries before, Mennonites had not kept well-tended church records. From accounts published by the Pennsylvania German Society, he picked up bits of scattered data. He made good use of family and county histories and of colonial records in the Pennsylvania State Archives in Harrisburg and Philadelphia before proceeding to New York. In the Shenandoah Valley, he managed to charm a prominent local attorney and former Confederate general named John Roller enough to gain access to his personal library. The collection, which Smith thought might have been the most extensive collection of books on Pennsylvania German history in the entire nation, proved largely void of useful information on Mennonites. Even so, by the time he judged his research to be mostly finished, he found that altogether he had accumulated an abundance of data beyond what he needed to finish his thesis. He carefully kept much of it in reserve for the production of the "complete history of the Mennonites in America" he had promised.[14]

Before Smith finished grad school, his dedicated historical spadework began to produce results for the church, starting in 1905. It quickly became evident that, despite all the attention it garnered and its definitive, all-encompassing title, Hartzler and Kauffman's big book on *Mennonite Church History* of that year was fundamentally lacking as a general history of the church. Four years later Smith airily dismissed it, along with Cassel's book, as not "trustworthy" except in regard to recent events. Even in its treatment of recent history, it was suspect. Hartzler was an able administrator and Kauffman a rising power in the church, but neither was a real scholar. They focused almost all of their attention on the MC Mennonites because they were "the original body of Mennonites who retained their organization" since arriving in America. Not that the founding of the General Conference church did not provide useful lessons. Its founder, John Oberholtzer, they said, possessed some admirable qualities, especially his passion for church union and his "aggressiveness." It was merely unfortunate that he also "manifested a self-will and lack of consideration for the judgment of his brethren," which—in lines that were indubitably Kauffman's—did not allow for the emergence of "an aggressive conservatism which would have proven a power in the development of the church." Figuring out the authorship of key parts involved some guesswork, because neither author had written large chunks of their book. From their introduction it was clear that Kauffman and Hartzler had asked MC Mennonite district conferences to write their own histories, and that they had just included these chapters under the names of their authors. Smith himself had contributed a chapter of his own on developments among European Mennonites after the immediate waves of Anabaptist persecution had ended.[15]

Perhaps it escaped Kauffman's editorial purview, or it may have been that, in 1905, doctrinal lines had not yet entirely calcified. Either way, a careful reading of Smith's analysis in Kauffman's book reveals patterns of thought that the latter would find unacceptable just a few years hence. To be sure, in some ways Smith helped set the tone and framework for much of the bedrock historical writing that would emerge in the Mennonite Church over the coming decades. For example, he quickly wrote the debacle at Münster, where a fanatical wing of Anabaptists attempted with violent force to set up a theocratic state, out of the main current of the Mennonite historical narrative. He also emphasized the central historical importance of the Schleitheim Confession, reducing it to three central principles: an acceptance of adult baptism, a rejection of the sword, and the necessity for Christian withdrawal from the world. These three principles, he said, still composed the "essence of Mennonitism." Other aspects of Smith's analysis, however, seemed to break entirely new conceptual ground. The religious toleration ultimately granted to the Dutch church did not come, he said, as an unabashed boon. "Worldliness" soon set in: many Dutch Mennonites grew wealthy; some married outsiders and left the faith. The remaining Dutch Mennonites soon realized they needed an educated Mennonite ministry. The lesson here seemed to be that "a church without educated leaders could not hold its own in a progressive age." In an American Mennonite church still largely led by lay pastors, many of whom were proud of the fact they had been selected by the lot and suspicious of a "hireling ministry," bold declarations like this would have been controversial.[16]

More provocative still was Smith's sketch of church governance. Stemming back to their earliest days, Smith wrote, "the system of church discipline among the Mennonites was congregational." The hierarchical church structures Kauffman was then busily constructing were, Smith gently suggested, not consistent with the Mennonite historical tradition; in its founding, their church lacked a strong central leadership and left most decisions to individual churches. "Consequently," he wrote, "the history of the church is almost entirely a history of separate congregations." The faint but still discernible implication, perhaps, was that the General Conference Mennonites, without bishops but with their strong congregational polity, had it right.[17]

An even more important early statement of Smith's on Mennonite history came in June 1906 in a major address he gave at the important GC Mennonite congregation First Mennonite Church of Philadelphia, undoubtedly as he passed through the city on his research trip. He made such a hit that night that his address caught the eye of Kauffman, who promptly printed it in serial form in his new church organ, the *Gospel Witness*, and then published it as a separate pamphlet for wide dissemination across the Mennonite Church. Similarly favorable mention in the GC denominational organ, the *Mennonite*, certainly drew the attention of many General Conference Mennonites, as well. With that kind of extended audience, the address functioned for Smith as something of an official, scholarly coming-out. As Robert Kreider would observe almost a century later, it was "the inaugural address of an historian," and one marked by a "brash, youthful, confident spirit." The tone fit the content of the address perfectly. He spoke that night, Smith informed the audience, on the subject of "the Mennonites in History," by which he meant to offer not a distillation of Mennonite history but to explore their significance in history. As he proceeded, it quickly became clear that he would offer his church nothing less than a grand and exciting usable past.[18]

Kreider was right: Smith was self-assured and maybe even a bit brash that evening. He exhibited these qualities in the first minutes of his address, moving immediately to demolish a theory of Anabaptist origins that many Mennonites had treasured for centuries. This was the comforting hypothesis that Anabaptists had taken the heart of their teaching from the Waldenses, who in turn had received it from numerous medieval sects, who themselves had received the teaching from other groups in a direct chain of thought stemming back to Christ's apostles. Coffman had apparently accepted the theory, as referenced in his momentous "Spirit of Progress" address. So had Hartzler and Kauffman; the first part of their writing on Anabaptism plainly built from such ideas. In Smith's chapter in their book, as he carved out a moderate path in the historiography, he had preferred to remain ambiguous about them. "The enemies of the church confound them with the Münsterites," he had explained in 1905, while "the friends go to another extreme and trace them exclusively to the Waldenses. The truth is, that the 'brethren' as they called themselves, many of whom were the descendants of the ancient Waldenses, and having largely of the faith of that body of people, were reorganized by Menno." In Philadelphia, now a year later, Smith's ambiguity was gone, torpedoed by his scientific commitment to empiricism. He definitively declared that "this hypothesis, beautiful in theory, is still nothing but a theory, and there is very little evidence to substantiate its claims." In this address, Smith instead located the origins of Anabaptism in Zurich with Swiss radicals like Conrad Grebel and Felix Manz, years before scholars like John Horsch and Harold S. Bender made such ideas *de rigueur* for the Mennonite Church. (Bender would later do much with such concepts, but at that point in 1906 he was about eight years old).[19]

The major part of Smith's address—and surely the reason for its widespread appeal—was the way it set up the Mennonites as no longer an obscure people at the margins of their society but as the founders of key religious and intellectual developments in the entire history of Western civilization. He accomplished this end through his development of three major points. First, he claimed for his people the title of the great trailblazers of the principle of religious liberty. "The Mennonites alone are the actual lineal descendants" of the original Swiss Anabaptists, he asserted, though other Christian traditions may lay legitimate claim to Menno as their spiritual founder. Skillfully Smith inter-knit his tradition into the popular iconography of American civil religion. The "little band of Mayflower colonists has been lauded to the skies," he pointed out; "Plymouth Rock has become immortal." But the Anabaptist dedication to liberty of conscience preceded that of the Mayflower migrants by a century, and clearly inspired the legendary Pilgrims. Their ancestors, Smith told his Mennonite audience, "antedate the Puritan, the Baptist, the Quaker and all the other agents that did so much to secure the free play of conscience upon English and American soil. None of these agents have made a single addition to Mennonite doctrine on this subject, and none have suffered more than Mennonites for the sake of conscience." Of course, they still waited the "final victory" of the idea, he admitted, but, reflecting the optimism of the times, he never doubted such progress would finally arrive within the course of human history.[20]

Second, Smith asserted, "in still another way must the Mennonites be considered as pioneers—that for the total abolition of warfare between Christian nations." Jesus had taught this ideal and it had permeated the early church until the "great calamity" wrought by the emperor Constantine. After his lamentable embrace of the sword, the church degenerated into "a fighting church." Yet fidelity to Christ's true teaching endured, he informed his audience, preeminently among their Anabaptist ancestors. Indeed, the Mennonite church was "the mother of all modern peace societies." Proper credit also belonged to the Quakers, he added, though George Fox was deeply familiar with Mennonite teaching and thus Quakers and Mennonites were "closely and vitally connected. In America they ran the same course," fighting "side by side" for freedom from military service (though, Smith admitted, the "more passive" Mennonites "allowed the Quakers to do most of the fighting"). All other Christian peace groups subsequently built on this Mennonite and Quaker foundation, thereby preserving this basic Christian message to the present day, when, he proclaimed, they may be finally witnessing the dawn of "the reign of universal peace." The signs were all around them, he told his audience with exuberant progressive optimism. They were seen in the increasing economic disincentives for war, in the growth of peace societies, and in the 1898 Hague Peace Conference. It all proved that the Mennonite peace position "is sound and that their ideal is gradually becoming a reality."[21]

There was yet, he continued, a third "and more obvious sense in which the Mennonites have been pioneers in the onward rush of civilization." They had been literal pioneers in whatever places where their loyalty to their faith had led them. Such pioneering had occurred in their early eighteenth-century migration from Switzerland to Prussia, in their subsequent migration from Prussia to southeastern Russia, and especially in their transatlantic trek from western Europe and Ukraine to the American frontier. Smith simply translated Frederick Jackson Turner into a Mennonite idiom. In the history of their country, he informed his audience, the Mennonites had always been located in "the front ranks of pioneers" and "among the earliest settlers" on the outward edge of the frontier. Moreover, "just as the westward expansion of civilization has kept the race young and hopeful," it had worked the same effects among Mennonites. In fact, Smith seemed poised to do Turner one better. The frontier, Turner had said, was the incubator of democracy, of instinctive American individualism, and of the power of common people. But centuries before there was an American frontier, Smith noted, the faith of the Anabaptists "was that of the common man." The followers of Menno may not have been big theologians, Smith reasoned, but they knew the Scriptures by heart and refused to get caught up with doctrinal disputes. This is why, "in creed and dogma, they have been the most liberal of denominations" and had been "able to live out the plain commands of the Master more consistently than those higher in station."[22]

Having sketched out such a stirring past, Smith did not hesitate to draw out its implications for Mennonites in the present. He closed his address with an emphatic call to action. Lest someone think he had "unduly magnified the position which our forefathers occupied in history," Smith hastened to assure the crowd that he had remained true to his scientific training as an objective historian. "I have tried to confine myself to the realm of fact," he maintained, "and do not think I have colored the picture too highly." In fact, they did their heritage a disservice if "we were to deliberately close our eyes to our past mistakes." He could identify two of them. For one, the persecution in centuries past had often rendered Mennonites too passive in the present, too willing to allow allies like the Quakers to exert a much greater influence on society. "The nonresistant spirit has frequently become an unaggressive spirit," he concluded. It was high time for the Mennonite church to "embrace a more *positive* nonresistance [italics in the original]" and project the lessons of their tradition outward into a society that so desperately needed them. A second "source of weakness," Smith continued, has been the Mennonites' historic hostility to higher education. He was eager to see the Mennonite church recover its lost influence and power. But this could only happen, he informed the church, by overcoming their "lack of self-confidence," by embracing higher education, and most of all by learning their true history. It was only 1906. Smith had just turned thirty-one years old. He remained a bachelor, still in grad school, as yet unsure as to where his career would take him. But he had nonetheless managed to set the agenda that would draw his best energies for all his remaining years.[23]

"The Finest Brown Eyes I Have Ever Seen"

It was inevitable, perhaps, that in Smith's increasing habitation of the realm of high ideas, he would leave the world of farm and family further and further behind. The old home place itself had changed locations in his absence. In November 1899, almost two years after Magdalena's death, John Smith had surprised his children, now mostly grown, by suddenly wooing and marrying an area widow named Lydia Albrecht, thereby becoming a stepfather to her eleven-year-old daughter, Agnes. Shortly afterward the new family had moved to a farmstead a half mile farther west toward town on the Metamora Stage Road. Henry Smith still maintained ties with home, returning periodically for visits of up to a week and participating in the familiar routines of chores and church. In her diary entries for July 1907, for instance, Agnes Albrecht, by then a teenager, noted that Henry had helped her with the wash and the next day had enjoyed dinner at the home of his older brother Sam. In May 1906 he had gone with the family to church for a Bible meeting and apparently afterward had delivered an impromptu lecture on Mennonite history. The following September he was back in the community with camera in hand to photograph an old church.[24]

Sometimes the value that Henry placed on familial bonds seemed to surprise his family. In a letter to his father, for example, Smith apparently confessed he had missed the doings at home. "I did not think that you get lonesome for home because you are gone so much," John Smith replied. Already by the time of Henry's high school years his family had struggled to understand him. The gap would have widened to Grand Canyon dimensions when he returned home from graduate school. Perhaps as late as May 1902, as Henry finished up at the University of Illinois and made plans to start after his MA in history at Chicago, his father reported on a conversation he had enjoyed recently with a local school superintendent, still believing his son was interested in returning to Woodford County to teach rural school. There "would be a chance for you with other applicants," the elder Smith had written happily. "So please let us know whether you would take that school if you could get it." Paul Whitmer once visited the Smith family home near Metamora about the time when Henry Smith was finishing up his doctorate. The elder Smith found a moment to pull Whitmer aside to beg his frank assessment. Tell me, John Smith inquired, "do you think Henry will ever amount to anything?" Just "give him a little more time," Whitmer assured. "I think he will." Undoubtedly Henry's siblings found their scholarly brother equally hard to fathom. "You said you didn't like your board very well," Sam Smith wrote him in the autumn of 1905, responding to complaints Henry had apparently voiced about his lodging at Snell Hall. "Well you better come home and help us shuck corn and we will give you good board and believe it would do you some good for a change. We have about 50 acres to shuck."[25]

The emotional and cultural distance between C. Henry Smith and his family would have suddenly and dramatically widened in July 1906, as he worked away at his research in Mennonite history. He had traveled from Philadelphia to New York City to look into some old church records he had heard were there. The whole few days he worked there in New York, however, buried deep in the public library, he "was possessed with a spirit of restlessness" and a powerful longing to return to Philadelphia that he could not understand. When he did make it back to Philadelphia, he found waiting for him a telegram from his older brother Joe, informing him that his father had suddenly died. John Smith was only sixty-three and had experienced, the coroner determined later, a heart attack. "In apparent robust health and with no warning his end was near," a local paper summarized later. He had felt some pains in his chest that day, but had eaten a good meal and gone to bed before suddenly experiencing a shortness of breath and dying at about 9:00 p.m. The Smith family had delayed the funeral, frantically contacting the press and even the police in trying to find Henry. He rushed home and arrived midweek on the night train from Chicago, having missed, the day before, the largest funeral in the history of Woodford County. Sixteen hundred people had solemnly filed past his father's body.[26]

Before heading east again, Smith spent a day morosely traipsing around in search of his old boyhood haunts and finding few of them. "Everywhere there was evidence of improved farming," he recalled later. Land prices had shot further upward, inducing local farmers to remove even more of the old woodlots along Partridge Creek, tear down old structures, and drain more of their fields, thus eradicating the small streams and all their wildlife that had so charmed him as a boy. Smith found it entirely unsettling. Afterward "my visits back would become increasingly brief and rare." His brothers noted the growing distance as well, and worried about it. "I am just a little afraid about your going to school so long," Sam confessed to him the next spring. "You know there is danger of knowing too much for our own good . . . I want you never to leave the plain teaching of the Bible." He offered Henry a job, still thinking it would be good for him to come home and shuck corn. Older brother Joe was similarly concerned. In the spring of 1906, he visited Henry in Chicago, taking in the university and spending time with him in his tiny room in Snell Hall. Before leaving, Joe suddenly pulled out his wallet and handed his brother a five-dollar bill. "Not that I needed the money particularly," Smith wrote later, "but it was his way of expressing his sympathy for me because of the dreary life he thought I was leading."[27]

Henry Smith, however, did not find life in Chicago dreary at all. In fact, he rather liked it. The "only thing" that can "be said in favor of a great big city," he informed a friend back in rural Illinois in 1908, is that "a man can do absolutely as he pleases and nobody is any the wiser." In the anonymity of the big city, Smith began to do absolutely as he pleased with increasing frequency. His friend Steiner could issue all the blistering denunciations he wanted to about the lurid evils of the theater (in such places, Steiner warned, the mind ran "unrestrained toward the goal of moral corruption"). Smith liked to think for himself, however, and discovered that such places were fun. He began to make regular excursions to the theater district and the grand opera house downtown, where "I heard all the great stars, both European and American, in the operatic world." He also took in epic performances of the great legends of American theater—Ethel Barrymore, Julia Marlowe, David Warfield, and others—in the last golden age before the coming of the movies. He did remain enough of a Mennonite country boy to be periodically uncomfortable. For instance, during his year teaching high school in Indianapolis in 1907–8, he wandered downtown one winter afternoon with nothing to do, and a passing friend talked him into attending a play that ended with the heroine shooting her sister and husband in the full glare of the floodlights. Smith immediately regretted going. The play was "full of crime and wickedness," he admitted a short time later. "There is really no excuse for anything like it on the stage." After that, he pledged, he would confine his theatergoing to "grand or light opera." Still, he was aware of the change that had come over him. He took a wicked pleasure in watching rural folk come into the city for the first time and try to decipher a restaurant menu "with a lot of foreign names." "I ought not to make fun of my own tribe," he confessed to a friend, "but it really is amusing." He saw a couple of farmers recently, he said, who reminded him of a younger version of himself.[28]

No doubt the Amish farm boy Henry Smith would have been secretly thrilled if a crystal ball could have somehow revealed to him the dashing, sophisticated man-about-town he would become. In Chicago the urbane C. Henry met up with a medical school intern and one-time Elkhart Institute student named Orie Yoder. The two quickly became fast friends. Among Smith's effects is a photo taken of the two of them from about this time, Yoder seated and Smith behind with his hand on Yoder's shoulder, both clad in high collars, sharp ties, and smart bowler hats. Nearly every evening of Smith's last two years in Chicago, the two would head out, presumably similarly attired, for long strolls in

"Orie Yoder and Me." Smith (right) *and his friend Orie Yoder, Chicago, 1907–08. BUASC.*

Jackson Park along the Lake Michigan lakefront, "discussing our mutual friends," he recalled in 1925, "or planning our careers." Among those shared associates they discussed together was a rural schoolteacher Yoder knew downstate. She had, Yoder insisted to Smith, "the finest brown eyes I have ever seen." And in the lovely Chicago springtime in March 1908, Yoder set into motion a chain of events that would bring their days of bachelor bonhomie to their natural end.[29]

Laura Ioder, Yoder doubtlessly told Smith, was smart, educated, and beautiful, but for Smith one of her most attractive qualities would certainly have been her lineage. Like him, she was a thoroughbred Mennonite. Her father, William Ioder, was the son of Amish Mennonite immigrants from Bavaria who had settled near the small hamlet of Tiskilwa in rural Bureau County, Illinois. Her mother, Fannie Stauffer Ioder, had been born to Amish parents in Alsace, France, and had migrated with them to Bureau County as a child. Both families had been instrumental in the founding of the budding Amish Mennonite Willow Springs congregation in the countryside four miles from Tiskilwa. From the beginning, the congregation had experienced trouble with certain members who had bucked against Amish dress restrictions, but at the same time showed an openness to other cultural innovations. In 1873 they erected their first meetinghouse, and in the 1880s made the important shifts to Sunday schools and English in their worship services. They also forged warm and productive ties with the nascent ecclesiastical structures of the emerging Western District Conference of the Amish Mennonite church, hosting, among other visiting speakers, Bishop John Smith from Metamora in 1892. William Ioder seems to have been a faithful member, but devoted the bulk of his attention to matters of family and farm, both of which flourished. He began his life as an adult with the inheritance of a 160-acre farm. By 1885 he had expanded it to nearly six hundred acres through financial acumen and general industriousness, gaining a local reputation as an expert stock-raiser with an eye for fine horses. "Financially," summarized a local historian in 1885, "Mr. Ioder has been a very successful man." He also did not allow possible church sanctions to limit his participation in community affairs, serving in several minor political offices and openly associating with the county Democratic Party. Nearly a century after his death, his granddaughter could still recall stories of his faithfulness to his church and his generosity to the poor. The Ioders, Elaine Bowers said, were "interesting, gentle, kind and gracious people. . . . They were people who lived what they believed and taught their children." They also shared an additional quality. "All the Ioders had eyes," she recalled, "dark, shiny, pretty eyes."[30]

William Ioder and Fannie Stauffer married in 1873 and proceeded to have children, nine in all, seven of whom survived to adulthood. In 1901 they augmented their family further by adopting an orphaned toddler named Margaret Yarrington. Laura Louise was born in 1880, exactly in the middle, with three older brothers and four younger sisters. They all grew up together on the expansive Ioder farm three miles east of Tiskilwa, all of them, their parents made sure, graduating from Tiskilwa High School,

Laura Ioder, 1904. BUASC.

making the six-mile round trip daily on horseback. Laura taught rural school for three years after graduation. Then she took what would have been, for a Mennonite farm woman at the turn of the century, a bold and remarkable step: she went to college. She completed two years at Knox College, not far away in Galesburg, Illinois, before returning home to Bureau County to set out on her own, teaching primary grades in Wyanet, Illinois, a dozen miles from home. According to the *Bureau County Tribune*, Laura Ioder was "one of Tiskilwa's well and favorably known young ladies, having a large circle of friends in this community." Her niece Elaine Burress Bowers recalled her as a kind and "sophisticated" woman who was educated, well-traveled, and who "liked all the nicer things in life." She had a beautiful singing voice and was a great cook. In later days, in her annual visits back to Bureau County as an older woman, "it was like the princess came home. . . . You always put out your best dishes." The young schoolteacher who Smith began to court, however, sometimes pushed up against the edges of acceptable domesticity. She could handle her father's fine horses and liked to go fishing for catfish with male friends even after she was engaged. When Smith once described to her with careless jocularity how a male friend of his foolishly allowed himself to "be led around by a girl," she reminded him sharply of how it looked from a woman's perspective, "how a girl will leave her home and family and all that is so dear to her and go with the one she loves to the end of the earth, if need be." After one of Smith's visits to Bureau County as their courtship deepened, a friend of hers casually said, "Laura, if you ever marry Mr. Smith you will have to polish up a little." "I told her," Laura relayed to Smith pointedly, "that if Mr. Smith ever marries me he will take me just as I am."[31]

The actual circumstances of their first encounter are lost to history. In September 1907, writing in the rapturous bliss of a man whose beloved had just accepted his marriage proposal, Smith referred to their "chance meeting" in Chicago the previous spring. He had heard Laura would be in the city then, he confessed, and had tried to reach her by phone, "hoping to get you to come to the university or get some other excuse to see you." It would be a stretch, however, to believe their meeting had been mere chance. Smith had no doubt heard that Laura would be in Chicago from his pal Yoder, who himself had begun to make regular trips to Bureau County, ostensibly to see a brother living there. "But," as Smith informed Laura a bit later, "I doubt he loves his brother quite as much as he lets on." The real reason for Yoder's trips, both knew, was his interest in a good friend of Laura's named Sadie Albright. It's a fair guess that the two women had come to Chicago together. In the background of their visit, Yoder dexterously pulled the strings available to him with all the romantic cunning of a character from Shakespeare.[32]

In March 1907, a few days after Smith first started writing Ioder, Yoder also approached her with advice as to how to handle his friend. "I know the gentleman well enough to be able to tell you just how to work him (I think) and keep him interested until you have formed opinions," Yoder told her. "And in the mean time you may rest assured that I shall at times give him extreme joy in telling him what a fine girl I think you are." Above all else, Yoder cautioned, "you must not let him suspect that I ever spoke of him in any other than just a casual way. . . . You know a fellow always likes to think he is playing his own games but as you also know he is a dead easy mark when there is a girl in the case. So you must not come too easy." Nor was this their first exchange of letters on the subject of the young professor Smith. Earlier Laura had apparently written Yoder wondering if Smith's attentions were just a "passing interest." They were not, Yoder assured her: "I feel sure that it is within your power to make this interest in this case permanent." He outlined a number of reasons why. Smith was approaching the end of his schooling, he reasoned, and would soon be anxious to exchange a rooming house for a real home. Moreover, having studied at the Elkhart Institute, and writing to a college-trained Mennonite woman, Yoder knew how to advise Laura from within the tiny but emerging new subculture of educated Mennonites, for whom the pool of like-minded marriage partners was still woefully small. "You must see that there are reasons why you should appeal to him peculiarly as you might not to many others and as very few can appeal to him," Yoder pointed out. "To be more explicit you are no doubt aware that his nearest relatives and many of his friends live in the country and are Mennonites. You would be in a position to understand this and appreciate why in some cases they are different from other people, while to many people they must seem ridiculous. Again you have had a great deal of experience with people who are not exactly of the farm and have had some college training."[33]

The able Miss Ioder soon found herself in a position to put this insightful advice to good use. After her "chance" meeting with Smith in Chicago, she dropped him a short postcard, giving him what he readily admitted later was "a good excuse to write you but I would have written anyway I think." Yoder was right: she had caught Smith at a propitious moment. That same month he had begged off from an invitation from Byers to rejoin the Goshen faculty, saying he needed another year to make up his mind about several personal matters. "When I go back to Goshen I want to stay," he explained, "and if that is the case I want to be sure that I have burned all my bridges behind me and that I have settled all the vital questions of my life." At least some of those vital questions, Byers learned, concerned a certain woman in Bureau County. The Mennonite academic world was a small one, and rumors about her had already reached Goshen. Smith acknowledged "how easily a man can become the subject of unpleasant gossip," but hastened to explain. "I agree with you," he told Byers, that the lady he had referred to "is an excellent young woman, cultured, with good sense and in many ways attractive." Smith thought he "would be pretty well received if I cared to make her acquaintance," but assured Byers he had no such intentions. "I don't know that I am in a particular hurry to settle down although I suppose I am old enough," he shrugged with manly indifference. "There are several other things I want to do first, including a trip to Europe and the publishing of my book, both of which I want to do as soon as I get enough money."[34]

It was all bluster. The letters Ioder began to receive from Smith had a contrasting tone: alternately supremely confident and shyly vulnerable, and altogether quite attentive. Immediately he began showing intense interest in her further teacher training, repeatedly recommending that she attend a pedagogical session

Newly hooded Dr. C. Henry Smith, with his University of Chicago doctorate, June 1907. BUASC.

the next summer at Normal. Forget the university at DeKalb, he said; "Normal is the place to go to." He described its beautiful campus and excellent teachers without a hint of the contempt for the place that later permeated his autobiography, especially recommending to her its medieval history course. Smith boosted Normal so sincerely and innocently he almost obscured another reason he had for recommending it to Ioder: that he, coincidentally, would be teaching a summer session there at the same time. By mid-May he dropped the pretenses. "I have been looking forward with pleasure to an opportunity for becoming better acquainted with you," he beseeched, "and I certainly hope I may have the pleasure of seeing you at Normal this summer. Won't you come?" At the same time, he worried he was writing her too much, assuring her that "whenever you want me to slow up you let me know and I'll try to put on the brakes." Ioder assured him that "you need not put on any 'brakes' (for the present at least)." She sent him copies of her students' poetry and then violets in the mail to remind him of springtime in the Illinois countryside. Smith sent her a picture of himself and

Courting days: Laura Ioder at Miller Park, Bloomington, Illinois, 1907. BUASC.

nearly managed to sound casual in requesting a photo of her in return. The pace of his correspondence temporarily subsided in late May as he underwent the ordeal of his final PhD comprehensive exams. "Well it is all over and I am about all in," he sighed to her in relief. "I had four days of it in succession and it was not at all an easy matter." He stayed around in Chicago that June just long enough to participate in graduation ceremonies, receiving his doctoral hood and taking in the commencement speaker, British ambassador Lord Bryce, before hurrying to Normal, where Ioder had started classes. Things apparently went very well between them there. By August, with the session ended, their relationship had deepened substantially to the point that, on just one day, he sent her four separate letters. Still, it was hard to know where Ioder, at least, thought things had progressed. She had listened carefully to Yoder's advice and was certainly capable of reading Smith's signs. Still, her letters to "My Dear Mr. Smith" that summer read like correspondence with an old platonic friend. She chatted gaily to him about her friends and doings in the village of Wyanet, even recounting the visits paid to her by various and earnest male suitors. At any rate she seemed thoroughly unprepared for what Smith did next.[35]

In early September 1907, Smith prefaced a letter to Ioder with the hope that what he had to say "won't take your breath away . . . but I have been wondering whether I dared ask you whether you cared enough for me to marry me sometime." He had wanted to wait until he saw her next to ask her, he admitted, but he didn't know when that would be and, in light of the attentions she was receiving from other men, "I don't want to wait." He was forthright and to the point: "I have learned to love you very much during our acquaintance and I hope that feeling will not be entirely unreciprocated." Sometime that spring or summer, he had received a job offer to teach at the University of Arizona, and Smith's family had never known why he had turned it down. As late as 1962, his nephew Willard Smith could only say that "for some reason he changed his mind." But Laura Ioder knew why. "If it had not been for you I might be in Arizona now," Smith wooed. "But I didn't want to be too far away from Illinois just yet. Now don't you think that I ought to be rewarded for my faithfulness?" All he could do was wait for her reply in return mail. "If you want to make me happy say 'yes,'" he concluded. "If you say 'no,' 'misery' won't half express my condition."[36]

At first she did not say yes. "The contents of your letter did almost take my breath away," she replied immediately. "I have been thinking of scarcely nothing else to-day and really hardly know how to answer." She couldn't say no, she admitted, but was not ready to say yes, telling him plainly that "I have learned to love you but whether I love you enough to give up my girlhood and freedom I can hardly tell." She wished he had proposed in person, she told him, and had not dreamed it would come "so early in our friendship." Smith admitted his disappointment, but handled the initial rejection gracefully. He knew he was pushing things fast, acknowledging that he was "a little more reserved in many respects than some." Still, he hoped that his proposal "will not make you feel less of me nor weaken my chances of winning your full love and confidence." Ioder's affirmation came sooner than he had anticipated. Her next letter was nine sentences long, but it was all he wanted. "There isn't any use of keeping you waiting because I know I do love you and we can live happily together," she consented. "You have my heart. Take good care of it." Smith could hardly contain his joy. "Your heart is in safe keeping," he proclaimed to her, "and I shall give you in return all my love unreservedly. All I have is yours."[37]

In the months to come the couple carefully negotiated their way through a great many more details, some in an air of fun, like Smith's irregular exercise, spotty church attendance (for which Ioder gently chided him), and the failure of the other to write often enough. There was also the matter of the wedding. Smith pushed for an earlier date, while Ioder preferred to wait a bit longer. As far as he was concerned, Smith declared in January 1908, "a year from next summer is the limit sure," though, considering the details of new dress she wanted, he said, "perhaps I (we) better wait until my salary is a little larger." Unlike Ioder, Smith also preferred the old Mennonite tradition of what he called "'sly marriages . . . I would just as soon get married suddenly without letting anybody know about it as not" (though, in this small arena of contention, he was bound to lose). Both struggled with how much to tip their heart to each other. "I hope you are as anxious to see me as I am to see you," Ioder wrote Smith six months into their engagement, while he closed one letter admitting that "I think of you often and often find myself dreaming about the future."[38]

In her visits with her aunt Laura and uncle Henry, Elaine Bowers recalled them as quite guarded and formal with each other in public. "If they had a passion and excitement and romance in their lives," she said, "I couldn't see it." It would have been bizarre for them to have acted otherwise. They reflected the influence of both their Amish Mennonite background and the Victorian culture of Gilded Age America, neither of which would have encouraged much open display of affection. In the privacy of their early correspondence, however, they reflected a different spirit: the petty jealousies of young lovers and the periodic irritations common to all human beings, but also a growing intimacy and undisguised longing for each other's company. There seems little doubt that Laura and Henry Smith soon developed a deep companionship that would bring them immense joy and sustain them through the considerable trials that would come their way. Orie Yoder was right. In their education, their life outlook, and their manner of navigating the meeting ground between Mennonite and American culture, they were entirely suited for each other. A few years before they met, Smith had already launched himself into a career-long effort to publicize the contributions Mennonites could make to society, and early in their relationship Ioder signaled her full endorsement of such efforts. "I sometimes get tired of telling people, I am a Mennonite," Ioder wrote her new professor friend in April 1907 from her rooming house in Wyanet. "People here hardly know what we are. A great many thought I was a Baptist because I never take communion." Their commitment to this shared project, and also to each other, would only deepen in the coming years.[39]

More immediately, Smith moved to address the final major life decision yet remaining to him: the matter of permanent employment. As he prepared to finish his doctorate in spring 1907, he told Byers he needed another year before coming back to Goshen because "I am up against, all at once, practically all the vital questions that a young man is called upon to solve in life." Byers soon read such references as code language for Laura Ioder. In order to stay within a short train trip from Bureau County, and also "to get some teaching experience in another institution," for the 1907–8 academic year, Smith accepted a job teaching at an elite high school in Indianapolis. From an office in the state capitol, he taught classes in government and oversaw the student senate, but this was not compensation enough for working with young and largely disengaged students. By January, in his letters to Ioder, he was already counting the days until the summer. Consequently, when Byers again contacted Smith about a faculty position, "we had little difficulty," he recalled later, "in persuading him to return to Goshen at half the salary."[40]

Byers was misinformed; in actuality, Smith spent much of that intervening year actively searching for another position. The reason, Ioder understood, was his deep unhappiness with Goshen salaries. In March 1907 Smith attempted to set up an appointment with Normal's president about a possible permanent job there. The following May he remarked to Ioder that he had just returned from the Palmer House Hotel in downtown Chicago "to see the President of the University of Washington. Nothing doing though I guess." He also planned to attend the upcoming annual meeting of the Chicago chapter of the Normal Alumni Association, hoping to corner university officials in attendance and lay out his qualifications for a position. By the following spring, with all other options apparently exhausted, Smith passed word to Byers that he would be coming back to Goshen. This time, it was clear, he would stay.[41]

"There is a story afloat back there that you have said you would not go back to Goshen single," Yoder informed his old friend in March 1908. "How about it: have all preparations been made to bring your bachelor days to a close soon? Well, I'll tell you 'Hank,'" Yoder pushed, "you should do that thing very soon." Certainly, the entrance of Laura Ioder into Smith's life was the major personal development for him in these Chicago years. A moment of banter a year or two earlier, however, best reveals how foundational this period had been for his intellectual growth. It happened in a bull session in a dorm room in Snell Hall, and was recorded in the yearbook. "The long-haired philosophers had gathered in room 56," read the 1907 *Snell Hall Cooler*. Smith had paused long enough in his doctoral work to join in the fun, affording his fellow YMCA friends an opening for commentary on his physical appearance and his life project. The hot topic of conversation that evening had apparently revolved around "Some Improved Methods of Running the Universe." One of the fellows had held forth at some length on the supposed greatness of the state of Texas. "Henry Smith then showed," summarized the yearbook, "that all the bald heads as well as all the progress of the United States could be directly traced to the Mennonites of Pennsylvania."[42]

5
How to Write the Mennonite Story

Smith had a fairly lengthy list of important tasks facing him in the summer and fall of 1908 as he wrapped matters up in Illinois and threw himself back into teaching at Goshen. Yet his major efforts would have been focused on his book manuscript, which he was laboring to get into print. The issue required particular care because the world of Anabaptist scholarship was in the midst of energetic revision. At that point it stood poised to welcome several major new scholarly players whose differing and sometimes clashing interpretations would reflect a parallel and related struggle occurring in the Mennonite churches of North America. While the scholarly debate over proper Anabaptism would encompass a variety of related issues, fundamentally it issued from the same question riveting the churches of whether to widen or narrow permissible boundaries: in scholarship, in personal matters like dress and behavior, even in the realm of private thought.

Scholarly Conversation about Anabaptism Develops

"Anabaptist historiography was formerly the privilege of its enemies," Harold Bender once summarized magisterially. Harassed, persecuted, and martyred by the thousands in their own day, over the subsequent centuries Anabaptists fared little better at the hands of most European historians, who lumped them together with Thomas Müntzer, instigator of the Peasant Wars in Germany, and the crazed enthusiasts in 1534 who grouped around Jan van Leyden and the ensuing horror of Münster. Such perspectives set the dominant scholarly tone for discussions of Anabaptism well into the latter part of the nineteenth century. In his student days a half century before, recalled the Zwingli scholar Walter Kohler in 1925, Anabaptism was seldom discussed, and when it appeared, it was immediately associated with words like "fanatic." Scholars inculcated with the noble standard of objectivity noted the difficulties that this dominant reading imposed. When he set out in these years to research Anabaptist origins, the scholar Belfort Bax found the available information "somewhat scant" and further "vitiated by the fact that much of it comes from bitterly hostile sources."[1]

By the time Smith was born, however, the scholarly tone in Anabaptist studies had begun to change, and his lifetime roughly paralleled a renaissance in the historiography of the field. Through the latter nineteenth century and into the twentieth, Bender noted, an increasing number of new books appeared in Europe and North America on different aspects of the movement, at times averaging nearly a major book every year. Sparked by the publication of new archival resources, especially court records, scholars developed a number of contrasting perspectives. Some scholars, like Bax, for instance, came at the field with a Marxist lens. The entire thrust of Bax's narrative led directly to Leyden and the Münsterites, who, he claimed, were "the forerunners of modern socialism." There were continuations of the older depictions of Anabaptists as heretics and fanatics. But now a series of energetic Anabaptist defenders emerged in the scholarly literature. Following the cherished historical progression laid out in revered Mennonite documents like van Braght's *Martyrs Mirror*, these apologists depicted the Anabaptists as inheritors of ancient medieval traditions passed down from groups like the Waldenses, and downplayed the movement's connections to apostles of apocalyptic violence like Müntzer and van Leyden. Such interpretations found allies in the developing new field of German sociology. Ernst Troeltsch, for example, carefully differentiated between Anabaptists as a "sect" over against "spiritualists" like Müntzer. Finally, Baptist scholars like Richard Heath and Albert Henry Newman instead explored Anabaptism as part of an effort to document the movement as the foundation of their denomination.[2]

This context renders perfectly understandable that key moment for Smith, early in his graduate school career, when he came across a book on Baptist history in the Chicago Divinity School library and discovered it claimed Menno as the author of that faith. The book he picked up may well have been either Heath's or Newman's, for both portrayed Anabaptism as something like a Baptist usable past. Heath, for example, depicted Zurich radicals like Grebel and Blaurock in lyrical, saintly tones, describing at length the extreme importance they attached to adult baptism and establishing how widespread the practice was among these "German Baptists," or just plain "Baptists" (words synonymous for Heath with *Anabaptist*). Newman's analysis proceeded along the same lines, repeatedly equating infant baptism with ignorance and superstition.[3]

Smith would later object to the way Baptists appropriated Menno Simons into their spiritual family tree, but the extant body of English-language scholarship on Anabaptism did appear to influence his thinking in several other ways. First, it may have been Heath, among others, who awoke him to the ideological potential of the Anabaptist devotion to freedom of conscience. As Heath wrote in the soaring crescendo of his closing paragraph, this critical doctrine was the cornerstone of freedom in all of "Christendom"; it was "the eternal conscience of the universe." Second, Heath and Newman, as well as Bax, located the origins of Anabaptism in a number of related but different sources. All described at length the importance of the Zurich radicals of 1525, but all also located Anabaptism in a much wider circle of Reformation figures than certain Mennonite scholars would allow a decade or two later. For the Baptist scholars, the figure of Balthasar Hubmaier was especially important as a forerunner of their denomination, but their Anabaptist pantheon also included reformers like Hans Denck and Hans Hut. Heath noted that the Zurich radicals were ecumenical and inclusive enough to write friendly letters of overture to Müntzer, whom they called "brother Thomas." Similarly, Bax made much of the typologies of Anabaptists written by their enemies like Heinrich Bullinger and accorded them much weight, identifying in the end a "network of Anabaptist communities or congregations," a "loose confederation" among German groups, which, while insisting on infant baptism, allowed a considerable variety of other theological positions.[4]

For Smith's Mennonite contemporaries, however, scholars like the Baptists and Bax would have been of minor importance. The great new wellspring influencing the way Mennonites in the later nineteenth century read Anabaptism sprung from sources closer to home, principally Ludwig Keller, a German archivist with a multifaceted spiritual agenda, and his chief disciple, an intense young Bavarian Mennonite named John Horsch.

Ludwig Keller, John Horsch, and a New Turn in Academic Dialogue

The world from which Horsch came—German Mennonitism in the later nineteenth century—was a subculture desperate, as was Horsch himself, for a historical identity. Most German Mennonites had been educated in Lutheran schools, and uncounted numbers with no Mennonite church nearby worshiped with the Lutherans. Even most German Mennonite pastors had been educated in other theological traditions, since no Mennonite seminaries existed. The cost of this neglect of their theology and tradition had become clear to European Mennonites by the 1880s. As a Dutch pastor wrote to Keller in 1885, "The Mennonites have fallen into a mundane, petty pedestrian rut" and greatly needed a "revival." Thus Keller's cascade of books on Anabaptist history—on Münster in 1880, a biography of Denck in 1882, a larger history of the Reformation sympathetic to Anabaptism in 1885—considerably recharged the Mennonite historical imagination. Not that Keller was an Anabaptist himself. His interest in them came out of his larger academic and personal project of establishing a line of "old evangelical" groups that existed, he thought, from the time of the apostles through the Waldenses. Keller wanted to establish the Anabaptists as a further central component of this historical stream and began working with European Mennonite pastors toward this end. In the same manner, he was also contacting, as the historian Abraham Friesen later noted, "Baptists, Quakers, Templars, Waldenses, and anyone else he could place in his 'old evangelical' category." In 1885 Keller received a letter from seventeen-year-old Horsch, who was eager to locate a rare tract by Denck and more eager, it soon appeared, to sit at Keller's feet. Soon Horsch began doing Keller's bidding on a variety of tasks, ranging from locating old Anabaptist documents to pushing copies of Keller's Denck biography into as many Mennonite hands as he could. There seemed little doubt, as a sympathetic biographer summarized later, that he had "almost completely adopted Keller's new vision."[5]

Because of the important role that Horsch would later play in Smith's life, he bears some careful attention here. Like Smith, Horsch had been raised on a Mennonite farm, the physically frail son of a Mennonite bishop who was a prominent leader of the Swiss-descended Mennonite clan of southern Germany. Unlike John Smith, however, the elder Horsch was also a deeply patriarchal figure who elected to keep his son fastened to the farm rather than encourage his obvious love for the world of books and ideas. In his late adolescence, about the time he plunged into his collaboration with Keller, Horsch was completing a term at the Bavarian state agricultural college and contemplating his response to the German military draft. Horsch was a dedicated Mennonite and military service was unthinkable, but so was a life following his father's dictates on the farm. Instead he chose a third option. In late 1886, as he approached his twentieth birthday, he secretly boarded a ship in Rotterdam and fled to the Mennonite enclaves in the American Midwest. Like other aspiring young Mennonite intellectuals in the late Gilded Age, Horsch soon found his way to Elkhart, Indiana, and employment with John Funk, first clerking his bookstore and then translating documents from German to English. Horsch was thus positioned to follow a trajectory—not dissimilar from that of Smith, Byers, and other young intellectuals of their generation—toward a firm embrace of progressivism in a Mennonite vein. There were moments when he even anticipated some of their key positions. Before emigrating, for example, he had waxed enthusiastically to Keller in 1886 about organizing some kind of grand conference of Mennonites from across Europe and America, an early variant of a Mennonite union movement, where they would pray and "stay focused on the great goal of renewal . . . in the spirit of old-evangelical theology." In a feature article in Funk's German-language edition of the *Herald of Truth* a year later, he condemned the petty Mennonite fixation on outward signs of faithfulness as a barrier to Mennonite unity.[6]

Having gained Funk's confidence, Horsch edited the *Herold der Wahrheit* from 1887 to 1895. He soon found the position afforded him a nearly unlimited forum for publishing at will on Anabaptist history and theology. Even while sporadically attending three small colleges and never completing a degree, he soon emerged, in the words of the Anabaptist historian Robert Friedmann, "an astonishingly prolific writer." His imprint appeared in nearly every issue of the *Herold der Wahrheit*: in old Anabaptist documents, in excerpts from Keller's writings, in short biographical sketches of early Anabaptist leaders, and increasingly in his own historical and theological essays. Nearly all of Horsch's work reflected, with only slight, periodic deviation, the views of his mentor. Initially dismayed over Horsch's emigration, Keller soon realized that his disciple's new position afforded him an almost unlimited potential for spreading his teaching widely among American Mennonites. This proceeded along several main lines of analysis. One was a heavy emphasis on the critical nature of mystical Anabaptist leaders like Denck. In 1888, for instance, Horsch edited and Funk's publishing house issued one of Denck's tracts that Keller thought was a particularly moving distillation of the "old evangelical" vision. Moreover, Horsch's channeling of Keller repeatedly stressed the historical continuities between figures like Denck, the emerging Anabaptist movement, and other "old evangelical" groups like the Waldenses.[7]

Smith's Entrance into the Conversation

By the first decade of the twentieth century, as Smith took up his analysis of early Anabaptism, there seems little doubt that Mennonite historical consciousness, as he received it, deeply reflected the new Keller-Horsch consensus on Anabaptist historiography. In his influential "Spirit of Progress" speech, for example, Coffman repeated such teachings. In their *Mennonite Church History* in 1905, Hartzler and Kauffman began their story with the gospel of John and the rise of Rome, and then traced the kernel of Anabaptist teachings through various medieval sects to the faith of Peter Waldo. Citing Keller and Horsch among others, these two early MC writers on Anabaptism presented a pluralistic Anabaptist family tree, including the Zurich radicals as well as men like Hubmaier and Denck ("a man of the most irreproachable life"), while admitting to some theological differences among different Anabaptist camps.[8]

Smith's initial entrance into the scholarly conversation about Anabaptism as a grad student displayed his grasp of its main assumptions while also indicating, very early on, his willingness to question them. Before Jameson redirected his research agenda from Europe to America, the very first item on Smith's research agenda had been the relationship of the Anabaptists and Mennonites to the Waldenses. Already by 1904 he had some of his own ideas about Anabaptist origins that ran at variance with early Mennonite efforts to separate themselves from the debacle at Münster. As he pointed out to Jameson that October in his case for a fellowship at Chicago, some of the Zurich radicals had been taught by apostles of violence like Nicholas Storch and Müntzer; several had even been baptized by Storch. "We are not quite as free from the Münsterites as our friends claim for us," he noted, and "not quite as related as our enemies try to make out."[9]

In January 1905, still pushing for a grad fellowship, Smith submitted to Jameson a lengthy paper on Anabaptist origins. He was pleased, he explained, that he had not read Bax's book until he had finished the paper, given how Bax foreshadowed some of his own thinking that he had reached independently. If anything, Smith told Jameson, Bax "minimizes the influence . . . of Münzer upon the Swiss." This paper undoubtedly formed the basis for a detailed, twelve-thousand-word article Smith published the following summer, serialized in the pages of the new Mennonite Church organ, the *Gospel Witness*. In it, Smith showed a remarkable ability to thread his way carefully through complex and competing arguments while underscoring the freshness and importance of his own. Certainly he described at length the disputation in Zurich in 1523–25 between Zwingli and radicals like Grebel and Felix Manz. He recognized the rebaptisms conducted by Manz and others as "the decisive step in the development of the new movement" because they signified "the complete severing of church and state." He approvingly summarized a Horsch pamphlet on the Schleitheim Confession as a fine representation of the peaceful views of the movement, and called Keller "probably the best and most sympathetic modern critic of Anabaptists [sic] lore." At the same time, he broke decisively with Keller's contentions that minimized the influence of Müntzer. The basic teachings of Anabaptism as Smith read them—opposition to infant baptism, the total separation of church and state, and a church body made up exclusively of like-minded believers—led him to believe that Müntzer and the Zurich radicals had much more in common than otherwise. To be sure, Smith admitted, they differed on the matter of violence, but that disagreement had not detracted from the love the Swiss felt for Müntzer nor minimized his influence on their grasp of "the essentials of the faith." Likewise he broke with Keller's dominant insistence on longstanding Anabaptist connections with their supposed Waldensian forebears. This idea was problematic, he pointed out, because even the best apologists for that view (he named Keller specifically) could establish similarities of thought between the two groups but no evidence of direct historical causation.[10]

Having rooted the origins of Anabaptism in Switzerland with heavy influence from Saxony, Smith described at length a "second stage" in the emergence of the movement. It proceeded, he said, from Denck to Hubmaier to Hans Hut to Melchior Hoffman, each of whom "stamped his own personality on the trend of Anabaptist development" and "modified slightly the common interpretation of the doctrines." Yet identifying even these main figures overly simplified the complex nature of the movement, Smith said, agreeing with Bullinger that there may have been as many as forty different sects, all of whom agreed on "the essentials." The trouble with them, he wrote, "was that they got hold of a little truth and went wild over it," many displaying "fanatical tendencies." Smith recognized the centrality of peacemaking in the emerging movement, but repeatedly left it off his phrasing of key Anabaptist beliefs. Only as he neared his conclusion did Smith take pains to condemn the excesses of Münster, and only then with the immediate qualifier that "the germ at least of the most fanatical outgrowth of Anabaptist doctrine was found in the teachings of the most conservative."[11]

At that point in the emerging scholarly discussion, it seemed only to have been Smith's evenhanded treatment of Müntzer that had given *Gospel Witness* editor Kauffman pause. When he introduced Smith's lengthy piece that May, Kauffman had briefly noted that "on some things the conclusions arrived at in this article are somewhat different from some of our own views, but we print the article for its historical worth, and invite each one of our readers to give it careful study." To make sure readers got the point, Kauffman interjected an editor's note after Smith's first installment, telling them that "while Müntzer was sound on many of the tenets of his faith," the Swiss had later rightly "repudiated his heresies."[12]

What was novel about Smith's approach in 1905 was the way he carefully tacked between two poles of scholarly debate; he offered, as he put it to Jameson, a "'middle of the road'" position. At that moment in time, none of the rest of Smith's claims—his large and inclusive Anabaptist family tree, for instance, or his particular summary of Anabaptist "essentials," which did not include nonresistance—occasioned any great academic uproar. He was merely distilling the historiographical consensus of his day, much of which went back to the *Martyrs Mirror*, and which was shared by socialists like Bax, Baptist historians like Heath and Newman, and Anabaptist writers like Kauffman, J. S. Hartzler, and the early John Horsch. "Anabaptism is like a tree with many roots," Smith concluded, which developed in a direct line "from Müntzer, through Grebel, to Münster." Seventy-five years later a subsequent generation of historians would grandly advance such "polygenesis" arguments as a monumental breakthrough in Anabaptist historiography.[13]

Accepting the pluralistic roots of Anabaptism as a matter of course, Smith instead underscored the importance of his contribution along different lines. Scholars have uncovered a multitude of origins of Anabaptism, he said, and "the difference lies not so much in the facts they present as in the interpretations of these facts or oftentimes in the willful, or ignorant suppression of various facts." One could hardly blame these scholars for such practices, he quickly added. "The trouble with most of the historians had been, and is largely today, that they are theologians or at any rate strict churchmen in the narrow sense of the term and were thereby incapacitated to write a fair unprejudiced history." Driven by the strict dedication to objectivity in which he had been schooled, Smith thus signaled that, from the very beginning of his scholarly career, he would reject approaches to Mennonite history that he saw as expressive of theological agendas. It was time, Smith implied, for a new breed of empirically trained professional historians to take over the writing of Anabaptist-Mennonite history. In such a phrasing, in the Mennonite world at that particular point in time, once again he could only mean himself. It was altogether a stunning suggestion for an emerging young scholar who had only just then been admitted to a doctoral program. But in 1905, he was just getting started.[14]

The Mennonites of America and Smith's Narrative Capacity

Not long after arriving back in Goshen that autumn of 1908, Smith completed a goal he had been aiming at for years: the publication of his doctoral thesis. He had no choice, he explained in 1925, but to issue it himself. The Mennonite Publishing House had put out Hartzler and Kauffman's book a few years before and was uninterested in a similar project, though they did consent to print the book. It was their loss. In his book, Smith managed to gather between two covers all the influences that had been working on him through his academic career to that point. The work denotes a significant milestone in the development of his thought and would prove even more significant for his church. A half century later Bender would recognize Smith's narrative as "the only comprehensive work on American Mennonite history." Smith would write little that would compare with it, in terms of scope and importance, until the last decade of his life. Hence, *The Mennonites of America* deserves careful scrutiny here.[15]

Smith had been careful to secure an editor for the book, *Gospel Herald* editor Daniel H. Bender, who had taken his job seriously. Amid preparations to assume the presidency of the new MC Mennonite college in Hesston, Kansas, he had been "exceedingly busy," Bender wrote Steiner in April 1909, "editing the Smith history." Smith's introduction was dated November 14, 1908, and the book appeared the next year. A paragraph of acknowledgments noted his debts to several academic colleagues: Funk for use of his library, General Conference Mennonite scholars Henry P. and Christian Krehbiel for their oversight of his material on the GC Mennonites, and his Goshen College colleague Daniel Gerig for his "critical suggestions." He dedicated the book to his parents. Curiously, for a revised doctoral thesis, Smith did not mention debts to any of his graduate school professors, perhaps because only a small portion of the book had been done under their oversight. In 1909 the Mennonite Publishing House printed a separate and bound copy of a doctoral dissertation by C. Henry Smith, which had been submitted to the history department at the University of Chicago. It consisted of three chapters: "Germantown," "The Pequea Colony," and "Mennonites and the State," a doctoral dissertation totaling 147 pages, including an expansive bibliography. It was for this level of output that the University of Chicago had awarded him a doctorate. Smith transferred all this material verbatim into the 1909 book, along with 331 pages of new material in fourteen new chapters he had somehow found time to produce. When one considers that he began his serious research just three years before, and in between had been occupied with a diversity of other projects—completing his PhD comprehensive exams, teaching high school, and wooing Laura Ioder—his level of scholarly productivity seems astounding.[16]

While the 1909 book thus made no mention of Smith's mentors, it nonetheless fully reflected his training and self-identification as a proud, professionally trained product of the University of Chicago, with all the influences that had permeated that context. Years later he described himself to his nephew Willard as a political historian, but understood that orientation included a full consideration of subordinate academic realms like cultural, intellectual, social, and religious history. Such an outlook appeared in the very organization of his text. Chapter titles reflected ecclesiastical-political groupings like "The Amish," "Franconia," and "During the Revolution." His analysis paid careful attention to such matters as the incorporation and governmental affairs of Mennonite colonies, the shifting tides of European immigration, and the Mennonite relationship with the U.S. state, especially during periods of war. Equally indicative of Smith's training was the aura of scientific objectivity that he imagined as undergirding the text. "I have tried to be impartial towards the various branches of the church," he pledged at the outset, "and have given each the amount of space which according to my judgment its importance deserved."[17]

As Smith's Chicago professors had apparently insisted and as his title indicated, the bulk of his focus was on American Mennonites, but he did begin his analysis with two chapters (about sixty pages of nearly five hundred in the total text) on their Anabaptist background. In the first paragraph of chapter 1, he quickly dismissed as "merely a waste of time" scholarly theories of Waldensian, medieval, or any other supposed origins of Anabaptism earlier than the events in Zurich in 1523–25. In most other ways, however, his material on Anabaptism deviated only slightly, with one major exception, from his thinking on the topic in 1905. (Many passages from that earlier paper, in fact, appeared in his 1909 book verbatim.) For example, he had not changed his mind on the many-sided nature of early Anabaptism. Figures like Grebel, Blaurock, and Manz were central in their development, he narrated, but so were Denck, Hubmaier, Hoffman, and Hut. In this manner Smith reaffirmed the early twentieth-century version of the polygenesis origins of Anabaptism, and for a simple reason. "Anabaptism was above all intensely individualistic," he explained, and "it manifested a variety of tendencies according to the spirit and opinions of its chief leaders." When Smith himself summarized basic Anabaptist beliefs, they included an insistence on church-state separation (symbolized by adult baptism), a self-exclusion from society, and, at least among "the majority of the Swiss," a refusal to take up the reins of government and a rejection of the sword. In fact, he stated, the rejection of the sword as stipulated in the Schleitheim Confession was "the position taken by Menno Simons and by all those Anabaptists who were later known as Mennonites."[18]

What differed in Smith's thinking from four years earlier, however, was his reading of the degree to which Müntzer and the apocalyptic episode at Münster had influenced the early movement. One can only speculate as to what had changed his mind. It could not have been original research into Anabaptist origins, since he himself would not venture to Europe for such purposes for almost two decades. The changing scholarly and ecclesiastical winds blowing in the Mennonite Church, as illustrated by Kauffman's 1905 editorial comments and subsequent career, may have played a role. Whatever the reason, in 1909 he downplayed the connection between what he distinguished as a mainstream Anabaptism from Müntzer and the chain of events that led to van Leyden and Münster. While the critical and "purely religious" events were unfolding in Zurich, Smith outlined, a parallel "largely political and social" movement, led by Storch and Müntzer, was underway in Saxony. As he had done in 1905, Smith described the warmth that Grebel and other Swiss leaders manifested toward Müntzer, but now, citing Keller, stressed their suspicions of Müntzer's views of the state. Whether Müntzer and his followers should be "regarded as Anabaptists," Smith reasoned, depends on one's "interpretation of the term Anabaptist." If the movement is defined so broadly as "to include all those different radical sects which followed in the wake of the Reformation" and rejected key tenets like infant baptism, then the answer is yes, Müntzer belonged in the Anabaptist fold. If the term is read largely through the lens of the Swiss, he said, then the answer is no. The intellectual and churchly lens through which Smith was increasingly beginning to operate was becoming clear. "The nonresistant, peaceful type, with which we are most concerned and which maintained its identity all through this time," he cautioned, "must not be confused with the fanatical, chiliastic elements of the movement." That element led directly to Münster, "one of the most familiar as well as most disgraceful episodes in Anabaptist history," and one that Smith refused to recount. Instead he devoted a chapter to Menno Simons, whom he saw as not the founder but the central organizer of the scattered Anabaptists and "one of the great heroes of the Reformation."[19]

Having dispensed with the Anabaptist background, Smith made even shorter work of the subsequent history of European Mennonites, quickening the pace of his narrative to cover the two centuries after Menno's death in 1559 in about sixteen pages. That the Mennonite story in North America was his central concern was also affirmed by the sudden appearance of footnotes. Only in the last part of his life would Smith be openly critiqued for neglecting to include proper citations of his scholarly sources, but it is clear here that his laxity stemmed back decades. The incongruity between Smith's carelessness with his sources and his otherwise deep dedication to scholarship is puzzling. To be sure, he did tell readers where, in general, he had obtained his material. He included a brief bibliography, for instance, on the sources he used for his arguments about Anabaptism, both in his 1905 *Gospel Witness* article and now in his 1909 book. He may have meant such brief appendices as signs to readers that his material on that topic was entirely derivative. Such larger, "covering references" appear elsewhere in the 1909 text. As he commenced his treatment of Mennonites in Ontario, for example, he reported that "for the facts of this chapter the author is largely indebted to the work of Ezra Eby," footnoting Eby's title and date of publication. Likewise, Smith might have intended the sudden appearance of detailed footnotes in various other places as cues to readers that from that point on they would be reading original research. Yet such subtle signals do not explain why he periodically, throughout much of the text, let several pages elapse with no citations at all. Or else he offered incomplete citations, like direct quotations with simply the mention of the author with little or no documentation in support. A real publisher might have caught this scholarly negligence, and perhaps some of the fault lies with the still-developing nature of the American historical profession. Such excuses would be less understandable in the future.[20]

It is entirely possible that few of Smith's readers paid much attention to his footnotes, absorbed as they must have been by the sweep and power of his narrative. It was Smith's overarching histories—starting in 1909, with successor volumes in 1919 and especially 1941—that cemented his reputation, as Bender acknowledged upon Smith's death, as the preeminent American Mennonite historian of his generation. Smith's books came to exert a paradigmatic hold on the historical imagination of American Mennonites for several interrelated reasons.

A main one would have been their undeniable inclusiveness. Mennonites had lived in North America for two centuries, but not until Smith's book appeared did they have in hand a comprehensive overview of their historical experience that stemmed back to their Anabaptist origins and included the myriad church groupings of the Amish and Mennonites. *The Mennonites of America* proceeded both chronologically and topically. Hence, Smith focused chapter-long analyses on important periods like the Mennonite and Amish experience during the American Revolution and the Civil War, interspersed with longer treatments of eighteenth-century migrations to eastern Pennsylvania and the Lancaster region, as well as further Mennonite migratory streams across the nineteenth-century American Midwest. In doing so, he included analyses of the Amish, the General and Central Conferences, and even smaller groups like the "New Amish" / Apostolic Christians, the Reformed Mennonites, and Henry Egli and his followers. He also described the Russian immigration of the later nineteenth century and the subsequent growth of the General Conference church.[21]

Though Smith would correct this later, he did not yet grasp, in 1909, the complexity of the Russian Mennonite world or its history. In thematic chapters on matters like "Principles, Customs and Culture" and "Literature and Hymnology," for instance, he leaned toward subtopics he knew better. Amish and (MC) Mennonite hymns, for instance, received especially detailed treatment, but he said nothing about those from the Russian Mennonite tradition. While he dutifully described the origins of Swiss-German related groups like the Wisler and Holdeman Mennonites, he overlooked completely the much larger group of the Mennonite Brethren and their emergence in nineteenth-century Ukraine. At the same time, however, he briefly mentioned relatively recent developments like the General Conference Mennonites' missions to the Arapaho and to India. Moreover, even as Smith remained secure in his position at the (MC) Mennonites' first college, his thinking about several key issues began to demonstrate a remarkable GC shading. For instance, already in 1909, he subtly read the congregational polity of the General Conference church as indicative of Mennonites as a whole. "In church government," he asserted, "the Mennonites have always followed the congregational type."[22]

Second, Smith's histories lured in readers because of narrative capacities he had been developing for years. All those long days on the Illinois prairie, perched on a corn planter with his nose in a book, echoed now, decades later, in his compelling prose. As Smith had already been demonstrating in shorter pieces in the Mennonite press, he had an ability, unparalleled in the English-speaking Mennonite world of his day, to draw readers into his stories with the intimate air of a fellow traveler on a long and monumental journey. His warm and authoritative voice became more apparent once he left the complex historiographical thicket of Anabaptism and ventured onto what was then largely untrodden historical terrain: the Mennonite story in North America. He worked a variety of angles to intensify the spell of his writing. There was his keen eye for telling detail and his ability to synthesize complex data into a rich and compelling account. In his narrative on the founding of Germantown, for example, he made sure to mention how these early Mennonite pioneers made their way to an "elevated spot between the Delaware and Schuylkill rivers," along an "Indian path" that was "lined with laurel bushes." Within a decade or two, the settlers had "erected larger and comfortable stone houses, some of which are still standing," in a colony then strewn with "blooming peach trees." Smith's transitions often affirmed his mastery of the material in a manner designed, he hinted, to reveal its hidden secrets. "In order to understand the causes of this steady inflow of Palatinates," he informed readers as he nudged his narrative into Lancaster County, "it is necessary that we know something about the conditions prevailing at that time in the land from which they came." In like manner he shared the limitations of his sources ("of the early incidents leading up to this settlement . . . we know nothing above what we are able to glean from these land records") or "what we can know" despite those limitations. At times Smith deliberately spoke an insider's language, sharing details that only fellow inhabitants of his subculture would understand. When he relayed Amish history or hymnody, he would sometimes quote his sources in their original German without bothering to translate, knowing most of his readers would not need translation. As he walked readers through rural Lancaster County, he instructed them that "the nucleus of the colony evidently was where the present Brick church stands near Willow Street." Smith reinforced the companionable tone of his writing by shifting from past to present tense in the mode of a travelogue ("near each of these buildings were laid out the earliest graveyards.... Here lies buried old Hans Herr") and by periodically shifting to the first person, which heightened the drama ("so far as I have been able to discover, this is the oldest marked Mennonite grave in the county"). Mennonites who picked up Smith's book to learn about their American past would have soon settled comfortably into the hands of a master storyteller.[23]

Third, Smith's Mennonite readers would have been drawn to his text because of an angle that he had been pursuing for several years: analysis of the Mennonite historical tradition as a major taproot of Western civilization. The "great religious movements" of the English Baptists and early Quakers "owed their rise at least in part," he asserted, to Dutch Anabaptism, and "the Mennonite church may be considered the mother of the modern Baptist denomination," as well as that of "the Dunkards." To be sure, Smith was an honest enough historian to include certain less savory stories he had uncovered in the Mennonite past. There was, for example, the Yoder ancestor who bound off his children as indentured servants in order to facilitate his family's immigration to America. While inconvenient, such details also accentuated the overall heroic tone of his narrative. Thus Smith embellished, with enough telling detail, his major agenda: to establish a mythic Mennonite past that could intertwine neatly with the mainstream American one. Once again he borrowed tones from Turner. "The Mennonites and Amish have everywhere appeared among the pioneers," he insisted; "wherever new lands have opened up for settlement there Mennonites have been among the first to put up their log cabins and sod shanties." In like manner, Smith read the coming of the Russian Mennonites in the 1870s into the same rugged frontier myth, describing at length the many hardships they endured to emerge nonetheless as "among the most prosperous people in the western states." He seemed to take particular delight in elevating the Mennonite tradition over the Quaker one. For years, school textbooks had told of the great Quaker contributions to the founding of the country, of their establishment of religious liberty and early protestations against slavery. Smith read the relevant records and thought he could discern a preceding Mennonite influence. Certainly, he admitted, the first written public protest against slavery emerged from a Quaker context, but he insisted its early signers included more Mennonite names and it was really more of a Mennonite document. "It is but fitting," he claimed, "that the Mennonites who in the old world were among the first advocates for the entire liberty of soul, should in the new one be the first to raise their voice in public protest against the bondage of the body."[24]

In other words, Smith labored energetically to fit his first book into what he had embraced as his life project. Here, as elsewhere, he would produce a usable Mennonite past for an audience that he thought was now primed for it. He was acutely aware of the vast cultural distance that separated his Mennonite subculture from the progressive mainstream. As a teenager at Metamora High School, he had burned with embarrassment at the ridicule he had received from his classmates, for the "big ungainly, homemade bonnets and caps" worn by the women, or for the way that grown Mennonite men greeted each other with a holy kiss. He had quietly noted the "small role" Mennonites played in the world, "especially as compared with other church groups. No Amish-Mennonite had ever been president. I never found the name in our school texts. Hardly ever were they mentioned in the big metropolitan dailies, and seldom even in our local papers."[25]

Two decades later Smith found himself uniquely situated, a full-blooded Mennonite now with a Chicago PhD, to address such slights. He was a prominent leader of the first wave of Mennonites who had successfully traversed that cultural gap and were busily constructing educational enterprises to assist their people in doing likewise. In his 1906 address and pamphlet, his 1909 book, and throughout his subsequent academic career, Smith was actively engaged in helping his Mennonite people "invent" (to draw from a more recent scholarly phrasing) their ethnicity. In contrast to straight-line theories of immigrant assimilation, this was a process, ethnicity scholars Kathleen Neils

Conzen and David Gerber have argued, that "suggests an active participation by the immigrants in defining their group identities and solidarities.... In inventing its ethnicity, the groups sought to define the terms, modes, and outcomes of its accommodation to 'others.'" Conzen and colleagues point out that the process accelerated with oncoming waves of immigration through the nineteenth century, as Irish and especially German immigrant groups helped legitimate new notions of American pluralism. It was a project that seemed especially suitable for America of the Progressive Era, with its celebration of the great American "melting pot" and corresponding pressures toward cultural conformity.[26]

Smith seems to have understood that it had fallen to him to construct a history appropriate to the task. No longer, he told his Mennonite people, did you have to remain a "queer people" on the margins. The courage and dedication of our ancestors, read his subtext, gave birth to foundational American principles like freedom of individual conscience, for which more accepted and more recognizably American groups had later received the credit. It was time to set the record straight. As he approached the end of his narrative, Smith brought such themes to a crescendo. "Taken all in all," he declared, "there are few people more industrious, frugal, thrifty, peaceful and law-abiding than the Mennonites." "While as a denomination they may fall behind others in their attainments in the world of culture," he concluded, "yet in possession of the sounder virtues they are surpassed by none. They are sober, honest, industrious, peaceable and religious—withal among the most useful citizens of the land." For English-speaking, literate, history-conscious Mennonites—the kind of Mennonites among whom the pace of acculturation had begun to quicken—no wonder Smith's writings met with the kind of reception they did.[27]

Finally and equally importantly, in Smith's 1909 book, he clearly set out to fashion a usable past not only for the church as a whole but particularly for Mennonites who called the church to embrace the changes of the day. Like many of his fellow Mennonite educators, Smith's personal, ecclesiastical, and academic commitments had set him firmly within the pulse of two significant and overlapping movements: one American and one peculiarly Mennonite. In traversing the cultural ground from the edge to the center of their society, educated Mennonites had absorbed, in one form or another, the reform passions of the day.

Put another way, they had become progressives. In Mennonite circles by the first decade of the twentieth century, reform commitments had dovetailed with and commonly been preceded by a ready embrace of other, more explicitly religious imports, like revivals, Sunday schools, and then church-based higher education. Through such channels, people like Coffman and Steiner—and especially disciples like Smith, Byers, and their academic allies—had clearly become exponents of a second kind of peculiarly Mennonite progressivism.

For Mennonite progressives in their collegiate redoubts, the two movements—national reform and a Mennonite variant—were so intertwined as to be scarcely distinguishable from each other. They would remain so until Mennonite progressivism began to meet resistance. In 1908, with such resistance only in its nascent stages, Smith could write with the calm and unquestioned assurance that the future belonged to the progressives. The examples in his text are legion. There was, for instance, his ready usage, always in positive tones, of the word *liberal*. After a disapproving account of the origins of the Egli Amish for their original exclusivity, for example, Smith informed his readers that a "second generation of the Egli branch has assumed a more liberal attitude toward the old church . . . and so the two are again working in harmony in the interests of a broader Christianity." It was precisely because of such traits that Joseph Stuckey received far better treatment in Smith's hands than he had in the analyses of Mennonite Church leaders like Kauffman and Hartzler. After outlining the conflict among Amish bishops over Joseph Joder's universalism, Smith merely characterized Stuckey as "more liberal-minded" than other ministers, "especially the easterners," who were "still addicted to formalities which have since been discarded." If such people had just left the Illinois Amish Mennonites alone to deal with Stuckey's objections in their own manner, he concluded regretfully, the split in the church may never have occurred. The two groups, after all, shared basic doctrinal commitments and just differed slightly in matters of dress. Under direction of people like Valentine Strubhar and Emmanuel Troyer, "all of them comparatively young men and talented," he concluded approvingly, "the church is making steady progress both in numbers and spiritual life."[28]

Smith's history as a usable past for Mennonite progressives is especially seen in his subtly negative reading of Mennonite schisms and in the antidote he offered for it. "No other religious body" had displayed the schismatic tendencies of the Mennonites, he admitted. He ascribed this trend to a number of reasons: to the pervasive Anabaptist-Mennonite individualism, to their deep religious commitments, and finally to their lack of education, since "as a class Mennonites have come from the humbler walks of life." Certainly the original Anabaptists, "Grebel, Hubmaier and Denck," had been educated, and so had their Mennonite followers like Menno and Philips. But their followers had been "common people, with little learning outside of a more or less thorough knowledge of the Bible." Hence, for long centuries, "learning disappeared among the Mennonites," and with it went a Mennonite ability, he implied, to discern essentials from nonessentials, to separate surface manifestations of faith from what really mattered.[29]

The Mennonite neglect of education, Smith continued, had persisted until the early eighteenth century, when pioneer schoolmasters like Christopher Dock began to address it. Even so, for another century the few Mennonites who had pursued higher education had left the church, which "intensified the prejudice against such training, and at the same time robbed the church of the very element which ought to have helped it most to higher ideals of service and culture." But farsighted church leaders soon realized that in order to stem this tide (which threatened to confine their denomination to persistent religious insignificance), they needed to create higher educational agencies of their own. Smith carefully walked readers through the emergence of such institutions, beginning with the GC colleges at Wadsworth, Ohio, Halstead and Bethel, in Kansas, and then to Goshen College. The emergence of the latter, he admitted, had been shaky, since there was "very little sentiment" in favor of it across the Mennonite Church (i.e., MC), and it only existed because of "a few of the more liberal-minded leaders of both branches of the main body" like Coffman, J. S. Hartzler, and Byers. Its future was not assured, Smith admitted, but "the awakening of the entire church to the need of educating its young people is only one of the evidences of renewed life." Given that Smith's book would function for decades as the basic overarching history of the church, the fact that several subsequent generations of Mennonites would be reading a basically progressive history is of no small consequence.[30]

In this manner, the kind of new Mennonite ethnicity Smith developed contained at its center a critical distance from it. As the historian Steve Nolt has described, early Anabaptists may have stressed separation from the world, but over time economic and community ties had cemented their descendants to it in ways they could not have imagined. In this manner "Mennonite faith often became part of a church member's ethnicity," particularly among the Swiss-South German Mennonites immersed in Pennsylvania German culture, or later, among the heavily Germanic immigrants from Russia on the Great Plains. As an Amish Mennonite growing up in a smaller Mennonite population dispersed among the assimilated Americans of the Midwest, Smith may have been especially primed, as Nolt has suggested, to begin to cobble together a "Mennonite ethnic identity in institutional and ideological terms." In exploring Mennonite culture, for example, Smith acknowledged that his people's traditional isolation had helped preserved their peculiar customs but also "engendered conservatism," which tended to fossilize them. It was this kind of dysfunctional ethnicity that lay behind the many superficialities that divided Mennonites, he argued—the "minor customs and practices" focused in many cases on differences in dress. Fortunately, he concluded, "there are . . . several centers which radiate influences which are making for unification."[31]

While objections to Smith's progressive reading would not be long in coming, the extent of his contribution was recognized immediately by influential people across the English-speaking Mennonite landscape, from Byers, Gerig, and men of increasing authority in Smith's churchly circles. Writing in the *Christian Monitor*, Daniel Bender praised Smith's prodigious research and scholarly objectivity. The ink on the book could scarcely have dried before J. S. Hartzler (though not his academic partner) testified that he had examined the text and heartily recommended it as "worthy of a place in every Mennonite home." Kauffman's perspective, expressed in the new *Gospel Herald*, was more restrained but still noted that Smith's book "is full of historical data of rare value and gives evidence of painstaking care on the part of the author." At the opposite end of the Mennonite ecclesiastical spectrum, General Conference Mennonites found much to applaud, and in a manner that similarly displayed agendas percolating in their church. Philadelphia pastor and influential eastern Pennsylvania Mennonite leader Nathanial Grubb, for example, especially admired Smith's ability to describe key Mennonite schisms without casting aspersions on the sincerity of their leaders, "as has been done" (in a clear slap at Hartzler and Kauffman) "by certain so-called historians." The GC denominational organ the *Mennonite*, as well as Illinois and Central Conference leader Valentine Strubhar, commended Smith's book in particular for the wider intellectual grounds it furnished for possible Mennonite unity.[32]

Except for the published accounts, many of the testimonials had apparently been secured by Smith himself to help provide a way out of a financial tight spot he had landed in through his academic confidence and his naiveté. With no publisher to advise him as to significant details like a realistic price and print run for the extant market, in the summer of 1909 he bullishly ordered five thousand copies printed and priced them steeply at $2.50 each (about $59 in 2014 dollars). "I went into the venture blindly," he confessed in 1925, "and trusted to luck." As late as the eve of the Second World War, Robert Kreider recalled from his childhood in interwar Bluffton, three thousand of the books remained unsold. Smith unloaded the other two-fifths of his inventory not so much from luck as through "a remarkable set of book agents" he had found: seven Goshen College students whom he had convinced of the wads of cash they could make by selling the book across various Mennonite communities that summer of 1909. Smith managed the campaign via regular letters to the boys that radiated pep, encouragement, and also the cultural stereotypes of the times. "So cheer up Reuben if you get turned down all day," he instructed. "Grin and bear it. Did you ever hear of a Jew failing? Did you ever hear of a Jew who cared a rap about what people said about him [?]. That is what you will run up against all through life. . . . So let's keep at it boys and watch the number crawl up," he added, closing his letters with cheery slogans like "Yours for a big business" or "Yours for a 250 week." While in the end Smith was satisfied that "most of the boys averaged well in their commissions," they met with varied receptions. One unfortunate lad spent a week among the Amish Mennonites of Archbold, Ohio (where, Smith recognized, neither Goshen College nor the book's author was terribly popular), and managed to sell, for his trouble, a grand total of four volumes. Another entered the fertile territory of central Illinois and, aided by a glowing endorsement in the *Metamora Herald*, peddled more than a hundred, many to Smith relatives.[33]

The episode is worth noting for a couple of reasons beyond the significant financial blow it must have been to him (and the raised eyebrows it no doubt drew from his wealthy in-laws). For one, it seemed to have taught him something about the world of business, and it was not altogether uplifting. Watching the experience of the students, he confessed to his sales team, "I have myself learned more about human nature and its weaknesses and its meannesses . . . than I ever knew before." His salesmen met some potential customers whom Smith had thought his good friends, but he discovered that "when you meet them in business are regular traitors." Altogether, Smith concluded, "you never really know people until you have business relations with them." He would carefully file away such insights for the future. At the same time, the pressing need to sell thousands of books also reveals something about the way Smith himself began to function as a businessman. Take, for instance, his talking points to his sales team about how to characterize their competitor volume, the Hartzler-Kauffman book on Mennonite Church history. Certainly, he was gracious. He urged the students to tell customers that his own book was a "supplement" to their book, not a replacement, and that "both are needed for the complete story." Customers should also know, he instructed, that Smith had helped write the earlier book. Behind the collegiality, however, were more negative nuances. Collegiality was one thing, but business was another. "H & K book written hurriedly in six months, Smiths was written in 5 years," the talking points read. Smith had traveled to major research libraries, they were to say, while Hartzler and Kauffman had not. "H & K book a church history only," while the Smith book covers not only Mennonite religious life but also their music, customs, principles, and all other aspects of their lives. Most important of all, Smith instructed his student salesmen to tell potential customers that his would be "the last book that will be published on the subject for 50 year(s)."[34]

Had Smith's last claim been true, then the publication of *The Mennonites in America* would have had all sorts of interesting and weighty implications, both for how the Amish and Mennonite people understood their shared past and also for Smith himself and his place in the church. As he built up to the climax of one of his closing chapters, he assured his readers that the future contributions of Mennonite higher education were more promising than they had imagined. The Mennonite colleges, he rhapsodized, "ought to do much to bring about a better understanding between, if not an entire unification of at least all the more progressive wings of the Mennonite denomination." It is possible that, by that moment in time, Smith laid down such lines innocently and confidently. Perhaps he had not yet imagined that such analyses would be read as controversial, even inadmissible, by an emerging and rival group of church leaders. By 1909, however, he would not be able to proceed in such innocence much longer.[35]

6
The Way of Exile

Laura Ioder and C. Henry Smith were married at dawn the day after Christmas 1908. The wedding was held in the parlor of her parents' farmstead outside of Tiskilwa, and the couple then honeymooned by visiting kinfolk across the wintry landscape of central Illinois. Shortly after arriving back in Goshen, they proceeded to build a new home on a lot they purchased from Noah and Emma Byers, who lived next door, and they launched into their new life together. Smith's five final years at Goshen were "happy ones," Willard Smith later summarized, and with good reason. Sure, salaries were low—Smith made about $800 annually, Byers admitted later, about half of what he had earned teaching high school in Indianapolis—but living expenses were lower still. Beginning his Goshen teaching career at about the same time, Paul Whitmer rented a home for eight dollars a month, which allowed him to buy furniture, live comfortably, and save about $100 a year besides. Moreover, for Smith and his set of like-minded colleagues, more important than salary was the meaning in the work itself. "The pleasure of watching the evolution of green, awkward country boys and girls into young men and women of culture and influence," he declared in 1925, "is one of the compensations for the small pay and hard work involved in educational pioneering." By that point he could easily recite what to him were a string of Mennonite success stories, which he had helped make possible. There was, for example, the long-haired Amish lad who arrived in college wearing hooks instead of buttons, who ultimately became a professor of English in a prestigious state university. There was the Pennsylvania farm boy who rose from humble roots in a conservative Mennonite community to become a true "captain of industry" with a million-dollar fortune.[1]

Having determined, as Smith told Byers, "all the vital questions of my life," his vocational calling appeared to have solidified. Seemingly settled in Goshen for good, he could perform a vital role for the church, one that all his training, education, and the hundreds of smaller life decisions had now seemingly predestined him to play. It would have been plain to Smith that his fellow Mennonites harbored a marvelously rich historical tradition. Once they finally shed their reticence born from centuries-long rural isolation, they were called to share that tradition with their society, which stood to benefit immensely from it. At the same time, Smith and his professor colleagues would prepare a vanguard of educated young people who would guide the church to become the beacon of progressive influence that the times demanded. In his research and writing as the preeminent Mennonite historian of his day, it would be Smith's particular job to lay out the necessary markers from their past to assist the church in its transition to an exciting new era of change.

There was, however, an alternate potential Mennonite response to an era of social and cultural transformation. Rather than embrace change, the church could try to hold it at bay, erect the walls higher, and tack partway back in an Old Order direction. In 1908 Smith and his fellow progressive Mennonite educators had begun to grasp this possibility only dimly. When it became clear that key people Smith had heretofore regarded as allies would frame the MC Mennonite response to change along these lines, he would be faced with a difficult personal choice. He could follow along reluctantly—quieting his conscience, modifying his dress and behavior, and accepting significant limitations on his thinking and scholarship. Or he could refuse to accept that agenda and instead embark down a different path. In the context of the Amish Mennonite and MC Mennonite world in which Smith had been born, raised, and nurtured, it was a direction that could only be read as the way of exile.

"The Ascendancy of Social Christianity"

Goshen was, of course, quite unlike Chicago, with all of its burning problems and cultural enticements. Yet for progressive Mennonites like Smith, enough was happening there to accentuate the urgency of the transition Mennonites needed to make. In October 1907 the sparkling new Jefferson Theater, which sat more than a thousand patrons, was rebuilt in downtown Goshen in the ashes of the fire that had consumed it the previous year. The leading actors and actresses of the day soon made their way to the Maple City. The spring of 1908 saw the worst flood of its history hit the city, sweeping away key bridges and crippling the electrical grid for four days. By itself such natural forces demonstrated anew the need for an efficient and beneficent state, personified in the fall of 1908 by a visit to Goshen by Republican presidential candidate William Howard Taft. The forces of progress appeared in other guises, as well. In August 1911, with the whistle at the town waterworks heralding its approach, local people came running from their houses and craning their necks to witness what the *Goshen Daily News* proclaimed a "glorious" and "dashing" spectacle: an airplane coming at them from the east at about 350 feet high, the first such craft ever to pass over the city. An old-timer speaking that afternoon in a city park recalled the moment when, as a boy, he had arrived in the state in a covered wagon, now marveling at the wonder he had lived long enough to see.[2]

Smith and his colleagues worked hard to prepare their Mennonite students to meet the challenges of the new age. He soon fell back into his old groove, though now with the increased responsibilities accompanying his rare and elevated status as a Mennonite with a doctorate.[3] Within a year of his return, the *Goshen College Catalogue* listed him as teaching fourteen separate courses, ranging from a three-semester sequence in American history to medieval, British, and modern European history, to church history, to three classes in political science. In addition to this numbing regimen, he served on the faculty's "Public Occasions" committee and also functioned as faculty dean. This was an uncertain time for student enrollments; their numbers fluctuated from almost four hundred in 1907 to half that total six years later. But Byers and his dean doggedly pushed the institution ahead anyway. In 1906 Byers had inaugurated a $21,000 capital campaign that resulted in the construction of a new women's dormitory the following year. Within two years of Smith's arrival back in Goshen, at the commencement exercises of 1910 he could take pride in witnessing the first Goshen students to graduate with bachelor's degrees. Meanwhile, as in years past, the YPCA continued what the *Catalogue* termed its "aggressive Christian work" with the student body.[4]

Goshen College faculty circa 1909. Smith, back row, second from left. Boyd Smucker is standing to the right of Smith. Paul Whitmer, middle row, second from left. Noah Byers, front row, far left. Irvin Detweiler is standing to the immediate left of Byers. Mennonite Church USA Archives.

Smith, Byers, and others also made sure that an absolute, unswerving commitment to free intellectual inquiry propelled Goshen campus life. Smith, of course, had been loudly and insistently extolling this since arriving to teach at the Elkhart Institute a decade earlier. As far as the college's leadership could tell, this agenda would not meet much resistance from the church, at least as they experienced it locally. Byers and particularly college administrator J. S. Hartzler had played key roles in the founding of a Mennonite congregation to serve the college community, a process that had commenced not long after the institution had relocated to Goshen from Elkhart. While technically a creation of the Mennonite Church (i.e., MC), in its leadership, orientation, and functioning the new campus Mennonite church was really a union congregation between that body and the college's other major constituent group, the Amish Mennonites. It emerged from a series of meetings in the fall of 1903, during which the new congregation appointed Byers to head the Sunday school and Smith to function as "chorister." When Smith returned to Goshen in 1908, he quickly gravitated to the same positions of leadership, agreeing once again to head choral efforts and also to serve on the finance committee. With this kind of college-based church leadership (the congregation physically met in the college's Assembly Hall until 1950), it came as no surprise that, in the words of an early history of the church, the "entire membership" of the congregation "was in full sympathy with the spirit of the progressive cause."[5]

It soon proved impossible for such progressive Mennonite intellectuals to confine their concerns only to campus. When area prohibitionists began a local option campaign to drive the saloon from Elkhart County, both Byers and Smith lent a hand. By early 1911 Byers had been elected treasurer of the county Dry organization, and Smith had been tapped to deliver a major address at a key meeting. Naturally their campaign followed the contours of similar efforts that had percolated across the evangelical landscape now for decades. That March, the Goshen Dry forces intensified the local excitement by bringing to town the fiery fundamentalist preacher and ex-ballplayer Billy Sunday for an election-eve, men-only rally at the Jefferson Theater. With Byers on the stage next to him, Sunday denounced the Wet forces in the style for which he had become famous. They were "liars, dirty, black hearted liars," Sunday roared out to the packed house of 1,300 men. "When members of all churches join together to tell the saloon to go to hell, it will go to hell." But Sunday's fiery passion was not enough to overcome the power of Elkhart County saloons; the next day the Wet forces carried Elkhart, Goshen, and the county. In 1912 the Dry troops rallied again, and this time Smith took a central role. Already he had developed a habit, which he would follow much of the rest of his life, of carefully clipping out articles from various publications and filing them away in small envelopes for future consultation. The clippings reveal the degree to which his Chicago mentors like Charles Merriam had inculcated in him the methodologies of proper social science research. He clipped and filed dozens of different stories, mostly from newspapers in Elkhart County and Berne, Indiana, that argued both for and against Prohibition from a variety of angles: its impact on businesses and the family, for instance, or its relative effectiveness. In Elkhart County politics, however, there was no doubt which side he was on. As the campaign intensified, the Dry campaign printed and distributed to every Goshen home a special small newspaper containing personal attacks on the opposition's leaders. At the top of the list of names of the anti-saloon executive committee was "C. H. Smith."[6]

Nor did these Mennonite activist intellectuals confine their efforts to what were by now traditional causes like Prohibition. In the spring of 1910, Smith published a long article, serialized in three separate issues, in the influential (MC) Mennonite publication *Christian Monitor* called "The Forces that Make for Peace." The article contained little data on Mennonites but stressed the need for effective arguments for peace as a counter to war propaganda. Smith clearly intended his arguments as a contribution to such a literature, and he framed them perfectly in line with the confident optimism of his age. Ranging over a broad panorama of human history and sociology and once again building from an acceptance of theistic evolution, he hammered away at the central lesson of how "our growing spirit of humanitarianism has driven the practice of war to its last resort." The fact that Smith had originally delivered his piece as a speech to the Goshen chapter of the Women's Christian Temperance Union serves as a potent reminder of the multifaceted nature of progressive reform. But at no other time did Smith better illustrate this aspect of the reform crusade—and also his growing ability as an activist—than in 1911–12, with his energetic leadership of the Goshen-area campaign of the Men and Religion Forward Movement (MRFM).[7]

The Men and Religion Forward Movement originated in New York City in 1910 as a joint outreach of three interdenominational Protestant organizations, most notably the International YMCA, which quickly began planning for what promised to be one of the great evangelical crusades of the century. Within a year research teams had examined social conditions in nearly a hundred cities across North America, while the parent coalition secured funding from corporate titans like Rockefeller and J. P. Morgan. With that kind of focus from the beginning, as the movement picked up steam it proceeded along two parallel tracks. Alarmed at what its leaders perceived as a steady exodus of men from the Protestant churches, the central thrust of the MRFM would be winning back men and boys for Jesus. This traditional evangelical agenda would be manifested in activities like personal evangelism, missions work, and Bible study. Given the prominent leadership roles assumed in the movement by Social Gospel stalwarts such as Raymond Robins and Charles Stelzle, however, the movement's second line of attack would be avowedly social. The MRFM would emphasize, read its central declaration, "the modern message of the Church in social service and usefulness." To be sure, a quiet subtext of the campaign also involved goals like blunting the appeal of Catholicism in the nation's burgeoning urban centers and, as the historian Gail Bederman has charged, reinforcing male control of the church. Once the eight-month public phase of the movement began in 1911, it seemed sure to draw the enthusiasm of progressive Christian intellectuals like Smith. As its planners envisioned, the movement would take place in over seventy cities simultaneously, each with its own local chair and team charged with thoroughly investigating social conditions in their communities and bringing men back to Christ by a powerful blend of evangelism and social justice.[8]

Smith seems to have been involved in the Goshen MRFM movement from the beginning, and by June 1911 had been appointed its president. The local campaign soon provided another illustration, as the Social Gospel leader Walter Rauschenbusch phrased it, "of the ascendancy of social Christianity." On a personal level, it gave Smith a chance to harness his social science training to the agenda of the larger church and also further to develop his latent capacities for inspiring others. Before long he had helped to mobilize men from a broad coalition of Goshen Protestant churches and set them to work on an array of committees ranging from evangelism, finance, and publicity to "Boys Work" and "Social Service." Local MRFM activists, which included Byers and other progressive allies like Amish Mennonite bishop Jonathan Kurtz, conducted surveys of community needs, ran Bible studies, talked with area hospitals and the YMCA, and brought in an expert to lecture on the "sex question." Another team of researchers carefully investigated the extent of the "liquor traffic" across the county. Then, in November, the campaign went public with a big banquet and rally at the Knights of Pythias Hall in downtown Goshen. Smith presided over the meeting and introduced the first in a series of noted area dignitaries. They fired up the crowd before giving way to the keynote speaker, dean Shailer Matthews of the University of Chicago Divinity School, whom Smith may have secured through his grad school connections. Matthews held forth at length on the subject of "Masculine Christianity." While "a woman's religion is a good thing for a woman," he admitted, the church really needed not "sissies" or "mollycoddles" but fighting Christian men who would strike hard against the forces of evil.[9]

Meanwhile, as leader of the local campaign, Smith seized the opportunity to reflect broadly and publicly on the social responsibilities of the church. "The Christian principles of love, service and sacrifice are the only solutions for our great national problems," he told a rapt audience gathered in a Lutheran church in nearby Millersburg in December. There was, for instance, the "negro problem" and the festering issue of rapid immigration. Proceeding in the informed tones of a trained social scientist, he rattled off statistics in support of his points, like the fact that the proportion of foreign-born exceeded the native-born population in nineteen different states, that two-thirds of factory workers were foreigners, and that Catholic Church membership had grown by 50 percent in the past decade alone, compared with 6 percent among the Protestants. Other developments caused him similar alarm. Labor was becoming "more dissatisfied," he noted, and surely there was "something wrong" when half the nation's wealth was owned by 1 percent of the population. "Christianity is bound to win" in the end, he proclaimed, but only if the church threw itself into the social issues of their day, for "you cannot save a man's soul until you save his body." Altogether the young professor thoroughly impressed his audience. It was clear that evening, summarized a local newspaper, that "Mr. Smith is a fluent and forceful speaker."[10]

Undoubtedly Smith's Goshen years were busy ones. If a new marriage, a heavy teaching load, college administration, and widespread civic activity were not enough, he continued to send a fair torrent of articles to the Mennonite denominational press. He described the Amish of Illinois in the *Mennonite Yearbook*, and acquainted readers of the *Christian Monitor* with the heroic life of pioneer Mennonite educator Christopher Dock. In his popular writing on such Mennonite historical subjects, Smith elaborated on the same basic theme that had dominated his writing for the past decade: the richness of Mennonite history and its tremendous utility for the present. In a brief serialized biography of Menno Simons, he told readers that what Tolstoy preaches today merely echoes Menno's message of four centuries ago. Menno's fame will grow, he predicted, as civilization continues in its current path and "rids itself of the monster war." For "the truth is" that, in their dedication to the "simple truth" of the Sermon on the Mount, "the Mennonites are not behind the rest of the world but . . . they are ahead of the world and the world is trying to catch up."[11]

Already by 1909, however, Smith was beginning to learn that he and his fellow Mennonite progressives were ahead of many of the Mennonite laity and that a powerful set of more traditionalist leaders had not caught up with his vision. The great Mennonite quickening, it appeared, had about run its course, and new dynamics at work in the Mennonite world began to push in a different direction. Such developments would have profound implications for Mennonite intellectuals of all stripes, including the framers of Mennonite history.

Leaders Resist the "Whirlpool of Worldliness"

By the mid-1890s, Theron Schlabach has summarized, "Mennonite leaders began trying to bring the quickening and acculturation processes under control." Fifteen years later they had succeeded, though a new set of captains was in charge. Battles had raged over control of a variety of the new institutions the quickening had wrought: the orphanages, the publishing house, the missions committees, and the Bible conferences. These conflicts had been driven, in part, by a generational struggle. By the time Smith settled back into Goshen, certain winners and losers had emerged. John Funk epitomized the losers. The old Elkhart bishop, Leonard Gross noted, had been an able journalist and even better activist; his response to the 1870s arrival of ten thousand Mennonite migrants from Ukraine had bordered on the heroic. But his authoritarian tendencies had intensified through the 1890s, as younger activists pried loose his fingers from the levers of power. The process had been messy at times. After tensions at Funk's Prairie Street congregation had escalated, for instance, a larger group of MC congregational authorities removed him from power. By 1907 his Mennonite Publishing Company, ravaged by a devastating fire and the failure of an area bank, had plunged into bankruptcy. Meanwhile, a younger set of activists headed by Daniel Kauffman established a rival center of power in Scottdale, Pennsylvania, where they began publishing a competing Mennonite periodical called the *Gospel Witness*. Within a year Funk conceded the struggle, sold his interests, and in the private pages of his journal increasingly gave way to despair.[12]

Kauffman and his comrades astutely made a rhetorical connection to Funk's old paper, renamed the new Mennonite Church organ the *Gospel Herald*, and quickly moved to consolidate their power. Coffman might have managed the leadership transition process with more pastoral gentleness had he lived into the new century, but even some of his protégés like Steiner, cautioning younger people to not allow "their enthusiasm [to] run away with them," began to see the wisdom of pulling back on the reins of change. Through the first decade of the new century, as Smith labored away at Mennonite history, other emerging new Mennonite leaders created a series of ecclesiastical structures that centralized their authority. Key new churchly mechanisms appeared: a board of education in 1905, a board of missions the next year, and a publication board in 1908. Preceding and propelling them all was a churchwide general body, the rudiments of a new Mennonite denomination called the Mennonite General Conference, which took shape in 1898. These structures would furnish positions of power to Steiner and many in his younger leadership cohort. Yet within a decade after the creation of the Mennonite General Conference, above all these new churchly authorities the towering figure of Daniel Kauffman reigned supreme.[13]

By 1909 Kauffman had relocated to Scottdale, where he would function as editor of the *Gospel Herald* until a year before his death in 1944. At one point he managed to work simultaneously on twenty-two different church boards or committees. He achieved this control for a variety of reasons. He seemed to possess a talent for church infighting and also a ready ability to enlist God's sanction for his actions: "no one present doubted that God was with us," he noted later about the creation of the Mennonite General Conference. He also strengthened his hand immeasurably through his parallel construction of an authoritative Mennonite corpus of Bible doctrine. From the days of the Anabaptists through the nineteenth century, Norman Kraus argues, Mennonites had accepted the moral authority of the Bible and emphasized "faithful obedience to its precepts," but had not necessarily regarded it as factually inerrant or as "authoritative doctrine." From the turn of the century and especially from 1908 on, Kauffman set out to remedy this perceived deficiency. Beginning in 1898 with his *A Manual of Bible Doctrine*, and then continuing later with a seven-hundred-page series of massive, edited texts called *Doctrines of the Bible*, Kauffman and his allies began to lay out a doctrinal catechism for the Mennonite Church that would deepen in its rigidity in the ensuing years. Rooted in

Daniel Kauffman at his typewriter, circa 1913. Daniel and Crissie Shank Photographs, HM4-329SC, Mennonite Church USA Archives.

a new view of the Bible as utterly authoritative and factually inerrant, it furnished a step-by-step plan of salvation and a codified explanation of divinely inspired rules to guide Mennonite theological thinking and proper behavior. It also, Mennonite scholars later noted, subtly elevated the primacy of doctrinal precepts like salvation over now secondary-level considerations like ethics or nonresistance.[14]

In all these developments, Kauffman and his allies saw themselves as acting in the best interests of the church at large. Too much unfiltered borrowing from outside society—as some of the Mennonite progressives like Smith would demonstrate—could be problematic for the church. "See the relentless war which is being waged against us," Kauffman editorialized in Funk's *Herald of Truth* in 1896, as he built support for the creation of the Mennonite General Conference. "See how many of our young people are carried away into the whirlpool of worldliness. . . . Why can't we get together, understand each other better, and do something?" Nor is it fair to interpret the codified rules and the ecclesiastical and theological structures that Kauffman's cohort constructed solely as some kind of oppressive system foisted down from above onto a captive Mennonite Church. Such structures provoked vigorous dissent and a fair stream of exiles into other Mennonite groups, but it is easy to lose sight of the fact, Gross points out, that many other Mennonites accepted them unreservedly. Kauffman's *Doctrines of the Bible* books sold well and were reissued in a third edition as late as 1928.[15]

The closing-down of the quickening and the new, hierarchical Mennonite Church that emerged are critical here for another reason. They underscore the fundamental irony that permeated the intellectual and ecclesiastical world in which Smith and his allies and adversaries lived out their adult lives. Both church progressives and their conservative antagonists would battle hard for the supremacy of their vision of a normative and supposedly untainted Mennonitism, but both would do so through often uncritical borrowing of outside worldviews. Take, for example, the many Mennonite Church regional bodies that began systematically printing meeting minutes and rule books, the rationalized administrative procedures, the many mission boards and church agencies, and, most critically of all, the bureaucratic, centralized structures of the Mennonite General Conference. All these mechanisms were created by an educated Mennonite leadership to strengthen their church's capacity to resist and regulate change. At the same time, such developments not coincidentally mirrored the operative structures of other Protestant church groups, which had created and utilized such structures as a means of defining and legitimating themselves as denominations.[16]

The parallel Mennonite ecclesiastical structures would set the parameters of Smith's professional and ecclesiastical world for the rest of his life. Similarly, the emergence of a powerful new theological and cultural force would significantly reshape the face of American Christianity. For Smith, Byers, and most of their academic and churchly allies, this force would function as the great foil to their vision—the antithesis to their thesis—from the beginning of the century to well past Smith's death in 1948. This was a creative Mennonite adaptation of another outside import: the transdenominational religious movement known as Protestant fundamentalism.

Fundamentalism began percolating in late Gilded Age America partly as a response to the apparent triumph of the Darwinian revolution and the rise of liberal theology, and partly to the accompanying sense among many evangelical Protestants that something had gone terribly wrong in their country. In the hands of its foremost recent interpreter, George Marsden, the movement was not merely reactive. Instead, far from a "temporary social aberration," fundamentalism was "a genuine religious movement or tendency with deep roots and intelligible beliefs." Its origins were multifaceted and developed concurrently in many different wellsprings in the American religious landscape. It was seen in the holiness movement, in dispensationalist premillennialism, and in the warm, pietistic revivalism of Moody's campaigns. For many religious conservatives, the movement's headquarters was the Bible institute Moody established in Chicago, but it was too dynamic and variegated to be located in any one place. Instead, it took many forms as it poured like a river across most major Protestant denominations: in the theological heresy trials riveting the ranks of the Northern Methodists, Presbyterians, and Lutherans, or in the Niagara Bible Conferences in New York, where disciples of dispensationalist Cyrus Scofield pored through his reference Bible with the intensity of rabbis examining a Talmudic text. Given the movement's multifaceted nature, generalizations about core fundamentalist beliefs are shaky, but certain key affirmations seem to have been widely shared. These included, as summarized by William Trollinger, a resolute commitment to "the supernaturalness and literal accuracy of the Bible, the supernatural character of Christ, including his bodily resurrection and imminent return to earth, and the necessity of Christians separating themselves from 'the world.'" In 1910 the movement acquired a name when two wealthy evangelicals in Los Angeles funded the publication of twelve booklets called *The Fundamentals*, which summarized conservative evangelical theology and lent coherence to the movement. It was bound together by its unflagging and bitter determination to oppose theological modernism in its every manifestation—a theology, one Moody Bible Institute president averred, that was simply "a revolt against the God of Christianity"—and also the threat that such a belief system posed to traditional American culture. As such, fundamentalism was both a theological and cultural movement of resistance. Many who claimed the new title of fundamentalist harbored no illusions about where the headquarters of the opposition lay. One of the financial sponsors of *The Fundamentals* openly intended his booklets as a reply to "those infidel professors in Chicago University."[17]

Given the rapidly shrinking cultural distance from their evangelical Protestant neighbors, Mennonites encountered fundamentalism in one form or another quite early on. Many warmed to it immediately and without reservation, others with more discrimination. Militant fundamentalism among MC Mennonites took hold especially strongly in Virginia's Shenandoah Valley and exerted a powerful influence there through much of the twentieth century. For this reason, Kauffman embraced it partly because of conviction and partly to guard his own right flank. Even so, he was at times critical of the national movement for its uncritical embrace of nationalism and militarism. Mennonites in the American Midwest encountered fundamentalism quite early, especially in the powerful influence of Moody Bible Institute (MBI), which permeated Mennonite circles particularly in rural Illinois. Both Coffman and Steiner commented favorably on Moody's revival campaigns and readily attended lectures by leaders of the emerging fundamentalist movement at his Bible institute, including expositions on his dispensationalist framework by Scofield. Mennonite students at MBI would later become so numerous as to compose something like a "Who's Who" of Illinois Mennonites. Of course, just because they attended the institute did not mean such Mennonites bought the whole fundamentalist package—especially not, Willard Smith cautions, in the movement's early days. This generalization seems especially accurate for some future Illinois Mennonite leaders like Emanuel Troyer and Lee Lantz, who later emerged as firm progressive allies of Smith, Byers, and others at Bluffton. Part of MBI's attraction for such people may just have been its theological conservatism, tempered by memories of Dwight Moody's Civil War–era pacifism.[18]

Because the emerging, more militant brand of twentieth-century fundamentalism did not translate easily into a Mennonite idiom—many, like Kauffman, found its affinity for militarism distasteful—some Mennonite scholars guardedly apply or even avoid the term *fundamentalist* to describe Mennonites. Paul Toews, for instance, insists that Mennonite fundamentalism "is really something more akin to denominational conservatism than American fundamentalism." Certainly, for many Mennonites, a major reason for its attractiveness was not so much its theology as its ready means of strengthening the bonds of separateness from American culture. Undoubtedly this was a major aspect of its appeal to people like Kauffman. For this emerging group of powerful Mennonite Church leaders, the line between theological and cultural liberalism was probably a fuzzy one. As the Mennonite historian Guy Hershberger later recognized, any cultural or theological trend such leaders disliked or found threatening could simply be banned as the fruit of "modernism." In this manner, writes Kraus, "a good deal of the excitement over liberalism was simply imported from the outside and superimposed upon the very real problem of cultural adaptation and reapplication of scripture which faced the Mennonite Church." Mennonites and Amish Mennonites alike soon heard new messages echoing down from pulpits across the church. "Henry Weldy of Wakarusa Ind. Preached here Sunday," Emma Smith wrote her brother Henry in 1910 from the farmstead near Metamora. "He was awful strict. He spoke against tobacco saloons pictures standup collars flashy ties albums lace curtains and everything else you could think of. I never heard a preacher speak like he did."[19]

Fundamentalism, many in the MC leadership realized, could easily become a powerful means of simultaneously resisting the seductions of outside culture while reinforcing the new hierarchies. Nowhere was the process better revealed than in the increasingly tough restrictions that the new hierarchy placed on permissible Mennonite dress. The restrictions had appeared in the late Gilded Age; in his revivals Coffman had reinforced the wearing of the bonnet by Mennonite women and the collarless "plain coat" by men as a symbol of new religious devotion. But the process intensified in the first two decades of the new century, paralleling and emerging from the new authority patterns. In 1911 the General Conference established an official dress committee (including, among others, Kauffman), and its 1913 report (authored by Kauffman) spelled out with increasing specificity the expected standards of Mennonite dress. Mennonite sociologists later read such mechanisms as textbook examples of "defensive structuring": efforts to reinforce cultural walls in an era of sweeping socioeconomic and demographic change. Likewise, later analysts writing in the deepening vein of Mennonite feminism recognized in such mechanisms an unmistakable effort by a male Mennonite leadership cohort to reinforce patterns of female subordination. Women's suffragists, Kauffman declared in 1920, were "enemies of the Bible," for "the Bible teaches woman's subjection, this order must be obeyed." In such efforts, Christian fundamentalism fit hand in glove. Plain dress became a Mennonite symbol that one had been saved.[20]

Certainly, fundamentalism was attractive to new leaders because it reinforced the means of Mennonite cultural separation. It remains difficult to believe, however, that many Mennonites could so widely adopt the forms of fundamentalism without also absorbing its theological content. From about 1908 on, except for a stress on Mennonite distinctives like dress, the comprehensive body of Bible doctrine that Kauffman and his allies developed and integrated into the fabric of the Mennonite Church bore uncanny resemblance to a similar body of teaching reverberating across the wider world of American Protestant fundamentalism. Kauffman's *Gospel Herald* approvingly cited and reprinted articles by leaders of the national fundamentalist movement like Reuben Torrey and William Bell Riley. The language and concepts of the movement increasingly peppered the *Gospel Herald* as well, such as the slogan of the Niagara Bible Conference and denunciations of liberal theology, higher criticism, and evolution. The doctrines were soon reflected in the wider Mennonite Church. By 1913 individual MC district conferences began passing resolutions expressing key fundamentalist concepts like the infallibility and the verbal and plenary inspiration of the Bible. Meanwhile, from 1909 to 1944 the Mennonite Publishing House in Scottdale promoted and sold in its catalog the Scofield Reference Bible, the intellectual anchor of dispensationalist premillennialism. And in this ready absorption of and identification with the national movement of Christian fundamentalism, the new leadership of the Mennonite General Conference also took to heart its great crusade against theological liberalism. Many of its most zealous Mennonite adherents took their cues accordingly and stood ready to wage relentless war against the perceived modernist enemy in whatever guise it should appear. They alerted themselves to the language of liberalism and the channels of its influence: its academic and popular journals, its colleges and seminaries. They especially watched for the signs of its emergence in their own ranks. By 1909 a self-selected coterie of Mennonite antimodernist crusaders stood ready to give battle.[21]

Locking Horns with John Horsch

In 1908, shortly before Kauffman relocated to Scottdale, he was preceded there by a chastened John Horsch, who had recently emerged from a personal and spiritual wilderness and now stood ready to fight against their common enemies. He had undergone quite a journey since his years as Ludwig Keller's eager tool for influencing the Mennonites of North America. Through the early 1890s, Horsch had continued to work closely with Keller to propagate his mentor's vision in his capacity as editor of Funk's *Herold der Wahrheit*. But this relationship came to an end for reasons scholars can only speculate. It may have been because of Keller's frustration with a Mennonite unwillingness to embrace his teachings completely. Perhaps the break also reflected Horsch's deepening engagement with the subculture of American revivalism. Whatever the cause, it is clear that correspondence between the two men ended in 1893. Two years later, unhappy with personal relationships in Funk's publishing house and disillusioned with the Mennonite church, Horsch severed his relationship with Funk. For years afterward he drifted, hovering at times on the edge of poverty, cobbling together student stints at the University of Wisconsin, teaching school in Illinois, and editing a German-language farm journal. The new century found him in Berne, Indiana, and then in the Cleveland area, typesetting and editing with a small firm called the Light and Hope Publishing Company of the Missionary Church Association. Meanwhile he pointedly refrained from membership in any church until joining a Baptist congregation near Cleveland. It was there in 1908, the story goes, that Steiner came upon him, supposedly remarking to Aaron Loucks, the general manager of the Mennonite Publishing House in Scottdale, that "this man is a Mennonite at heart, and we must get him back into the service of the church." Shortly afterward Horsch moved to Scottdale, where he would make his living editing German-language publications for the publishing house until his death in 1941. Ever the driven writer, Horsch almost immediately resumed his former career as a scholar and apologist for Anabaptism, though now possessed by a new theological framework.[22]

At some point in Horsch's dark spiritual sojourn (perhaps as early as 1902), he adopted nearly completely the doctrine and worldview of fundamentalism. Within a month of his arrival in Scottdale, at the invitation of Kauffman, Horsch published in the *Gospel Herald* a sweeping denunciatory description of the new modern theology. Horsch and Kauffman clearly intended the piece as a wake-up call to the Mennonite churches—to quote the article's title—on "the Dangers of Liberalism." Highlighting a University of Chicago theologian whose writings he judged especially alarming, Horsch posed a rhetorical question: "What use is there in writing about Liberalism in the *Gospel Herald*" in light of a prevailing view he had encountered, "that there is little danger of modern unbelief finding its way into the church"? In other denominations, Horsch answered, "the New Theology has 'come in unawares' through the agency of a few men, while others seemed to be asleep." The avenue of entry appeared to be a willingness to accept free intellectual inquiry, which "is clearly contrary to the principles of the Gospel." Soon he was warning of "The Consequences of Higher Criticism," which had enveloped the Protestant churches of Germany in "a loathsome spectacle of disintegration, of death by the slow process of suicide." By 1911 he was attacking a German Mennonite pastor for his apparent embrace of free thinking and his description of the Mennonite church as "undogmatic." In his condemnation of unfettered intellectual inquiry he knew well whereof he spoke, he admitted fifteen years later in a surprisingly revealing letter to Charles Clayton Morrison, editor of the liberal vehicle the *Christian Century*. "I am a Mennonite and a fundamentalist," Horsch declared flatly to Morrison, also admitting that "for a long period I have been a modernist and have tried modernism in actual experience."[23]

From Horsch's subsequent writing on Anabaptist history, it is evident that he later equated his years of service to Keller as an apprenticeship in modernism. Immediately upon arriving in Scottdale, he reapplied himself to his life's work, characterized by his future son-in-law Harold Bender as "reviving the church through writing." Thereafter Horsch would use his prodigious talents as a writer and publicist on behalf of two major causes: the furtherance of Anabaptist-Mennonite history, and an equally energetic service to the cause of Christian fundamentalism by a ceaseless attack on modernism, especially on a perceived Mennonite strand he thought he could identify. Indeed, he soon discovered that the two enterprises could easily be conflated. Already by 1910 his new faith commitments had triggered a significant rereading of the origins and development of early Anabaptism. From that point on, Horsch (and leading thinkers of the "Goshen School" of Anabaptist historiography, who would later take their cues from him) insisted the origins of Anabaptism could be precisely and solely traced to the Swiss Brethren, the young radicals like Manz, Grebel, and Blaurock, who broke with Zwingli at Zurich in the winter of 1524–25. The figure of Hans Denck—whom Horsch, as Keller's disciple, had lionized with such devotion for years—suddenly no longer belonged in the Anabaptist pantheon, for "Denck advocated a rationalizing view of the scriptures" ("rationalizing" almost surely signifying *liberal*) and embraced an unbiblical grasp of justification. At the same time, Horsch's newfound reading of Anabaptist history through the framework of fundamentalism led him to view with disfavor scholars who did not take a similar approach. In 1911 he focused his lens on the star history professor at Goshen.[24]

Smith and Horsch had established a relationship by correspondence as early as January 1908, when they exchanged letters exploring their mutual interest in books on Anabaptism. From the very beginning, they were cordial in their personal exchanges. Still living at that time in a Cleveland suburb, Horsch seemed deferential to Smith's expertise, admitting that "on the history of the Mennonites in America, I have done little, if any, original work." (Smith seemed to agree with Horsch on that point; in the otherwise extensive bibliography to his 1909 *The Mennonites of America*, he included not a single reference to Horsch's voluminous writings on Anabaptism.) Within three years, however, Horsch's new religious framework furnished him the tools he needed to judge Smith's reading of Anabaptism, and he took square aim at it in a blistering article on "The Anabaptist View of Toleration." He did not mention Smith by name. Yet from Horsch's opening lines on—"In the opinion of a number of recent writers the Anabaptists, including the early Mennonites, were the champions of the modern liberalistic view of toleration"—it would have been clear to any educated Mennonite which writers he principally had in mind. In Smith's writing on Anabaptism, he had, of course, been emphasizing their prizing of freedom of conscience and demand for religious toleration. "The very thing" that Anabaptists battled so hard for, Smith stressed in 1909 in *The Mennonites of America*, "was individual freedom in matters of religion." At the same time, Smith also stated, an inch further down the page, that the Anabaptists established the Bible as "the final authority on all matters of faith and discipline." It may have been that Horsch simply missed the qualifier, but at any rate he had read Smith's stress on the first half of that equation. In line with the commitments to proper doctrine permeating the MC world and operative within fundamentalism more broadly, Horsch judged as a "baseless assertion" the claim that "the Swiss Brethren and early Mennonites held conscience to be the final authority, instead of the Holy Scriptures." He made clear, of course, that his definition of Mennonites was inclusive only of those from Switzerland, South Germany, and the Netherlands. Others—including "the 'Denckians,' the rationalistic Anabaptists of the South"—did not qualify as members of the church, and all soon disappeared anyway. Real Mennonites certainly "had a system of well-defined doctrine," and claims otherwise were little more than aspects of "the modern liberalistic aversion to doctrine and creed."[25]

Smith responded immediately to Horsch's charges, publishing within a month a piece in the *Christian Monitor* on "The Early Mennonites as Bible Students." While not mentioning Horsch by name, he almost certainly meant it as a direct rebuttal. He reiterated the Anabaptists' deep knowledge of the Scriptures and their ardent devotion to Bible study. Then he drew out the obvious point of the lesson for Mennonite readers. "The Mennonites recognized no authority above the Bible," Smith reiterated, "and they were right. History proves there is always a tendency to make philosophy, tradition and dogma—in other words, the explanations of man, take the place of the Bible itself as the guide to spiritual life." There was, he continued, another common error during the Reformation "from which we might derive profit." In the eagerness to read Scripture correctly, many people "often overemphasized certain passages of scripture at the expense of others. References were frequently taken out of their context. . . . This is still a danger we need to avoid."[26]

Smith and Horsch would cross swords again soon enough. For Horsch's kind of thinking quickly began to gather enough denominational momentum to bring the possibility of profound change to Mennonite colleges.

Theological Reverberations at Mennonite Colleges

By their very purpose and being, Mennonite colleges challenged church conservatives. To the many Mennonites who prized a lay pastorate and distrusted a "hireling ministry," college programs designed to train pastors were particularly suspect. Especially for the MC and Amish Mennonites east of the Mississippi, the traditional association of the farm with spiritual purity and subsequent distrust of intellectual pursuits rendered the phrase "Mennonite higher education" something of an oxymoron. James Juhnke states it well. "The Mennonite colleges," he writes, "were crucibles of contradiction. They stood not only between traditional, German-speaking Mennonitism and progressive, English-speaking Americanism but also in the midst of the double transition from farm to town to city." Almost automatically, every Mennonite college soon found itself in a deep and pervasive conflict with many Mennonites in the pews. One could pick almost blindly among the writings of Mennonite intellectuals and church leaders and find a hundred disparate quotes that would illustrate this tension. "The function of the small college is to distribute among the masses the necessary enlightenment," Smith insisted in 1925. To Kauffman, in contrast, the Mennonite college existed as a means by which "our young people [can] be protected from the dangers of the sinful and selfish world." It fell to presidents of Mennonite colleges to straddle this gap. Most found this a nearly impossible task, and one that rendered their terms relatively short.[27]

In Goshen Noah Byers found himself caught in a balancing act that grew more delicate with each passing year. In affirming the call John E. Hartzler felt for evangelistic work, for example, he embraced in a single sentence the opposite poles then operative in American Protestantism, suggesting to Hartzler he take summer courses "at the Moody institute or University of Chicago, or both." Byers was fully cognizant of the task at hand. "There is a strong reactionary spirit among some of the leaders," he informed his prize student, "and while it is a good thing and nobody wants to fight it, yet I think we need some who will emphasize other features of the general cause, in order that we may keep a proper balance in the work as a whole." He maintained a polite relationship with Kauffman, cordially receiving his suggestions for improvements needed at the college—which included keeping faculty and students away from all worldly amusements, fashionable dress, intercollegiate athletic encounters, musical instruments, and any "trace of higher criticism or any other form of infidelity," Kauffman said. As long as Goshen College kept those things at bay, Kauffman affirmed, "I bid you Godspeed." After an MC committee on dress had investigated the college in 1907, Byers found it politic to begin wearing the plain coat. Late in 1908 he sent out a circular letter to twenty MC pastors whose support was critical for the college, including Kauffman and Steiner, inviting them to pinpoint sources of congregational unhappiness. A majority of the respondents agreed that Goshen suffered from two problems in particular: fashionable faculty dress and the prevalence of musical instruments, both of which Byers carefully defended. Yet he could not mask his growing frustration. "You will find me reasonable when I am counseled with in a charitable manner," he informed this group of important pastors, "but inclined to resent being dictated to by those who will not listen to explanation." He had bought too deeply into the professional ethos to give much ground to traditionalist critics on key academic issues. "You can't fool the people, when they go to school they want to get good work by trained men," he groused privately to Steiner.[28]

Moreover, Byers's efforts at damage control with conservatives would be continually undermined by the larger climate of free personal expression and intellectual excitement that he, Smith, and others had been responsible for creating. Photographs of bare-limbed Goshen students in athletic and swimming gear caused him immense trouble when circulated among the deeply conservative Mennonites in Virginia's Shenandoah Valley. College fundraisers found that concerns about inappropriate student dress significantly hampered their efforts.[29]

For the increasing numbers of Mennonites who had begun to resonate to fundamentalist arguments, even more ominous was the appearance on campus of two University of Chicago professors in 1908, one of whom lectured on literary approaches to Bible study. While professors and students found the lectures "interesting and inspiring," summarized a Goshen College historian in 1955, they also served as a lightning rod for further criticism. Some of it came directly to Byers from Horsch, who had joined other conservatives in watching Goshen with a critical eye. "It is not merely some of the men of the University of Chicago whose attitude is incompatible with the principles of biblical Christianity," Horsch instructed Goshen's president, "but *it is University itself* [emphasis in the original]." "I know the attitude of the 'liberals' in this matter," he maintained. "They say: read all the books you can, the more you read or hear of theological do[ctrines], whether they be sound or unsound . . . the better." The sense of alarm felt not only by Horsch but by many other conservative critics undoubtedly deepened when an influential Goshen professor like Smith appeared on stage in downtown Goshen in 1911 with Shailer Matthews, dean of the University of Chicago Divinity School and by then the very symbol of modernism for fundamentalists across the church. Goshen's president sharply defended his college against such attacks, warning Horsch against "the danger of getting the spirit of the Pharisee and the Persecutor." Byers especially objected to Horsch's guilt-by-association inferences, telling him plainly that "I cannot help but feel you are unduly prejudiced against men, simply because they are associated with the University of Chic[ago]."[30]

The premier Chicago alumnus on Goshen's faculty was, of course, its history professor. Undoubtedly Smith watched the way the winds were blowing across the MC landscape and did not like them. Even before he had arrived back in Goshen in 1908, his friend Orie Yoder had cautioned him to "be very careful." In his 1909 book, Smith warned of the growing power of Mennonite bishops and the opportunity it afforded "a few men of strong personality to dominate the conference and dictate the policy of the church." The coming years at Goshen would provide Smith with a multitude of what would have struck him as appalling and personal illustrations of this point. Years later he distinctly recalled his disgust at arriving at church one Sunday morning to witness Byers being called to account for his "sin" in serving as judge at an educational exhibit at the county fair. He would have read Horsch's 1911 article on toleration as an attack both on his scholarship and on his theological soundness. He would have likewise noted Horsch's new place of employment and the powerful new allies he was making. It would have been clear to Smith by then the limitations such new authorities would put on the free expression of ideas, which he understood as the very heart of academic life. Whether the usable past he was then constructing for his church would be appreciated at Goshen, or even allowed, was increasingly in question. "The germ" of Anabaptist teaching, he asserted in 1909, was "that no outside authority, either lay or ecclesiastical, has the right to force any religious system upon the people." Read in this light, it is clear that Smith's emphasis on such ideas may have emerged, at least in part, as a kind of ideological preemptive strike against the new forces of fundamentalism he saw rising in his church. Neither did Smith appreciate the way that the more conservative MC district representatives had been granted increased authority on Goshen's board of trustees. It may have been for this reason he had disagreed with Byers back in 1905 about strengthening their influence. He had watched the Central Illinois Conference—with which he had increasingly begun to identify—petition the board for representation. Had it been granted, he was confident that the Central Conference would have embraced Goshen as its denominational school. Instead, "too conservative to admit outside participation," Smith said, Goshen's trustees had turned them away.[31]

Undoubtedly Smith reacted negatively to the changes afoot in the Mennonite Church for more private and personal reasons, as well. The religious changes swirling through it in those years—the lengthy expositions of authoritative doctrine, the expressive new language of fundamentalism—excited many Mennonites, but not all. Certainly they did not enthrall Smith. He had come to his God in a manner that was increasingly out of date: not through the emotional persuasion of a revivalist, or through the intellectual appeal of a doctrinal catechism, but through the ancient bonds of the Amish Mennonite community. "Mennonites did not believe in protracted meetings," he wrote in 1925. "We arrived at our convictions through a gradual period of education in the home and church, and through our growing consciences." In reading his extensive correspondence with Laura Ioder in the critical life moment of their courtship, one is struck by the absence in his writing of nearly anything resembling God-talk. The only time he referred to the workings of God at all was in his joyful moments in September 1907, after Ioder's acceptance of his marriage proposal, when he had reflected back on their "chance" meeting the previous spring. "If there is such a thing as the special interference of providence in the affairs of men," he theorized wondrously, "I believe there was something of the providential in our meeting and subsequent career." Or, for another example, witness his words of condolence to his friend J. R. Thierstein in the mid-1920s, when he had just returned from Europe and received the word about the tragic death of Thierstein's teenage son. Amid words of sympathy, he suggested that "life is a strange compound any way of bitter and sweet experiences, but no doubt in the divine plan of things each has its place and every sorrow has its compensations if we only knew them." Throughout his life Smith seems to have maintained a belief in the power of God. Yet he was increasingly out of step with many in his church when he did not express it or perhaps even understand it in the increasingly prevalent style of popular evangelicalism.[32]

Having learned as an Amish Mennonite child how to buckle to church authorities, Smith could have chosen to adapt to the new trends, to don the required new gear and squelch outward expressions of dissent. But he also knew the personal unhappiness such a course would have brought his life partner. In 1925 Bender would note to Horsch that among the Goshen student body, "a number of the young girls, especially from Illinois, are quite 'dressy.'" It is clear that this trend went back decades and that Laura Ioder Smith was part of it. In the fall of 1907, after she had accepted Smith's marriage proposal and saw which direction his career was headed, she asked her fiancée with apprehension about the dress customs of "the church you belong to . . . and say—at Goshen one must wear a little white cap. Tell me about their rules there, won't you?" The prospect of dress codes would have brought her some anxiety, because Mennonite women in rural Bureau County enjoyed more freedom. A month before Smith's wedding, his sister Emma wrote to tell him that she had just met one of the Ioder sisters at a Bible conference, and "she seemed a very proud girl." "I hope Laura isn't that way," Emma said to her brother. But to Emma, Laura probably would have seemed proud (or worldly) as well. Laura's younger sister Clara, nicknamed "Mace," had attended a Bible conference in Tiskilwa the previous year. This was evidently an ecumenical gathering among Illinois Mennonites, for Mace had run into over a hundred "strangers," some of whom were from the Metamora area. (One of the strangers Mace had met, Laura wrote Henry, was "your sister"; Mace had found her "very sweet.") Mace had reported, Laura said, that "the meetings were very good also very Mennonitey. . . . The women were 'cappy and some of the men tie-less.'" The presence of caps and the absence of ties was a noteworthy matter to the Ioders. They wanted no part of such dress codes, and, not long after Laura's marriage, they acted on their convictions. A fair number of the members at the old Willow Springs congregation had reached a breaking point with the increasingly tough MC dress restrictions. In the fall of 1911, they invited a Central Conference bishop named Lee Lantz to hold revival meetings in the area. Shortly afterward Lantz assisted them in withdrawing from Willow Springs and forming Tiskilwa Mennonite Church, which soon joined the Central Conference church. Church records from the time show that Laura's brother William and sister Mary supported the new congregation financially. In November 1914 her now-widowed mother and brothers Julius and Almer were listed as members, and her brother William retained his membership there until his death in 1957. Elaine Bowers remembered once, as a child, asking her Ioder aunts—her aunt Laura, along with aunts Mace and Mary—why they had left the old Willow Springs church. Because "we wanted to wear hats," came their reply.[33]

For all of these reasons, Smith surely would have regarded with some dismay the theological and ecclesiastical winds then blowing in the Mennonite Church. They also explain why he, Byers, and their academic allies would have been attracted to a countervailing trend then rapidly escalating in the Midwest. By 1909 Smith had already come up with a name for it, and began watching it favorably. He called it "the unification movement."[34]

The Mennonite Union Movement

Movements toward Mennonite unity had been percolating in fits and starts for the previous half century. Under the guidance of its founder John Oberholtzer, the General Conference Mennonite Church had originally been founded in part with such an aim in mind. Since then, appeals for increased cooperation among the various groups had sounded periodically in Mennonite settlements in the Midwest. Tellingly, in a speech to the Illinois Mennonite Conference in 1893, Bishop John Smith had voiced such a plea, and according to Willard Smith, the 1910 founding of the Central Illinois Mennonite Conference had also propelled the vision forward. That same year, I. A. Sommer, editor of the GC denominational organ the *Mennonite*, circulated a suggestion that representatives from different Mennonite groups meet together to talk through their various similarities. The idea won warm endorsement from Mennonites from a number of groups, including important Central Conference leader Aaron Augspurger. But it also drew fire, particularly from Horsch, who immediately blasted any talk of Mennonite unity in an editorial in the *Gospel Herald*. While admitting Mennonite unity to be a good thing, at least theoretically, Horsch instead stressed the many grounds of difference among Mennonites, especially highlighting the current GC membership in the Federal Council of Churches as a vehicle that would "open the door for modern liberalism" among Mennonite congregations.[35]

Byers, however, pushed the idea forward. At that point still an important MC leader, he sent an editorial to the *Mennonite* that endorsed Sommer's idea. He particularly called for the journal's editors to facilitate the creation of a committee from "at least five of the larger branches of Mennonites" to discuss Mennonite commonalities—Horsch, Byers affirmed, had already furnished a good list of discussion topics—"before an open general meeting to which all Mennonites of America shall be invited." Kauffman initially considered participating and then decided against it. He issued a cautious early affirmation of the union idea in 1910, recognizing that "there is still a bond of love between most of" the Mennonite groups and hoping that "time, prayers and an overruling Providence may bring about more things of a similar nature." Within a year, however, Kauffman changed his mind after an MC church leader he respected had asked him "whether it was true that I was about to join the Oberholtzers." Kauffman's personal decision to oppose the union movement, along with Horsch's editorial, probably killed any chance of official MC involvement in the union efforts. This was a weighty development, since an alternative course in 1910 might conceivably have accelerated the ultimately successful movement, eight decades later, toward MC-GC integration. Yet it did not set back the subtle scheming of Goshen's president. By the fall of 1912, Byers was busily engaged in networking with a new set of partners in a project that would have sweeping impact on the course of Mennonite higher education.[36]

Byers's venture began innocently enough. In 1909, with Goshen becoming the first of the Mennonite colleges to award bachelor's degrees, he wrote to the presidents of the other schools—J. W. Kliewer at Bethel and Samuel Mosiman at Central Mennonite College in Bluffton—asking them for the names of their recent graduates in order to facilitate their matriculation at Goshen. The proposal seemed, as Byers explained it, a win-win proposition all around. At the time, the other Mennonite schools were junior colleges, and Goshen needed students; this way these young people would complete their education at a Mennonite school. Byers also would have known, however, that the other schools were planning a four-year course for their own students. He could not have been much surprised when the other presidents did not even deign to reply.[37]

Three years later, however, Byers had come up with an idea that would simultaneously advance the cause of Mennonite unity and Mennonite higher education, and find him a new academic position to boot. Nascent stirrings of Mennonite institutional collaboration were already underway, in fall 1912, in the joint creation by professors at Bethel and Bluffton of a new Mennonite Historical Society and in efforts to find repositories for church records. Byers had immediately signaled Goshen's eager participation. Then, within a month, he sought dramatically to widen these cooperative efforts. No doubt he was sincerely convinced of the need for Mennonite unity, but he also must have known that his days as Goshen's president were numbered. His former student and friend Paul Whitmer had been approached the previous spring by a representative of Goshen's trustees, wanting to know if he would assume the college presidency. Shocked at what appeared to him as "an unethical maneuver to replace a man whose term of office had not yet expired," Whitmer rejected the offer and certainly would have passed word to Byers. By November 1912, in light of such developments, Byers was clearly thinking big. He wrote to Kliewer, wondering if the time had come for different Mennonite church bodies to cooperate more closely together in educational efforts, especially to create the first Mennonite seminary, perhaps at Bethel. A month later, Kliewer and Mosiman privately met Byers in a Chicago hotel room to extend the thinking further. They laid plans for a large meeting with like-minded individuals from an alliance of Mennonite groups at Warsaw, Indiana, the following May. In the meantime, the focus of Byers's thinking had shifted from Bethel to Bluffton. He noted to Mosiman all the advantages he saw in the latter location and quietly took the train down from Goshen to Bluffton to see the school and deepen the planning. He signaled to Bluffton's president that he would be happy to serve under him as dean. On the eve of the big meeting in Warsaw, all the pieces seemed to be falling into place. "You can count on several of our best men" for the Bluffton faculty, Byers assured Mosiman, "and some hearty support from some progressive members in our branch. I believe the movement is timely and can be worked."[38]

Foremost among the "best men" on Goshen's faculty planning to move to Bluffton was Smith. At some point he had become convinced that progressives had no future at Goshen. His enthusiasm for Byers's maneuvers was illustrated by his active participation in them. By spring 1913 he was working steadfastly with Byers in various aspects of the planning, sounding out others in the small circle of Mennonite college professors about a possible move to Bluffton and signaling his eagerness to meet with Mosiman personally. He played a key role in the Warsaw meeting, where delegates from five Mennonite groups (MC, GC, Central Conference, Defenseless Mennonites, and Mennonite Brethren in Christ) agreed to sponsor a joint college and seminary. Minutes from the meeting recorded Smith as stating that "nothing will make for final unification as some institution of this kind" and that a seminary "is the one thing we really need." He brought forth the resolution, subsequently affirmed unanimously, that that the new school become established in connection with one of the existing Mennonite colleges. Likewise, Smith served as secretary of the important meeting in Chicago the next month, where the same delegates voted to create "Bluffton College and Mennonite Seminary" to replace the old Central Mennonite College. At the Chicago meeting, Mosiman was elected president of the new institution, Byers was named dean, and Smith, Byers, and Whitmer were officially appointed to the faculty. In August, despite his position as a new Bluffton professor, Smith was in Berne, Indiana, to serve in the official role as secretary to the first meeting of the board of trustees for the new Bluffton College, where he participated in drafting the reshaped institution's new bylaws.[39]

The next day Smith stayed in Berne to partake in the fruition of Byers's proposal of 1910, the long-anticipated meeting of the "First All-Mennonite Convention in America," where he delivered a major paper on Mennonite history in America. The paper was largely a rehash of themes he had been developing since 1905: it reviewed Mennonites as the archetypal American pioneers, as the mother denomination for other American church groups, and some of the earliest activists in the world peace and antislavery movements. But Smith also used the occasion to signal his growing intellectual commitment to the cause of Mennonite unity. Mennonites, he admitted, had been an extremely schismatic group, an attribute he attributed to their lack of education and culture, and their "strong bent toward individualism." Cautioning his listeners, in good academic style, to be open-minded and rid themselves of "all preconceived sentiments," he asked if the differences of the past are "today sufficiently great to keep the body divided?" The answer, of course, was no. In detailing the past, Smith furnished his response to some of the changes that had swept through the MC church and that had induced him to leave it so publicly. The key points of Mennonite doctrine that they all had in common, he pointed out—adult baptism, nonresistance, the simple life, and refusal to swear oaths—had been established in 1632 in the Dordrecht Confession. It had been the other "minor points of detail . . . often in everyday life and custom" that had needlessly kept Mennonites apart. As such, "they illustrate a tendency to which the entire Mennonite body has always been subject—namely the danger of mistaking custom and tradition for fundamental principles." For "the spirit of the age demands co-operation. And if the Mennonite church is ever to fulfill the mission to which she is entitled in light of her past history she, too, must cease to be divided." In their actions in Berne the past few days, Smith and Byers had publicly modeled such sentiments, moving as prominent MC educators into leadership positions in a GC college. The very name they preferred for the reborn institution also reflected their reading of the demands of the moment. They should rename it, Byers told Mosiman, "Union College."[40]

While Mennonites in Bluffton were indubitably thrilled with these developments, to many at Goshen they were disastrous. Thirty years later they still reverberated in the college's 1955 history as a "stunning blow to students and alumni." In losing treasured instructors and leaders like Byers and Smith, Goshen said goodbye to its longtime president and academic dean, and in Smith's departure they lost their sole PhD. Moreover, oratory professor Boyd Smucker also announced he would move to Bluffton, as did Whitmer (though he changed his mind after a visit from a contingent of Goshen faculty, who persuaded him to replace Smith as dean). Goshen students immediately drew up a petition of protest to the Mennonite Board of Education. One wonders if Byers had misgivings. Scarcely ten years earlier, he had ventured to Steiner that "the Dunkards have made a big mistake in organizing so many 'colleges' when they can hardly be said to have one that deserves the name. . . . Not for the next 100 years does the Mennonite church want more than one college." Now he had played a key role in the weakening of one and the reinvigoration of another. Yet Smith seemed to have had no second thoughts. "Goshen will not suffer any," he reassured Mosiman at least twice, though he did admit to Goshen's incoming president John E. Hartzler that some of the college staffers "have not been so kindly disposed to us during the summer." He sold his Goshen home to Hartzler and asked Mosiman to look for a large one in Bluffton that could accommodate all the Smith furniture.[41]

Two statements, one from Horsch and another from Smith, served to illustrate the resulting dynamics that reverberated among the Mennonite churches. They also indicated that not just 120 miles of farmland but a huge ecclesiastical chasm would soon separate the two Mennonite schools. Conceding to Kansas Mennonite leader H. P. Krehbiel that the departing Goshen professors were "good teachers," Horsch still smoldered with indignation at their move. "This seminary scheme which was laid out 'in darkness' and in secret (as far as our church is concerned)," he wrote, "has been the means of killing what sentiment there was among us in favor of union." As early as 1913, Horsch had reached his major conclusion about Goshen's ecclesiastical rival. "Bluffton College," he informed Krehbiel, "has been the principal seat of the modern religious views among Mennonites." Smith had already delivered his verdict on recent events four years earlier in the concluding lines of his *The Mennonites of America,* in which he accurately depicted two polar opposite positions that would frame Mennonite debate in the years ahead. "The Mennonite denomination is passing through a critical period in its history," he stated. "The two questions of most vital importance to the future of the church are its relations to the unification movement, and to the question of a more liberal education for its young people." The Mennonite church, he prophesied, "will never take the position which rightly belongs to it in the religious world until it passes favorably upon both of these questions."[42]

7
The "Most Liberal Wing"

Smith arrived in Bluffton in the early fall of 1913, excited to join what he would six years later call "the latest and most ambitious venture in the Mennonite field of education." He was undoubtedly relieved to have left the MC world. Here at Bluffton he would not encounter what had so wearied him at Goshen: a "board of farmer preachers who were afraid to let go of old traditions," as he phrased it in 1925. He would face "no censorship of the books that went into the library." General Conference Mennonites welcomed him as automatically as they embraced Mennonites of all stripes, in line with their church's founding mission. The GC commitment to ecumenicity explained both the remarkable pluralism of their church and why the church so quickly endorsed the union movement. In the forty years from 1890 to 1930, the church would grow from 44 to 159 separate congregations, ranging from urban and highly acculturated Swiss Mennonites in eastern Pennsylvania to the heavily Germanic and semiautonomous Dutch-Russian communities on the Great Plains. Moreover, the GC church signaled a remarkable level of openness to outside society, which Smith would have found liberating. In 1908 the group had officially joined the Federal Council of Churches and certainly seemed to epitomize what he described in 1909 as the Mennonites' "most liberal wing." That kind of environment was clearly where he wanted to be.[1]

In early August 1913, five thousand people, among them the state's progressive Democratic governor, rallied on campus to celebrate an event grandly titled "Bluffton Home Coming and College Day." Governor James Cox certainly warmed to the spirit of the occasion. As he approached the village on the train, he told the huge crowd, his traveling companion, a rising Cleveland politician and local native named Cyrus Locher, had suddenly pointed out the window and told him "'yonder are the spires of Bluffton College.' And when I came here," Cox declared, "it seemed to me that this is the most elegant spot in all the world." But it fell to Noah Byers to really encapsulate the promise that the day held for many Mennonites. The words he chose reveal with crystal clarity the consciousness he shared with his colleagues about who they were and what they were about. He had, Byers admitted, left the helm of one college for "a subordinate position here." He did so "because of my confidence in the future of Bluffton College" and because of the people he had encountered in Bluffton. "United progressive Mennonites. These are significant words," Byers announced. "The union of different sects in this great work is surely in line with the best spirit of the age, and surely we can count on high heaven to bless this movement."[2]

Over the next few decades, as one of the chief intellectual architects of the union movement, Smith would discover something both of its promise and its limitations. In 1913 he could proceed with blithe confidence that the vision of normative Mennonitism that he and his colleagues were so busily promoting could be framed in perfect harmony with progressive American culture. He would discover within a half dozen years, however, that the spirit of the age could abruptly embrace a darker chord and grow hostile to even united and progressive Mennonites. When that happened, Smith would be confronted with some hard lessons about reshaping the contours of Mennonite belief in order to fit them into the defining parameters of outside ideas.

Laboratory for the Union Movement

From 1913 to Smith's death, Bluffton would remain his home and his base of academic operations. Soon after his arrival there, he would have discovered something of its internal dynamics. GC Mennonites, he soon learned, were not immune from the conflicts that seemed to permeate all the new ventures in Mennonite higher education. Central Mennonite College had been founded a dozen years earlier as a project of the Middle and Eastern District Conferences of the GC church, primarily as a means of educating their young people, though the board had nearly immediately ruled that the college "shall be open to all." The church had situated its new school in Bluffton because it had the largest Mennonite population of the four midwestern towns vying for it, and a large congregation whose ancestors had emigrated from the Jura Mountains region of Switzerland before the Civil War. Church leaders had watched the headstrong young president of the new Central Mennonite College, a University of Chicago grad named Noah Hirschy, plunge the institution into a destructive conflict with the old Swiss church. A great part of it was due to Hirschy's personal issues, namely his dogmatic worldview and resistance to cooperative relationships with the Swiss church's preachers. But Hirschy's troubles also emanated, Smith would have learned, from local objections to his seemingly liberal theology that he had learned at places like Chicago. Hirschy's departure from Bluffton in 1908 eased tensions, and his successor, Samuel Mosiman, worked assiduously to patch up relations with the college's mother church. Even so, by itself Central Mennonite had a shaky future. Mosiman knew its founding church bodies were probably too small to sustain a college. Hence he would have greeted Byers's overtures in 1912 with a mixture of joy and relief. The union movement—with the infusion of new students, funds, and Mennonite denominational energies it promised—held out the hope of long-term institutional survival.[3]

Indeed, if there ever was a testing laboratory for the validity of the union movement, it was at the newly emerging Bluffton College. As an Amish Mennonite who had transferred his teaching career from an MC to a GC college, Smith was something of an ecumenical Mennonite pioneer. Even so, he could not have been entirely prepared for the polyglot Mennonite mixture he encountered in his new home. For one, the college and especially its mother church were still deeply and ethnically Swiss-German. For a full quarter century before 1910, the *Bluffton News* carried a regular column called "The German Settlement," which reported faithfully on the foibles and happenings of the local Swiss-German community for the convenience of English-speaking readers. Hirschy observed from afar in 1917 that the college "has largely lost its German life and tone," but its constituency was still so ethnically German that administrators printed its monthly newsletter, the *College Record*, bilingually until shortly before Smith arrived.[4]

The college's reinvigoration by the union movement in 1913 brought further leaven to this rich ethnic mix. The dominant strain of the GC church came to be represented on the faculty by scholar-preachers like Jacob Langenwalter and Jacob Thierstein. They arrived from Mennonite communities on the Great Plains in 1914 and 1915, respectively, the former to serve as seminary dean and the latter as professor of German. Bluffton's president and first lady seemed to embody several different ethnic strains at once. Mosiman had been raised at Trenton Mennonite Church, a wealthier and more cultured Mennonite community in Butler County, Ohio, which would contribute several more key people to Bluffton, including biology professor M'Della Moon, English professor Wilbur Howe, and Olga Berky, wife of chemistry professor H. W. Berky. In 1909 Mosiman surprised the community by bringing back to Bluffton from a GC church conference a new bride, the former Emilie Hamm of the Prussian Mennonite community of Beatrice, Nebraska. Emilie Mosiman soon emerged as the very embodiment of aristocratic, cultured Mennonite elegance in Bluffton. She joined others from the Trenton contingent in speaking High German, and made it her life's work to properly inculcate the rough farmhands in the student body in the ways of polite manners and refined living. In 1914 the college welcomed to its faculty a Bible professor from something of the opposite end of the Mennonite ecclesiastical and cultural spectrum, Rev. Jasper Huffman of the Mennonite Brethren in Christ Church (MBIC) and editor of its journal, the *Gospel Banner*. The MBIC had been born some decades earlier out of an attraction by many Mennonites to the holiness strains of rural evangelical subculture, and it was unclear how Huffman, with his pious rectitude, would fit in to Bluffton's eclectic mix. But the college needed Huffman's denomination for its students, its money, and as further validation of the union movement. For its part, with no college of its own, the MBIC needed Bluffton. Huffman had represented his church in some of the early reorganization meetings in 1913 (where he had seemed, Mosiman noted, "really enthusiastic") and had served as its representative on the board of trustees until his resignation to take up a position on the faculty. Finally, the college's faculty was to be further enriched by an ongoing stream of exiles from the MC academic world. These included Smith and Byers, of course, but also Boyd Smucker in 1915, and then Paul Whitmer. Mosiman and Langenwalter had been wooing Whitmer, but he had remained steadfastly committed to Goshen until he reached a breaking point with the increasingly stringent MC rules. Finally, when he heard the choice put plainly to either "conform or get out," Whitmer chose the latter course and arrived in Bluffton in 1917.[5]

All the new arrivals, Smith among them, would make their homes in a bustling little village of about two thousand people. Bluffton's pastoral elegance may have charmed the governor in 1913, but it masked a remarkable level of business activity. The great northwest Ohio oil boom had subsided before the turn of the century, but in the decade before Smith arrived and continuing after it, other budding entrepreneurs launched a number of new concerns. Traditional enterprises like lumber and grain milling remained active along Big Riley Creek east and north of Main Street, but they were soon augmented by a number of other small but busy industries making washing machines, hand gloves, and, later, gasoline engines and electrical implements. In 1906, the Interurban, a kind of intercity streetcar, arrived in Bluffton, providing the village its third separate railroad, though the increasing number of new automobiles appearing on its streets—in 1910 the *Bluffton News* counted "at least seventeen"—offered a glimpse of the ultimate source of the railroads' demise.[6]

C. Henry and Laura Smith moved directly to put down solid roots in their new community. By early 1914 Mosiman had acquired a five-acre tract of land across Little Riley Creek on the south edge of campus, and had it replotted into building lots facing the creek along a new street, soon appropriately called "Campus Drive." On it, he envisioned, would soon rise a women's dormitory and professors' homes. Within a year, along the new drive and directly west of the future dorm site, the Smiths constructed a handsome, two-story, shingled house with a broad front porch facing the creek and campus. As in Goshen, they had acquired the land from Noah and Emma Byers, who once again would be their neighbors in a home they constructed right next door. There were a number of advantages living so close to campus. The Smith and Byers homes, for instance, were apparently connected to the college's heating plant. Once the dorm appeared—the stately, pillared Ropp Hall was dedicated in December 1914—Smith would occasionally jaunt across a street and past a small cornfield (later a parking lot) to take meals in the college dining hall in its basement. Smith and Byers came to serve as an advance guard for a small neighborhood of Bluffton professors.

Laura's handwritten caption in the Smith photo album: "Early Bluffton Days." Smith in front of his new home, 1914–15. BUASC.

The Smith (front center) and Byers homes (behind it) along Campus Drive, Bluffton, 1915. This photo was undoubtedly taken from the newly completed Ropp Hall. BUASC.

Directly across the back of the Smiths' lot stood the Mosimans' fine brick home with its pillars and expansive front porch. Next door to Mosiman was the home of Jacob Thierstein. Diagonally across Lawn Street from Mosimans resided Boyd and Mary Smucker, and in 1918, when John E. Hartzler also made the switch from Goshen to Bluffton, he and his spouse, Mamie, would purchase a residence next door to the Smuckers.[7]

Likewise, the Smiths also established a local church home. When they first arrived in Bluffton and probably for some years afterward, along with the Byers and Smucker families they seem to have attended Zion Mennonite Church four miles west of town, an MC congregation and the home church of their old friend Menno Steiner. Though Steiner had died in 1910, the congregation doubtlessly carried the residue of his activism. Noah Byers transferred his membership there soon after his arrival and within two years had been appointed superintendent of the Zion Sunday school. Not long after Whitmer came to Bluffton, he assumed the congregation's pastorate.[8]

While the Smiths attended Zion, however, in 1914 they transferred their membership from the college congregation in Goshen to a Central Conference congregation two states away, East White Oak Mennonite Church near Normal, Illinois. One can only guess at the reason. Certainly the Central Illinois Conference would have been alluring (it dropped "Illinois" from its official name in 1914). Officially founded as a separate body in 1908 and dedicated to what it described then as a "conservative and orthodox position," the conference retained enough of the progressive outlook that had informed its founding by the old Amish Mennonite bishop Joseph Stuckey three decades before. Its congregations were immersed in Sunday schools, mission efforts, relief work, orphanages, and the other activities of quickened Mennonites. Importantly for Smith, it was one of the five Mennonite bodies in the union movement that rallied behind the reorganized Bluffton College, and it proceeded to direct its funds and its young people toward Bluffton. East White Oak in particular was a progressive and Bluffton-oriented congregation. It welcomed Bluffton fundraisers and its energetic long-time pastor from 1899 to 1928, Emmanuel Troyer, served for years on the college's board of trustees. Already by 1909 Smith described Central Conference pastors like Troyer in glowing terms and soon began participating in its gatherings. Even before Smith left Goshen he had agreed to serve as the editor of the "Educational Section" in the conference's monthly journal, the *Christian Evangel*. He had barely arrived in Bluffton, in October 1913, when he gave an address on the college's work at the annual meeting of the Central Conference, and likewise delivered lectures on Mennonite history and "The Value of Good Literature" at the 1915 and 1919 meetings, respectively.[9]

Smith would have been drawn to East White Oak and the Central Conference for many of these good reasons, but an additional one was probably the peculiar dynamics at Zion in 1914. It may have been a progressive church but it was still an MC congregation, and thus subject to its denomination's increasingly tough dress restrictions. Soon after the Goshen contingent arrived, certain Zion members began objecting to MC guidelines on women's headdress apparel. To Laura this would have seemed a replica of her family's struggle at Willow Springs. In establishing their membership with a Central Conference congregation, the Smiths located themselves beyond the reach of MC church discipline. At the same time, however, the Smiths' decision to place their membership in a congregation three hundred miles away may have limited the pastoral care they needed when dealing with the kind of personal crisis they faced in 1916.[10]

Mennonites, historians argue, had acculturated to some of the cultural mores of the Victorian age, but not to the point where they would commonly repress their sexuality. Both Henry and Laura had come from large farm families and, like any other couple in an era without accessible and reliable birth control, had undoubtedly assumed they would have children relatively soon. This may have been one reason that Laura had first demurred on Smith's marriage proposal and then pushed back their wedding date. "Whether I love you enough to give up my girlhood and freedom, I can hardly tell," she had initially explained at age twenty-seven. It is impossible to know, of course, why no Smith children appeared in their first four years of marriage at Goshen or in their next three years together in Bluffton. But by March 1916, at age thirty-six, Laura was certainly in the early stages of pregnancy. Writing Smith from a visit to her family back in Tiskilwa, she told her spouse that she had both lost her appetite and begun vomiting every morning. "It scares me," she confessed, "to think of eight months more and the worse, at last . . . I am not looking forward to the event." She also demonstrated that she had not lost any of her assertiveness or her unwillingness to think quietly about traditional evangelical teaching about gender. "I do not see why it has to be so one-sided anyway," she remarked. "Because Eve sinned?" She instructed her husband to begin thinking of baby names and get a trellis constructed, "so the whole countryside will not see me every time I step outside of [the] door." But there would be no Smith children. Ioder women had suffered from a series of miscarriages and stillbirths, and in August, Smucker noted to Mosiman, "Mrs. Smith is seriously ill at the hospital. Premature child birth." The Smiths' infant son died at or shortly after birth. The couple buried him at the Zion church cemetery, not far from the grave of their old friend Menno Steiner. Thirty years later they were still making small contributions to the cemetery's upkeep.[11]

The loss of their infant son was undoubtedly a huge emotional blow to both of them, and in particular may have exacerbated the kind of personal emotional issues that troubled Laura. There had been, Laura's niece Elaine Bowers commented, a long history of mental illness in the Stauffer side of the Ioder family. Embarrassed by the public stigma attached, the Ioders did their best to keep it private, and succeeded with more distant relatives. When Smith's niece Ruth Smith Dick, in old age, reviewed her memories of her uncle Henry and aunt Laura, she was unaware that Laura had any health issues at all. Within the immediate Ioder family, however, it was impossible to keep quiet. Bowers heard rumors that several Stauffer ancestors had taken their own lives, and with the generation of Ioders she knew, the illness was more than rumor. Laura's brother Almer had it severely enough to be confined at times to an asylum, as was her sister Mary. The illness manifested itself as well in Laura's sister Mace, and in Laura.[12]

Laid low for months at a time, Laura worried particularly about her salvation, her niece Elaine Bowers recalled—whether she was "good enough to make it to heaven." She used words like "sick" or told family she was in one of her "blue funks." By the 1940s a more precise psychiatric terminology had penetrated the rural Midwest. During the war Bowers, by then a nursing student at Bradley Polytechnic in Peoria, visited her uncle Henry and aunt Laura in Ohio. As he picked her up from the train station and drove her to Bluffton, Smith found a moment to shift the conversation. He wondered what she knew, Bowers recalled, about this word "depression." Was it a term she recognized? The Ioder family could only hope that the husbands of these Ioder sisters would stand by them in their recurrent times of black crisis. In Laura's case they let their fears rest. They knew, Bowers said, that Smith "was good to her."[13]

Smith probably coped by doing what he did best: immersing himself in his academic career and frantic busyness. He could certainly count on job security. The first two decades of the twentieth century, argues one scholar, were a transitional time in American higher education. The old, multipurpose college was ceasing to exist, and its replacement, the small liberal arts college, was just being born. As one of the few Mennonites with a doctorate, Smith was well positioned to help engineer this shift in Mennonite higher education. Bluffton, for example, was growing. New buildings rose, not just a women's dorm but also one for men, Lincoln Hall, in 1924. In 1915, after an extensive fundraising canvas of the local community, the college erected its second academic building, Science Hall. The college's student numbers steadily climbed through the 1920s, with a slight dip during World War I, from almost 200 students to the 250–300 range. To teach them, when he arrived in 1913, Smith joined a faculty of fifteen instructors, some of whom—like a newly arrived chemistry instructor named Herbert Berky and a pianist named Pearl Bogart—he would work with until he retired. In 1915, now with the title of "professor of history and social sciences," Smith plunged into a wide-ranging teaching schedule. From the fall of 1921 to the spring of 1922 alone, he offered courses in American, English, nineteenth-century, medieval, and "current" history; American and European government; the French Revolution; international law; and something called the "Physical Factors of Society." It must have been exhausting. "The teachers are over-burdened with work," Thierstein complained to Mosiman in 1915. "The mass of subjects offered, for instance, under the names of Professors Langenwalter, Byers, Smith and myself, is too much for any one man." If this were not enough, by the fall of 1913 Smith was appointed to the publication and advertising, athletics, and library committees of the faculty, and had been appointed editor of the *College Record*. In 1917 he also served as faculty secretary.[14]

One of Smith's early classes at Bluffton College. He is standing behind the class at right. BUASC.

Outside the classroom, Smith worked with his colleagues to inculcate in students what they called the "Bluffton Spirit," a campus culture thoroughly steeped in the national climate of progressivism. Expressive of the progressive culture on other campuses, Bluffton soon developed an honor code and structures of student government. Before the war, Dean Byers led a revision of the curriculum to one with a fairly heavy immersion in the liberal arts. Enjoying a freedom that would soon not be permitted at places like Goshen, oratory professor Smucker directed regular plays, including productions of Shakespeare and an old Smith favorite, Tennyson's *Enoch Arden*; in the 1916–17 academic year, he introduced an intercollegiate debate competition. Students debated the wisdom of a national child labor amendment and the Treaty of Versailles, and hosted a speaker advocating Prohibition. Smith, Byers, and others stoked enthusiasm for the national missions agency, the Student Volunteer Band, and especially for the YMCA-YWCA. Smith apparently enjoyed informal interaction with students. He agreed to serve as faculty advisor to the class of 1919, thereby opening himself to gentle ribbing in the student newspaper the *Witmarsum*. A 1916 photo and tribute to him in the paper reveals that he had, on the approach of his fortieth birthday, lost at least half of his hair and also some of his athletic abilities. "When the gentle zephyrs of summer blow," a *Witmarsum* writer noted, "Dr. Smith appears upon the tennis courts at stated periods, and indulges in more or less violent exercise but most of us have given up all hope of seeing him as an athletic star."[15]

Meanwhile Smith continued to develop local interest in his life's work, Mennonite history, lecturing in 1914 on Menno Simons at Grace Mennonite Church in nearby Pandora and joining with others in 1918 to organize a local Mennonite historical society. He taught a course on Mennonite history at the seminary, which forty years later Whitmer still recalled as having been "well-received" by the seminarians. It was through Smith's teaching there that he landed one of his prized and most influential students. In August 1916, a bright and able recent Bethel College grad named Edmund Kaufman was planning on a career in the mission field, but wanted first to complete a year in seminary. He had just about eliminated Bluffton from consideration. He knew its seminary was a small-scale affair, with only two full-time professors (Huffman and Langenwalter) and just a few graduate students. Late that August he attended the Second All-Mennonite Convention in Carlock, Illinois. Smith was almost certainly back in Bluffton, attending to his wife and the crisis stage of her pregnancy (this was probably the only such convention he did not attend). Huffman was there, however, and delivered a solid affirmation of the call to plain dress, which left Kaufman appalled. Langenwalter persuaded him to come to Bluffton anyway, but Kaufman's doubts were magnified when the seminary dean placed him in an undergraduate Bible course with the promise of a special discussion section for the four seminarians. Back in his room, Kaufman refrained from unpacking his bag, thinking he might transfer to Oberlin.[16]

What changed Kaufman's mind, his biographer James Juhnke later summarized, were classes with Byers on the psychology of religion and especially on the Social Gospel with Smith. Indeed, Smith quickly emerged as Kaufman's academic mentor and would serve informally in this role for decades. The immediate extent of his influence on the emerging young GC leader is seen in Kaufman's master's thesis, which he produced that year under Smith's direction. Kaufman set out to examine GC Mennonites in Kansas through the lens of the Country Life Movement, a Progressive Era initiative (specifically by Theodore Roosevelt) to deal with the problems and address the potentialities of rural America. The 180-page thesis was not, Juhnke admits, "a polished work." However, in approaching his material through the dual lenses of history and the social sciences, Kaufman helped to define Mennonites sociologically while at the same time underscoring the influence of his advisor. In his preface he thanked both Langenwalter and Smith, but the latter's fingerprints were all over his thesis (even to the point of his sloppy documentation). His summary of the Anabaptist family tree, for example, was very broad, inclusive of not just the Swiss Brethren but also Hubmaier, Denck, and Hoffman. He compared the Mennonites' Germantown to the sacral importance that English-speakers assigned to Plymouth Rock. In full Smithian fervor, Kaufman described Mennonites as archetypal pioneers and abolitionists, acknowledging their inherent individualism and bemoaning their separatist tendencies ("Mennonites always were in danger," he explained, "of confusing custom and tradition with principles," though fortunately "the prominent tendency of today is toward union"). His sociological survey of Kansas Mennonites likewise identified the kind of positive trends so prized by his advisor, among them Mennonites' current embrace of higher education and the contributions they stood to make to outside society, once they could get beyond their commitment to rural isolation.[17]

No doubt Smith was delighted with what he read, and also with Kaufman's subsequent rise to prominent leadership in the GC church. Kaufman's work and trajectory would have further confirmed for Smith the attractiveness of his historical vision for many Mennonites. After he became more firmly settled in Bluffton, however, Smith made efforts to expand his influence beyond Mennonite circles. Mennonites were beginning to realize, Kaufman wrote in his thesis, that it was a "Christian duty . . . to take active part and do constructive work also along the line of politics and government." At the very time he wrote these words, his main professor was modeling them.[18]

"Dr. Smith Is Looking After Things"

Even amid the pressing demands of his new job, Smith kept his eye on political and social trends and further honed his ability to speak publicly about them. Periodically he made speeches in local churches on issues of current importance. In 1920, for example, he delivered an impassioned address on behalf of Prohibition at a church near Bluffton. Not long after he arrived in the community in 1913, he outlined the "Modern Trend in Education," which suggested that his attitudes toward his profession had not changed much in fifteen years. Education was a "freeing process," he told the crowd, and teachers needed professional training in part because they were leaders. Charles Merriam, one of Smith's professors at Chicago, argued that "participation in politics was the only base for an experimental approach to the study of politics." Smith had not forgotten his lessons. In November 1915 he was elected to the Bluffton Village Council as a Democrat.[19]

Given the fervent commitment to the Republican Party saturating his childhood in rural Illinois, Smith's partisan switch was in some ways surprising, and he never accounted for it. Undoubtedly he had been won over by the soaring progressivism of current president Woodrow Wilson. If so, he also followed the trend of President Mosiman and many in his immediate peer group (excluding Byers, who in fall 1917 waged an unsuccessful campaign for a seat on the village council as a Republican). Kaufman and other Bethel College intellectuals had swung toward Wilson before World War I, and a Bluffton College student at the time later recalled that nearly all the Mennonites in the Bluffton area "were by and large Democrats, and therefore pretty faithful to Wilson." In his single term on the council, Smith quickly demonstrated that party labels did not matter much in village politics. Immediately after taking the oath of office he was elected president pro tem, and then over the coming months filled his weekday evenings with prosaic matters like grading streets, regulating motor vehicle traffic, and dealing with town drunks. His progressive idealism probably came more into play in an attempt he led to submit a charter to the voters, in the fall of 1917, to "draw up a new form of government." But the motion never appeared on the ballot, apparently having lost on a procedural vote, and Smith did not stand for reelection. He did serve a partial term on the local school board in 1922–23, most of which occurred while Smith took a temporary teaching position at Bethel College out of state. After that he was finished as a politician, but not with civic involvement. From 1919 to nearly the end of his life, Smith preferred to channel his civic energies through the better-remunerated avenue of business.[20]

Mennonites, historians argue, have traditionally harbored ambivalent attitudes toward business enterprise. They did not condemn small-scale merchant activity and certainly were not above acquiring lots of land, but historically they shrank from unrestrained capitalist fervor. In

1891, for example, the Amish Mennonite Western District Conference (Smith's childhood church body) passed a resolution against going beyond "lawful" rates of interest, though by the 1870s they had become more accepting of basic financial institutions like banks. The Smiths showed an early willingness to acculturate in such areas. In his memoir, Smith described how his father, during his childhood, invested in land in Kansas, quickly adding that he lost money on the deal. But he did not always lose money, and in this manner the elder Smith passed on to his children the idea of expanding one's financial capital. Moreover, Henry Smith may have been prodded into such activities by genuine financial need. Professorial salaries were low across the board in America and declined especially sharply in the years after World War I. In 1928, for example, a history professor not far away at Wittenberg College had an annual salary of $3,000, the top level in the college, an amount that did not enable him to afford a small car or even a radio. In 1920, Smith had also reached Bluffton's top faculty salary level: exactly half that amount, $1,500 per year (an amount equal in 2013 dollars, by one estimate, to $17,500). Nor could Bluffton professors count on the regularity of their paychecks. In March 1916, just as Smith was absorbing the news that he would soon become a father, Mosiman admitted to a local attorney that the faculty had not been paid in three months.[21]

In the face of their pressing economic needs, who could blame bright and talented Mennonite intellectuals for doing what they could to supplement their pitiful incomes? But Smith seems to have been more successful than most. He began with a substantial leg up. His father-in-law, William Ioder, had done very well as one of the leading farmers and stock-raisers in Bureau County, Illinois. "He was industrious, economical, and very generous," read his obituary in a local newspaper, and "the owner of a handsome fortune." Ioder was generous in particular with his eight surviving, and now adult, children. Before or upon his death in 1914, his granddaughter recalled a century later, he had enough financial resources to pass on to each of them a farm of their own. Longtime Bluffton residents can still recall Smith saying in jest that he "got all my money from my wife."[22]

Smith knew what to do with such capital. Already by 1914 Smith was financially comfortable enough to make a contribution of $200 (better than a fourth of his regular annual salary) to the college's campaign for a new science hall. Two years later he was clearly receiving income from tenants on at least one farm, and by the end of the decade he also owned property nearer to home in southeast Lima. By the 1930s his correspondence indicates he was renting out working farms in Michigan, Indiana, and perhaps elsewhere. While traveling in Arizona years later, Willard Smith suddenly remembered with regret that he had once turned down an offer from his uncle Henry for some acreage of free land near the town of Casa Grande if he would only assume the back taxes.[23]

Already by his Goshen years, Smith had begun to branch out into other financial enterprises, often in concert with Byers and other professor friends. Smith and Byers together invested in a milk-condensing plant in Goshen, which apparently did very well. In the early 1920s, Smith, Thierstein, and Smucker bought stock in an auto transmissions facility in Lima, which did not. Around the same time, Smith and his partners sunk substantial funds into a dairy and condenser in nearby Findlay. The group—consisting of the above professors, plus Byers and W. S. Gottshall, the conservative pastor of Ebenezer Mennonite Church west of Bluffton—initially seemed to have great hopes for the Findlay operation. Their confidence was such that, in 1920, the *Bluffton News* reported, Smucker resigned his position as college "field secretary" (fundraiser) to take up a position with the Findlay dairy, and three years later Smith and Byers were listed among its "directors" (likely meaning majority stockholders). Smucker mortgaged his home and some of the partners sunk astounding sums of money into it, given that they were hard-pressed college professors. "Fool that I was I borrowed nearly two thousand dollars, so that I might invest $2400.00 in this business," Thierstein later wrote, reflecting ruefully on an amount that was probably twice his annual salary. But soon it all went sour. A state department of inspection had condemned the dairy building, Smith reported to Thierstein (who had by then relocated to Bethel). This required a $20,000 investment to get it up to code, an amount that heavily deflated the stock price of the operation, and local banks began to deny the operation credit. Altogether Smith seems to have felt a bit badly about it. "My loss has been the biggest share of the original investment," he admitted to Thierstein. "I am very sorry the way the thing turned out especially for our Bluffton group, but there is still a chance for the stock to pick up if it is managed right." Starting in 1927—again with Byers, Smucker, college business manager H. A. Alderfer, and a similar set of professors and allied investors—Smith became a major shareholder in an operation called the "Bluffton Silver Black Fox Farm." The pelts brought decent dividends for several years until the Great Depression killed the demand.[24]

Unlike others in the Bluffton group, however, Smith had the financial wherewithal to ride out the bumps. He had resources in land and, soon after the end of the First World War, had become heavily involved in not one but two local banks. Not that he probably knew much about the business, though one of the undergraduate courses he had taken while a grad student at Chicago was "Money and Banking." His first foray seems to have emerged from informal conversations he and Bible professor Huffman had enjoyed together, when they admitted to each other that they both had a "bee" in their "bonnets" to get into banking. Finally they decided to act. After a careful canvas of the area, the two shortly concluded that the village of Pandora, seven miles northwest of Bluffton, offered decent people, fertile area farms, "business initiative," and all the other requirements they were looking for. In December 1918 they pulled together an initial set of stockholders—which included Huffman, Whitmer, and both C. Henry and Laura Smith—and applied to the state for a charter. The following June, First National Bank opened for business in a converted house in the center of Pandora with an initial capitalization of $30,000 and Smith appointed its president. He would serve in this capacity until 1934, and would remain on the bank's board of directors until a month before his death.[25]

Six months after opening his bank in Pandora, Smith jumped into a similar enterprise in Bluffton, probably to help meet a genuine community crisis. In November 1919 John Bixel, a heretofore upstanding area citizen and president of Bluffton's First National Bank, suddenly absconded with most of the bank's funds. Bixel fled to Columbus and would soon land in the state penitentiary, but in the meantime the rapid disintegration of his bank had potentially devastating local consequences. Funds were already scarce in the community in the immediate aftermath of the war, and the bank's stockholders faced substantial losses. "Dr. Smith and Revs. Huffman and Whitmer los[t] their ten shares apiece, i.e. $1600," Thierstein wrote to Mosiman, who was temporarily out of town, adding that "this is pretty hard on the latter two" (by itself a telling comment on Smith's finances). Moreover, many local organizations had funds tied up in Bixel's bank, including the college, which had deposits there for over $2,000. On this point, Thierstein advised Mosiman, he needn't worry, because "Dr. Smith is looking after things." But the community needed help. Eleven days after Bixel's bank crashed, a group of area citizens (Smith almost certainly among them) met to take over its assets and create a successor institution. Within a month they received a charter for the new bank, called Citizens National, with an initial capitalization of $50,000 and Smith as its president.[26]

The new bank officially opened its doors on the last day of January 1920, giving away free apples to its new customers. Nearly a year later, the bank was doing well enough to erect a handsome new building on a corner lot along Main Street in Bluffton's downtown. It would be a while before Smith saw much return on these investments. Neither bank registered any profit in 1921, Huffman admitted, though the Pandora one might have done so had a major customer not lapsed into bankruptcy, "incurring quite a loss on us." Yet the potential for real earnings was there. Moreover, Smith discovered that one financial acquisition led, almost organically, to another. In his appointment as president of Citizens National, for example, he soon acquired a financial stake in the *Bluffton News*, and became the legal president of a Ford dealership a block north on Main Street called the Dixie Motor Car Company. Smith himself would not sell any Model Ts, but thought enough of the honorific title to include it, along with his bank presidencies, on a rough resume he sent a decade later to Harold Bender.[27]

In 1932 a trade journal called *American Banker* ran a feature story on Smith called "Bank President a College Professor." It was the kind of story that its readers assuredly would have appreciated: of a respectable bank president in a solid Ohio town who doubled, bizarrely enough, as a history professor. Smith also undoubtedly enjoyed the story, but he knew who he was. Titles like bank president were flattering but really signaled, he soon learned, more of a figurehead and oversight role; the cashier did most of the actual work of managing a small bank. No doubt Smith's secondary occupation as a successful local businessman was satisfying on a number of levels. The wealth it produced made his

Citizens National Bank following its construction, early 1920, along Main Street in downtown Bluffton. The cupola of First Mennonite Church, adjoining the bank to the west, is on the far right of this photograph. BUASC.

far-flung research and tourist travels possible, and also underwrote his primary identity; local people would have seen Smith as a prominent local banker and key figure of Main Street. But Smith knew his real calling was as a college history professor and a leading Mennonite progressive intellectual.[28]

Seeing the "Hand of God in American History"

Smith understood that his duties as a Mennonite educator included expressing that role both inside and outside of the classroom. Through the second and into the third decades of the new century, he continued to send a fair torrent of articles to lay readers of the Mennonite denominational press. Taken as a whole, these writings are worth noting for a couple of reasons. First, the wide number of different topics he wrote about indicates something of the range of his thought while simultaneously reinforcing his wholehearted embrace of the worldview and solutions of progressive reform. Second, as his experience in the Great War would reveal to him in an unmistakable way, they illustrate the dangers of uncritical borrowing of outside worldviews and ideas.

Smith never lost his primary interest in Christian and Mennonite history, but especially in these years the extensiveness of his commentary on a variety of matters really was remarkable. These ranged from observations about the growth of the modern peace movement, to the need to eradicate the common housefly, to the importance of conserving natural resources. In the latter piece, he offered an early, detailed, forthright plea for the early conservation movement, noting the steady dwindling of American timber and mineral resources and the need for better watershed management and soil conservation efforts. He read deeply in progressive sociology and examined trends in such interrelated fields as juvenile delinquency reports, public health statistics, and the socialization of children to compile a lengthy overview of current thinking on children's issues. In particular he embraced the growing professionalization of play and the concurrent reform drive for more play spaces, now called "playgrounds," for urban children.[29]

As these examples illustrate, in nearly all of Smith's popular writing in these years, he repeatedly evidenced the thorough degree to which he had internalized the worldview of American progressivism. For instance, in a short piece simply titled "Progress," he sketched out the amazing advances humankind had seen in just the past half century, heralding the coming "age of gasoline, as important in its own way as either steam or electricity." He noted the "unseen wonders in the new field of bacteriology," especially the "germ theory of disease," which had rapidly diminished the threat of typhoid, yellow fever, diphtheria, and many other diseases that "for countless ages had been the terror of mankind." We live, he told the Mennonite laity, in a wonderful age of progress. Moreover, in these developments and others, as a dedicated progressive, Smith offered as the premier solution the intervention of a beneficent state. As an antidote to the "reckless and careless exploitation" of the nation's natural wealth, for instance, he argued that "to the national government then these interests can be most safely committed." Similarly, in outlining the social crises affecting poor, urban children, he continually highlighted the current governmental efforts in ameliorating them. In so doing he clearly accepted an emerging progressive approach to reform and one that ran so contrary to the evangelical crusades of the previous century. Instead of effecting social reform by first focusing on individual transformation, Smith and other progressives readily accepted the alternative course: that by changing one's environment one could change society. "They say you can not [sic] make people good by legislation," he remarked to the readers of the *Christian*

Evangel. "That statement needs modification. You can make them well by legislation, and in that way greatly contribute to their goodness."[30]

Smith's absorption of progressive analyses and solutions likewise informed a thoughtful 1912 exploration of American socialism. Though acknowledging the small number of Christian socialists, Smith made it clear that he did not embrace their movement because of the overall "anti-christian" [sic] nature of socialism. Even so, he was balanced and sympathetic. He carefully described concepts like the labor theory of value and Marxist economic determinism for Mennonite readers, summarized socialism's current political strength as reflected in recent state and municipal elections, and underscored its commitment to achieving its goals through the normal channels of American democracy instead of through extra-legal violence. "The party gains its adherents," he told readers, "not from the foreign element but from native American stock as well." Here as elsewhere Smith demonstrated his emergence as a new kind of Mennonite public intellectual, drawing from a careful reading of such disparate intellectual threads as economic theory, rural sociology, current political trends, and eighteenth-century thinkers like Thomas Malthus. "Although there is much that is harmful in socialism, yet it also advocates many reforms that are needed," he concluded in true progressive manner. "The only remedy for socialism is adequate social reform which will remove the glaring inequalities which exist among the people."[31]

In these analyses and others, Smith performed a vital function for his people. As Mennonites drew closer to outside society, they needed intellectuals like Smith to help them discern which of the outside intrusions provided a healthy invigoration of their tradition and which did not. At times Smith performed this role nobly for his church. Other times he failed. Nowhere was his dysfunctional borrowing more painfully evident than in his uncritical channeling of Progressive Era nationalism and racism.

"The pilot of history has dealt kindly with the American nation," Smith declared in the *Christian Evangel* in 1914, and elaborated on that premise in a lengthy, four-part narrative overview of "The Hand of God in American History." It was a remarkable display of how deeply and uncritically he had accepted what would be later called American civil religion. According to Smith, God's providential intervention lay behind nearly every fortuitous turn in the national story, from Columbus's timely landfall in the Caribbean in 1492, to the tide of European settlement led by the sturdy "Anglo-Saxon race," to the Louisiana Purchase, and then to the Civil War. "The only explanation for Lincoln," Smith reasoned, "is that he was providentially raised to save his country in this great crisis." The god Smith described in this account was clearly a white American god. "If the American nation is to survive and fulfill the mission for which an allwise Providence has thus far prepared for it," he told readers, "it must keep pure both its Anglo Saxon blood and Christian ideals." There were many dangers threatening its racial purity, he claimed. Not only are "we . . . threatened by an invasion of the yellow race on our western coast," but the massive influx of the "ignorant and inferior races" of southern and eastern Europe and the "prolific" breeding rates of "inferior . . . Negroes," if allowed to proceed unchecked, "will outnumber the intelligent Teutonic element."[32]

Smith would have come to his prizing of white racial purity by drinking from a number of different intellectual and cultural wells. His Gilded Age childhood and adolescence had coincided with the rise of a new kind of radical racism that swept the country, holding that recently freed blacks were reverting to their "natural" state of animal savagery. This theory was promulgated not only by the emerging political champions of white supremacy in the post-Reconstruction South as a buttress for their new policies of Jim Crow segregation, but also by Harvard intellectuals and many political and cultural leaders across the North and Midwest. By the turn of the century, evangelical Protestantism was shot through with racism and ethnocentrism. The YMCA, for example, preached a conservative approach to racial policies predicated upon African American separation from whites. Racist understandings of the supposed inferiority of nonwhite peoples helped propel the great missionary drives in Progressive Era Protestantism, as well as its support for American imperialism. Likewise, racist understandings thoroughly permeated academia. Scholars have written of a "near unanimous racism of northern historians" that lasted well into the twentieth century. The millions of new immigrants pouring into the country, Massachusetts Institute of Technology president Francis Walker famously declared in 1896, were "beaten men from beaten races" and unfit for self-government. Of course the politicians of the Progressive Era shared such ideas and acted on them. They worked closely with the paralleling nativist movement to endorse immigration restriction policies and write them into legal code, actions that Smith wholeheartedly endorsed in 1914. When achieving national political power, they constructed a progressivism that, in the words of one scholar, was "for whites only." Theodore Roosevelt commonly used crude racial epithets in his private speech, worried about maintaining white racial purity, and was happy to leave white Southerners in charge of U.S. racial policies. At best, Roosevelt represented a paternalist racial policy. Wilson, Smith's great political champion in these years, was even worse, reinstituting Jim Crow across government offices in Washington, D.C. He unhesitatingly showed the racist film *Birth of a Nation* at the White House, affirming as "all so true" its ugly mythologizing of the Ku Klux Klan.[33]

Historically, most Amish and Mennonites did not live in close proximity to many people of color, and their attitudes tended to reflect a kind of ingrained racist paternalism as opposed to extreme racism. Even so, as the quickening brought Mennonites into more engagement with outside society, many of them reflected white American racial attitudes. Early MC urban mission efforts conducted their work on a segregated basis. In a lengthy 1905 explication of "The Negro Question," which appeared without noticeable controversy in the *Goshen College Record*, one writer damned interracial marriage, argued that African Americans were "an alien and lowly race" that slavery had civilized, and declared black suffrage "one of the most astounding blunders of the nineteenth century." In the 1920s, J. E. Hartzler supplemented his income as Witmarsum Seminary president by giving popular lectures. In an advertising blub for one of them, he promised to explore "how the colored races of the world are multiplying faster than the white race. Shall the white race become extinct?" As late as 1940, the Virginia Mennonite Conference voted to segregate communion cups for the few Mennonites of color, and in 1943 Kauffman would warn about the threats of "hordes of colored (and renegade) white races" deluging the numbers of white Christians who practiced birth control.[34]

Not surprisingly, Smith reflected this body of cultural teaching. For instance, writing to his fiancée in September 1907 about the city of Indianapolis, where he had just arrived to establish his residence, he noted in passing that "it is pretty far south and has a lot of niggers."

Likewise, as a sophisticated intellectual he commented favorably on a new movement then gaining much positive traction among the country's educated classes: eugenics, or selective race breeding. Again writing in the polished tones of a trained social scientist, Smith summarized new studies of heredity as explicated by eugenicist thinker Francis Galton, outlining how "statistics show that degeneracy is on the increase" and how, through more careful race breeding, "society must in some way protect itself" from the growth of its "feeble-minded, alcoholic, syphilitic, congenital criminal" and other kinds of demographic burdens.[35]

Given the prevalence of racism in American society, and also Smith's eager embrace of his role as a principal intermediary between it and his Mennonite people, perhaps it would have been surprising had he not internalized such racist thinking. In the context of his day, he appeared something of a racial moderate, and at any rate it was not a major aspect of his thought. Even so, with a little more critical distance from society, Smith might have been able to discern something of the darker side of progressivism. He certainly missed this aspect with regard to racial issues. In 1917–18 the lesson was driven home to him in an unavoidable way on another front. In those traumatic years he learned what it was to be a pacifist Mennonite in a nation engaged in holy war.[36]

Progressive Mennonites Chastened by War

The First World War posed a tremendous challenge to Mennonites of all stripes, not least its progressive intellectuals. As historian Gerlof Homan has outlined, after the outbreak of war in late summer 1914, Mennonite reactions tended to mirror those of other Americans in that their sympathies were partly determined by their cultural identities. In the Mennonite communities on the Great Plains, cultural ties with Germany remained strong. Initially, at least, German-language Mennonite newspapers rang with cries of sympathy for Germany and collected funds from Mennonite congregations for the German Red Cross. East of the Mississippi, where the Mennonite migration from Europe had largely occurred a century or more before, the response ran toward shock and affirmations of American neutrality. The *Gospel Herald* blamed the war on human greed and national jealousies, while the GC organ the *Mennonite* censured all participating nations. In a series of 1915 articles that ran simultaneously in the *Christian Evangel* and the MC publication the *Christian Monitor*, Smith seemed to encapsulate the initial reactions of most midwestern and eastern Mennonites. He plunged readers into a detailed historical narrative, beginning with European balance-of-power politics in the later nineteenth century; through the Balkan policies of Russia, England, and Germany; and then to the foreign policy calculations that had led the belligerent powers to war declarations once the Balkan powder keg blew. His tone was exemplified in the third paragraph of his opening piece, where he noted that now, "to our humiliation, even the Mennonite has raised his sword against fellow-Mennonite." It was nationalism, not racism that caused the war, he declared, for "the English and the Germans are both members of the Teutonic branch of the great Aryan race." As to war blame, he displayed none of the pro-German sympathies then resonant in the Mennonite communities in Kansas, concluding in July that "all nations are to blame, although some are more guilty than others," especially Austria, Germany, and Russia, and then France and England, in that order.[37]

Meanwhile, as Smith deepened his analysis of the war's causes, his political hero Wilson edged the country ever more inescapably toward American involvement. The march toward war particularly escalated in the summer of 1915, as Germany sunk the passenger liner *Lusitania* off the coast of Ireland and followed with unrestricted submarine warfare against neutral vessels on the high seas. Two years later Wilson asked for and received from Congress a war declaration against Germany. Ominously, for all potential war objectors, including Mennonites, it appeared that their government would prosecute the war in a manner that would involve them. The president quickly signaled his intention to brook little dissent from the war on any level. In one of the bigger ironies of the nation's history, when its soaring, idealistic, progressive president led them to war—a devout Presbyterian who had appointed a pacifist, William Jennings Bryan, as secretary of state—his policies moved the country toward something resembling a police state. In draconian legislation, like the Espionage Act of June 1917 and the Sedition Act a year later, the government received powers to enforce dramatic restrictions of American freedom of expression. War dissenters were mobbed and lynched across the country, the attorney general banned from the mail anything he deemed seditious, and ordinary Americans received jail sentences for dissenting publicly against the war. In doing little to restrain the vigilante actions that sprung up in many communities, government officials from the president on down seemed to give them official sanction. Some pacifists abandoned the cause and fell dutifully in line behind the war. Others regarded their former progressive champion Wilson with deep bitterness and a sense of personal betrayal.[38]

Mennonites quickly found themselves woefully unprepared to deal adequately with this escalating crisis. Their immense ethnic, theological, and ecclesiastical divisions rendered a coherent response impossible. Individual Mennonite groups tried to clarify church teaching on nonresistance and to manage relationships with government officials on their own. The MC church reaffirmed traditional nonresistance in the so-called Yellow Creek statement of 1917. The GC church created an official exemption committee, chaired by Mosiman, to provide some leadership, but its strong congregational polity mostly left district conferences and individual congregations to map out their own responses. Despite the absence of significant participation from key Anabaptist-Mennonite groups like the Old Orders and the MC church, at its August 1916 meeting in Carlock, Illinois, the All-Mennonite Convention quickly pulled together a statement purporting to speak for the entire church. Affirmed by participants and sent to Wilson, it reiterated Mennonite opposition to all war and particularly their objections to participation in military training. By December, with an eye on conscription legislation that Congress would soon consider, the convention prepared a separate statement asking for complete Mennonite exemption. Huffman took it to Washington, D.C., the following spring and presented it to Wilson administration officials and various Congress members, all of whom received it politely and with bland, generalized pledges of their sympathies with the Mennonites' position. But they offered nothing concrete, undoubtedly confused by the fact that Huffman was merely one of three Mennonite delegations in Washington at the moment, each operating independently of the others, and also probably by his astoundingly inaccurate assurances that Mennonites would gladly participate in any military activity short of actually bearing arms.[39]

During and after the congressional debate over the conscription bill, as Mennonite leaders negotiated with war secretary Newton Baker and other governmental officials, they received broad—and, as it turned out, false—assurances that Mennonite nonresistance would be respected in policy. But the actual conscription bill the president signed into law in April 1917 allowed no exemption for reasons of conscience. It drafted all pacifists into the military, where they were assigned a yet-undefined noncombatant role. Waves of shock and dismay rippled across Mennonite communities and rose to a crescendo as the church saw the kind of treatment that military officers soon meted out to Mennonite draftees. Isolated away in army camps, Mennonite young men had to sort out on their own how much their consciences could cooperate with military orders. Those who chose a stricter course—refusing to don the uniform, for example, or to obey routine orders—faced brutal treatment, especially in western states. They were pummeled with fists, raked raw with brooms, or made to stand at attention for hours at a time. For this reason, later historians wondered if the church had in fact been caught up in something like a "conscription trap," lulled by wily governmental officials into official cooperation with policies that achieved government objectives but that gave little official sanction to Mennonite principles. That kind of analysis was articulated at the time. "The non-resistant denominations have been duped by these politicians," a former Bluffton student, now a noncombatant soldier, wrote Mosiman in October 1917. "I guess the best is to stand firm."[40]

Nor would such tests of conscience come only to their draftees, Mennonites soon discovered. Following the cues of their national leaders, Americans quickly launched into a vicious, high-strung campaign against a perceived German enemy at home and abroad. As a definably ethnic German group who were also pacifist, Mennonites were doubly suspect. Across the country, their churches were daubed with yellow paint, draped with American flags, or even, in two instances, burned to the ground. Individual Mennonites were mobbed and threatened with lynching when they refused to buy war bonds. Because they had signed the Yellow Creek statement, 181 MC Mennonite deacons and bishops faced an indictment from a zealous U.S. attorney in Cleveland for ostensibly violating the Espionage Act.[41]

As Mennonites increasingly found themselves targets of popular wrath, no doubt it was particularly discomfiting to the church's progressive intellectuals. For years they had been beckoning their church toward heightened engagement with outside society, assuring it that they had special contributions to make in the national drive for progress, and that Americans would welcome them. By 1917 Smith had been energetically preaching such a message for nearly two decades. Now he could only watch as the tides of persecution crept closer. In April 1918 vandals visited his home congregation back in Metamora, writing ugly slogans—"We buy no Bonds" and "We are Slackers"—in bright yellow paint and in letters three feet high. The outlines of the letters shone through new paint and were discernible for years afterward. Emmanuel Troyer, Smith's pastor at East White Oak, placed a U.S. flag over the church's pulpit, apparently as a means of warding off such humiliations. By spring 1918 patriots had begun to assemble in Allen County, Ohio. Official vigilante groups formed: the "Yellow Dog Clubbers' Club," and another called the "Lima Vigilantes Corps," which began visiting homes of suspected traitors in the community and advising them to "display their patriotism." Local citizens who were judged as insufficiently patriotic were forced to salute publicly or kiss the flag. The school board in Lima, the county seat, barred the teaching of German, and two thousand people cheered as high school students tossed hundreds of German textbooks onto a bonfire. German Township west of Lima officially changed its name to American Township. Blocks from Smith's home, forty Bluffton High School students took German language textbooks and papers and burned them on the banks of Big Riley Creek. Smith's friends Boyd and Mary Smucker were so nervous about the anti-German hysteria that they changed the spelling of their five-year-old son's name from the German-sounding "Karl" to the more American "Carl."[42]

Soon patriots in the community and elsewhere began to finger Mennonites as an especially potent source of possible disloyalty. In June 1918 a Lima newspaper urged mob action against the pacifists in Bluffton. Three hundred local citizens visited two Mennonite churches in the countryside west of Lima, the Salem and Pike congregations, draping American flags across their entryways. The college was also being carefully watched by higher authorities from farther away. In

April, Langenwalter wrote Mosiman, two "secret service men" showed up to "find out why we had 'appointed a censor on patriotic news in the *Witmarsum.*' Dean Byers and Drs. Smith and Thierstein waited on them and fully satisfied them," Langenwalter reported, calling in the *Witmarsum*'s student editors for "some very sane advice."[43]

There could not have been many ostensibly disloyal utterances in the *Witmarsum*, for the newspaper, along with the rest of the college community, mostly rang with enthusiasm for the American war effort. Students raised money for the Red Cross, the glee club traveled to Camp Sherman to entertain the troops, and both the *Witmarsum* and the yearbook, the *Ista*, celebrated military accomplishments. Five professors served in some military capacity, either in straight army ranks or through the umbrella sponsorship of the YMCA, which so seethed with war enthusiasm it functioned something like an auxiliary unit of the military. Byers, for example, spent much of 1919 in France, teaching psychology under Y auspices at an army university. Presumably such students and professors might have expected some kind of disciplinary sanction from college authorities, given that activities of this sort plainly violated the peace principles of the college's founding church. But they would receive no punishment from Mosiman. Devoted to institutional survival in a hostile climate and persuaded of the rightness of the Allied cause, Bluffton's president counseled a much more accommodative course to the national crusade than would many Mennonites elsewhere. He urged Mennonite draftees not to involve themselves in "hairsplitting" over military orders to don "the uniform and such things," and he damned as "wicked and foolish" advice from other church leaders that they do so. He joined other allies like the *Mennonite* editor Silas Grubb and the Berne, Indiana, leader J. F. Lehman in enthusiastically endorsing war bond purchases, and he readily permitted such drives at the college.[44]

Smith's course of action with regard to the war is somewhat elusive, but in most ways he seems to have followed the path laid out by Mosiman and Byers. On the one hand, a student who ended up in straight military ranks remembered later that the only teaching of traditional nonresistance he had received before he enlisted had come from the Goshen transfers on the Bluffton faculty: Smith, Byers, and Whitmer. On behalf of the All-Mennonite Convention in 1916, Smith worked with Mosiman and Byers to draft the statement asking for Mennonite military exemption that their colleague Huffman took to Washington.[45]

On the other hand, Smith made wartime choices that other Mennonites certainly would have seen as unmistakable compromises of their peace position. He apparently served as an official, for example, on the county draft board. In October 1917 a war bonds official wrote to thank Mosiman for the splendid assistance he had received from several Bluffton professors in a recent Liberty Loan drive in Allen County, especially praising Smith for his energies. The following spring, Smith journeyed to the Great Lakes naval training station in Chicago to give a series of lectures at the YMCA unit there. In June 1918 Smith heard from a nephew serving as an army noncombatant in Alabama how "us objectors here . . . are treated real nice," and how pacifist draftees who took a tougher line "went intirely to far [sic] when they said they would do nothing." Smith's progressive commitments quickly led him to analyses of wartime developments that were profoundly sympathetic to the government line. In 1920, for example, while admitting that abuses of objectors occurred at the hands of a few zealous officers, Smith wrote admiringly of "the liberal policy of the War Department" in regard to conscientious objectors. "Fortunately for the Mennonites," he said, "both President Wilson and Secretary Baker displayed the greatest consideration for the scruples of sincere objectors." He did describe at length the particularly ugly brutalities inflicted on Mennonite draftees at Kansas's Fort Leavenworth, "tortures that would have done credit to the medieval Inquisition." But "the large majority of the Mennonites at Fort Leavenworth had little cause to complain of their treatment as prisoners." Smith would have had little patience with any talk of a "conscription trap" sprung onto innocent Mennonites by duplicitous government officials. Indeed, he insisted in 1922, Wilson and Baker "were inclined to give the conscientious objector respectful consideration and undoubtedly stretched the Conscription Act to the limit to meet the situation."[46]

Historians argue that the First World War was altogether a traumatic experience for most American Mennonites, plunging them into, as Juhnke has noted, a profound moral crisis emanating from their recognition that they were not yet fully accepted as American citizens.

All of Smith's progressive filters could not render him immune from the same kinds of unsettling conclusions. In fact, the war years marked a subtle but clear transition in his thought. It is possible to overstate the shift. He shed little of his enthusiasm for the kind of tempered acculturation into American society he had been advocating for two decades. Soon after the war, he would model it by his rapid construction of a business career that soon rendered him a pillar of Bluffton's downtown. Even so, the Mennonite experience in the war years clearly caused Smith to emerge with a much more tempered progressivism and with new ideas of how best to effect social change.[47]

At times Smith's new tone appeared with dramatic suddenness. Already by 1915, for example, before Mennonites found themselves on the receiving end of American intolerance, Smith had read enough of the bloodletting in Europe to begin to back away from his exuberant progressive projections about the coming great age of peace. He could be astonishingly brazen about it. "We were told," he told the readers of the *Christian Monitor*, as if he himself had not been one of the principal ones doing the telling, "almost everywhere on the platform, in the press, in the pulpit that the day of universal peace foretold in the Old Testament had finally dawned. War would be no more." The soothsayers had all been insistent: the financiers, who had assured that war was too costly; the philosophers, "who had told us the world is getting too humane"; the advocates of military preparedness, who had said that a big military apparatus would assure peace. "But in spite of all those declarations that war is an impossibility," Smith lectured knowingly, "we are face to face with the humiliating fact that we are engaged not only in the bloodiest war of all history, but for which, even if we should grant that some wars are justifiable, there is not the slightest excuse." His prescription for the way forward was religious as before, but now in a notably nonpolitical way. "The lesson which the pacifist needs to learn from this war," he declared, "is that human nature has not changed in the last two thousand years and that war cannot be eliminated from the earth by peace organizations, by international agreements, not by a show of military force, but only by a complete transformation of the human heart."[48]

By the war's end, Smith's faith in the basic goodness of liberal democracy had likewise begun to unravel. He could excuse the brutality against objectors as the fault of overzealous officers who had escaped the purview of the noble Wilson, but in 1920 he had to acknowledge how quickly their non-Mennonite neighbors had warmed to the ways of popular wartime hatred, detailing the near-lynchings and mob violence by the "self-styled Vigilance Committees" against innocent Mennonites only attempting to follow the dictates of their faith. The future, he warned the All-Mennonite Convention in 1922, would bring more such trials. No more could they expect exemptions from military service as they had enjoyed at times in Europe, for "as governments grow more democratic the securing of special privileges grows increasingly difficult." Wars of the future "will require such a complete mobilization of the man power and economic resources of the nations that conscription will be inevitable from the start." Such a turn of events, Smith prophesied, "will bring in a new problem for such Mennonites as believe that all war is wrong and have the courage to act on that belief."[49]

In sum, the war ushered Smith toward a much darker worldview and the erosion in his progressive faith in the curative powers of democracy. Moreover, it pushed him to begin advocating a look inward for his church. Before the next time of testing came, he advocated, "the world needs . . . right thinking as well as a converted heart and here Mennonites, Quakers and those who think war is fundamentally wrong should find a fruitful field for constructive teaching relative to the injustice of war." Even as he proclaimed these words, Smith himself had commenced such a new teaching, beginning with a new textbook in his field of expertise.[50]

The Mennonites: A Brief History

During the war years the educational committee of the GC church approached Smith and asked him to prepare a "short general history of the Mennonites" suitable for use in college classes and also across the church. Moreover, the war, as Smith noted in his preface, had stimulated interest in Mennonites among the public at large. At any rate, "such is the excuse for this book." He was steadily at work on his textbook by the spring of 1918, and it was published it two years later with the Mennonite Book Concern in Berne, "affectionately dedicated" to Laura. He made his standard claims for his impartiality and underscored them by acknowledging his debt to a wide range of scholars and church leaders across the Mennonite landscape of North America, including not only key GC figures but also a few MC writers like Funk and John Horsch. Perhaps the scholarly patina of Smith's prestigious doctorate buttressed his claims of objectivity, but the commissioners and purposes of the text betrayed its ultimate agenda. Freed from the agendas and hierarchies he had been answerable to in 1909, in his 1920 book Smith could further amplify his reading of a Mennonite usable past that was both mythical and progressive, and do so now in a way that openly presented the GC experience as normative. *The Mennonites: A Brief History* accomplished these ends in several ways.[51]

First, Smith's 1920 book was more balanced in its coverage overall. It was shorter and more concise than his 1909 book (340 as opposed to nearly 500 pages), with half that amount devoted to the Anabaptist story in Europe (in contrast to his relatively scant, 65-page treatment of their ancestors in 1909). His treatment of Anabaptism differed slightly from his thinking on the topic ten years earlier. In 1920 as before, Smith traced its origins to radical movements in Zurich and Saxony, both broadly labeled Anabaptist, but now he subtly downplayed the connection of the Swiss Brethren with Müntzer, outlining how Grebel and his comrades were initially sympathetic to Müntzer until they realized he would attempt to secure church reform through force, after which "they repudiated all connection with him." The two movements, Smith now stressed, "were entirely different in spirit and method, and essential aims. They should not be confused." In like manner, in 1920 he devoted more attention to the rise of "chiliastic" leaders like Hut, Hoffman, and then Matthys. These movements he characterized as a declension from the original "peaceful group of evangelical Christians" with which he was primarily concerned ("nearly all of whom later became known as Mennonites"), though of course the association gave rein to the movement's enemies to lump them all together as fanatics. These movements merely shared a commitment to separation and a rejection of infant baptism, he noted, and refused to get drawn into "merely a quarrel as to terminology" whether or not all should be included under the general term *Anabaptist*.[52]

In 1909, however, Smith had been more willing to include Müntzer and the Swiss Brethren as branches of the same movement, and one can only speculate on reasons for his nuanced shifts ten years later. They may have been to guard himself against further attacks from scholars like Horsch, though he certainly knew they were coming. For example, Smith persisted in his heroic portrayals of Anabaptists like Hubmaier and Denck, figures he well knew that Horsch had since thrown out of the Anabaptist canon. Likewise sure to draw fire from MC scholars were Smith's repeated depictions of the inherent individualism of the Anabaptists and their great pioneering of religious toleration, though once again he anticipated the objections of his critics. "Mennonite theology has never been fundamentally philosophical, but decidedly Biblical," he affirmed. Mennonite readers who thrilled to the carefully wrought dispensationalism of Cyrus Scofield could not help but catch the implications of Smith's insistence that their Anabaptist ancestors had "never concerned themselves with fine spun theories and philosophical distinctions made by the theologians of the day." Instead, Smith just listed the "usual orthodox beliefs" Mennonites held in common with other Protestants, and then elaborated on several distinctive group beliefs that were "sufficiently individualistic to merit extended attention." Among these, all highlighted in bold print, he included baptism, the Lord's Supper, footwashing, nonresistance, and the ban.[53]

Second, Smith's 1920 history was especially more attentive to the GC threads of the Mennonite story. In the past decade, Smith had clearly learned a lot about the Russian Mennonite experience, and he presented it in its Ukrainian complexity, narrating in detail key developments like the growth of the Chortitza and Molotschna colonies and then the schismatic births of the Kleine Gemeinde and the Mennonite Brethren church. As befitted his audience, his tone was generally sympathetic, though he left little doubt about his preference for sober piety as opposed to less respectable religious expression. Some of the Kleine Gemeinde, for example, displayed an "excessive emotionalism," which, "as is frequently the case . . . finally led to serious immorality." The Mennonite Brethren, on the other hand, retained good "Mennonite fundamentals." Among them "the spirit of fanaticism did not last long," and overall "the movement had a beneficial effect on the old church in emphasizing the need of a deeper spiritual life and more vital religion." Once again Smith found in the past a means for subtle commentary on the present. In the apocalyptic wanderings of Claas Epp, for instance, he saw a useful lesson for followers of certain

American religious groups, suggesting that "even at the present time perhaps there is more teaching of this sort than is wholesome." Smith's careful attention to the Russian Mennonite experience was also comprehensive enough to permeate the boundary between history and current events, outlining the ominous developments he had been able to piece together through published letters now coming out of Ukraine. Readers shared in his shocked horror about the anarchy and armed banditry sweeping through the old Russian colonies at the recent war's end, the rise of the radical "Bolsheviki," and their disturbing implications for faithful Mennonites.[54]

In other ways Smith's 1920 book reflected many continuities with his analyses of 1909 and earlier, marginally modified now with more attention to GC groups and a slightly less triumphalist tone. Here as before readers would have been carried along by his powerful narrative skills and engaging periodic shifts to the first person ("our information regarding the history of the colony is scant. We do know, however . . ."). Confident now he was writing for an educated American Mennonite audience, he could employ familiar markers from U.S. history to illustrate his points. Daniel Pastorious, for example, the founder of the Germantown settlement, appears here as "the John Smith of the new colony." Smith often concluded chapters with long lists of the common Mennonite names in the area of focus, reinforcing the book's purpose as an introductory text for students. The similarities with the 1909 book were evident, too, in his inexcusable lack of any citations and, in 1920, not even an index, as if students did not need such scholarly staples.[55]

More positively, he returned at length to the old Smithian themes of a Mennonite usable past: how the Dunkard and Quaker traditions were derivative from the Mennonite one, and the Mennonites as the prime founders of concepts like church-state separation and religious toleration. In like manner he restated a progressive usable past. Smith once again reserved his highest praise for the change agents (of the calm and practical kind, at least) and the outside innovations they engendered, particularly their missions efforts and institutions of higher education. He did, however, modify the main lines of the heroic narrative in two major ways. One was more purposefully to write the Russian Mennonite experience into it. For example, "just to the south" of the

Molotschna colony, he told readers, "were still to be found bands of wild, half-wild nomadic Tartars who hated the frontier settlers as our Indians did the American pioneers." Moreover, in such deliberate efforts to integrate the Russian Mennonite story into the North American Mennonite experience, Smith not only further expanded his inclusive reading of Mennonite history, but deepened his efforts to integrate more Mennonite complexities into the pluralistic ethnic landscapes of North America. Second, with the massive cataclysm of world war now in the immediate background, Smith had to adjust his confident old projections of how the world was surely learning peacemaking from the Mennonites. Among the many great "fundamentals of religious and civil liberty" in which "Menno and his co-workers were centuries ahead," Smith noted, was "the desirability at least of universal peace." Similarly, Smith continued to develop a treatment of Mennonite ethnicity through a progressive ideological lens. "The greatest hope of a reformed Manitoba," he told readers, lay in the hope that cloistered Russian Mennonite colonies might shed their isolation and deepen their social and religious affiliation "with other more liberal Mennonite groups." Likewise, south of the border, the union movement "has not made much progress among the more conservative elements of the older American Mennonites. Old customs and traditions are too strongly entrenched."[56]

Finally, despite the fact that he was not a member of the General Conference Mennonite Church, in 1920 Smith began to treat the GC experience as normative for all Mennonites. This analytical line was revealed in his repeated stressing of the inherent individualism of the Mennonites, their prizing of toleration, and their strong patterns of congregational autonomy. In fact, he asserted, "in the field of *church government*, Mennonites were the original Congregationalists. Each congregation was an independent unit [italics in the original]." With this as something like the Mennonite default position, Smith contrasted it with the "primitive episcopacy" among the MCs, "that is a bishop for every church." His treatment of the MC church appears ever so slightly disdainful today, but was surely deafening in certain circles in 1920. The "Old Mennonites," Smith summarized, "are still quite conservative on all matters of church policy. . . . Dress regulations are quite rigid, especially for the women." The union movement, he noted, had made little headway among them, for "old customs and traditions are too strongly entrenched," rendering them unable to be "greatly influenced by any liberal or progressive movement outside their own body." Smith damned MC scholarship with faint praise. He noted Horsch's 1916 biography of Menno as "the most important recent study" of that great Mennonite leader, "next to the comprehensive book by Vos." In terms of general histories of the church, Smith included just one book by MC scholars, Hartzler and Kauffman's work, merely mentioning that it was "printed at Scottdale in 1905."[57]

The reactions to Smith's book were almost predictable. The GC church passed a general resolution thanking Smith and urging that a copy of it soon find its way to "every Mennonite home in the land." Mennonites of a certain persuasion loved it. Twenty years later Thierstein recalled to Smith that, in just a few hours of work over two successive afternoons in the immediate vicinity of Bluffton, he sold thirty copies. Mennonites of other persuasions were less enthused, though Kauffman's *Gospel Herald* was balanced and a bit gracious. Smith's book, a small review read, "is attractively bound, written in a pleasing style and is well arranged. . . . The book being written from the standpoint of a progressive Mennonite," the reviewer observed, "the reader will find in the discussion of the issues a different viewpoint from that which one more conservative would present," but admitted that "the student of history will find much that is valuable and accurate." Undoubtedly Smith would have been surprised by the review. Perhaps the chasms in the Mennonite world were not as wide as he had imagined.[58]

By the time Smith neared the end of his first decade in Bluffton, he had many reasons to feel good about the life he had found there. He had quickly taken his place as a leader of Bluffton's academic community with a fine home across from the south edge of campus. In the intervening years he had emerged as a solid member of the community, a respected civic leader and bank president with a second office on Main Street. Now, with the publication of his second book, he had established himself as the dean of Mennonite history in North America. He seemingly enjoyed full and unhampered freedom to interpret the Mennonite past in line with the progressive vision he embraced.

Privately, though, he must have been unsettled. The ordeal that Mennonites had undergone during the war years had begun to reveal to him that progressivism was not the source of renewal for the church that he had supposed. Popular democracy had an ugly side, and war could not be wished or legislated away. "There is but one power that can completely transform the human heart," he told a large Mennonite assemblage in 1922, "and that is the regenerating power of the grace of God." By then he knew how he himself could best contribute to such an enterprise. All the accolades over his 1920 book were nice, but he confessed to his friend Thierstein that "I wrote it too hurriedly." He needed to get back to the basics of his discipline, visiting archives and sifting through the dusty annals of the past. "I am beginning to get interested again in Mennonite history and feel that I wasted about ten years of my life that I should have used in gathering material on the subject," he wrote Thierstein. "But perhaps it isn't too late yet."[59]

8
Forays down a Winding Road

In the early 1920s, Smith discovered that his banking and other investments provided the means to pursue a lifelong urge to travel. Even before the war, he had begun to satisfy that yearning, and after the war he commenced the process in earnest. In the eight years after the 1922 Bluffton College commencement ceremonies, he would be gone from Bluffton for most of two of them and complete three extensive trips abroad: two summer-long sojourns in Europe and a shorter trip to Mexico. "A winding road has always had strong fascination for me," he wrote in 1925 in the aftermath of his first trip to Europe. "You can never tell where it leads nor what surprises may lie just ahead." Yet Smith was too much of a scholar and Mennonite church intellectual to travel just for the sheer joy of discovery. Like nearly everything else he was engaged in, he would do his best to ensure his travels likewise contributed to the development of a Mennonite usable past.[1]

"A Lesson in Toleration"

Amid all else Smith would be involved in through the coming decade, it is easy to overlook how busy he remained at his job. The 1925 *Bluffton College Bulletin* listed his official position as professor of history and government, which required him to teach eleven different courses in history and five in political science. In addition, it noted his service as secretary of the faculty and a member of the athletics, graduate studies, library, recommendations, and publications and advertising committees. As usual, he carried on whatever duties came his way as an informal booster of the "Bluffton spirit": accompanying seniors on their "sneak day" to Lake Erie in 1923 and on a "bobsled party" in 1924, serving as a judge for an intercollegiate debate, and speaking at vespers services and Y meetings. He was less enthralled with other aspects of student life. Back in 1917 the trustees had appointed him to an official administrative committee, and its first act of business was to thank the student athletic association for not renewing their campaign to bring back intercollegiate football. It seemed worldly and violent, and had alienated the conservative churches. Students nonetheless pushed relentlessly for a decade to have the sport reinstituted. The trustees finally relented and reestablished football in the fall of 1923. Smith was not a fan. "I think debating is more important than athletics, and I would rather win in debating than in football," he complained to his friend Thierstein. More often than not, when Bluffton College appeared in the local papers, "it is usually football or something else of that sort, which is not the best kind of advertising."[2]

Smith's lack of sports enthusiasm notwithstanding, students seemed to appreciate him. Decades later, amid a busy career as a high school administrator in Illinois, a former student took a moment to pen to Smith some of his most vivid memories of his college years in the 1920s: of his fellow students gathering "yellow tablet armchairs" in the "history room in the old college building" and watching Smith "pull your books and notes out of a green cloth bag and . . . listen to you expound the intricacies of the law of diminishing returns or elaborate on the effect of the frontier on American history." Smith's "greatest assets," commented the *Witmarsum* in 1924, "are his personality, his spirit of helpfulness, [and] his Christian character." Not only has he "made the study of history a real vital factor in college life," but "his presence and encouragement has helped many a wayworn student over the rocks of discouragement and doubt." Smith would have a lot of students to help, for the college continued to grow. The fall of 1921 found the dining hall in Ropp "crowded to overflowing," Mosiman reported, with numbers climbing upward nearly every year. The next fall, Smith observed, the student body numbered more than two hundred, and, "better than I expected," twenty more in the seminary. Some things apparently did not change. In 1923–24 the new student numbers necessitated the construction of a new men's dorm, Lincoln Hall. It would be, Smith wrote to Thierstein, "a good home for the boys. If only it were paid for we would be alright. Financially the college is about like it has been—hard up, about the hardest for some time."³

Financial considerations had apparently driven Thierstein to relocate to Bethel College in Kansas, but other developments brought to Bluffton new friends and old. In 1921, after years of wooing, Mosiman finally persuaded Jacob Quiring to join the seminary faculty. Quiring was at once a prized and risky addition. A native of the Mennonite colonies in Ukraine who had worked for years as a GC "Home Missionary" both there and across the American Great Plains, Quiring was a graduate of both Moody Bible Institute and the University of Chicago. He had been influenced more by the latter than the former, however, and his increasing willingness to share with students the new approaches to Bible study he had learned at Chicago would cause Mosiman much grief. But within a week of his arrival, Smith observed, he "seems to be getting into the spirit of the work. . . . I think I will like him very much." In 1926 Russell Lantz arrived in Bluffton to teach choral music after a harrowing experience during World War I imprisoned as an absolutist objector at Fort Leavenworth. He moved next door to the Smiths in subsequent years and became a good friend. Developments at the seminary brought to town another Smith companion. In 1921 its leaders decided officially to separate from the college. This occurred for prosaic reasons. If it incorporated apart from the college, Whitmer thought, it might attract graduates from other Mennonite schools, who could now attend without fear they had joined a rival to their alma maters. Shortly after the decision, Whitmer recruited J. E. Hartzler for the seminary presidency, and the two managed to kindle some real excitement in progressive Mennonite congregations. Within weeks of the official incorporation of the new "Witmarsum Seminary," upward of $20,000 had arrived in support. Hartzler himself soon arrived in town, settling in a fine home a block away from Smith. The two would travel Europe together and renew an old friendship from Goshen days.⁴

In 1922, Smith elected to spend a year teaching at yet a third Mennonite college. "Yes I am thinking of spending a year at Bethel in doing some research on the Russian Mennonites and doing some teaching also," he apprised Thierstein. "I think it will give me a chance to look up some of the subjects which can be studied only in the west." He had been there at least once before, lecturing on Mennonite history during a special Bible week the previous January. A full academic year at Bethel promised to accomplish several important objectives: research, certainly, but with an experiential dimension that encompassed much more than merely archival digging. When Smith arrived in south-central Kansas in early fall 1922, he entered a profoundly different ethnocultural landscape. Large numbers of German-speaking Russian Mennonites had begun arriving there about the time of Smith's birth a half century before. They had brought with them a cultural acuity and sense of institutional initiative they had developed through a century of autonomy on the plains of southern Ukraine. They were eager to maintain the bonds of cultural separation, meaning that Smith's home for the year would be an intensely Germanic community. At the same time, these Mennonites were more open to innovation, more used to self-government, and more eager to build institutions than the Mennonites Smith had known in the East. Bethel College was the oldest Mennonite college in the country, home not only to old friends like Thierstein and Jacob Langenwalter but also to people Smith would have immediately recognized as kindred spirits: progressive intellectuals trained at top universities where they had become devotees of intellectuals like John Dewey and politicians like Woodrow Wilson.[5]

When Smith arrived at Bethel, however, he encountered a community that was just recovering from two different kinds of trauma, one of which he would have immediately recognized and the other with which he would soon become painfully familiar. For one, their experience in the recent war had brutally shattered their German cultural affinities as their main boundary of separation with a burgeoning American society. The Bethel faculty quickly dropped German from the curriculum, editors of Mennonite German-language newspapers found themselves under investigation, and the nearby Mennonites were attacked for refusing to buy war bonds. In a year at Bethel, Smith would have been frequently reminded of the low tolerance that democracies sometimes have for dissent. Equally discomfiting was the ugly experience that had occurred at Bethel because of intolerance closer to home. In 1916, as the war intensity heated up, a German professor named Gustav Enss had suddenly charged the academic dean, Jacob Balzer, with teaching modernism. The trustees dismissed Enss two years later, but this only accelerated the controversy. Enss simply moved to the pastorate of a nearby Mennonite congregation, where he could repeat and broaden the charges against other Bethel faculty and administrators. He also corresponded with John Horsch, who aided his efforts from Scottdale. Students and area congregations subsequently lined up on both sides, and the affair ultimately resulted in the purging from Bethel of most of its progressive professors. Bethel was a long way physically from Bluffton, but Smith might have read this confrontation as an ominous sign for Mennonite educational institutions.[6]

None of Bethel's recent difficulties seemed to have marred Smith's experience. In April 1924 he confessed wistfully to Thierstein that "we still have a warm feeling for the place because of our year's stay there." The Bethel academic year began that September with a featured lecture by Smith titled "Sidelights on Pennsylvania Mennonites." He breezed through what would have been well-trodden ground for him, outlining the Mennonites as the archetypal American pioneers and leaders in the antislavery movement before closing by calling students to research an "unexplored field": their own Kansas Mennonite tradition. He lectured again on early Anabaptism during "special Bible week" in January 1923. In the meantime, in his classes, the historian Keith Sprunger observed, he "brought some fresh, up-to-date approaches to teaching history at Bethel, especially Mennonite history, which heretofore had been rooted in traditionalist German church history." His classes also seemed replicas of his longtime staples at Bluffton, which would have left him lots of time for research. In May 1923 the community was sad to see him go. "His experience with us has been one of mutual profit," wrote the *Bethel College Monthly*, "and an experience long to be remembered."[7]

Smith also jumped on the opportunity afforded him by a year in Kansas to serve as something like a traveling evangelist for the union movement. He had learned there of the deep division permeating Mennonite communities in the West. Indeed, he noted from back in Bluffton in 1925, "It will be a little more difficult . . . to get cooperation in the west than here because there are not as many cooperating branches as here." Smith addressed this problem forthrightly in a lengthy address to the Ministers Meeting of the GC's Western District Conference in Goessel, Kansas, probably in the spring or summer of 1923. The church's receptivity to his message was underscored by the fact that it was serialized and published simultaneously the following fall in both the *Mennonite* and the *Christian Evangel*.[8]

Smith began in the tones of a trained social scientist, setting up a demographic problem, which, moving into the rhetorical pose of a revivalist, he then fully answered. The basic issue he laid out was that "although the Mennonite church is a very old church, it has not grown as rapidly as one might expect." With an eye fixed on his recent research, he held up the Russian Mennonites as the best possible test case. They had expanded their numbers fourfold from their arrival in the 1870s. If the entire global Mennonite church had mirrored the same rate of increase, Smith calculated, its size would easily approach nearly two million instead of the half million Mennonites he estimated existed currently. What had gone wrong? Certainly the heavy persecution the church had experienced was part of the problem. But Smith especially stressed two other causes of the slow Mennonite growth rate, both of which led directly to the meat of his message. The church had failed to grow, he claimed, in large part because it lacked the schools and a dedication to higher education that could help retain its young people. An even greater problem, he suggested, lay in the Mennonite penchant for divisions over "matters of practice rather than fundamental doctrines." They all shared equal devotion to key doctrinal principles. Instead, the splits were over silly things, like buttons, bonnets, and the tilt of one's head during baptism. The tendency had begun in Europe, but now "it remains for the Mennonites of America—free, democratic, individualistic America to excel in divisions." At last count, he pointed out to the pastors and beyond them the GC and Central Conference churches, there were seventeen different Mennonite bodies in America, "most of them claiming to be the only true followers of Menno." Many refused to interact with each other: "not only not cooperating, but worse, still, working at cross purposes and destroying each other's influence for good." Smith could not resist a subtle commentary on elements of the fundamentalist subculture thoroughly permeating sectors of the Mennonite world. He did not name the particular parties, but astute listeners would have known to whom he was referring. It would be better, Smith pled, "to rest some of the fundamental doctrines on a Scriptural basis and let it go at that, rather than attempt to square them with some cut and dried philosophical formulas . . . which may in turn be the cause of endless confusion. . . . What the Mennonite church needs today," he insisted, "is that its broken body should be healed and made whole." And "what the Mennonites need perhaps above all else is to get acquainted with each other." Fortunately, he assured the ministers, that trend was already underway: in the colleges, at Witmarsum Seminary, and at the All-Mennonite conventions.[9]

The Mennonite union movement in the first half of the twentieth century has largely been treated dismissively by scholars. What analysis it has received has been critical. Juhnke, for example, calls the All-Mennonite conventions "misnamed," since Old Order and conservative groups did not attend and proceedings there did not speak for them. Willard Smith, C. Henry's nephew, admitted that the movement was dominated by church progressives, whose calls for unity proceeded from a prior acceptance of progressive positions. These are legitimate critiques. Yet to leave it at that, and thus place the union movement on the margins of historical narratives, is to disregard a development of signal importance in the Mennonite story of twentieth-century America. The drive by a great many Mennonites to straddle their ethnocultural and theological differences would ultimately be consummated, albeit imperfectly, in the latter half of the century. This later success may well have been delayed much further without the passionate, sincere, fumbling efforts of the earlier movement. And by the mid-1920s, C. Henry Smith had emerged as something like its godfather.[10]

In early September 1925, the Fifth All-Mennonite Convention gathered at the West Market Street Mennonite Church in Nappanee, Indiana. Smith had attended three of the previous four meetings and seems to have participated in them energetically. Now, as the convention's chair, he led off proceedings with a stirring keynote address called "The Next Step." According to the official minutes, it "was well received and in a large measure determined the temper of the convention." Delegates would have been thrilled with it, for Smith encapsulated in folksy but soaring cadences the hopes that had propelled the movement from the beginning. He began, prosaically enough, with the story of receiving a telescope for his sixteenth birthday. As he started to focus his new instrument on the stars, he told his audience, he realized the universe was far bigger than he had ever imagined. It had millions of stars, each the center of its own solar system. It was unfathomably immense: "how it humiliates us. And against such a background as this how insignificant seem the little differences of opinion which exist among us mortals." In fact, he declared, the "greatest lesson I learned from my little telescope" did not concern astronomy. Instead, it had taught him "a lesson in toleration."[11]

It was toleration that the Mennonite church demanded, Smith affirmed at Nappanee in 1925. Certainly, he admitted, this was a "relative term. It never meant anarchy," proceeding with no discipline. This was what "certain Mennonite leaders" were insisting it meant, though "I know of no Mennonite who holds such views." Neither was toleration a "one sided virtue. It involves obligations as well as privileges": obligations to respect the views of others even if one disagreed with them. Perhaps it was too much to hope for some kind of "organic unity" to emerge among modern Mennonites, he admitted, though he suggested that he himself embodied it. Perhaps Mennonites would never achieve a total unanimity in faith and practice, Smith admitted, but they could move toward an amiable and warm "confederation" for achieving in "education and publication" what they had already begun to accomplish in efforts like mission and relief. This was the fifth time they had all met together to discuss such issues, he concluded. Through such encounters "we have learned to know each other better—and suspect each other less. We have learned by this time that we are at heart one in purpose and fundamental faith." It was time, Smith declared, his voice rippling out across the crowd, to extend such a lesson further. At the same time, he was a diligent enough student of current Mennonite affairs to know how difficult such a course would be.[12]

By the mid-1920s, having spent a year on the southern plains and won the affection of many in that part of the church, Smith had polished his credentials as a leading Mennonite public intellectual and an astute commentator on churchly affairs. Just one particular criterion remained to be accomplished. For two decades Smith had been writing about the European origins of his faith, and he had been dreaming about visiting the key sites since his years in grad school. With the summertime flexibility enjoyed by college professors, he certainly had the time. Thanks to their banks and other investments, the Smiths clearly had the money. It was time to go to Europe.

Talent as a Travel Writer

Ever since he was a child, packed with the other Smith kids into the six-seater buggy for a trip down into the "timber" west of Metamora, he had been drawn inexorably to the open road. He had scraped together enough funds from a meager Goshen salary to do some traveling west even before his starting his doctorate, and clearly hungered to go again. As Smith's fiancée, Laura Ioder caught his longing, telling him that "I will not object to a little traveling," though hoping he would not "do all your going before we are married." Ioder could not, of course, have known what awaited her. By 1911, Smith was reporting to the readers of the *Christian Evangel* of his "Rambles through Historic New England" in a lengthy article of the same title. In summer 1917, as the rest of the nation geared up for world war, he and Laura shot off west in a tour of some of the great national parks, camping in places like Yosemite Valley and hiking the depths of the Grand Canyon. Smith described at length for Mennonite readers the magnificent vistas they took in, as well as their encounters with friendly fellow tourists and less congenial bears. The two seem to have made at least part of the trek by car, since Smith's published narrative describes, for instance, the hairpin turns on the road in its descent into Yellowstone. (It may have been on that trip that Laura developed her preference for train travel.) The summer of 1919 found Smith navigating the Yukon River valley by train and steamboat as far north as Whitehorse and Dawson City. That time, apparently, Laura stayed home.[13]

In June 1924, the Smiths headed east instead of west. They caught a train in Bluffton with connections to Detroit, and then a Canadian Pacific Railway line to Quebec. There they secured berths on the SS *Montroyal*, a sixteen-thousand-ton steamer bound for Liverpool. Throughout the journey, Smith developed an uncanny knack as a travel writer, sending home regular dispatches that were published on the front page of the *Bluffton News*. Like the best in that tradition, sometimes his exaggerations went overboard. "Incidentally," he told readers authoritatively in his first installment, "the St. Lawrence route by way of Montreal is an excellent introduction to European travel." One could scarcely have guessed that it was his first such trip. But generally Smith's travel prose sparkled. Witness, for example, his description of the yaw a ship makes that leads passengers into seasickness. "A ship at

The Smiths and their first automobile, a 1916 Chalmers. BUASC.

Smith (right) heads up the Yukon in the summer of 1919. Laura's handwriting in Smith photo album: "Traveling companions on Northwestern, en route to Klondike." BUASC.

sea," Smith wrote, "goes thru [*sic*] three motions—nautically defined as pitching, rolling, vibrating, which in plain English means that she rears up and down length ways, swings back and forth sideways, and at the same time wiggles all over." He was proud to report that the waves troubled him only slightly; out of twenty meals on the six-day voyage, "I made a perfect score" in devouring all of them, while Mrs. Smith, the village of Bluffton was informed, managed to keep down only seven. Even so, "yesterday we decided that the next trip to Europe we would go by way of north west [sic] Canada, then down the Yukon to Nome, Alaska and wait for the Behring straight [sic] to freeze over, and then cross over by dog sled and come into Europe the back way over the trans-Siberian Railroad. It might take a little longer, but it would be decidedly more comfortable."[14]

In the hands of such a guide, Bluffton readers could settle back, let Smith take them by the elbow, and whisk them along on his whirlwind trip to Europe. They were with the Smiths as they toured England's Lake District, which Dr. Smith enlivened with literary tidbits about Wordsworth and Sir Walter Scott. They made their way through the streets of London, worshiped with the Smiths at Westminster Abbey, and beheld the Rosetta Stone at the British Museum. On the continent they scurried through the streets of Amsterdam and Paris, took in the sights at the Louvre, climbed the Eiffel Tower, and left Mrs. Smith to survey the "lace shops" of Brussels while accompanying the professor to the site of the battle of Waterloo. Smith described with awe and sadness what tourists saw then at Verdun: vast landscapes of dead tree trunks, shell holes now green with grass, and mile after mile of crumbling trenches laden with wooden crosses. At the American military cemetery near the battlefield of Belleau Wood, readers stood quietly with Smith as he cast his eyes over the stretching rows of graves a half dozen years old. Before coming home to start classes in September, Smith intimated to his audience that the great killing fields had left many problems unresolved, describing the seething resentment of Germans at the French military occupation they encountered as they made their way up the Rhine.[15]

The Smiths' 1924 European trip was strictly for pleasure, and he did not try to mask it. They made no apparent efforts to contact the Mennonites in Amsterdam, and as they entered the Mennonite ancestral birthplace of Switzerland, almost exactly four centuries after the Anabaptist movement had started there, they did not visit the key historic sites. "There are two Switzerlands for the traveler," Smith explained, "One the Switzerland of tradition and history—Zurich, Geneva and Berne; the other, Switzerland as the pleasure ground of Europe . . . We visited the latter, leaving the former for some other

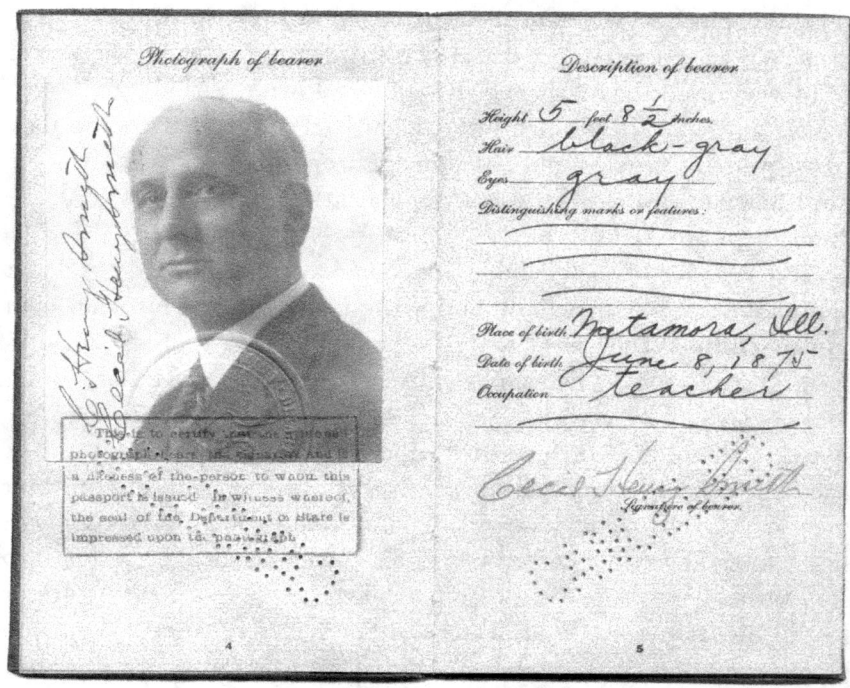

Smith's passport on his 1926 European trip. Note his signature as "Cecil Henry Smith." BUASC.

time." Two years later Smith made up for it in another trip to Europe more explicitly harnessed to academic and educational purposes. He accomplished it by reconnecting with the great religious siren of his adolescence and young adult years, the YMCA.[16]

From the end of the war through the 1920s, scholars recount, large sectors of the old coalition of progressive reformers made the same kind of broad intellectual pivot that Smith did on a personal level: from great optimism about the social possibilities the war offered to dismay with what it brought. Many broke, at some point along the way, with their old reform hero Wilson (in contrast to Smith, who in 1924 led the campus in a memorial service to Wilson upon the president's death). They entered the postwar period, as did Smith, with a much more chastened progressivism, still imbued with fervor for reform but much less sanguine about its possibilities and without their old, confident optimism about a golden future achievable by human action. The YMCA, by now a thorough vehicle of liberal Protestantism, reflected these shifts. Y campus chapters shifted their foci from individual moral reform to issues of systemic economic injustice and especially to international educational efforts, with a new stress on peacemaking. Through the 1920s, many chapters commonly gave birth to or dovetailed their work with campus peace clubs.[17]

Few people better embodied the basic shifts and new agendas of postwar progressive Protestantism than the indefatigable national Y leader Sherwood Eddy. Smith had doubtless followed his career since his own days as a campus Y leader: Eddy's passionate energies as one of the great young leaders of the Student Volunteer Movement, the Y's overseas mission arm; his years as the Y's traveling secretary in Asia; and his peripatetic speaking tours on American college campuses. He broke with his initial support for the war, fully embraced the Social Gospel, and developed some commitments as a peace Christian. By the early 1920s, Eddy had become convinced that in its refusal to join the League of Nations and its postwar embrace of Warren Harding's "normalcy," the United States was abdicating its moral authority and the position of global leadership the war had prepared it to play. Eager to shape public opinion to counter such trends, he developed an initiative he called the "American Seminar." Beginning in 1921, Eddy took select groups of Americans on summer tours of Europe, where they met, seminar-style, with national political and cultural leaders he had had come to know personally through two decades of international Y work. With short breaks for sightseeing, participants proceeded from London to various other European capital cities: Berlin, Paris, Vienna, Prague, and the League of Nations headquarters in Geneva, interviewing prominent political leaders and receiving lectures on current political and social trends at every stop. Eddy's seminars worked as he intended, soon attracting a wide range of U.S. public-opinion shapers, including luminaries such as the theologian Reinhold Niebuhr, *Christian Century* editor Charles Clayton Morrison, and college presidents, educators, civic leaders, and church leaders from across the ranks of liberal Protestantism.[18]

The American Seminar seemed perfectly designed to excite the intellectual passions (and loosen the wallets) of wealthier Mennonite progressive intellectuals like Smith and Hartzler. In January 1926 the *Bluffton College Bulletin* announced that the two "have been admitted to the Sherwood Eddy Seminar which makes annual tours to Europe for the study of particular national and international problems," noting that "membership of the party is restricted to persons who will be actively interested in promoting better international relationships upon their return." Eddy admitted 120 people to the 1926 tour but still had to turn some away, which might explain why Laura did not go. Smith and Hartzler set sail out of New York City on June 23 on the SS *Berengaria* and immediately plunged into what must have been a heady experience. After a transatlantic crossing laced with meetings and lectures, they began first in London, staying in the famous settlement house Toynbee Hall. Before heading to the continent, they heard from a stream of speakers and dignitaries including conservative and liberal members of Parliament, British industrial and labor leaders, and England's prime minister Stanley Baldwin. In Germany they were granted an audience with president Paul von Hindenburg and in Czechoslovakia with president Tomas Masaryk. Along the way, they heard viewpoints that Smith certainly would have found interesting and provocative. In London, for example, a tempered but still unabashed imperialist named Philip Kerr, the secretary for the Rhodes Trust, conceded that the age of imperialism would end as soon as "primitive people" were ready for it. The economist, politician, and Marxist theoretician Harold Laski told the seminar that, having just visited the U.S., he feared that Tocqueville's predictions were coming true: that "an aristocracy of business more powerful, more grim, more relentless than the older territorial aristocracy . . . has come into being."[19]

While seminar participants heard diverse perspectives, several themes seemed to emerge repeatedly: the attempts by European political and intellectual leaders to come to terms with the tremendous carnage of the war, the hopes they invested in the new League of Nations as a means for averting another such cataclysm, and their sadness and frustration with the lack of American participation in it. Smith received and repeated the message. To stand as he did at the League of Nations headquarters building in Geneva, he wrote in a special dispatch to his hometown newspaper, the *Metamora Herald*, and not see an American flag waving there alongside those of fifty-five other member nations—this triggered a keen sense of disappointment for "any American who for the time being can forget his political prejudices and remember only his interest in a better world order." Other lengthy analyses he sent to

The SS Berengaria, on which Smith and Hartzler sailed for Europe, along with other members of Sherwood Eddy's 1926 American Seminar. BUASC.

the *Christian Exponent*, a new journal being published by a group of MC dissidents, indicated that many of his older, progressive inclinations were still intact but were being gradually overlaid with an increasingly internationalist orientation. For example, Smith judged England as needing to rid itself of its inefficient pampering of labor and "many of her old social traditions and cumbersome and wasteful methods of work if she is to compete with countries that are unencumbered with survivals of medievalism." Likewise hampering England's progress, he noted with lingering prohibitionist sentiment, was its "enormous drink bill." France was shuddering to enormous high rates of postwar inflation and waiting for the U.S. to bail it out, though Smith thought it would be foolish for his country to do so. Germans, he told readers, were adjusting to much grimmer standards of living than they had known before the war. Both that country and also Czechoslovakia, he stated, were pinning their hopes on the goodwill and active financial intervention of the United States and the new League of Nations.[20]

Amid the intellectual high tonic of the Eddy Seminars, however, Smith did not lose sight of the main academic project of his adult life, to which he kept returning like a homing pigeon through the decade of the 1920s. When the seminar ended, Hartzler returned home alone. Smith stayed on in Europe a full six weeks more for archival research on original Mennonite source materials and finally to take

The 1926 Eddy American Seminar participants and a group of international law students in the League of Nations Assembly Hall in Geneva, Switzerland. With magnification, Smith can clearly be identified slightly in front of a pillar at the upper end of the hall. BUASC.

in the key sites of Anabaptist history (he had arranged for a local pastor to cover his classes). Following through with the pledge he had made as a Chicago grad student to secure that history the "greater publicity" he thought it deserved, he worked with the *Mennonite* to publish an account of his travels, not "a serious attempt at an exhaustive treatise on Mennonitism," but instead a "pilgrimage to the homes of our Mennonite forefathers" for lay readers. It is indicative of the wide following that Smith had cultivated in the GC church that the editors agreed to an extensive, ten-part serialized narrative that ran on the journal's cover pages from January through August 1927. What is particularly fascinating about the series is that Smith clearly took a new tack in the way he presented Mennonite history to people in the pews. Here the history appears divorced from his earlier progressive agendas. Instead, Smith's newer writing presented a Mennonite history as intrinsically interesting in itself and laden with potential enrichment for the church.[21]

The last stop of the Eddy tour was Geneva, so this is where Smith began, carrying with him a letter of introduction to European Mennonites from GC church president H. J. Krehbiel. He first described for readers his initial visit to a Mennonite congregation in the Emmenthal, in the old Canton of Berne, from which their ancestors had been cruelly driven centuries before in accounts he had described so vividly in his books. Harnessing all his talents as a travel writer, he moved skillfully between references to one or another incident in European Anabaptist-Mennonite history and contemporary settings in the bucolic Swiss and German countryside or the busy streets of Amsterdam. For Mennonites who did not know much about their historical or cultural tradition or appreciate its richness, it is hard to imagine a better guide. Smith took readers across the home country of their faith with a trained and patient eye, describing their surviving churches and architectural styles. He noted Mennonite names on shops or street signs that would be sure to delight their distant relatives with similar names now scattered across the American Midwest. Readers walked with him in his search for historical Mennonite documents in old congregational storerooms and rare Anabaptist texts in dusty shops in forgotten country towns. He described the flow of his conversations with this café owner or that old Mennonite pastor, and the new scholarly leads they offered. He knew how to connect with his audience, sometimes switching from his historical vignettes to observations of the comparative difference between European and American farming technologies, aided by a richly endowed storehouse of memories from his childhood on the Illinois prairie.[22]

In their imaginations Mennonite laity traveled with Smith from Zurich to the Palatinate and to his meeting with German Mennonite pastor and historian Christian Neff. Smith was happy to meet Neff, who, along with a comrade named Christian Hege, were about a third of the way through assembling and editing their monumental *Mennonitisches Lexikon*, a three-volume compilation of all extant information about Mennonites. Smith inserted an advertisement for the project in his story, telling readers that the book was "undoubtedly the most ambitious Mennonite publication since the appearance of the Martyr's Mirror," and making sure to remind readers that the GC church had, the previous fall, sent $200 to help Neff and Hege in their efforts. He once again caught passage down the Rhine to the one-time Mennonite town of Crefeld, from which the founders of the Mennonite congregation in Germantown, Pennsylvania, had emigrated centuries before. He then finished the series with an intricately detailed description of his sojourn among the Dutch Mennonites, narrating his search for old Mennonite documents like a detective and conveying in marvelous detail something of the richness and complexity of the Mennonite community there.[23]

Smith returned home to Bluffton five weeks into the school semester, undoubtedly both exhausted and exhilarated. Presumably he had satisfied his rambling itch enough to keep him home at least a little while. Meanwhile, his travels in Europe, with one eye focused on international events and the other on Mennonite history, clearly reinforced the subtle but significant shifts in his thinking that had been percolating since the war. These shifts would have been discernible to his various audiences at the time. Once again, for example, he spoke to a dilution of his old progressive faith in the powers of American democracy and in the possibilities for a warless world. In a speech he gave at a local high school in November 1925, he told students to not depend too much on the constitution, that it had no "magic power." Shortly after his return home from the Eddy Seminar, an adult Sunday school class at First Mennonite Church in Bluffton heard from him that Europe seemed a more polite society, with less crime and more respect for law and for human life. London police officers, he observed, carried no guns. In a 1929 address called the "Progress of Peace," which Smith delivered at Grace Mennonite Church in nearby Pandora, he outlined the increasing destructiveness of war, now with its poison gases and aerial attacks. He took some heart in new measures taken to combat these horrors, mentioning the League of Nations, the recent Washington Conference on Disarmament, the birth of the World Court, and the just-concluded Kellogg-Briand treaty and its attempt to outlaw war. But the real significance of such efforts, he said, was in other issues, like the "right thinking" they suggested: that war itself was a crime. It was not caused by corrupt human nature, he told the congregation, but by "wrong ideas of national dignity" and by misplaced thinking on "the necessity, inevitability, glory, justice and benefits of war." There were ways, he continued, of combating such evils, primarily educational ones. We need to be intelligent, he concluded, to be optimistic, to be "wide awake—vote right," and above all else, we need to "demilitarize our hearts."[24]

Moreover, Smith's visits to the actual sites of Anabaptist history apparently worked alongside his reevaluation of his formerly unalloyed progressivism to affect an emerging new approach to Mennonite history. As he ushered Mennonite readers across their faith's birthplaces, gone were any references to Mennonites as quintessentially American or as farsighted progressives; missing was a depiction of their history as a kind of a ticket for full admittance to American society. Instead, as a new set of scholars had begun to do in Goshen at about the same time, the kind of new Mennonite historical consciousness that Smith conveyed here promised to contribute to Mennonite self-definition on its own terms. At that point it was confined to articles in the GC Mennonite press. But he would take up these themes with more depth and care when he turned his attention to longer projects.

9
Diverging Readings of Anabaptist History

Through the 1920s, as Smith kept up a frantic teaching schedule, traveled extensively, and supervised two banks, he thoroughly knit his mind once more back into the fabric of Mennonite history. Even much of his travel abroad was for research or explicitly educational purposes, and in between his trips he spent nearly every other summer either buried in various archives or intensively immersed in writing. All these efforts bore fruit. Before the end of the decade, he would write two more major books, edit a third, complete a lengthy private memoir of his growing-up years, and furnish a running commentary on his journeys to the Mennonite popular press.

The tumultuous Mennonite world of the 1920s, however, was in no mood to receive anyone's historical narratives dispassionately. In coming to Bluffton, Smith had removed himself from the immediate authority of the bishops and other hierarchs of the Mennonite Church. The congregational polity of the General Conference church did not lend itself to the emergence of such officials, and even as he retained his membership in a Central Conference congregation, with his 1920 book Smith cemented his reputation as something like the official historian of the GC denomination. Yet Smith was fooling himself if he thought he could remain immune from the theological and ideological conflicts raging around him. He persisted in seeing himself as a historian thoroughly committed to the lofty ideal of objectivity. "I have no ax to grind, no preconceived ideas to find justification for," he would insist in supreme exasperation to his most vigorous attacker. "I am merely an honest searcher after the truth." The Mennonite world of the

1920s would not allow such a removed position. The theological and ecclesiastical fight between Mennonite fundamentalists and progressives was rising to a fever pitch, and it would place diverging readings of Mennonite history at the very center of the storm.[1]

Two New Books and Thematic Shifts in Writing

In the fall of 1924, after soliciting the opinions of the faculty as to the right people for the job, Mosiman asked Smith, along with math professor Edmund Hirschler, to head up the effort of producing Bluffton College's official history for the celebration of its quarter-century anniversary. They intended this book, announced an official "publication committee," as a signal contribution to the history of Mennonite higher education, produced at a time when many of the founders were still around and "able to speak as eye-witnesses" to the college's historical development. By the following June, the two professors managed to produce an edited tome of nearly three hundred pages, proceeding in the same manner as most of Smith's other books: from a straight chronological narrative of basic historical events to an exploration of key themes in the latter part of the text. Because the book represented the contributions of eleven different authors, ranging from Mosiman and Hirschy to Byers, Smith, Whitmer, and other faculty, and because the chapter authors were not identified in the book, it is impossible to know which chapter or chapters Smith himself wrote. But one can guess. The author of the chapter explaining the transition from Central Mennonite to Bluffton College, for example, wrote in a style and an analysis that was decidedly Smithian. It narrated how cooperation among Mennonites had been difficult because "we have been quite clannish and provincial," factors that stymied "any worthwhile contribution to the Kingdom" until it became evident that Mennonites needed "one strong institution to train a leadership for a united and progressive Mennonite denomination."[2]

Smith would have realized that Mosiman and his colleagues meant the college history assignment as an honor, but undoubtedly it also interrupted his work on other projects. In his year at Bethel, he returned to a research tool he had begun as a grad student: sending out a mimeographed letter to contacts across the Mennonite world seeking information about founding Mennonite families. He ventured to one archive or another to see what he could dig up himself. The summer of 1922 found him back in John Funk's personal library at Elkhart. In the summer of 1925, he traveled to the Minnesota state library in Minneapolis and then on to Winnipeg, Manitoba, for research into the Russian Mennonite experience. The following Christmas season he was back for more work in Goshen. In the meantime, he began sharing something of his findings with the wider church, publishing a summary of noteworthy statistics in the *Mennonite* and then a detailed explication of letters he found on the early Amish movement for readers of the *Christian Exponent*. By early 1927, even having taken time out for two summers of travel in Europe, Smith had somehow completed drafts of not one but two major books, finished within six months of each other, in March and October. Both of them quickly emerged, Robert Kreider has noted, into "benchmark studies" that opened up new historical terrain for scholars of the North American Mennonite experience.[3]

"I was glad to hear that the Western District Conference was interested in a history of the Russian immigration," Smith wrote Thierstein late in 1925. "I find it an interesting story and I should think that those of Russian descent would be interested in it." He wondered why "no one has written it up yet for a doctor[']s thesis." But by then, Smith himself was writing it. He published *The Coming of the Russian Mennonites: An Episode in the Settling of the Last Frontier* less than two years later, dedicated to his students in his Mennonite history class at Bethel in 1922–23, and intending it, as with much else he wrote, for both Mennonite and American audiences. (While paying close attention to the Mennonite experience on the Canadian prairie, he could not divorce himself from his American perspective, referring more than once to matters "on this side of the international boundary line.") One reason why Smith was able produce the book so quickly is that the first fifth of it was a close paraphrase of his 1920 book, with many passages and some entire pages copied verbatim. In other ways as well, Smith's writing was all of one piece. Like his previous books, it had the same professional carelessness, lacking an introduction, a conclusion, and, once again, citations, index, or bibliography (though in the text itself Smith at least mentioned by name the various newspaper accounts, government documents, and sometimes even particular correspondence from which he drew). This new book also followed the same general pattern of his older ones. It proceeded from a detailed summary of European (in this case, Ukrainian) conditions, to a detailed accounting of the different migration streams to the U.S. Great Plains in the 1870s, and then to the establishment of various Mennonite settlements in the new country, all in the same master pioneer motif.[4]

Most importantly, like Smith's older books, this one was woven by the same skilled historian and with many of the same thematic threads. Once again readers could settle back into the hands of a master narrator. The power of Smith's storytelling was exhibited even in his chapter titles: "Spying out the Promised Land," "A Petition that Miscarried," "Beginning the Great Trek," and the like. Again he entranced readers with his immense powers of descriptive writing. Witness, for example, his portrayal of the impact of the desolation of the great West: "the mournful whistling of the hot winds as they blew across the sunburnt prairies. Nothing but seared grass and browned prairie flowers, and a far-flung sky in every direction. . . . Was it for this she left her comfortable home in the beautiful village of Annafeld, amid the green fields near Simferopol?" Here, too, he displayed his encyclopedic knowledge of different Mennonite migration streams from various corners of southern Ukraine in the 1870s, a microcosmic focus that extended down even to the transatlantic treks of different Mennonite congregations, correlating them with individual steamships and migration routes. Once again Smith utilized his strengths as both a political and social historian. For example, he integrated the arrival of Russian Mennonites into both the sociopolitical conditions in Russia in the 1870s—the new "Russianization" government programs that induced many Mennonites to leave—and parallel conditions on the American frontier, like the Panic of 1873 and the great grasshopper plague about the same time, which created incentives in the western states to attract new settlers. Once again he brought in the perspectives of a trained social scientist, sketching out Russian Mennonite material culture and its technological innovations, such as the big brick stoves, which worked better in their new environment than those of their Canadian and American neighbors. Here was more of Smith's richly detailed Mennonite ethnic mosaic, pressing the case for Mennonite inclusiveness within the church and to the North American societies beyond it.[5]

At the same time, by the later 1920s, Smith's historical writing had begun to display subtle new thematic shifts. While more restrained, the old progressive Smith made periodic appearances. He beamed approvingly, for instance, at the Halstead, Kansas, church as "one of the most progressive congregations in the entire Western District Conference," and assured readers that the current generation of Mennonites "coming up through the public schools is as thoroughly American as are the descendants of the Mayflower passengers." He plugged the union movement, calling on western Mennonites to work more cooperatively together. Even so, Smith's prewar optimism and unabashed boosting of progressive culture were absent, as evidenced in particular in his treatment of the war years. While still holding Wilson blameless for wartime civil liberties violations, Smith described them in detail and implied that buying war bonds was a compromised position. Likewise, he displayed sudden sympathies for the position of the absolutists, defending them against charges of cowardice and carefully explaining their logic. When one reads between the lines, it appears as if Smith suggests that theirs was the most faithful Mennonite position of all.[6]

By and large, Smith's effort met with glowing reviews. Writing in the *American Historical Review*, the esteemed ethnologist Marcus Hansen admitted he wished for "more footnotes. But the book itself is practically a source," he asserted, and mostly judged Smith's work a valuable analysis of how "a peculiar social organization [was] broken down by the forces of American environment." Closer to home, Goshen's new young history professor Guy F. Hershberger likewise found much to praise in a lengthy and detailed treatment in the new journal *Mennonite Quarterly Review*. Since 1909, Hershberger said, Smith had been regarded as "the leading authority on American Mennonite history," and that he did nothing to mar that reputation in this most recent offering. While critiquing Smith for his periodic misspellings and his carelessness with citations, Hershberger detailed Smith's accomplishments at length, claiming it "adds another milestone to the author's record as a scholar and a historian."[7]

Commissioned by the Pennsylvania German Society and emerging in 1929, Smith's *The Mennonite Immigration to Pennsylvania in the Eighteenth Century* in many ways appears a mirror image of his Russian Mennonite book. It, too, lacked an index or bibliography. The first hundred or so pages built heavily on previous work, again with much overlap and many of the same passages from his 1920 text. It also followed the same schematic pattern of his other books, with two chapters on the Anabaptist background, a chapter on the process of Mennonite immigration, and then a detailed description of the early Mennonite colonies across Pennsylvania before it turned to a thematic overview of matters like Mennonite doctrine, literature, hymnody, and relationship with the state. He persisted in his development of a progressive reading of Mennonite ethnicity. For example, curiously for someone who had grown up Amish, he displayed a marked inability to understand their folkways, merely ascribing them to the centuries of persecution that have rendered many of their customs "fossilized to the present day." Smith did not seem to have changed his thinking about the essential nature of Anabaptism except perhaps to have deepened in his grasp of its basic individualism. The early Anabaptists, including such stalwart leaders as Denck and Hubmaier, he explained, formed a church that, following the New Testament example, was "democratically controlled" and "as free and voluntary as a social club . . . admitting the charter members through the act of baptism." The debacle at Münster "gave all Anabaptists an evil name," but once these fanatics died out, "only the peaceful evangelical groups remained," which Menno Simons knit into a coherent church. None of this seemed to break new ground for Smith. Transplanted centuries later into the American environment, he related, these followers of Menno emerged as archetypal Americans. He also inserted again his concern for minority rights in a democracy.[8]

So what was new or noteworthy for Smith in this 1929 book? This became clear as he turned from Anabaptist origins to analyze the Mennonite experience in the sixteenth-century Palatine. Gradually footnotes appeared, and then a brief explanatory note that the data in the chapter "has been taken directly from the archives at Karlsruhe." A few pages later he began footnoting material he found in Mennonite archives in Amsterdam. In chapter 4, his treatment of Germantown, he began regular and detailed referencing of all his material, first briefly and then with long, discursive notes that elaborated on his text and explored additional subtleties. In other words, amid the same spritely writing and engaging narrative, here in his fourth major book, Smith suddenly began employing all the disciplinary expectations of a trained, professional historian. He included and cited long lists—such as of ship passengers and early Mennonite settlers to various pockets of eighteenth-century Pennsylvania—rendering his book a valuable reference for future genealogists. He demonstrated his capacity to analyze sources critically, examining letters, for example, to and from impoverished Palatinate Mennonites and a Dutch Mennonite relief committee in the early eighteenth century. In places he seemed so entranced by the documents that he was almost captured by them, his analysis proceeding letter by letter. In other instances he was able to lift himself above his sources and pay close attention to context and interpretation, wondering, for instance, why Mennonites seemed to disembark from ships last (as evidenced by the fact that their names were clustered together at the end of ship lists) and what that suggested about group psychology.[9]

Finally, Smith could not resist weaving into this treatment of the Mennonite past a subtle commentary on current church battles. In explaining the traditional Mennonite resistance to a salaried pastorate, he even invented a new word. "An uneducated ministry, of course, had its drawbacks," he noted. "It was one of the most important causes of the unprogressiveness of the Mennonite church during the century . . . and of the stagnation of their religious and social life." Yet in this he was entirely consistent with a trend in historical analysis that he had pursued almost from the beginning of his career. For about a quarter century now, Smith had read Mennonite history through a lens that treated the progressive—particularly the GC—perspective as normative. The references, for instance, to the "inquisitorial committees" and to the "farmer preachers afraid to let go of old traditions" peppering his 1925 autobiography were not just personal memories but a coded discourse on the present. The same kind of veiled commentary slipped through nearly all his public work in the 1920s: his popular writing, his historical analyses, and his speeches in GC circles and to the All-Mennonite gatherings. Certainly Smith did not primarily have fellow progressives in mind as those Mennonites who most needed, as he had outlined at Nappanee in 1925, a "lesson in toleration." The proper targets of such commentary understood perfectly to whom Smith was referring. They were people of influence and considerable resources, and they were capable of a sustained, powerful, and highly effective response.[10]

Debate about Liberalism Buffets Bluffton

Even if fundamentalism had never taken hold in the MC church and someone like John Horsch had never existed, Bluffton would have been in for a difficult time in the 1920s. Bethel's experience during the war had demonstrated fundamentalism's widespread appeal among many GC Mennonites and its alarming consequences for Mennonite colleges. Suspicions that Bluffton was infused with theological and cultural liberalism had percolated across the college's constituency since the days of Noah Hirschy, and critics found various ominous trends as the years wore on. Already by 1913 a key leader of the Mennonite Brethren in Christ was voicing his perception to Mosiman that the college was "tainted with 'higher criticism.'" By 1920 the MBIC, along with the Defenseless Mennonites, had officially withdrawn their support from the college. This move cost Smith the collaboration of his banking partner, seminary professor Jasper Huffman, who declared that if he had stayed at Bluffton he would have forfeited all influence with the MBIC. In 1922 he left for another position elsewhere. More dangerous for Bluffton was the possible loss of support from the Central Conference, which was increasingly penetrated by the fundamentalist teaching from Moody Bible Institute. Their unhappiness with the college had escalated through the war years for a number of reasons, not just its perceived theological liberalism but its undeniable compromises of nonresistance during the war. Mosiman vigorously defended such behavior in a lengthy exchange of letters with key Central Conference leader Aaron Augspurger, even trying to appeal to Augspurger's premillennialist theology to justify his support of the Allies. Augspurger would have none of it. "We may be blockheads out here in Ill[inois]," he growled, "but there is one thing which we refuse, and that is to be softsoaped and swallowed whole."[11]

Fundamentalist agitation against Bluffton College in the GC church soon came to be led by two influential pastors closer to home. Already by 1920, pastor P. R. Schroeder of First Mennonite of Berne, Indiana, had decided that both Bethel and Bluffton were unsafe for the church's youth and began to push Moody instead. "He terms us heretics," summarized a Bethel professor whom Schroeder was attacking. Similarly, by the end of the war, William S. Gottshall, pastor of Ebenezer Mennonite Church two miles west of the college on the Columbus Grove road, had begun to wage an energetic campaign on behalf of fundamentalism in general and against Bluffton in particular. From his position as chair of the GC Home Missions Board, he regularly brought the board to meet at Moody, tried to win the endorsement of a fundamentalist statement of doctrine by the larger GC church, and pushed hard for the establishment of a fundamentalist school to counter Bluffton. No doubt Gottshall was sincere in his convictions, but the intensity of his anger at the college may have been at least partly fueled by personal matters. Some of Gottshall's private correspondence seethed with bitter resentment at perceived slights from college people and other personal grudges that went back years. At the same time, when his campaign against Bluffton seemed most intense, Gottshall was part of the group of partners Smith had pulled together to invest in the money-losing Findlay dairy operation. One can only wonder if this also played a role in his deepening sense of alienation.[12]

Certainly Gottshall and Schroeder's program boded ill for Smith and his colleagues. Yet critical developments, which had especially weighty implications for Mennonite progressive intellectuals, were concurrently unfolding in MC circles. Scholars of the MC tradition have recounted how deeply this branch of the church fastened itself to fundamentalist doctrine and worldviews, albeit in a Mennonite vein, before and after the First World War. In 1921 the Mennonite General Conference officially adopted a long list of "Christian Fundamentals," which blended commitments to traditional Mennonite nonresistance and nonconformity with equal devotion to fundamentalist doctrinal stances such as the inerrancy of Scripture. Widely attended "Fundamentals Conferences" in 1924 and 1927 served to promulgate premillennialist teachings, while Kauffman's *Gospel Herald* relentlessly promoted the movement from its pages.[13]

The rising power of MC fundamentalists had a deep and pervasive impact on Bluffton progressive intellectuals through the 1920s, not least because their institution served as the great, glaring symbol of liberal error against which so many conservatives reacted. One of the reasons for this development lay in the close association many Bluffton people formed with a group of young MC rebels and a church journal they founded. The roots of this movement went back to the war, when about forty dedicated MC young people, many of them Goshen grads, journeyed to France with the Quakers to engage in reconstruction work. Their experiences proved deeply transformative, moving many toward a passionate embrace of the social implications of the gospel and an indignant dismay at the refusal of their church leaders to encourage their commitments. Officially calling themselves the Young People's Conference (YPC), the dissidents soon focused their list of grievances on what they saw as the autocratic nature of MC leadership. MC bishops quickly discerned a lack of fundamentalist phraseology in the movement, grasped that it posed a challenge to their authority, and moved in short order to squelch it.[14]

Bluffton progressives naturally regarded the YPC movement with hope and sympathy. Byers attended the first key organizing conference, at Clermont, France, in June 1919, where he was elected to its executive committee. Smith was kept apprised of the movement by a former student, J. D. Augsburger, who informed him that "we must have more freedom of conscience" and "we demand a more democratic ruling method in our church." After the YPC disintegrated in 1923, many of the dissidents continued to push for reform in a biweekly journal, the *Christian Exponent*. In its short life from 1924 to 1928, it quickly became the dominant forum for the writings of MC progressives. While its editorial group included Bluffton people like Byers, Hartzler, and Whitmer, it primarily remained the project of many former YPC activists and thus was chiefly rooted in the MC church. Even so, Horsch reflected a perception probably held by many in the MC hierarchy when he informed an ally that "really the Exponent is the mouthpiece of the Bluffton crowd."[15]

The promise of the YPC movement was crystallized in a memorable gathering in June 1922 at Byers's home congregation, the Science Ridge church near Sterling, Illinois. Most of the MC hierarchy pointedly stayed away, despite strenuous efforts by the YPC leadership to get them there. "The church cannot permit an independent movement of this kind," Horsch fulminated in the *Gospel Herald*. While thus unable to serve as a forum for working through differences across the wider MC church, the three-day gathering was noteworthy because of the large number of MC progressives it attracted. This was serious business, and the sessions were long and intense. The list of different speakers for the three-day meeting numbered close to fifty and included a wide variety of progressive intellectuals: not just "Old Goshen" professors like Smith and Byers, but noted younger pastors and activists like J. C. Meyer, Lester Hostetler, Amos Kreider, Raymond Hartzler, and Jesse Smucker, as well as Mennonite Central Committee leader Orie Miller and Goshen dean Noah Oyer. Smith delivered an overview of Mennonite history, especially focusing on the contributions that Mennonites had made to their society. Mennonite principles, he suggested again, had served as a foundation of it. This was all old and well-trodden rhetorical ground for Smith. The real value he would have found in the conference was probably in the hallway conversations and the opportunities for personal networking it afforded. He was undoubtedly meeting some of these younger progressives for the first time. And it was most likely at Sterling where he first encountered the emerging MC leader and promising young scholar Harold Bender.[16]

In a great many ways, Bender had emerged out of a historical trajectory that had primed him to function as a close colleague and maybe even a disciple of someone like Smith. His father, George Bender, had been another one of the bright, young, quickened Mennonites recruited by John Funk to work in his enterprises in Elkhart. Through Harold's childhood there, the Benders joined an emerging urban Mennonite middle class. In Harold's adolescence his father was treasurer of the MC mission board, housed where the Benders lived. Hence the Bender children grew up in one of the major MC nerve centers, with prominent church leaders commonly staying in their home. Along with his family, Harold attended the Prairie Street congregation, where his pastor, J. E. Hartzler, nurtured him in MC progressivism. In Bender's college years at Goshen from 1914 to 1918, nearly coterminous with Hartzler's presidency, Goshen's high culture and progressive ideas had not yet been eradicated by the rising power of MC fundamentalists. Bender quickly emerged as a noted campus leader, courted John Horsch's daughter Elizabeth, and became close friends with future YPC activists like J. C. Meyer and especially Jesse Smucker. As a seminarian at Garrett and Princeton, and then at Tübingen in Germany, he deepened his interest in biblical studies, but it was also in Germany where he fell in love with Mennonite history.[17]

Mennonite historical study had been an interest of Bender's even before he immersed himself in the historic sites of Anabaptism. He first began to consider working in the field as a Garrett Seminary student in 1921, and that May, seeking a thesis topic, he wrote to two scholars he identified as dominant in the field, Horsch and Smith. Horsch dismissed Bender's initial ideas on possible topics and mostly warned him against "liberalistic" theology at Garrett. Smith's response was more thoughtful and constructive. He briefly summarized something of the historiography, suggested several possible thesis topics worth exploring and pledged to help the seminary student find useful material. Bender soon came to regard Smith as a valuable academic resource. No doubt the two enjoyed fruitful conversation in June 1922 at Sterling. Bender made sure to stop by Bluffton for a meeting with Smith that September as he traveled from Garrett to Princeton. He tried to tap Smith for another speaking slot at a YPC meeting scheduled for June 1923 (though Smith politely declined because of research commitments). In sum, an early foundation seemed to have been laid for a mutually helpful collaboration between these two Mennonite scholars, one senior and one junior, and it glittered with potential for Mennonite history writing. For decades Smith had been exploring Mennonite history as a means of church renewal, and already Bender seemed a likely comrade in that project. This initial moment of promise, however, soon foundered on the widening theological and ecclesiastical fissures dividing the Mennonite church at large.[18]

In the six years after the end of World War I, the conflict wrought by fundamentalism reached a climax in the MC church. It raged with particular destructive force in the Indiana-Michigan Conference, where church authorities enforced dress restrictions with increased vigor. The eye of the storm was at Goshen College. Hartzler's removal from its presidency in 1918 seemed to epitomize the control that MC fundamentalists now had over the Mennonite Board of Education. In a campaign to find the right conservative leader for the college, in the next five years they hired and dismissed four presidents and three deans. About an eighth of Indiana-Michigan Conference membership left for neighboring Mennonite congregations, including a large group of talented ministers who soon composed a nucleus of progressive pastoral leadership in the GC church. Morale plummeted among Goshen students and faculty. Three-quarters of the student body elected not to return to Goshen in the fall of 1922 before the Board of Education decided to close the school for the entire 1923–24 year to purge it of its supposed "modernists."[19]

Goshen's disaster appeared to many at Bluffton as a wonderful moment of promise. In 1921 the MC General Conference had approved a resolution advising Mennonites to steer clear of Bluffton because of its shaky supposed adherence to "the fundamentals of the Christian faith." In the wake of Goshen's turmoil, however, its alumni association recommended that Goshen students transfer to Bluffton. A great many of them did, along with a new cluster of Goshen professors. In November 1923 Smith noted the appearance of about fifty Goshen transfers in the Bluffton student body, a happy sign that they "will not be lost entirely to Mennonitism." Individuals in the church who saw Bluffton College as the enemy put the best possible face on it. "Bluffton remains the dumping ground for your refuse," Gottshall noted gleefully to Horsch. But Bluffton leaders determined to make the most of their golden opportunity. Byers sent out a circular letter informing people that "Goshen has started rebuilding at Bluffton," while Witmarsum Seminary president Hartzler issued a similar missive to all the ministers of the GC's Middle District Conference, urging them in capital letters, "DON'T ROCK THE BOAT." "This is the year that we win or lose with the Old Church," he instructed. "We may have their students and their money for Bluffton." Indeed, he read the exciting developments as a culmination of the hopes of the All-Mennonite conventions since 1913. "The union movement represented at Bluffton," he jotted to Mosiman, "is beginning to look to many as the only solution for Mennonitism in America." In the fall of 1924, when Goshen reopened, Bluffton's student body stood at 262 students, Bethel's at 236, and Goshen's at just 70. Bender caught the danger quite clearly, worrying that Bluffton might emerge as "an all-Mennonite college which would ultimately take the place of Goshen College."[20]

This was the immediate context that informed Bender's 1924 arrival on the faculty of the reopened Goshen College and that would shape the Mennonite historical renaissance he fashioned there. As Bender's biographer, Albert Keim, related, he came back to Goshen a cautious and chastened progressive (if indeed the term still applied at all). His leadership of the YPC had hewed to a moderate and temperate course, but he had still bucked the MC old guard enough so that new Goshen president Sanford Yoder took a risk even hiring him. Bender had to assent to difficult stipulations, agreeing to wear the plain coat and to forswear writing for the *Christian Exponent*. Most disappointing to him was his assignment to teach history, not Bible and theology; his YPC activism had too unsettled the fundamentalists on Goshen's board. But Bender soon discovered that teaching history afforded him a certain freedom to, as Juhnke phrased it, "use modern methods of critical analysis which he dared not use in biblical studies." Concessions to conservatives came easily to Bender for other reasons, as well. His theology gravitated toward fundamentalism, Keim suggested. His favorite professor in grad school had been the eminent J. Gresham Machen at Princeton, who combined his work as an Old Testament scholar with a role as a major defender of fundamentalism in its national struggle against modernism. The alarms by Horsch and others about the spreading influence of Mennonite "modernism" were concerns that Bender genuinely shared. Moreover, he was by nature someone reluctant to take risks, instinctively willing to defer to authority, and predisposed to give ground on smaller issues in pursuit of larger objectives.[21]

Bender's emotional makeup, his conservative instincts, and his reading of the larger ecclesiastical dynamics operative in the MC world all played significant roles in the way he shaped Mennonite history writing at Goshen and how he responded to someone like Smith. There were other factors at work, as well. Bender was an energetic defender of his alma mater, and Bluffton clearly represented a threat to its institutional health. He worried about Goshen's inability to match Bluffton's fundraising totals and "the strong competition Bluffton is giving us in Ohio." It angered him when he perceived Bluffton to be infringing on Goshen's institutional turf, hotly telling the editor of *Christian Exponent* that Bluffton's official policy "in practice is one that is frankly antagonistic to Goshen." An even more powerful pull on Bender's scholarship and worldview was his close relationship with Horsch, whose daughter Elizabeth he had married in 1923. "Throughout Bender's life," Keim writes, "John Horsch had a profound influence on his development as a historian." One wonders if Bender, after his own father's death in 1921, allowed his father-in-law to perform something of that role. This could be seen in their voluminous correspondence, which Bender addressed to "Father Horsch." While Bender distinguished Horsch's theology, which he liked, from his bitter polemical attacks, they also shared similar worldviews. "I am more convinced than ever," Horsch wrote to Bender, "that Bluffton has denied the old Bible faith and stands for modernism." When the offer came to teach at Goshen, Horsch pleaded with his son-in-law to take it, telling him "your God-appointed cause is to go to Goshen," where he could combat the "liberalists" and win the church for fundamentalism.[22]

Bender quickly signaled his enthusiasm for this agenda. He won plaudits from MC fundamentalists with his hard-hitting, nine-page review of J. E. Hartzler's published doctoral dissertation. Admittedly, Hartzler was not a brilliant scholar. Smith had read a draft of the book, responded with discomfort, and urged his friend to get a good editor. But Bender's review of his old pastor's book—as described by Keim, "a devastating and intemperate attack on a fellow Mennonite scholar"— took criticism to a new level. It also shored up his credentials with conservatives and allowed him to press on with his real agenda: Mennonite history as a means of church renewal.[23]

Bender had scarcely arrived at Goshen before he recharged the lethargic Mennonite Historical Society and then began laying out a case for a stronger denominational focus on Mennonite history with a series of articles in the *Gospel Herald*. He diligently began collecting rare Mennonite books and documents. Along with a German Mennonite scholar named Ernst Correll, whom he had brought back to Goshen with him from his graduate study in Europe, he began planning a celebratory scholarly conference in Goshen in June 1925 to mark the four-hundredth anniversary of the beginning of the Anabaptist movement among the Zurich radicals. All of these efforts were but precursors for the birth of Bender's great vehicle for Mennonite historical renaissance, the 1927 founding of the *Mennonite Quarterly Review* (*MQR*). In his opening issue, he proclaimed to "THE YOUTH OF THE MENNONITE CHURCH" that "THE GOLDEN AGE of the Mennonite Church is not past; it is just ahead." Powered by a new appreciation of their heritage, it was time for Mennonite young people, Bender cried, to "Get the vision, follow the gleam, bend your back to the burden, consecrate yourself to the task."[24]

In all his efforts at recharging Mennonite memories, however, Bender would not or could not separate his scholarship from other agendas operative in his world. The *MQR*, for instance, would come to serve as a central scholarly journal in the field of Mennonite history, but its very birth was saddled with the more pressing contemporary agenda: to enlist that history as a counterweight to the influence of the *Christian Exponent* and as a weapon against the perceived "modernists" at Bluffton. At least, this is how Bender justified it to people like Horsch and Kauffman. "We shall need such a journal more in the future," he reasoned with Horsch, "as a means of binding the thinking of our young people together and leading them away from the influence of the Bluffton element and our other liberal leaders." He had barely arrived at Goshen and begun seeing himself as a historian when he signaled that he had readily adopted Horsch's interpretive framework on the Swiss Brethren and broken with the reading that had been advanced for decades now by Smith. "Our forefathers," Bender concluded in a 1924 piece he published (without his name attached) in an early issue of the *Christian Exponent*, "were not a loose society of tolerant individualists, but closed communities with strict discipline and a fixed faith and firm rules of conduct. They were scarcely modern liberals." Smith's take on these new currents in Mennonite historical scholarship appeared in a feature article in that same issue of the *Exponent*. "I believe that history can teach us great lessons," he stated, "but I do not believe that any historian has the right to twist historical facts in such a way as to reflect his own prejudice and bias. He should present the facts in their true light and let the reader judge for himself as to what those facts teach."[25]

It was evident to a number of people in the MC world at that moment—to Bender, in his efforts to kindle a Mennonite historical renaissance, and to church authorities advancing the cause of fundamentalism—that they would need to deal with Smith in some way. He was a prominent figure and established scholar who could not be easily undermined. Indeed, Bender drew both from Smith's eminence and from Bluffton's perceived threat to justify his pursuit of a doctorate in history, telling Horsch that they could not allow their liberal rivals to get ahead in "advanced degrees and scholarship." "C. H. Smith is the only historian among us who has the degree," Bender reasoned, "and in the world the degree counts for something." Smith's corpus of work constituted a direct challenge to MC scholars. They had been grappling with how to respond to it for almost twenty years. Daniel Kauffman detected "a number of points" in Smith's 1909 history that needed "straightening out," and Horsch had been offended by aspects of Smith's historiography in his 1920 book. Horsch did not care, for instance, for the way Smith had dismissed his Menno Simons biography in comparison to the new one by Vos. Smith, Horsch suspected to Bender, had never read Vos. He likewise found ominous overtones in the way Smith had emphasized the affection Grebel apparently had for Thomas Müntzer. Already by 1911 MC scholars had begun to consider producing a Mennonite history textbook of their own to counter Smith's. The discussions went nowhere then but reemerged in 1927 in the wake of Bender's rekindling of MC historical work. Bender initially began pushing Horsch to write such a text but soon thought the entire project unwise. "It will be difficult to give excuse for writing another book alongside of C. Henry Smith's book," he concluded. "This book is intended to be used . . . as a general handbook on Mennonite history, and despite its evident lack in some places it will be difficult to do much better in a book of the same size and type without giving the impression of rivalry."[26]

Yet Horsch had no intention of surrendering an overarching interpretation of Mennonite history to the likes of Smith. At the same time Bender launched his efforts at MC historical renewal, with its lingering promise of collaborative history across Mennonite denominational lines, Horsch undermined it by escalating his desperate struggle against Mennonite "modernists." They were, in his mind, centered at Bluffton, and Smith was a primary offender.

"Interpreting History to Justify His Own Point of View"

In 1923 Horsch returned from a year-long visit to his kinfolk in Germany shocked at the apparent liberal drift of the German Mennonites. In short order he churned out a harsh new polemic, *The Mennonite Church and Modernism*, to renew the fight against similar trends he discerned at home. Howls of outrage soon echoed across the Mennonite world from the distinguished church leaders he had denounced as modernists, and with good reason. In retrospect, it is hard to read Horsch's methods—which even Gresham Machen gently reproved him for—as entirely scrupulous. One of the victims of his attacks summarized these techniques as "taking isolated passages out of their contexts, making constant misinterpretations, judging of motives without proper evidence . . . making serious and unsubstantiated charges against individuals, drawing entirely unwarranted conclusions from certain statements and reading into them meanings which the authors never intended or thought of, [and] refusing to accept statements in good faith." Nearly a century later, scholars still hypothesize about what drove Horsch to such a campaign. Certainly, as Sawatsky notes, "Horsch's overriding concern was to save the church he loved." Combined with what Keim calls his "bleak view of human nature," this commitment fed his mindset in which liberalism appeared a wholly evil enemy that deserved no quarter. Some of his contemporaries (including, at times, Bender) tried to slip more shades of gray into his world. "There must be some further motive" to your attacks, wrote one Illinois Mennonite to Horsch, "beyond the well-being of our beloved denomination . . . there is too much personal feeling permitted to enter into it." In actuality, suggests Keim, more personal relationships might have eased Horsch's rhetorical aggression. Introverted and lacking in social skills, Horsch rarely traveled far from Scottdale. It is hard to find evidence, for instance, that he and Smith ever personally met. The "modernists" he assailed were mostly just names on paper, unattached to relationships with real, living persons, which might have caused him to temper his words.[27]

Whatever the reason, by 1926 Horsch had completed a number of blistering pamphlets against modernism and a major book, *Modern Religious Liberalism*, which went through three editions and sold ten thousand copies in the wider circles of Protestant fundamentalism. More damaging to his Mennonite enemies were two pamphlets aimed directly at them: *The Mennonite Church and Modernism* and *Is the Mennonite Church of America Free from Modernism?*, which, in concert with allies like Gottshall and Schroeder, he worked assiduously to spread widely across the church. For all Horsch's smoke, there was a bit of fire, manifested at Bluffton in the person of Jacob Quiring. Excited by the new, higher critical teachings in biblical scholarship he had learned in graduate school in Chicago and Berlin, the Russian scholar naively thought he could share them with his Bluffton students, perhaps unaware of the furor it would trigger across the church. Strangely, however, Quiring appeared a relatively minor figure in Horsch's lineup of prominent modernists. Horsch aimed his major blasts at other Bluffton figures, principally Hartzler, Mosiman, Byers, and Smith. Hartzler, for instance, had told the All-Mennonite Convention of 1919 that Christians should believe something not just because the Bible said it, but because what the Bible said was true. Thus Hartzler, claimed Horsch, denied the authority of Scripture and accepted "modernist reasoning." In a defense of Mennonite pacifism in the *Christian Exponent*, Byers had suggested that many people had embraced Wilson's great moral platitudes and afterward had descended back to their "own level of character." Byers was implying, Horsch reasoned, that soldiers possessed high moral character, thus indicating his acceptance of "modernist idealism." Smith's guilt seems to have rested primarily in his assertion, which Horsch quoted, of the Anabaptist devotion to freedom of conscience and of their fundamental, underlying individualism. Of course, this was erroneous, Horsch said, elaborating on his oft-repeated insistence that Anabaptists assigned priority to doctrine and creed. But there was more to it, he asserted in *The Mennonite Church and Modernism*, than a quibble over proper historical interpretations. "The opinion that it is not the Church's business to uphold a definite creed . . . is called individualism," he informed the church. "It is readily seen that individualism is but another word for modernism."[28]

John Horsch. MennoMedia.

The late historian Rodney Sawatsky made much of the way Horsch labeled Smith's reading of Anabaptism as modernist. Given how Smith's body of writing had been adopted in 1920, he said, as "virtual identity symbols of the General Conference Mennonite Church," in attacking Smith as a modernist, Horsch meant by extension to delegitimize the entire thrust of GC historiography that Smith had been so central in creating. Sawatsky had a point, though it is hard to know the degree to which Smith saw himself, in 1924, as a GC historian. What is clear is that he viewed himself as a historian committed to the ideal of objectivity, and understood that he had been unfairly assaulted by someone who was not. The American historical profession in these years, argues Peter Novick, was characterized by decorum and collegiality. Most book reviews were gentle and criticism was generally muted. Horsch's kind of attacks were not done in Smith's world, and they left him aghast. In contrast to Hartzler and Byers, however—who, having been publicly censured, hotly defended themselves in the same sphere—Smith chose to respond to Horsch privately, and in a remarkably restrained and dignified manner.[29]

Smith pointed out to Horsch that he had misquoted him and had wrought much mischief in doing so. He denied having written, as Horsch had claimed, that Mennonites interpreted the Bible for themselves and were thus free to act in matters of faith only as their consciences dictated. Instead, Smith insisted to Horsch here, copying from his *The Mennonites: A Brief History*, he had written that "Mennonitism is the essence of individualism, and consequently Mennonites as a BODY were never committed to ONE particular confession of faith etc [emphasis in the original]." In actuality, both men were correct: each was quoting a different passage in the Smith text and the confusion perhaps emanated from the fact that in his pamphlet Horsch had, like Smith, eschewed proper citations. But Smith insisted that his qualifiers spelled all the difference. "When I say that Mennonitism is the essence of individualism," he explained, "I mean merely that Mennonites taught that the individual himself is responsible to God, without the mediation of any priest as the Catholics taught, or the mediation of the state as the Lutherans taught. . . . But where you can find any ground for the claim that I am teaching a kind of religious anarchy . . . is beyond my comprehension." "Now brother Horsch," Smith emphasized, he had devoted a great deal of time and money to Mennonite history, only "because of my interest in the subject, and I assure you that my purposes in the cause are as lofty as yours."[30]

In his response, Horsch evidently pointed out that he had indeed quoted Smith correctly, for Smith followed up with a forthright apology for accusing Horsch of misquoting him, admitting that he "may have been rather severe in my last letter to you," but that he had written it "on the spur of the moment" after reading Horsch's book. Smith still proceeded to spell out carefully how, it seemed to him, Horsch had deliberately misinterpreted his writing to imply to readers that "consequently I must be unsound in the faith and need to be regarded with suspicion. That is undoubtedly the impression that your readers will get from your book . . . I never held the views you say I do and . . . I can't see by what particular twist of logic you can twist that meaning out of what I said if you read all of what I said instead of taking a few disconnected sentences," something which "a man of your training" should understand. Smith confessed, in closing, that "this may seem a little harsh, but not more so than the language you use in your book against the men you name." Moreover, Smith added, he had communicated his objections privately, "not spread broadcast among the public with the attempt to injure the reputation of the person concerned." This was clearly, in his mind, the way that professional scholars treated each other.[31]

Horsch renewed the private dialogue eighteen months later, commending Smith for his remarks on tolerance to the 1925 All-Mennonite Convention. He wondered to Smith, however, whether he approved of "the work of proselyting [sic] and propaganda against the position of our communion," then underway at the hands of "certain men of Bluffton, Ohio," which disregarded Mennonite denominational differences as "not worthwhile." In dismissing such lines of separation, Horsch suggested, the union movement "practice[d] toleration toward those within their communion but not toward outsiders." Smith responded with a thoughtful, four-page reply that laid out their areas of disagreement while remaining scrupulously within the bounds of professional decorum. His entire first paragraph, for example, elaborated on his view that "there is so much room for honest and sincere men to differ on matters of interpretation," admitting that he himself had "been mistaken so often in little matters of judgment." He repeatedly seemed to take extra pains to smooth any hard feelings his honest disagreement might evoke, employing long phrases like: "my own impression, however, is, if you will pardon me for telling you what my opinion is in the matter without in the least criticizing you." Yet Smith made it clear that that the two did deeply disagree. While in Smith's mind Horsch viewed the church as "the body of preachers and especially bishops, rather than the entire laity," Smith held to a conception of the church very much something of the opposite, almost like a democratic interest group, in which "the group as a whole, the entire body should have an equal vote in all matters of belief and policy and then it is the business of the minority to abide by the will of the majority. That is what I believe to be democracy, and if I am not mistaken that was the basis of the apostolic church, and also of the first Anabaptist congregations."[32]

Smith may have begun to temper his progressivism, but he was still a progressive who read the church through the lens of liberal democracy. He also remained fully committed to the union movement. As to Horsch's question of proselytizing, for instance, Smith explained there was no need for Mennonites to engage in such behavior among themselves because doctrinally they all believed the same things. Smith remained at heart a progressive social scientist, chalking up peoples' differences primarily to external conditions. Mennonites, he told Horsch, just differed on small issues, "customs and practices which have been the result of differences of environment." His colleagues in Bluffton, by the way, were not "proselyting" at all, but rather defending themselves "against the attacks made upon their views in the book you wrote and which the Publishing House scattered through all the churches."[33]

It is hard not to be sympathetic with Smith here. Scholars have explored how the Mennonite "modernism" Horsch found was mostly illusory. Theron Schlabach has characterized Horsch's crusade as "aiming elephant guns to kill flies." Smith tried to help Horsch make finer distinctions. The way you phrased it, Smith pointed out, modernists included everyone from "an avowed infidel" like Clarence Darrow to someone like himself, whom Horsch had charged with heresy only because he had suggested that Anabaptist church polity was congregational. "There certainly ought to be a wide difference between the two forms of modernism," Smith suggested, "but you do not discriminate." Most of the Bluffton people Horsch tagged as modernists were similarly better characterized as progressives. Horsch, however, seemed unable or unwilling to make such distinctions, and he continued to press his campaign with full vigor.[34]

This confrontation between the two leading Mennonite historians of the first part of the twentieth century ensued primarily because they proceeded from two profoundly different worldviews. At the same time, ironically, they were drawn together by their joint commitment to Mennonite history. They were mediated in this now by Bender, who understood that his great Mennonite historical renaissance needed to proceed ecumenically, as difficult as the task might be. This, as he tried to explain to Horsch, required working closely with Smith. He was the major Mennonite historian in the field, and enjoyed resources that the MC scholars merely dreamed about. Whitmer casually informed Horsch that Smith had "imported from Germany and Holland many hundreds of dollars' worth of Anabaptist and Mennonite books since the war." He had paid for the copying of key manuscripts "by librarians in different parts of Europe. He probably has the best Mennonite historical library in America." Within months of Bender's arrival back in Goshen to teach history, he wrote to Smith for a list of all the master's theses on Mennonite subjects held at Bluffton College's library, and also to apprise Smith of the big plans he and his Goshen partner Ernst Correll had come up with to translate and critically edit all the correspondence of the early Swiss Anabaptist leader Conrad Grebel. In so many ways, Smith and Bender seemed cut from the same academic cloth, and if left alone might work together quite fruitfully. Bender and Correll quickly pushed into high gear their Mennonite book-collecting, a project that had long captivated Smith. Bender was to let Smith know "if you run across anything in the way of either new or old books on Mennonite history." Smith jotted to Bender, "I am making it a policy of buying everything that has any connection with the subject if the price isn't prohibitive." For his part, Bender knew these Mennonite historical projects needed money, and Smith had plenty of it. Smith's enthusiastic response to the Grebel idea probably moved Bender to approach him about possibly funding the publication of a manuscript by a German scholar named Johann Loserth on the early Anabaptist leader Pilgram Marpeck. Smith demurred, thinking it would be better to send out an appeal for funds for the project by a Mennonite historical society, like the one at Scottdale, rather than to secure funding from an individual. That way, he suggested, the project could garner the backing of the wider church. "Smith's answer is what I had expected it to be," Horsch grumbled. "I am inclined to think it is a satisfaction to them that we come to them at Bluffton when we are in trouble."[35]

Smith understood quite well Bender's ecumenical limitations and generally responded graciously. He really liked, for example, what Bender had told him of a possible "federation of Historical societies for the publishing of a quarterly journal," suggesting the project would really take off with a board made up of representatives from the historical societies of different Mennonite branches. "If you can get the cooperation of John Hors[c]h and S. F. Coffman," he remarked to Bender knowingly, "I am quite sure it could be accomplished." Smith's general affability was particularly tested in one trying episode in the spring of 1925. In their plans for the celebration of the four-hundredth anniversary of the founding of the Swiss Brethren in Zurich, Bender and Correll had lined up an impressive array of speakers from different parts of the Mennonite world. Smith had quickly agreed to deliver an address, and they had also, they thought, secured Horsch's presence. A few months before the celebration, however, Horsch began to waver, urging Bender to remember that Smith "is one of the 'crowd' which has set itself the aim to liberalize and modernize the Mennonite church." Bender begged his father-in-law not to put them in an "embarrassing situation." Smith was not part of the modernist group at Bluffton, Bender said, urging Horsch to "draw a line between him and Quiring or Hartzler, and others. Smith takes no part in such matters." Horsch was unmoved. "The church is at the present time engaged in a death struggle with liberalism," he reminded Bender. "It is a time of crisis for the church. All that crowd wants us to do is to compromise our position. I do not feel free to have part in a meeting where a Bluffton professor would have a part." Bender had no choice but to disinvite not only Smith but, to be consistent, all the GC speakers from the celebration. The result was a shortened and somewhat mediocre program and the obstruction of a potentially meaningful event, Keim wrote, "which might have begun to bring Mennonite historians together." Smith seemed able to put the event behind him quite quickly. He remained confident, he assured Bender, that "some day [sic] such cooperation in a common cause as you proposed will be possible."[36]

There was one moment, however, where Horsch's obstinacy seemed to push Smith to a breaking point. In the spring of 1926, he apparently informed Bender that Horsch's attacks had rendered his colleagues at Bluffton (and presumably also himself) unwilling to proceed in joint fundraising for Loserth's Marpeck book. One can only speculate about what had crystallized Smith's anger, but the appearance that year of another searing attack pamphlet from Horsch is a good guess. In *Is the Mennonite Church Free from Modernism?* Horsch reiterated and elaborated on his charges of two years before, only now mostly substituting Quiring for Smith in his catalog of dangerous modernists. Bender liked Horsch's pamphlets very much—*The Mennonite Church and Modernism* had received, he told Horsch, his "hearty *Zustimmung* throughout"—but nonetheless needed to get Smith back on board with the program. The decision not to support the Marpeck project, he wrote Smith, had left him shocked and dismayed. "I can understand the lack of good feeling for Mr. Horsch," Bender admitted, "but it seems very strange to me that personal feeling should enter into the consideration of this perfectly harmless historical work . . . Have you folks gotten one man 'on the brain' as badly as that," Bender wanted to know. He urged Smith to "separate Mr. Horsch's historical work from his theological writing" and vouchsafed for his skills as a scholar: his grasp of the sources, his capacity for hard work.[37]

Then Bender played his strongest card, appealing to Smith's devotion to the union movement. If you deny your cooperation now, on such a project as this, Bender rose to a crescendo, then "I shall count the statements issuing from your group regarding cooperation as quite worthless, indeed as mere propaganda to win proselytes. If Mennonites as near in space, in time, and in origin as Ohio and Indiana cannot cooperate to further common historical goals, the movement for cooperation and union is a mere farce." Smith let his moment of anger pass, and Horsch, remarkably, agreed to cooperate as well. Within months both historians issued strong fundraising appeals on behalf of the Marpeck manuscript to their circles of influence, Smith in the *Christian Exponent* and Horsch in the *Gospel Herald*. Meanwhile, Smith resumed his ready cooperation with Bender's program in Goshen, reviewing an extensive bibliography of Mennonite writings he had put together, agreeing to come to Goshen to speak to its historical society, and suggesting the libraries of their respective institutions coordinate their acquisition of Mennonite historical materials.[38]

There was, of course, a great irony to the entire conflict raging between Mennonite progressives and fundamentalists in these years.

Both understood themselves as defending something like the essence of Mennonitism, large elements of which they had borrowed from the outside. At the same time, they spent a good deal of time and energy accusing the other side of borrowing and in this manner betraying the church. Mosiman, for example, had advised a fundamentalist critic that he did not feel bound "to join in the fight of the Baptists and the Presbyterians with the 'Fundamental Party' . . . I feel that the Colleges have a mission to guard the faith delivered to the Saints from being mixed up with all sorts of modern fads." In the contesting views of history that emerged, Smith's worldview certainly seemed more nuanced than Horsch's, more aware of its internal frailties and possible misinterpretations, less sure of its firm grasp on the truth. Yet these were differences in degree, not in kind. When Smith momentarily advised Bender in 1926 to forget about his cooperation on the Marpeck project, he had accused Horsch of "interpreting history to justify his own point of view." This was exactly what Smith had been doing for decades, albeit more subtly and blinded to it because of his self-image as a professionally trained, objective historian. Since nearly the start of his academic career, Smith had been reading Mennonite history through a progressive, GC lens. Meanwhile, MC historians like Horsch—and increasingly, now, Bender—read Mennonite history through a fundamentalist, MC lens. In such a context, it is hard to imagine anything else emerging but alternative, as opposed to collaborative, histories.[39]

Smith did not record the emotional residue that the struggle with church fundamentalists—the ceaseless attacks, the concerted efforts to wreck church institutions and damage personal reputations—had left him with. One expects he was weary and angry. Perhaps that is what lay behind lines like this one, which he inserted in his *Coming of the Russian Mennonites*. He had been discussing the abuse leveled onto Mennonite draftees in the Great War as they attempted to remain faithful to their pacifist consciences in isolated army camps. It was in such young people—and not, he implied, in church hierarchies, revival meetings, or even in Scripture—where might be found "the salvation of the world."[40]

In 1928 and then especially in 1929, Smith removed himself from the conflicts by once again hitting the road. In summer 1928, he signed on to another educational study tour. Consisting largely of teachers, ministers, and social workers, and organized out of Boston by an international educator named Hubert Herring, the group focused its attention on social and political conditions in Mexico. Entering at Laredo in early July, they spent most of a month in Mexico City, where they listened to lectures, interviewed local officials, and witnessed the unrest that swept through the capital after the assassination of Mexican president-elect Obregon. Smith authored the section of the seminar's final report on Mexico's agricultural sector, and his conclusions suggested he still retained a degree of his old progressive optimism. The people of Mexico, he summarized, were in a heady transition from a medieval stage to a "modern progressive state," and the lot of its poor peasants was steadily improving. Such conditions, he concluded, invited the sympathy of other democracies instead of their criticism.[41]

In June 1926, the Bluffton College board of trustees opened the door for a much longer period of travel—and of rest for its overworked faculty—when it ruled that longer-serving professors, principally Hirschler, Berky, Smith, and Byers, in that order, would be granted year-long leaves of absence. Smith was suddenly presented for the first time with the prospect of a sabbatical, and had the financial means to use it well. He arranged for use of research facilities at the University of Southern California, and in August 1929, he and Laura packed up their car for an entire academic year away. He dusted off his skills as a travel writer, once again treating *Bluffton News* readers to a richly detailed narrative of their adventures on the road. By late October they were happily ensconced in Los Angeles, where, Smith reported to Bender, "We are enjoying California very much." But the best was yet to come. On New Year's Day 1930, the two sailed out for a short visit to the exotic locale of Hawaii. This made such a deep impression on the Smiths that, once Henry returned home, he lectured about Hawaii—its flora and fauna, its racial multiculturalism, its unique history and culture—with enough regularity to print off a little self-promotion brochure called "Hawaii: The Paradise of the Pacific."[42]

The immediate Mennonite world the Smiths left behind, however, reverberated to less happy chimes. In summer 1929, at the GC general conference meeting in Hutchinson, Kansas, GC fundamentalist leader P. R. Schroeder, along with the board of deacons of First Mennonite Church of Berne, Indiana, formally charged Bluffton

The Smiths depart Hawaii, spring 1930. BUASC.

College with teaching modernism, with Horsch's pamphlets as supporting documents. Suddenly here was a development that could inflict some real damage upon the college within the GC church. Even more ominous was the increasingly precarious state of college finances, accentuated now by alarming developments occurring along Wall Street in New York City. In 1928, in order to reach the half-million-dollar endowment required for full academic accreditation, Mosiman launched a full-throated, high-pressure fundraising campaign. A year later it had, by one measurement, reached total success. The college now had in hand, its president grandly announced, the requisite amount of money, and full academic accreditation seemed assured. He did not publicize, however, the small technicality that most of the money the college needed had been pledged, not actually yet donated; in fact the college had in hand a little over $5,000. Once the pledges came in, it would be a new day for Bluffton. But in October 1929, the nation's financial nerve center along Wall Street suddenly plunged into convulsions. One hopes the Smiths enjoyed the orange blossoms of Los Angeles and Hawaii's balmy breezes, because when they came back to Ohio, they would return to a world in turmoil.[43]

10
The Mennonite Intellectual in a Time of Crisis

When Smith returned home from Hawaii in spring 1930, he returned to an institution that seemed to be floating above the economic turmoil engulfing the rest of the country. Student numbers were again trending upward; the following September they reached the three-hundred mark. That spring the college received word that it had been admitted to the smaller of the accrediting agencies, the Ohio College Association, and that its prospects for admission into the major North Central Association seemed very good. In June it celebrated one of the most memorable commencement days in its history, dedicating a sparkling new library, the gift of a wealthy Pennsylvania apple-grower named C. H. Musselman. The past year, Smith informed readers of the *Mennonite Year Book* in 1931, "has been the best in the history of the school." With Byers enjoying his own sabbatical in 1930–31, Smith would have taken particular pleasure in the energetic work of the new acting dean, his old student Edmund Kaufman, who led the faculty through a major new curricular overhaul before leaving for Kansas the next year to teach at Bethel College and ultimately take up its presidency.[1]

Elsewhere, however, as the Great Depression deepened, the nation shuddered to levels of unemployment and poverty that it had never before experienced. The collapse of Wall Street in the brutal autumn of 1929 was shortly followed by waves of bank failures across the country. November and December of 1930 witnessed over six hundred such closings, with frantic depositors descending on teller windows to demand their savings. From 1929 to 1932, the national income declined by half, tens of thousands of people lined up daily for bread, and the New York City school system counted some twenty thousand malnourished children sitting listlessly in its classrooms. Even tiny Bluffton distributed federal relief supplies and gained a new high school football stadium and a new hospital at the hands of the Works Progress Administration.[2]

Of course such conditions soon swept up Smith, his banks, and his college, as well. As a pillar of Bluffton's Main Street, Smith would be integrally involved in keeping the town's finances solvent. For similar reasons, he would be thrust into the center of the desperate struggle that ensued when Depression conditions combined with fundamentalist attacks to threaten the future of Bluffton College. These were roles he could perform competently. He would be less prepared when fate and friendship thrust him into a different kind of crisis: a faculty fight so far-reaching and destructive he would wonder, at one acute moment, if he still had a job. For these reasons, while the Depression largely left Smith's finances untouched, he still would have later looked back on the 1930s as an especially difficult and bitter time. He would redeem it by expanding another kind of role, one that he had been pioneering for his church for decades. In the 1930s, Smith would emerge even more centrally as one of the premier Mennonite public intellectuals of his day.

Deepening Confrontations in the Church

Among the many challenges both Smith and his college would face in the 1930s was the continuing barrage of fundamentalist criticism. Horsch, for example, did not rest. In four separate issues of the *Mennonite Quarterly Review* (MQR) in 1930–31, he outlined a lengthy review of Anabaptist theology called "The Faith of the Swiss Brethren." In a clear slap at Smith, he wrote that any supposition that Anabaptists prized freedom of conscience over a greater devotion to church authority was "absurd." Like Smith, Horsch continued to develop his own form of a Mennonite usable past, here offering, as Bender ally Robert Friedmann recognized later, an extended "proof that the Anabaptists were essentially Fundamentalists." He continued to war with alternative ideas. In 1928, for instance, Kaufman completed his doctorate in theology at the University of Chicago (a choice no doubt influenced by his mentor Smith) and soon approached Bender about publishing his thesis in the new Studies in Anabaptist and Mennonite History book series. Kaufman was an able scholar, and his study—an examination of the Mennonite experience in America through the vantage point of Ernst Troeltsch's sect-cycle theory—was solid work. Bender was initially favorable and telegraphed Kaufman a publication offer. But then he heard from Horsch, who complained that Kaufman approached his subject like a sociologist rather than as a person of faith. "Is not the book written from a Modernist viewpoint?" Horsch pressed. After arguing briefly with Horsch, Bender knuckled under and withdrew the offer.[3]

Smith increasingly responded to the debate with Horsch by checking out of it. When Kaufman's thesis finally appeared, at the hands of the publication board of the GC church, Smith ignored Horsch and gave it a glowing review in the *Mennonite*. It is, he declared, "likely the last word on the subject . . . a complete, scholarly and unbiased history." Or take the short popular biography of Menno Simons that Smith published in 1936. Because he clearly intended it for the lay reader, his lack of citations, or even an introduction or conclusion, is somewhat more understandable. Instead he covered Menno's life in fifty-six pages, along with another twenty or so pages on current-day Mennonites, in his straightforward, engaging, narrative history. He offered up another version of his Mennonite usable past, arguing that Menno was "centuries ahead of his day" on basic touchstone ideas of Western civilization like church-state separation, religious toleration, and the need for universal peace. He also proceeded, once again, as if nothing Horsch wrote mattered. In a veiled swipe at the conservative evangelical movement of his own day, Smith informed readers that Menno came to faith on his own, "not swept from his moorings by the enthusiasm of a great popular religious uprising." He reiterated his view of the extremely democratic nature of early Anabaptism, and deviated not a whit from his formulation of Anabaptist founders from three decades before, including not only Marpeck and Grebel but also Hubmaier and Denck (who, in 1934, Horsch was once again writing out of Anabaptism as an "Anabaptist liberal").[4]

Smith could afford to ignore Horsch, but his lack of membership in the GC church limited his ability to intervene in its internal struggle with fundamentalism, even as that religious movement posed direct threats to people and institutions he prized. In 1933 the church met again for its conference meeting, this time in Bluffton, where one of the primary agenda items was to take up the modernism charges that people like Schroeder and Gottshall had filed against Bluffton College in 1929. In the end, nothing came of the effort. With Depression economics having defused combative spirits, the conference accepted an inconclusive report from an investigating committee, and the forces of GC fundamentalism, Whitmer observed, "became a silent protest instead of an open revolt." Smith attended the conference at Bluffton, meeting a few blocks from his home at First Mennonite Church. Yet, along with MC Mennonites like Bender and Orie Miller, he was officially listed as a "guest." In spring 1930, a coalition of fundamentalist pastors across the GC church did succeed in forcing the resignation of Bible professor Jacob Quiring, and later that summer were able to achieve the closing of Witmarsum Seminary. Witmarsum admittedly had a lot of problems besides conservative opposition. The Depression had withered its already shaky financial base, and, as Smith knew, it was not being served well by its president, J. E. Hartzler. At one point he had been giving $100 annually to the seminary, Smith informed Whitmer, but ceased because he felt Hartzler (as Whitmer pointedly summarized to the seminary president) was "loafing on the job and using the seminary in a purely selfish way." By 1929, Hartzler's new plan was to try to pull together all Mennonite groups behind a united Mennonite seminary in Chicago, or affiliate it with an established seminary like Hartford. Hartzler was his "good friend and a likeable man," Smith wrote to seminary board chair Emmanuel Troyer, but had embarked on a "suicidal policy." "No body [sic] knows better than Hartzler," Smith said bluntly, "that it is mere foolishness to talk about united Goshen, and Bluffton, and Conservative old Virginia at the present time." When Hartzler resigned the presidency in summer 1930, its board agreed to close it for no more than five years, but it would not reopen. The prospect cheered church conservatives. He had avidly hoped, Bender wrote Horsch that July, "that the Seminary at Bluffton will die a natural death." Yet as Mennonites surrendered the training of their pastors to other denominations, Smith knew the cost to the church, and he would feature it prominently in his speeches and popular writing as the decade wore on.[5]

A schism at East White Oak, the Central Conference congregation where Smith had placed his official membership, reminded him of fundamentalist threats from another direction. In 1928, Pastor Troyer gave way to a Moody Bible Institute grad named Reuben Zehr, who immediately began reshaping the church in line with the teaching he had absorbed at fundamentalist-oriented Moody. Increased tension with the Central Conference soon resulted. In 1933, the conference officially suspended Zehr until he agreed to work more cooperatively. Zehr responded by pulling the congregation out of the conference, reestablishing it as the independent East White Oak Bible Church. Two states away, Smith was on the sidelines of the conflict but indicated his take on it by withdrawing his membership, probably about that time, from East White Oak. One would have expected him finally to join First Mennonite in Bluffton, where he and Laura worshiped regularly. Robert Kreider, whose father Amos pastored the church from 1931 to 1934, remembers them both sitting in a customary pew and Dr. Smith sometimes lecturing to church youth on Mennonite history. The Smiths instead placed their membership with Carlock (Illinois) Mennonite Church, pastored by another Central Conference progressive, R. L. Hartzler. Meanwhile, as with the lack of a Mennonite seminary, Smith's reading of the danger that fundamentalist Bible colleges posed to traditional Mennonite faith would emerge as an increasingly common theme in his public speeches.[6]

Even if Smith had been an official member of the GC church, or was living in closer proximity to East White Oak, there was probably little he could have done to stop the congregational schism, deflect the modernism charges, or save Witmarsum Seminary. Instead, as the Depression deepened, he bent his energies toward rescuing what other parts of his world he could: namely, Bluffton College and the financial lifeblood of the village of Bluffton.

Happy Days at Lake George

As a prominent local banker, Smith had his fingers on the financial pulse of both the college and Main Street. He would have known, early in the decade, that both were in trouble. By the fall of 1931, fifty local banks had failed in northwest Ohio, seven of them in the Bluffton area and two of them depositories of college funds. The failure of the

Commercial Bank of Bluffton created a good deal of hardship across the village. Its depositories (among them the village government) apparently lost their personal savings, and its failure froze the construction of the new high school. Smith moved fast. He quickly arranged a deal with state banking examiners to have the $50,000 in capital of his Citizens National Bank (CNB) reduced by 20 percent, until CNB shareholders could approve a resolution increasing its capital to the $100,000 or so it would have once it absorbed the assets of the Commercial Bank. By early November 1931, with the deal falling into place, Smith sent a "cordial letter" to former Commercial Bank customers, inviting them to make CNB their "banking home" and promising to pay an immediate initial dividend of 40 percent on their lost deposits. With over $100,000 in capital, he assured them, CNB was "one of the largest and safest banks for a town of the size of Bluffton in this part of the state." Shortly before Christmas he confidently reported to a state official that "the public seems well pleased with the whole procedure thus far," but privately he knew it had been a near miss. "We were pretty badly scared for a while," he admitted to a cousin, "because when one bank fails in a neighborhood the people get scared and begin to draw their money out of all neighboring banks and that may soon put a bank out of business even though it may be perfectly sound in normal times."[7]

In the first days of March 1933, on the eve of the inauguration of president-elect Franklin Roosevelt, the same situation threatened to play out again. A bank panic started in Michigan, proceeded to Maryland, and then unrolled across the upper South. Governors proclaimed "bank holidays" to avert mob action. By inauguration day, such proclamations had shuttered banks across half the country. Smith published a special advertisement in the *Bluffton News*, informing CNB depositors that, in accordance with emergency state banking legislation just passed in Columbus, like other Ohio banks CNB had enacted a temporary prohibition of all withdrawals of over 3 percent. "There is no need for alarm," he soothed, but knew things could unravel quickly. Runs on more banks did not ensue that week in Bluffton or elsewhere in the country, prevented not by small-town bankers like Smith but by the power of an emboldened federal government. The day after his inauguration, President Roosevelt proclaimed a national banking holiday while staffers quickly cobbled together the Emergency Banking

Act, the first of many measures of the newly dubbed New Deal. In Bluffton, Smith suspended operations of CNB in accordance with the law and then reopened it ten days later upon a green light from the Federal Reserve. "News of the bank's reopening spread rapidly thru [sic] town," reported the *Bluffton News*, "and was greeted everywhere with approval. . . . That the Bluffton bank was permitted to resume business at the earliest possible date under the federal mandate is in itself eloquent testimony of the sound condition of the local institution." The following August, the bank managed to avert a physical threat to its survival when gangster John Dillinger and his men entered the lobby one day about noon, brandishing pistols. They told the teller it was a holdup and made off with $2,100, spraying Main Street with gunfire as they sped away. Smith was not in the bank at the time, but hustled over to assure depositors that the loss was covered by insurance.[8]

Three blocks west of Main Street, the college faced trials of its own. The bank failures of the summer of 1931 not only ruined Mosiman's initial plan to restructure the college's substantial bond indebtedness, but other area banks holding college bonds requested payment. As the school year began, the college paid outstanding bonds with interest totaling $10,000, emptying its treasury. This left no funds for payment of matters like salaries or other bonds, which came due like falling dominoes over the next few years. In fall 1933, with no funds at hand and no other option, the college defaulted on its bonds. Mosiman sent letter after letter to various bondholders begging for more time and assuring them that the college would meet its obligations when able. But that moment seemed unreachable. For by 1935 the college found itself more than a quarter million dollars in debt (over $4.2 million in 2013 dollars), staying alive only on the goodwill of its creditors.[9]

Smith was quickly thrust into the center of this escalating crisis. By the fall of 1931, he was serving on an official "retrenchment committee" of the faculty, and the following spring tendered a number of suggestions to the board about how further to reduce college expenditures, including substantial faculty salary reductions. Before long the trustees began to ask him to sit in on their meetings and in 1934 extended a call to him to serve as the college's treasurer and business manager. Smith declined, but did agree to serve on the board's finance committee along with a special subcommittee on fundraising. His most important assignment, beginning in late summer 1934, was chairing a special group called the "underwriters committee." This was a group of five men of means, including a Bluffton College trustee and fellow banker from Berne named Elmer Baumgartner, who would tackle an initial total of $94,000 of outstanding bond debt, trying to buy up the defaulted bonds at forty cents on the dollar. In Smith's papers are dozens of notes of transmittal from various college bondholders, along with his rough tallying of which particular bonds were outstanding and which were safe in his bank. Eager to help the college, some bondholders settled gladly. Others did so with hesitation, knowing that a real alternative was to receive nothing at all. Still others, communicating through their lawyers, insisted on receiving the full amount. By June 1935 the committee could point to some real gains, with over half the bonds in friendly hands. But it was a difficult process, and Smith knew the likely result if they should fail. "Just now we are trying to get a number of men [to] underwrite the bond issue," he wrote R. L. Hartzler before the committee commenced its work, "and that must be done immediately if the school is going to go on at all." Worse yet, progress would come much harder as many of the principals, Smith included, found themselves locked into a bitter personal conflict. [10]

Like many small institutions, Bluffton College, with two hundred and some students and less than two score professors, was a small, close-knit world. Through Smith's career it remained a place where, as a student in the 1930s put it, "we all knew each other including all the professors, their wives and children, and the dogs and cats." Relationships among the small faculty and smaller staff tended to be close, and people performed a multitude of roles in each other's lives: as colleagues, fellow church members, and neighbors. Many of them, like Smith, Mosiman, Byers, Smucker, and others, constructed their homes adjacent to each other and regularly hosted one another for supper. For some years in the later 1920s and early 1930s, a fair number vacationed together at property the college owned along Lake George, in Clare County, Michigan, about halfway up the "Big Mitten" of the Lower Peninsula. At some point during the Depression, the college began giving land to faculty there in lieu of back salary, a process that led to summer homes for the Smuckers and also presumably for Smith, since in 1932 the college sold him land along the lake for a dollar. Many Bluffton

College people thoroughly enjoyed the locale and each other's company. It was "a little harmless lake (3 miles by ½ I guess)," Emilie Mosiman wrote in August 1928 to her friend, college librarian Edna Hanley. There Laura Smith found relief from her hay fever, Emilie reported, and "the days pass quickly with writing, reading, washing handkerchiefs, boating, canoeing and playing rook in the evenings" with the Smiths. "We even had a delightful picnic with the Smuckers at a beautiful place called Pine Point. Dr. Smith found a muse there and has made it his sanctuary, writing poetry or history or what." In the Smith photo album exists one of the few extant photos of Smith clad in something else than a suit and tie, instead wearing rustic old clothes and a cap, holding a rake, and standing next to Laura in a rocker, a contented grin on his face.[11]

Laura's handwritten caption in the Smith photo album: "Happy Days at Lake George." BUASC.

In the early 1930s, many of these relationships began to disintegrate as this extended faculty family divided into two rough but distinct factions. While personality conflicts were central, they also reflected differences in ethnicity and social class. One side was clearly led by Samuel and Emilie Mosiman. Both came from backgrounds that were, by Mennonite standards, prosperous, even wealthy: he from the established Mennonite community of Trenton, in Butler County, Ohio, and she from a prominent Prussian Mennonite community in Nebraska, where she had immigrated with her family as a child. In Bluffton they had become socially close to faculty families with whom they shared similar ties, like home economics professor Elizabeth Boehr, from Emilie's Prussian community in Nebraska, and fellow Trenton Mennonites like biology professor M'Della Moon, English professor Wilbur Howe, and

Olga Berky, wife of chemistry professor H. W. Berky. For decades Emilie Mosiman led a crusade to teach manners, etiquette, and fine living to the Mennonite farmhands who made up much of Bluffton's student body. In her flowing dresses and flowery hats, and accompanied by her husband in his Prince Albert suit, she was perfectly suited to the role.[12]

The stretching process of acculturation had not entirely erased the social distance that would have existed between these GC Mennonites and faculty from Amish or MC Mennonite backgrounds—Smith, Byers, Lantz, Smucker—whose tradition had stressed humility and plain dress and warned against the dangers of pride. Sometimes these cultural differences expressed themselves over differences of policy. "There has always been a strong resentment against this group which they call the Goshen bunch on the part of the General Conference group here," explained Smith to a Bluffton College trustee in 1935, when the conflict reached its peak. "I think it goes back to the football days when the Goshen group [was] coming from a school that did not allow football [and] did not favor too much athletics. Berky and Miss Boehr are the two who are stirring up the trouble." But such policy differences were probably more of a symptom, rather than a cause, of a deeper social and cultural gap. It was manifested in subtle ways. Emilie Mosiman, Robert Kreider recalled, "did not hide her disdain" for the Goshen transfers on the faculty, whom she referred to as "a pushy lot, Mennonite Jews." Kreider's mother "never ceased to feel that in Mrs. Mosiman's eyes, she and her family were of lesser class." Three-quarters of a century later, near the end of his life, Boyd Smucker's son Donovan still admitted to lingering feelings of antipathy for the aristocratic Mosimans, whom he had watched as a boy, holding forth in their fancy clothes on the front porch of their fine, pillared home across the street.[13]

No doubt this latent tension was rubbed raw by the personal suffering that many Bluffton faculty families experienced during the Depression. Steadily through the decade, faculty agreed to accept half or two-thirds of their salaries and sometimes made do for months at a time with none at all. Berky's daughter Margaret recalled her mother, who had been raised in a well-to-do Mennonite family in Trenton, crying softly when her father returned home from work with word that there would be no salary again that month. Such families canceled life insurance policies, did without cars, and survived on shaky lines of

Laura and the Smiths' 1936 Pontiac. BUASC.

credit from Bluffton grocers, big garden plots, or periodic leftovers from the student dining room in Ropp Hall. Smith's personal wealth sheltered him from such deprivations, and his colleagues knew it. Margaret Berky Houshower remembers Smith, on his way to the bank from his home or the college, regularly walking by the Berky children as they played in their yard. He would often stop to chat, ask them about their games, and sometimes on a Sunday afternoon take them for rides in the country in his big, plush car. To the Berky kids this was a special treat because their family could not afford a car of their own.[14]

It is possible to overstate the cleavages of social class and cultural distance on the Bluffton faculty. Such tensions had not prohibited many of them from socializing together, as in the happy days at Lake George. Amos Kreider came from an MC background before he arrived in Bluffton in 1931 from the Goshen faculty to take up the pastorate at First Mennonite Church. Despite their ethnic dissimilarity with the old Swiss church, his son Robert remembered, the Kreider family was warmly embraced by the congregation. As someone of Amish Mennonite background and also relatively wealthy and cultured, Smith in particular seemed capable of rising above the division and perhaps even mediating it. Houshower recalled that the relationship between her father, H. W. Berky, and Smith was mostly cordial and collegial. At one key moment in the 1930s, Smith came to the defense of Mosiman in a manner that suggests something of a real emotional bond between the two men, and also of other aspects of Smith's temperament.[15]

As the economic crisis deepened, Bluffton's longtime president had become increasingly embattled. In 1932 he had felt compelled to issue an extensive and firmly worded statement to the faculty to dismiss campus gossip accusing him of misappropriation of funds. But rumor escalated, propelled in part by Dr. Peter Epp, a Mennonite refugee from Ukraine whom Mosiman had found penniless in 1925 and hired on at the college to teach German. In the early 1930s, apparently having lost faith in Mosiman, Epp began documenting evidence of the president's financial mismanagement. In 1934 he managed to get fifteen minutes in front of the trustees to present his case. These men, he said later, were "decidedly hostile" to his arguments, and so was Smith. When Epp told Smith of his brief against Mosiman, Epp said afterward, "he attacked me vehemently and among other remarks he hurled the following words at me: 'they picked you up when you could not get anywhere.'" Gratitude and loyalty were apparently qualities Smith prized deeply. While admirable, in the mid-1930s they implicated him in a faculty fight so destructive it appeared for a moment as if it might bring his distinguished career to an end.[16]

Sometime in the early 1930s, Smith's close friend Byers began an intimate personal relationship with college librarian Edna Hanley. In a world as small as Bluffton, it was impossible to keep hidden, even had the pair been inclined to be more discreet. By early 1932, Mosiman had heard about it from a variety of sources, board members had asked him about it, and faculty had told him that "we can stand the sacrifice of salary, but we can no longer stand the hurt that comes from scandal." Smith did his best to downplay the affair. He knew of "all these rumors floating about," he told college trustee Dr. Benjamin Thutt, but accounted them to "interested parties who have an axe to grind. Of course there is no question about the fact that where there is smoke there is a little fire," he admitted, "but the fire is a very small part of the ugly gossip that seemingly some people delight in promoting." Smith identified the "man who seems to be the chief instigator in the matter" as Berky, who had launched a campaign to get Byers fired. Bad blood had existed between Berky and Byers, Smith said, for a dozen years or more. But to fire Byers now, Smith told Thutt, promised to usher in a "general faculty scrap." Instead, he advised, "by far the best way to handle the situation would be to make an *honest* effort to hush up the matter and let it go [italics in the original]" for a year or so, when Byers had promised to resign the deanship voluntarily.[17]

Matters initially played out as Smith suggested. In May 1932 trustees granted Hanley a leave of absence for a year and no doubt sighed with relief when she accepted a permanent position as a college librarian in Georgia. Reflecting the ingrained sexism of the day, Byers was not forced out. Instead, in January 1933, he submitted his resignation as dean and returned to faculty ranks, effective the following June. The whole episode might have blown over quietly had not Byers and Hanley continued their relationship long-distance. Living next door to Byers, the Smiths could not escape emotional involvement. Laura Smith and Emma Byers had been neighbors for decades, and, one suspects, good friends. Of course Laura would have shared her friend's humiliation and did not hide her feelings, or her neighborly observations, from her spouse. In July 1936, with Smith away in Europe, she wrote to him that Hanley was once again visiting Bluffton. "This is the third time she is here . . . The tongues will be wagging again soon. Too bad they do not try to keep things quiet." By the summer of 1933, Berky was again maneuvering to see Byers fired. As Smith had feared, this had deeply polarized the faculty, which was "divided into factions," wrote faculty spouse Sylvia Pannabecker to relatives in 1933. "The Old Mennonites and Central Illinois seem to be on one side and the rest on the other." At this delicate moment—with Smith, Mosiman, and others desperately trying to placate angry bondholders and keep the college alive—the conflict became transferred onto the level of college presidential politics. When that happened, the academic careers of Smith, Byers, and others briefly hovered at the edge of a precipice—along, perhaps, with Bluffton College.[18]

In 1934 Samuel Mosiman was sixty-seven years old and beginning to think about retirement. Some trustees, not deaf to those in the community blaming Mosiman for the college's financial crises, seemed ready to hasten his exit. In July they designated a respected Pennsylvania minister (and Bluffton College and Witmarsum Seminary grad) named Arthur Rosenberger as associate president, clearly assuming that Mosiman would groom him as his successor. Smith pled with one trustee, his new pastor R. L. Hartzler, to give Mosiman more time before showing him the door. This would be wise, Smith suggested, partly because of Mosiman's important work with bondholders and partly to be sensitive to the proud president's feelings, not to mention those of his many and powerful supporters on the board. "The whole matter has possibilities of some friction," Smith observed in the seasoned air of someone used to college governance, "and I think we ought to manage it in a way that in the long run will be best for the college."[19]

The problem, Hartzler replied, is that the trustees gave Mosiman an open-ended exit date, and he showed signs of leaving it open for a very long time. But his departure, it turned out, came sooner than he expected. At what would have been a momentous board meeting in February 1935, for reasons still not entirely clear, the board suddenly moved to install Rosenberger as president and retain Mosiman on full salary as president emeritus. Mosiman pledged his public support but behind the scenes he was wrathful, pledging to his supporters on the faculty he "would not go out with a besmirched character." Angry letters and telegrams poured in to the trustees in protest. Smith kept a close eye on developments. Mosiman's supporters on the faculty, he told a trustee, quickly circulated a petition of protest to the board, with the apparent concurrence of the president and Emilie. The ultimate goal of this effort seemed to be to win Mosiman his job back and remove a few professors "to satisfy a personal grudge." Yet the petition did not seem to be gaining steam, and in the end, Smith thought, Mosiman "will calm down eventually and get on the band wagon and ride along with the procession. I don't think he will march but I think he will ride."[20]

Then, in April, faculty politics took a dangerous new turn for Byers and also for Smith, whose dogged defense of his old friend clearly implicated him in the whole matter.[21] At the move of the board's faculty committee, the trustees' executive committee appointed an "official investigating committee to investigate and ascertain the facts relative to certain damaging reports circulating about certain faculty members and report their findings to the next meeting of the board of trustees with recommendations." The way Smith reported the meeting to a trustee, the executive committee had been "dominated by Dr. Mosiman" who "spent most of the day" trying to persuade the trustees to axe several professors who had not been fully supportive of his policies. Smith was apparently among them, and the consequences were potentially serious. The now ex-president still had clout with the trustees. One of the three trustees on the investigative committee, Berne banker Elmer Baumgartner, had already indicated privately to Mosiman that he favored a general "house-cleaning" of the faculty. In early April the executive committee agreed to a motion by Baumgartner to reappoint a list of professors for the upcoming school year. The names of Smith, Byers, and Bible professor Irvin Detweiler (another Goshen transferee and Byers's cousin) were not on the list.[22]

Smith at age sixty, 1935. BUASC.

From the volume and tenor of Smith's correspondence on this episode (and also from the fact that he uncharacteristically kept carbons of it), it is clear he had been stung deeply. The three professors under a cloud sent off a polite but tough appeal to the trustees, indicating their refusal to meet with the investigating committee because of procedural irregularities in the way it had been constituted and also because they doubted its fairness. While its members were "men of the highest integrity and fair-mindedness," the statement read, they were "closely connected with those making the charges" and thus would find it "impossible" to render "an unbiased decision." Smith mounted a private offensive of his own. "I was considerably hurt when I learned of your action dropping me and two others from the faculty roll of the college," he wrote one trustee. "[Y]ou certainly handed us a lemon in the investigating committee you selected," a group so biased on behalf of Mosiman it seemed incapable of reaching anything else but a preordained verdict. It was led by men, he wrote to another trustee, who "either are not Mennonites or if so do not stand for Mennonite principles," and it was directed against professors who "have stood for Mennonite principles and for making the college a Mennonite college." Moreover, the timing could not have been worse. Right at that moment, Mosiman was trying to manage the critical process of repurchasing college bonds, and he desperately needed the involvement of "the group he is now trying to get rid of." "I am amazed," Smith bristled sarcastically, "at Dr. Mosiman's far-reaching business sagacity." If these men were fired, Smith warned his friend Thutt, a general faculty exodus would follow and "then they might as well close the doors" of the college.[23]

In the end, it is hard to know how close Smith actually came to losing his job. Both Thutt and Baumgartner assured Smith they held him in great esteem and had no intention of dropping him from the faculty. However, they also understood Smith to have said that if Byers was fired, he would also resign from the faculty, and they wanted to see if this really was the case. At any rate, the new president soon signaled that it was time to put an end to the conflict and move on. At the end of April, Rosenberger presented to the board a new set of rules, which he asked each faculty member to accept. They included the pledge that each would cooperate with the administration, would "have a willingness to forgive," and would "refrain from speaking about any other faculty members in unfavorable terms." Finally, each Bluffton professor, Rosenberger required, "shall keep in mind his high moral responsibility as a Christian educator and keep himself above all shadow of suspicion." All would proceed under the understanding that their position expired annually, and they would be rehired based on their willingness to do their jobs and on their "acceptability to the churches of the supporting conferences." Each Bluffton professor, now including Smith, Byers, and Detweiler, indicated their accord by attaching their signature to the new rules. The trustees then reappointed the entire—and presumably now chastened—faculty.[24]

For Smith it had been a discomfiting, ugly little episode. No doubt it afforded all involved some grounds for reflection. What Smith took away from it seems to have been a deeply felt sense of the level of prejudice and distrust among different Mennonite groups that reverberated across even his own little corner of the Mennonite world. It was no coincidence, he wrote to several trustees, that the men doing the accusing and investigating were all General Conference Mennonites, while "the men under suspicion are either members of the Central Illinois Conference or former old Mennonites." It was nothing more than a personal vendetta, based on "so many false accusations and rumors," clearly designed, in his mind, "to get rid of the Goshen college group." For Smith and others, the unpleasant faculty conflict of the 1930s might have provided grist for some darker thoughts about the larger promise of the union movement. If what happened at Bluffton was any indication, unity seemed a fragile concept even among like-minded progressive Mennonites. What kinds of prospects did the episode hold out for the movement as a whole?[25]

In the meantime, the financial future of Bluffton College was still uncertain, and Smith continued to be central to its rescue. In fall 1935 he began serving on a new board group, the refinance and adjustment committee, which met six different times in the space of about a month in places ranging from nearby Lima to Chicago, in a desperate search for a way to put the college on a more solid financial footing. That December the committee told the larger board that the college was "facing a real crisis." Considering and then rejecting one idea—that the college file for bankruptcy—the committee finally put together a renewed campaign to buy back college bonds. In the end, the college's future was only assured when Mosiman visited each of the disgruntled claimants personally and persuaded them to sign on to the new accord. He completed the process by the later 1930s shortly before succumbing, in January 1940, to cancer. It seemed a fitting coda to a spate of sad and bitter years in Bluffton.[26]

"Think More Peace and Talk Less War"

Despite the turmoil, through the decade Smith pushed doggedly on, teaching, writing, and especially speaking. The memories that echo back of him from these years are not ones of an angry or embattled figure but instead convey more gentle images: of a warm and generous uncle, a good neighbor, and a passionate and dedicated classroom teacher.

"As I reflect upon our contacts with Uncle Henry," Smith's nephew Tilman wrote decades later, "I realize they were lifelong and quite intimate." For a host of Smith nieces and nephews, there seemed little doubt that Henry remained, as Willard Smith put it, "a favorite uncle."

When he visited them in their younger years, he always brought small gifts—books, pencils, erasers—and sometimes bigger ones. When Tilman graduated from Hesston academy, his uncle Henry gave him five dollars. When Smith asked his nephew later what he had bought with the money and Tilman replied nothing, Smith handed him another five dollars and told him to go spend it. As the Smith kids grew older, their uncle's generosity kept pace. When Smith attended her wedding in 1941, his niece Ruth Smith Dick recalled, he presented her with a gift of $300 (over $4,000 today). As a child, Dick recalled, "It was always an event" when Uncle Henry came back home to central Illinois. "He was the first one from around here who went very far. . . . He was kind of a celebrity." Her father, Sam, would take the day off work, and the Smith kin would gather at brother Joe's home in Eureka. Ruth and her sisters would hover around Henry's knees, squabbling about which one would get to hold his hat. "He was very gentle and talked very fast," she recalled, "and he was always interested in what we girls" were doing. If his visit lasted over a weekend, he would usually accompany the family to church back at Metamora or Roanoke, "and it was sort of an occasion when he did."[27]

To fellow townspeople in Bluffton, Smith flickers in their distant memories as an everyday acquaintance and friendly neighbor, though someone who was sometimes a bit on the formal side. Three-quarters of a century later, some recalled the way he strode the streets of the village, sometimes with a cane or twirling an umbrella, tipping his hat to folks he passed on the sidewalk. Paul Klassen, son of Smith's faculty colleague John Peter Klassen, remembered Smith as more of a banker and man-about-town than a college prof. "He didn't show any trace of a humble Old Mennonite background . . . he was a distinguished city man." Yet Smith seems to have taken a special interest in kids. When he and his childhood buddies played football on a Bluffton vacant lot, Robert Kreider remembered, Smith was the only adult to stop and watch their games. To young Kreider, he always appeared as "a benign, friendly sort of person. You just felt a warmth there." Smith was a "sustaining member" of the local Boy Scout Council, and even today Camp Berry, a Boy Scout facility in neighboring Hancock County, has a plaque denoting appreciation for Smith's service as council president for the remarkably long span of 1923–34. As someone of means in the

C. Henry Smith speaking at a 1935 Smith family reunion in Eureka, Illinois. BUASC.

community, Smith periodically seized on the opportunity this afforded him to affect young people in other ways. Bluffton College student Jim Miller, for instance, was a Bluffton native who had worked through much of his adolescence as a paperboy. He had assiduously saved up the remarkable sum of $800 to pay for his college education, only to see the sum disappear in 1931 when Bluffton's Commercial Bank failed. A friend suggested he stop in at Citizens National Bank and see Dr. Smith. "How much do you think you need?" Smith wanted to know. When Miller replied a hundred dollars, Smith simply replied, "I think we can do that," writing out a note for Miller to take to the cashier. He also arranged to pay Miller a portion of his lost Commercial Bank funds, enabling him to stay in school at Bluffton during the depths of the Great Depression. Decades after he graduated, a history major wrote to express his appreciation for the multitude of roles Smith had played in his life, as his "major professor, father, confessor and guarantor of one or two of my notes."[28]

Student memories of Smith in the 1930s devolved primarily from his presence in the classroom. "He did a lot of lecturing," Miller remembered, but with a presence that "demanded attention and respect." To Donovan Smucker he was simply "an excellent teacher." Smith would come into the class with few notes, Richard Weaver recalled, and deliver polished lectures, pointing at maps, connecting history with current events, and often illustrating his points with anecdotes from his travels. He developed an effective style of his own: pacing back and forth in front of the class, gesticulating energetically but never shouting or raising his voice, and habitually taking his glasses on and off while he talked. He treated students formally, calling them "Mr." and Miss," but still managed to put them at ease, meeting with them outside of class for extra help if they requested it. A half century after his 1932 graduation, Harry Yoder recalled to classmates that "it is still a pleasure to picture C. Henry Smith leaning on the window sill on his right elbow and let the dates and descriptions of historical events flow in such a way that helped many of us fit life together."[29]

Through the 1930s and well into the war years, Smith continued to offer this same service not only to his church but to the wider society beyond. His public agenda increasingly reflected his academic one. In a short introduction to a 1937 book on Christian peacemaking by his friend Henry P. Krehbiel, Smith underscored this connection. Perhaps indicating his grasp of the thinking of the theologian Reinhold Niebuhr, whose book *Moral Man in Immoral Society* had appeared shortly before, Smith pointed out the variance between the behavior of individuals and that of the state. Killing someone individually, he pointed out, is murder, while doing so in war "is an act of highest patriotism . . . individually we are fairly good Christians; collectively in our international relations we are pagans." But Smith rejected the Niebuhrian compartmentalization between individual and social ethics. "Wars will cease when we become as good Christians collectively as individually," he asserted; "the road to universal peace is the road of education." Or take the remarks Smith delivered in Berne, Indiana, in August 1930 to the Seventh All-Mennonite Convention. Assigned the topic of Christian peacemaking, along with Quaker peace leader Clarence Pickett, he served as one of two keynote speakers on the last day of the meeting. In an informal but cogent little address, Smith reviewed the great piles of "inflammable stuff lying about Europe out of which wars are made," and also the many factors that then seemed to mitigate the possibility of another global cataclysm. (Subsequent events proved him a poor prophet, given his assurance to the convention that "there is not much danger of a general war in the near future." The current generation of world leaders had so absorbed "the horrors of the last war, it is not likely that they can be driven into another.") But he was continuing a thought process commenced in the previous decade and stemming out of his own soul-searching about the fundamental factors that made for war and how to combat them. War is, he repeated, "the result of wrong thinking" about its inevitability and justice. Most wars, Smith said, "find their source in the head, not the heart. The solution must be found in a comprehensive program of education." Smith fleshed out a concept of education that was more than the mere fact memorization he had imbibed as a youth. As he worked his way intellectually toward how to solve the age-old human problem of warfare, the notion of education as a great means of peace socialization increasingly emerged in the forefront of his thinking. To cultivate faith in a warless world, he told the crowd at Berne that August of 1930, it fell to "each one in his own small way and in his own little corner to help mould [sic] public opinion on the futility of modern warfare." In the 1930s, Smith would emerge even more centrally as one of the premier Mennonite public intellectuals of his day.[30]

Smith drew from a number of different intellectual currents. An inveterate newspaper clipper, he likely often sat at his breakfast table with scissors in hand, cutting out story after story from a wide variety of major media sources of his day. These ranged from financial analyses like *Barron's Financial Chronicle* and the *Wall Street Journal* to mainstream publications like the *Saturday Evening Post*, liberal Protestant beacons like the *Christian Century* and the *World Tomorrow*, and daily newspapers like the *New York Times* and especially the *Cleveland Plain-Dealer* (to which he remained devoted, despite the repeated efforts of Bluffton paperboy Miller to induce him to switch to the *Toledo Blade*). His files still bulge with hundreds of such clippings, each stuffed into a small envelope with one or another scribbled subheading. He was an eclectic reader. He collected data on current demographic movements at home and abroad, the intricacies of American politics, and economic trends like inflation rates, public debt, and foreign trade. He filed away dozens of pieces by conservative *Wall Street Journal* columnists like gold standard devotee Frank Kent and fervent anticommunist William H. Chamberlain. He particularly seemed to treasure the writings of the liberal journalist Dorothy Thompson, foreign affairs columnist for the *Saturday Evening Post*. He remained on the mailing list of his old YMCA heroes Sherwood Eddy and Kirby Page, now leading pacifist intellectuals, as well as that of Helen Keller, by then a thoroughgoing socialist. In 1942 Smith was a member of the World's Christian Fundamentals Association and in 1944 sent a small contribution to aid the work of the American Civil Liberties Union. Until the radical pacifist group the Catholic Worker finally culled its mailing list in 2007 (sixty years after Smith's death), a regular copy of its organ, the *Catholic Worker*, still came addressed to Smith care of the Bluffton College history department.[31]

Through the Depression and into the war years, Smith moved with renewed dedication to share his reading and thinking with groups both inside and outside the Mennonite world. In this manner he created a new model for the public contributions of the Mennonite intelligentsia. Not that he labored alone. Farther west there was already a small but vigorous collection of such scholar-activists, and its key leaders were Smith students. A whole raft of younger Mennonite historians, Willard Smith said, regarded him as "the master." Nowhere was this truer than at Bethel College, where, as Bethel historian Keith Sprunger noted, Smith was "much revered." Smith's most prominent disciple at Bethel remained its president. In 1941 Willard Smith was engaged in a phone interview with Edmund Kaufman for a teaching job at Bethel, when the president discovered Willard's family ties. He immediately exclaimed, "Well, if you are a nephew of C. Henry Smith I won't have to come to see you. I am ready to hire you over the telephone." In the end, Willard would ultimately settle into a long and fruitful teaching career in the Goshen College history department. But Smith secured another tie to Bethel in 1934 when Emmett Harshbarger, one of his students from the early twenties, finished his doctorate at Ohio State and arrived there to teach. Soon Kaufman and Harshbarger began displaying the kind of public engagement they had learned from their mentor. In particular this was found in the set of conferences called the Kansas Peace

Institutes, which ran in consecutive summers at Bethel from 1936 to 1940, endeavoring to spread Christian peace teachings in the lower Midwest. The ranks of these activists were augmented in 1941 by the arrival on the Bethel faculty of another of Smith's prized students, Winfield Fretz.[32]

This kind of activism faced more institutional constraints in Mennonite communities elsewhere. Goshen certainly harbored a fair group of sparkling intellectuals like Bender, the English professor Edward Yoder, and especially the bright, young ethicist and historian Guy F. Hershberger. Yet the MC hierarchy continued to exercise tight control over their public associations. Through the 1930s, MC fundamentalists agitated militantly against their denomination's involvement on any level with the peace movement then percolating in the wider circles of liberal Protestantism. Horsch, for instance, scornfully dismissed the approach and program of Mahatma Gandhi, whose teachings on nonviolence were being read with increasing excitement by American pacifists. Gandhi's ideas were only a "pitiful perversion" of Jesus's message, Horsch judged; "no thinking person can take him seriously." As far as Lancaster Conference bishop John Mosemann was concerned, a major part of the work of the MC peace committee was to simply "show the utter fallacy of the modern peace movement." This hostility meant that an emerging young set of MC thinkers and activists—Hershberger, for example, or the emerging MC peace leader Orie Miller—had to limit their ecumenical associations carefully. Miller could only attend meetings of the Continuation Committee of Pacifist Churches in the status of an "observer." Likewise, when in 1936 Bender attended—and to a large degree, led—the Mennonite World Conference in Amsterdam, he could do so only in an unofficial capacity. These men would need to proceed cautiously as they nudged their church toward a greater sense of responsibility for the world's pain and need.[33]

Bluffton, of course, was not bound by such strictures, and Smith eagerly strengthened ties between Mennonite progressives and the liberal Protestant peace movement. He corresponded briefly with Toyohiko Kagawa, the great leader of interwar Japanese pacifism, and sent him three of his books on Mennonite history. Likewise he exchanged mutually admiring letters with the Quaker scholar Richard B. Gregg, then popularizing Gandhi's teachings for American audiences, and also with

Kirby Page. When Gregg and later Page visited the Bluffton campus for lectures, the Smiths were happy to host them at their home on Campus Drive.[34]

In Bluffton the major voice on peace, politics, and international affairs remained Smith himself. Already by mid-decade, new academic dean Jacob Schultz reported to the trustees, Smith or some other professor had a regular forum in chapel, where he "interprets an event of outstanding significant importance." By the later 1930s, this role seems to have been assumed by Smith alone. Every Friday, students from the time remembered, Smith took the pulpit in chapel to elaborate to the student body his take on current events. "He was our conduit to the outside world," Margaret Weaver put it. Even by the war's end, as he approached his seventies, he remained a regular speaker at chapel, Lois Sommer Kreider remembered: "he would bring us up to date on what was happening in the world. It was full of narrative material, of imagery, and it was smooth." To students in particular he possessed immense credibility as a world traveler, someone who had penetrated far beyond the close confines of the rural Mennonite world and conversed knowledgeably with people in the corridors of power. Nor was this special expertise confined to international affairs. Among his personal effects is a ribbon inscribed "Delegate, State Democratic Convention, Columbus, O., Aug. 19–20, 1932." Six years later Smith again took advantage of the opportunity to listen closely to the power elite in another Sherwood Eddy Seminar, this one in New York City and Washington, D.C. Along with assorted other professors, ministers, and civic leaders, he heard from a host of the nation's major political and cultural lights: publishers like Henry Luce of *Time* magazine and Oswald Garrison Villard of the *Nation*; New Deal stalwarts such as Harry Hopkins, interior secretary Harold Ickes, Eleanor Roosevelt, and postmaster general James Farley; Congress of Industrial Organizations (CIO) chieftain John L. Lewis, and Supreme Court justice Hugo Black. In New York City he listened to the insights of leading liberal clergyman Harry Emerson Fosdick and, on a visit to Harlem, those of cult leader Father Divine. Perhaps the highlight for the group was an audience with President Roosevelt, whom Smith clearly heard say, with the war clouds again gathering, that "as long as I am president there will be no war involving the United States."[35]

Throughout the 1930s and well into the war years, Smith shared the fruits of his reading and experiences with audiences of his own. In the early 1930s, he began systematically inserting a half sheet of paper into his typewriter and pounding out speech outlines in a series of bullet points, at some point going back and scribbling in dates and locations for some (but not all) of them. In doing so he left a record of an astoundingly busy public speaker. For the past two decades, he had been addressing outside audiences three to four times a year. But in the 1930s and into the World War II years, he intensified his efforts and easily doubled that pace. By war's end his written record of speeches delivered since 1930 numbered over 110. Each message was different but reflected some common themes. To Mennonite audiences he offered something of his older version of a usable Mennonite past, refashioned now to meet the exigencies of the day, particularly in terms of the growing dangers to their peace position. To non-Mennonite or secular audiences, he spoke on a wide range of political and foreign policy issues, but found subtle ways of interlacing his remarks with Mennonite themes.

Mennonite groups never tired of hearing their story told by someone most regarded as the preeminent Mennonite historian of the day. For instance, in spring 1934 Smith journeyed to the Wadsworth and Salem congregations in central Ohio to walk audiences through the Mennonite heritage and "essentials." He touched on a number of themes he had been preaching for decades: the origins of their church as a voluntary body of believers, the pioneer struggle, their commitment to nonresistance, and their influence on early Baptists and Quakers. Yet he closed both speeches with a worried eye to the future, stressing the increased danger to their peace tradition posed by the militarism increasingly found in the public schools as well as the Bible schools. He reinforced the importance of peace education as a preeminent vehicle for youth socialization, telling his audience at Salem to take the Sermon on the Mount seriously because "ideas rule . . . heads must be right as well as hearts." For the future they faced would be difficult. In June 1934 he warned Mennonite young people at a special "Young People's Retreat" in Meadows, Illinois, that nations engaged in total war would be aiming for complete mobilization of their societies, making things hard on dissenters. We "will need to follow our convictions and take the consequences," he declared; more of us will land in jail. It will take more courage to stay out of the next war, he told a special 1935 "peace convention" at the Silver Street Mennonite Church near Goshen. Mennonites of all ranks will need to sacrifice for their beliefs. The stands for conscience made by individual Mennonites in the last war, he suggested to another congregation in 1938, provided the best model for the future. "Those who were willing to die made possible the exemptions for all."[36]

Smith also outlined the growing threat he perceived to the Mennonite peace position in the Mennonite popular press. His major bit of writing along this line took shape in 1938 in an overview of the Mennonite historical peace witness at the request of the GC Peace Committee, which published it in a little pamphlet and distributed it across the church. In *Christian Peace*, a distillation of four hundred years of Mennonite peace statements and actions into thirty-two compact pages, Smith broke little new intellectual ground, but his glance to the future summarized many of the arguments he was making in oral form elsewhere. Democracies, he warned readers, are generally less tolerant of minority rights than totalitarian states, and America was exemplifying this trend by making the state "the supreme object of loyalty and worship." This was evident to Smith in the Supreme Court's 1931 *Macintosh* decision, which began to assume a central place in his writings and speeches. Douglas Clyde Macintosh, a Yale theologian born in Canada, had applied for citizenship but saw his naturalization rejected because he stated he would only take up arms for his new country if he felt the cause morally justifiable. By a narrow 5–4 vote, the court affirmed the denial of his citizenship because of that qualifier. The decision met with quick and explosive denunciation in the liberal Protestant press as a dangerous violation of the basic American right to freedom of conscience. The *Christian Century* blasted it as "monstrous" and "incredible," comparable in importance to the Dred Scott case before the Civil War, and told readers that it amounted to an official, national sanctification of the "Cult of the Omnipotent State." To Smith the implications of the *Macintosh* ruling were dire and ominous. Fundamentally they meant that "conscience must give way to the dictates of the state." Under such reasoning, he pointed out, the Pilgrims themselves would have landed in jail.[37]

Mennonites faced dangers to their peace position from a variety of directions, Smith explained: from the increased militarization of the schools and especially—a new thought for him—the "disintegrating influence" of "the changing social and economic order." Decades earlier he had welcomed acculturation as mutually beneficial for Mennonites and for a progressive society no longer beyond the boundaries of their world. The searing Mennonite experience in the Great War and his ruminations on their developments since then led him to a much darker assessment. In older days, he reasoned, Mennonites could protect their distinct traditions and beliefs through rural isolation and a distinct language, "but all of this is rapidly being changed now. With the coming of the automobile, rural telephone, compulsory high school attendance, increased contacts with city life, college training, all of these distinctive features of earlier Mennonitism are being ironed out . . . some of the fundamentals are in danger of being lost also."[38]

Yet the "greatest menace of all" to traditional Mennonite peace commitments, Smith concluded, was the "subtle influence creeping into the church from certain short-cut Bible schools" that "do not believe in peace." Mennonite ministers who were trained in such schools returned "with a weakened loyalty to the distinctive and fundamental principles of Mennonitism. There is no quicker way to drive nonresistance out of the church than by letting these Bible schools train our ministers and leaders." Smith's premier solution was obvious. We need our own colleges and seminary to socialize our young people and our preachers, he insisted to Mennonite congregations from eastern Ohio to Illinois. "Unless the leadership of the church get wholeheartedly back of its training schools," he concluded to readers of *Christian Peace*, "Mennonitism is doomed."[39]

When Smith appeared in front of non-Mennonite audiences, he deftly harnessed the same set of speaking skills and expressed, more subtly, many of the same perspectives. Through the 1930s Smith played an active part in the activities of the Lima branch of a national civic-leadership group called the Torch Club, serving in 1932–33 as the local chapter president. His speeches so impressed one member that he wrote to a national officer of the group, urging that Smith be given a speaking spot at the club's national convention. "He speaks without notes," testified this member, "having a good, rapid working memory, as well as a rapid manner of speech. A good questioner, he also enjoys the after-dinner bombardment from the membership, having much in reserve for side-lights to be brought out after the address." Smith demonstrated a remarkable ability to lecture on a wide range of topics. He sifted through the relative advantages of the direct primary and then talked through the Treaty of Versailles with the Lima Democratic Women's Club. He outlined "Europe Today" to the Lima Delphian Club and Japan's policies in Manchuria for another Lima civic group. In a 1935 address called "Boot-Strap Economics" at two local high schools, Bluffton and nearby Mt. Cory, he told students to be wary of "quacks in economics" like Depression-era populists like Dr. Townshend and Huey Long. He closed with some practical advice: "Read widely. Don't believe it all. Make up your own mind. Be willing to cooperate. Keep your head." A careful reading of speech bullet points indicates his early enthusiasm and then growing disillusionment with the New Deal. In a 1934 address to the Bluffton Farmers' Institute, he made a case for more government regulation of the economy and told the group, admittedly "strange for a banker," to "spend all you can afford." In 1935 he admitted to Bluffton chapel students that "I am for Roosevelt." By 1938, however, in an address to the "Women's Federation" of Bluffton, he stressed that the Depression had not been solved, complained of "too much experimentation," and warned of the "encroachment" of an increasingly powerful federal government.[40]

Smith managed to express subtly to secular groups the same ideas he had been pushing in Mennonite circles, especially in his treatment of foreign affairs. To be sure, the popularity of the interwar peace movement in the mid-1930s afforded him an opportunity. In 1931 a large majority of Protestant clergy polled by the *World Tomorrow* agreed that the church should never again support international conflict, and in April 1935 over sixty thousand students on American university campuses mounted large peace demonstrations. Yet Smith persisted with the same message after that movement had peaked and public opinion began shifting toward war. In a 1938 talk on "Hitlerism" to a Putnam County group, he used the title of Sinclair Lewis's chilling novel on the coming of fascism to America, *It Can't Happen Here*, to suggest very much that it could, referring to the *Macintosh* ruling as evidence. He awoke a variety of groups to the possible approach of totalitarianism and war. Considered as a matter of Darwinian theory, he told the Lima Federation of Women's Clubs in 1935, war was not inevitable. The causes of conflict were found in such evils as imperialism, nationalism (a point he supported by a long list of bellicose quotes from British, French, Japanese, and especially American figures), and also the growing trend to make the state "an object of worship." "Will there be war?" Smith discussed with the Lima Torch Club in 1936. The signs were pointing that way, he admitted, but part of the answer depended on their response to the warmongers. His advice? "Think more peace and talk less war." War was "caused by wrong ideas and ideals," he told the Parent Teachers Association of Bluffton in 1937, not by "human passions." Proper teachers could socialize young people in a more positive direction. The "task of education" was to "develop [a] conviction of wrong." In a commencement address to the Luckey (Ohio) High School class of 1939, Smith informed graduates that "Uncle Sam" was "not a rich Santa Claus." In fact, there was no Uncle Sam: "we are the government." And as such, he declared, we must change our beliefs about war.[41]

In 1936 Smith expressed many of these same ideas in the international arena, seizing an opportunity to address German and Dutch Mennonites in what would be, it turned out, his last trip to Europe. Though he may not have known it, he was fortunate to have had the opportunity to go. Bender had quickly maneuvered himself into the thick of the planning for the Mennonite World Conference in Amsterdam that year. Assigned to pick eight American attendees, two from each of the four major U.S. Mennonite groups, Bender appropriately selected General Conference church president Peter R. Schroeder to go. For the other GC slot, to speak on the theme of "Mennonites and Culture," Bender wanted Edmund Kaufman. After some hesitation, Bethel's president decided he could not do it. Less than six weeks before the conference, Bender then turned to Smith, who accepted immediately.[42]

On June 17, a month later, Smith sailed for Europe with Bender, Schroeder, Orie Miller, and the three others in the U.S. delegation aboard the SS *Deutschland* of the Hamburg-America Line. By all accounts the conference was a significant event for the international Mennonite church. Over two thousand people attended the opening session in Amsterdam. Smith's paper came two days later in front of a smaller

At Elspeet, Netherlands, with the 1936 Mennonite World Conference. Left to right: *German Mennonite leaders Christian Neff and Emil Haendiges, American General Conference Mennonite president Peter R. Schroeder, Mennonite Central Committee chair Peter C. Hiebert, and Smith. BUASC.*

but still substantial audience of 350 people at a Dutch Mennonite conference center in the town of Elspeet. Undoubtedly due, at least in part, to the relatively limited time Smith had been given to prepare his address, it lacked much of an introduction or conclusion, or even a certain coherence. Smith moved quickly through a summary of basic Anabaptist belief commitments—religious toleration and freedom of conscience—and then to how Mennonites pioneered these ideas in the New World, serving as ideological ancestors to later, derivative groups like the Baptists and the Quakers. Only in the last third of the address did he get around to exploring his ostensible topic: Mennonite cultural contributions in Europe and America. He contrasted the substantial artistic and literary contributions of European Mennonites with their American cousins' relative dearth. This was due, he implied, to the sociocultural isolation that North American Mennonites had imposed upon themselves, though this distance now seemed to be breaking down.[43]

These were all old ideas for Smith by now. The real significance of his remarks in Elspeet was more due to their context. Over the previous century, nonresistance among Dutch and German Mennonites had deeply eroded. During the First World War, many had readily entered military ranks, and several Dutch Mennonites (including Jan Gleijsteen, an Amsterdam bookseller whom Smith had come to know), had done short stints in prison for advocating conscientious objection. The European planners of the Mennonite World Conference had even rejected proposed speech topics like "Peace" and "Use of Force" because they were "too political" and likely to cause division. Yet Smith seized upon the occasion to issue a ringing endorsement of nonresistance as normative for all Mennonites. To Mennonite congregations back home, such a point was a regular and uncontroversial staple of his speeches, but among European Mennonites such words undoubtedly assumed a greater import. Peacemaking had been a central part of their shared faith since the beginning, Smith reminded European Mennonites, though now among most of them it had become a "dead letter." They had "given up the old faith," he declared flatly, and "it remains for the American Mennonites to carry on." For most of their history in North America, Mennonites had fortunately dealt with governments that had "always shown a high regard for the tender consciences of Mennonites on this question." Yet things were changing. They faced dangers to their freedom of conscience from a number of quarters, he warned: from the U.S. Supreme Court (read: *Macintosh*), from compulsory military drill in state universities, and especially from "the dangerous, militant, millenarianism taught in certain short-cut so-called prophetic Bible schools." Mennonite ministers who attend those schools return to their communities, Smith admitted, with a weakened commitment to basic Mennonite doctrines, nonresistance included. "And for this reason the founding of a Mennonite Seminary where fundamental Mennonite principles are taught and practiced is an absolute pre-requisite to the preservation of the faith of the fathers."[44]

One of the delights of the Elspeet meetings, Smith later informed the readers of the *Mennonite Yearbook*, was that they allowed for "a free and frank exchange of views on all questions discussed." Given the context of the times, no doubt there was a lively discussion after his address. For him, the conference and the weeks following were a rich and meaningful time. After Elspeet, the conference participants journeyed a hundred miles north for a worship service in Menno Simons's hometown of Witmarsum. Then the American delegation, Smith

At Elspeet, 1936: Harold S. Bender (left), MCC leader Orie O. Miller (center), and Smith. BUASC.

certainly among them, met with Gleijsteen, an official from The Hague Peace Palace named Jacob ter Meulen, and a small group of Dutch Mennonites to strategize together about how to revivify their peace position. With all official business concluded, Smith took off for some sightseeing and networking of his own, visiting old friends and Mennonite scholars like Christian Hege and then reconnecting with Bender to visit Mennonite families in the Heidelberg region whom Bender knew from his grad student years there. While he worried the entire time, he confessed privately to Laura, about what he would do if his hosts asked him to speak in German, he seemed greatly to enjoy traveling with Bender. Altogether Smith's 1936 trip further deepened his ties with key Dutch and German Mennonites. When, two years later, Robert Kreider (then a nineteen-year-old senior at Bethel College) bicycled across the same region, he carried along Smith's Menno Simons biography as a kind of tour guide. Along the way, in his visits among the European Mennonite settlements, he kept running into Smith's "old friends" who spoke of him with great admiration and respect.[45]

In 1936, however, amid the warm encounters with European Mennonites, Smith could not help but pick up discomfiting signals as to the tenor of the times. "Everybody is strong for Hitler here," he wrote home to Laura from Germany, even to the point of replacing ordinary greetings with the worshipful "Heil Hitler." And he was deeply troubled by the routine anti-Semitism he observed: the increasingly long list of discriminatory practices spelled out against Germany's Jews, or the roadside signs, as he approached towns, proclaiming "Jews not wanted here." These were ominous omens for a Mennonite intellectual still committed to the ways of peace. When Smith returned home, he undoubtedly resumed his speaking schedule with increased urgency.[46]

Smith boarding the SS Europa *at Bremen, Germany, bound for home, 1936. BUASC.*

"We Must Save Democracy and Religion"

As the difficult decade of the 1930s came to an end, Smith could look back on some victories, both personally and for the causes for which he had long labored. Morale among Bluffton professors, Bluffton College president Rosenberger noted later, seemed to have bottomed out about 1935 and then entered an upswing, no doubt aided by the regular payment of salaries again. Like other professors, Smith would have been dismayed by Rosenberger's increasing ill health and saddened by his resignation in 1938, but would certainly have been pleased by the subsequent elevation of Lloyd Ramseyer, one of his former students, to Bluffton's presidency. Smith continued to work collegially across the Mennonite ecclesiastical divide, particularly with Bender. In 1938, after a nudge from his colleague Ernst Correll, Bender finally asked Smith to serve on the editorial board of the *Mennonite Quarterly Review* (*MQR*). He had held off tendering the offer in years past, Bender grumbled to Correll, because of Smith's persistent disinclination to publish in the journal. But Smith seemed delighted, Correll reported, by his appointment. There were even signs of a thaw in Smith's personal relationship with MC fundamentalists. As he reworked his general

Mennonite history for one more big book, Smith approached Horsch to ask if he would read and critically comment on several chapters. Horsch, perhaps to his surprise, agreed. Smith also wrote Horsch to suggest he work on a Mennonite encyclopedia, perhaps coedited with Daniel Kauffman and Bender, and to commend him for a recent pamphlet he had published on nonresistance. In response to one lay reader, who wrote Smith in 1938 to ask about the Anabaptist relationship with the Waldenses, he referred her to Horsch, calling him "perhaps the best informed historian of the Mennonite Church on that particular field."[47]

It is possible to overstate the extent of this rapprochement. A few of the private reasons for Smith's *MQR* appointment, Correll made clear, was that both he and Bender wanted to secure Smith's financial underwriting of further scholarly projects, and also, someday, his extensive personal library for Goshen. Smith and Edmund Kaufman had agendas of their own. He had heard of Smith's possible appointment to the *MQR* board, Kaufman wrote his mentor, and urged him to consider it in light of a competing historical journal that the GC church had planned. "The Goshen set-up is not bad," Kaufman offered, "only that it refuses to touch any present-day Mennonite problems and limits itself to old and dusty subjects which are, of course, safe." He also warned Smith against a new general Mennonite history he had heard that Bender and Horsch were producing "to duplicate yours and, if possible, to come out before yours does." Smith agreed that "there is a need for a good general history of the Mennonites and of course it can't be written from John Horsch's point of view." But Smith told Kaufman not to worry. His own revised volume was coming along quickly enough, and if the GC church did produce a competing quarterly to Goshen's journal, it would be easy enough for him to resign from the *MQR* board. Altogether Smith's differing level of esteem for the two other major MC historians of his day seemed to be summarized in a comment he made to Harshbarger, who was planning a trip to Europe and wondered if Smith could help him with entrées into the European Mennonite world. Smith was glad to oblige, furnishing a lengthy list of his friends and contacts in Dutch and German Mennonite circles. "These are the men most interested in Mennonite affairs," Smith concluded in regard to Mennonite leaders in south Germany, informing Harshbarger matter-of-factly, "I think most of them know either personally or by name at

Bluffton College Faculty, circa 1939–40, on front steps of Science Hall. Smith, front row, third from left; *art professor J. P. Klassen*, front row, far right; *Bluffton president Lloyd Ramseyer*, second row, far left; *chemistry professor H. W. Berky*, top row, far left; *and music professor Russell Lantz (Smith's neighbor)*, top row, third from right. BUASC.

least a number of Americans including HS Bender who has spent several summers in Europe and is well known because of his relief work, and they know John Horsch because he has been attacking the theology of most of them."[48]

Smith still retained a measure of respect for Horsch, and one suspects he had that and more for Daniel Kauffman. Three decades before, Smith had relocated to Bluffton and Kauffman to Scottdale, and there had not been much positive interchange, personal or ecclesiastical, between those two centers of Mennonite thought in all those years. But the relationship between the two men had predated that divide, stemming back to a time, forty years before, when both had been tapped by the legendary revivalist John Coffman and served together as eager agents of the quickening he had brought to the Mennonite Church of their youth. Now in his last years, Kauffman reached out across the chasm with an affection born of older times. In December 1939, looking out his window into a driving snowstorm, Kauffman jotted a small note to Smith. The snow blowing in from the west had caused him to wonder, Kauffman mused, if "northwestern Ohio has moved over into western Pennsylvania. It would be nice if one of these storms would carry C. Henry Smith on its wings."[49]

In the fall semester of 1937, Smith reduced his teaching load from three-quarters to half time. While he remained busy with his bank and continued to work on his book manuscript, one expects he was looking ahead to retirement. But in January 1939, Smith received a letter from Jacob ter Meulen, the director of the library at the Palace of Peace at The Hague, and one of the Dutch Mennonites he had met in 1936 who were desperately trying to rekindle their church's peace commitments. "We are suffering here from the terrible political crisis in which we live," Ter Meulen told him. "You will understand that the meetings of our small groups of Mennonites against military service are the more necessary." The following September, Germany invaded Poland, triggering what many had feared for so long: a second world war.[50]

A few days later, the parent-teacher association in Beaverdam, Ohio, asked Smith to come in and speak on the subject of "Education and War." He reminded the crowd that war "settles nothing" and they needed to do all they could to make sure America stayed out of it. The people rule in America if they are alert, Smith reminded them. So they should write their congressional representatives, write the president, "keep cool," and "look out for propaganda." Most of all, "we MUST SAVE DEMOCRACY AND RELIGION," he emphasized, "but [we] can't do it by war. War destroys both. People can save both if they are vigilant." Given what Smith had been doing with his life, it was no time for him to ease quietly into his golden years.[51]

11
The Final Mennonite History

On June 8, 1940, Smith traveled to Goshen College to deliver the keynote address at a special luncheon inaugurating the new facility housing Mennonite historical collections. This event was part of the festivities dedicating the college's brand-new library. Assigned by Bender to lecture on the "Progress in Mennonite History in America," Smith would have proceeded confidently; the topic was an old favorite. He sketched out some of the early histories done by Mennonite pioneers, highlighting the handicaps they faced—their lack of records, language barriers, and rural isolation—before focusing on a breakthrough in Mennonite history writing in the late nineteenth century. Mennonite history and institutions, Smith narrated, developed simultaneously in the hands of "progressive young people" like Funk, Coffman, George Bender (with a nod to his host's father), and Noah Byers. While noting that "the story of the modern period has not yet been written," he closed by highlighting some dangers to Mennonite peace doctrines that seemed especially threatening: increasing intermarriage with outsiders and the onset of peacetime military training. He offered the same solutions to these dangers that he held up in front of nearly every Mennonite audience he addressed. We can only preserve our past and our current solidarity, he affirmed, by increased attention to Mennonite education and by a seminary for our ministers.[1]

Perhaps lost in the august tenor of the proceedings was the private significance of the day. It was Smith's sixty-fifth birthday. That such a senior scholar would cap off a fine career by keynoting that occasion seemed appropriate, and Smith seemed increasingly willing to perform such roles. By 1940 he was overseeing his magnum opus in its final stages before publication, and the next year he would turn over his magnificent personal library not to Goshen (as Bender had hoped) but to Bluffton. It was "a worker's library, not an antiquarian's library," he told Bender in print, in which he had deposited copies of books he had garnered from Mennonite archives across Holland and south Germany. He himself would be the librarian of the collection, his agreement with Bluffton specified, and he would have "sole charge of the books for as long a period as he is willing and able."[2]

The last eight years of Smith's life, however, would not facilitate such an easy retirement. His forthcoming book would trigger one last public struggle with his colleagues in Mennonite academia about the proper form and uses of Mennonite history. More importantly, far from the quiet spaces of college libraries, larger forces were moving that would draw even tired old Mennonite academics into their wake. Two days before Smith's birthday on that June day, British forces had been evacuated at Dunkirk. By the end of the month, German armies would take Paris, sweep to the coast, and begin preparing for a cross-channel invasion of England. A year and a half later, America would enter the conflict. As a result, along with other Mennonites, Smith would once again be plunged into a difficult struggle over what it meant to be people of peace in a nation at total war. Up to the very end of his life, he would push hard, as a thought leader of his people and as a leading Mennonite public intellectual, to map out alternative courses for both his church and his country.

"This Gradual Sliding into War"

As America drew closer to the European war, Smith's public advocacy intensified. Many Mennonite audiences were interested in a message on peace. "War today is the world's greatest economic folly and its greatest collective sin," he told one such gathering in June 1940 in Meadows, Illinois. Their tradition of nonresistance, he confirmed, was the "solution of all social ills." Yet even while isolationist sentiment rose and pacifist expression declined across the Midwest, Smith found a variety of speaking invitations coming from non-Mennonite groups, at least up until Pearl Harbor. For example, tapped as a discussion leader for a statewide convention of Baptist youth in Lima in December 1939, he called his charges to stay true to the bedrock principles of their church like religious toleration and church-state separation. Their tradition, he told Baptist teenagers, called them to keep their distance from creeping American militarism and nationalism, seen in recent threats such as the *Macintosh* decision, and to treasure dissenters like the absolutist conscientious objectors of the last war, for whom we "ought to be thankful."[3]

Moreover, Smith happily discovered access to a wider medium of influence: the airwaves. Early in 1939 the college's publicity department entered into an arrangement with WLOK radio in Lima to broadcast half-hour segments from the college chapel. Some of the programs consisted mostly of numbers by campus musical groups, but in others Smith began to be featured regularly in a special *Background of the News* series. Before long, the program's director reported, people across the state were tuning in. Smith took the assignment seriously, as evidenced by the fact that, for these addresses, he typed out not just little bullet-point outlines but entire transcripts of his remarks. Now he could share with a larger audience his detailed grasp of global power politics, along with, more subtly, his perspectives on war and peace.[4]

At times he proved himself less than astute. While Hitler was "drunk with power" and there was "no telling where he will stop," he suggested to listeners in March 1939, "my guess is that there won't be war, and Hitler will get pretty much what he wants." After the war began the following fall, he walked his radio audience through the various partitions of Poland through history, wondering if "the liquidation of these small states may be a necessary step in the building of a stable order in Europe. It is the means of reaching this objective, rather than the objective itself that we deplore." The national distinctions were "acquired, artificial differences of culture, religion and language, easily ironed out through a process of education." Other times his analysis proceeded on stronger grounds. In an exploration of Russia's military sweep into the Baltics, he outlined the Soviet state as a traditional great power acting in a manner consistent with Russian history, noting, along the way, his own political foresight. "I said twenty years ago," he reminded his listeners, "that as soon as the Russian Communists found themselves safely and securely in the saddle and at reasonable peace with the world; and Russia again had reached a state of normalcy, the old urge toward the Baltic and the Dardanelles would again be revived. That prophecy has now been fulfilled."[5]

Through much of 1940, Smith turned increasing attention to American politics, worrying about the centralization of American power as Roosevelt campaigned for a third term. He highlighted the implications of the *Macintosh* case and the general dangers to democracy at home and abroad for audiences ranging from WLOK radio to a group called the "Reformed Brotherhood" to the Rotary Club in nearby Ada. Steadily and almost imperceptibly, he suggested to his radio listeners that traditional safeguards of American liberty—the separation of powers, the direct primary, and the regular turnover of officeholders—were being undermined; "even in our own beautiful Ohio the voter often has no real vote." By the eve of the election he had broken decisively with Roosevelt. He had to be more circumspect over the radio, but not so back on campus. The New Deal, he summarized for the college YMCA, had the nation headed directly toward: "1. Bankruptcy, 2. Dictatorship, 3. War." Styling himself an anti–New Deal Democrat, he was "perfectly willing," he told the students, "to exchange a trained business man for the job" instead of "the social welfare directors, the college professors and the politicians who have plunged to an all high debt of 60 billions without showing any results." He intended to vote that fall for the Republican candidate Wendell Willkie.[6]

In his analysis of foreign affairs and especially in the solutions he offered, Smith continued to take his cues from the leaders of liberal Protestantism, although in repeatedly stressing the magical cure-all of education, his analysis retained its Smithian hues. One long-term solution for the problem of war, he thought, was greater international cooperation, like a renewed League of Nations. After outlining to the Lima Torch Club the possible advantages and disadvantages of such an international union, he left no doubt about where he stood. Such an instrument would do away with war and usher in economic growth, he concluded, using all caps in his notes for emphasis, for "NATIONALISM [IS] THE GREATEST ENEMY TO WORLD PEACE AND PROSPERITY." As a second and nearly universal solution for the world's deepening crisis, Smith repeatedly pointed to a public and engaged Christianity. It was only through such a means that Hitler could be defeated, Smith suggested to the ministerial association of Findlay. Indeed, if a "Christian" peace had been crafted at Versailles two decades before, Hitler never would have appeared. We need to complete the Sermon on the Mount, he informed a missionary conference in Bowling Green, Ohio, for "Christianity has not been tried" since the year 310 (when the emperor Constantine made Christianity the state religion and abandoned the pacifism of the early church). To a group of Illinois Mennonites in June 1940, he prescribed a "new type of patriotism, based on the proposition that all men, regardless of color, race or nationality, are brothers." It was not their job to "save the British Empire, or to prevent Japan from getting the East Indies, but to preserve freedom," he suggested. Echoing but inverting Niebuhr's famous dictum, Smith told WLOK listeners that "world peace will be assured only when nations will learn to be as generous and unselfish as individuals are supposed to be," for "national selfishness is always more selfish than individual selfishness." Reversing this was "a matter of education. . . . The economic forces back of national policies are constant; and so ideas must change."[7]

As for an immediate means to deal with the threat of fascist militarism, however, Smith had little to say. In none of his wartime writing or speeches did he make even scant reference to the stark evil of the Holocaust or Japan's orgy of rape and massacre at Nanking. In this he likewise reflected the wider thinking of liberal Protestant pacifism, which, as even a sympathetic pacifist historian later agreed, offered "no immediate solutions to cope with the aggressive world of angry power relationships it confronted." Smith's advice to Illinois Mennonites and Findlay ministers was not to worry. Totalitarianism was usually just temporary. It is only born out of despair, he assured an audience in June 1940, and now that Germany and Russia have won, "the need for totalitarianism no longer exists and people who are democratically minded will no longer permit dictatorship." For "even dictatorship must rest on [the] will of people."[8]

As America drew closer to the war, on the air, in churches, and in meeting halls, Smith took pains to rebut the growing rationales for U.S. intervention. Roosevelt's program of extending aid to England, popularly characterized as "Lend Lease," Smith suggested to a church in nearby Cridersville, was a sham. "Battered airplanes, exploded bombs, boys blown to bits"—none of them would be returned to the U.S. It would be impossible for Hitler to invade the U.S., he told Findlay ministers, and there was "no evidence" for such a desire in his book, *Mein*

Kampf. Roosevelt's policies were steadily pushing the country toward war, Smith insisted to WLOK listeners in November 1941, thus making a mockery of any supposed neutrality. In fact, "this gradual sliding into war" was much more advantageous than a formal declaration, since it "relieves both the president and the Congress, as well as the general public, from the responsibility of making the painful and fateful decision that would bring us into this terrible conflict." Three weeks before Pearl Harbor, he warned that war seemed to be approaching. With American sanctions now taking a severe toll on the Japanese economy, its government dominated by militarists, Smith anticipated that the Japanese pro-war clique may well "take the chance, desperate though it may seem," of launching war against the United States. On December 10, three days after the attack, with the ruined hulks of the U.S. Pacific Fleet jutting out of Pearl Harbor and Roosevelt calling the nation to war, Smith cautioned his radio audience to harbor no illusions about what was coming. The immense productive capacity of the United States left no doubt, he assured listeners, that it would ultimately prove victorious. But getting there could be hard. "This war," he warned, "may be long, hard fought, and extremely costly."[9]

The Crisis of Waning Nonresistance

While Smith devoted his energies to a one-Mennonite campaign to avert the war, other leaders of his church busied themselves with a more prosaic task: negotiating with the state for protection of their peace commitments during wartime. What resulted was a conscientious objector (CO) program, paid for and administered by the historic peace churches but under the direct supervision of Selective Service. COs would be officially recognized and directed into—as stated by the 1940 draft bill in an important phrase—"work of national importance under civilian direction." Officially called Civilian Public Service (CPS), for most objectors it meant forestry and soil conservation work in isolated camps, and, later on, work with the mentally ill in mental hospitals. As the war went on, Quaker and especially secular objectors criticized CPS work as meaningless, its unpaid aspect as "slave labor," and denounced the peace churches for serving as an arm of an oppressive state. Great majorities of Mennonites felt differently. Civilian Public Service was such a far cry from the traumatic collective experience they had endured in the last world war that a wide spectrum, from the program's creators to individual objectors in the camps, regarded it with gratitude. Particularly in the summer and fall of 1941, as the draft geared up and COs began leaving their farms and colleges for CPS camps, most Mennonites, historian Paul Toews has summarized, were "euphoric" about the program.[10]

Mennonite peace commitments once more quickly relegated them to a tiny minority in their country. After Pearl Harbor nearly all other Americans, including most liberal Protestants, rapidly fell in line behind the war. The *Christian Century*, for example, affirmed the war as a "guilty necessity." As before, wartime presented an uncertain climate for Mennonite colleges. President Ramseyer pursued a different course than had his Bluffton predecessor in the last world war, plainly signaling in various ways that this time Bluffton College would remain firmly committed to the ways of peace. Students took their cues accordingly, and persisted with a student culture expressive of Mennonite commitments. They formed a war relief committee, and the peace club remained active, bringing pacifist leaders like A. J. Muste and John Nevin Sayre to campus and raising support for CPS. Faculty adjusted easily with regard to smaller matters, voting to end the spring 1942 semester two weeks early and allowing seniors to substitute comprehensive exams for remaining coursework if drafted earlier. The bigger problem concerned what professors would do as draft calls accelerated and college enrollment dropped. (Smith merely taught less and spent more time at his bank.) Yet remaining an unpopular minority in a nation at war, the college discovered, brought unexpected benefits, as well, like a strengthened Mennonite presence and consciousness. As an example, dean Jacob Schultz informed other Mennonite college administrators in 1942 that enrollments had already tripled in Smith's class on Mennonite history.[11]

Smith continued to find young people engaging and was especially curious about their reading of the war. In a wartime visit to Bluffton, Laura's niece Elaine Bowers, by then a nursing student at Bradley Polytechnic in Peoria, recalled her uncle Henry as a warm and polite host. He talked a good deal about his academic field but also peppered her with questions about her take on the war and what Bradley students thought about it. He knew, she said, his own views about such matters were different from hers, but nonetheless "he was gracious to me and respectful." During the war, Smith received letters from former students now in military service who shared their war experiences with no other apparent assumption than that their old professor would find them interesting.[12]

Even so, there was no mistaking what such correspondence signified about the fundamental crisis facing the church. As young men made their decisions about the draft, individual Mennonite branches began keeping careful track, as did MCC, which mounted some larger surveys later in the war to be able to get a firm handle on the fidelity of Mennonite young men to the ancient church teaching on nonresistance. What they found was both illuminating and shocking. Among Mennonite draftees as a whole, only 46 percent had opted for conscientious objection. Almost 40 percent—many of them men whose pastors had evaluated as in good standing with their church—chose straight military service. More than 14 percent chose noncombatant roles, serving as medics and the like (a position still rejected by the churches). Among the GC Mennonites, only a quarter of the draftees declared themselves COs, and an even lower number of Bluffton College students—22 percent—did so. Mennonite pastors and church leaders of all stripes could only respond with deep and focused alarm.[13]

Smith could not have been very surprised. He had been warning for years, in person and print, that outside forces like militant nationalism and fundamentalism were eating away at Mennonite peace commitments. Even so, he plunged into the struggle to meet the crisis that the draft numbers signified. His basic analysis remained largely the same. Take, for example, a 1942 article he published on the front page of the *Mennonite*, wondering if the GC church was losing its peace commitments. He took as his lead a recent comment by Winfield Fretz, suggesting that the rural environment was more conducive to preserving such basic Mennonite principles. On the one hand, Smith agreed. Fretz was right: famers were more independent and less subject to "social pressure" than city folk. On the other hand, Smith said, he himself knew of many rural Mennonite churches that were indifferent or hostile to the peace teaching of their wider church conference. In explaining why, he listed his same old suspects: the fact that young people aren't taught correctly by their elders (solution: Mennonite education), and the fact that many Mennonite ministers are trained in outside seminaries (solution: a Mennonite seminary). He took square aim at evangelical subculture as a prime culprit, underscoring the kind of two-track theology that elevated doctrinal essentials from ethical nonessentials, which many Mennonites had begun to accept. "Contrary to a widely held view in certain circles," he explained, "conversion has an intellectual content. It involves the head as well as the heart."[14]

Smith took the same message back out onto the road, venturing in March 1942 back to Bethel College to serve as the guest lecturer during their Bible Week. Kaufman had beckoned, suggesting that "the war is producing a state of mind which would make our people particularly receptive to your message." Smith plunged in, outlining the "modern disintegrating forces" eating away at their peace commitments: the high school, the attractions of secular, urban life, and the influence of militaristic Bible schools. Then he prescribed his familiar remedies. The entire trajectory of a long and detailed foray into Mennonite history seemed to be to stress to students the applicability of the martyr stories to their own day. "Democracy and Christianity are going to be saved by the martyr, not by the soldier," he summarized. "The blood of the martyr has always been the seed of the church." Once again Smith urged his audience to take the long view, admitting that Mennonite solutions to a world aflame with war had no immediate bearing. Hitler, he suggested, was "not the pacifists' problem." Pacifism was "not a remedy to end war but to end the war system and prevent war." The most important thing Mennonites should do now was to get behind CPS with all their might. It was the "greatest opportunity in their history," Smith told his Bethel audience, to "testify to their peace testimony without compromising their conscience." During the war years, then in his late sixties, Smith would practice what he preached, traveling hundreds of miles to isolated CPS camps across the eastern states to buck up morale and lecture on Mennonite history: to Medaryville, Indiana; Ypsilanti, Michigan; Sideling Hill and Wells Tannery, Pennsylvania; Hagerstown, Maryland; and Luray and Grottoes, Virginia.[15]

Smith expanded his capacity for church service in the cause with a decision he made in 1940. The onetime Amish Mennonite farm boy completed his full journey across the Mennonite ecumenical landscape when, at age sixty-five, he officially joined the General Conference

Mennonite Church. Undoubtedly the move came because of a factional dispute in the Carlock congregation in spring 1940, which triggered the resignation of its pastor, Smith's friend R. L. Hartzler. Reading between the lines of Hartzler's carefully worded explanation for his decision, he had apparently become another casualty of the running fight between fundamentalism and progressivism in the Central Conference. This same conflict had no doubt been the root cause, eight years before, of the Smiths' decision to transfer their church membership from East White Oak to Carlock. (Indeed, in explaining his resignation decision, Hartzler even compared the Carlock situation to East White Oak.) Apparently fleeing fundamentalism once again, in December 1940 both Smiths transferred their membership from Carlock to First Mennonite of Bluffton.[16]

Settling into this new congregation would not have been a jarring transition for the Smiths; they had been worshiping there for at least fifteen years. Even so, the entire episode seems to have further intensified Smith's antipathy, already fully stoked, for Mennonite fundamentalism. When in 1943 Smith received word of the founding of a new school, Grace Bible Institute in Omaha, by GC fundamentalists, he shot off a letter to its board asking if the school intended to operate by the ancient Mennonite doctrine of nonresistance. Or take a letter Smith wrote that fall to a friend in a Mennonite congregation that was considering calling an area man to their pulpit. Smith admitted he did not know this young man personally, only that he had come from a neighboring, conservative Mennonite church whose ministers "have been on the outs with most of the other Mennonite churches" in the area (probably a reference to the Ebenezer church). But he did know that the pastoral candidate had attended Moody Bible Institute, and for Smith, that was enough. In his advice to his friend, Smith almost seemed to regard Moody like a kind of cancer. "I think you will find that the Moodyites, and the city missionaries," Smith suggested, "never make very good pastors for country churches, and especially if you want your church to remain a Mennonite church." Referring explicitly to the rupture of the East White Oak church, Smith stated, "I don't want to influence any body [sic] in their choice but I have seen so much damage done to Mennonite churches by these Moodyites who are too religious to go to their own schools I am suspicious of all of them."[17]

Now an official member of the GC denomination, Smith soon discovered that it facilitated his leadership in several church initiatives during the war. Soon he was serving as secretary of the peace committee of the GC's Middle District Conference (MDC). Working closely with the committee chair Donovan Smucker (his old student and now a Mennonite pastor in Wadsworth, Ohio), he threw himself into the work, sending off a regular stream of letters to conference pastors, pleading with them to complete their draft census forms, expand their home-canning operations and other fundraisers for the CPS camps, sell civilian bonds and peace stamps, and the like. It was discouraging work. Congregations were ever behind in meeting these obligations, and many seemed uninterested in the committee's agenda. In speaking before the delegates to an MDC annual meeting in August 1942, Smith noted that upward of 80 percent of MDC draftees were choosing straight military service; the peace doctrines of the conference seemed to be vanishing before their eyes. All of us, he confessed, "ministry and laity alike must share the responsibility for [the] indifference and blindness to the forces of disintegration that have been at work among us." He hammered away with the same solution. "The remedy," he prescribed, "must be sought in a united and determined program of education" as a primary means of socialization, and from every available angle: "the home, the pulpit, the Sunday school, the religious press," and Mennonite schools.[18]

Soon after joining the GC church, Smith also found himself tapped to serve, along with Smucker, as an official delegate from the denomination to a National Study Conference on the Churches and a Just and Durable Peace. A project of the Federal Council of Churches chaired by the influential international lawyer and Presbyterian lay leader John Foster Dulles, the commission materialized in 1940 as a major vehicle for liberal Protestantism to exercise its leadership in wartime America and to formulate a national moral vision for the postwar world. Toward these ends, by 1945 the commission had hosted two national conferences and innumerable local ones, worked extensively with government officials, and published scores of pamphlets and articles. Its first national meeting, in Delaware, Ohio, in early March 1942, chaired by Dulles, attracted the national press and drew from the energies of more than 370 delegates—clergy, professors, religious editors, missionaries, and university and seminary presidents—representing thirty Protestant denominations. Discussion focused on thirteen "Guiding Principles" and culminated in a series of strongly worded resolutions, all of which would have had Smith nodding vigorously in agreement. These included a nonpunitive peace imposed on the war's losers, and greater patterns of economic sharing and international brotherhood as antidotes to the racism, imperialism, and selfish global economic policies that delegates held were the primary causes of the war. The delegates also called for some kind of postwar international union to ensure that such principles were enforced. Smith scribbled extensive (and nearly illegible) handwritten notes on the proceedings and listened intently enough to catch on to a major controversy mostly occurring behind closed doors. This occurred when *Christian Century* editor Charles Clayton Morrison introduced a resolution, subsequently rejected by the steering committee and omitted from the final report, proclaiming that "the Christian church is not at war." The phrase soon began appearing as a bullet point in Smith's speech outlines, one of many ideas from the conference that resonated deeply. His ideas for a "durable peace," he described to the Lima Torch Club two months later, included no harsh penalties leveled again on a defeated Germany, open markets, a general withdrawal from Asia by the West, and a new League of Nations. "If we win," he prescribed, "we must make the world not only safe for us but all the world." Torch Club members responded to such ideas blankly, receiving Smith's comments without discussion and not turning the lectern over to him again for two years.[19]

Conferences and speaking engagements were exciting, but to shepherd his church most usefully through the trials of war, Smith returned to what he did best: writing and popularizing Mennonite history. During the war years, he diligently sketched out something like a wartime usable past. This occurred most notably in the pages of the GC's weekly organ, the *Mennonite*, where Smith's articles on Anabaptist-Mennonite history and life began to appear regularly again. In 1943 and 1944, he treated lay readers to a small series on the Anabaptist origins of their faith, with a special stress on the life and teachings of Menno Simons. Smith focused other pieces on the particular wartime message he thought his readers needed most to hear. In "God and War" he worked to undermine the religious sanctions with which many

American Christians were cloaking the war. He revived a reading of Dwight Moody as a Civil War–era pacifist, laid out in another piece an overlooked but real reservoir of public peace sympathies, and in two other issues furnished readers with an annotated bibliography of peace-related books that ran to nearly sixty titles.[20]

Smith's most explicit harnessing of his popular Mennonite history writings to his church's wartime needs came with his contribution to an MCC initiative, a course called "The Mennonites and Their Heritage." With the war having revealed the deficiencies in Mennonite socialization, leaders quickly realized that CPS could serve as a massive Mennonite school—a place to conduct, as one historian phrased it later, a kind of a "churchwide teach-in" on Mennonite life, doctrine, and history. Its foundation would be six core courses, each with its own booklet. Bender, the author of the booklet on the Anabaptist heritage, was also the series editor, and he assigned Smith to write up a brief summary of Mennonite history in America. He produced a draft by January 1941, and a year later was engaged in final editing, with MCC ready immediately to send out a thousand copies into the camps.[21]

Under pressure to produce a quick and concise little booklet satisfactory to all parties, Smith's interpretive overlay in his *Mennonites in America* pamphlet was relatively light, particularly in part A, on the history of the early settlements. He managed to summarize early migrations and Mennonite expansion across Pennsylvania before 1800 in eleven pages and cover the Russian Mennonite migration in just four. His brief descriptions of heroic Mennonite pioneers and early Mennonite objections to slavery, so pleasing to the dual Mennonite-American identities of his readers, raised objections from nobody. But part B, his encapsulation of the "origin, history, peculiar emphasis and contributions of the various Mennonite branches," required a more delicate touch. Bender explained, in a little editorial note in the text, that time constraints had precluded each group submitting its own brief self-description. So they would all have to trust Smith "to present an interesting, sympathetic and fair treatment" of each group; he begged "the forbearance of any who feel that the treatment does not measure up to the ideal."[22]

Even before the publication of his booklet, Smith saw that his readers' forbearance had limits. Bender circulated a draft of Smith's work to other groups, and while all judged Smith "eminently fair and unpartizan [sic]" in his descriptions, some thought he had overemphasized schisms and minor differences. The Holdeman Mennonites rewrote some aspects of Smith's summary. The Brethren in Christ objected so "strenuously," Bender relayed, that they sent in their own sketch. Smith responded to all such criticism agreeably, and particularly to this latter one. Creating the intellectual grounds for Mennonite unity was a project he had been pursuing now for about thirty years. But Smith ran into immediate problems with Bender in regard to his treatment of Bender's MC branch. They were, Smith hastened to explain, "the largest and most important group." In fact, "the whole church up to the time of the schisms was Old Mennonite . . . so they remain the main trunk of the church still after all the different wings split off. To give them a separate heading wouldn't fit in logically." Anyway, he assured Bender, he allotted them "more space" than he gave to other groups and thus their "subordinate position in the classification may not be noticed." Bender did notice, and his editorial hand remained firm. His set of Mennonites received their own separate little chapter in Smith's published booklet titled "The Mennonite Church," though he retained Smith's subheading ("sometimes called the 'Old' Mennonites") and acceded to this nomenclature, along with the little terminological caveat: "though that is not their official name, and is not recognized by them."[23]

In the end, the series was a smashing success. By 1945, Bender reported to the authors, MCC had already issued two runs of the series of four thousand copies each and was planning a third edition of a thousand more. Robert Kreider (who, as CPS educational director, was in a position to know) thought that CPS men generally found Smith's and Bender's booklets the "most interesting and stimulating" of the lot. On this project as in others, Smith and Bender had worked together amicably, and their minor interpretive tangle amounted to nothing. But in fall 1942, Smith would discover that this same historiographical debate, considerably amplified, would play out on a more public stage, sparked by the publication of his last and largest book.[24]

Smith's Magnum Opus

Smith had been planning on publishing a new, definitive edition of his Mennonite history for a long time. As early as 1922, he ventured to his old friend Thierstein that "there is a great deal of material that can still be had for the writing of a final book on the subject." In 1925 he estimated that such a project would take him two or more years; in the end, it took him almost twenty. It occupied his lone sabbatical year in 1929–30, and, when time allowed, he had labored away since then. In 1941 his great magnum opus, *The Story of the Mennonites*, finally appeared, published by the Mennonite Book Concern of Berne, Indiana, and dedicated, once again, to Laura.[25]

Besides the relentless busyness of Smith's teaching, speaking, and banking, there had been a good reason for his delay. From the mid-1920s a great outpouring of new work had emerged on Anabaptism, establishing it as a key component of the Reformation. As a result, his 1941 book differed from his 1921 and 1909 versions in one major way: the length and depth of coverage it provided, especially on Anabaptist history. The entire book, index excluded, totaled 817 pages, and Smith did not even turn his attention to developments in North America until page 535. Because of his persistent, maddening refusal to cite his sources, include maps, or even a bibliography (he was writing for the "general reader," he explained again, and did not want to "clutter up the text" with references), it is difficult to know exactly what of the new scholarship he consulted. But his massively expanded treatment of Anabaptism in the 1941 version suggests he had immersed himself in a bulk of it. This bore fruit in the depth and detail with which he conveyed the movement: his elaboration of various martyr stories, for instance, or his encyclopedic treatment of early Dutch Mennonite groups, distinguishing between Flemish, Frisians, Waterlanders, Upper Germans, Jan Jacobs-folk, and "Uko-Wallists."[36]

Smith's 1941 book differed from his earlier version in two other ways. First, in the 1941 book, a slight patina of anti-Catholicism appeared, again probably reflecting his continued immersion in the liberal Protestant press. At a few places in the text he described the Anabaptists' Catholic persecutors as particularly intolerant and cruel, referring to Jesuits as especially "bigoted." More importantly, his lack of concern about the ultimate length of the text allowed him to extend his story as close as he could to the present day, up to 1939 and the commencement of the "present war." He could cover in detail important developments in recent Mennonite history like the cataclysm occurring in the

Mennonite world in Ukraine from the end of the Great War onward: the massacres perpetuated by the anarchist leader Nestor Machno and his men ("fiends in human form") and the ensuing destruction of the Mennonite colonies in Stalin's terrors. In this contemporaneous focus, he retained his critical capacities, relaying in some depth the acceptance of the "un-Christian racial theory of Hitler" by some German Mennonites and the loss of nonresistance across Europe, as well as the recent efforts by certain Dutch Mennonites to recover it.[27]

In nearly all other ways, however, Smith's 1941 Mennonite history bore remarkable resemblance to his previous books. It had the same organizing scheme: part 1 on Europe, organized regionally, part 2 on the Mennonite experience in the Americas, organized largely chronologically, with two closing chapters, "Culture and Progress" and "Keeping the Faith," exploring Mennonite cultural themes like education, missions, hymnology, and nonresistance. It had the same commitment to objectivity, promising to "cover the whole Mennonite movement . . . without favor or prejudice." It offered the same fine writing and narrative sweep to captivate lay readers, and also, in its long lists of Mennonite surnames from various regions, to satisfy lay genealogists. Once again he delivered a treatment of Mennonite ethnicity that would cement a secure place for his people on the spectrum of North American pluralism, but also an ethnicity read through a lens that was unabashedly progressive. In nearly all other ways, Smith's latest and last interpretation chimed to the same chords he had been sounding now for forty years. He reiterated his basic reading of Anabaptism as fundamentally individualistic and democratic. This did not mean, he immediately qualified again, that Anabaptists were "religious anarchists" or "indifferent to fundamental beliefs." But they remained congregational to the core, eschewing authoritarianism and merely inviting dissenters to worship elsewhere. He emphatically insisted now on a huge gulf separating the scriptural and sober Anabaptists from the "fanatics" of Münster, though he remained a careful enough historian to put events there in context. Otherwise he reaffirmed the same inclusive reading of Anabaptist leaders that he had maintained now for decades, embracing a set of leaders that ranged from Marpeck and the Swiss Brethren to Denck, Hut, and Hutter.[28]

Smith's 1941 book remained consistent with his previous ones in three other key ways. First, here again lay readers would have thrilled to his heroic depictions of their Mennonite forbears as centuries ahead of other Christians: in their advocacy of civil and religious liberty, their anti-slavery convictions, their commitment to the ways of peace, and their pushing out into new territories as true American pioneers. Second, here again he offered an elaborate statement, though this one more nuanced and self-critical, of a Mennonite usable past. He reiterated his old point that Mennonites did not suffer much for their nonresistance in the autocratic eighteenth-century European states. It is only modern democracies that "are inclined to show little patience with the conscientious scruples of minorities." But he was also capable of regarding his basic reading of Mennonite individualism in a critical way, suggesting that schisms among Dutch Mennonites served as an apt illustration of what could happen when this tendency was "directed by unbalanced leadership."[29]

Finally, as ever, Smith persisted in offering a usable past that was enlightened and progressive. He could not resist, for example, taking another shot at the "extreme emotionalism" of groups like the Mennonite Brethren. While over time they "outlived their earlier fanatical practices," they still remained "easy marks for the more or less fanatical religious movements common among an unstable religious people." As for the MCs, Smith could write about them as he pleased, for Bender was not the editor of this book. He placed them only in a subsection of a chapter on various nineteenth-century Mennonite divisions and let his interpretive hand proceed freely. While highlighting the "enlightenment" these Mennonites owed to "a few far seeing leaders" like Funk and Coffman, and admitting that the "Old Mennonites in the main have adopted a rather progressive program of church activities," they remained, Smith declared, committed to "many of the traditional religious and social practices and customs of by gone [sic] days." Recently a "new doctrine" of nonconformity, almost assuming "the importance of a fundamental tenet of faith," has set in with such rigidity as to "isolate" this Mennonite group "from the rest of the religious world." Yet the passing of such "social taboos," which MC youth were presently demanding, would make it possible for the denomination to enter into a "new alignment into perhaps two or three groups on the real issue of religious liberalism and conservatism rather than on the basis of superficial peculiarities and customs." Once again he wrote in a manner reflecting his commitment to Mennonite unity on the basis of a progressive agenda. Smith divided Mennonites into a tripartite schema of "Conservatives, Liberals and Moderates," though immediately adding that "all are still conservative in their theology, and true to the teaching of Menno Simons." As Toews phrased it, "in Smith's reading, the liberating elements became the main story." Smith's chapter on GC Mennonites, for example, concluded with his familiar solutions. If we want to "preserve what is worthwhile of Mennonitism," he advised, we will need to "overlook insignificant details like the cut of a coat. . . . A united Mennonitism will come with more enlightened church leadership, and that will come from our common colleges and a common theological seminary."[30]

With the economy and Mennonite finances still locked in the Great Depression, by the time Smith began approaching the Berne publishers in 1940, it quickly became clear that he would need to advance them $500 of his own funds to subsidize its publication. Upon the book's appearance a year later, he was jarred by the typographical errors the publishers had allowed, and he doubted, he confessed to his friend John Umble of Goshen's English department, whether many people would buy it. But he was wrong. Smith's book began selling briskly upon its publication. By spring 1942 it had sold well enough to pay off the initial investment, and in late 1944, with only ninety-five copies left from an initial run of a thousand, the Berne house was preparing another printing. Most reviews were overwhelmingly positive. The book received fulsome praise from journals ranging from the *Friends' Intelligencer* and the *Union Seminary Review* to the Mennonite Brethren in Christ organ, the *Gospel Banner*. Melvin Gingerich told readers of the *Mennonite* that Smith's magnum opus "is the book for which those interested in Mennonite history have long been waiting." Even the MC publication the *Christian Monitor*, while thinking that "at least some will deplore the rather condescending attitude" Smith displayed toward their group, still judged that the book "deserves a place in the library of everyone interested in Mennonite history." Smith also received private signals that people in his academic corner appreciated his work. The chair of the GC publications board, not surprisingly, loved it, while several Goshen scholars—Umble, Guy Hershberger, and a new Bender ally and recent European refugee named Robert Friedmann—sent like affirmations.[31]

Goshen scholars would also have other, less positive responses, though they would not emanate from John Horsch. Through the 1930s, Albert Keim summarized, Horsch had resounded with indignation at the unjust peace imposed on Germany at the end of the war, and had "rejoiced at Hitler's success in redressing those grievances." At the same time, he had increasingly struggled with heart trouble. In spring 1940 he suffered a stroke, perhaps triggered by a shocked emotional reaction to Germany's blitzkrieg across Europe and its brutal invasion of the Netherlands. In October 1941 he died, further traumatized by European events and a failing heart.[32]

Thus, by the time Bender began preparing his most direct and central response to Smith's reading of Mennonite history, it was clear that the mantle of leading what historians would later call the "Goshen School" had finally passed to him. "Dr. C. Henry Smith's The Story of the Mennonites is now off the Berne Press," Bender's associate, the young Goshen Bible professor John C. Wenger, wrote him in July 1941. "You got a review copy this morning (for MQR). No pictures, no footnotes, no bibliography," Wenger could see at a glance. "But 800 pages of smooth writing, with Smith carelessness to boot!" Bender and his associates would soon sit down to consider Smith's work carefully. Their review, and Smith's response, would set off what Toews would later call "one of the finer Mennonite historiographical exchanges," in which two alternative readings of Mennonite history and historiography would be laid bare in stark outline. While they would cross scholarly swords on a number of points, fundamentally the debate revolved around a few key matters that Smith and his MC colleagues had been debating now, in one form or another, for decades: whether individualism or "brotherhood" was a basic shaping characteristic of Anabaptist history or current Mennonite faith, and whether the MCs or the GCs were the best carriers of that vision. In addition, Bender and his colleagues would raise a third key issue that penetrated to the heart of Smith's understanding of his craft since his days in grad school: whether strict empiricism was the best intellectual vehicle for producing the kind of history that Mennonites required.[33]

Bender and Correll led off in the October 1942 issue of *MQR* with a jointly authored, keenly detailed, five-page review of Smith's book. They began with paragraphs of high, sincere (and politic) praise. This "dean of American Mennonite historians," working under the handicaps facing any Anabaptist-Mennonite historian—a multitude of necessary languages, inadequate archives scattered over three continents, a minimum of available background monographs—has now produced, they summarized, "probably the crowning volume of his long career, a scholarly, well-written and readable history of the Mennonites, the best, we dare say, which has been written to date in any language." They lauded him for his narrative ability and his capacity to lay out an "objective and fair treatment of various schisms" that produced the different Mennonite groups. Some of their smaller criticisms—typographical errors and misspelled place names, his weak bibliography, sketchy index, and lack of citations—no doubt irked Smith but could not have surprised him. Other critiques devolved more from matters of interpretation, which he likewise knew were coming. Bender and Correll did not care for Smith's broader inclusivity of Anabaptist leaders—his favorable treatment of Denck, for instance, and the "undue space and emphasis" he accorded to Hans Hut, especially contrasted with his comparative neglect of Marpeck. They did not like what seemed to be Smith's prejudicial tone in his descriptions of the emotional piety of some Mennonite groups, nor his dwelling on the "oddities" of the Amish. And they certainly did not appreciate the comparatively short shrift he gave to MC Mennonites, especially his implication that the Mennonite future rested primarily with the GC church. Many people, Bender and Correll maintained, "hold out that the soundest promise" for the Mennonite future lay instead with the moderates Smith described, "with their stronger group solidarity, their greater steadfastness under test, their greater sense of historical tradition, and their stronger resistance to 'worldly' influences."[34]

The heart of the Bender and Correll critique revolved around the inadequacy of Smith's basic reading of Anabaptism. Bender restated a primary objection to Smith's reading of history that he and Horsch had been making since the mid-1920s: his overemphasis of the Anabaptist fidelity to individual conscience and corresponding inattention to their "group solidarity and discipline." He compounded this problem in this book, they argued, by neglecting to adequately explore "basic principles of Anabaptist faith and life," as well as their social ethics. But here Bender pushed this critique even deeper. Smith needed, he and Correll suggested, to "penetrate beneath the surface to the inner life of the group." The charge was vague; both scholars seemed to be struggling themselves for a word or phrase to capture it. The best they could produce was that they thought Smith should do more with "the history of ideas or inner history" of Anabaptism, and should recover "an interpretation of their inward experience and its relation to outward conduct." And it was here, Smith realized as he mulled over the review, they were asking him to go beyond where a properly trained, empiricist historian should go.[35]

Perhaps Kreider's characterization that Smith was "deeply hurt" by the review is an overstatement, but he was clearly rankled. Even the seeming grace of Bender and Correll's closing lines—in which they congratulated "our good friend, Professor Smith," hoping that sales of his book will soon allow "a second and improved edition"—contained, as Keith Sprunger noted, a real barb. Smith was still sputtering with indignation two months later. "I was rather put out [when] I first read Bender's review," he admitted privately to Kaufman that December, "by his cock sureness and dogmatic finality." He suspected the criticism came from plain old intra-Mennonite prejudice. "I have noticed," Smith wrote, "that when they review a book written by a Goshenite or an Old Mennonite they speak of it in highest praise, never even mentioning typographical error or points of view, but they take a special delight in pointing out all the flaws in any book by a non-old Mennonite." He was reminded of Bender's zeal "in tearing apart Dr. Hartzler's book some years ago." By the time Smith finished drafting his official response to Bender and Correll, he was composed and collegial. But in six packed pages of the *MQR*, he left no doubt that he thought them wrong on nearly every count.[36]

Smith found some of the charges easier to rebut than others. He thanked his critics for catching his "minor errors," which were due to "poor proofreading" and "misprints," and which would be easily corrected in the second printing. So would be "several expressions" he had employed with regard to different Mennonite groups, which created an unfortunate impression of some bias on his part. He vigorously

Smith in his Mennonite Historical Library at Bluffton College, 1944. BUASC.

defended his extolling of Denck and inclusion of Hut as Anabaptist leaders, in the process injecting a brief lecture on historical objectivity. "The fact that Hut was not orthodox according to the saner standards of that day or this does not justify the historian in neglecting him," he instructed Bender. "Saint and sinner must both be given their dues in an accurate account of historical events." Neither did he regret the relative way he had treated GC and MC Mennonites, except, he admitted, he wished he had given Bender's branch its own chapter heading. To Smith it seemed a good moment to reiterate the relative importance of the GC church. "The General Conference story," he explained, "is one of new episodes and ventures" among Mennonites. "Introductory new movements and departures demand more space than the main current which runs along the main groove with little unusual to record."[37]

Finally, Smith turned his attention to Bender and Correll's charge that his stress on Anabaptist individualism had somehow overlooked something of their "essence." All he was trying to say, he patiently clarified again, is that "conscience is not a collective matter; but individual." Catholics followed their priests "unconditionally" while "the Mennonite followed his own conscience, his individual conscience." Their demand that historians probe beyond this to some kind of "inner emotional life of the movement," Smith told his two critics, would soon run up against the practical reality "of the paucity of source material on these matters. If one were to indulge very deeply in these realms, he would soon find himself in the field of mere speculation, rather than history, where we would have mere opinion rather than fact."[38]

The Goshen scholars greatly appreciated the exchange. "You may be assured that none of us in any way objects to what you say," Bender wrote Smith privately in October 1943 as Smith's rebuttal appeared, "even though we might enjoy the privilege of debate with you over a few points." Actually, Robert Friedmann informed Smith, Bender liked his book enough to be using it, along with Horsch's last work, in Goshen classes. Friedmann soon took the lead in the entire discussion. He was an interesting character—a Jewish intellectual from Austria, brought to Bender's attention by Horsch, who had come to the Mennonite faith through an academic monograph on the Hutterite movement. Fleeing the Nazis, he had arrived in New York in 1939 with the help of the Quakers. Through correspondence and then a visit, Bender befriended him and in 1940 raised money to bring him to Goshen to organize the new Mennonite historical library. Before long he was corresponding politely with Smith about matters *Mennonitica*. In November 1943, in the same tone of earnest, friendly collegiality, Friedmann sent a long letter to Smith that forecast the points he would make a few months later, with much deeper elaboration, in the pages of *MQR*.[39]

Friedmann's published contribution to the historiographical discussion was at once erudite and deferential, proceeding through a swirl of Anabaptist historiography and history. He reiterated the great contribution of Smith's "excellent history . . . the first Mennonite history of high quality that historians should possess in order to write history." He had two central objections to Smith's reading. There was, he told Bender (in this exchange, both Friedmann and Smith addressed the editor of *MQR*), the old troubling matter of Smith's dogged insistence on the basic individualism of the Mennonites. Friedmann was aghast at Smith's description of the Anabaptist church, which, he quoted, as "merely the fellowship of congenial and like-minded believers." What church does not at least claim to be that? Smith's choice of the adjective *merely*, Friedmann claimed, revealed his shallow understanding of the nature of the church. The Anabaptists saw the church as a great deal more, he declared, a "real brotherhood," an "essential fellowship." That was "the Central [sic] idea of Anabaptism, the real dynamite in the age of Reformation." Moreover, to Friedmann, Smith's failure to grasp that point was indicative of his deeper problems in other areas, like the elusive inner history that Bender and Correll were struggling with, and the core concept of historical objectivity. "Mennonite history," Friedmann asserted, "is not simply another history in which a sympathetic but academic objectivity is all that is required." In fact, the whole empiricist paradigm was flawed, because "no written history can be or ought to be as objective as other sciences are supposed to be." Hence, Smith's "relativistic objectivity" was an inadequate tool for understanding Anabaptist-Mennonite "essentials." To truly grasp the Mennonite past, scholars needed to capture "the deeper spiritual attitudes" for which no English word sufficed, though Friedmann thought the Germans had a term: "the almost untranslatable word *Geistesgeschichte*." The foundational problem with Smith's history, Friedmann reasoned, is that it had too much empiricist focus on the "external depicting of happenings and individuals" and not enough *Geistesgeshichte*.⁴⁰

"I am very much interested in Dr. Friedmann's commentary on the shortcomings of my *Story of the Mennonites*," Smith began his published reply in the same issue of *MQR*. "As to just what those shortcomings are I am not quite sure," he confessed, but they seemed to include, listing Friedmann's charges like a bill of indictment, "too much academic and relativistic objectivity, a lack of religious concern and understanding, too factual . . . the lack of that final spiritual penetration which alone makes history meaningful, the lack of some intangible, indefinable something which the German historians call *Geistesgeshichte* but which American historians have not been able to comprehend and for which there is no suitable word in English." He proceeded in the mode of a senior scholar responding to the bothersome questions of a junior one. His patience seemed taxed, his tone slightly caustic.⁴¹

Since Friedmann objected most centrally to Smith's commitment to empiricism, in his rejoinder Smith addressed the issue directly, furnishing for the first time in many years a window into his understanding of the nature of history. Over the previous decades, the American historical profession had moved some in its understanding of objectivity—and so, Smith revealed here, had he. Before the Great War and accelerating after it, emerging new giants of the American history professoriate like Charles Beard, Carl Becker, and James Harvey Robinson began articulating new philosophies of history (elements of which, decades later, intellectual descendants would refashion into the new thinking of "postmodernism"). There was no basic truth about the past, the new philosophy went, a history "as it really happened" that historians-as-scientists could somehow discover if only they were somehow objective enough. Instead, historians themselves reflected their own times and wrote out of a specific context, producing truths that were only relative to each other. As Crane Brinton, one of these "New Historians," explained in 1939, "the historian can get rid of the incubus of absolutism implied in the 'as it really happened' and accept all the advantages of a frankly relativistic position."⁴²

Up to then, Smith's previous corpus of work had offered scant evidence that he had followed much of this new historiographical turn. In his one bit of writing on "The New History," published under that title for Bluffton alumni in 1932, he grasped that fellow historians had widened their scope beyond the narrow traditional confines of nationalistic, political history and begun to integrate social and economic analyses into their writing. Yet he also described the New Historian as properly wedded to the "scientific attitude of mind" and "just as objective in his quest after truth . . . as the chemist with his test tube"—as if little had changed in historical thinking since his days in graduate school.[43]

In his response to Friedmann, now, a dozen years later, Smith revealed that his understanding of historiography had become more complex. He knew it was inadequate, he told Friedmann, merely to revisit "the bare facts of life of a people" without interpreting them. "Too much objectivity often leaves history dry and bare—bones without meat." Having established this point, Smith immediately moved the other way, warning of "the equal danger of too much subjectivity, which . . . too often degenerates into mere personal opinion without sufficient basis in fact." To him this was, of course, exactly the approach his Goshen colleagues were asking him to take, and why he rejected it so emphatically. Even so, it was clear that his commitment to the "bare facts" had been shaken. The historian, he grasped, must fill facts with meaning. Of course the task was dangerous. "*Geistesgeshichte* is merely often a particular interpretation of fact," he informed Friedmann, "and sometimes a distortion of fact, from a special point of view, and with a definite aim in mind." For a century, both knew, German historians had produced their "political histories from a decidedly nationalistic viewpoint, with results which unfortunately are only too evident to us today." Church histories had been written for hundreds of years from a "church-state point of view," which read Anabaptists solely through the lens of heresy and thereby justified their extermination. The fact that current historians were now viewing Anabaptists as great models of religious toleration did not happen only because these scholars had found new original documents, "but rather because they have changed their original assumptions." The larger point was that all history emerged not as the product of some scientifically achieved objective truth, but as the contextually driven reading of a particular historian.[44]

The matter had potentially revolutionary and explosive implications, which Smith was only beginning to realize. He was aware, he told Friedmann, that "Mennonite history may be written from other viewpoints, and with many objectives," including "regional histories, histories of different branches, histories of persecutions and migrations, doctrinal histories, literary histories," as well as "histories of the changing essence of Mennonitism." In this Smith was not only subtly reflecting a new relativistic framework, but he seemed to be again approaching here what a later generation of Mennonite scholars would, with the breathless thrill of a new discovery, grandly label *polygenesis*. At that point, he employed it for a more practical and immediate end—as the exclamation point to his entire discussion with his Goshen colleagues. "As to the perfect general history as visualized by Dr. Friedmann, covering the whole of Mennonite life and experience," encapsulating "the proper spirit and real essence of Mennonitism through the changing centuries, impartial to all shades of belief," Smith concluded with a flourish, "that history will never be written."[45]

When Smith, late in life, finally began to admit the limits of strict empiricism and to recognize the tenuous and contextually driven nature of historical knowledge, it was a point he seemed to concede only grudgingly. As leveled by Friedmann, the admission by itself seemed to render him guilty of the damning heresy of "relativist objectivity." This has been adeptly summarized by Theron Schlabach as the position in which "historians are conscious of their beginning assumptions and those assumptions' importance, yet apply rigorous rules of evidence and logic so as to end up with conclusions that no fair-minded critic can dismiss as merely conjecture or propaganda to fit an a priori stance." Seventy years later, with the intellectual tenability of a pure objectivity shattered and the radical relativism of extreme postmodernism a beckoning alternative, what in 1948 seemed as Smith's heresy today appears an intellectually respectable way forward.[46]

Bender's most direct response to Smith came in late December 1943, when he stood up at in front of a group of scholars assembled in the Men's Faculty Club at Columbia University and read his presidential address to the American Society of Church History. He titled it "The Anabaptist Vision." Anabaptism, he told the church historians, could be understood as devolving from three central teachings. First, the Anabaptists treasured a life of discipleship patterned on the example of Christ. Second, they saw the church as a true community of believers expressing an absolute nonconformity to worldly ways. Finally, central to Anabaptist practice was "the ethic of love and nonresistance as applied to all human relationships." Mennonite historians have devoted a substantial amount of attention to Bender's statement, mounting entire academic conferences on it and analyzing it from nearly every possible angle. Fewer have grasped that, among its other purposes, in his piece Bender was also continuing the conversation with his intellectual sparring partner C. Henry Smith. Not that he was quick to admit it. In a paper that furrowed deeply into Anabaptist historiography, he cited Smith exactly once, referring to his 1941 *The Story of the Mennonites* in a general, overview reference on the extant literature. Yet the paper appeared in the same *MQR* issue as the Friedmann-Smith discussion of historiography; as Keim noted, Bender almost certainly had Smith's lengthy rejoinder to his critique of *The Story of the Mennonites* in front of him as he developed his argument.[47]

Throughout his piece, Bender further developed his critique of Smith's historiography. He once again refuted, for instance, Smith's inclusive reading of Anabaptist founders. Reiterating an argument that he and especially Horsch had been developing for almost two decades, he now fastened into Mennonite consciousness a historical reading of the Swiss-South German Anabaptists as the original and normative Anabaptists. In like manner, Bender's insistence of the essential "brotherhood" commitments of these original Anabaptists functioned as a clear antidote to Smith's depictions of their basic individualism. His treatment of Smith's basic progressivism was more ambiguous. On the one hand, Gerald Mast argues, Bender's statement proceeded in a basic "progressive plot" that, in true Smithian manner, lauded Anabaptism as an advance guard of the spread of enlightenment concepts like religious toleration and democracy. On the other hand, Bender emphatically rejected the kind of heightened social and political engagement that Smith drew from this recognition, calling Mennonites instead to witness to their society through the creation of a markedly different but definably Christian social order. Finally, in the same *MQR* issue in which his colleague Friedmann critiqued Smith so centrally for overlooking the inner Anabaptist essence, Bender deepened the critique with an extensive development of the concept of Anabaptist discipleship. As important as it was, merely recognizing "the Anabaptist contribution to the development of religious liberty," he said, "fails to define the true essence of Anabaptism. In the last analysis, freedom of religion is a purely formal concept, barren of content; it says nothing about the faith." Given the contours of Bender's current conversation with Smith, to whom could such lines be directed other than Smith?[48]

Bender tried to continue the discussion in private correspondence, though there is no evidence Smith responded. When Smith's *The Story of the Mennonites* came up for a reprint in 1945, the only change he made was to split off his section on "The Old Mennonites" into a separate chapter and add an extensive, concluding footnote on the CPS system and the record of Mennonite objectors in the current "suicidal global war." Perhaps Smith merely felt the discussion had run its course. There were also other matters demanding his attention: his advancing age, for example, and the need to find a way into retirement. There was also a commitment he felt, old age or no, to help his Mennonite people find their way through the war's end and the approach of an exhausted peace.[49]

Retirement, the *Mennonite Encyclopedia*, and the "Final Mennonite History"

As the war drew to its close in cataclysmic violence, Smith kept up his schedule of part-time teaching, part-time banking, and as much activism as he could manage. He and Smucker kept on doggedly with their MDC peace committee work, pushing congregations for donations to CPS and calling conference pastors to exert themselves against peacetime conscription proposals. More rewarding was an opportunity to again serve, along with Smucker and also now Bender, as Mennonite delegates to the culminating conference of the Commission for a Just and Durable Peace. With Allied armies now pulling closer to Germany, the FCC commission wanted to reinforce an internationalist outlook among American churches. This was becoming an especially pressing concern in light of proposals for the creation of a new international agency (ultimately the United Nations) that had emerged in autumn 1944 from a gathering of international representatives at the Dumbarton Oaks mansion in Washington, D.C. In January 1945 Smith and the Mennonite group joined another 450 influential Protestant delegates in Cleveland, with Dulles again chairing, for three more days of intensive discussion. In the end, they produced an official report,

"Message to the Churches," that laid out a variety of recommendations for a Christian peace in the postwar world similar to those produced by the Delaware meeting three years before, but now specifically including church support for the emerging new United Nations. As at the Delaware meeting, much of the real debate at the conference was sparked by a minority of pacifist delegates—"idealists," Smith called them, and he was one—who took their cues from Quaker leader E. Stanley Jones. None of the delegates endorsed the Dumbarton Oaks proposals without reservation, but these "idealist" pacifists were especially critical. Smith encapsulated their objections in his report on the conference to GC president C. E. Krehbiel. "Dumbarton Oaks is a step in the right direction and we should go along with it," he advised, "but it needs a good many improvements, especially in the direction of a wider democracy. . . . The present proposal is nothing more than a power alliance of the big three powers so organized as to give these powers the right to dominate all the rest."[50]

With the approach of peace seeming to free up the local political climate, Smith again seized opportunities to insert his Mennonite take on these and other matters into area public discussion. As the Germany war effort collapsed in April 1945, he reminded the Lima Ministerial Association that their supreme loyalty lay with Christ instead of the state, and urged them to educate the public for non-vindictive peace. He pushed a group of Presbyterians in nearby Ada, Ohio, to support the new UN, work toward universal disarmament, and raise their voices against early proposals for universal military training. Some of his subpoints suggested that his own vision of Christian social concerns had expanded in necessary ways. While undoubtedly also a product of his years of reading and rethinking, after the Durable Peace conferences Smith began to tell audiences that among the agenda items in "a wise Christian peace" was doing away with racial discrimination. He also began speculating publicly about the kinds of international developments coming in the postwar world. Previously he had proved himself a haphazard prophet but now anticipated some ensuing developments with remarkable prescience. Looking ahead to the coming peace in 1944, Smith told an audience in Ottawa, Ohio, that "it won't be a better world" and that certainly it would be a poorer one. Already by spring 1944 he forecast to the Lima Torch Club that the postwar

Soviet Union "will dominate the peace table" and "will get what she wants," namely, the international boundaries that had existed before 1914 and now a row of "friendly buffer states." In July 1945 he was more specific, suggesting to the group that Russia would soon enter the war against Japan and that an age of Russian empire was approaching (maybe someday, he thought, a Chinese one, too). Casting his eyes around the world, Smith saw the British Empire in clear decline, the Italian one finished, and France afraid of losing its colonies, particularly in Indo-China.[51]

For Smith personally, the end of the war and the ensuing increase in Bluffton student enrollment numbers must have accelerated his thinking about retirement. He had already been working it through, signaling to Ramseyer in early 1944 he would happily step down as soon as the college located a "suitable replacement." Ramseyer quickly identified this person as Robert Kreider, then still in CPS administration, and began pushing the young man for a commitment to Bluffton before he had even begun his doctoral studies. Meanwhile, one more interesting opportunity came Smith's way. Beginning in 1940, when the old Witmarsum Seminary board agreed to relinquish its institutional existence to a new GC one, the prospects for a Mennonite seminary had begun to stir once again. Momentum built steadily through the war years, pushed by Bethel's Kaufman. By summer 1945, a new Mennonite Biblical Seminary had been created, affiliated with a Church of the Brethren seminary in Chicago, and eighteen students stood ready to begin classes. That August its first president, Abraham Warkentin, contacted Smith, asking if he would be interested in commuting up to Chicago for six weeks that fall to give the seminarians a short course in Mennonite history. Of course he squeezed it in. Given all that Smith had been saying across the church for the past fifteen years, it is hard to imagine something that would have delighted him more. Even so, Smith's energy for teaching seemed to be ebbing. First-year student Burton Yost took Mennonite history under him back on campus that academic year and recalled him being "quite relaxed," mostly sitting at a table along with the students, getting up now and then to write something on the board, not lecturing much but instead just engaging students in discussion of his *The Story of the Mennonites*. Sometime late in the spring 1946 semester, Smith told colleagues he was through.[52]

Faculty and students at the new Mennonite Biblical Seminary in Chicago, 1945. Smith seated, front row, second from right. BUASC.

In early June 1946, on Smith's seventy-first birthday, he and Laura headed into the college library, ostensibly for a meeting, where they were surprised by a collection of Bluffton College faculty and friends from the bank who threw a combination birthday and retirement party for the old professor. Letters of appreciation came in from former students now launched into various careers. Some were teaching high school or college; one was serving as the dean of men at Bucknell. Yet all wanted to thank Smith for what he had meant in their lives. "Really, you will never retire," one wrote. "Your influence and teaching will be as endless as the American diplomacy you spoke of, and never so devious." For its part, the college bestowed emeritus status and, a year later, in its June 1947 commencement exercises, awarded both Smith and Byers honorary doctorates. Smith tried to downplay the fuss. In a letter to J. C. Meyer, an old comrade in the Young People's movement a quarter century before, he grew wistfully introspective. "As I look over the past years," he reflected, "I have been convinced that one should have only one chief interest in his life work. I made the mistake some years ago in adding business to my interests, and so in dividing my activities I became neither an outstanding teacher nor a brilliant banker, but mediocre in both fields." While admitting that one could learn a great deal from practical experience outside of academia, "if I were to live my life over again," he confessed to Meyer, "I would cut out all the business connections and stick to my subject and perhaps I might have gotten somewhere."[53]

Smith soon discovered that he did not know quite how to retire. He had no hobbies or grandchildren with which to occupy himself. "Retirement" soon came to mean cutting back his teaching to a single annual class on Mennonite history, perhaps spending less time at the bank, and keeping at his familiar activities. He agreed to serve as a coeditor of a new magazine, *Mennonite Life*, which had been started at Bethel by their new historian, a former refugee from Ukraine named Cornelius Krahn. Periodically through the war years, Smith had been investigating one or another aspect of his hometown history and writing up little sketches for the *Metamora Herald*. In 1947 he paid the college bookstore to print them up in a little pamphlet. At war's end the GC Peace Committee asked him to contribute a chapter on the history of the Mennonite peace position to a new study manual on nonresistance they were developing for use in youth Sunday school classes. Smith readily agreed, and two years later was sending out the booklet, *The Power of Love*, to MDC ministers, urging them to get it in front of their youth. But the major focus for Smith's energy in these immediate postwar years was a project that emanated from a casual conversation with fellow scholars over lunch, led directly to the creation of a small "guild" of like-minded colleagues, and then quickly ballooned into a huge undertaking. This was the *Mennonite Encyclopedia*.[54]

The momentum began in late December 1944 at the American Historical Association's annual meeting in Chicago when Smith, along with Fretz and Gingerich, met for lunch with Bender and Hershberger, who were attending the concurrent meetings of the American Society of Church History. The conversation naturally turned to their mutual interest in Mennonite scholarship. The five professors "shared notes," Keim summarized, "and the chemistry between them must have been creative." They agreed to call a selected circle of like-minded colleagues to a meeting in Bluffton the following summer. In the meantime Bender and Fretz would produce a blueprint for a new organization called the Mennonite Scholars Guild. The selection of Bluffton for its inaugural meeting surely was a sign of deference to Smith. So was his immediate election as president of the new group, renamed the Mennonite Research Fellowship, when they reassembled in August 1945 in the Walnut Grill Room of the Pine Restaurant, along Main Street in Bluffton.[55]

Smith's title and new position aside, to some degree the gathering represented a generational transition in Mennonite studies that was clearly underway. Except for Smith, all others present were younger or middle-aged men. Bender, Hershberger, Wenger, Umble, and Sanford Yoder came from Goshen, along with Friedmann, who had landed a faculty job in Michigan. Bethel sent Kaufman, Warkentin, Gingerich, Fretz, and Krahn. Yet all stood positioned to benefit from the fresh new possibilities of Mennonite ecumenicity that had emanated from such shared wartime ventures like CPS. The new body, they decided, would be open to anyone with a membership in a Mennonite congregation who held at least a master's degree and "cordial loyalty" to Mennonite principles. It was not a social club, but instead would be "an intimate fellowship of Mennonite research men who have demonstrated their ability." Though not intentionally, it was also apparent, given the gendered language they used, that this fellowship would be an all-male guild, reflecting the fact that the field of Mennonite studies in the mid-century decades was the near-exclusive purview of male scholars. The first project that this self-styled "fellowship of craftsmen" would tackle, they decided, would be something that Smith and Bender began discussing within days of that creative lunch meeting in Chicago. They needed to help German Mennonites complete their long-delayed *Lexikon*, which had languished during the 1930s and the war. At the meeting in Bluffton in August, the new group appointed a subcommittee, including Smith, to investigate the state of the project in Europe and the possibly of issuing an American edition.[56]

In this manner Smith quickly became drawn into a huge, consuming project. Once the committee looked into the state of the *Lexikon*, they quickly realized that the project involved much more than what Smith had originally envisioned, merely a translation of the German volumes into English. The data in the *Lexikon* by now was too outdated, and its treatment of North American Mennonites was much too shallow. Doing the project well would require a huge amount of new writing and a deep investment of their pooled resources, as well as a new name, the *Mennonite Encyclopedia*. Smith began working quite collaboratively and closely with Bender, who appreciated, he told the committee, Smith's abundant enthusiasm for the project and the way he prodded the rest of them to get going with the revisions. (Smith was, admittedly, the only one among them who no longer had a full-time job). But they made steady progress regardless: in December 1945 in Chicago, where they began considering matters like editors, individual writers, and possible topics; then in March 1946 in Kansas City, where they created an interim editorial board of eight scholars and appointed Smith and Bender as coeditors. Bender managed to pull the various Mennonite publishing houses together into a joint publishing committee. Then, while in Europe in September 1946, he negotiated with German Mennonites for full American rights. As a key leader in the project, Smith found himself on the road a fair bit too, repeatedly boarding trains from Bluffton-area depots for meetings in Goshen, Chicago, Kansas City, and Newton, Kansas. The entire process incurred delicate maneuverings in the nascent new frontiers of Mennonite ecumenicity. With Bender away in Europe with MCC in 1946-47 and Smith left in charge, Wenger wrote Bender a private letter expressing his concern over Smith's pushing for more writers from the General Conference. Yet by January 1948, the committee had finalized its editorial board, with Smith and Bender now as official coeditors, and had established an editorial council with representatives from thirteen different Mennonite groups.[57]

Smith at Bluffton College May Day festivities, 1947. BUASC.

In the meantime Smith kept up diligently with his ongoing commitments, the most prominent of which was his 1947 presidential address, "The Final Mennonite History," to the new Mennonite Research

Fellowship. The fact that he began by underscoring to his listeners that he meant his title as ironic by itself spoke to the increasing complexity of his historiographical worldview. By it, he told his audience, he did not mean to suggest he had "in mind the last final word in the field of Mennonite history." He knew that "historical evolution is a continuing and never ending process" and that "the final history in this sense will never be written." He only meant to explore, he explained, the ongoing work in the field. In the first part of the address, delivered to the fellowship at Goshen, he surveyed the present state of the field, noting the need for a variety of new work: regional and local Mennonite histories, studies of different groups, more biographies of key leaders, and especially more work in the "cultural field." Nodding at Friedmann, who was engaged in a thorough study of Mennonite devotional writing, he conceded that "the devotional literature opens up a fruitful field of study, very essential for an understanding of the real spirit and development of the Mennonite movement." Smith framed a central question for the second part of his address. "Having all the essential facts placed at his disposal by the specialists," he wondered, "what are some of the problems facing the final historian who attempts to put these facts together and interpret them in a final general history of the whole[?]" In this manner he returned explicitly to his historiographical debate with Bender and others four years earlier in the pages of *MQR*, even quoting part of his rebuttal at length. While admitting his suspicion of "the philosopher turned historian," he plainly could no longer retain a commitment to pure empiricism, and he struggled to find an intellectually acceptable way forward beyond it. A final Mennonite history, "covering the whole field of Mennonitism," Smith thought, "must be objective and thoroughly impartial as to the different branches." At the same time, he noted it should without question reflect a legitimate bias toward the historic doctrines that all groups shared. "That much of propaganda and subjectivity I would regard as permissible," he allowed. Then, almost as if the admission unnerved him, he tacked quickly back in the opposite direction, offering that "objectivity may be carried too far; but so may subjectivity. Mere opinion should never be substituted for plain fact." These were tough intellectual issues about which Smith could not see his way clear, and with which he wrestled to the end of his days.[58]

Smith had spent his adult life busily constructing a usable past for his people, and in 1947 he received a thrilling indication of the practical difference it could make now in the real world. It had to do with yet one more brutal chapter in the ongoing tragedy of the Russian Mennonites. As German armies began their retreat from Ukraine in 1943, some 35,000 remaining Mennonites, most of whom had greeted the German soldiers as liberators from Soviet oppression, retreated westward with them. Hundreds died along the way from hunger or caught in the crossfire between the armies. At the end of the war, Soviet authorities insisted on repatriating most of the survivors (about 22,000) and promptly "resettled" them in Siberia. But by 1946–47, MCC staffers in Europe succeeded in prying loose smaller groups of these refugees, ultimately totaling about 10,000, for a happier future in Paraguay, one of the few countries that would admit them. A key question revolved around their ultimate national origins. If these refugees were classified as Germanic, then international authorities would not permit their escape into the West. If MCC could prove, however, that they really were of Dutch extraction, Soviet arguments carried less weight. In 1947, the question focused on a group of Ukrainian Mennonite refugees housed on a Dutch ship MCC had chartered, the *Volendam*, plus another thousand or so trapped in Berlin waiting permission to board it. Bender, Krahn, and a young MCC staffer (and former student of Smith's) named William T. Snyder prepared an extensive brief trying to establish the Dutch national origins of these refugees. The brief quoted extensively from Smith's books, among other sources, as evidence, and included his *The Coming of the Russian Mennonites* as an attachment. At one point in the small drama Smith telegraphed Goshen with more evidence, and Bender hand-delivered the brief to a U.S. State Department official with whom he had been working. Shortly afterward the State Department accepted these arguments, and the *Volendam*, with the thousand additional refugees from Berlin now aboard, sailed for the West. Bender could only think of a biblical metaphor. "The Lord changed the heart of Pharaoh," he exulted to Correll.[59]

In late February 1948, Smith's old friend and traveling companion John E. Hartzler, now teaching at Hartford Seminary, wrote in his congenial, breezy style to impulsively lay out a proposal. "Say, C. Henry," Hartzler inquired, "in all seriousness, what you say, you and I go to Holland and western Europe this summer? What you say?" But for Smith there would be no more European trips. His uncle Henry, Willard Smith recalled, was not the sort of person who dwelled much on his health, and even close friends and relatives received just a few guarded references. In a letter to his sister Ella in July, for instance, Smith touched briefly on health matters, mostly concerning Laura, who "is fairly well just now. But we can never tell just how long it will last." As for himself, Smith casually acknowledged to Ella that "I am feeling my years somewhat. I had an operation several months ago and am getting along fairly well." Such little admissions, however, were masks. In reality Smith was quite ill. The operation he mentioned, in late fall 1947, was in conjunction with a deepening cancer of the prostate. Smith seems to have told no one; for much of his illness he kept it even from Laura. But quietly he began pulling his affairs together. It was only in retrospect, Willard wrote later, that people close to him grasped "the significance of the detailed preparations he had made."[60]

Through much of 1948, Smith plowed ahead, checking things off his little to-do lists as if nothing had changed. In May he wrapped up yet one more Bluffton College class on Mennonite history. He continued his pursuit of the details of Mennonite history, mailing inquiries to various scholars about extinct GC congregations in Ohio. He lent his energies to Bluffton in what ways seemed to be needed. Ramseyer remained in hot pursuit of Kreider as Smith's replacement, informing the young grad student that "Dr. Smith is very anxious that we find someone who can take over with Mennonite history where he has left off. Our invitation to you to join the history faculty has his whole hearted [sic] and enthusiastic approval." Smith sent Kreider a follow-up note echoing Ramseyer's pleas. In August he penned a letter to Kaufman to ask why no Bluffton faculty had appeared on the program of a recent academic conference Bethel had hosted. He maintained his banking interests, remaining president of Citizens National Bank up to the day of his death.[61]

On the other hand, Willard Smith was right: hindsight revealed the thorough manner in which Smith prepared for his coming end. He resigned from the GC historical committee. He prepared his personal papers for archiving, a task that involved, among others, going through his speech outlines and scribbling on most of them the location, audience, and an approximate date. (There was, for example, this telling notation, at the top of an address entitled "What is wrong with England?": "Chapel—May 19, 1948. Perhaps the last time.") He worked away steadily at the sixteen articles he had been assigned for the *Mennonite Encyclopedia*. At some point Smith updated his will, an interesting document that reveals his clear desire to perpetuate his priorities. After providing abundantly for Laura and leaving $1,000 to his brother Sam and $300 each to his twenty-one nieces and nephews (about $12,000 and $3,000, respectively, in 2013 dollars), the will created the "C. Henry Smith Charitable Foundation," which would direct funds into a variety of core Smith concerns. It would have a lot of money to work with: upward of $70,000 (over $830,000 today), "the largest Bluffton estate ever devoted to philanthropic commitments," one area newspaper summarized when the will was later admitted to the probate court in Lima. Smith's foundation provided scholarship money for all the descendants of his parents to attend either Bluffton or Goshen Colleges. It directed funds toward the purchase of books and manuscripts for the Smith collection at Musselman Library and to permanently endow the peace oratory contest at the five American Mennonite colleges. Interest accrued in 1960, Smith stipulated, would be directed toward the publication of his autobiography, entitled *The Education of a Mennonite Country Boy*. The rest of the fund's resources would be allocated by a board of directors (one of which would be Laura, as long as she lived), toward the ever-necessary task of education as peace socialization, expressed in the "dissemination among the Mennonite colleges and churches . . . of the traditional non-resistant peace doctrines as taught by the Mennonite church."[62]

Finally, as his illness deepened, Smith had one more major item on his agenda: to ensure that his reading—or, at least, a GC reading—of the Mennonite story would continue after his death. He had lived his adult life in a time of a deep gulf between different branches of the church. This divide was reflected in, and also perhaps in part propelled by, the different ways these groups constructed their pasts. He had been working agreeably and fruitfully with Bender, but he was still of no mind to surrender to him the construction of an overarching Mennonite history. This "will be the case," he warned Krahn in April 1948, "if Bender ever finished the proposed general history now proposed by the

Old Mennonites." Smith laid out two options. One would simply be for Krahn or Melvin Gingerich to write a "suitable college text for our schools." The other possibility Smith envisioned (though not necessarily preferable, he stated clearly) would be for Krahn to rework his *The Story of the Mennonites*. The revisions he suggested revealed his basic agreement with many of the criticisms had he had received from his Goshen colleagues during the war. Besides bringing the entire story up to date with ensuing developments, they included "a somewhat lengthier treatment of the Old Mennonites," a "longer and revised treatise on the Mennonite Brethren," and "perhaps more mention of the devotional literature," which was probably how he meant to speak to some kind of inner Anabaptist essence. Either way, Smith reinforced to Krahn, they cannot "allow the Old Mennonites to write the text for our schools, which undoubtedly they will do, especially if there is no other text."[63]

As his illness worsened, Smith put on a brave front, but close friends knew the hard truth. At one point in these last months, Bluffton College choir director Russell Lantz and his wife, Mabel, neighbors from two doors down, stopped by the Smith home to lend their support. In the midst of the visit, Laura recalled fourteen years later, Lantz suddenly "broke down and cried and sobbed." Mabel told him to pull himself together. "'Now Russ,' she scolded, 'we came over to help Mrs. Smith and you act like that.'" Smith kept pushing himself. Sometime in September he mailed off the last of his *Mennonite Encyclopedia* articles, and on September 14 he drove out to Pandora to attend a shareholders' meeting at First National Bank, which he and Bible professor Jasper Huffman had founded thirty years before.[64]

Late in September Smith invited Ramseyer and the college librarian over to the Mennonite historical library at Musselman and walked them through his collection of books and papers. Ramseyer suggested to Kreider that "something unusual" was in Smith's mind, for it seemed as if he was delivering "what seemed to be final instructions concerning the upkeep of the library." He thought about it briefly, but when the old professor entered the hospital a few days later, Ramseyer wondered if Smith had somehow known "he would not be with us long." A surgery in early October revealed that the cancer had metastasized dramatically. Then it was only a matter of time. On October 17, propped up in his bed at Lima Memorial Hospital, Smith scrawled his last letter. It was to the GC board of publications to deal with two more pressing items of business. Smith seemed confused about the grim state of his health. He suggested to the board the names of a couple of men who might serve to replace him on an interim basis since, he estimated, with his recent operation it would probably be six months before he could resume service. More importantly he asked the board to give Krahn full authorization to revise his *The Story of the Mennonites*. About dusk the next day he suffered a massive, sudden heart attack. Over his lifetime the old professor had written a million words and had traveled untold thousands of miles, but it was at that point he found his final road home.[65]

The funeral was held a few days later in the sanctuary of First Mennonite Church. Pastor Jesse Smucker officiated ably, Lantz brought the college choir over for a hymn, but the most interesting words came from Bender. Smith meant a great many things to all of them, he summarized to the crowd, "a fine teacher, a noble scholar, a gifted writer." He lingered on two of Smith's characteristics in particular. Of course we remember him, he said, as a "cherished friend." The memories of Smith he evoked in illustration—their time together at the Mennonite World Conference, their "hours of happy historical shoptalk"—left no doubt he was clearly speaking quite personally here. But Bender focused the heart of his comments on Smith as a scholar. "Dr. Smith," he declared, "was unquestionably the greatest of the historians produced by the Mennonites of America." Bender's elaboration of the point spoke volumes to the struggles that had consumed Smith's adult life. For half a century, Smith had devoted his best efforts into the construction of a usable past for his Mennonite people. Given what was occurring in the Mennonite world of his time, and how central history became to Mennonite self-definition, the writing of their history would transpire on an increasingly contested intellectual terrain. Bender was an honest enough historian at least to allude to it. "To us as younger Mennonite historians he will remain a challenge to complete objectivity," he admitted. Smith had, moreover, been a "valiant fighter," he said, for "the best in our Mennonite heritage, particularly for our testimony of peace and nonresistance" and also for "a better understanding and eventual reunion of all our divided Mennonite brotherhood." Filing out of the church, the crowd carried Smith's body to Maple Grove Cemetery, just west of town on the Columbus Grove road, and laid it to rest along faculty row, near the graves of Samuel Mosiman and Jacob Quiring, and almost within sight of the college library.[66]

One by one, over the ensuing decade or two, nearly all of Smith's peers in that founding generation of "Mennonite educational pioneers" would make their way along the same path: Byers in 1962, Hartzler the next year, Paul Whitmer in 1966. Laura would live on for yet another quarter century after Smith's death, appearing to the neighborhood as the friendly old widow at 303 Campus Drive. She and Mrs. Hauenstein (who bought the Byers house next door) would laugh and clap, Richard Weaver remembered, at the visits and little theatrical performances neighborhood kids mounted for them. But behind closed doors she battled her depression, at one point undergoing electroshock therapy, and became increasingly isolated as the years wore on. Until home economics professor Edna Ramseyer moved to Kansas in 1965, she visited Laura almost daily, and faculty spouses also looked after her. One of them, Alice Ruth Ramseyer remembered, visited her one day and opened her refrigerator to find it containing little more than a box of chocolates. "I do have some good friends," she assured Smith's sister Ella in 1967, but sometimes could not help letting her mind run back toward the past. "Do you realize," Laura wrote, "Henry has been gone 19 years—Oct. 18—that is a long time to live alone—and now I do not feel too well." Sometime early in the next decade, she was no longer able to manage on her own, and kinfolk came out from Illinois to help her move into the Mennonite Memorial Home on the other side of campus. In 1973, at the age ninety-two, her frail health finally gave out, and the remaining Ioders buried her next to her spouse at the cemetery west of town.[67]

There remained one more chapter to be written in the drama of these human lives, and it would be an ongoing one. Smith and his academic cohort left their earthly legacy in the hands of individuals they would have surely judged as the most appropriate imaginable. They passed it, of course, into the care of the historians.

12
Epilogue

For decades after Smith's death, a firm scholarly consensus developed holding that Bender's Anabaptist Vision had won the day. It emerged rapidly into, as Sawatsky summarized, "the trade name for twentieth century Mennonite self-definition." Not only did MC Mennonites embrace the statement, the scholarly consensus holds, the GCs ultimately did as well, though not without resistance. Through the 1950s, Bethel's Kaufman continued to advance Smith's progressive reading of Anabaptism. So did Krahn, in his work editing *Mennonite Life*, and particularly in his appointment as Smith's successor as associate editor—not, Bender insisted, as coeditor—of the *Mennonite Encyclopedia*. Krahn pushed hard for equal coverage of GC matters in the project and especially butted heads with Bender on whether to call his group The Mennonite Church, with the clear, pejorative implication that all other Mennonite bodies were mere derivations, if not deviations, from this mother church. (On this issue as others, Krahn lost.) In the end, however, the consensus continues, GC Mennonites realized the spiritual poverty of the optimistic liberal pacifism promulgated by Smith. Most of them quickly came to affirm Bender's reading as an attractive middle path between it and a dogmatic fundamentalism. In this manner, with both liberal and conservative options discredited, Bender's Anabaptist Vision came to serve, in Toews's phrasing, as the great "identifying incantation for North American Mennonites."[1]

This argument is persuasive on many levels. Bender's statement was rapidly published, reprinted, and reread across the Mennonite landscape.[2] The fact that nearly three-quarters of GC draftees during the war disregarded their church's ancient teaching of nonresistance did suggest that a reliance on "individual conscience" alone was a losing strategy, and even some younger GC progressives admitted to the spiritual and intellectual attractions of Bender's history. Yet like most neat and tidy generalities, this one can be questioned, in this case through the complexities presented by Smith's life and thought.[3]

The claim, for example, that GC Mennonites embraced Bender's vision because of the perceived inadequacies of Smith's naive liberal optimism proceeds under the erroneous assumption that his thought remained static, frozen in place circa 1915. Moreover, the intellectual dominance of the Goshen school would itself be challenged and overthrown. The revisionists came in successive waves from the 1960s on. Important and sweeping changes in Mennonite studies were brought by James Stayer and his colleagues, who convincingly demonstrated that Anabaptism emerged simultaneously in at least three different centers across Reformation Europe, and thus largely put to rest the Horsch-Bender monogenesis founding myth of Swiss Brethren origins. In this manner they recovered a pluralistic understanding of Anabaptist origins that Smith (and for that matter, John Horsch as well, before he became born again) had articulated sixty years before.[4]

Most importantly, the version of the Anabaptist-Mennonite past that Smith had spent his adult life constructing did not suddenly just vanish into some kind of scholarly black hole. Rodney Sawatsky was a superb and insightful scholar. But when he doubted that "Mennonites, especially after World War II, were even aware of an alternative" understanding of their past other "than that emanating from Goshen," he was simply mistaken. Smith's history endured for many of the same reasons that had propelled its popularity in the first place: it offered Mennonites a well-written, compelling narrative synthesis of their past that performed the same function of inclusion and legitimation for them that it had for the past half century. Of course *The Story of the Mennonites* changed with the times. Krahn followed the instructions Smith had given him in his last months and adjusted it accordingly. In the third edition in 1950, Krahn updated the story to include the complexities of the World War II years and immediately afterward. He also added a much-needed bibliography. A fourth edition in 1957 saw fewer revisions, but spoke to student needs with the welcome addition of some illustrations and maps. In 1981 Krahn, by then emeritus professor at Bethel, came out with a fifth edition so extensively revised it became, in Keith Sprunger's words, "a hybrid, partly Smith, partly Krahn"—exactly as Smith seems to have anticipated. Not only did Krahn update the narrative further in light of the continued unfolding of events, he began to slightly change its tone and emphasis. Writing in an era when polygenesis explanations of Anabaptist origins had taken hold, Krahn's reading pushed the pluralist understanding beyond what even Smith had dared, including people like Müntzer, Matthys, and Claas Epp back in the Mennonite family. He subtly downplayed Smith's stress on Anabaptist individualism and likewise eased away from his depiction of Mennonite history as a linear march of progress toward a more enlightened, educated future.[5]

Even with these changes, Smith's voice continued to be heard past the end of the twentieth century. His worries to the contrary, MC Mennonites never did produce a competing book. Admittedly, by the time Krahn produced the fifth edition, another introductory volume to Mennonite history had become available. Edited by Cornelius Dyck, a GC Mennonite born in Ukraine, it incorporated the new consensus on the pluralist origins of Anabaptism. It was also an ecumenical effort, with six of twenty-two chapters written by MC scholars and the rest produced by Dyck or other scholars of the GC or Mennonite Brethren traditions. Meanwhile, Smith's text continued to influence Mennonite historical thinking. In the early 1980s it remained, commented one reviewer of Krahn's fifth edition, "the most comprehensive survey of Mennonite history." For long decades it functioned as the standard vehicle through which students in hundreds of Mennonite history classes absorbed the topic, both in Mennonite colleges and many of the new Mennonite high schools emerging in the postwar years. The experience of one such student probably speaks for thousands of others. When John Kampen arrived at the high school academy at Rosthern Junior College on the plains of Saskatchewan in the early 1960s, he recalled, it was through *The Story of the Mennonites* that he learned of his church's past. He responded well, Kampen said, to Smith's book: "it certainly gave me a progressive view of Mennonite history." He never even read Bender until years later at the Mennonite seminary in Elkhart. When Sprunger looked into the matter of Smith book sales in the mid-1990s, Faith & Life Press in Newton (successor to the Berne publishing house) reported total sales of Smith's *The Story of the Mennonites* at 8,300, with hundreds of copies still selling every year and extensive orders coming in "for classroom use in Canada." The book is still in print, available now through Wipf and Stock Publishers in Oregon.[6]

Smith's legacy endures, however, in more ways than just his last book. It was evident in the broad sweep of his life. There is, for one, his decades of service as one of the prime levers towards Mennonite union. The books he produced, so doggedly inclusive of Mennonites from a variety of different historical trajectories, by themselves advanced the cause of Mennonite ecumenicity. As an Amish Mennonite from Swiss-South German origins, Smith produced some of the first extensive historical literature in English on the Dutch-Russian Mennonite stream, prodding their descendants on the Great Plains to begin to recapture their Russian immigrant story. The more explicit Mennonite union movement failed to deliver on its promise, at least immediately. Any Mennonite association largely boycotted by conservatives could hardly claim the name "All-Mennonite." In Smith's article on the "All-Mennonite Convention" for the *Mennonite Encyclopedia*, he acknowledged that no new meetings occurred after 1936. From a Bluffton perspective, with a majority of the smaller Mennonite bodies having removed their affiliation with the college because of "modernism" suspicions, the great hopes for the college as an embodiment of Mennonite unity had clearly faded. The union movement of 1913, Ramseyer bluntly informed the Bluffton College trustees in 1944, was dead. On the other hand, even as its demise seemed apparent, inter-Mennonite cooperation was springing up anew, as Smith also noted in his *Encyclopedia* article, in areas like shared work in peace and famine relief. Such efforts would dramatically intensify during the war in the joint venture of CPS, and the service ethic resulting from the war would propel yet more ecumenical Mennonite cooperative efforts: Mennonite Voluntary Service, Mennonite Disaster Service, Mennonite Mental Health Service, and a shared seminary. These accelerated patterns of inter-Mennonite cooperation would finally culminate, half a century later, in a development which in Smith's era would have been unthinkable: the integration of the MC and GC church bodies. One can only wonder if such a trajectory would have unfolded like it did without the persistent efforts of pioneers like Smith, who kept the vision of

Mennonite unity alive through decades of cultural fragmentation and theologically driven distrust.⁷

Second, Smith modeled for his people the role that an engaged, Mennonite public intellectual could play. As a twenty-year-old schoolteacher in rural Illinois, sending off wandering little essays to M. S. Steiner's *Young People's Paper*, he began to realize something of the excitement of wielding a public voice, a practice that grew in power and influence as his career and confidence developed. He discovered that his position as a Goshen professor afforded him a useful platform to speak to the multitude of social concerns that permeated his consciousness at the height of the Progressive Era. For long decades in a parallel position at Bluffton, he performed the same critical service for his people: crisscrossing the church with speech after speech, widening the Mennonite field of social responsibility, and nudging his people to conversation on new issues, especially about new forms of peace witness. It was a role made possible only by a deep, private engagement with the social and political currents of his day and a wide-ranging personal curiosity determined to resist, as he proclaimed in a chapel address back at Elkhart Institute in 1899, any boundaries on absolute freedom of thought. Smith retained this public engagement and intellectual curiosity to his last days. In October 1948, as he departed for Lima Hospital for what would be the final time, he left notes on his desk about the relationship Mennonites might have had with the Dutch painter Rembrandt and an outline for a new talk in the Bluffton College chapel on the trial of Nazi war criminals then underway at Nuremburg. The beneficiaries of Smith's devoted intellectual engagement were not just Mennonites, but different audiences in a myriad of settings as he consistently carried a Mennonite voice into the public sphere. Down the road, others from the church would take up the same role, creating a line of Mennonite public intellectuals that included Hartzler, Kaufman, and Harshbarger, in Smith's day, extended later to bright lights like Guy Hershberger, J. Lawrence Burkholder, and John Howard Yoder, and then, more recently, to scholars and activists like Douglas Hostetter, Lisa Shirch, and John Paul Lederach. To a great degree, the founder of this tradition was C. Henry Smith.⁸

Of course Smith's intellectual vision had flaws. He could not escape them; he engaged public issues as a product of his time. In absorbing so enthusiastically the outside current of progressivism, he helped pull into the Mennonite world patterns of thinking that should have stayed outside it. One thinks with disappointment here, for example, of the evident racism and ethnocentrism of his younger years, positions he carried with him into middle age. Likewise, especially in his articles for the laity, as Kreider put it, Smith "seemed to accept uncritically the American mythology of progress, manifest destiny and the superiority of American civilization." Admittedly, such worldviews were widely shared by other Mennonites of the day, and while succeeding generations may have escaped the intellectual confines of a previous one, they themselves remained bound by the strictures of their own. Even so, through much of his adult life, Smith may have been blinded more than most to the contextually driven nature of his worldview by his unswerving commitment to the gospel of objectivity and a fetish for "the facts." It was a personal, churchly context, as much as a national one, that may have shaped his treatment of Anabaptism in particular. Suppose the Mennonite Church of Smith's young adult years had not been trending in such a clear authoritarian direction, and Smith himself not reacted to it so strongly out of an evident infatuation with the liberating effects of education. Would he have been so quick, one wonders, to stress Anabaptist individualism and to depict the early movement as free and democratic as a social club?[9]

The question invites a reconsideration of the critique that Bender and Friedmann had mounted, the matter of Smith's view of the church. A dense fog of ambiguity still surrounds this point; his spiritual life was a topic that the adult Smith was consistently silent about. As a result, one is mostly left with further questions. It is hard to know, for instance, how to read the fact that for most of his adult life, Smith kept his official church membership in congregations two states away. Did that decision betoken a shallow understanding of the nature of church? Or did it simply reflect a residual commitment to the union movement of 1913, and a determination to make sure the Central Conference maintained a presence on Bluffton faculty rolls? Two points seem clear in response. First, throughout his life Smith retained the emotional residue of an Amish Mennonite childhood, with its distrust of open expressions of piety and its emphasis on lived Christianity. No doubt because of this heritage, he refused to reflect on his personal faith publicly, and especially not through the language of the outside import of fundamentalism, despite the fact that such refusals left him vulnerable to reckless charges of "modernism." Second, another reason he refused to bring such considerations into his scholarship was due to his underlying commitment to empiricism. "I have noticed," he told Bender in 1943, "that when our Mennonite historians enter into the realm of speculation and sociological interpretation they are inclined to dig so deeply into the rootage from which they think Mennonitism springs that one hardly recognizes any connection with things Mennonite." He would prefer to remain in pursuit of just the facts, even as he finally began to realize just how elusive a quarry they were.[10]

On the other hand, even with the limitations imposed by Smith's personal context, it is remarkable how many of his insights seemed on target. This was seen not just in his (sometimes) uncanny ability to peer ahead into shifting geopolitical currents but, more importantly, in the safe and constructive way forward he outlined for his church. He remained a flexible enough thinker to shed some of the more problematic parts of his progressive worldview. For instance, his shocked horror at what Nazism represented helped him grasp the anti-Christian nature of racism. Long before this, World War I had become a major, searing turning point in his thinking, as he increasingly began to recognize. He suggested to readers of the *Mennonite* in January 1944 that up until World War I, "most of us would have said that the age of the martyrs was past, that the world had become too civilized to engage in such atrocities. But recent history has shown us that we were wrong." This was a profoundly chastened progressivism, a shift that had begun to occur for Smith not long after the first global cataclysm had ended. He quickly shed his view of a beneficent democratic state as the prime agent of social progress, instead increasingly worrying about its authoritarian tendencies both abroad and at home.[11]

Similarly, from the mid-1920s on, Smith began to regard the process of acculturation with a much more critical eye. This did not mean he was ready to sign on to a reinforcement of the Mennonite rural community, a new thrust in the Mennonite church that activist scholars like Hershberger and Fretz were fashioning about the time of the Second World War. Smith airily dismissed this as "a back to the farm movement." Instead, for the last quarter century of his life, he relentlessly advanced the same familiar solutions as antidotes to the assimilative pressures of modern life. He pounded away with a need for a new denominational seminary in front of nearly every Mennonite audience he addressed (the lack of which, though he was too gracious to say it, registered a profound cost to the church, one that was measureable as the World War II draft census results came in). For Smith, education altogether was a major Mennonite answer to the myriad of problems they faced. Education was more than merely conveying information; it was, to Smith, a major vehicle for socializing Mennonite youth and thus securing the church's future through subsequent generations. "We must look to religion and education using that term in the broadest sense . . . as the two forces that will lead us to a brighter future," he declared in the *Mennonite*. To Bender he was equally forthright, writing in the pages of *MQR* that "if we are going to preserve the faith of our fathers in these days of the radio, the automobile, rural mail and the centralized high school I am firmly convinced that it will come through a process of the right kind of education and perhaps reeducation in our church schools and colleges."[12]

In an adult lifetime spent writing about these matters and speaking relentlessly about them across the church, Smith hammered out a clear and compelling answer to the basic theological question confronting his people in the twentieth century: what it meant to be a Mennonite in the modern world. It was a nuanced but still markedly different vision than the one increasingly advanced by Bender and Hershberger, who argued that the proper Mennonite posture was best found in maintaining, as Toews summarized it, "a distinctive Christian social order." Instead of standing apart from other North Americans, Smith called Mennonites to engage them with their ideas. Rather than creating an alternative model for outsiders to follow, Smith consistently urged his people to share with their society the values that their peculiar history had gifted them with—peacemaking, religious toleration, the sanctity of individual conscience—and that it so desperately needed.[13]

Mennonite history was, of course, critical to this vision and it was there that Smith's life work registered perhaps its deepest impact. He most centrally served his people through his pursuit of his vocational calling, the role of a Mennonite historian. His books were the first broad syntheses of the Mennonite past available to the church:

accessible, engaging narratives that explained to an emerging and educated generation where they had come from and how they might move forward. In a time when Mennonites had begun to emerge from rural isolation and more directly confront the assimilative pressures of modern North America, his history provided them with the kind of invented ethnicity they required to secure a legitimate and respected place in the pluralistic ethnic and religious landscapes they inhabited.

Given what Smith had to work with, it was altogether a remarkable accomplishment. When he began serious research into the Mennonite past, there were none of the denominational archives or historical libraries that exist today. He worked only from a few scattered collections of materials existing in the hands of isolated individuals. The entire library available to researchers or students at the new Goshen College, Smith discovered when he arrived to teach there, consisted of a single row of books on a lone shelf at the back end of a classroom. Hence, producing Mennonite history for the church thus required Smith and his peers to function not only as pioneer scholars but pioneer book collectors and archivists. After half a lifetime of such efforts, during which Smith amassed and turned over to Bluffton a remarkable private library that his financial acumen had made possible, he still lacked a vast bulk of the academic resources that scholars of a later generation take for granted. "Even as late as 1940," Kreider has noted, when Smith sent his magnum opus off to press, he "probably had not one-tenth of the books, periodicals and documents a scholar has today in telling the same story." Despite such obstacles, he furnished Mennonites with a usable past in the critical moment at which they began to shed their rural isolation and find their way into an accepted place on the American denominational landscape. In their books and popular writings—the stream of articles on Mennonite history in the pages of the *Mennonite* or the *Gospel Herald*, and the historical travelogues that Smith and Bender sent back from their pilgrimages to Anabaptist sites across Europe—Smith and his few scholarly colleagues cemented into modern Mennonite consciousness the importance of their history.[14]

The body of historical work that Smith produced could only have emanated from a deep well of affection for his subject, and it was a fascination for Mennonite history that many of his people found contagious. His enthusiasm gained him a reputation in his church that still echoes down across the years. In 2010 Richard Weaver recalled a remark about Smith his uncle had made to his father more than a century before. Smith had been in Elkhart County only a short time, but long enough to establish a reputation. Sometime near the turn of the twentieth century, the two Weaver brothers were standing together on the streets of Goshen and noticed the young scholar at an opposite corner. "That man there," Weaver's uncle declared, pointing at Smith, "knows more about Mennonite history than anyone else." Edmund Kaufman relayed a similarly revealing anecdote from about the same time that occurred in a different corner of the Mennonite world. Once when he and his father were harvesting wheat in rural Kansas, he saw his father stop to talk with a passerby. The fellow shortly pulled out a book from a satchel he was carrying and handed it over to Kaufman's father, who scrutinized it carefully and then apparently bought a copy. "As a youth I was impressed with this experience and concluded that this book must be important to rate so much attention during harvest season," Kaufman said. "Indeed thereafter it was considered, next to the Bible and the *Gesangbuch mit Noten*, a very precious possession of our family." This was how he first encountered Smith's 1910 history, *The Mennonites of America*.[15]

The rich Mennonite historical consciousness that Smith, his colleagues, and his adversaries nurtured into being became immensely fruitful for the church. As early Mennonite theologizing diverted into a sterile and destructive microcosm of the larger fundamentalist-modernist conflict wracking American Protestantism, history became a safer landscape where Mennonites could understand and define themselves. Mennonite historical writing was certainly not immune to the conflict raging in the background. The ready Mennonite absorption of outside ideas over the course of Smith's life ensured that the history he offered would be contested, at times fiercely. While he personally shied away from ecclesiastical infighting, other MC exiles like Hartzler and the *Christian Exponent* writers, Sawatsky notes, "turned Smith's reading into a primary weapon" in their battles with their church.[16]

Smith's basic underlying training as a historian served both him and his church well in these struggles. When Bender arrived to teach at Goshen in 1924, he was disappointed to learn that he would be assigned to teach history instead of his true love, Bible and theology. He emerged as a fine church historian, but his writings had a theological agenda, a tendency he never displayed more clearly than in his celebrated "Anabaptist Vision" (which was delivered, not coincidentally, in front of an academic body formed as a counterweight to the overt empiricism of the American Historical Association). As a theological—some would say mythical—statement, Bender's vision pared down Anabaptism to a few magnetic essentials. Moreover, in enshrining a heroic founding generation as the apogee of the Anabaptist-Mennonite story, it reinforced, Paul Toews has charged, a mid-twentieth-century Mennonite tendency to read all of their history from the Anabaptists forward in a fundamental mode of declension. This interpretive stance took such a central hold on the Mennonite imagination that it allowed an emerging new generation of Mennonite scholar-activists to accuse Bender of betraying the Anabaptist heritage in the denominational structures he had been so central in creating.[17]

Problematic as it was in its own lights, Smith's commitment to the unreachable ideal of objectivity did lead him to resist rooting his historical narratives in the kind of explicitly theological agenda advocated by people like Bender and Friedmann. Instead, Smith approached his material first and foremost as a historian and a storyteller. Anabaptist-Mennonite theology could not be abstracted, he insisted, from the particular sociocultural and ethnic contexts in which these individuals lived. His histories were also laden with his agendas, of course, but they also proceeded in the difficult messiness of people who were both heroic and broken, and who acted in accordance with the contextual complexity of their times. Smith was interested, Gerald Mast put it, "in the long story as it unfolds—generation to generation, century to century, continent to continent. For him Anabaptism is not so much an underlying or original essence to which we continue to be accountable in disappointing ways but rather the actual Mennonite church's life of faithful and sometimes faithless struggle." In eschewing a theological agenda, Smith could perhaps better understand his people as flesh-and-blood individuals caught in the particular realities of their day and responding to them accordingly.[18]

Bender and Friedmann critiqued Smith for overlooking some kind of unitary, bedrock Mennonite "essence" that functioned at the core of their history. Yet in the end Bender's Anabaptist Vision—that great attempt at establishing a self-legitimating spiritual and intellectual foundation—foundered on the same shoals that Smith had spent his adult lifetime navigating: the basic pluralism of the Anabaptist-Mennonite experience. Given their fractious, schismatic historical trajectory, what else could Mennonite history be if not contentious? Perhaps the problem lay in attempting to locate some kind of Mennonite essence in a single group or historical experience.

There could not and would not be a single, overarching narrative that could knit fragmented Mennonites together, no one unitary vision recovered by some pure, objective approach. Instead, there could only be elements that emerged, sometimes simultaneously, in a number of different places. Any Mennonite essence was by nature partial and divided, and could be located only in competing arguments. It was found in Bender's Anabaptist Vision, to be sure, and also in the furious passions of John Horsch, typeset in an inky printing office in Scottdale. It was found in a thousand churchyard conversations in Mennonite meetinghouses from Lancaster to Winnipeg to western Kansas. It was found in the Mennonite history of C. Henry Smith.

Notes

Preface

1. On this acculturation process, see Calvin Redekop, *Mennonite Society* (Baltimore: Johns Hopkins University Press, 1989); and Perry Bush, *Two Kingdoms, Two Loyalties: Mennonite Pacifism in Modern America* (Baltimore: Johns Hopkins University Press, 1998), 129–52. Following the lead of the sociologist Milton Gordon, I am defining *acculturation* here as a process by which a subgroup adapts some but not all of the cultural traits and mores of a mainstream culture, using what it has adopted to strengthen its own worldview. See Milton Gordon, *Assimilation in American Life* (New York: Oxford University Press, 1964).

    On the Amish, see, for example, Donald B. Kraybill, *The Riddle of Amish Culture*, rev. 2nd ed. (Baltimore: Johns Hopkins University Press, 2001); and Kraybill and Carl F. Bowman, *On the Backroad to Heaven: Old Order Hutterites, Mennonites, Amish and Brethren* (Baltimore: Johns Hopkins University Press, 2001).

2. C. Henry Smith, Opening Address, "The Next Step," *Report of the Fifth All-Mennonite Convention, Held in West Market St. Mennonite Church, Nappanee, Indiana, Sept. 2–3, 1925*, 12; "A Communication from C. Henry Smith Concerning the Review of His Book 'The Story of the Mennonites'" [sic], *Mennonite Quarterly Review* (hereafter abbreviated *MQR*) XVII (October 1943), 250; Ohio Department of Public Health, Certificate of Death, C. Henry Smith, October 18, 1948.
3. Robert Kreider, email message to author, September 19, 2010.
4. C. Norman Kraus, "American Mennonites and the Bible, 1750–1950," *MQR* XLI (October 1967), 324–27, quoted 326; James C. Juhnke, *Vision, Doctrine, War: Mennonite Identity and Organization in America, 1890–1930* (Scottdale, PA: Herald Press, 1989), 279–80.

Chapter 1: Geography of a Prairie Childhood

1. Cornelius Krahn, preface to *Mennonite Country Boy: The Education of C. Henry Smith* by C. Henry Smith (Newton, KS: Faith & Life Press, 1962), 5–7; Smith, *Mennonite Country Boy*, quoted p. 11. For examples of enthusiastic responses, see J. B. Sommer to Smith, May 11, 1948, and Mary Ann Sommer to Smith, April 28, 1948, box 10, file 28, C. Henry Smith Papers, MS 1, Bluffton University Archives and Special Collections, Bluffton University (hereafter

abbreviated BUASC); and H. G. Good to Smith, Smith Papers, February 11, 1948, box 3, file 28, BUASC. Some, like Paul Whitmer, were so moved by Smith's memoir they decided to write their own. See Paul Whitmer, foreword to "The Autobiography of Paul Whitmer," n.p., 1952 (copy at BUASC).

2. On the way that neighboring non-Mennonites ("Yankees") referred to their Amish and Mennonite neighbors as "Dutch," see Smith, *Mennonite Country Boy*, 39.

3. Smith, *Mennonite Country Boy*, quoted 12; Keith L. Sprunger, "C. Henry Smith's Vision of Mennonite History," *Mennonite Life* 50 (March 1995), 7 ("nearly all Smith's books," Sprunger writes here, "began with a chapter on the origins and beliefs of the Anabaptists, distilled into some sort of essence or fundamentals"). For a brief synopsis of Smith's exchange with Bender in 1943, see Sprunger, 8–10. I will consider this exchange in much more detail in chapter 11.

4. On nineteenth-century Amish and Mennonite migration to the American Midwest, see Theron F. Schlabach, *Peace, Faith, Nation: Mennonites and Amish in Nineteenth-Century America* (Scottdale, PA: Herald Press, 1988), 33–46; and V. Gordon Oyer, "Plain or Fancy: Butler County and the Nineteenth-Century Amish in America," *Illinois Mennonite Heritage Quarterly* (hereafter abbreviated *IMHQ*) XXX (Winter 2003), 45, 53, 54–59.

5. On Amish religious life in Alsace-Lorraine, see Steven R. Estes, *Living Stones: A History of Metamora Mennonite Church* (Henry, IL: M & D Printing, 1984), 16–18; and Kenneth Ulrich, "Roanoke Mennonite Church History," *IMHQ* XXVIII (Spring 2001), 1, 4. On Willow Springs and Science Ridge, see Willard H. Smith, *Mennonites in Illinois* (Scottdale, PA: Herald Press, 1983), 69–70, 43–45; and Harry F. Weber, *Centennial History of the Mennonites of Illinois* (Scottdale, PA: Mennonite Publishing House, 1931), 222–25.

6. Estes, *Living Stones*, 25–32, 47–9; Smith, *Mennonites in Illinois*, 60–65; Lydia Leman Hohulin, "A French Connection: Tracing the Roots of My Leman, Smith and Belsey Families," *IMHQ* XXXVII (Spring 2010), 9–12.

Similarly, later Mennonite institutions would be tied to these Amish immigrants with other ties than merely Smith's. For example, an enterprising Amishman named Christian Ropp settled along the Mackinaw in 1836. He proved such a capable tinkerer in farm machinery that he accumulated quite a fortune, part of which his son John would later pass on to Bluffton and Goshen Colleges. In turn, a student dormitory—Bluffton's Ropp Hall—would be named in his honor; see Smith, *Mennonites in Illinois*, 66–67.

7. Ardys Serpette, "Christian and Catherine Bechler Smith," *IMHQ* XXXI (Winter 2004), 41, 49–51; Estes, *Living Stones*, 32–3; Hohulin, "A French Connection," 13–15 (Smith genealogy); Smith, *Mennonite Country Boy*, 15; Smith to George H. Summer, March 13, 1932, Smith Papers, MS I, box 10, file 4, BUASC (Smith's search for family records).

The Massanaris knew the box contained the land deed signed by U.S. president Martin Van Buren. They did not know then of other documents in the box: birth and death records of Smith ancestors. Even if they had found them, they could not have read them, since no one in the family could read French (John J. Smith, email message to author, May 19, 2010). These Smith

family documents now are open to the public at the Illinois Mennonite Heritage Center in Metamora, Illinois.
8. Smith, *Mennonite Country Boy*, 14–15. For anecdotes on Christian Smith, see Serpette, "Christian and Catherine Bechler Smith," 49, and Estes, *Living Stones*, 32, 56.
9. Smith, *Mennonites in Illinois*, 44 (Smith quoted); Estes, *Living Stones*, 53–56, 60–61 ("meat everyday," 56); Richard Jensen, *Illinois: A Bicentennial History* (New York: Norton, 1976), 85–6 (farm price statistics); John Mack Faragher, *Sugar Creek: Life on the Illinois Prairie* (New Haven, CT: Yale University Press, 1986), 61–65, 88–91. On free labor ideology, see Eric Foner, *Free Soil, Free Labor, Free Men: The Ideology of the Republican Party before the Civil War* (New York: Oxford University Press, 1970), 11–39. For death rates in later Gilded Age Illinois, see: 1880 U.S. Census, Population and Housing Statistics, "Statistics of Mortality: Of Ratios, and Deaths from Certain Specified Causes: Illinois (35)," www.census.gov/prod2/decennial/documents/1880a_v12-05.pdf (site discontinued); 1880 U.S. Census, Population and Housing Statistics, "Statistics of Mortality: Table 2: deaths, by states and territories, with distinction of sex and color, 7, 10," www.census.gov/prod2/decennial/documents/1880a_v11-01 (site discontinued); Martha Smith obituary, written by "C.H.S.," undated, Smith Papers, Box 1, file 51, BUASC.
10. Smith, *Mennonites in Illinois*, 63–66; Estes, *Living Stones*, 36–38, 58 (Smith Bible quotation).
11. Ferne Smith, "Christian Heroes: Chapter I: The Story and the Life of Bishop John Smith," *Youth's Christian Companion* 17 (September 20, 1936), 303 (John Smith quoted). For Smith biographical details and anecdotes, see J. J. Camp, "Bishop John Smith, 1843–1906," *Gospel Herald* XXII (November 28, 1929), 715; Smith, *Mennonites in Illinois*, 345 (commutation fee); Estes, *Living Stones*, 62, 84–5, 163; and Smith, *Mennonite Country Boy*, 15–17.
12. On the transformation of Illinois agriculture in the Gilded Age, see Smith, *Mennonites in Illinois*, 30–31; Jensen, *Illinois*, 86–87 ("frozen" quoted 87); Estes, *Living Stones*, 35; Steven J. Diner, *A Very Different Age: Americans of the Progressive Era* (New York: Hill and Wang, 1998), 103 (farm price increases).
13. Smith, "Christian Heroes," 303 (Smith land investments); Obituary for William Ioder, clearly from a Bureau County, Illinois, newspaper about 1914 (copy provided to author by Elaine Bowers of Princeton, Illinois, in author's possession); Faragher, *Sugar Creek*, 63–64 (new ploughs). On Amish migration out of the creek into the prairie and formation of the Roanoke congregation, see Estes, *Living Stones*, 148–49; Roanoke Mennonite Church, *Centennial Year, 1875–1975* (Roanoke Mennonite Church, 1975), 1–2; and H. R. Schertz and Harold Bender, "Metamora Mennonite Church (Metamora, Illinois, USA)," *Global Anabaptist Mennonite Encyclopedia Online* (hereafter abbreviated *GAMEO*), 1957, http://www.gameo.org/encyclopedia/contents/M4888.html.
14. Estes, *Living Stones*, 145–46; Wilma Schertz, "Smith Family Genealogy, 1865–1979," n.d., n.p., Illinois Mennonite Heritage Center, Metamora, Illinois.
15. Smith, *Mennonite Country Boy*, 18–30. *Fraktur* refers to a kind of ornamental, illuminative writing. Dating back to medieval Europe, it became especially prized by Mennonites of both Dutch-Russian and Swiss/South-German

ethnic traditions. On this see Cornelius Krahn, Harold S. Bender, Ethel Ewert Abrahams, Mary Jane Lederach Hershey, and Carolyn C. Wenger, "Fraktur (Illuminated Drawing)," *GAMEO*, 1989, http://gameo.org/index.php?title=Fraktur_(Illuminated_Drawing)&oldid=121064.

16. For example, one August day Smith's sister Ella jotted to him, "John Camp is thrashing today"; Ella Smith to Henry Smith, August 5, Smith Papers, August 5, 1902, box 1, file 44, BUASC. For Smith's explanation of "thrashing," see *Mennonite Country Boy*, 39.

17. Smith, *Mennonite Country Boy*, 34–47, quoted 39; Diner, *A Very Different Age*, 103 (farm work hours); J. Sanford Rikoon, *Threshing in the Midwest, 1820–1940: A Study of Traditional Culture and Technological Change* (Bloomington: Indiana University Press, 1988), 25, 39–48, 115–18.

18. Smith, *Mennonite Country Boy*, 61–69, quoted 61; Michael McGerr, *A Fierce Discontent: The Rise and Fall of the Progressive Movement in America, 1870–1920* (New York: Oxford University Press, 2003), 26–32 (on the larger context in the rural Midwest).

19. Robert Kreider, "C Henry Smith—Part One: Always an Amish-Mennonite Farm Boy," *IMHQ* XXI (Spring 2004), 9. For Kreider's family roots on the Illinois prairie, see Robert Kreider, *My Early Years: An Autobiography* (Kitchener, ON: Pandora Press, 2002), 46–59.

20. Smith, *Mennonite Country Boy*, 121–28.

21. C. Norman Kraus, "American Mennonites and the Bible, 1750–1950," *MQR* XLI (October 1967), 317; Susan Fisher Miller, "John S. Coffman's Mennonite Revivalism," in Stephen L. Longenecker, ed., *The Dilemma of Anabaptist Piety: Strengthening or Straining the Bonds of Community?* (Penobscot, ME: Penobscot Press, 1997), 99. On the lure of local revival meetings, see John Umble, "John S. Coffman as an Evangelist," *MQR* XXIII (July 1949), 125–26.

22. Smith, *Mennonite Country Boy*, 123–24, 129–30 (quoted 124, 130); Smith, *Mennonites in Illinois*, 172 (on John Smith as pastor); Smith to Bender, May 16, 1931, H. S. Bender Papers, Hist. Mss I-278, box 12, file 5, Archives of the Mennonite Church, Goshen, Indiana (hereafter abbreviated AMC).

23. For Amish rule changes as a response to social change, see Schlabach, *Peace, Faith, Nation*, 95–97, 208–17, Estes, *Living Stones*, 74–75, and Paton Yoder, *Tradition and Transition: Amish Mennonites and the Old Order Amish, 1800–1900* (Scottdale, PA: Herald Press, 1991), 102–9, 213–18. Also on changing Amish and Mennonite dress, see Melvin Gingerich, *Mennonite Attire through the Centuries* (Breinigsville, PA: The Pennsylvania German Society, 1970), 32–34, 52–60. Smith, *Mennonite Country Boy*, 129.

24. Schlabach, *Peace, Faith, Nation*, 214–20; Yoder, *Tradition and Transition*, 137–83, quoted 171. On the formation of the Amish Mennonites and their discipline, see Smith, *Mennonites in Illinois*, 167–78, and Estes, *Living Stones*, 177–78.

25. On Stuckey and the formation of the Central Conference, see Samuel F. Pannabecker, *Faith in Ferment: A History of the Central District Conference* (Newton, KS: Faith & Life Press, 1968), 24–42; Estes, *Living Stones*, 150–51; Smith, *Mennonites in Illinois*, 88–102, 185–87; Schlabach, *Peace, Faith, Nation*, 219; William B. Weaver and Harold S. Bender, "Stuckey, Joseph (1825–1902),"

in *GAMEO*, 1959, http://gameo.org/index.php?title=Stuckey,_Joseph_(1825-1902); and Weaver, "Central Conference Mennonite Church," in *GAMEO*, 1953, http://www.gameo.org/encyclopedia/contents/C458857.html.

26. Estes, *Living Stones*, 152–53, 178–96 (on Stuckey and the Partridge Creek Amish); Smith, *Mennonites in Illinois*, 172–73, 182, 186, and Melvin Gingerich, "Ten Leaders of the Western District Amish Mennonite Conference," *Mennonite Historical Bulletin* 1 (October 1940), 1–2 (Smith's leadership); Yoder, *Tradition and Transition*, 192–93 (on general rapprochement with Stuckey).
27. Martha Smith to Henry Smith, May 1, 1899, Box 8, MS 1, File 2, Smith Papers, BUASC, and September 11, 1899 (on hats), Box 10, File 28; Yoder, *Tradition and Transition*, 175 ("liberal Amish"); Smith, *Mennonite Country Boy*, 122; Estes, *Living Stones*, 154 (Joseph Smith anecdote). *Frau* translates, literally, to "Mrs." Other Amish Mennonite women in the area were also pushing to keep their hair covered with a hat instead of more restrictive devotional coverings; see Weber, *Centennial History of the Mennonites of Illinois*, 228–29.
28. Smith, *Mennonites in Illinois*, 235–38, and Estes, *Living Stones*, 175–76, 200–201; Smith, *Mennonite Country Boy*, 128 ("Uncle Chris's beard"), 66–67.
29. Schlabach, *Peace, Faith, Nation*, 65–70 (development of Sunday and singing schools); handwritten note from C. H. Smith, n.d., attached to clipping of Simon Hertzler obituary, Smith Papers, Box 51, "printed material—clippings," BUASC ("one of the bright spots").
30. Smith, *Mennonite Country Boy*, 48–55, 80–82; Jensen, *Illinois*, 80 (Illinois school reforms).
31. Smith, *Mennonite Country Boy*, 70–71, 92–93.
32. Ibid., 96–101, 105, quoted 95, 105; "Books I have Read, April 30, 1893," in wire-bound notebook, box 6, file 6, "addendum," Smith Papers, BUASC; W. L. Whitmire to Smith, February 12, 1895, box 9, file 19, Smith Papers, BUASC.
33. Smith, *Mennonite Country Boy*, 103–5, quoted 104, 105.
34. Robert L. Geiger, "The Crisis of the Old Order: The Colleges in the 1890s," in Geiger, ed., *The American College in the Nineteenth Century* (Nashville: Vanderbilt University Press, 2000), 265–66 (new growth of high schools); Smith, *Mennonite Country Boy*, 106, 35–36, 115–16, 101–3; "Many hours ahead of all the other Chicago dailies," (Chicago) *Inter-Ocean* (November 12, 1888): 1.
35. Smith, *Mennonite Country Boy*, 117–18; Estes, *Living Stones*, 83 (Smith Lincoln encounters); "Debate," dated January 15, 1893, in wire-bound "Folio" notebook, Smith Papers, MS 1, box 6, file 6, "addendum," BUASC.
36. Smith, *Mennonite Country Boy*, 119–20, 138–41, quoted 140.
37. Ibid., 119 (quoted), 136–37 (quoted), 142–44.
38. Ibid., 118, 109 (quoted).
39. Ibid., 110. On Amish Mennonite suspicion of high schools, see Yoder, *Tradition and Transition*, 230–31, and Smith, *Mennonites in Illinois*, 251.

Chapter 2: Becoming C.

1. Norman H. Clark, *Deliver Us from Evil: An Interpretation of American Prohibition* (New York: Norton, 1976), 1–5 (quoted 1, 3, Presbyterian quoted 4). For statistics on alcohol consumption, see Clark, ibid., 18–22, and W. J.

Rorabaugh, *The Alcoholic Republic: An American Tradition* (New York: Oxford University Press), 6–21 (early nineteenth-century alcohol consumption). Also on the early Prohibition movement, see McGerr, *A Fierce Discontent*, 84–85.

2. For changing Amish and Mennonite attitudes on alcohol and interest in temperance, see Schlabach, *Peace, Faith, Nation*, 167–70; Estes, *Living Stones*, 165–66; Yoder, *Tradition and Transition*, 224–66; and Nathan E. Yoder, "Mennonite Fundamentalism: Shaping an Identity for an American Context," (PhD diss., University of Notre Dame, 1999), 90–94. Jason Martin, "A Statistical Study of the Herald of Truth, 1864–1900," Goshen College student paper, 1962, 1–4, in files of Mennonite Historical Library, Goshen College, Goshen, Indiana (hereafter abbreviated MHLG). Smith, *Mennonites in Illinois*, 398–99 (on John Smith and Western District Conference).

3. Clark, *Deliver Us from Evil*, 93–97; Thomas R. Pegram, "The Dry Machine: The Formation of the Anti-Saloon League of Illinois," *Illinois Historical Journal* 83 (Autumn 1990), 174–77, quoted 176 (on the local option development).

4. Pegram, "The Dry Machine," 183; John Smith, email message to author, November 13, 2009; Ella Smith to Henry Smith, May 18, 1899, Ella Smith Oyer Collection, AMC; "twenty-five snakes" in wire-bound "Folio" notebook, box 6, file 6, "addendum," C. Henry Smith Papers, MS 1, BUASC.

5. Pegram, "The Dry Machine," 185 (Illinois ASL); Clark, *Deliver Us from Evil*, 88–93, quoted 92, 88 (larger ASL success); Perry Bush, "Economic Justice and the Evangelical Historian," *Fides et Historia* XXXIII (Winter/Spring 2001), 20–21 (on Willard).

6. Bush, "Economic Justice and the Evangelical Historian," 21; Sydney Ahlstrom, *A Religious History of the American People*, vol. 2 (Garden City, NY: Doubleday, 1975), 321–22. Also on this politicized evangelicalism and its effects in the Gilded Age Midwest, see Richard Jensen, *The Winning of the Midwest, Social and Political Conflict, 1888–1971* (Chicago: University of Chicago Press, 1971), 58–71; and Herbert G. Gutman, "Protestantism and the American Labor Movement: The Christian Spirit in the Gilded Age," in Gutman, ed., *Work, Culture and Society in Industrializing America* (New York: Random House, 1977), 79–118.

7. Schlabach, *Peace, Faith, Nation*, 295–6 (quoted 296); Theron Schlabach, "Reveille for *Die Stillen im Lande*: A Stir among Mennonites in the Late Nineteenth Century," *MQR* LI (July 1977), 213–15 (on this "quickening").

8. On Funk, see Juhnke, *Vision, Doctrine, War*, 41–42, and Smith, *Mennonites in Illinois*, 228–30; Martin, "A Statistical Study of the Herald of Truth, 1864–1900," 3–4.

9. Miller, "John S. Coffman's Mennonite Revivalism," 95–97.

10. Ibid., 99–104 (quoted 104); Sem Sutter, "John S. Coffman, Mennonite Evangelist," University of Chicago seminar paper, 1974, 3–12, Horsch Mennonite Essay Contest Papers, I-3-3.5, Box 20, AMC (convert quoted 9); Umble, "John S. Coffman as an Evangelist," 128–30, 135–36 ("Funks" and "sinful Funks" quoted 129); Yoder, *Tradition and Transition*, 251–55 (Amish bishop quoted 254).

11. On Steiner, see John Umble, *Mennonite Pioneers* (Scottdale, PA: Mennonite Publishing House, 1940), 71–89 (Steiner quoted 86); Esther Meyer, "Steiner, Menno Simon," in *GAMEO*, 1959, http://gameo.org/index.php?title=Steiner,_Menno_Simon_(1866-1911); Schlabach, *Peace, Faith, Nation*, 298–99; Yoder, *Tradition and Transition*, 244–46 (on Coffman's ecumenicity). For Steiner's missions enthusiasm, see Yoder, "Mennonite Fundamentalism," 94–95.
12. Noah Byers, "The Times in Which I Lived—I," *Mennonite Life* 7 (January 1952), 44–46; J. E. Hartzler, "Autobiographical Notes," *Mennonite Historical Bulletin* 42 (April 1981), 3–4.
13. Daniel Kauffman, *Fifty Years in the Mennonite Church* (Scottdale, PA: Mennonite Publishing House, 1941), 2–3 (quoted 3). Also on Kauffman see Yoder, "Mennonite Fundamentalism," 116–20, and Brenda Martin Hurst, "The Articulation of Mennonite Beliefs about Sexuality, 1890–1930," (PhD diss., Union Theological Seminary, 2003), 86–87.
14. John S. Coffman diary, March 13–14, 1889, box 1, file 5, and Coffman diary, February 17–19, 1893, box 2, file 1, John S. Coffman Papers, Hist. Mss 1–19, AMC; Coffman to Steiner, February 23, 1893, M. S. Steiner Papers, Hist. Mss I-33, box 2, file 8, AMC. For an overview of Coffman's trips to central Illinois, see Estes, *Living Stones*, 191–94.
15. Coffman to Steiner, February 23, 1893; Smith, *Mennonite Country Boy*, 109–10.
16. Hurst, "The Articulation of Mennonite Beliefs about Sexuality," 27–35; Schlabach, "Reveille for *Die Stillen im Lande*," 215.
17. Schlabach, *Peace, Faith, Nation*, 301–2; Schlabach, "Reveille for *Die Stillen im Lande*," 215–20 (quoted 220); Smith, *Mennonite Country Boy*, 51 (on Sankey hymns). For the Chicago Mennonite Mission, see Juhnke, *Vision, Doctrine, War*, 25; Smith, *Mennonites in Illinois*, 262–64; and Yoder, "Mennonite Fundamentalism," 95–97.
18. Schlabach, "Reveille for *Die Stillen im Lande*," 220–22; Juhnke, *Vision, Doctrine, War*, 14–23; Schlabach, "The Humble Become 'Aggressive Workers': Mennonites Organize for Mission, 1880–1910," *MQR* LII (April 1978), 113–26 (Kauffman quoted 115).
19. Schlabach, *Peace, Faith, Nation*, 163–66, 301; Juhnke, *Vision, Doctrine, War*, 143–44; "Salutatory," *Young People's Paper* I (January 6, 1894), 1 (this editorial has no listed author, but since Steiner was the paper's main editor it seems safe to assume the words are his); M. S. Steiner, *Pitfalls and Safeguards* (Elkhart, IN: Mennonite Publishing Co., 1899), 11–13, 17–31, 40–41, *passim*; Sutter, "John S. Coffman, Mennonite Evangelist," 13.
20. Estes, *Living Stones*, 202 (Metamora contributions to the Chicago mission); Yoder, *Tradition and Transition*, 235 (Western District Conference resolution); Agnes Albrecht Gunden Diary, entries dates January 1, 1906, December 20–27, 1906, April 13, 1908, September 24, 1908, Agnes Albrecht Gunden Collection, Hist. Mss. I-332, box 1, files 1–2, AMC; Smith to Steiner, January 26, 1895, Steiner Papers, Hist. Mss I-33, box 4, file 5, AMC; Smith, *Mennonite Country Boy*, 158.

Given the Smith family's devotion to Coffman, it's doubtful that Smith was referring to him here. Instead, reflecting his heightened anger at such

"Puritanism" in 1925, he may have had in mind contemporary culprits like Daniel Kauffman, or instead may have just been happy to let his intended small audience of friends fill in the blank.
21. Hurst, "The Articulation of Mennonite Beliefs about Sexuality," 34–36 (on Coffman's wedding of faith and reason); Smith, *Mennonites in Illinois*, 251 (Steiner's pushing).
22. For the roots of Elkhart Institute, see John S. Umble, *Goshen College, 1894–1954* (Scottdale, PA: Mennonite Publishing House, 1954), 1–2, and Susan Fisher Miller, *Culture for Service: A History of Goshen College, 1894–1994* (Goshen, IN: Goshen College, 1994), 17–18; Smith, *Mennonite Country Boy*, 149.
23. Smith, *Mennonite Country Boy*, 147–53 (quoted 151, 152). There is some ambiguity about exactly which summer it was when Smith attended Elkhart Institute as a student. In *Mennonite Country Boy* (p. 150), he states clearly he arrived for classes in May 1894, yet Umble states (p. 1) that the institute did not begin offering classes until that September.
24. Henry Smith, "Reading and Home Education," *Young People's Paper* II (March 5, 1895), 34; Smith, "The True Aim of Education," *Young People's Paper* II (April 27, 1895), 66.
25. Smith, *Mennonite Country Boy*, 146–47, 153, 162 (quoted 162).
26. Henry Smith to Ella Smith, October 18, 1896, Ella Smith Oyer Papers, MS 112, Box 1, File 9, BUASC; W. J. Thayer to J. M. Bame, May 24 (1897), Box 1, file 7, Smith Papers, BUASC; "Philadelphia Officers," *ISNU Index*: 1898, box 1, file 6, p. 13, Smith Papers, BUASC; Smith, *Mennonite Country Boy*, 163–64, 166–70, 173–74 (quoted 168).

"Judged by his extra-curricular involvements" at ISNU, Robert Kreider observed, "Smith appears to have lost some of his inferiority complex"; Kreider, "C. Henry Smith, Part One," 10.
27. Smith, *Mennonite Country Boy*, 164–65, 169–70.
28. Ibid., 174–75 (quoted 175); Serpette, "Christian and Catherine Bechler Smith," 50.
29. Smith, *Mennonite Country Boy*, 176.
30. C. Henry Smith to Martha Smith, June 13, 1897, Ella Smith Oyer Papers, MS 112, Box 1, File 18, BUASC; Smith, *Mennonite Country Boy*, 171 (quoted); "Y.M.C.A." *ISNU Index*: 1898, 39–40 (quoted), box 1, file 6, Smith Papers, BUASC.
31. David P. Setran, *The College "Y": Student Religion in the Era of Secularization* (New York: Palgrave Macmillan, 2007), 16–22, 42–63 (YMCA-YWCA history). On Eddy, see Rick L. Nutt, *The Whole Gospel for the Whole World: Sherwood Eddy and the American Protestant Mission* (Macon, GA: Mercer University Press, 1997), 14–16.
32. Smith, *Mennonite Country Boy*, 171–72 (quoted); Byers, "The Times in Which I Lived—I," 44–47. Also on the Smith/Byers meeting see Miller, *Culture for Service*, 23–25.
33. Miller, *Culture for Service*, 17–19; Umble, *Goshen College*, 2–4.
34. Byers, "The Times in Which I Lived—I," 46–47; Miller, *Culture for Service*, 25–26; Umble, *Goshen College*, 196–97.

35. N. E. Byers, "Professor C. Henry Smith, Ph.D., Litt. D., Student and Teacher as I knew Him," box 20, file 16, Smith Papers, BUASC; Coffman to Smith, April 4, 1898, box 2, file 37, Smith Papers, BUASC; Smith, *Mennonite Country Boy*, 176–78; John Smith to Henry Smith, March 1898 and August 28, 1898, box 6, file 50, both in Smith Papers, BUASC.
36. Smith, *Mennonite Country Boy*, 179–84 (quoted 181, 182, 184); Umble, *Goshen College*, 1; *Catalogue of the Elkhart Institute*, 1899–1900 (Elkhart: Elkhart Institute, 1899), 5, MHLG; John C. Smith to Henry Smith, November 28, 1898, box 6, file 52, Smith Papers, BUASC; Samuel Smith to Henry Smith, December 28, 1898, box 8, file 6, BUASC; Katie Smith to Henry Smith, December 18, 1898, box 6, file 61, BUASC.
37. Smith, *Mennonite Country Boy*, 184–86; Umble, *Goshen College*, 11, and *Catalogue of the Elkhart Institute*, 1899–1900, 17 (on Smith's position in the Bible Department); Byers, "Professor C. Henry Smith, Ph.D.," 3; C. Henry Smith, "Department of English," *Institute Monthly* 11 (September 1899), 12–13. Miller, "John S. Coffman's Mennonite Revivalism," 96 (on Heatwole); Lewis Heatwole to C. Henry Smith, December 20, 1899, box 3, file 55, Smith Papers, BUASC.

    Smith almost certainly was referring to Daniel Greenleaf Thompson, *The Philosophy of Fiction in Literature* (New York: Longmans, Green and Co., 1880). See, for example, 29–45.
38. Smith, *Mennonite Country Boy*, quoted 184; on J. E. Hartzler, see Miller, *Culture for Service*, 40–41, 54–55; for Smucker, see Joseph Smith to Henry Smith, October 21, 1901, box 10, file 28, Smith Papers, BUASC; Paul Whitmer, "Autobiography," 23–34, 48.
39. Umble, *Goshen College*, 195; Julia Kasdorf, *Fixing Tradition: Joseph W. Yoder, Amish American* (Telford, PA: Pandora Press, 2002), 38–44, 47, 55–66.
40. On the Ys and early Elkhart Institute activities, see Umble, *Goshen College*, 18, 195; Miller, *Culture for Service*, 26–29; Edmund G. Kauffman, *General Conference Mennonite Pioneers* (North Newton, KS: Bethel College, 1973), 242 (March 1899 event).
41. C. Henry Smith, "Bondage," *Institute Monthly* I (April 15, 1899), 50–51. For "educational pioneering," see Smith, *Mennonite Country Boy*, 179.
42. Smith, *Mennonite Country Boy*, 186–87, 189; Byers, "Professor C. Henry Smith, Ph.D.," 4; Byers to Steiner, February 2, 1901, Steiner Papers, box 7, file 11, AMC.
43. Smith, *Mennonite Country Boy*, 143; entry for "Charles Henry Smith," in *The Semi-Centennial Alumni Record of the University of Illinois*, ed. Franklin W. Scott (Champaign-Urbana: University of Illinois, 1918), 189; Passport for Cecil Henry Smith, 1926–1936, box 1, file 24, MS1-1, Smith Papers, BUASC.

    When Smith's political science professor Charles E. Merriam entered the Chicago aldermanic primary in 1909 as "C. Edward Merriam," for example, his campaign manager told him to drop the "C" because it made him look too much like a professor. See Barry Karl, *Charles E. Merriam and the Study of Politics* (Chicago: University of Chicago Press, 1974), 61.

Chapter 3: The Democracy of Learning

1. Miller provides a concise, analytical summary of Coffman's important address; see *Culture for Service*, 3–5.
2. Coffman's "Spirit of Progress" speech was published in M. S. Steiner, *John S. Coffman: Mennonite Evangelist* (Spring Grove, PA: Mennonite Book and Tract Society, 1903), 112–17; 2 Cor 6:17.
3. Coffman, "The Spirit of Progress," in Steiner, *John S. Coffman*, 118–23 (quoted 118).
4. Ibid., 126–30 (quoted 126, 128, 130).
5. Miller, *Culture for Service*, 9–10.
6. Steiner, *John S. Coffman*, 135–38.
7. Diner, *A Very Different Age*, 1–7; Arthur S. Link and Richard L. McCormick, *Progressivism* (Arlington Heights, IL: Harlan Davidson, 1983), 11–13; Ella Smith to Henry Smith, April 26, 1901, Ellen Smith Oyer Collection, MS 112, box 1, file 13, BUASC.
8. For economic inequality in the Progressive Era, see Diner, *A Very Different Age*, 4–5; McGerr, *A Fierce Discontent*, 6–10, 68; and Link and McCormick, *Progressivism*, 11–25, 29–47, 58–66, 72–103 (on the crises of 1893, see 15–20).
9. For useful summaries of the historiography of progressivism, see Link and McCormick, *Progressivism*, 3–11, and Robert D. Johnston, "Re-Democratizing the Progressive Era: The Politics of Progressive Era Political Historiography," *Journal of the Gilded Age and Progressive Era* 1 (January, 2002), 68–92.
10. Jean B. Quandt, *From the Small Town to the Great Community: The Social Thought of Progressive Intellectuals* (New Brunswick, NJ: Rutgers University Press, 1970), 5–19; Robert Crunden, *Ministers of Reform: The Progressives' Achievement in American Civilization, 1889–1920* (Chicago: University of Chicago Press, 1984), 4–5; Richard F. Hamm, "The Prohibitionists' Lincolns," *Illinois Historical Journal* 86 (Summer 1983), 93–116. On the depth and power of Lincoln memories in the twentieth century, see Scott Sandage, "A Marble House Divided: The Lincoln Memorial, the Civil Rights Movement, and the Politics of Memory, 1938–1963," *Journal of American History* 80 (June, 1993), 135–67.
11. "Lincoln-Douglas Day," undated clipping, clearly from the *Metamora Herald* in about 1907–08, in Smith Papers, Hist Ms. I, box 43, file 28, BUASC; Willard Smith, *The Trail to Santa Fe*, 119; Byers, "The Times in Which I Lived–I," 46; Miller, *Culture for Service*, 41 (on Smucker). Whitmer, "Autobiography," 24–25. On Hirschy, see Kauffman, *General Conference Mennonite Pioneers*, 176, and Perry Bush, *Dancing with the Kobzar: Bluffton College and Mennonite Higher Education, 1899–1999* (Telford, PA: Pandora Press U.S., 2000), 47.

   On the larger professionalization of recreation in the Progressive Era, see Roy Rosenzweig, *Eight Hours for What We Will: Work and Leisure in an Industrial City, 1870–1920* (Cambridge, MA: Cambridge University Press, 1983), 140–48.
12. Helen Lefkowitz Horowitz, *Campus Life: Undergraduate Cultures from the End of the Eighteenth Century to the Present* (Chicago: University of Chicago Press, 1987), 5–6, 69–71, and Lawrence R. Veysey, *The Emergence of the American University* (Chicago: University of Chicago Press, 1965), 263–68 (growth of

U.S. university system); Burton J. Bledstein, *The Culture of Professionalism: The Middle Class and the Development of Higher Education in America* (New York, NY: Norton, 1976), 34–39 (rise of an educated professional culture).

13. For undergraduate culture, see Horowitz, *Campus Life*, 7–8, and Bledstein, *The Culture of Professionalism*, 288–90; Veysey, *The Emergence of the American University*, 268–70 (on percentage of university attendance).

14. For Thierstein, see Kauffman, *General Conference Mennonite Pioneers*, 284–88. Scott J. Peters, *The Promise of Association: A History of the Mission and Work of the YMCA at the University of Illinois, 1873–1997* (Champaign, IL: University YMCA, 1997), 1–2 (Draper quoted).

   In actuality, the jump from high school principal to college president may not have been as dramatic as it first appears, in light of the fact that in their first years many of these new Mennonite "colleges"—Central Mennonite, Freeman, Elkhart Institute—mostly taught high school classes.

15. Smith, *Mennonite Country Boy*, 193; Smith to Ella Smith, September 16, 1900, Ellen Smith Oyer Collection, MS 112, box 1, file 9, BUASC. Roger Ebert, ed., *An Illini Century: One Hundred Years of Campus Life* (Champaign, IL: University of Illinois Press, 1967), 55–56, 70–71, 73–74.

16. Smith, *Mennonite Country Boy*, 192–95; Smith to Ella Smith, September 16 and November 26, 1900, Ellen Smith Oyer Collection, MS 112, box 1, file 9, BUASC.

17. Smith, *Mennonite Country Boy*, 193–94 (quoted 193); Peters, *The Promise of Association*, 28; Solberg, *The University of Illinois*, 280 (the University of Illinois YMCA); Setran, *The College Y*, 74.

18. Bradley J. Longfield, "From Evangelicalism to Liberalism: Public Midwestern Universities in Nineteenth-Century America," in *The Secularization of the Academy*, eds. George Marsden and Bradley Longfield (New York: Oxford University Press, 1992), 46–51 (quoted 47); Winton Solberg, "The Conflict between Religion and Secularism at the University of Illinois, 1867–1894," *American Quarterly* 18 (1966), 183–99; Setran, *The College Y*, 87–92. For the Illinois Ys, see Solberg, *The University of Illinois: The Shaping of the University* (Chicago: University of Chicago Press, 2000), 281–82, and Peters, *The Promise of Association*, 22–26 (membership quoted 22).

19. Setran, *The College Y*, 115–16, 124, 135 (quoted 135); Peters, *The Promise of Association*, 363–69; "Students' Hand-Book, compliments of the Christian Associations of the University of Illinois," 1901–02, box 52, file 36, Smith Papers, BUASC, 16–20 (quoted 19). For Harper, see Michael Lee, "Higher Criticism and Higher Education at the University of Chicago: William Rainey Harper's Vision of Religion in the Research University," *History of Education Quarterly* 48 (November 2008): 517–28.

20. William R. Hutchinson, *The Modernist Impulse in American Protestantism* (Durham: Duke University Press, 1992), 115, 186–93; Ahlstrom, *A Religious History of the American People*, 235–42; Winthrop S. Hudson, *Religion in America*, 3rd ed. (New York: Scribner's, 1981), 266–67, 273–79 (Matthews quoted 277).

21. Hudson, *Religion in America*, 266–67; Ahlstrom, *A Religious History of the American People*, 242–49; George Marsden, *The Soul of the American*

University: From Protestant Establishment to Established Nonbelief (New York: Oxford University Press, 1994), 257.
22. Setran, *The College Y*, 117–19 (Setran quoted 120, Y official 119); C. Henry Smith, "The Language of the Bible," *Institute Monthly* II (April, 1900), 117–18.
23. Smith, "The Meaning of Education," *Herald of Truth* XXXIX (August 1, 1902), 234–35.
24. Smith, *Mennonite Country Boy*, 195–96; Emma Eliza (Smith) to C. Henry Smith, March 10, 1901, C. Henry Smith Papers, MS I-I, box 2, file 2, BUASC.
25. Smith, *Mennonite Country Boy*, 196.
26. Maureen A. Flanagan, *America Reformed: Progressives and Progressivisms, 1890–1920s* (New York: Oxford University Press, 2007), 4–7.
27. On the origins of the University of Chicago, see Frederick Rudolph, *The American University and College: A History* (Athens: University of Georgia Press, 1990), 349–53 (quoted 350); James P. Wind, *The Bible and the University* (Atlanta, GA: Scholars Press, 1987), 18–19, 105–08; Marsden, *The Soul of the American University*, 236–40 (quoted 36 on faculty raid); Richard J. Storr, *Harper's University: The Beginnings* (Chicago: University of Chicago Press, 1966), 73–77; Thomas Goodspeed, *A History of the University of Chicago: The First Quarter-Century* (Chicago: University of Chicago Press, 1925), 206–8, 410–12. For McLaughlin, see Herman Belz, "In Retrospect: Andrew C. McLaughlin and Liberal Democracy: Scientific History in Support of the Best Regime," *Reviews in American History* 19 (1991), 445–46; on Jameson, see Morey D. Rothberg, "'To Set a Standard of Workmanship and Compel Men to Conform to It': John Franklin Jameson as Editor of the *American Historical Review*," *American Historical Review* 89 (October 1984), 958–62.
28. Goodspeed, *A History of the University of Chicago*, 207 (Judson quoted); Smith, *Mennonite Country Boy*, 196–99 (quoted 196); Smith to A. K. Parker, University Registrar, "To whom it may concern," January 17, 1906, C. Henry Smith Papers, MS I-3, box 2, file 2, BUASC; Estes, *Living Stones*, 238–39.
29. On the larger climate of reform dominating American universities in the Progressive Era, see Roberts and Turner, *The Sacred and Secular University*, 56–57, and Rudolph, *The American University and College*, 356–61. For scientific approaches, see Deborah Haines, "Scientific History as Teaching Method: the Formative Years," *Journal of American History* 63 (December 1977), 9035.
30. Donald Gorrell, *The Age of Social Responsibility* (Macon, GA: Mercer University Press, 1988), 46–47, 247 (Judson quoted); Karl, *Charles E. Merriam and the Study of Politics*, 39–40, 45–48, 50–54, 61–83. For Smith's classes under Merriam, see his professional resume, untitled and undated, box 52, file 32, in Smith Papers, MS I, BUASC.
31. Marsden, *The Soul of the American University*, 242, 248–49, 256 (quoted); Wind, *The Bible and the University*, 141–42; Gorrell, *The Age of Social Responsibility*, 124–27 (on civil religion in the Social Gospel movement).
32. Smith, *Mennonite Country Boy*, 199–200.
33. Ibid., 201.
34. Umble, *Goshen College*, 6; Miller, *Culture for Service*, 32–33.
35. Anthony Deahl, *A Twentieth-Century History and Biographical Record of Elkhart County, Indiana* (Chicago: Lewis Publishing Co., 1905), 148–50; Byers

to Steiner, August 14, 1899, M.S. Steiner Papers, Hist. Mss. I-33, box 6, file 1, AMC; Byers to Steiner, November 23, 1901, box 7, file 11, and Byers to Steiner, January 10, 1903, box 8, file 3 (Byers quoted), Steiner Papers, AMC; Miller, *Culture for Service*, 33.

The Wadsworth Institute had accomplished much good, serving as the major training ground for a number of progressive Mennonite educators and preachers in the Midwest. But its collapse because of factional infighting would serve as a prod to the establishment of enduring and successful Mennonite higher educational institutions, Central Mennonite Colleges among them. On this point see Bush, *Dancing with the Kobzar*, 29–30, 45, 55.

36. For Goshen groundbreaking, see Byers, "The Times in Which I Lived—II," *Mennonite Life* (March 1952), 78–80; Miller, *Culture for Service*, 33; "Start Goshen College," *Goshen Democrat* (June 17, 1903), 1; "With Ceremony for Goshen College," *Goshen News*, clipping dated 1903, box 43, file 28, Smith Papers, BUASC; Umble, *Goshen College*, 27–28 (East Hall), 34, 40–41 (student enrollment numbers); Smith, *Mennonite Country Boy*, 202; Byers to Steiner, May 18, 1903, Steiner Papers, Hist. Mss. I-33, box 8, file 3, AMC; Whitmer, "Autobiography," 49.

This is one of the few occasions where Smith's recollections deviate slightly from the historic record. In his autobiography (p. 201), he said he "was invited to deliver the address of the day." The *Goshen Democrat* account cited above makes it clear that the keynote address was actually delivered by John Blosser, president of the college board of trustees.

37. Smith, *Mennonite Country Boy*, 204.

38. Umble, *Goshen College*, 45–46, 215, 242; Noah Byers to Intercollegiate Peace Association, April 6, 1956, Hist. Mss 4-MS-C-V, box 1, file 28, Byers Papers, BUASC.

39. On the reorganization of the Goshen College board, see Umble, *Goshen College*, 33–34, Smith, *Mennonite Country Boy*, 209–10, Byers, "The Times in Which I Lived—II," 80, and Miller, *Culture for Service*, 345–50; Byers to Steiner, July 12, 1901, Steiner Papers, box 7, file 11, AMC.

40. Smith, *Mennonites in Illinois*, 256 (John Smith as trustee); John Smith to Henry Smith, March 10, 1901, C. Henry Smith Papers, MS I, box 6, file 50, BUASC; John Smith to Henry Smith, April 12, 1901, Ellen Smith Oyer Collection, MS 112, box 1, file 14, BUASC; Daniel Coffman to Henry Smith, October 19, 1900, C. Henry Smith Papers, MS I-3, box 2, file 2, BUASC.

41. Smith, *Mennonite Country Boy*, 206–09 (quoted 209); C. Henry Smith, "A Remarkable Book," *Goshen College Record* 7 (September 15, 1904), 391–92; Smith, "Mennonite History," *Goshen College Record* 7 (January 15, 1905), 451–53, reprinted in *Family Almanac* (1905), 6, 8.

Funk's library, Smith wrote his old Chicago professor Jameson that fall, "is the most rare and complete one on the subject in this country west of Pennsylvania." See Smith to Jameson, October 25, 1904, Hist. Ms. I, box 1, file 20, Smith Papers, BUASC.

Chapter 4: In the Service of a Usable Past

1. Smith, *Mennonite Country Boy*, 211.
2. Smith to Jameson, October 25, 1904. These four letters from Smith to Jameson are found in photocopied form in Smith's papers at the Bluffton University archives; the originals are with Jameson's papers at the Library of Congress. Also on this exchange see Sprunger, "C. Henry Smith's Vision of Mennonite History," 5.
3. Smith to Jameson, October 26 and November 2, 1904, Hist. Ms. I, box 1, file 20, Smith Papers, BUASC. On Jameson's background, see John Tracy Ellis, "Jameson and American Religious History," in *J. Franklin Jameson: A Tribute*, ed. Ruth Anna Fox and William Lloyd Fox (Washington, DC: The Catholic University of America Press, 1965), 11–22. Sprunger, "C. Henry Smith's Vision of Mennonite History," 5–6 (quoted 6).
4. Smith, *Mennonite Country Boy*, 212–13; Harry Pratt Judson, "Award of Fellowship," April 16, 1906, box 1, file 9, Smith Papers, BUASC.
5. For Snell Hall as a Y house, see Storr, *Harper's University*, 166–67; *The Snell Hall Cooler, 1906*, 8, 12 (quoted), box 52, file 35, Smith Papers, BUASC; Noah Byers, "Professor C. Henry Smith, Ph.D., Litt. D: Student and Teacher as I Knew Him," unpublished memoir, box 20, file 16, Smith Papers, BUASC (Smith in the UC choir). For a list of Smith's courses at Chicago, see his professional resume, done sometime in the mid-1910s, box 52, file 32, Smith Papers, BUASC.
6. Peter Novick, *That Noble Dream: The "Objectivity Question" and the American Historical Profession* (Cambridge, MA: Cambridge University Press, 1988), 21–45; Dorothy Ross, *The Origins of American Social Science* (Cambridge, MA: Cambridge University Press, 1991), 57–60, 266–68 (Ranke quoted 267); Roberts and Turner, *The Sacred and Secular University*, 44–55 (quoted 55); Rothberg, "To Set a Standard of Workmanship," 958; and Wind, *The Bible and the University*, 18 (on Adams at Hopkins).
7. Smith, *Mennonite Country Boy*, 214, and H. A. Trexler to C. Henry Smith, February 9, 1946, box 8, file 58, Smith Papers, BUASC (memories of McLaughlin); Smith resume, box 52, file 32, Smith Papers, BUASC. For McLaughlin's scholarship, see Belz, "Andrew C. McLaughlin and Liberal Democracy," 447–59 (quoted 447, 459).
8. Eileen Ka-May Cheng, "Exceptional History? The Origins of Historiography in the United States," *History and Theory* 47 (May 2008), 203–4, 212; Haines, "Scientific History as Teaching Method," 902 (on the Committee of Seven); Belz, "Andrew C. McLaughlin and Liberal Democracy," 455–56 (on McLaughlin's commitment to objectivity); Michael J. Birkner, "A Conversation with Philip S. Klein," *Pennsylvania History* 56 (October 1989), 252; Willard Smith, *The Road to Santa Fe*, 86–87.
9. Smith to Jameson, October 25, 1904; C. Henry Smith, *The Mennonites of America* (C. Henry Smith, 1909), 14; Smith, *Mennonite Country Boy*, 214–15; Smith to Mrs. Rodolphe Petter, February 13, 1938 and to Rodolphe Petter, February 27, 1938, both in Rodolphe Petter Collection, Hist. Mss. 31, box 6, file 47, Mennonite Library and Archives, Bethel College, North Newton, Kansas (hereafter abbreviated MLA).

10. "Haines, "Scientific History as Teaching Method," 909–12 (Darwinian frameworks); "General and Local History," undated clipping from an Elkhart County newspaper, Smith Papers, box 8, file 17, BUASC; Novick, *That Noble Dream*, 98–99 (Jameson's civic history); Smith to Byers, November 28, 1907, Goshen College President's Office Records, V-04-14.1, box 1, file 35, AMC.
11. Steven R. Estes, "C. Henry Smith: Dean of American Mennonite Historiography," Goshen College student paper, 1979, 18–20 (quoted 18), MHLG; J. Herbert Fretz, "Cassel, Daniel K. (1820–1898)" in *GAMEO*, 1953, http://gameo.org/index.php?title=Cassel,_Daniel_K._(1820-1898)&oldid=120940; Harold S. Bender, "Historiography: North America," in GAMEO, 1956, http://gameo.org/index.php?title=Historiography:_North_America&oldid=120154; James C. Juhnke, "Gemeindechristentum and Bible Doctrine: Two Mennonite Visions of the Early Twentieth Century," *MQR* 57 (July 1983), 208–12 (on Wedel).
12. C. Henry Smith, "Mennonite History," *Family Almanac* (1905), 8; J. S. Hartzler and Daniel Kauffman, *Mennonite Church History* (Scottdale, PA: Mennonite Book and Tract Society, 1905); Emma Smith to Henry Smith, November 22, 1904, box 6, file 44, C. Henry Smith Papers, BUASC.
13. Simon Baechler to C. H. Smith, September 21, 1904, and Amanda Troyer to Smith, September 16, 1905, box 17, file 10, C. Henry Smith Papers, BUASC.
14. John Funk, "To Whom It May Concern," October 24, 1904, box 10, file 9, Hist. Ms. I, C. Henry Smith Papers, BUASC; Smith, *Mennonite Country Boy*, 214–18, 222–25 (quoted 214, 225).
15. Smith, *The Mennonites of America*, 461; Hartzler and Kauffman, *Mennonite Church History*, 8–9, 290–94, 326–29 (quoted 327).
16. Smith, "The Mennonites of Europe," in Hartzler and Kauffman, *Mennonite Church History*, 91–96.
17. Smith, "The Mennonites of Europe," 96.
18. Editorial comment, the *Mennonite* XXI (July 12, 1906), 1; C. Henry Smith, *Mennonites in History* (Scottdale, PA: Mennonite Book and Tract Society, 1907), 8; also serialized in the *Gospel Witness* II (November 21 and 28, December 5 and 12, 1906), 530, 546–47, 562, 578; Kreider, "C. Henry Smith—Part Two: Premier Mennonite Historian—Master Story-Teller," *IMHQ* 31 (Summer, 2004), 20–21.
19. Hartzler and Kauffman, *Mennonite Church History* 15–89; Smith, "The Mennonites of Europe," in Hartzler and Kauffman, ibid., 90; Smith, *Mennonites in History*, 10–11; Kreider, "C. Henry Smith—Part Two," 21; Sprunger, "C Henry Smith's Vision of Mennonite History," 6 (Smith's rejection of Waldensian origins).

    Admittedly, Smith also included in this pantheon of Anabaptist heroes names that Horsch would soon vehemently reject, like Hans Denck and Balthasar Hubmaier. I will explore this clash of ideas below.
20. Smith, *Mennonites in History*, 12–19 (quoted 16–18).
21. Ibid., 19–28 (quoted 19, 24, 25, 26, 28).
22. Ibid., 28–36 (quoted 28, 31–32, 33, 35).
23. Ibid., 36–41 (quoted 36, 37–39, 41).

24. Wilma Schertz, "Smith Genealogy," 1865–1979; Willard Smith, *The Trail to Santa Fe*, 12; Agnes Albrecht diary entries, May 9 and September 19, 1906, July 24–25, 1907, Hist. Mss. I-332, Agnes Albrecht Gunden Papers, Box 1, files 1-2, AMC.
25. John Smith to Henry Smith, September 25, 1902, C. Henry Smith Papers, MS I, box 6, file 49, BUASC; John Smith to Henry Smith, May 21 [1902?], Ella Smith Oyer Papers, MS 112, box 1, folder 14, BUASC; Smith, *Mennonites in Illinois*, 253 (Whitmer anecdote); Samuel Smith to Henry Smith, October 31, 1905, box 8, file 6, BUASC.
26. Smith, *Mennonite Country Boy*, 219; "John Smith Dies Suddenly," undated obituary, probably from the *Metamora Herald*, C. Henry Smith Papers, box 60, file 4, BUASC; Agnes Albrecht diary entries July 10–11, 1906, Hist. Mss. I-332, Agnes Albrecht Gunden Papers, Box 1, file 1, AMC.
27. Smith, *Mennonite Country Boy*, 216–22 (quoted 219, 216); Sam Smith to Henry Smith, May 14, 1907, box 8, file 6, Smith Papers, BUASC.
28. Smith to Laura Ioder, January 19, 1908 ("the only thing"), January 26, 1908 ("full of crime"), all in Smith Papers, Hist. Mss. I-I, box 1, file 8; September 16, 1907 ("foreign names"), Smith Papers, Hist. Mss. I-I, box 1, file 7, BUASC; Steiner, *Pitfalls and Safeguards*, 100; Smith, *Mennonite Country Boy*, 216–17 (quoted 216).
29. Smith, *Mennonite Country Boy*, 215 (quoted 227).
30. For biographical data on William Ioder, see "William Ioder," in *A History of Bureau County, Illinois*, ed. H. C. Bradbury (Chicago: Word Publishing, 1885), 558–59 (quoted 559), and *Voters and Taxpayers of Bureau County, Illinois* (Chicago: H. F. Kett and Co., 1877), 266, both at Bureau County Historical Society, Princeton, Illinois. On Willow Springs, see Smith, *Mennonites in Illinois*, 69–70, 185, and Weber, *A Centennial History of the Mennonites of Illinois*, 222–34; Elaine Burress Bowers, interview with author, May 13–14, 2010.
31. Bowers, interview; copy of Ioder family history, n.p., loaned to author by Elaine Bowers; obituary for William Ioder, undated but about 1914 from a Bureau County newspaper, copy in author's possession; "Tiskilwa News," *Bureau County Tribune* (January 1, 1909); Smith to Laura Ioder, January 19, 1908, box 1, file 8; Ms. I-I, Smith Papers, BUASC; Ioder to Smith, January 10, 1908, box 7, file 11, and May 24, 1908, box 7, file 13, Smith Papers, BUASC.
32. Smith to Ioder, September 16, 1907, Smith Papers, Hist. Mss. I-I, box 1, file 7 ("chance meeting"), March 20, 1907 ("he usually tells"); Bowers, interview.

In the end, the two couples made a neat romantic foursome. Yoder ended up marrying Sadie Albright (or Albrecht), and in turn was related to the Ioders by marriage, since his new brother-in-law was Albert Albrecht, who married Laura's sister Mary. Yoder and Sadie Albright had two sons together and lived out their lives in Peru, Illinois, where Yoder practiced medicine; Bowers, interview.

33. Orie Yoder to Laura Ioder, March 24, 1907, box 1, file 10, Smith Papers I-I, BUASC.
34. Smith to Byers, March 3 ("when I go back to Goshen") and April 1, 1907 ("how easily a man"), Goshen College President's Office Papers, V-04-14.1, box 1, file 35, AMC.

35. Smith to Ioder, March 20 ("Normal is the place") and May 1, 1907 ("whenever you want me to"), May 9, 1907, all in box 1, file 4, BUASC; May 15 ("I have been looking forward") and June 2, 1907 ("it is all over"), both in file 5, Smith Papers, I-I, BUASC; Ioder to Smith, May 5, 1907, box 7, file 4, March 20, 1908, box 7, file 12, Smith Papers, BUASC.
36. Smith to Ioder, September 4, 1907, Smith Papers, box 1, file 6, BUASC; Willard H. Smith, "C. Henry Smith: A Brief Biography," in Smith, *Mennonite Country Boy*, 238.
37. Ioder to Smith, September 6 ("contents of your letter") and September 13, 1907 ("there isn't any use"), box 7, file 4, Ms. I, Smith Papers, BUASC; Smith to Ioder, September 10 ("a little more reserved") and September 15, 1907 ("your heart"), both in box 1, file 7, Smith Papers, BUASC.
38. Ioder to Smith, September 3, 1907, Smith Papers, box 7, file 4, March 27, 1908 ("I hope you are as anxious"), box 7, file 13, January 3 and January 31, 1908, box 7, file 11, BUASC; Smith to Ioder, January 16 ("I think of you often") and January 26, 1908, both in box 1, file 8; February 2, 1908 ("sly marriages"), box 1, file 9, Smith Papers, I-I, BUASC.

    According to Schlabach, many Mennonite couples in the nineteenth century tried to keep news of their engagement quiet; see Schlabach, *Peace, Faith, Nation*, 80.
39. Bowers, interview; Ioder to Smith, April 7, 1907, box 7, file 3, Smith Papers, BUASC.
40. Smith to Byers, February 24, 1907, Goshen College President's Office Papers, V-04-14.1, box 1, file 35, AMC; undated newspaper clippings, "New Instructor Engaged," and "The Manual Training High School Senate," box 43, file 28, Smith Papers, BUASC; Byers, "Professor C. Henry Smith," 5–6.
41. Ioder to Smith, January 10 and February 28, 1908; Smith to Ioder, March 20 and May 16, 1908 ("to see the President").
42. Yoder to Smith, March 20, 1908, Smith Papers, box 9, file 37, BUASC; "A Reunion of the Sages," *Snell Hall Cooler*, 1907, p. 18, box 52, file 35, Smith Papers, BUASC.

Chapter 5: How to Write the Mennonite Story

1. Harold S. Bender and John S. Oyer, "Historiography: Anabaptist," in *GAMEO*, 1989, http://gameo.org/index.php?title=Historiography:_Anabaptist&oldid=121134 (Bender and Kohler quoted); C. Arnold Snyder, *Anabaptist History and Theology: An Introduction* (Kitchener, ON: Pandora Press, 1995), 398; Belfort Bax, *Rise and Fall of the Anabaptists* (New York: American Scholar Publications, 1903), 2.
2. For the new Anabaptist apologetics, see Bender and Oyer, "Historiography: Anabaptist," and Snyder, *Anabaptist History and Theology: An Introduction*, 399. Richard Heath, *Anabaptism: From Its Rise at Zwickau to Its Fall at Muenster, 1521–1536* (London: Alexander and Shepheard, 1895), 32–36, 92–98; Albert Henry Newman, *A History of Anti-Pedobaptism* (Philadelphia: American Baptist Publication Society, 1897), 86, 101, 105–6; Bax, *Rise and Fall of the Anabaptists*, 391.

3. On Heath's purpose in establishing a Baptist usable past, see the preface by editor George Gould in Heath, *Anabaptism*; Newman, *A History of Anti-Pedobaptism*, 62, 86.
4. Heath, *Anabaptism*, 25–30, 86–91, 193–94 (quoted 194); Newman, *A History of Anti-Pedobaptism*, 91–92, 101–9, 128–30, 162–67; Bax, *Rise and Fall of the Anabaptists*, 28–65 (quoted 64).
5. Abraham Friesen, *History and Renewal in the Anabaptist/Mennonite Tradition* (North Newton, KS: Bethel College Press, 1994), 41–46, 54–86, 113–17 (quoted 61; Dutch pastor quoted 44). On the rapid emergence of Horsch as a Keller disciple, see Friesen, ibid., 112–27, and Robert Friedmann, "John Horsch and Ludwig Keller," *MQR* 21 (July 1947), 161–64 (quoted 164).
6. Harold S. Bender, "John Horsch, 1867–1941: A Biography," *MQR* 21 (July 1947), 131–33. Friesen, *History and Renewal in the Anabaptist/Mennonite Tradition*, 117, 126 (quoted 117).
7. Friedmann, "John Horsch and Ludwig Keller," 165–71 (quoted 166); Bender, "John Horsch, 1867–1941: A Biography," 134–35; Friesen, *History and Renewal in the Anabaptist/Mennonite Tradition*, 123–28.
8. Coffman, "The Spirit of Progress," in Steiner, *John S. Coffman*, 121–22; Hartzler and Kauffman, *Mennonite Church History*, 15–77 (quoted 70). For Keller's influence among Russian-descended General Conference Mennonites in Kansas, like their leading intellectual Cornelius Wedel, see Juhnke, "*Gemeindechristentum* and Bible Doctrine," 211.
9. Smith to Jameson, October 26, 1904, box 1, file 20, Ms. I-I, Smith Papers, BUASC.
10. Smith to Jameson, January 20 and 27, 1905 (quoted), box 1, file 20, Smith Papers, BUASC; C. Henry Smith, "The Anabaptists," *Gospel Witness* I (May 31, 1905), 40–71; 1: 10 (June 7, 1905), 78; 1: 13 (June 13, 1905), 102; 1: 14 (July 5, 1905), 110 (quoted).
11. Smith, "The Anabaptists," *Gospel Witness* I: 15 (July 12, 1905), 118 (quoted); I: 16 (July 19, 1905), 126 (quoted); I: 17 (July 26, 1905), 134 (quoted); I: 15 (August 2, 1905), 142.
12. Daniel Kauffman, editorial notes, *Gospel Witness* I: 9 (May 31, 1905), 68, 71.

    Kauffman and several associates in Scottdale, Pennsylvania, founded the *Gospel Witness* that January as a competitor paper to Funk's *Herald of Truth*. Within three years they would succeed in wresting control of Funk's paper away from him. Renamed the *Gospel Herald*, it would function for the rest of the century as the denominational organ for the Mennonite Church. See Harold S. Bender, "Gospel Witness (Periodical)" in *GAMEO*, 1956, http://gameo.org/index.php?title=Gospel_Witness_(Periodical)&oldid=122977; and Juhnke, *Vision, Doctrine, War*, 126–27.
13. Smith to Jameson, October 26, 1904; Smith, "The Anabaptists," *Gospel Witness* (August 2, 1905), 142.

    The late Rodney Sawatsky recognized Smith as a predecessor of the Anabaptist polygenesis school two decades ago. See Rodney J. Sawatsky, "The One and the Many: The Recovery of Mennonite Pluralism," in *Anabaptism Revisited*, ed. Walter Klassen (Scottdale, PA: Herald Press, 1992), 142–45; and

Sawatsky, *Authority and Identity: The Dynamics of the General Conference Mennonite Church* (North Newton, KS: Bethel College Press, 1987), 45–47.
14. Smith, "The Anabaptists," *Gospel Witness* (August 2, 1905), 142.
15. Smith, *Mennonite Country Boy*, 225; Estes, "C. Henry Smith: Dean of American Mennonite Historiography," 20–21; Harold S. Bender, "Mennonites of America, The (Monograph)," in *GAMEO*, 1957, http://gameo.org/index.php?title=Mennonites_of_America,_The_(Monograph)&oldid=92769.
16. Bender to Steiner, April 3, 1909, Steiner Papers, Hist. Mss 1-31, box 14, file 1, AMC; Smith, *The Mennonites of America*, 14–15 (quoted); C. Henry Smith, "Mennonites of America" (PhD diss., University of Chicago, 1909).
17. Smith, *The Mennonites of America*, 7, 9–10; Estes, "C. Henry Smith: Dean of American Mennonite Historiography," 24–26 (on Smith's self-conception as a political historian).
18. Smith, *The Mennonites of America*, 17–52 (quoted 7, 33, 354–55).
19. Ibid., 25–64 (quoted 25, 28, 41, 44, 64). In his rejection of Waldensian origins, Smith may also have just been following the currents of contemporary Anabaptist scholarship. About the time Smith was researching his book, Walter Kohler warned Anabaptist scholars against Keller's theory as inadequately grounded in historical evidence; see Friesen, *History and Renewal in the Anabaptist/Mennonite Tradition*, 133.
20. Smith, *The Mennonites of America*, 81ff (for detailed footnotes), 265 (quoted). For examples of "covering" references or incomplete notes, see 193, 276, 307, 329, 332. On the immature nature of the American historical profession at the time, see Novick, *That Noble Dream*, 48–55. Whatever the reason, the carelessness was not the fault of Smith's professors at Chicago; the three chapters he transferred from his dissertation were all fully footnoted.
21. Harold S. Bender, "C. Henry Smith: A Tribute," in Smith, *Mennonite Country Boy*, 232; in general, see the table of contents in Smith, *The Mennonites of America*, and 243–48, 390 (quoted), 403–4, 431–42.
22. Smith, *The Mennonites of America*, 305–14, 386–446 (quoted 390).
23. Ibid., 96–108, 135–91, 239, 433 (quoted 104, 106, 107, 147, 174, 176).
24. Ibid., 71–4, 120–23, 172, 178–9 (quoted 72, 73, 120, 290, 341). For the prominence given to Quaker contributions in a popular children's textbook of the time, see D. H. Montgomery, *An Elementary American History* (Boston: Ginn and Co., 1904), 44–48.
25. Smith, *Mennonite Country Boy*, 136–37.
26. Kathleen Neils Conzen et al., "The Invention of Ethnicity: A Perspective from the USA," *Journal of American Ethnic History* 12: 1 (Fall 1992), 1–3, 6–7 (quoted 3).
27. Smith, *The Mennonites of America*, 384–85, 408. Conzen et al. suggest that it was particularly immigrants who had settled in urban areas upon whom the assimilative pressures were greater and whose needs for "ethnicization" were intensified. See Conzen et al., "The Invention of Ethnicity," 9–10.
28. For Smith's confidence in a progressive future, see Sprunger, "C. Henry Smith's Vision of Mennonite History," 7–8; Smith, *The Mennonites of America*, 247–52 (quoted 248, 252).
29. Smith, *The Mennonites of America*, 291, 397–98 (quoted 397).

30. Ibid., 397–403 (quoted 399, 401, 402–3).
31. Steve Nolt, "A 'Two-Kingdom' People in a World of Multiple Identities: Religion, Ethnicity and American Mennonites," *MQR* 73 (July 1999), 487–99, quoted 487, 497; Smith, *The Mennonites of America*, 389 ("engendered conservatism"), 454–5 ("minor customs and practices").
32. Hartzler, "To whom it may concern," June 25, 1909; comments from Byers and other notables in the *Gospel Herald* and *Mennonite* were included in an undated, typewritten memo called "Testimonials," and a handwritten, undated postcard from Strubhar, box 10, file 17, Ms. I-I, Smith Papers, BUASC.
33. Smith, *Mennonite Country Boy*, 225–26; Kreider, "C. Henry Smith—Part Two," 19; "Report #3" and "The Weekly Report," in Smith Papers, MS I, box 38, file 13, BUASC; "Henry Smith issues Work," undated clipping from the *Metamora Herald* (notation in Smith's handwriting), Smith Papers, box 43, file 28, BUASC. Real cost estimates from U.S. Bureau of Labor Statistics in http://www.bls.gov/data/inflation_calculator.htm.
34. Smith quotes on the nature of business are in "Report #3"; his instructions to his sales team in undated memo, "Canvas," box 59, file 12, Smith Papers, BUASC.
35. Smith, *The Mennonites of America*, 403.

Chapter 6: The Way of Exile

1. *Bureau County Tribune*, January 1, 1909, 7; Tilman Smith to C. Henry and Laura Smith, December 23, 1938, box 9, file 62, Ms. I, Smith Papers, BUASC (Smiths' honeymoon); C. Henry Smith to John E. Hartzler, October 7, 1913, J. E. Hartzler Papers, Hist. Mss. I-62, box 2, file 3, AMC; Byers, "The Times in Which I Lived—II," 79; Whitmer, "Autobiography," 67; Smith, *Mennonite Country Boy*, 203.
2. *Goshen: Sesquicentennial Edition, 1831–1931* (Goshen, IN: News Printing Company, 1981), 48–50; "Birdman through Goshen; Two Aviators Are Dashed to Death in Chicago," *Goshen Daily News*, August 13, 1911, 1.
3. Besides Smith there were, by 1908, only two other Mennonite scholars—Noah Hirschy and another biblical scholar named Samuel Mosiman—who had obtained doctorates and who remained yet within the church. Both had received their doctorates the previous year from German universities, and both were teaching in Bluffton. On these men, see Bush, *Dancing with the Kobzar*, 32, 60–61.
4. 1909–1910 *Goshen College Catalogue* (Goshen, IN: Goshen College, 1909), MHLG, "Faculty," and pp. 34–37, 104 (quoted); Umble, *Goshen College, 1894–1954*, 39, 58 (student numbers), 43–45 (capital campaign); Miller, *Culture for Service*, 36 (bachelor's degrees), 28–29 (Y work).
5. Miller, *Culture for Service*, 36–39 (campus climate); Theron Schlabach, *Goshen College Mennonite Church: An Overview* (Goshen, IN: College Mennonite Church, 1979), 17–21; Goshen College Mennonite Church, meeting minutes, December 8, 1904, April 27 and June 5, 1909, 2–3, 45, 49, College Mennonite Church Papers, Hist. Mss. III-14-1.1, "Church Minutes Book, 1904–1924," AMC; Jonathan M. Kurtz, "The Goshen Congregation (1903–1924)," College Mennonite Church Papers, box 1, file 7, AMC (quoted 6).

6. "Local Option League Meeting," *Goshen Daily News*, February 15, 1909, 1; "Launch Campaign for City Option," *Goshen Daily News*, February 16, 1911, 1; "Only Men Next Monday Night," *Goshen Daily News*, March 22, 1911, 1; "Billy Sunday Closes Fight," *Goshen Daily News*, March 29, 1911, 1 (Sunday quoted); "Wet: Goshen 146, Elkhart 468," *Goshen Daily News*, March 29, 1911, 1; "Special Newspapers," unnamed newspaper clipping with handwritten notation by Smith, "Goshen, Indiana 1912," box 1, Smith Papers, MS I, BUASC. For Smith's clippings on the Prohibition campaign, see box 20, file 8.
7. Smith, "The Forces that Make for Peace," *Christian Monitor* II: 3–5 (March, April, May 1910), 468–69, 502, 511, 532–33, quoted 532.
8. For overviews of the MRFM, see Gary Scott Smith, *The Search for Social Salvation: Social Christianity and America, 1880–1925* (Lanham, MD: Lexington Books, 2000), 336–40; Gary Scott Smith, "The Men and Religion Forward Movement of 1911–12: New Perspectives on Evangelical Social Concern and the Relationship between Christianity and Progressivism," in *Modern American Protestantism and Its World: Historical Articles on Protestantism in American Religious Life*, ed. Martin Marty (New York: K. G. Saur, 1992): 171–74; and Gorrell, *The Age of Social Responsibility*, 155–60 (MRFM statement quoted 156). On its efforts at the masculinization of Protestantism, see Gail Bederman, "'The Women Have Had Charge of the Church Long Enough': The Men and Religion Forward Movement of 1911–1912 and the Masculinization of Middle-Class Protestantism," in *A Mighty Baptism: Race, Gender and the Creation of American Protestantism*, eds. Susan Jester and Lisa McFarlane (Ithaca, NY: Cornell University Press, 1996), 107–37.
9. "Big Mass Meeting at First M.E.," *Goshen News Times*, June 3, 1911, 1; Gorrell, *The Age of Social Responsibility*, 155 (Rauschenbusch quoted); "Gathering Data and Statistics," *Goshen News Times*, October 12, 1911, 1. Smith notes on the Goshen MRFM are found in an untitled and undated spiral notebook, box 42, file 3, Smith Papers, BUASC; "Advocated Awakening," *Goshen News Times*, November 11, 1911: 1 (Matthews quoted).
10. Smith notes on a speech, with the notation in Smith's handwriting, "Delivered at Millersburg, Ind., Dec. 19, (1911?) on behalf of Men & Religion Movement," in Smith Papers, box 42, file 3, BUASC; "Forward Movement Meeting," undated newspaper clipping but clearly on this Millersburg address, box 42, file 28, Smith Papers, BUASC.
11. C. Henry Smith, "The Amish in Illinois," *Mennonite Yearbook and Directory, 1907* (Mennonite Board of Missions and Charities, 1907), 19–24; Smith, "Christopher Dock: The Pious Schoolmaster of the Skippack," *Christian Monitor* 1 (January 1909), 18–19; Smith, "Menno Simons," *Christian Monitor* 1: 8–9 (August and September 1909), 241–43, 274–76 (quoted 275).
12. Schlabach, "Reveille for *Die Stillen im Lande*," 226 (quoted); Schlabach, "The Humble Become 'Aggressive Workers,'" 121–22. For Funk's struggles, see Yoder, "Mennonite Fundamentalism," 154–56 and Juhnke, *Vision, Doctrine, War*, 125–27. Leonard Gross, "The Doctrinal Era of the Mennonite Church," *MQR* LX (January 1986), 89–91.

13. For new MC hierarchical institutions, see Hurst, "The Articulation of Mennonite Beliefs about Sexuality," 143–45, and Schlabach, "The Humble Become 'Aggressive Workers,'" 121–22 (Steiner quoted). Also on Steiner's growing caution, see Yoder, "Mennonite Fundamentalism," 268.
14. On Kauffman see Paul Erb and Leonard Gross, "Kauffman, Daniel (1865–1944)," in *GAMEO*, 1989, http://gameo.org/index.php?title=Kauffman,_Daniel_(1865-1944)&oldid=112855. For Kauffman's committees, see Schlabach, "The Humble Become 'Aggressive Workers,'" 124. Kauffman quoted in Hartzler and Kauffman, *Mennonite Church History*, 368 (given the subsequent course of events, it seems logical to assume these words are Kauffman's); Kraus, "American Mennonites and the Bible," 313–16 (quoted 315, 313); also see Kauffman, *Fifty Years in the Mennonite Church*, 3–4. For Kauffman's Bible doctrines, see Gross, "The Doctrinal Era of the Mennonite Church," 87–89, 92, and Juhnke, "*Gemeindechristentum* and Bible Doctrine," 214–19. On the separation between doctrine and ethics, see J. Denny Weaver, *Keeping Salvation Ethical: Mennonite and Amish Atonement Theology in the Late Nineteenth Century* (Scottdale, PA: Herald Press, 1995), 218–20; Schlabach, *Peace, Faith, Nation*, 318–19; and "Paradoxes of Mennonite Separatism," *Pennsylvania Mennonite Heritage* II (January 1979), 12–17.
15. Gross, "The Doctrinal Era of the Mennonite Church," 96, Kauffman quoted 87.
16. Schlabach, *Peace, Faith, Nation*, 308–10; Juhnke, *Vision, Doctrine, War*, 28–30, 119–20. "We are now in the 'organization' period of our church life," Steiner wrote in 1910. "Everybody seems to have been taken in by the fever throughout the church." At the same time, he added thoughtfully, "the thing is being overdone"; quoted in Juhnke, 120.
17. George Marsden, *Fundamentalism and American Culture: The Shaping of Twentieth-Century Evangelicalism, 1870–1925* (New York: Oxford University Press, 1980), 3–8, 32–85ff (quoted 5–6). Also on the rise of fundamentalism, see Hudson, *Religion in America*, 279–85, 366–68; Ahlstrom, *A Religious History of the American People* II, 277–87; William Vance Trollinger Jr., *God's Empire: William Bell Riley and Midwestern Fundamentalism* (Madison: University of Wisconsin Press, 1990), 4–5 (quoted 5); and Paul Toews, "Fundamentalist Conflict in Mennonite Colleges: A Response to Cultural Transitions?" *MQR* 57 (July 1983), 242–43. Gorrell, *The Age of Social Responsibility*, 128–29 (Moody president and *Fundamentals* sponsor, quoted 128).
18. On Mennonite embrace of fundamentalism, see Juhnke, *Vision, Doctrine, War*, 262–63, Yoder, "Mennonite Fundamentalism," 110–11, and Smith, *Mennonites in Illinois*, 303–4. On Illinois Mennonites and MBI, see Smith, 304–10. For Kauffman's criticisms of the fundamentalist movement, see Kauffman, "Unfundamental Fundamentalists," *Gospel Herald* XXXIV (February 25, 1932), 1026–27.
19. Paul Toews, "Fundamentalist Conflict in Mennonite Colleges," 245. Juhnke, likewise, is more comfortable writing of "conservative Mennonite anti-Modernists"; see Juhnke, *Vision, Doctrine, War*, 258–60 (quoted 260). Guy F. Hershberger, "The Times of Sanford Calvin Yoder: The Mennonite Church and the First Fifty Years of Goshen College," in *An Evening to Honor Sanford*

Calvin Yoder (Goshen: Goshen College, July 1974, MHLG), 16–17; Kraus, "American Mennonites and the Bible," 327 (quoted); Emma Smith to Henry Smith, February 14, 1910, box 6, file 44, Smith Papers, BUASC.

20. For increasing MC dress restrictions, see Hurst, "The Articulation of Mennonite Beliefs about Sexuality," 179–86; Juhnke, *Vision, Doctrine, War*, 130–32; Hershberger, "The Times of Sanford Calvin Yoder," 17. For feminist analyses, see Donald B. Kraybill, "Mennonite Woman's Veiling: The Rise and Fall of a Sacred Symbol," *MQR* LXI (July 1987), 325–26; Marlene Epp, "Carrying the Banner of Nonconformity: Ontario Mennonite Women and the Dress Question," *Conrad Grebel Review* 8 (Fall 1990), 237–46; and Sharon Klingelsmith, "Women in the Mennonite Church, 1900–1930," *MQR* LIV (July 1980), 177–82 (Kauffman quoted 180).

21. Kraus, "American Mennonites and the Bible," 318–27.

22. On the Keller-Horsch relationship, see Friesen, *History and Renewal in the Anabaptist/Mennonite Tradition*, 126–28, and Friedmann, "John Horsch and Ludwig Keller," 171–72. Horsch biographical details in Bender, "John Horsch, 1867–1941: A Biography," 135–41 (Steiner quoted 138), and Harold S. Bender, "Horsch, John (1867–1941)," in *GAMEO*, 1953, http://gameo.org/index.php?title=Horsch,_John_(1867-1941)&oldid=123472.

23. For Horsch's embrace of fundamentalism, see Friesen, *History and Renewal in the Anabaptist/Mennonite Tradition*, 128–31; Kraus, "American Mennonites and the Bible," 325; and Yoder, "Mennonite Fundamentalism," 190–91 (Horsch in 1902). Daniel Kauffman to John Horsch, April 14, 1908, Horsch Papers, Hist. Mss. I-8-1, box 2, file 6, AMC; John Horsch, "The Danger of Liberalism," *Gospel Herald* I: 12 (June 20, 1908), 178–79; Horsch, "The Consequences of Higher Criticism," *Gospel Herald* II: 7 (May 13, 1909), 99–100 (quoted 100); John Horsch to Charles Clayton Morrison, November 15, 1926, Horsch Papers, I-8-1, box 7, file 9, AMC. Likewise, in a sympathetic review of Horsch's theology, John C. Wenger later noted that "One of the handicaps he had to overcome was the liberal theology he imbibed during his early years in America"; Wenger recalled Horsch himself saying that "as a young man the reading of modernistic literature had a detrimental effect on my religious thinking." See John C. Wenger, "The Theology of John Horsch," *MQR* XXI (July 1947), 151.

24. Bender, "John Horsch, 1867–1941: A Biography," 141; Friesen, *History and Renewal in the Anabaptist/Mennonite Tradition*, 130–32 (Horsch quoted on Denck, 131).

25. John Horsch to C. Henry Smith, January 8, 1908, box 3, file 70, Smith Papers, BUASC; Smith, *The Mennonites of America*, 18–19, 46–47 (quoted 47); John Horsch, "The Anabaptist View of Toleration," *Christian Evangel* I: 11 (May 1911), 221–23.

26. C. Henry Smith, "The Early Mennonites as Bible Students," *Christian Monitor* 3: 6 (June 1911), 174.

27. Juhnke, *Vision, Doctrine, War*, 171; Smith, *Mennonite Country Boy*, 204; Miller, *Culture for Service*, 102 (Kauffman quoted).

28. Noah Byers to John E. Hartzler, John E. Hartzler Papers, Hist. Mss I-62, box 1, file 2, AMC; Kauffman to Byers, November 12, 1908 (quoted) and January 25,

1909, Byers Papers, box 1, files 27 and 24, AMC; Umble, *Goshen College*, 51 (Byers and the plain coat); Byers to "Dear Brethren," January 20 and February 5, 1909, M.S. Steiner Papers, Hist. Mss I-31, box 14, file 1, AMC. Also on Byers's circular letter, see Yoder, "Mennonite Fundamentalism," 182–83.

29. Miller, *Culture for Service*, 48.
30. Umble, *Goshen College*, 45, 216 (quoted); Horsch to Byers, April 14, 1908 and Byers to Horsch, April 20, 1908, Horsch Papers, Hist. Mss. I-8-1, box 2, file 6, AMC.
31. Yoder to Smith, November 9, 1907, box 9, file 37, Smith Papers, BUASC. Smith, *Mennonite Country Boy*, 211; Smith, *The Mennonites of America*, 393, 19; C. Henry Smith, "Report of a Meeting held at Warsaw, Indiana, May 29, 1913, of a group of the various branches of the Mennonite Church to consider the founding of a Union College and Seminary," July 9, 1940, unpublished manuscript, BUASC.
32. Smith, *Mennonite Country Boy*, 130; Smith to Laura Ioder, September 16, 1907, box 7, file 4, BUASC; Smith to J. R. Thierstein "and wife," October 15, 1926, Thierstein Papers, Hist. Mss. 19, box 5, file 38, MLA.
33. Smith, *Mennonites in Illinois*, 326 (Bender quoted); Emma Smith to Henry Smith, November 1, 1908, C. Henry Smith Papers, box 6, file 44, and Laura Ioder to Henry Smith, November 1, 1907 ("tell me about their rules"), Smith Papers, box 7, file 8, and Dec. 12, 1907 (Mace comments), box 7, file 10, BUASC. On Tiskilwa Mennonite Church, see Harry F. Weber, *Centennial History of the Mennonites of Illinois* (Scottdale, PA: Mennonite Publishing House, 1931), 229–30, 480, and Smith, *Mennonites in Illinois*, 100. For Ioder membership records, see "Building Account" for 1912 and 1913, in Financial Ledger Book, Tiskilwa Mennonite Church, and members list for November 1914, in "Tiskilwa Mennonite Members over the Years, Compiled from old Church Records," n.p., December 1985, both in Tiskilwa Mennonite Church Papers, G-1-04, Illinois Mennonite Heritage Center, Metamora, IL. Bowers, interview, May 14, 2010.
34. Smith, *The Mennonites of America*, 455.
35. Sawatsky, *Authority and Identity*, 3–4, and Smith, *Mennonites in Illinois*, 462–63 (early Mennonite union efforts); Umble, *Goshen College*, 52 (Sommers's suggestion); John Horsch, "In What Fundamentals do Mennonites Agree?" *Gospel Herald* III: 8 (May 26, 1910), 114–15.
36. Smith, *Mennonites in Illinois*, 463, and Noah Byers, "Mennonite Unity," *Mennonite* XXV: 32 (August 18, 1910), 4 (Byers's involvement). Daniel Kauffman, "In What Fundamentals do Mennonites Agree?" *Gospel Herald* 1910, reprinted in Daniel Hertzler, ed., *Not by Might* (Scottdale, PA: Herald Press, 1983), 24; Kauffman to John E. Hartzler, May 8, 1911, Hartzler Papers, box 1, file 6, AMC.
37. Bush, *Dancing with the Kobzar*, 63; Byers, "The Times in Which I Lived—II," 81; Noah Byers to Samuel K. Mosiman, June 3, 1909, box 1, file titled "Letters, Resolutions leading to the Merger of Central Mennonite College into Bluffton College," Ms. 1-A-a, Noah Hirschy Papers, BUASC.
38. Henry P. Krehbiel to Noah Byers, September 27, and Byers to Krehbiel, October 18, 1912, both in H. P. Krehbiel Papers, Hist. Mss. 12, box 10, file 67,

MLA (on efforts to create a joint archive). For Byers's resignation, see Whitmer, "Autobiography," 71–72, and Miller, *Culture for Service*, 51. On Byers's vision for Bluffton, see Bush, *Dancing with the Kobzar*, 63–65, and C. Henry Smith and Edmund Hirschler, eds., *The Story of Bluffton College* (Bluffton, OH: Bluffton College, 1925), 117–18; Mosiman to Kliewer, March 13, 1913, and to J. F. Lehman, March 14, and Byers to Mosiman, May 9, 1913, box 1, file titled "Letters, Resolutions leading to the Merger of Central Mennonite College into Bluffton College," Ms. 1-A-a, Noah Hirschy Papers, BUASC.

39. For Smith's role in the creation of Bluffton College, see Byers to Mosiman, May 9 and 15, and July 16, 1913, and "First meeting of the Board of Trustees of Bluffton College," Berne, Indiana, August 18, 1913, all in Hist. Mss. 1-A-a, Noah Hirschy Papers, box 1, file titled "Letters, Resolutions leading to the Merger of Central Mennonite College into Bluffton College," BUASC; Extracts of Warsaw meeting minutes and list of attendees in Mosiman to "Dear friend," June 12, 1913, H. P. Krehbiel Papers, Hist. Mss. 12, box 4, file 27, MLA; P. R. Schroeder, "Notes taken at a Session of Members of various Mennonite conferences at Warsaw, Indiana," attached to Smith, "Report of a Meeting held at Warsaw, Indiana, May 29, 1913," unpublished manuscript, BUASC; "Cooperation in Higher Education," *Christian Evangel* III: 8 (August 1913), 314–16.

40. C. Henry Smith, "A Review of the early History of the American Mennonites," in *Echoes: A Book Containing the Report and Addresses of the First All-Mennonite Convention in America* (Hillsboro, KS: Publication Committee, 1913), 38–50 (quoted 47, 48–49, 50), MHLG. Union College suggestion in Byers to Mosiman, June 19 and April 10, 1913, box 1, file titled "Letters, Resolutions leading to the Merger of Central Mennonite College into Bluffton College," Ms. 1-A-a, Noah Hirschy Papers, BUASC.

41. Bush, *Dancing with the Kobzar*, 65 (Bluffton reactions); for Goshen reactions, see Umble, *Goshen College*, 54 (quoted), and Miller, *Culture for Service*, 51. Byers to Steiner, January 10, 1903, Steiner Papers, Hist. Mss. I-33, box 8, file 3, AMC; Smith to Mosiman, July 10, 1913, box 1, file titled "Letters, Resolutions leading to the Merger of Central Mennonite College into Bluffton College," Ms. 1-A-a, Noah Hirschy Papers, BUASC; Smith to Hartzler, October 6, 1913, Hartzler Papers, box 2, file 3, AMC.

42. Horsch to Krehbiel, July 15, 1913, Krehbiel Papers, Hist. Mss. 12, box 4, file 27, MLA; Smith, *The Mennonites of America*, 455.

Chapter 7: The "Most Liberal Wing"

1. C. Henry Smith, *The Mennonites: A Brief History* (Berne, IN: Mennonite Book Concern, 1920), 303; Smith, *Mennonite Country Boy*, 210. On the GC vision and geography, see Juhnke, *Vision, Doctrine, War*, 49–51; Sawatsky, *Authority and Identity*, 3–4; Sawatsky, "The One and the Many," 143–45; and Rodney Sawatsky, *History and Ideology: American Mennonite Definition through History* (Kitchener, ON: Pandora Press, 2005), 51. Smith, *The Mennonites of America*, 352.

2. "The Governor of Ohio Addressed 50,000 People on the College Campus," and "Bluffton Educational Advantages, Address delivered by N. E. Byers at

Bluffton Home Coming and College Day, Aug. 5, 1913," *College Record* XII (September 1913), 86–88.

3. Bush, *Dancing with the Kobzar*, 37–56, 65, quoted 35.

4. Edgar Schumacher, preface to *Life in the Bluffton and Pandora, Ohio Community, 1877–1910: Excerpts from the* Bluffton News, ed. Edgar Schumacher (Swiss Community Historical Society, 1997); Bush, *Dancing with the Kobzar*, 84 (Hirschy quoted).

5. For Thierstein and Langenwalter, see Edmund G. Kaufman, *General Conference Mennonite Pioneers* (North Newton, KS: Bethel College, 1973), 181–84, 233–34; "John R. Thierstein, Ph.D.," and "Rev. Jasper A. Huffman, Professor of New Testament Language and Literature," *Bluffton College Bulletin* II (November 1915), 5–6; Bush, *Dancing with the Kobzar*, 61 (on Mosimans); oral interview with Margaret Berky Houshower, March 23, 2010 (on the Trenton connection). For MBIC, see Harold S. Bender, "Mennonite Brethren in Christ," in *GAMEO*, 1957, http://gameo.org/index.php?title=Mennonite_brethren_in_christ&oldid=115157. Huffman described in Mosiman to Langenwalter, January 22, 1914, Hirschy Papers, "Corr. of 1913 from Central Mennonite College to Bluffton College," BUASC (Mosiman quoted); "Cooperation in Mennonite Education," *Christian Evangel* III (August 1913), 316; "First Meeting of the Board of Trustees at Bluffton College," August 18, 1913, Board of Trustees Meeting minutes, I-B, BUASC. For Smucker, see David J. Rempel Smucker, *Bid Me Discourse: Boyd David Smucker (1879–1936): Orator and Mennonite Educator* (David J. Rempel Smucker, 2011), 53–55; on Whitmer, see Langenwalter to Whitmer, February 9, 1915, and Whitmer to Langenwalter, February 15, 1915, both in Jacob Langenwalter Papers, Hist. Mss 29, box 1, file 2, MLA; Whitmer, "Autobiography," 77–83 (quoted).

6. Fred Steiner, ed., *Town at the Fork of the Rileys Revisited: Historical Sketches of Old Shannon and Bluffton, Ohio* (Bluffton: Bluffton News, 1986), 21–24, 31–32; *Bluffton News*, March 31, 1910, in *Life in the Bluffton and Pandora, Ohio Community*, ed. Edgar Schumacher, 164. For a visual representation of the community Smith was entering, see Robert Kreider et al., "The Swiss Settlement at the Turn of the Century: A Photographic Essay," *Mennonite Life* 43 (December 1988), 20–47.

7. Mosiman to Langenwalter, January 31, 1914, Hist. Mss I-a-b, Samuel K. Mosiman Papers, box 8, MHLB (Campus Drive addition). Property Deed, from Emma and Noah Byers to Laura I. Smith, March 1, 1915, in Smith Papers, MS I, box 59, file 34, BUASC; Laura to C. Henry Smith, Smith Papers, December 23, [1916?], box 7, file 1, and February 19, 1916, box 7, file 14, BUASC; Bush, *Dancing with the Kobzar*, 70 (on Ropp Hall); Smucker, *Bid Me Discourse*, 61, 67–69 (faculty neighborhood).

8. Smucker, *Bid Me Discourse*, 60; Noah and Emma Byers, "Church Record," membership records, First Mennonite Church, Bluffton, Ohio, copy in author's possession. On Zion, see John Umble, *Ohio Mennonite Sunday Schools* (Goshen, IN: The Mennonite Historical Society, 1941), 178–80.

9. Smith church membership noted on brief, undated resume accompanying Smith to Bender, May 16, 1931, Bender Papers, Hist. Mss. 1-278, box 12, file 5, AMC. For East White Oak, see Weber, *Centennial History of the Mennonites*

of Illinois, 469–70, Rev. Peter Schantz, "Information for East White Oak," Hist. Mss. I-665, Harry F. Weber Papers, box 2, file 13, AMC. For the Central Conference, see Willard Smith, *The Mennonites of Illinois*, 97–110 (conference quoted 103). C. Henry Smith, *The Mennonites of America*, 252; *Bluffton College Record* 12 (October 15, 1913), 91; "Our Policy," *Christian Evangel* I (January 1911), 24; *Bluffton College Record* 12 (October 15, 1913), 91; *Program of the Central Conference of Mennonites, held at Goshen, Indiana, Aug. 25–27th, 1915* (n.p., MHLG); *Annual Meeting of the Central Conference of Mennonites, held at Bethel Church, Pekin, Ill, Aug. 27, 28 and 29, 1919* (n.p., MHLG).

10. Smucker, *Bid Me Discourse*, 60.
11. Schlabach, *Peace, Faith, Nation*, 75–80 (Mennonite and Amish sexual attitudes); Laura Ioder to C. Henry Smith, September 6, 1907 and March 6, 1916, Smith Papers, box 7, file 4, and box 7, file 14, BUASC; Smucker, *Bid Me Discourse*, 69 (Smucker quoted); Zion Mennonite Cemetery Association Records, Zion Mennonite Church Papers, 3-Ch-OH-1, BUASC. Laura's niece Elaine Bowers suspected there may have been some genetic marker in the Ioder family behind such childbirth complications. Laura's mother lost two children prematurely or in infancy. Likewise, her sister Clara only gave birth to one daughter, who died in infancy. Data taken from Bowers interview, undated obituary for Fanny Ioder, and unpublished Joseph Stauffer family history (copies in author's possession).
12. Ruth Smith Dick, interview with the author, May 14, 2010; Bowers, interview.
13. Smith Dick, interview; Bowers, interview. While some of Smith's extended family apparently did not know about Laura's illness, it was common enough knowledge in Bluffton, as I learned from numerous informal conversations with various longtime residents.
14. Roger Geiger, "The Crisis of the Old Order: The Colleges in the 1890s," in *The American College in the Nineteenth Century*, ed. Roger Geiger (Nashville: Vanderbilt University Press, 2000), 264–76; Bush, *Dancing with the Kobzar*, 63 (student numbers), 70 (campus buildings). Berky and Bogart in "The Faculty," *College Record* 12 (September 1913), 1; *Bluffton College Bulletin*, II (November 1915), 5. C. Henry Smith, "Bluffton College Semester Class Record, for term beginning Sept. 1920," box 20, file 19, Smith Papers, BUASC; Thierstein to Mosiman, June 22, 1915, box 8, file titled "J. R. Thierstein," Mosiman Papers, BUASC; faculty meeting minutes, September 24, 1913, Bluffton College Faculty Meeting Minutes, box 1, I-E-a, BUASC; Bluffton College Board of Trustees, meeting minutes of May 31, 1917, Board of Trustees Meeting minutes, I-B, BUASC.
15. Bush, *Dancing with the Kobzar*, 67, 71–72, 75–77 (BC progressive culture); Rudolph, *The American University and College*, 369–70 (progressive climate nationally); Smucker, *Bid Me Discourse*, 80, 85–86. On campus "Y" enthusiasm, see 1915 *Ista*, 78; 1918 *Ista*, 158–59; 1919 *Ista*, 104; 1919 *Ista*, 59, 61; on the Student Volunteer Band, see 1919 *Ista*, 59; *Witmarsum* III (March 1916), 4.
16. *College Record* 1:11 (December 1914), 4; *Bluffton College Bulletin* 5: 2 (March 1918), 3; Whitmer, "Autobiography," 99–100; James C. Juhnke, *Creative*

Crusader: Edmund G. Kaufman and Mennonite Community (North Newton, KS: Bethel College, 1994), 64–65.

17. Juhnke, *Creative Crusader*, 65–70 (quoted 65); Edmund G. Kaufman, "Social Problems and Opportunities of the Western District Conference Communities of the General Conference of Mennonites of North America" (MA thesis, Bluffton College and Mennonite Seminary, 1917), ii, 2–18, 130–31, 164–66 (quoted 17–18).

18. Kaufman, "Social Problems," 87.

19. "Anti-Saloon Speech," handwritten outline for a speech delivered at "Pleasant Hill Church Bluffton, Oct. 20," and "Modern Trend in Education," handwritten outline for a speech delivered in Rawson, Ohio, October 24, 1914, both in brown leather planner, Smith Papers, box 1, file 6, BUASC; Karl, *Charles E. Merriam and the Study of Politics*, 40.

20. "Dean Byers Is Running for Town Council," *Witmarsum* V: 8 (November 3, 1917). "Mennonite Democratic Party enthusiasm in Juhnke," *Creative Crusader*, 77–78; Bush, *Dancing with the Kobzar*, 67; and transcript of oral interview with Wilmer Shelly, in *Sourcebook: Oral History Interviews with World War One Conscientious Objectors* (Akron, PA: Mennonite Central Committee, 1986), 202. Bluffton Village Council Minutes, Bluffton Village Hall, Bluffton, Ohio (see minutes for the meetings of January 3, April 4, September 4, and October 16, 1916, January 15 and June 4, 1917, January 7, 1918, and passim; A. D. Luginbuhl to Smith, 1922, box 2, file 7, Ms. I, Smith Papers, BUASC. The procedural vote on Smith's charter revision attempt occurred in early September 1916, just as he was dealing with the death of his infant son. One expects he was inattentive to council politics at the time.

21. For Amish and Mennonite business attitudes, see Schlabach, *Peace, Faith, Nation*, 46–58 (Amish Mennonites, quoted 50), and Yoder, *Traditions and Transition*, 228–29. Smith, *Mennonite Country Boy*, 30–31; Novick, *That Noble Dream*, 169–70 (Wittenberg anecdote). Smith salary in Bluffton College Board of Trustees meeting minutes of February 2, 1930, Board of Trustees Meeting minutes, I-B, MHLB; Mosiman to James Halfhill, March 9, 1916, Mosiman Papers, box 1, file titled "Merger of Central Mennonite College to Bluffton College," MHLB. The $1,500/$17,500 comparison is found in an inflation calculator by the U.S. Department of Labor, Bureau of Labor Statistics, http://www.bls.gov/data/inflation_calculator.htm.

22. Undated obituary for William Ioder, copy in author's possession (quoted); Bowers, interview. "I got all my money from my wife" is from Alice Ruth Ramseyer, interview with the author, January 12, 2012. I also heard this anecdote from longtime local resident Samuel Diller, whose parents were Bluffton-area contemporaries of Smith's.

23. "Give $16,398 to Science Hall," *Bluffton News* (November 5, 1914); Laura to Henry Smith, March 6, 1916 ("Have you heard anything about your farm[?]," Laura asked her spouse. "I hope he sold the oats when you told him to.") Willard Smith, *The Trail to Santa Fe*, 127; Dave [sic] Flick to J. R. Thierstein, November 15, 1924, Thierstein Papers, Hist. Mss. 19, box 4, file 29, MLA.

24. Flick to Thierstein, November 15, 1924; J. R. Thierstein to C. L. Parker, January 8, 1926 ("fool that I was" and data on Goshen condenser), box 4, file 26;

Gottshall to Thierstein, February 11, 1924; Smucker to Thierstein, December 5, 1923, box 4, file 29; Findlay Dairy Company, "Notice of Stockholders Meeting," December 1923; Smith to Thierstein, January 3 ("my loss has been the biggest share"), and April 13, 1924, all in Thierstein Papers, Hist. Mss. 19, MLA; Smucker, *Bid Me Discourse*, 75.

Losing the dairy was also a hard blow to the unfortunate Smucker. "I have never been so hard up as I have been this past year," he admitted to Thierstein in December 1923. "I borrowed every cent of money I put in the dairy and heavily mortgaged my home and never got a cent of it back . . . with my four boys and usual irregularity in salary it keeps me on the jumps all the time"; Smucker to Thierstein, December 5, 1923. He was soon able to get his Bluffton College job back; Smucker, *Bid Me Discourse*, 75.

The fox farm was located down West Elm Street from the college on the site of the current Mennonite Memorial Home. Smith, the second-largest single investor, owned thirty-six shares, more than twice the amount of most others. The farm was finally dissolved in 1938. Keith Sommers of Bluffton kindly allowed me to consult a ledger book on the operation. This document is currently in the possession of the Swiss Historical Society of Bluffton.

25. On Chicago courses, see Smith's professional resume from the mid-teens, box 52, file 32, Smith Papers, BUASC; "Banking Began in Corner of Store," *150 Years along the Riley: A History and Events of Riley Township and Pandora, Ohio, 1832–1982*, ed. Don Schneck (Riley Township Sesquicentennial, August 1982), 71; "A Better Bank," pamphlet on the history of First National Bank of Pandora, 1954, copy in author's possession (quoted); Nita Crawford of First National Bank of Pandora, interview, February 25, 2010.

26. "Bank Closes Doors; Shortage in Accounts," *Bluffton News*, November 13, 1919, 1; "Shortage will reach $125,000," *Bluffton News*, November 20, 1919, 1; "Bixel begins Prison Term," *Bluffton News* (December 4, 1919), 1; "Citizens Bank to open Jan. 31," *Bluffton News*, January 22, 1920, 1; Thierstein to Mosiman, November 12, 1919, Mosiman Papers, I-A-b, box 8, file titled "J. R. Thierstein," BUASC; "History of the Founding of The Citizens National Bank of Bluffton, Ohio, Presented at the 50th Anniversary Dinner, by Mr. James West, President," January 20, 1970 (copy provided by current bank president Michael Romey, in author's possession).

27. "History of the Founding of The Citizens National Bank of Bluffton, Ohio"; Huffman to Thierstein, December 7, 1921, Thierstein Papers, box 3, file 22, MLA; "Bankrupt bank given permit to sell stock," *Lima Daily News*, February 19, 1920; "Old-Fashioned Value" (advertisement), *Lima News*, June 22, 1970; Smith to Bender, May 16, 1931.

28. "Bank President a College Professor," *American Banker*, October 25, 1932, clipping, box 43, file 11, Smith Papers, BUASC; Crawford interview.

29. C. Henry Smith, "Christianity as a World Movement," *Christian Evangel* II: 14–15 (August–September 1911), 360–63, 409–12, 428; Smith, "The Mennonites," *Christian Evangel* I (March 1911), 212–24; Smith, "The Progress and Cause of Peace," *Christian Evangel* I (February 1911), 70; Smith, "The House Fly and Typhoid Fever," *Christian Evangel* I (February 1911), 71; Smith, "Conservation of Natural Resources," *Christian Evangel* II: 11–12 (June–July

1911), 267–71, 314–16, 332; Smith, "Conservation of Childhood," *Christian Evangel* III (May 1913), 191–98.

30. Smith, "Progress," *Christian Evangel* I (April 1911), 166; Smith, "Conservation of Natural Resources," 315; Smith, "Conservation of Childhood," 192–94 (quoted 193). On Progressive Era acceptance of the primacy of environmental factors in human behavior and the necessity of a beneficent state, see Link and McCormick, *Progressivism*, 21–22, 68–69.
31. C. Henry Smith, "Socialism," *Christian Evangel* III: 4–7 (April–May–June–July 1912), 157–58, 205–11, 269–71, 317–19 (quoted 318, 271, 319).
32. C. Henry Smith, "Some of the Providences of American History," *Christian Evangel* IV: 4–6 (May, June, July 1914), 186–88, 226–28, 262–63 (quoted 186, 187, 226, 227).
33. On national racism in the Gilded Age, see Joel Williamson, *A Rage for Order: Black-White Relations in the American South since Emancipation* (New York: Oxford University Press, 1986), 78–90; Ahlstrom, *A Religious History of the American People* II, 325–29 (on larger Protestantism); Setran, *The College Y*, 137–40 (on racism in the Ys); Novick, *That Noble Dream*, 74–81 (quoted 76). For Progressive Era racism, see Matthew Frye Jacobson, *Whiteness of a Different Color: European Immigrants and the Alchemy of Race* (Cambridge: Harvard University Press, 1998), 68–90, 215–20 (Walker quoted 72); McGerr, *A Fierce Discontent*, 189–96, 213–17 (C. Vann Woodward, "for whites only," quoted in McGerr 216); James Loewen, *Lies My Teacher Told Me* (New York: Simon & Schuster, 2007), 19–21 (Wilson quoted 21).
34. Schlabach, *Peace, Faith, Nation*, 304–5 (Mennonite paternalism); C. E. Bender, "The Negro Question," *Goshen College Record* VII (March 1905), 489–95 (quoted 490, 492); "President John Ellsworth Hartzler," undated advertisement for popular lectures, probably mid-1920s, Hist. Mss. 5, John E. Hartzler Papers, BUASC; Tobin Miller Shearer, *Daily Demonstrators: The Civil Rights Movement in Mennonite Homes and Sanctuaries* (Baltimore: Johns Hopkins University Press, 2010), 6–7 (Kauffman quoted 7).
35. Smith to Ioder, September 16, 1907; Jacobson, *Whiteness of a Different Color*, 77–78 (national popularity of eugenics); Smith, "Conservation of Childhood," 195–97 (quoted 196). For Smith and other progressive Mennonite intellectuals, this kind of racism and ethnocentrism may have been a natural and corresponding parallel to their invention of Mennonite ethnicity in positive ways. "Certainly immigrants were tempted to play the game of arguing," Conzen et al. point out, "that someone else's ethnicity might be undesirable, but that theirs should be tolerated, even cultivated, for the sake of the positive contributions it had to make." See Conzen et al., "The Invention of Ethnicity," 6.
36. Smith's racial middle ground is best evidenced in a 1907 comment he made to Ioder. Early in their relationship, Ioder remarked to Smith that she had been attending a book club discussion, and one of the recent popular novels the club had read was Thomas Dixon's supremely racist best-seller *The Leopard's Spots*. Smith replied that in his opinion, "the book is very much colored with Dixon's prejudice against the negro. He really wrote the book as a contrast to Uncle Tom's Cabin, and The Leopard's Spots is just about as true historically in one direction as Uncle Tom's cabin is in another." See Ioder to Smith, May 5, 1907,

box 7, file 4, Ms. I-I, Smith Papers, BUASC; Smith to Ioder, May 9, 1907, Ms. I-I, Smith Papers, box 1, file 4, BUASC. On Dixon, see Williamson, *A Rage for Order*, 106, 112–13.

37. For Mennonite initial reactions to WWI, see Juhnke, *Vision, Doctrine, War*, 210–12, and Gerlof Homan, *American Mennonites and the Great War, 1914–1918* (Scottdale, PA: Herald Press, 1994), 39–40. C. Henry Smith, "The Great War," *Christian Evangel* V (March–October 1915), 104–6, 188–90, 226–28, 264–68, 305–7, 346–48, 392–94 (quoted 104, 266); *Christian Monitor* VII (February–September 1915), 52–3, 80–81, 113–14, 149–50, 178–79, 207–8, 241–42, 274–75.

38. David M. Kennedy, *Over Here: The First World War and American Society* (New York: Oxford University Press, 1980), 5, 10–11, 24–26, 45–92; Joseph Kip Kosek, *Acts of Conscience: Christian Nonviolence and Modern American Democracy* (New York: Columbia University Press, 2009), 30–36 (Wilson's move toward war and liberal/pacifist reactions).

39. Juhnke, *Vision, Doctrine, War*, 212–13, 229–30 (official Mennonite denominational responses); Homan, *American Mennonites and the Great War*, 41–42, 46 (All-Mennonite statement and Huffman's visit to Washington).

40. Homan, *American Mennonites and the Great War*, 47–59 (conscription bill), 99–122. For Baker's role and the "conscription trap," see Juhnke, *Vision, Doctrine, War*, 230–32, and Allen Teichroew, "Mennonites and the Conscription Trap," *Mennonite Life* 30 (September 1975), 10–12. On persecution of Mennonite draftees, see Homan, ibid., 99–122, and Juhnke, ibid., 208–9, 233–41. Harvey Beidler to Mosiman, October 29, 1917, box 12, file titled "War, 1917–19," Mosiman Papers, BUASC.

41. Homan, *American Mennonites and the Great War*, 57–80.

42. Estes, *Living Stones*, 216–17, and Homan, *American Mennonites and the Great War*, 90 (Metamora); Homan, *American Mennonites and the Great War*, 72 (East White Oak); "Lima Vigilantes Warn Alleged Disloyalists," *Lima Daily News*, May 10, 1918; "Yellow Dog Clubbers' Club Is to Be Organized Tonight," *Lima Daily News*, June 20, 1918; "Dunhauer Girl Is Made to Kiss American Flag," *Lima Daily News*, November 8, 1918; "Employee of Lima Packing Plant Forced to Salute American Flag," *Lima Daily News*, March 29, 1918; "German Books Burn as 2,000 Persons Cheer," *Lima Post-Gazette*, April 18, 1918; "German Township Is Officially American," *Lima Daily News*, August 27, 1918; Smucker, *Bid Me Discourse*, 57–58.

43. Homan, *American Mennonites and the Great War*, 71–72; Mosiman to Aaron Augspurger, June 11, 1918, box 7, file titled "Rev. Aaron Augspurger," Mosiman Papers, BUASC; Langenwalter to Mosiman, April 20, 1918, box 8, "J. H. Langenwalter," Mosiman Papers, MHLB.

44. Bush, *Dancing with the Kobzar*, 84–87 (Mosiman quoted 85). On the war enthusiasm of the national YMCA, see Setran, *The College Y*, 154–55; Homan, *American Mennonites and the Great War*, 87, 90–92, 132 (Mosiman's pro-war enthusiasm).

45. Shelly interview in *Sourcebook*, 200; Jasper Huffman to R. H. Richert, December 9, 1916, H. P. Krehbiel Papers, Hist. Miss. 12, box 5, file 29, MLA.

46. "United States World War I Draft Registration Cards, 1917–1918," index and images, FamilySearch (https://familysearch.org/pal:/MM9.1.1/K6XY-LCR, Waldo M. Niswander, 1917–1918; my thanks to Jan Emmert for this detail); William Clegg to Mosiman, October 30, 1917, box 12, "War, 1917–19," Ms. I-A-b, Mosiman Papers, BUASC (Smith as war bond salesman); *Bluffton College Bulletin* V: 4 (June 1918), 1 (Smith lecturing at Great Lakes naval station); Lester Smith to "Dear Uncle," June 9 and June 27, 1918, C. Henry Smith Papers, box 8, file 1, BUASC; Smith, *The Mennonites: A Brief History*, 288–89, 293–94; Smith, "Mennonites and War," in *Report of Fourth All-Mennonite Convention, Held in Eighth Street Mennonite Church, Goshen, Indiana, Sept. 6–7, 1922*, n.p., p. 82, MHLG ("respectful consideration").
47. James Juhnke, "Mennonite Benevolence and Revitalization in the Wake of World War I," *MQR* 60 (January 1986), 16–17.
48. Smith, "The Great War," *Christian Monitor* 7 (August 1941), 241.
49. Smith, *The Mennonites: A Brief History*, 296–97; Smith, "Mennonites and War," 81–83 (quoted 81, 83).
50. Smith, "Mennonites and War," 84.
51. "A Text Book on Mennonite History," *Bluffton College Bulletin* V (March 1918), 3; Smith, *The Mennonites: A Brief History*, preface.
52. Smith, *The Mennonites: A Brief History*, 14–38 (quoted 19, 35, 36).
53. Ibid., 13, 28–30, 66, 320–28 (quoted 322, 324).
54. Ibid., 147–85 (quoted 163, 167, 174, 183).
55. Ibid., quoted 194, 196.
56. Ibid., quoted 57, 152, 262, 281.
57. Ibid., quoted 252, 281, 329, 330, 314.
58. "Report of the Publication Board," in *Minutes, Reports and Papers of the 22nd Session of the General Conference of the Mennonites in North America, meeting at Perkasie, Pennsylvania, Aug. 29–Sept. 5, 1920*, n.p., 79–80, BUASC; Thierstein to Smith, June 10, 1940, Smith Papers, box 8, file 48, BUASC; "Book Review, *The Mennonites*, by C. Henry Smith," *Gospel Herald* XIX (July 1, 1920), 270.
59. Smith, "Mennonites and War," 83; Smith to Thierstein, November 14, 1925, and March 6, 1922, J. R. Thierstein Papers, Hist. Mss. 19, box 4, file 35, and box 3, file 23, MLA.

Chapter 8: Forays down a Winding Road

1. Smith, *Mennonite Country Boy*, 27.
2. "Catalog Number" of the 1925 *Bluffton College Bulletin* XII (April 1925), 16, 824; *Witmarsum* XI (October 23, 1924), sneak day; *Witmarsum* XI (February 23, 1924), bobsled party; *Witmarsum* XI (March 8, 1924); *Witmarsum* XII (October 4, 1924); *Witmarsum* XI (November 10, 1923), campus speaking. Board of Trustees minutes dated February 1, 1917, Bluffton College Board of Trustees Minutes I-b, no box number, BUASC; Smith to Thierstein, April 13, 1924 and November 14, 1925, Thierstein Papers, Hist. Mss 19, box 4, files 30 and 35, MLA.
3. Milton F. Sprunger to Smith, June 4, 1946, Smith Papers, Hist. Mss. I, box 10, file 22, BUASC. "Faculty Sidelights," *Witmarsum* XII (October 11, 1924), 6.

Student numbers in Bush, *Dancing with the Kobzar* 94–95 (Mosiman quoted 94). Smith to Thierstein, September 18, 1922, Thierstein Papers, Hist. Mss 19, box 3, file 24, MLA.

4. Bush, *Dancing with the Kobzar* 73–74, 92 (Quiring and Lantz); Smith to Thierstein, April 13, 1924, Thierstein Papers, box 4, file 30, MLA; Whitmer, "Autobiography," 101–6 (Hartzler).

5. "The Special Bible Course," *Bethel College Monthly* 27: 1 (January 15, 1922), 1; Smith to Thierstein, March 6, 1922, Thierstein Papers, box 3, file 23, MLA. On Bethel in the early 1920s, see Juhnke, *Vision, Doctrine, War*, 83–94, and James C. Juhnke, "Gustav. H. Enss, Mennonite Alien," *Mennonite Life* 36: 4 (December 1981), 10–11.

6. Juhnke, *Vision, Doctrine, War*, 218–24, and Homan, *American Mennonites and the Great War*, 64–71 (WWI-era persecution). On Enss and "modernism" charges at Bethel, see Juhnke, "Gustav H. Enss, Mennonite Alien," 11–12, and Sawatsky, *History and Ideology*, 62–64.

7. Smith to Thierstein, April 13, 1924; "The Opening of the School Year," *Bethel College Monthly*, 27:7 (September 1922), 1 (Smith lectures); Sprunger, "C. Henry Smith's Vision of Mennonite History," 4; handwritten, undated note on professorial teaching loads, Bethel College Presidential Papers, Hist. Mss. III-I-e, box 1, file 151, MLA; "The Faculty," *Bethel College Monthly*, 28: 5 (May 1923), 3 ("his experience with us").

8. Smith to Thierstein, November 14, 1925.

9. C. Henry Smith, "Lessons from Mennonite History," *The Mennonite* 28 (October 4, 1923), 1–2; (October 11, 1925), 5–6; (October 25, 1923), 3; (November 1, 1923), 6, published simultaneously in the *Christian Evangel* XIII (September 1923), 208–9, 215; (October 1923), 227, 239; (November, 1923), 257; (December 1923), 28–81, 287.

10. For summaries of the "All-Mennonite Conventions," see Juhnke, *Vision, Doctrine, War*, 229 (quoted), 294–95; Smith, *Mennonites in Illinois*, 463; Homan, *American Mennonites and the Great War*, 35.

11. C. Henry Smith, Opening Address, "The Next Step," *Report of the Fifth All-Mennonite Convention, held in West Market St. Mennonite Church, Nappanee, Indiana, Sept. 2–3, 1925*, 1, 11–12.

12. Smith, "The Next Step," 13–15.

13. Smith, *Mennonite Country Boy*, 27, 205–8; Ioder to Smith, March 27, 1908, box 7, file 13, Ms. 1, Smith Papers, BUASC; C. Henry Smith, "Rambles through Historic New England," *Christian Evangel* I (October–November 1911), 458–60, 476, 507–8, 512, and II (February 1912), 76–79; C. H. Smith, "The Grand Canyon," *Christian Evangel* VII (September1917), 208–9; "Yellowstone Is a Wonderland," *Christian Evangel* VII (October 1917), 230–31; "Yosemite Falls Surpass Niagara," *Christian Evangel* VII (November 1917), 354–55; Smith to Thierstein, September 18, 1922 (on Laura's train preference); "Alaska Has No Summer Nights," *Christian Evangel* IX (October 1919), 238–39; "Visitors Here from the South Seeing Sights," *Dawson Daily News*, box 19, file 8, undated clipping in Smith Papers, BUASC.

14. C. Henry Smith, "French Canadians Cling to Own Tongue and Customs," *Bluffton News*, July 24, 1924; Smith, "No One Immune from Sea Sickness

on Ocean Voyage," *Bluffton News*, July 31, 1924; "Passenger List, S.S. *Montroyal*," from Quebec to Liverpool, Friday, June 27, 1924, box 3, file 6, Smith Papers, BUASC.

15. Smith, "Rural England Is Land of Small, Well-Kept Farms," *Bluffton News*, August 7, 1924; Smith, "London Is City Filled with Historic Interest," *Bluffton News*, August 14, 1924; Smith, "Visit French Battlefields Made Famous in World War," *Bluffton News*, August 21, 1924; Smith, "See Paris, City of Royal Splendor and Art Center," *Bluffton News*, September 11, 1924; Smith, "Occupied Germany Pays for Entire Nation's Sins," *Bluffton News*, October 2, 1924 (German resentment).

16. Smith, "Finds Familiar Family Names in Switzerland," *Bluffton News*, August 24, 1924.

17. On changing attitudes among postwar progressives in Kennedy, see *Over Here*, 30–36, and Kosek, *Acts of Conscience*, 303–7, 41–43; "Honor Woodrow Wilson at Memorial Service," *Witmarsum* XI (February 9, 1924); Setran, *The College Y*, 195–96, 223–28 (on developments in the Y).

18. Rick L. Nutt, *The Whole Gospel for the Whole World: Sherwood Eddy and the American Protestant Mission* (Macon, GA: Mercer University Press, 1997), 14–18, 22–24, 33–37, 99–101 (early travels), 121–24, 134–38, 145–46 (Eddy's break with the war system), 153–54 (embrace of the Social Gospel), 201–4 (American Seminars). Also on Eddy, see Kosek, *Acts of Conscience*, 19, 57.

19. *Bluffton College Bulletin* XIII (January 1926), n.p.; Nutt, *The Whole Gospel for the Whole World*, 204 (on the 1926 seminar); newspaper clipping from the *Metamora Herald*, September 24, 1926, box 43, file 28, MS I, Smith Papers, BUASC (Smith embarks for Europe). On the range of speakers and perspectives on the 1926 seminar, see mimeographed seminar papers in charcoal gray notebook titled "C. Henry Smith, Bluffton, Ohio, USA," box 2, file 6, Smith Papers, BUASC, Kerr quoted 3, Laski 95.

20. *Metamora Herald* clipping, September 24, 1926; C. Henry Smith, "England," *Christian Exponent* III (August 27, 1926), 278–79; Smith "France," *Christian Exponent* III (September 24, 1926), 309–10; Smith, "Germany and Czecho-Slovakia," *Christian Exponent* III (October 8, 1926), 329–31.

21. *Bluffton College Bulletin* XIII (October 8, 1926), n.p.; C. Henry Smith, "A Pilgrimage to the Homes of Our Mennonite Forefathers: I. Switzerland," *The Mennonite* XLII (January 20, 1927), 1.

22. H. J. Krehbiel to C. Henry Smith and Krehbiel, "To Whom it May Concern," both dated June 10, 1926, box 36, file 1, both in Smith Papers, BUASC; Smith, "A Pilgrimage to the Homes of Our Mennonite Forefathers: I. Switzerland," continued in *Mennonite* XLII (January 27), 6–7, and 5 (February 3), 6–7.

23. Smith, "A Pilgrimage to the Homes of Our Mennonite Forefathers: II. The Palatinate," *Mennonite* XLII (February 24), 1–2 (quoted 2); Smith, "A Pilgrimage to the Homes of Our Mennonite Forefathers: III. Down the Rhine to Crefeld," *Mennonite* XLII (June 2 and 9), 1–2, 2–3; "IV. In the Land of the Wooden Shoes" (July 21, 28, and August 4, 1927), 1–2; Albert N. Keim, *Harold S. Bender, 1897–1962* (Scottdale, PA: Herald Press, 1998), 158 (on Hege, Neff, and the *Lexikon*).

24. For these remarks, see collections of speech outlines: "Constitution," delivered to (Bluffton?) High School, November 15, 1925, Smith Papers, box 38, file 8; untitled address given to "Travel Class" (at First Mennonite Church, Bluffton), December 31, 1926, box 4, file 6; "Progress of Peace," delivered to Grace Mennonite Church, Pandora, Ohio, January 13, 1929, box 28, file 9, BUASC.

Chapter 9: Diverging Readings of Anabaptist History

1. C. Henry Smith to John Horsch, June 8, 1924, Horsch Papers, Hist. Mss. I-8-1, box 3, file 5, AMC.
2. Smith and Hirschler, eds., *The Story of Bluffton College*, 3–4, 110–15, quoted 3, 110, 113, 115.
3. C. Henry Smith to "Dear Friend," no date but on Bethel College letterhead, box 28, file 11, Ms. I, Smith Papers, BUASC (Smith used many extra copies of this letter for scratch paper); Smith to Thierstein, September 18, 1922 (in Funk's library); *Bluffton College Bulletin* XII (November 1925), n.p.; Smith to Thierstein, November 14, 1925 (in Minneapolis and Winnipeg); Smith, "A Few Statistics," *Mennonite* 38 (February 8, 1923), 5–6; Smith, "Some Old Letters," *Christian Exponent* I (April 11, 1924), 118–19, I (May 9, 1924), 145, I:12 (June 6, 1924), 178–79, I: 15 (July 18, 1924), 226–27; C. Henry Smith, foreword to *The Coming of the Russian Mennonites* (Berne, IN: Mennonite Book Concern, 1927), 9; Smith, foreword to *The Mennonite Immigration to Pennsylvania in the Eighteenth Century* (Norristown, PA: Pennsylvania German Society, 1929), 10; Kreider, "C. Henry Smith—Part Two," 22.
4. Smith to Thierstein, November 14, 1925; Smith, *The Coming of the Russian Mennonites*, 10, 53–4ff, 79–80, 125–26 (quoted 203). For examples of the overlap between these two books, compare *The Mennonites: A Brief History*, 151, 155, 157–58, with *The Coming of the Russian Mennonites*, 21, 25–26, 32, 36.
5. Smith, *The Coming of the Russian Mennonites*, table of contents, 58, 60–61, 96–99, 114, 198–99 (quoted 67, 134–35).
6. Ibid., 151, 229, 282–92 (quoted 157, 247).
7. Marcus L. Hansen, Review of C. Henry Smith, *The Coming of the Russian Mennonites: An Episode in the Settling of the Last Frontier*, in *American Historical Review* 34 (January 1929), 401–4; Guy F. Hershberger, review of C. Henry Smith, *The Coming of the Russian Mennonites: An Episode in the Settling of the Last Frontier*, in MQR IV: 1 (January 1930), 72–77 (quoted 72, 76).
8. C. Henry Smith, *The Mennonite Immigration to Pennsylvania in the Eighteenth Century* (Norristown, PA: Pennsylvania German Society, 1929), 10–21, 247–49 (quoted 12, 17, 248, 287, 307). On Smith's borrowing here from his earlier book, compare pp. 108–09, 112–13, 114–15, 120–22 of *The Mennonites: A Brief History* with pp. 92–93, 98–9, 102–3, 107 of *The Mennonite Immigration to Pennsylvania*.
9. Smith, *The Mennonite Immigration to Pennsylvania*, 29–54, 75–122, 138–39, 182–90, 208–10, 220–21 (quoted 54).
10. Ibid., 372.

11. Bush, *Dancing with the Kobzar*, 87–88, and A. S. Bechtel to Mosiman, July 18, 1920, Mosiman Papers, I-A-b, box 9, file, "Corresp–A.S. Bechtel," BUASC (on tensions with Central Conference; Augspurger quoted 87). On BC tensions with MBIC, see Bush, ibid., 88, and S. K. Mosiman to A. A. Friesen, July 6, 1922, Samuel Mosiman Papers, I-A-b, box 5, file "Mosiman/Canadian Board of Colonization," BUASC (on Huffman).
12. E. D. Schmidt to J. R. Thierstein, November 16, 1920 ("he terms us 'heretics'"), and W. S. Gottshall to Thierstein, February 11, 1924 (Smith investor group), both in Thierstein Papers, Hist. Mss. 19, box 2, file 17 and box 4, file 30, MLA; Sawatsky, *History and Ideology*, 64–65 and Bush, *Dancing with the Kobzar*, 89 (on Gottshall); Gottshall to Allen H. Miller, October 12, 1927, Papers on the Charges of Modernism against Bluffton College, I-D-e, box 1, file, "Berne Church of Deacons," BUASC (Gottshall's resentments).
13. For increasing MC fundamentalism, see Smith, *Mennonites in Illinois*, 313, Sawatsky, *History and Ideology*, 67–68, 80–81, and Yoder, "Mennonite Fundamentalism," 340–45. As an example of the embrace of fundamentalism in Kauffman's *Gospel Herald*, see "Fundamentalism in Christian Living," *Gospel Herald* 21 (February 21, 1929), 985–86.
14. Anna Showalter, "The Mennonite Young People's Conference Movement, 1919-1923: The Legacy of a (Failed?) Vision," *MQR* 85 (April 2011), 191–201 (quoted 208); Keim, *Harold S. Bender*, 98–100, 163.
15. J. D. Augsburger to C. Henry Smith, March 9, 1919, Smith Papers, box 1, file 51; BUASC; Sawatsky, *History and Ideology*, 75–76 (on the larger influence of the *Christian Exponent* and Bluffton involvement); John Horsch to Harold Bender, February 16, 1925, H. S. Bender Papers, Hist. Mss. I-278, box 2, file 7, AMC.
16. For the Science Ridge conference, see Keim, *Harold S. Bender*, 127–28, and Showalter, "The Mennonite Young People's Conference Movement," 208; John Horsch, "The Young People's Conference," *Gospel Herald* XV: 10 (June 8, 1922), 203; "Report of the Young People's Conference," *Christian Monitor* (September 1922), 658.
17. Keim, *Harold S. Bender*, 29–34, 43–48, 53–60, 113–16, 120–24, 145–60.
18. Ibid., 115–16, 118–19 (Horsch quoted 115); Smith to Bender, May 9, 1921, and April 14, 1923, both in Bender Papers, box 4, file 2, AMC.
19. For tensions at Goshen, see Sawatsky, *History and Ideology*, 66–68 and Miller, *Culture for Service*, 64–88; Whitmer, "Autobiography," 92–96 (Indiana-Michigan Conference).
20. Sawatsky, *History and Ideology*, 69 (MC General Conference and Byers quoted); Smith to Harry F. Weber, November 17, 1923, Smith Papers, box 1, file 10, BUASC; W. S. Gottshall to John Horsch, February 8, 1926, Horsch Papers, box 3, file 17, AMC; Hartzler to "The Ministering Brethren of the Middle District Conference," August 20, 1923, and to Mosiman, March 31, 1923, both in S. K. Mosiman Papers, Hist. Mss. I-A-b, box 1, file "J. E. Hartzler corresp.," BUASC; Bender quoted in Juhnke, *Vision, Doctrine, War*, 176. Also on Bluffton's response to Goshen's crisis, see Bush, *Dancing with the Kobzar*, 90.

The transfer of a third of Goshen's student body to Bluffton seems to have been the final blow that precipitated the closing of Zion Mennonite Church.

With many new MC students in town and the Zion congregation too far away for them to access it by foot, to serve these young people the congregation decided to hold services at First Mennonite in town. This drew the two congregations even more closely together, and in 1925 the Zion congregation decided formally to merge with the town church and raze its building. While continuing to hold their membership at East White Oak, it was almost certainly at this point when the Smiths began worshiping at First Mennonite, along with the Whitmer and Byers families, and others from the old Zion church. Umble, writing from an MC perspective, accounted the underlying cause to the fact that, given their close association with Bluffton College, Zion's leaders were "out of harmony with the Ohio Mennonite Conference." Whitmer and Byers, for their part, said they were expelled from the church. These diverging readings are themselves indicative of the polarization of the church about this time. See Umble, *Ohio Mennonite Sunday Schools*, 180–81, quoted 180; Whitmer to J. R. Thierstein, July 2, 1925, Thierstein Papers, box 4, file 31, MLA; Byers to A. J. Steiner, July 16, 1925, Hist. Mss. I-472, A. J. Steiner Papers, box 1, file 40, AMC.

21. Keim, *Harold S. Bender*, 101–6, 117–18, 163–66, 186–87, 204–5 (quoted 187); Showalter, "The Mennonite Young People's Conference Movement," 205–8; Juhnke, *Vision, Doctrine, War*, 279–81 (quoted 280). Also on Bender's conservatism, see Smith, *Mennonites in Illinois*, 319–20.

22. Keim, *Harold S. Bender*, 94–95, 135–37, 177–78, 203–5 (quoted 95, Bender quoted 178); Bender to Lester Hostetler, June 17, 1925, Bender Papers, box 2, file 9, AMC ("frankly antagonistic"); Horsch to Bender, February 16, 1925 (quoted). Also on the Horsch/Bender relationship, see Friesen, *History and Renewal in the Anabaptist/Mennonite Tradition*, 135–36, Horsch quoted 136.

23. For Bender's review of Hartzler, see Keim, *Harold S. Bender*, 186–87 (quoted 187); Sawatsky, *History and Ideology*, 88–89; Yoder, "Mennonite Fundamentalism," 306–7; and Miller, *Culture for Service*, 148–49.

24. Keim, *Harold S. Bender*, 180–88 (Bender quoted 188); Juhnke, *Vision, Doctrine, War*, 280.

25. Bender to Horsch, February 11, 1925, Horsch Papers, box 7, file 8, AMC; also on the *MQR* as a "modernist" counter, see Keim, *Harold S. Bender*, 184. "The Historical Approach" in "The Open Forum," *Christian Exponent* I (April 11, 1924), 127; Smith, "Some Old Letters," 119.

26. Bender to Horsch, December 28, 1926, quoted in Sprunger, "C. Henry Smith's Vision of Mennonite History," 9; L. J. Heatwole to Daniel Kauffman, January 9 and 23, 1911, and undated memo, "Mennonite Literature," all in Daniel Kauffman Papers, Hist. Mss I-20, box 1, file 6, AMC (Heatwole quoted Kauffman here); Horsch to Bender, July 30, 1921, Bender Papers, box 2, file 7, AMC; Friesen, *History and Renewal in the Anabaptist/Mennonite Tradition*, 133–34 (Horsch and Vos); Keim, *Harold S. Bender*, 191 (on the proposed Horsch/Bender history); Bender to Horsch, January 8 and 15, 1927, Horsch Papers, box 4, file 5, AMC (quoted January 15).

27. Keim, *Harold S. Bender*, 95, 199–202 (quoted 201); Sawatsky, *History and Ideology*, 47 (quoted); Wenger, "The Theology of John Horsch," 152; J. Gresham Machen to Horsch, January 7, 1925, box 3, file 11; Vernon Smucker

to Horsch, June 9, 1924, box 3, file 5 ("taking isolated passages out of contexts"); A. S. Bechtel to Horsch, April 24, 1926, box 3, file "corr A-B," all in Horsch Papers, AMC ("there is too much personal feeling").

28. Sawatsky, *History and Ideology*, 64–65, 76–77 (Horsch antimodernist pamphlets and book); Bush, *Dancing with the Kobzar*, 91–3 (Horsch pamphlets and Quiring). John Horsch, *The Mennonite Church and Modernism* (Scottdale, PA: Mennonite Publishing House, 1924), 17–18, 31–32, 71–77, 84–85, 111–14 (quoted 31, 72, 77, 79). Also on Horsch's attacks, see Paul Toews, *Mennonites in American Society, 1930–1970: Modernity and the Persistence of Religious Community* (Scottdale, PA: Herald Press, 1996), 66–67.

29. Sawatsky, *History and Ideology*, 79; Novick, *That Noble Dream*, 57–59, 200–204. For Byers's and Hartzler's responses to Horsch, see N. E. Byers, "A Reply," in "The Open Forum," *Christian Exponent* 1 (July 18, 1924), 239–40; J. E. Hartzler, "The Mennonite Church and Modernism," in "The Open Forum," *Christian Exponent* I (August 15, 1924), 271–72; N. E. Byers, "An Explanation," *Mennonite* 41 (May 1, 1926), 4–6.

30. C. Henry Smith to John Horsch, June 8 and 21, 1924, both in Horsch Papers, box 3, file 5, AMC. On these contrasting passages, see Smith, *The Mennonites: A Brief History*, 66–67, 320; and Horsch, *The Mennonite Church and Modernism*, 77.

31. Smith to Horsch, June 21, 1924.

32. Smith to Horsch, December 12, 1925, Horsch Papers, box 3, file 13, AMC.

33. Horsch to Smith, November 28, 1925, box 3, file 70, Smith Papers, BUASC; Smith to Horsch, December 12, 1925.

34. For the actual dearth of Mennonite modernism, see Theron Schlabach, *Gospel versus Gospel: Mission and the Mennonite Church, 1863–1944* (Scottdale, PA: Herald Press, 1980), 114, and Toews, "Fundamentalist Conflict in Mennonite Colleges, 244–48. Smith to Horsch, December 12, 1925.

   In a manner inconsistent with his otherwise sound and insightful scholarship, Nathan Yoder has recently resurrected Horsch's charges of Smith's supposed modernism through the same facile reasoning as Horsch. It is true that in his undergraduate years more than two decades before, Smith reflected an initial acceptance of liberal theology. Thereafter, however, his writing on such subjects stopped. Yoder instead locates the adult Smith's supposed modernism in certain isolated sentences of his popular writings that seemed to echo similar quotations from Shailer Matthews. He also finds it in Smith's demonstrated progressivism, which, like Horsch, Yoder carelessly equates with modernism. See Yoder, "Mennonite Fundamentalism," 192–95. Smith was guilty of emphatically rejecting fundamentalism; this did not automatically render him a modernist.

35. Paul Whitmer to John Horsch, August 15, 1924, and Bender to Horsch, January 16, 1925, both in Horsch Papers, box 3, file 5, AMC; Keim, *Harold S. Bender*, 181 (Bender and Correll's Grebel project); Smith to Bender, January 31 and March 9, 1925, and Horsch to Bender, February 16, 1925, all in Bender Papers, box 4, files 2 and 7, AMC.

36. Smith to Bender, May 10 ("federation of historical societies") and April 25, 1925 ("if you can get the cooperation"), both in Bender Papers, box 4, file

2, AMC; Horsch to Bender, March 6 ("he is part of the crowd") and 15, 1925, Bender Papers, box 2, file 7, AMC; Keim, *Harold S. Bender*, 183 (Keim quoted); Bender to Horsch, March 17, 1925 ("draw a line"), Horsch Papers, box 7, file 8, AMC.

Horsch harbored no apparent regrets from the incident. He admitted to Bender that Smith "is not so radically modernistic as Byers and others, yet he certainly holds to the Bluffton crowd and their victory would be his own. . . . I fail to see the consistency of cooperating in any endeavor with a crowd standing for the things for which Bluffton does stand." Bender continued to try to nudge Horsch toward greater cooperation with Smith on Mennonite historical matters, telling him "we can never get anywhere by withdrawing from the world." See Horsch to Bender, December 31, 1925, Bender Papers, box 2, file 7, and Bender to Horsch, January 16, 1926, Horsch Papers, AMC.

37. Sawatsky, *History and Ideology*, 82 (Bender quoted 77); Bender to Smith, June 4, 1926 (quoted), and Smith to Bender, May 27, 1928, both in Bender Papers, box 4, file 3, AMC; Bender to Smith, box 1, file 73, Smith Papers, BUASC.
38. Bender to Smith, June 4, 1926; John Horsch, "A Plan for Publishing the Source Material of Mennonite History," *Gospel Herald* 19 (July 26, 1926), 394; C. Henry Smith, "A Worthy Cause," *Christian Exponent* IV (August 2, 1927), 237.
39. Bush, *Dancing with the Kobzar*, 89 (Mosiman quoted); Bender to Smith, June 4, 1926 (Bender quoted Smith here).
40. Smith, *The Coming of the Russian Mennonites*, 292.
41. "Conditions in Mexico Subject at Vespers," *Witmarsum* XVI (September 23, 1928), 1; "No Revolution Coming in Mexico, Says Bluffton Man," *Bluffton News*, August 9, 1928, 1; "Party entering at Laredo July 3, 1928," box 18, file 8, Smith Papers, BUASC; Dr. C. Henry Smith "Report No. II: The Agrarian Situation," box 59, file 29, Smith Papers, BUASC.
42. On Smith's sabbatical, see Board minutes dated June 11 and September 30, 1926, Bluffton College Board of Trustees Minutes I-b, no box number, BUASC, and "Bluffton College Faculty Training," undated memo, S. K. Mosiman Papers, box 8, file "S.K. Mosiman Corr," BUASC. "Smiths Leave for Western Tour," *Bluffton News*, August 8, 1929, 1; "Motor Trip over the Santa Fe Trail," *Bluffton News*, October 31, 1929, 1, 7–8; Smith to Bender, October 20, 1929, H. S. Bender Papers, box 4, file 2, AMC; undated speech outline, "Hawaii," filed with "CHS Addendum," Smith Papers, BUASC; brochure "Hawaii: The Paradise of the Pacific," box 53, file 29, Smith Papers, BUASC.
43. On Schroeder's "modernism" charges, see Samuel Floyd Pannabecker, *Faith in Ferment*, 224–26, and Sawatsky, *History and Ideology*, 72. Bush, *Dancing with the Kobzar*, 95–98 (Bluffton College fundraising campaign and accreditation).

Chapter 10: The Mennonite Intellectual in a Time of Crisis

1. Bush, *Dancing with the Kobzar*, 97; Smith, "Bluffton College," in *Yearbook of the General Conference of the Mennonite Church of North America* (1931), 30; Juhnke, *Creative Crusader*, 140 (on Kaufman).
2. David Kennedy, *Freedom from Fear: The American People in Depression and War, 1929–1945* (New York: Oxford University Press, 1999), 65–66, 86–87;

Town at the Fork of the Rileys Revisited: Historical Sketches of Old Shannon and Bluffton, Ohio (Bluffton News, 1986), 34–35.

3. Toews, *Mennonites in American Society*, 90–91 (on Horsch; Friedmann quoted 91), 95–96 (on Kaufman); Horsch, "The Faith of the Swiss Brethren," *MQR* 5 (October 1931), 257; Juhnke, *Creative Crusader*, 122, 125–27; Horsch to Bender, July 1, 1929, Bender Papers, I-278, box 2, file 8, AMC. The *MQR* never reviewed Kaufman's book.

4. Smith, review of Edmund Kaufman, "The Development of the Missionary and Philanthropic Interest among the Mennonites of North America," *The Mennonite* 46 (December 10, 1931), 2–3; Smith, *Menno Simons, Apostle of the Nonresistant Life* (Berne, IN: Mennonite Book Concern, 1936), quoted 53, 12, 15; Horsch, "Hans Denk, The Anabaptist Liberal," *Gospel Herald* 27 (August 30, 1934), 471.

5. On the 1933 GC conference meeting, see Toews, *Mennonites in American Society*, 77–78; Whitmer, "Autobiography," 148; and Evening Meeting, August 28, in "Official Minutes and Reports of the 26th Session of the General Conference of the Mennonite Church," Bluffton, Ohio, August 23–30, 1933 (General Conference Mennonite Church, n.p.), 35. Bush, *Dancing with the Kobzar*, 99–100, and Samuel F. Pannabecker, *Ventures in Faith: The Story of Mennonite Biblical Seminary* (Elkhart, IN: Mennonite Biblical Seminary, 1975), 18–20 (closing of Witmarsum Seminary). Whitmer to Hartzler, February 8, 1926, MS 4, box 1, Paul Whitmer Papers, BUASC; Smith to Emmanuel Troyer, May 14, 1929, box 41, file 11, Ms. I, Smith Papers, BUASC; Bender to Horsch, July 20, 1930, Horsch Papers, I-8-1, box 5, file "corr 1920 A-B," AMC.

6. Smith, *Mennonites in Illinois*, 332–33 (East White Oak); C. Henry Smith membership record, Church Membership records, vertical file, First Mennonite Church, Bluffton, Ohio; Robert and Lois Kreider, interview with the author, March 9, 2010; Kreider, "C. Henry Smith, Part I," 7.

7. Bush, *Dancing with the Kobzar*, 103–4 (bank failures; for CNB's absorption of Commercial Bank, see Smith to Ira Fulton, November 8, 1931, to "Dear friend," November 2, 1931, to Charles Saffin, December 19, 1931 ("the public seems well pleased"), Fulton to Smith, November 12, 1931, J. W. Pole telegram to Smith, November 5, 1931, all in Smith Papers, box 17, file 11, BUASC; and Justin King, "'God willing there shall be a brighter day': Bluffton College, Modernism, Bonds and the Struggle for Survival," Bluffton University student paper, May 1, 2008, 1-E-ee, 2008, file 7, History Research Seminar Papers, BUASC. Smith to George Sommer, March 3, 1932, box 10, file 4, Smith Papers, BUASC ("we were pretty badly scared").

8. Kennedy, *Freedom from Fear*, 131–37 (national banking developments); "To Our Depositors," *Bluffton News*, March 2, 1933; "Bank Here Opens for Business Wednesday," *Bluffton News*, March 15, 1933; "Dillinger Robbed Our Bank in 1933," *The Town at the Fork of the Rileys Revisited*, 37–38. Smith also remained president of First National Bank, which closed like others in March 1933, but did not reopen until the following October. Reasons for the delay are unclear, as is the reason why Smith was listed as president of the bank that spring, but by October was listed as vice president; "Banking Began in Corner of Store," *150 Years along the Riley: A History and Events of*

Riley Township and Pandora, Ohio, 1832–1982, ed. by Don Schneck (Riley Township Sesquicentennial, August 1982), 71; Crawford, interview.

9. Bush, *Dancing with the Kobzar*, 103–4 (college bond crisis); Samuel Mosiman to C. R. Stuckey, October 15, 1931, file "Financial drives, Mosiman, 1916–33," Ms. I-D-I, Mosiman Papers, BUASC. The translation of 1935 dollars into 2013 dollars is made using an inflation calculator by the U.S. Department of Labor, Bureau of Labor Statistics, http://www.bls.gov/data/inflation_calculator.htm.

10. Faculty meeting minutes of October 31, 1931, box 1, file: "Faculty mins Sept. 13, 1926–June 4, 1935," Ms. I-E-a, BUASC (retrenchment committee); Bluffton Board of Trustees minutes, May 19, 1932, June 5, 1933, January 26, June 4, and October 18, 1934, and Finance Committee meeting minutes October 18, 1934, Board of Trustees Meeting Minutes, I-B, BUASC (treasurer); Mosiman to J. E. Hartzler, September 10, 1934, and to A. C. Alderfer, August 11, 1934, box 5, file "bond information," Ms. I-A-b, both in Mosiman Papers, BUASC (underwriters committee); "Underwriting Agreement," August 11, 1934, box 6, file 6, Smith Papers, BUASC; also see many copies of "Bond Purchase Agreement: Certificate of Escrow" in this same file and also Box 17, file 8. For larger overview of these developments, see King, "'God willing there shall be a brighter day,'" 27–29. Smith to R. L. Hartzler, July 29, 1934, box 1, file "Reports of incidental meetings," Ms. 3-B-e, R.L. Hartzler Papers, BUASC.

11. Student quoted in Bush, *Dancing with the Kobzar*, 115 (close faculty relationships); Smucker, *Bid Me Discourse*, 98 (Smucker home at Lake George); warranty deed, property title transfer from Bluffton College to C. H. Smith, July 5, 1932, box 41, file 2, Smith Papers, BUASC; Emilie Mosiman to Edna Hanley, August 30, 1928, box 1, file 9, Ms. 4-C-I, Emilie Mosiman Papers, BUASC. In addition, Margaret Berky Houshower, daughter of chemistry professor H. W. Berky, remembered spending a delightful summer week along Lake George, and Robert Kreider recalled that business manager H. A. Alderfer also owned property there; Margaret Berky Houshower, interview, March 23, 2010; Kreider, interview.

12. Houshower, interview; Kreider, interview; and Bush, *Dancing with the Kobzar*, 61 (faculty conflicts).

13. Bush, *Dancing with the Kobzar*, 61; Smith to Earl Salsman, March 28, 1935, box 41, file 11, Smith Papers, BUASC; Robert Kreider, *My Early Years: An Autobiography* (Kitchener, ON: Pandora Press, 2002), 143–44, 149 (quoted); Donovan Smucker, interview, April 3, 1998.

14. On Bluffton faculty economic deprivations in the 1930s, see Bush, *Dancing with the Kobzar*, 107; Houshower, interview; and Arthur Rosenberger to "Dear Friend," May 24, 1935, file "A. S. Rosenberger form letters, 1934–35," Ms. I-A-c, Rosenberger Papers, BUASC.

15. Kreider, interview; Houshower, interview.

16. On Epp, see Bush, *Dancing with the Kobzar*, 109–10, S. K. Mosiman, "Statement of the President to the Faculty of Bluffton College," October 4, 1932, Mosiman Papers, I-A-b, box 1b, file 1, BUASC, and Epp to Arthur Rosenberger, December 27, 1935, box 1, file "Dr. Peter Epp, 1933–36," I-A-c, Rosenberger Papers, BUASC (Smith quoted).

17. Bush, *Dancing with the Kobzar*, 108 (faculty quoted); Smith to A. C. Alderfer, undated but clearly from mid-April 1935, and Smith to B. F. Thutt, February 16, 1932, box 41, file 11 (quoted), both in Smith Papers, BUASC.
18. Bush, *Dancing with the Kobzar*, 108 (on Hanley and Byers); Laura Smith to C. Henry Smith, C. Henry Smith Papers, July 4 and July 8, 1936, box 7, file 15, BUASC; Sylvia Pannabecker to Lloyd and Lelia (Pannabecker), July 13, 1933, personal papers of Alice Ruth Pannabecker Ramseyer, copy in author's possession; Bluffton Board of Trustees minutes, January 27, 1933, Board of Trustees Meeting Minutes, I-B, BUASC (debt crisis in 1933). In 1950, the widowed Byers would leave Bluffton and move to Georgia to marry Hanley; see Bush, ibid., 109.
19. B. F. Thutt to R. L. Hartzler, July 26, 1934 (on Rosenberger), and Smith to Hartzler, July 29, 1934 (quoted), Hartzler Papers, 3-B-e, box 1, file "Reports of incidental Meetings," BUASC.
20. Hartzler to Smith, August 1, 1934, Hartzler Papers, 3-B-e, box 1, file "Reports of incidental Meetings," BUASC; Bluffton Board of Trustees minutes, February 8, 1935, Board of Trustees Meeting Minutes, I-B, BUASC; Bush, *Dancing with the Kobzar*, 110–111 (Mosiman quoted 111); Smith to A. C. Ramseyer, March 11 ("get on the band wagon") and to Earl Salzman, March 28, 1935 ("to satisfy a personal grudge"), box 41, file 11, Smith Papers, BUASC.
21. As late as four years later, a college fundraiser reported that his efforts were still hampered by "the smoldering antagonisms from the Mosiman, Smith, Byers feud"; quoted in Bush, *Dancing with the Kobzar*, 126.
22. Minutes of the Executive Committee, Bluffton College Board of Trustees, April 3, 1935, Board of Trustees Meeting Minutes, I-B, BUASC; Smith to A. C. Ramseyer, March 1, 1935 ("dominated by Dr. Mosiman"); E. W. Baumgartner to Mosiman, February 12, 1935, I-A-b, box 2, file 12, Mosiman Papers, BUASC ("house-cleaning").
23. "To the Board of Trustees of Bluffton College" from Detweiler, Smith, and Byers, undated, box 4, file 11, Smith Papers, BUASC; Smith to "My Dear Doctor," April 22, 1935 ("I was considerably hurt" and "far-reaching business sagacity"); Smith to A. C. Ramseyer, April 17, 1935 ("have stood for Mennonite principles"); Smith to "My dear Ben [Thutt]," April 22, 1935, box 4, file 11, Smith Papers, BUASC ("they might as well close the doors").
24. Thutt to Smith, undated but clearly from April 1935, Smith Papers, box 8, file 54; and Baumgartner to Smith, April 16, 1935, box 1, file 64, Smith Papers, BUASC; Minutes of the Faculty Committee, Bluffton College Board of Trustees, April 30, 1935, Board of Trustees Meeting Minutes, I-B, BUASC (Rosenberger statement, with signatures).
25. Smith to A. C. Ramseyer, April 17, 1935 ("get rid of the Goshen College group"); Smith to Thutt, April 22, 1935 ("men under suspicion").
26. Minutes of the Faculty Committee, Bluffton College Board of Trustees, December 10, 1935, Board of Trustees Meeting Minutes, I-B, BUASC. On bond repurchase campaign, see King, "'God willing there shall be a brighter day,'" 29–31, and Bush, *Dancing with the Kobzar*, 105, 111.

27. "Tilman Smith, "The Memories of Tilman R. Smith," unpublished mss., 1996–98, pp. 48–49, Tilman Smith Papers, Hist. Mss. I-741, box 28, AMC; Willard Smith, *The Trail to Santa Fe*, 74; Dick Smith, interview.
28. Paul and LaVonne Klassen, interview, January 23, 2012 (Smith walking Bluffton streets); Kreider, *My Early Years*, 167–68 (memories of Smith); Kreider, interview (quoted); Darrell Groman, email message to author, July 16, 2009 (on Camp Berry); Jim Miller, interview, September 28, 2011; Milton F. Sprunger to Smith, June 4, 1946, box 10, file 22, Smith Papers, BUASC.
29. Miller, interview; Smucker, interview; Richard and Margaret Weaver, interview, October 27, 2011. Memories of Smith as a teacher taken from Emerson and Evelyn Niswander, interview, March 21, 2010, and Winfield Fretz, interview, June 8, 1994. Harry Yoder recollections in "Bluffton College Letters, Class of 1932, Fiftieth Reunion, May 21, 1982," Ms. I-616, Roy Wenger Papers, BUASC.
30. C. Henry Smith, introduction to *War, Peace, Amity* by Henry P. Krehbiel (H. P. Krehbiel, 1937), viii–ix; C. Henry Smith, "The Outlook for International Peace," *Report of the Seventh All-Mennonite Convention, held at First Mennonite Church, Berne, Indiana, Aug. 27–28, 1930*, 85–91, quoted 86, 90–91.
31. Miller, interview; for clippings and mailings, see Smith Papers, boxes 51–52; World's Christian Fundamentals Association membership card in box 18, file 5; for ACLU, see S. W. Hubich to Smith, January 18, 1944, Smith Papers, MS I, box 1, file 39, BUASC.
32. Smith, *Mennonites in Illinois*, 254; Sprunger, "C. Henry Smith's Vision of Mennonite History," 9; Smith, *The Trail to Santa Fe*, 128–29; Toews, *Mennonites in American Society*, 118–20 (on Harshbarger); Fretz, interview.
33. For tensions among MC progressives and fundamentalists, see Sawatsky, *History and Ideology*, 99–118; Toews, *Mennonites in American Society*, 111–13; and Bush, *Two Kingdoms, Two Loyalties*, 39–42 (Mosiman quoted 40). Kosek, *Acts of Conscience*, 81–88 (pacifist enthusiasm for Gandhi); Horsch, "Gandhi, his teaching and his Attitude toward Christianity," *Gospel Herald* 24 (June 4, 1931), 211; Keim, *Harold S. Bender*, 252–53 (Bender's restrictions at the Mennonite World Conference).
34. Toyohiko Kagawa to Smith, May 25, 1939, box 4, file 13, Richard Gregg to Smith, October 6 and 18, 1935, and March 4, 1936; Kirby Page to Smith, August 27, September 16, and December 10 (all undated); and Mary Alma Page to Smith, October 23, 1941, box 5, file 54, all in Smith Papers, BUASC.
35. J. S. Schultz, "Semi-Annual Report" to the president and the board of trustees, February 8, 1935, 3, S. K. Mosiman Papers, I-A-b, box 3, file "BC Board of Trustees, 1933–34," BUASC; Weaver, interview; Kreider, interview; ribbon found in Smith Papers, box 61, BUASC; "Prof. C. H. Smith interviewed; tells of Nation's Leaders," *Witmarsum* XXV (May 6, 1938), 12 (Roosevelt quoted); "Providing employment is major problem of nation, say leaders," undated clipping, box 43, file 28, Smith Papers, BUASC. Also see Smith's handwritten notes on this seminar, box 20, file 6.
36. "Our Mennonite Heritage," delivered at "Salem Church, Dalton, O.," April 29, 1934, and "Essentials of Mennonitism," delivered at "Wadsworth, O.," May 6, 1934, both in Smith Papers, box 38, file 8; "War Experiences" and

"Dangers threatening our Peace Principles," Meadows, IL, June 9–10, 1934, both in Smith Papers, box 38, file 9; "Our Mennonite Peace Inheritance," delivered to "Silver Street Indiana Peace Convention," November 10, 1935, box 38, file 9; "Dangers threatening our traditional Peace Doctrines," delivered at Normal, IL, May 23, 1938, box 4, file 6, Smith Papers, BUASC ("those who were willing to die").

37. C. Henry Smith, *Christian Peace: Four Hundred Years of Mennonite Principles and Practice* (Peace Committee of the General Conference of Mennonites, 1938), 27–29, quoted 28–29; Ronald Flowers, "The Naturalization of Douglas Clyde Macintosh, Alien Theologian," *Journal of Supreme Court History* 25 (November 2000), 244, 247, 253–56, 258–61, *Christian Century* quoted 247, 160. Smith did not refer to the *Macintosh* case by name in *Christian Peace*, but did elsewhere. See, for example, Smith, "Brotherhood Topic for March: Separation of Church and State," *Mennonite* 53 (March 1, 1938), 2.

38. Smith, *Christian Peace*, 30.

39. Ibid., 31–32.

40. "Program-Roster" of the Lima Torch Club, 1938–39, Smith Papers, box 52, file 14; Howard Kay to C. K. Searles, October 4, 1937, box 4, file 20, Smith Papers, BUASC ("he speaks without notes"); Smith speech outlines: "Direct Primary: pro and Con," delivered to Lima Democratic Women's Club, March 7, 1933, box 38, file 8; "Mistakes of Versailles," delivered to Lima Women's Club, March 20, 1933, and "The Far East," delivered to "Lima Federation," July 5, 1935, both in box 4, file 6; "Boot-Strap Economics" delivered at Bluffton High School, October 14, 1935, box 38, file 9; "This Changing World," delivered to Bluffton Farmer's Institute, February 19, 1934, box 4, file 6; "Quest for Utopia," delivered in college chapel, March, 1935, box 38, file 9; "Political Trends," delivered to the "Woman Federation" of Bluffton, October 25, 1938, box 38, file 8; all in Smith Papers, BUASC.

41. For polling data and popularity of the peace movement in the 1930s, see Lawrence Wittner, *Rebels Against War: The American Peace Movement, 1933–1983* (Philadelphia: Temple University Press, 1984), 1–22, and Kosek, *Acts of Conscience*, 145–55. Smith, "Hitlerism," delivered to Putnam County group, April 20, 1938, box 4, file 6; "War—its cause and cure," speech delivered to the Lima Federation of Women's Clubs, March 29, 1935, box 38, file 9; "Germany Today," delivered to the Lima Torch Club, September 10, 1936, box 38, file 8; "Education for World-Mindedness," delivered to the Bluffton Parents Teachers Association, February 15, 1937, box 38, file 9; "Education in a changing world," commencement address, Luckey High School, May 24, 1939, box 38, file 9; all in Smith Papers, BUASC.

42. Keim, *Harold S. Bender*, 252–53 (Bender's leadership of Mennonite World Congress); Bender to E. G. Kaufman, November 20, 1936 and to P. R. Schroeder and C. E. Krehbiel, April 3, 1936, both in Kaufman Papers, III-1A-10, box 45, file 28, MLA; and Bender to Schroeder and Krehbiel, April 3, 1936, and to Kaufman, November 20, 1936 (Bender's efforts to line up speakers); Bender to Smith, May 17 and 20, 1936, box 19, file 11, Smith Papers, BUASC.

43. For the 1936 Mennonite World Conference, see Keim, *Harold S. Bender*, 253–54; Bender to Schroeder and Krehbiel, April 3, 1936; C. Henry Smith,

"Mennonite World Congress," in *Yearbook of the General Conference of the Mennonite Church of North America* (Berne, IN: 1937), 18–20; Smith, "Mennonites and Culture," *MQR* XII: 2 (April 1938), 71–76, 81–84.

44. Claude Baecher et al., *Testing Faith and Tradition: A Global Mennonite History: Europe* (Intercourse, PA: Good Books, 2006), 78, 84, 118–19, 124–25 (European context for the conference); Keim, *Harold S. Bender*, 252–53; Smith, "Mennonites and Culture," 74, 76–81, quoted 78, 80. Also on the tensions at the 1936 World Conference, see James Irvin Lichti, "The German Mennonite Response to the Dissolution of the Rhoen-Bruderhof," *Mennonite Life* 46: 2 (June 1991), 12–15.
45. Smith, "Mennonite World Congress," 20–21 (quoted 20); Keim, *Harold S. Bender*, 253–54; C. Henry to Laura Smith, July 13, 1936, Smith Papers, BUASC; Kreider, "C. Henry Smith—Part One," 7.
46. C. Henry to Laura Smith, July 13, 1936; Smith, "Hitlerism" address, 1938.
47. Arthur Rosenberger (likely author), "The Bluffton College Faculty and the Depression," undated memo, box 3, file "1935–1937 reports on college," I-A-C, Rosenberger Papers, BUASC; Bush, *Dancing with the Kobzar*, 123–24 (Rosenberger), 126 (on Ramseyer). Ernst Correll to "Lieber Harold [Bender]," November 6, 1937; Bender to "Lieber Ernst [Correll]," November 14, 1937, and Correll to Bender, April 30, 1938, all in Bender Papers, Hist. Mss. I-278, box 6, file 4, AMC; Smith to Horsch, December 27, 1937, May 28 and June 8, 1939, Horsch Papers, Hist. Mss. I-8-1, box 6, file 22, and box 7, file 3, AMC; Smith to Mrs. Rudolph Petter, February 13, 1938, Rudolph Petter Papers, Hist. Mss 31, box 6, file 47, MLA ("the best informed historian").
48. Correll to Bender, November 6, 1937 and April 14, 1938; Kaufman to Smith, February 24, 1938, and Smith to Kaufman, March 5, 1938, both in Kaufman Papers, Hist. Mss. III-1A-16, box 55, file 384, MLA; Smith to Emmet Harshbarger, July 27, 1939, Harshbarger Papers, Hist. Mss. 34, box 2, file 14, MLA.
49. Daniel Kauffman to Smith, December 21, 1939, box 4, file 15, Smith Papers, BUASC.
50. *Bluffton College Bulletin* XXXIV (June 1937), 3 (Smith's reduction of teaching load); Jacob ter Meulen to Smith, January 27, 1939, box 10, file 16, Smith Papers, BUASC.
51. Smith, "Education and War," delivered to Parent Teachers Association, Beaverdam, Ohio, September 11, 1939, box 38, file 9, Smith Papers, BUASC.

Chapter 11: The Final Mennonite History

1. H. S. Bender to Smith, April 3 and June 4, 1940, Smith Papers, MS I, box 1, file 73, BUASC; "American Mennonite Historians," address delivered at Goshen College, June 8, 1940, box 4, file 6, BUASC. Also see official program, "Dedication, Mennonite Historical Library and Sixteenth Anniversary Program of the Mennonite Historical Society," Mennonite Historical Library Room, Goshen College, June 8, 1940, box 52, file 28, Smith Papers, BUASC.
2. "On Mennonite Historiography: A Communication from Dr. C. Henry Smith," *MQR* XVIII (April 1944), 124; "Smith Mennonite History Library," *Bluffton College Bulletin* XXIX (July 1942), 1; "Memorandum of Agreement between

Dr. C. Henry Smith and Bluffton College," October 27, 1941, box 3, file 19, Smith Papers, BUASC.

3. "Mennonites and Their World" and "The Christian's Attitude in a Warring World," outlines for speeches delivered at "Meadows Retreat," June 1940, Smith Papers, box 38, file 9. For Baptist youth convention in Lima, see Ed Clark to Smith, July 26, 1939, and Helen Wicker to Smith, November 13, 1939 (Smith's discussion talking points attached), box 17, file 6, Smith Papers, BUASC. For data on shifting attitudes in wider society, see Wittner, *Rebels against War*, 29.

4. "Radio Broadcasts," *Bluffton College Bulletin* XXVI (November 1939); "Radio Programs Receive Attention," *Witmarsum* XXVII (December 1, 1939), 1.

5. "Radio Broadcast, March 25, 1939"; *The Background of the News*, October 28, 1939 ("the liquidation of these small states"); "Russia's Baltic Policy," November 17, 1939 ("I said twenty years ago"); both in WLOK radio address transcripts, box 39, file 9, Smith Papers, BUASC.

6. "Is Our Democracy Threatened?" delivered to the "Reformed Brotherhood," March 28, 1940, and "Dangers Threatening Our Democracy," delivered to the Ada Rotary Club, April 8, 1940, both in Smith Papers, box 4, file 6; WLOK radio address transcripts, "Is Our Democracy in Danger?" December 8, 1939, and "The Third Term Issue," March 27, 1940 (quoted); and "Anti New Deal Democrat," delivered to "College YMCA," October 23, 1940, box 39, file 9, all in Smith Papers, BUASC.

One can only speculate about the reasons for Smith's final break with Roosevelt. As an old Wilsonian progressive with individualistic impulses, and also as a small-town businessman, he was probably discomfited by the collectivist sense of many New Deal programs and Roosevelt's increasing affinity for big labor. Smith was also undoubtedly unhappy with what appeared as FDR's increasingly interventionist tilt as the war clouds gathered. Finally, it may have had something to do with genuine enthusiasm for a liberal businessman and former Democrat like Willkie. The same kinds of political shifts were also apparently underway with Smith's close friends and allies, like Kaufman and his nephew Willard. On Kaufman's embrace of noninterventionism, see Juhnke, *Creative Crusader*, 208–9; for Willard Smith's break with FDR after his second term, see *The Road to Santa Fe*, 196.

7. "Union Now," delivered to the Lima Torch Club, February 19, 1940," Smith Papers, box 4, file 6. "Christ or Caesar," address delivered to the "U.B." (United Brethren) Church in Cridersville, Ohio, October 19, 1941; "Need for Clear Thinking in a Crisis," address delivered to the Findlay Ministerial Association, November 3, 1941; "The World Situation and the Church," delivered to the "U.B. Missionary Conference," Bowling Green, Ohio, May 7, 1941; "The Most Important Event of the Week," delivered on WLOK Radio, November 13, 1941, Smith Papers, BUASC.

8. "The World We Live In," delivered at "Meadows Retreat," June 1940; box 39, file 9 ("a new type of patriotism"), Smith Papers, BUASC. On attitudes in wider liberal Protestantism, see Wittner, *Rebels against War*, 26–27, quoted 33; Kosek, *Acts of Conscience*, 155–56; and Gerald Sittser, *A Cautious Patriotism:*

The American Churches and the Second World War (Chapel Hill: University of North Carolina Press, 1997), 231.

9. "Christ or Caesar," October 19, 1941; "Need for Clear Thinking in a Crisis," November 3, 1941; "The Most Important Event of the Week," delivered on WLOK Radio, November 13, 1941; "The Japanese War," delivered on WLOK Radio, December 10, 1941; box 39, file 9, all in Smith Papers, BUASC. With this address, Smith's radio series seems to have ended, and one can only speculate why. It may have been that now, in a wartime environment, WLOK management quickly concluded that pointed commentary from a noted local pacifist was too controversial to remain on the air.

10. On CPS, see Bush, *Two Kingdoms, Two Loyalties*, 69–77, and Toews, *Mennonites in American Society*, 134–42, quoted 139, draft bill quoted 135. Wittner, *Rebels against War*, 70–86, explores the critiques of the program in larger pacifism.

11. Wittner, *Rebels against War*, 34–35, *Christian Century* quoted 42 (collapse of the interwar peace movement). For developments at Bluffton College, see Bush, *Dancing with the Kobzar*, 128–32. For enrollment numbers, see "Mennonite Colleges in War Time, A Conference for Administrators of Mennonite Colleges," Winona Lake, Indiana, August 7, 1942, 5, L.L. box 5, folder titled "L. Ramseyer Mennonite Committee for College, 1942–47," A-A-d, Ramseyer Papers, BUASC.

12. Elaine Bowers, interview; Dale Reichenbach to Smith, April 9, 1944, box 5, file 86, and James Griffith to "Dr. and Mrs. Smith," undated, box 9, file 53, Smith Papers, BUASC.

13. Toews, *Mennonites in American Society*, 173–75, and Bush, *Two Kingdoms, Two Loyalties*, 87–88, 97–98 (Mennonite draft decisions); Bush, *Dancing with the Kobzar*, 133 (Bluffton numbers).

14. Smith, "Is the General Conference Losing Its Peace Testimony?" *Mennonite* 52 (July 28, 1942), 1–2.

15. E. G. Kaufman to Smith, December 2, 1940, Smith Papers, box 4, file 8; Bethel College lectures, March 23–27, 1942: "Lessons from Mennonite History" ("modern disintegrating forces"), "Mennonite Origins," "Through Fire and Blood" ("democracy and Christianity are going to be saved by the martyr"), and "Keeping the Faith" ("pacifism not a remedy to end war," "not the pacifists' problem," and "greatest opportunity in their history"), all in Smith Papers, box 32, file 5. For Smith visiting CPS camps, see Charles Suter to Smith, June 16 and 25, July 20, and August 17, 1943, and Olen Britsch to Smith, August 25, 1943, all in box 10, file 24; William T. Snyder to Smith, July 27, 1943, box 8, file 15, BUASC; "Persecution," outline for speech delivered at Medaryville, Indiana, CPS camp, March 18, 1946, as yet unprocessed, BUASC.

16. C. Henry Smith membership record, Church Membership records, vertical file, First Mennonite Church, Bluffton. On Hartzler's situation at Carlock, see R. L. Hartzler to Rev. Allen Yoder, May 8, and to Rev. A. H. Miller, May 15, 1940, box 2, file "Carlock church," 3-B-e, both in R. L. Hartzler Papers, BUASC. Explicitly comparing his situation with the "E. White Oak affair," Hartzler said the root of his resignation partly went back to a visit to the church by "a certain 'fly-by-night evangelist'" who "came along and swept some folks off their

feet." He also noted that further congregational unhappiness resulted from his own clear resistance to teaching a religious worldview "which was violently at variance with our Mennonite faith in their disparagement of peace and extolling of militarism and their emphasis on eternal security."

While important to him personally, Smith's transfer of membership from the Central to the General Conference was not terribly radical. The two Mennonite bodies were rapidly growing closer together, and would merge shortly after the end of the war. On this, see Toews, *Mennonites in American Society*, 270–71.

17. On Grace Bible Institute, see Smith to Rev. Albert Schultz, July 6, 1943, Smith Papers, box 4, file 6; also see responses from individual Grace founders, all testifying to the institute's dedication to nonresistance: Paul Kuhlmann, July 14 (box 4, file 48), J. R. Barkman, July 16 (box 1, file 59), and C. H. Suckau, July 22, 1943 (box 8, file 4), BUASC. On Moody grad candidate, see Smith to Albert [no last name given], Oct. 12, 1943, Smith Papers, box 10, file 7.

18. For Smith's work with the MDC Peace Committee, see E. S. Mullet, C. H. Smith, and J. E. Amstutz to "Dear Brother," undated, and Mullet et al. to "Dear Pastor or Peace Secretary," July 14, 1942; Don Smucker, C. H. Smith, and E. S. Mullet to "Dear Pastor," September 18, 1942, and to "Dear Brother," July 10, 1943, and June 8, 1944; "Our Peace Testimony, Address at Middle District Conference, Summerfield, IL, Aug. 16–19, 1942"; all in Middle District Conference Papers, 3-A-b -3, 5, 6, 7, file "Peace Committee," BUASC ("the remedy").

19. For larger analyses of the Durable Peace conferences, see Robert Alan Johnson, "'A Uniquely Dangerous and Promising Time': America's Protestant Establishment Confronts a New World, 1941–1950," (PhD diss., Texas Christian University, 2001), 48–74 (Morrison quoted 67), and Dennis L. Tarr, "The Presbyterian Church and the Founding of the United Nations," *Journal of Presbyterian History*, 53: 1 (1975), 4–5. On its resolutions, see "The Churches and a Just and Durable Peace: A Report Adopted at the National Study Conference, Delaware, Ohio, March 3–5, 1942," *Christian Century* 59: 12 (1942), 390–97. For Smith as delegate, see C. E. Krehbiel to Smith, January 26 and February 3, 1942, box 4, file 41, Smith Papers, BUASC. Smith, "Keeping the Faith," address, and "The Delaware Conference," delivered in BC chapel, April 24, 1942, box 58, file 9, and "Debatable Assumptions in our Thinking about our War Efforts," address delivered to Lima Torch Club, May, 1942, box 38, file 7, Smith Papers, BUASC. For his notes on the conference, see box 59, file 8.

20. For Smith's "Byways of Mennonite History" series in the *Mennonite*, see in vol. LVIII, "Introduction" (October 5, 1943), 5–6; "Origins" (October 19, 1943), 5–6; "Menno Simons" (November 23, 1943), 5–6; "What Did Menno Simons teach?" (December 7, 1943), 4–5; "What Did Menno Simons Teach? False Brethren (The Münsterites)" (December 28, 1943), 12; in vol. LIX, "The Blood of the Martyrs" (January 11, 1944), 5–6; "The European Ancestral Home of the Pennsylvania Mennonites" (February 8, 1944), 6–7. For wartime topical articles, see Smith, "God and War," *Mennonite* 52 (December 15, 1942), 6; "Dwight L. Moody and War," *Mennonite* 53 (September 28, 1943), 1; "Keeping the Faith," *Mennonite* 54 (July 11,1944), 5; "A Five Foot Book

Shelf of Peace I," *Mennonite* 54 (October 3, 1944), 5; "A Five Foot Book Shelf of Peace II," *Mennonite* 54 (November 28, 1944), 10.
21. On the Mennonite Heritage Course, see Toews, *Mennonites in American Society*, 169–72 ("churchwide teach-in" 170), and Bush, *Two Kingdoms, Two Loyalties*, 77. Smith to Bender, January 4, 1941, and March 31, 1942, Bender Papers, Hist. Mss. I-278, box 23, file 1, AMC; Bender to Smith, April 3, 1942, box 1, file 73, Smith Papers, BUASC (Smith's involvement in the course).
22. C. Henry Smith, *Mennonites in America*, "Mennonites and Their Heritage," no. 2 (Akron, PA: Mennonite Central Committee, 1942), 3–10, 13–14, 19–24, Bender quoted 24.
23. Bender to Smith, March 27, 1941, box 1, file 73, Smith Papers, BUASC; Smith to Bender, January 4, 1941; Smith, *Mennonites in America*, 33.
24. Bender to Smith et al., January 17, 1945, box 1, file 73, Smith Papers, BUASC; Kreider, "C. Henry Smith, Part II," 22.
25. Smith to Jacob Thierstein, March 6, 1922, box 3, file 23 (quoted), and November 14, 1925, box 4, file 35, Thierstein Papers, Hist. Mss. 19, MLA; C. Henry Smith, *The Story of the Mennonites* (Berne, IN: Mennonite Book Concern, 1941).
26. Keim, *Harold S. Bender*, 321 (new developments in Anabaptist historiography); Smith, *The Story of the Mennonites*, 3, 177–87.
27. Smith, *The Story of the Mennonites*, 4, 27, 240–44, 313, 32–45, 359, 373–74, 477–531, quoted 344, 485. On the anti-Catholic undercurrents then percolating through liberal Protestantism, see Justin Nordstrom, *Danger on the Doorstep: Anti-Catholicism and American Print Culture in the Progressive Era* (Notre Dame, IN: University of Notre Dame Press, 2006).
28. Smith, *The Story of the Mennonites*, 4, 10–63, 79–86, 167–68, 278, quoted 29.
29. Ibid., 122–23, 135–37, 203–4, 214–15, quoted 136, 187.
30. Ibid., 427–34, 614–24, 697–98, 748–64, quoted 433–34, 620, 624, 698, 748; Toews, *Mennonites in American Society*, 97 (on Smith's progressive reading of Mennonite history).
31. On Smith's subsidy and other prepublication details, see Jacob Thierstein to Smith, July 15, August 21, and October 26, 1940, and to Berne Witness Company, April 10, 1941, all in box 8, file 48, and Fred Von Gunten to Smith, September 8, 1941, box 10, file 11. Smith to John Umble, John Umble Papers, Hist. Mss. I-46, box 4, file 5, AMC (Smith's initial preconceptions). On sales, see J. M. Suderman to Smith, August 7, 1942, box 10, file 12; Von Gunten to Smith, December 20, 1944, box 9, file 3; all in Smith Papers, BUASC. For reviews of Smith's book, see the *Union Seminary Review*, November 1941; the *Gospel Banner*, August 7, 1941; Melvin Gingerich in the *Mennonite*, October 14, 1941; and the *Christian Monitor*, September 1941; box 43, file 2, all in Smith Papers, BUASC. For private affirmations, see A. J. Richert to Smith, July 6, 1941, box 6, file 3; Guy Hershberger to Smith, August 5, 1941; Robert Friedmann to Smith, July 28, 1941, box 3, file 8, BUASC.
32. Keim, *Harold S. Bender*, 287–88, quoted 287. Even if Horsch's health had been better, Smith learned, his objections to Smith's book might have been mild. He had read it carefully in the months before his death, Edward Yoder relayed to Smith from Scottdale, and his primary criticism had merely to do with Smith's

fleeting treatment of the seventeenth-century Dutch social reformer Cornelius Plockhoy. See Edward Yoder to Smith, September 18, 1942, box 10, file 12, Smith Papers, BUASC.

33. On the "Goshen School," see Sawatsky, "The One and the Many," 146. "John [C. Wenger]" to "Harold [Bender]," July 7, 1941, Bender Papers, Hist. Mss. I-278, box 24, file 2, AMC. Toews, *Mennonites in American Society*, 96–98, quoted 98. Also on the Smith-Bender debate, see Theron Schlabach, "Discipleship, Generational Change and the Practice of Mennonite History," *MQR* 73 (July 1999), 428–29.
34. Harold Bender and Ernst Correll, "C. Henry Smith's *The Story of the Mennonites*," *MQR* 16 (October 1942), 270–75, quoted 270–73.
35. Bender and Correll, "Smith's *The Story of the Mennonites*," 272–73.
36. Kreider, "C. Henry Smith, Part II," 22; Bender and Correll, "Smith's *The Story of the Mennonites*," 275; Sprunger, "Smith's Vision of Mennonite History," 9 (Smith's indignation); Smith to Edmund Kaufman, December 21, 1943, Kaufman Papers, Hist. Mss. II-I-A, box 55, file 384, MLA.
37. "A Communication from C. Henry Smith Concerning the Review of His Book 'The Story of the Mennonites,'" *MQR* 27 (October 1943), 246–52, quoted 246–47.
38. "A Communication from C. Henry Smith," 248–49. Smith sent Kaufman an advance copy of his reply to Bender, and Bethel's president loved it, writing Smith to "express my satisfaction on the way you answered him . . . I hope he mends his ways. After all he will take it from you sooner than from someone else. He seems to be getting worse with age." Kaufman to Smith, December 16, 1943, box 4, file 18, Smith Papers, BUASC.
39. Bender to Smith, October 21, 1943, Smith Papers, box 1, file 73; Friedmann to Smith, September 27 and October 16, 1940, box 3, file 8; July 13, 1942, box 10, file 12; November 4, 1943, as yet unprocessed, BUASC. On Friedmann, see Keim, *Harold S. Bender*, 301–5.
40. Robert Friedmann, "On Mennonite Historiography and On Individualism and Brotherhood," *MQR* 18 (April 1944), 117–22, quoted 117–18, 121–22. Theron Schlabach is particularly insightful on Friedmann's critiques; see "Discipleship, Generational Change and the Practice of Mennonite History," 428–30.
41. "On Mennonite Historiography: A Communication from Dr. C. Henry Smith," 122–23.
42. For larger developments in American historiography, see Novick, *That Noble Dream*, 133–67, Brinton quoted 141; and Schlabach, "Discipleship, Generational Change and the Practice of Mennonite History," 433–35.
43. C. Henry Smith, "The New History," *Bluffton Alumnus* 1 (March 1932), 55–56, quoted 55.
44. "On Mennonite Historiography: A Communication from Dr. C. Henry Smith," 123.
45. Ibid., 123, 125.
46. Schlabach, "Discipleship, Generational Change and the Practice of Mennonite History," 433–43, quoted 434; Sawatsky, "The One and the Many," 141–45. I am especially indebted in my thinking here to Dr. Schlabach's analysis.

47. For the larger context of Bender's monumental Anabaptist Vision statement, see Keim, *Harold S. Bender*, 310–15; Harold S. Bender, "The Anabaptist Vision," *MQR* 38 (April 1944), 67–68, 68 n3, quoted 85.
48. Bender, "The Anabaptist Vision," 69 (quoted), 82–83. On Smith's book as one of Bender's major intellectual streams, see Keim, *Harold S. Bender*, 315; his entire analysis (315–22) is required reading here. On Bender's Anabaptist Vision as enshrining Swiss/South German Anabaptism as normative for Mennonites in a manner that became mythological, see Sawatsky, *History and Ideology*, 127–31, and Gerald Biesecker-Mast, *Separation and the Sword in Anabaptist Persuasion: Radical Confessional Rhetoric from Schleitheim to Dordrecht* (Telford, PA: Cascadia Press, 2006), 47. Also on the Anabaptist Vision, see Toews, *Mennonites in American Society*, 105.

    In subsequent articles, Bender and other allied scholars of the emerging "Goshen School" further fleshed out this Anabaptist Vision, with a further critique of Smith's historiography as an important subsidiary point. For instance, as he wrote in the *MQR* in 1950, the Anabaptist movement "was the opposite of individualism, having a full church order and discipline." On this point, see Sawatsky, *History and Ideology*, 131–32, Bender quoted 132.
49. Bender to Smith, June 15, 1944, Smith Papers, box 1, file 73, BUASC; C. Henry Smith, *The Story of the Mennonites* (Berne, IN: Mennonite Book Concern, 1941 and 1945), 817–19, quoted 817.
50. Smith to "Dear Brother," June 8, and Don Smucker, C. H. Smith, and E. S. Mullet to "Dear Brother," November 14, 1944, 3-A-b-3, 5, 6, 7, file "Peace Committee," Middle District Conference Papers, BUASC. For the 1945 conference, see Johnson, "'A Uniquely Dangerous and Promising Time,'" 101–14; Tarr, "The Presbyterian Church and the Founding of the United Nations," 13; Smith to C. E. Krehbiel, February 3, 1945, box 18, file 9, Smith Papers, BUASC.
51. Speech outlines: "The Church in a World of Sin," delivered to the Lima Ministerial Association, April 9, 1945; "Christ in the World Order," delivered to the Ada Presbyterian Brotherhood, April 26, 1946; "The Post War World," delivered in Ottawa, Ohio, March 21, 1944; "Cleveland Conference," delivered to First Mennonite Church, Bluffton, 1945; all in Smith Papers, box 38, file 9; "Has Russia Changed?", delivered to Lima Torch Club, May, 1944; and "Postwar Europe," delivered to Lima Torch Club, July 27, 1945; box 38, file 7; all in Smith Papers, BUASC.
52. Lloyd Ramseyer to Robert Kreider, February 4, 1944, and December 7, 1945, box 12, folder titled "Letters, 1943–50," I-A-d, Ramseyer Papers, BUASC; Bush, *Dancing with the Kobzar*, 147; Pannabecker, *Faith in Ferment*, 315–17 (Ramseyer's grooming of Kreider). On the founding of Mennonite Biblical Seminary, see Juhnke, *Creative Crusader*, 221–23. Abraham Warkentin to Smith, August 3 and 11, 1945, box 4, file 7, Smith Papers, BUASC; "Dr. Smith on Staff of New Seminary," *Witmarsum* XXXIII (October 13, 1945), 3 (Smith's class there). Burton and Elnore Yost, interview, June 14, 2013. "Honored on Retiring from College Faculty," *Bluffton News* (June 13, 1946), 1 (Smith's retirement).
53. "Honored on Retiring from College Faculty" (retirement party). D. B. Zook to Smith, June 4, 1946, and Milton Sprunger to Smith, same date, both in Smith

Papers, box 10, file 22; Ralph Page to Smith, June 5, 1946, box 5, file 81; Russell Oyer to Smith, June 5, 1946, box 5, file 12; Lloyd Ramseyer to Smith, May 28, 1947, box 5, file 81, BUASC; John L. Stipp to Smith, November 25, 1946 (quoted), and Smith to J. C. Meyer, June 25, 1946, both in C. Henry Smith Papers, Hist. Mss I-211, box 2, file 2, AMC; "C. Henry Smith and Noah Byers granted honorary degrees," *Mennonite* 62 (June 24, 1947), 14.

54. H. J. Unruh to Smith, July 10, 1945, box 18, file 3; Albert Gaeddert to Smith, May 6, 1946, box 10, file 12; promotional flyer for *Mennonite Life* in box 52, file 18; all in Smith Papers, BUASC (on *Mennonite Life*). C. Henry Smith, *Metamora* (Bluffton: College Book Store, 1947). For GC peace pamphlet, see Ernest Bohn, C. Henry Smith, and J. E. Amstutz to "Dear Brother," April 25, 1947, 3-A-b-3, 5, 6, 7, file "Peace Committee," Middle District Conference Papers, BUASC; and The Peace Committee of the General Conference Mennonite Church, *The Power of Love: A Study Manual Adapted for Sunday School Use and Group Discussion* (Newton, KS: The Board of Publication, 1947), 5, 38–57.

55. Keim, *Harold S. Bender*, 355–56.

56. Ibid., 355–56 ("fellowship of craftsmen" 355, "cordial loyalty" 356); "Minutes of the Organizational Meeting of the Mennonite Research fellowship," August 23, 1945; Fretz and Bender to Smith, May 15, 1945, and Bender to Smith, January 2, 1945, box 10, file 27, both in Smith Papers, BUASC.

57. On the transformation of the *Lexikon* into the *Mennonite Encyclopedia*, see Rachel Waltner Goossen, "From Anabaptism to Mennonitism: The *Mennonite Encyclopedia* as a Historical Document," *Mennonite Life* 37 (December 1982), 13–14, and Keim, *Harold S. Bender*, 357–59, 439. Bender to Mennonite Lexicon Committee, January 3, 1946, Hist. Mss. V-15, *Mennonite Encyclopedia* files, box 2, MLA; "Minutes of the Meeting of the Publishing Committee of the Proposed Mennonite Encyclopedia," March 23, 1946, box 10, file 27, Smith Papers, BUASC (for a general sense of Smith's travels in this period, see various meeting minutes in these files); "John C. [Wenger]" to "Harold [Bender]," August 15, 1947, Bender Papers, Hist. Mss I-278, box 4, file 2, AMC.

58. Smith, "The Final Mennonite History," presidential address delivered at Goshen College to the Mennonite Research Fellowship, 1947, box 28, file 12, Smith Papers, BUASC.

59. Keim, *Harold S. Bender*, 379–80, Bender quoted 380; Abraham Friesen, *In Defense of Privilege: Russian Mennonites and the State Before and During World War I* (Winnipeg: Kindred Productions, 2006), 327–330; Frank H. Epp, *Mennonite Exodus: The Rescue and Resettlement of the Russian Mennonites since the Communist Revolution* (Altona, MB: D. W. Friesen & Sons, 1962), 373–79; William T. Snyder to George Warren, April 5, 1948, and to Smith, April 12 and 13, 1948, with accompanying legal brief, all in Smith Papers, BUASC (these papers as yet unclassified). Subsequent efforts to establish this same point of Dutch origin would prove less successful; see Friesen, 332–37.

60. J. E. Hartzler to Smith, February 29, 1948, Smith Papers, MS I, box 3, file 48. Also on Smith's illness, see Cornelius Krahn to Smith, box 4, file 37, Smith Papers, BUASC; Willard Smith, "C. Henry Smith: A Brief Biography," appendix 2 in Smith, *Mennonite Country Boy*, 246; Henry to Ella (Smith Oyer),

February 16, 1948, Ella Smith Oyer Papers, MS 112, box 1, file 9, BUASC. Laura's ignorance of her husband's illness taken from Robert Kreider, email message to author, July 19, 2011. Robert and Alice Ruth Ramseyer also suggested to me that Laura knew little or nothing about her husband's illness until near the end, which they undoubtedly heard from Robert's father, Lloyd.

61. Smith to Ella (Smith Oyer), July 16, 1948; Smith to John Umble, April 17 and 29, 1948, Umble Papers, Hist. Mss. I-46, box 4, file 12, AMC (extinct congregations); Ramseyer to Kreider, May 28, 1948, I-A-d, box 12, folder titled "Letters, 1943–50," Lloyd Ramseyer Papers, BUASC; Kreider to Smith, July 8, 1948, Smith Papers, MS I-3, box 1, file 2, BUASC (follow-up note); Smith to Kaufman, August 18, 1948, Kaufman Papers, Hist. Mss. II-I-A, box 55, file 384, MLA.

62. Willard Smith, "C. Henry Smith: A Brief Biography," 246–47, 251–52; Smith speech outlines, box 4, file 6 (this inscription was possibly in Laura's handwriting); Walter Dyck to Smith, November 4, 1947, box 2, file 61 (Smith resignation); "Last Will and Testament of C. Henry Smith," undated draft, box 8, file 28; "$70,000 Smith Estate goes to Philanthropy," undated newspaper clipping, box 43, file 28 (Smith's will, quoted); all in Smith Papers, BUASC. Adjustments for inflation dollar estimates were made via an inflation calculator by the U.S. Department of Labor, Bureau of Labor Statistics, http://www.bls.gov/data/inflation_calculator.htm.

63. C. Henry Smith to Cornelius Krahn, April 10, 1948, Cornelius Krahn Papers, Hist. Mss I-165, box 1, no file number, MLA.

64. Laura Smith to "Laura and Frank [King]," March 3, 1952, box 19, file 5, Ms. 2, Laura Ioder Smith Papers, BUASC (Lantz anecdote); "C. Henry Smith: A Brief Biography," 246–47 (*ME* articles); Nita Crawford, interview.

65. Lloyd Ramseyer to Robert Kreider, October 20, 1948, box 12, folder titled "Letters, 1943–50," I-A-d, Lloyd Ramseyer Papers, BUASC ("something unusual"); Klassen interview (Smith's last days); Smith to "Dear Bernie [Bargen]," October 19, 1948, box 1, file 21, Smith Papers, BUASC; Edmund G. Kaufman, "Smith's Story," review of *The Story of the Mennonites* by C. Henry Smith, 3rd ed., revised and enlarged by Cornelius Krahn, *Mennonite Life* 4 (April 1951), 45; "Dr. C. Henry Smith Called," *Bluffton College Bulletin* XXXV (October 1948), 1.

66. "Dr. C. Henry Smith Called"; Harold Bender, "C. Henry Smith: A Tribute," appendix 1 in Smith, *Mennonite Country Boy*, 231–32.

67. Kaufman, *General Conference Mennonite Pioneers*, 198–99 (Byers's death), 247 (Hartzler); "Death Claims Retired Minister, Educator at Bluffton, Ohio," *Mennonite Weekly Review* (August 12, 1966), 1 (Whitmer). Edna Hanley Byers brought her husband's body back from Georgia to Bluffton and buried it across from Smith at Maple Grove Cemetery, in this manner rendering the two of them once more—in the same way they had been throughout much of their adult lives—neighbors. Laura's last years taken from Weaver, interview; Ramseyer, interview; and Kreider email July 19, 2011; Laura Smith to "Dear Ella or 'Ellen,'" July 31, 1967, Ella Smith Oyer Papers, MS 112, box 1, file 11, BUASC; Bowers, interview (Laura's death); "Mrs. Laura Smith Succumbs Sunday," *Bluffton News*, March 22, 1973.

Chapter 12: Epilogue

1. For the postwar dominance of Bender's Anabaptist Vision as normative for Mennonites, see Toews, *Mennonites in American Society*, 104–5, and Sawatsky, *History and Ideology*, 128–29, 132–33 ("the trade name," 133); Sawatsky, "The One and the Many," 145–46 (on Kaufman); Sawatsky, *Authority and Identity*, 48–51, and Waltner, "From Anabaptism to Mennonitism," 14–16 (on Krahn); Paul Toews, "Mennonites in American Society: Modernity and the Persistence of Religious Community," *MQR* 63 (July 1983), 240–41. For conflicted reactions from GC Mennonites and others to Bender's statement, see Sawatsky, "The One and the Many," 144–47, and Abe Dueck, "Canadian Mennonites and the Anabaptist Vision," *Journal of Mennonite Studies* 13 (1995), 71–84.
2. In 1965, for example, after a number of reprints of Bender's statement had already been issued, Herald Press published it again in a different format as a small pamphlet. It would go on to sell an additional 22,500 copies over the next quarter century. See John Roth, "In this Issue," *MQR* 69 (July 1995), 278.
3. On GC attraction to Bender's statement, see Sawatsky, *Authority and Identity*, 48–49, and Bush, *Two Kingdoms, Two Loyalties*, 69.
4. On the revisionists' reaction to the Goshen School, see Harold S. Bender and John Oyer, "Historiography: Anabaptist," in *GAMEO*, 1989, http://gameo.org/index.php?title=Historiography:_Anabaptist&oldid=121134; Sawatsky, "The One and the Many," 142–47; and Biesecker-Mast, *Separation and the Sword in Anabaptist Persuasion*, 38–40.

    As happens in scholarship, in this case the revisionists have likewise been subjected to revision. In the last two decades, a kind of "post-polygenesis" reading has emerged in Anabaptist historiography, largely at the hands of Stayer and his revisionist colleagues themselves. This recent scholarship has begun to stress the subtle primacy of the Swiss Brethren and "soften," in Werner Packull's words, the heretofore hard lines of demarcation they had laid down among different Anabaptist groups. For a concise summary of this historiographical shift, see Werner Packull, *Hutterite Beginnings: Communitarian Experiments during the Reformation* (Baltimore: Johns Hopkins University Press, 1995), 8–11, quoted 11.
5. Sawatsky, *History and Ideology*, 126 (quoted); Cornelius Krahn, preface to *Smith's Story of the Mennonites*, 5th ed., by C. Henry Smith, revised and enlarged by Cornelius Krahn (Eugene, OR: Wipf and Stock Publishers, 2004, reproduced by permission of Herald Press), xvii; Sprunger, "C. Henry Smith's Vision of Mennonite History," 11 (quoted). Keith Sprunger has astutely summarized Krahn's further revisions of Smith's book. See Sprunger, review of *Smith's Story of the Mennonites*, revised and enlarged by Cornelius Krahn, *Mennonite Life* 36 (September 1981); 29.
6. Cornelius J. Dyck, ed., *An Introduction to Mennonite History* (Scottdale, PA: Herald Press, 1981); Kreider, "C. Henry Smith Part II," 22 (classroom use); Paul Klassen, review of *Smith's Story of the Mennonites*, revised and enlarged by Cornelius Krahn, *MQR* 54 (July 1982), 298–99, quoted 299; John Kampen, email message to author, June 25, 2008; Sprunger, "C. Henry Smith's Vision of Mennonite History," 4.

7. C. Henry Smith, "All-Mennonite Convention," in *GAMEO*, 1989, http://gameo.org/index.php?title=All-Mennonite_Convention&oldid=90797; Bush, *Dancing with the Kobzar*, 140 (Ramseyer on the union movement). For new, postwar patterns of Mennonite ecumenicity, see Toews, *Mennonites in American Society*, 180–82, and Bush, *Two Kingdoms, Two Loyalties*, 165–68.
8. C. Henry Smith, "Bondage," *Institute Monthly* I (April 15, 1899), 50; Cornelius Krahn, "A Life That Made a Difference," *Mennonite Life* 5 (April 1950), 3 (notes on Smith's desk).
9. Robert S. Kreider, foreword to *Smith's Story of the Mennonites*, 5th ed., by C. Henry Smith, xi-xii. Toews, *Mennonites in American Society*, 104–5 (on Smith's individualism).
10. "A Communication from C. Henry Smith," 248.
11. C. Henry Smith, "Byways of Mennonite History," *The Mennonite* 54 (January 11, 1944), 5–6, quoted 6.
12. For the Mennonite Community Movement, see Bush, *Two Kingdoms, Two Loyalties*, 130–36. "A Communication from C. Henry Smith," 247 ("back to the farm movement").
13. Toews, *Mennonites in American Society*, 105. Subsequent developments among U.S. Mennonites suggested that in this area, as well, Smith may have been highlighting a constructive way forward. Within a decade of his death, led by scholar/activists like Hershberger, MC and GC Mennonites would begin proactively to witness to the state about a variety of social and political issues, which an older, two-kingdom model had previously defined as outside their sphere of concern. On this point, see Bush, *Two Kingdoms, Two Loyalties*, 187–256, and Theron Schlabach, *War, Peace and Social Conscience: Guy F. Hershberger and Mennonite Ethics* (Scottdale, PA: Herald Press, 2009), 447–71.
14. Kreider, foreword to *Smith's Story of the Mennonites*, xii.
15. Robert Kreider, email message to author, July 19, 2013 (Smith's affection for his people and their history); Weaver, interview; Edmund Kaufman, "Smith's Story," review of *The Story of the Mennonites*, by C. Henry Smith, 3rd. ed., revised and enlarged by Cornelius Krahn, *Mennonite Life* 6 (April 1951), 44.
16. On the growth of Mennonite historical consciousness, see Toews, *Mennonites in American Society*, 87–95; Kraus, "American Mennonites and the Bible," 324–27 (on the destructiveness of the fundamentalist/modernist conflict); Sawatsky, *Authority and Identity*, 65 (quoted).
17. Keim, *Harold S. Bender*, 165–66 (Bender's position in the Goshen history department); Mast, *Separation and the Sword in Anabaptist Persuasion*, 44 (Bender's context); Paul Toews, "The American Mennonite Search for a Useable Past: From the Declensive to the Ironic Interpretation," *MQR* 73 (July 1999), 476–81; Nathan Hershberger, "Power, Tradition and Renewal: The *Concern* Movement and the Fragmented Institutionalization of Mennonite Life," *MQR* 88 (April 2013), 155–72.

    For more recent popular restatements of Bender's Anabaptist Vision, see Stuart Murray, *The Naked Anabaptist: The Bare Essentials of a Radical Faith* (Scottdale, PA: Herald Press, 2010), and Palmer Becker, *What Is an Anabaptist Christian?* (Elkhart, IN: Mennonite Mission Network, 2008). The insights of Gerald Mast and Robert Kreider have deeply informed my analysis in these last several paragraphs.
18. Gerald Mast, email message to author, July 18, 2013.

Selected Bibliography

Manuscript Collections
Archives of the Mennonite Church, Goshen College, Goshen, Indiana (abbreviated AMC)
Harold S. Bender Papers
John S. Coffman Papers
College Mennonite Church Papers
Goshen College President's Office Papers
Agnes Albrecht Gunden Papers
John E. Hartzler Papers
John Horsch Papers
Daniel Kauffman Papers
Emma Smith Oyer Papers
C. Henry Smith Papers
Albert J. Steiner Papers
Menno S. Steiner Papers
John Umble Papers
Harry F. Weber Papers
Illinois Mennonite Heritage Center, Metamora, Illinois
Tiskilwa Mennonite Church Papers
John and Magdelena Schertz Smith Family Papers
Mennonite Historical Library, Bluffton University, Bluffton, Ohio (abbreviated BUASC)
Board of Trustees Meeting Minutes
Bluffton College Faculty Meeting Minutes
Noah E. Byers Papers
Raymond L. Hartzler Papers
Noah Hirschy Papers
Middle District Conference Papers

Emilie Mosiman Papers
Samuel K. Mosiman Papers
Lloyd L. Ramseyer Papers
Arthur Rosenberger Papers
Laura Ioder Smith Papers
Roy Wenger Papers
Paul Whitmer Papers
Zion Mennonite Church Papers
Mennonite Library and Archives, Bethel College, North Newton, Kansas (abbreviated MLA)
Bethel College Presidential Papers
Edmund Kaufman Papers
Cornelius Krahn Papers
Henry P. Krehbiel Papers
Jacob Langenwalter Papers
Mennonite Encyclopedia files
Rodolphe Petter Papers
Jacob R. Thierstein Papers

Books and Articles

Ahlstrom, Sydney. *A Religious History of the American People*. 2 vols. Garden City, NY: Doubleday, 1975.

Bax, Belfort. *Rise and Fall of the Anabaptists*. New York: American Scholar Publications, 1903.

Becker, Palmer. *What Is an Anabaptist Christian?* Elkhart, IN: Mennonite Mission Network, 2008.

Bederman, Gail. "'The Women Have Had Charge of the Church Long Enough': The Men and Religion Forward Movement of 1911–1912 and the Masculinization of Middle-Class Protestantism." In *A Mighty Baptism: Race, Gender and the Creation of American Protestantism*, edited by Susan Jester and Lisa McFarlane, 107–40. Ithaca, NY: Cornell University Press, 1996.

Belz, Herman. "In Retrospect: Andrew C. McLaughlin and Liberal Democracy: Scientific History in Support of the Best Regime." *Reviews in American History* 19 (1991): 444–61.

Bender, Harold S. "The Anabaptist Vision." *Mennonite Quarterly Review* 28 (April 1944): 67–88.

———. "Gospel Witness (Periodical)." *Global Anabaptist Mennonite Encyclopedia Online*. 1956. http://gameo.org/index.php?title=Gospel_Witness_(Periodical)&oldid=122977.

———. "Historiography: North America." *Global Anabaptist Mennonite Encyclopedia Online*. 1956. http://www.gameo.org/encyclopedia/contents/historiography_north_america.

———. "Horsch, John (1867–1941)." *Global Anabaptist Mennonite Encyclopedia Online*. 1953. http://gameo.org/index.php?title=Horsch,_John_(1867-1941)&oldid=123472.

———. "John Horsch, 1867–1941: A Biography." *Mennonite Quarterly Review* 21 (July 1947): 132–44.

Bender, Harold S., and Ernst Correll. "C. Henry Smith's *The Story of the Mennonites*." *Mennonite Quarterly Review* 61 (October 1942): 270–75.

Bender, Harold S., and John S. Oyer. "Historiography: Anabaptist." *Global Anabaptist Mennonite Encyclopedia Online*. 1989. http://gameo.org/index.php?title=Historiography:_Anabaptist&oldid=121134.

Bender, Harold S., and Richard D. Thiessen. "Mennonite Brethren in Christ." *Global Anabaptist Mennonite Encyclopedia Online*. 2013. http://gameo.org/index.php?title=Mennonite_brethren_in_christ&oldid=115157.

Biesecker-Mast, Gerald. *Separation and the Sword in Anabaptist Persuasion: Radical Confessional Rhetoric from Schleitheim to Dordrecht*. Telford, PA: Cascadia Press, 2006.

Birkner, Michael J. "A Conversation with Philip S. Klein." *Pennsylvania History* 56 (October 1989): 243–75.

Bledstein, Burton J. *The Culture of Professionalism: The Middle Class and the Development of Higher Education in America*. New York: Norton, 1976.

Bush, Perry. *Dancing with the Kobzar: Bluffton College and Mennonite Higher Education, 1899–1999*. Telford, PA: Pandora Press U.S., 2000.

———. "Economic Justice and the Evangelical Historian." *Fides et Historia* XXXIII (Winter/Spring 2001): 11–27.

———. *Two Kingdoms, Two Loyalties: Mennonite Pacifism in Modern America*. Baltimore: Johns Hopkins University Press, 1998.

Byers, Noah. "The Times in Which I Lived." *Mennonite Life* 7 (January 1952): 44–47; (April 1952): 77-81; (July 1952): 138-41.

Cheng, Eileen Ka-May. "Exceptional History? The Origins of Historiography in the United States." *History and Theory* 47 (May 2008): 200–28.

Clark, Norman H. *Deliver Us from Evil: An Interpretation of American Prohibition*. New York: Norton, 1976.

Conzen, Kathleen Neils, David A. Gerber, Ewa Morawska, George E. Pozzetta, and Rudolph J. Vecoli. "The Invention of Ethnicity: A Perspective from the USA." *Journal of American Ethnic History*, 12:1 (Fall 1992): 1–33.

Crunden, Robert. *Ministers of Reform: The Progressives' Achievement in American Civilization, 1889–1920*. Chicago: University of Chicago Press, 1984.

Diner, Steven. *A Very Different Age: Americans of the Progressive Era*. New York: Hill and Wang, 1998.

Dueck, Abe. "Canadian Mennonites and the Anabaptist Vision." *Journal of Mennonite Studies* 13 (1995): 71–84.

Dyck, Cornelius J., ed. *An Introduction to Mennonite History*. Scottdale, PA: Herald Press, 1981.

Ellis, John Tracy. "Jameson and American Religious History." In *J. Franklin Jameson: A Tribute*, edited by Ruth Anna Fox and William Lloyd Fox, 9–23. Washington, DC: The Catholic University of America Press, 1965.

Epp, Frank H. *Mennonite Exodus: The Rescue and Resettlement of the Russian Mennonites since the Communist Revolution*. Altona, MB: D. W. Friesen & Sons, 1962.

Epp, Marlene. "Carrying the Banner of Nonconformity: Ontario Mennonite Women and the Dress Question." *Conrad Grebel Review* 8 (Fall 1990): 237–57.

Erb, Paul, and Leonard Gross. "Kauffman, Daniel (1865–1944)." *Global Anabaptist Mennonite Encyclopedia Online*. 1989. http://gameo.org/index.php?title=Kauffman,_Daniel_(1865 -1944)&oldid=112855.

Estes, Steven R. *Living Stones: A History of Metamora Mennonite Church*. Henry, IL: M & D Printing, 1984.

Faragher, John Mack. *Sugar Creek: Life on the Illinois Prairie*. New Haven: Yale University Press, 1986.

Flanagan, Maureen A. *America Reformed: Progressives and Progressivisms, 1890–1920s*. New York: Oxford University Press, 2007.

Flowers, Ronald. "The Naturalization of Douglas Clyde Macintosh, Alien Theologian." *Journal of Supreme Court History* 25 (November 2000): 243–70.

Foner, Eric. *Free Soil, Free Labor, Free Men: The Ideology of the Republican Party before the Civil War*. New York: Oxford University Press, 1970.

Fretz, J. Herbert. "Cassel, Daniel K. (1820–1898)." *Global Anabaptist Mennonite Encyclopedia Online*. 1953. http://gameo.org/index.php?title=Cassel,_Daniel_K._(1820-1898)&oldid=120940.

Friedmann, Robert. "John Horsch and Ludwig Keller." *Mennonite Quarterly Review* XXXI: 3 (July 1947): 160–74.

———. "On Mennonite Historiography and On Individualism and Brotherhood." *Mennonite Quarterly Review* 18 (April 1944): 117–22.

Friesen, Abraham. *History and Renewal in the Anabaptist/Mennonite Tradition*. North Newton, KS: Bethel College Press, 1994.

———. *In Defense of Privilege: Russian Mennonites and the State before and during World War I*. Winnipeg: Kindred Productions, 2006.

Geiger, Roger L. "The Crisis of the Old Order: The Colleges in the 1890s." In *The American College in the Nineteenth Century*, edited by Roger Geiger, 264–76. Nashville: Vanderbilt University Press, 2000.

Gingerich, Melvin. *Mennonite Attire through the Centuries*. Breinigsville, PA: The Pennsylvania German Society, 1970.

Goodspeed, Thomas. *A History of the University of Chicago: The First Quarter-Century*. Chicago: University of Chicago Press, 1925.

Goossen, Rachel Waltner. "From Anabaptism to Mennonitism: The *Mennonite Encyclopedia* as a Historical Document." *Mennonite Life* 37 (December 1982): 13–19.

Gordon, Milton. *Assimilation in American Life*. New York: Oxford University Press, 1964.

Gorrell, Donald. *The Age of Social Responsibility*. Macon, GA: Mercer University Press, 1988.

Gross, Leonard. "The Doctrinal Era of the Mennonite Church." *Mennonite Quarterly Review* 60 (January 1986): 83–103.

Gutman, Herbert G. "Protestantism and the American Labor Movement: The Christian Spirit in the Gilded Age." In *Work, Culture and Society in Industrializing America*, edited by Herbert Gutman, 79–118. New York: Random House, 1977.

Haines, Deborah. "Scientific History as Teaching Method: The Formative Years." *Journal of American History* 63 (December 1977): 892–912.

Hamm, Richard F. "The Prohibitionists' Lincolns." *Illinois Historical Journal* 86 (Summer 1983): 93–116.

Hartzler, John. E. "Autobiographical Notes." *Mennonite Historical Bulletin* 42 (April 1981): 3–4.

Heath, Richard. *Anabaptism: From Its Rise at Zwickau to Its Fall at Muenster, 1521–1536*. London: Alexander and Shepheard, 1895.

Hershberger, Guy F. "The Times of Sanford Calvin Yoder: The Mennonite Church and the First Fifty Years of Goshen College." In *An Evening to Honor Sanford Calvin Yoder*, 6–40. Goshen: Goshen College, July 1974.

Hershberger, Nathan. "Power, Tradition and Renewal: The *Concern* Movement and the Fragmented Institutionalization of Mennonite Life." *Mennonite Quarterly Review* 87 (April 2013): 155–86.

Hohulin, Lydia Leman. "A French Connection: Tracing the Roots of My Leman, Smith and Belsey Families." *Illinois Mennonite Heritage Quarterly* 37 (Spring 2010): 9–15.

Homan, Gerlof. *American Mennonites and the Great War, 1914–1918*. Scottdale, PA: Herald Press, 1994.

Horowitz, Helen Lefkowitz. *Campus Life: Undergraduate Cultures from the End of the Eighteenth Century to the Present*. Chicago: University of Chicago Press, 1987.

Hudson, Winthrop S. *Religion in America*. 3rd ed. New York: Scribner's, 1981.
Hutchinson, William R. *The Modernist Impulse in American Protestantism*. Durham: Duke University Press, 1992.
Jacobson, Matthew Frye. *Whiteness of a Different Color: European Immigrants and the Alchemy of Race*. Cambridge, MA: Harvard University Press, 1998.
Jensen, Richard. *Illinois: A Bicentennial History*. New York: Norton, 1976.
———. *The Winning of the Midwest, Social and Political Conflict, 1888–1971*. Chicago: University of Chicago Press, 1971.
Johnston, Robert D. "Re-Democratizing the Progressive Era: The Politics of Progressive Era Political Historiography." *Journal of the Gilded Age and Progressive Era* 1 (January 2002): 68–92.
Juhnke, James C. *Creative Crusader: Edmund G. Kaufman and Mennonite Community*. North Newton, KS: Bethel College, 1994.
———. "Gemeindechristentum and Bible Doctrine: Two Mennonite Visions of the Early Twentieth Century." *Mennonite Quarterly Review* 57 (July, 1983): 208–12.
———. "Gustav H. Enss, Mennonite Alien." *Mennonite Life* 36 (December 1981): 9–15.
———. "Mennonite Benevolence and Revitalization in the Wake of World War I." *Mennonite Quarterly Review* 60 (January 1986): 15–30.
———. *Vision, Doctrine, War: Mennonite Identity and Organization in America, 1890–1930*. Scottdale, PA: Herald Press, 1989.
Karl, Barry. *Charles E. Merriam and the Study of Politics*. Chicago: University of Chicago Press, 1974.
Kasdorf, Julia. *Fixing Tradition: Joseph W. Yoder, Amish American*. Telford, PA: Pandora Press, 2002.
Kauffman, Daniel. *Fifty Years in the Mennonite Church*. Scottdale, PA: Mennonite Publishing House, 1941.
Kaufman, Edmund G. *General Conference Mennonite Pioneers*. North Newton, KS: Bethel College, 1973.
Keim, Albert N. *Harold S. Bender, 1897–1962*. Scottdale, PA: Herald Press, 1998.

Kennedy, David M. *Freedom from Fear: The American People in Depression and War, 1929–1945*. New York: Oxford University Press, 1999.

———. *Over Here: The First World War and American Society*. New York: Oxford University Press, 1980.

Klingelsmith, Sharon. "Women in the Mennonite Church, 1900–1930." *Mennonite Quarterly Review* 54 (July 1980): 163–207.

Kosek, Joseph Kip. *Acts of Conscience: Christian Nonviolence and Modern American Democracy*. New York: Columbia University Press, 2009.

Kraus, C. Norman. "American Mennonites and the Bible, 1750–1950," *Mennonite Quarterly Review* 61 (October 1967): 309–29.

Kraybill, Donald B. "Mennonite Woman's Veiling: The Rise and Fall of a Sacred Symbol." *Mennonite Quarterly Review* 61 (July 1987): 298–320.

Kreider, Robert. "C. Henry Smith—Part One: Always an Amish-Mennonite Farm Boy." *Illinois Mennonite Heritage Quarterly* 31 (Spring 2004): 1, 7–11.

———. "C. Henry Smith—Part Two: Premier Mennonite Historian–Master Story Teller." *Illinois Mennonite Heritage Quarterly* 31 (Summer 2004): 13, 16–23.

———. *My Early Years: An Autobiography*. Kitchener, ON: Pandora Press, 2002.

Kreider, Robert, et al. "The Swiss Settlement at the Turn of the Century: A Photographic Essay." *Mennonite Life* 43 (December 1988): 20–47.

Lee, Michael. "Higher Criticism and Higher Education at the University of Chicago: William Rainey Harper's Vision of Religion in the Research University." *History of Education Quarterly* 48 (November 2008): 508–33.

Lichti, James Irvin. "The German Mennonite Response to the Dissolution of the Rhoen-Bruderhof." *Mennonite Life* 46 (June 1991): 10–18.

Link, Arthur S., and Richard L. McCormick. *Progressivism*. Arlington Heights, IL: Harlan Davidson, 1983.

Longfield, Bradley J. "From Evangelicalism to Liberalism: Public Midwestern Universities in Nineteenth-Century America." In *The*

Secularization of the Academy, edited by George Marsden and Bradley Longfield, 46–73. New York: Oxford University Press, 1992.

Marsden, George. *Fundamentalism and American Culture: The Shaping of Twentieth-Century Evangelicalism, 1870–1925*. New York: Oxford University Press, 1980.

———. *The Soul of the American University: From Protestant Establishment to Established Nonbelief*. New York: Oxford University Press, 1994.

McGerr, Michael. *A Fierce Discontent: The Rise and Fall of the Progressive Movement in America, 1870–1920*. New York: Oxford University Press, 2003.

Meyer, Esther Steiner. "Steiner, Menno Simon." *Global Anabaptist Mennonite Encyclopedia Online*. 1959. http://gameo.org/index.php?title=Steiner,_Menno_Simon_(1866-1911)&oldid=121307.

Miller, Susan Fisher. *Culture for Service: A History of Goshen College, 1894–1994*, Goshen, IN: Goshen College, 1994.

———. "John S. Coffman's Mennonite Revivalism." In *The Dilemma of Anabaptist Piety: Strengthening or Straining the Bonds of Community?*, edited by Stephen L. Longenecker, 93–104. Penobscot, ME: Penobscot Press, 1997.

Murray, Stuart. *The Naked Anabaptist: The Bare Essentials of a Radical Faith*. Scottdale, PA: Herald Press, 2010.

Newman, Albert Henry. *A History of Anti-Pedobaptism*. Philadelphia: American Baptist Publication Society, 1897.

Nolt, Steve. "A 'Two-Kingdom' People in a World of Multiple Identities: Religion, Ethnicity and American Mennonites." *Mennonite Quarterly Review* 73 (July 1999): 485–502.

Nordstrom, Justin. *Danger on the Doorstep: Anti-Catholicism and American Print Culture in the Progressive Era*. Notre Dame, IN: University of Notre Dame Press, 2006.

Novick, Peter. *That Noble Dream: The "Objectivity Question" and the American Historical Profession*. Cambridge, MA: Cambridge University Press, 1988.

Nutt, Rick L. *The Whole Gospel for the Whole World: Sherwood Eddy and the American Protestant Mission*. Macon, GA: Mercer University Press, 1997.

Oyer, Gordon. "Plain or Fancy: Butler County and the Nineteenth-Century Amish in America." *Illinois Mennonite Heritage Quarterly* 30 (Winter 2003): 45, 53–59.

Packull, Werner. *Hutterite Beginnings: Communitarian Experiments during the Reformation.* Baltimore: Johns Hopkins University Press, 1995.

Pannabecker, Samuel F. *Faith in Ferment: A History of the Central District Conference.* Newton, KS: Faith & Life Press, 1968.

———. *Ventures in Faith: The Story of Mennonite Biblical Seminary.* Elkhart, IN: Mennonite Biblical Seminary, 1975.

Pegram, Thomas R. "The Dry Machine: The Formation of the Anti-Saloon League of Illinois." *Illinois Historical Journal* 83 (Autumn 1990): 173–86.

Peters, Scott J. *The Promise of Association: A History of the Mission and Work of the YMCA at the University of Illinois, 1873–1997.* Champaign, IL: University YMCA, 1997.

Quandt, Jean B. *From the Small Town to the Great Community: The Social Thought of Progressive Intellectuals.* New Brunswick, NJ: Rutgers University Press, 1970.

Redekop, Calvin. *Mennonite Society.* Baltimore: Johns Hopkins University Press, 1989.

Rikoon, J. Sanford. *Threshing in the Midwest, 1820–1940: A Study of Traditional Culture and Technological Change.* Bloomington: Indiana University Press, 1988.

Roanoke Mennonite Church. *Centennial Year, 1875–1975.* Roanoke, VA: Roanoke Mennonite Church, 1975.

Roberts, Jon H., and James Turner. *The Sacred and Secular University.* Princeton: Princeton University Press, 2000.

Rorabaugh, W. J. *The Alcoholic Republic: An American Tradition.* New York: Oxford University Press, 1979.

Ross, Dorothy. *The Origins of American Social Science.* Cambridge, MA: Cambridge University Press, 1991.

Rothberg, Morey D. "'To Set a Standard of Workmanship and Compel Men to Conform to It': John Franklin Jameson as Editor of the *American Historical Review.*" *American Historical Review* 89 (October 1984): 957–75.

Rudolph, Frederick. *The American University and College: A History.* Athens: University of Georgia Press, 1990.
Sandage, Scott. "A Marble House Divided: The Lincoln Memorial, the Civil Rights Movement, and the Politics of Memory, 1938–1963." *Journal of American History* 80 (June 1993): 135–67.
Sawatsky, Rodney J. *Authority and Identity: The Dynamics of the General Conference Mennonite Church.* North Newton, KS: Bethel College Press, 1987.
———. *History and Ideology: American Mennonite Definition through History.* Kitchener, ON: Pandora Press, 2005.
———. "The One and the Many: The Recovery of Mennonite Pluralism." In *Anabaptism Revisited*, edited by Walter Klassen, 141–54. Scottdale, PA: Herald Press, 1992.
Schertz, H. R., and Harold S. Bender. "Metamora Mennonite Church (Metamora, Illinois, USA)." *Global Anabaptist Mennonite Encyclopedia Online.* 1957. http://gameo.org/index.php?title=Metamora_Mennonite_Church_(Metamora,_Illinois,_USA)&oldid=117077.
Schlabach, Theron. "Discipleship, Generational Change and the Practice of Mennonite History." *Mennonite Quarterly Review* 73 (July 1999): 427–42.
———. *Goshen College Mennonite Church: An Overview.* Goshen, IN: College Mennonite Church, 1979.
———. *Gospel versus Gospel: Mission and the Mennonite Church, 1863–1944.* Scottdale, PA: Herald Press, 1980.
———. "The Humble Become 'Aggressive Workers': Mennonites Organize for Mission, 1880–1910." *Mennonite Quarterly Review* 52 (April 1978): 113–36.
———. "Paradoxes of Mennonite Separatism." *Pennsylvania Mennonite Heritage* II (January 1979): 12–17.
———. *Peace, Faith, Nation: Mennonites and Amish in Nineteenth-Century America.* Scottdale, PA: Herald Press, 1988.
———. "Reveille for *Die Stillen im Lande*: A Stir among Mennonites in the Late Nineteenth Century." *Mennonite Quarterly Review* 51 (July 1977): 213–26.
———. *War, Peace and Social Conscience: Guy F. Hershberger and Mennonite Ethics.* Scottdale, PA: Herald Press, 2009.

Schumacher, Edgar, ed. *Life in the Bluffton and Pandora, Ohio Community, 1877–1910: Excerpts from the* Bluffton News. Swiss Community Historical Society, 1997.

Serpette, Ardys. "Christian and Catherine Bechler Smith." *Illinois Mennonite Heritage Quarterly* 31 (Winter 2004): 41, 49–51.

Setran, David P. *The College "Y": Student Religion in the Era of Secularization*. New York: Palgrave Macmillan, 2007.

Shearer, Tobin Miller. *Daily Demonstrators: The Civil Rights Movement in Mennonite Homes and Sanctuaries*. Baltimore: Johns Hopkins University Press, 2010.

Showalter, Anna. "The Mennonite Young People's Conference Movement, 1919–1923: The Legacy of a (Failed?) Vision." *Mennonite Quarterly Review* 85 (April 2011).

Sittser, Gerald. *A Cautious Patriotism: The American Churches and the Second World War*. Chapel Hill: University of North Carolina Press, 1997.

Smith, Gary Scott. "The Men and Religion Forward Movement of 1911–12: New Perspectives on Evangelical Social Concern and the Relationship between Christianity and Progressivism." In *Modern American Protestantism and Its World: Historical Articles on Protestantism in American Religious Life*, edited by Martin Marty, 166–93. New York: K. G. Saur, 1992.

———. *The Search for Social Salvation: Social Christianity and America, 1880–1925*. Lanham, MD: Lexington Books, 2000.

Smith, C. Henry. *Christian Peace: Four Hundred Years of Mennonite Principles and Practice*. The Peace Committee of the General Conference of Mennonites, 1938.

———. *The Coming of the Russian Mennonites*. Berne, IN: Mennonite Book Concern, 1927.

———. *Menno Simons, Apostle of the Nonresistant Life*. Berne, IN: Mennonite Book Concern, 1936.

———. *Mennonite Country Boy: The Education of C. Henry Smith*. Newton, KS: Faith & Life Press, 1962.

———. *The Mennonite Immigration to Pennsylvania in the Eighteenth Century*. Norristown, PA: Pennsylvania German Society, 1929.

———. *The Mennonites: A Brief History*. Berne, IN: Mennonite Book Concern, 1920.
———. *Mennonites in America*. Mennonites and Their Heritage, no. 2. Akron, PA: Mennonite Central Committee, 1942.
———. *The Mennonites of America*. C. Henry Smith, 1909.
———. "On Mennonite Historiography: A Communication from Dr. C. Henry Smith." *Mennonite Quarterly Review* 28 (April 1944): [n.p.].
———. *Smith's Story of the Mennonites*. 5th ed., revised and enlarged by Cornelius Krahn. Eugene, OR: Wipf and Stock Publishers, 2004. Reproduced by permission of Herald Press.
———. *The Story of the Mennonites*. Berne, IN: Mennonite Book Concern, 1941.
Smith, C. Henry, and Edmund J. Hirschler, eds. *The Story of Bluffton College*. Bluffton College, 1925.
Smith, Willard H. *Mennonites in Illinois*. Scottdale, PA: Herald Press, 1983.
———. *The Road to Santa Fe*. Willard Smith, 1985.
Smucker, David J. Rempel. *Bid Me Discourse: Boyd David Smucker (1879–1936): Orator and Mennonite Educator*. David J. Rempel Smucker, 2011.
Snyder, C. Arnold. *Anabaptist History and Theology: An Introduction*. Kitchener, ON: Pandora Press, 1995.
Solberg, Winton U. "The Conflict between Religion and Secularism at the University of Illinois, 1867–1894." *American Quarterly* 18 (1966): 183–99.
———. *The University of Illinois, 1894–1904: The Shaping of the University*. Chicago: University of Chicago Press, 2000.
Sprunger, Keith L. "C. Henry Smith's Vision of Mennonite History." *Mennonite Life* 50 (March 1995): 4–11.
Steiner, Fred, ed. *Town at the Fork of the Rileys Revisited: Historical Sketches of Old Shannon and Bluffton, Ohio*. Bluffton: Bluffton News, 1986.
Storr, Richard J. *Harper's University: The Beginnings*. Chicago: University of Chicago Press, 1966.

Tarr, Dennis L. "The Presbyterian Church and the Founding of the United Nations." *Journal of Presbyterian History* 53:1 (1975): 3–32.

Teichroew, Allen. "Mennonites and the Conscription Trap." *Mennonite Life* 30 (September 1975): 10–12.

Toews, Paul. "The American Mennonite Search for a Useable Past: From the Declensive to the Ironic Interpretation." *Mennonite Quarterly Review* 73 (July 1999): 470–84.

———. "Fundamentalist Conflict in Mennonite Colleges: A Response to Cultural Transitions?" *Mennonite Quarterly Review* 57 (July 1983): 241–56.

———. "Mennonites in American Society: Modernity and the Persistence of Religious Community." *Mennonite Quarterly Review* 63 (July 1983): 227–46.

———. *Mennonites in American Society, 1930–1970: Modernity and the Persistence of Religious Community*. Scottdale, PA: Herald Press, 1996.

Trollinger, William Vance, Jr. *God's Empire: William Bell Riley and Midwestern Fundamentalism*. Madison: University of Wisconsin Press, 1990.

Ulrich, Kenneth. "Roanoke Mennonite Church History." *Illinois Mennonite Heritage Quarterly* XXVIII (Spring 2001): 1, 4–8.

Umble, John. *Goshen College, 1894–1954*. Scottdale, PA: Mennonite Publishing House, 1954.

———. "John S. Coffman as an Evangelist." *Mennonite Quarterly Review* 23 (July 1949): 123–46.

———. *Mennonite Pioneers*. Scottdale, PA: Mennonite Publishing House, 1940.

Veysey, Lawrence R. *The Emergence of the American University*. Chicago: University of Chicago Press, 1965.

Weaver, J. Denny. *Keeping Salvation Ethical: Mennonite and Amish Atonement Theology in the Late Nineteenth Century*. Scottdale, PA: Herald Press, 1995.

Weaver, William B. "Central Conference Mennonite Church." *Global Anabaptist Mennonite Encyclopedia Online*. 1953. http://gameo.org/index.php?title=Central_conference_mennonite_church&oldid=115173.

Weaver, William B., and Harold S. Bender. "Stuckey, Joseph (1825–1902)." *Global Anabaptist Mennonite Encyclopedia Online*. 1959. http://gameo.org/index.php?title=Stuckey,_Joseph_(1825-1902)&oldid=121587.

Weber, Harry F. *Centennial History of the Mennonites of Illinois*. Scottdale, PA: Mennonite Publishing House, 1931.

Wenger, John C. "The Theology of John Horsch." *Mennonite Quarterly Review* 21 (July 1947): 151–55.

Williamson, Joel. *A Rage for Order: Black/White Relations in the American South since Emancipation*. New York: Oxford University Press, 1986.

Wind, James. *The Bible and the University*. Atlanta: Scholars Press, 1987.

Wittner, Lawrence. *Rebels against War: The American Peace Movement, 1933–1983*. Philadelphia: Temple University Press, 1984.

Yoder, Paton. *Tradition and Transition: Amish Mennonites and the Old Order Amish, 1800–1900*. Scottdale, PA: Herald Press, 1991.

Unpublished Papers

Estes, Steven R. "C. Henry Smith: Dean of American Mennonite Historiography." Goshen College student paper, 1979. MHLG.

Hurst, Brenda Martin. "The Articulation of Mennonite Beliefs about Sexuality, 1890–1930." PhD diss., Union Theological Seminary, 2003.

Johnson, Robert Alan. "'A Uniquely Dangerous and Promising Time': America's Protestant Establishment Confronts a New World, 1941–1950." PhD diss., Texas Christian University, 2001.

King, Justin. "'God willing there shall be a brighter day': Bluffton College, Modernism, Bonds and the Struggle for Survival." Bluffton University student paper, 2008. MHLB.

Martin, Jason. "A Statistical Study of the *Herald of Truth*, 1864–1900." Goshen College student paper, 1962. AMC.

Schertz, Wilma. "Smith Family Genealogy, 1865–1979." Illinois Mennonite Heritage Center, Metamora, Illinois.

Smith, Tilman R. "The Memories of Tilman R. Smith." AMC.

Sutter, Sem. "John S. Coffman, Mennonite Evangelist." University of Chicago seminar paper, 1974. AMC.

Whitmer, Paul. "The Autobiography of Paul Whitmer." MHLB.

Yoder, Nathan E. "Mennonite Fundamentalism: Shaping an Identity for an American Context." PhD diss., University of Notre Dame, 1999.

Index

A

Adams, Herbert Baxter, 104
Addams, Jane, 94
Albrecht, Agnes, 60, 116
Allen County, Ohio, 55, 214, 216
All-Mennonite Conventions, 183, 198, 231, 251, 354
   and Bender, 257
   and Hartzler, 257, 263
   and Smith, 83, 198, 216, 218, 231, 251, 265, 292, 354
   and WWI, 212, 216
American Civil Liberties Union, 294
American Historical Association, 102, 105, 107, 341, 361
American Seminar, 237–41
Amish (Egli), 144, 149
Amish (Old Order), 13, 14, 42, 47, 73, 91, 155, 317, 363n1
   acculturation, 36–37, 48, 54, 58, 75–76, 366n23
   alcohol, 50, 368n2
   church, 34–35, 56, 364n5
   migration, 26, 364n4, n6, 365n13
   pioneers, 25–26, 28–34
   racial paternalism, 209
   religious life, 29, 35, 78
   settlements, 28–29, 110
   Smith's scholarship and, 141, 144, 146, 149, 162, 247, 250, 328
   tradition, 13, 17, 36, 50, 78, 91, 102, 366n17
   women, 65
Amish Mennonites, 24, 30, 32, 34–35, 47, 63, 69, 73, 75, 128, 151–52
   and business attitudes, 201
   and Coffman, 54–56
   community, 32, 34, 36, 40, 178
   cooperation with MC, 38, 158
   and education, 44, 47–48
   founding, 37
   fundamentalism, 169
   and higher education, 61, 68, 175, 179
   in Illinois, 24, 37, 121, 149
   language transition, 39, 53
   missions, 60
   and Prohibition, 50
   and the quickening, 52–53, 58–59, 61
   relationship with Stuckey Amish, 38–39
   religious life, 53–54, 58, 60, 78, 169, 178
   singing schools, 40
   Smith's heritage in, 72, 74, 128, 151, 156, 178, 189, 283, 354, 356
Anabaptism, 13, 100, 146, 171, 229, 235, 255, 323, 356
   and Coffman, 78, 113
   and freedom of conscience, 114, 172–73, 178
   in *Herald of Truth*, 53
   in *The Mennonite Immigration to Pennsylvania*, 250
   in *The Mennonites: A Brief History*, 219–20
   in *The Mennonites of America*, 141–43, 275
   in *The Story of the Mennonites*, 352–53

Anabaptist historiography, 106, 131–39, 145, 172–73, 323, 331–32, 336–38, 361, 352
  polygenesis readings, 139, 141, 353, 380n13, 416n4
  and Smith, 132–33, 136–39, 141–42, 219–20, 324, 332–33, 361
Anabaptist history, 108–11, 114, 219–20
  and Horsch, John, 172–73, 263, 275
  in *The Mennonites of America*, 141–43
  and Smith's 1926 trip to Europe, 240–41
  in *The Story of the Mennonites*, 323–24, 327–28, 331–32, 336–38, 352–53
  and Waldenses, 306
  during WWII, 320–21, 336–38
Anabaptist-Mennonite theology, 24, 114, 138–39, 172–73, 348, 361, 331–32
  and Amish Mennonites, 37
  Bender, 336–38
  and Coffman, 78, 113
  and Horsch, 173–74, 275
  Smith at Amsterdam, 302
Anabaptist origins, 102, 106, 132, 137–39, 144, 232, 320, 352
  "Anabaptist Vision, The" 335–37, 351, 361–62, 413n48, 416n2
  and Horsch, 172–74, 275
  and Kaufman, 199
  in *The Mennonites: A Brief History*, 219–20
  in "The Mennonites in History" address, 113
  in *The Mennonites of America*, 141–43, 275
  Smith in 1936, 275
  in *The Story of the Mennonites*, 352–53
Anti-Saloon League, 51–52, 82
Apostolic Christian Church, 144
Augspurger, Aaron, 181, 252

B

Baechler, Simon, 109
Balzer, Jacob, 228

banking crisis, 277–80
Baptists, 54, 92, 113, 129, 134, 146, 171, 270, 310
  historiography of, 132–33
  in Smith's writing, 95–96, 114, 139, 146, 297, 302
Baumgartner, Elmer, 280, 287–88.
Bax, Belfort, 132–33, 139
Beard, Charles, 333
Becker, Carl, 333
Bender, Daniel H., 140, 151
Bender, Elizabeth Horsch, 255, 258
Bender, George, 255, 309
Bender, Harold S., 17, 24, 36, 113, 172, 276, 295, 309–10, 337, 353, 358, 361
  and Anabaptist historiography, 131–32, 352
  Anabaptist Vision, 335–37, 351, 361–62, 413n48, 416n2
  arrival on Goshen's faculty, 257–58, 360
  childhood, 155
  cooperation with Smith, 267–70, 306, 347
  critique of *The Story of the Mennonites*, 327–32, 344, 356, 361
  education of, 255–56
  fundamentalist inclinations of, 258, 267, 270
  Goshen/Bluffton tensions, 257–58
  and Horsch, 173, 179, 258–59, 262, 268–69
  and Kaufman, 274–75, 301
  meeting Smith, 255
  and *Mennonite Encyclopedia*, 341–43, 351
  and Mennonite historical renaissance, 259, 267
  and Mennonite Scholars Guild, 341–42
  Mennonite union movement, 269
  1936 Mennonite World Conference, 301, 304
  Mennonites and Their Heritage course, 321–22
  progressivism of, 255
  Russian Mennonite crisis, 1947, 345
  at Smith's funeral, 349

and Smith's history, 140, 144, 260–61, 306–7, 325
    YPC leader, 255–56
Berky, Herbert W., 190, 196, 270, 282, 284, 307
Berky, Olga, 190, 282
Berne, Indiana, 159, 171, 183–84, 215, 280, 287, 292
    Mennonite publishing house in, 59, 219, 326–27, 353
Bethel College, 108, 182, 253, 257, 304, 341–42, 346, 353
    and Kaufman, 198, 200, 273, 301, 339, 351
    regard for Smith at, 294–95
    Smith visits, 200, 228–29, 246–47, 317
    in Smith's writing, 150
    and Thierstein, 202, 227
Bethel Mennonite Church, Garden City, Missouri, 56
Bixel, John, 203
Black Hawk's War, 26
Blaurock, George, 78, 133, 141, 173
Bluffton College, 168, 182, 194, 198–99, 200–1, 225–26, 233, 340, 346, 348
    attacked as "modernist," 252–53, 260–63, 265–67, 275–76
    ecumenicity, 188–89, 282–83, 288–89
    faculty, 189–90, 227, 305, 297, 346, 356
    faculty tensions, 279–83, 284–85
    Great Depression and, 282–83
    growth of, 196, 339
    history department, 294
    library, 267, 310, 330, 340, 348, 359
    progressivism at, 187–88, 197, 253, 295–96
    rebirth in 1913, 182–84, 187–90
    Smith's arrival, 187, 194, 245, 310
    in Smith's scholarship, 246
    students, 213, 291–92, 339
    as threat to Goshen, 258
    trustees, 271, 279, 285–88, 354
    and WWI, 215–16
    and WWII, 315–16
Bluffton Farmer's Institute, 300

Bluffton High School, 214, 300
Bluffton News, 202, 204, 206, 233, 271, 278–79
Bluffton, Ohio, 14, 55, 79, 83, 152, 191, 202–4, 223, 235
    banking crisis, 277–80
    Bender in, 256
    birthplace of Mennonite Encyclopedia, 341–43
    Great Depression and, 274
    memories of Smith, 290–91
Bluffton Village Council, 200
Bluffton Women's Federation, 300
Boehr, Elizabeth, 281–82
bond crisis, 279–80, 285
Bowers, Elaine Burress, 121–22, 128, 180, 195–96, 315
Brinton, Crane, 333
Bryan, William Jennings, 64, 211
Bullinger, Heinrich, 133, 138
Bureau County, Illinois, 25, 31, 121–24, 129, 179, 201
Burkholder, J. Lawrence, 355
Byers, Emma LeFevre, 69, 155, 191, 285
Byers, Noah, 84, 151, 155–56, 166, 168, 246
    appointed principal of Elkhart Institute, 68–69
    attacked as modernist, 263–64
    awarded honorary doctorate, 340
    and Bluffton faculty feud, 285–88
    as Bluffton professor, 196–97
    Bluffton Village Council race, 200
    burial, 415n67
    childhood and early education, 67–68
    and Coffman, 56, 67–69
    as dean of faculty at Bluffton College, 183, 188
    death of, 350
    departs Goshen, 182–84
    embrace of progressivism, 82, 135, 148–49
    and faculty of Elkhart Institute, 70, 72, 74, 80
    financial investments with Smith, 202–3
    Goshen capital campaign, 157

and Goshen College Mennonite
  Church, 158
and Goshen faculty, 98, 158
in "Goshen Group" on Bluffton
  faculty, 282
and Goshen Prohibition campaign,
  159
and Goshen trustees, 99
and Goshen's closing, 257
graduate study, 97
and Hanley, Edna, 284–85
hosts Smith at Goshen, 99
and Kaufman, 198
marries Emma LeFevre, 69
meets Smith, 67
Men and Religion Forward
  Movement, 161
and Mennonite union movement,
  180–85, 188
possibilities for relocating Elkhart
  Institute, 97
relocates to Bluffton, 185
resigns as dean, 285
sabbatical, 271, 273
and Smith's Goshen faculty position,
  124, 129–30
and Steiner, 97–99, 176, 185
tensions with conservatives as Goshen
  President, 175–77
in WWI, 215–16
and Young People's Conference,
  254–55
and Zion Mennonite Church, 193,
  398–99n20

C

Camp, John, 63
Carlock Mennonite Church, Carlock,
  Illinois, 277, 318
Cassel, Daniel, 107, 111
Catholic Worker, 294
Central Conference, 14, 152, 180, 230
  creation, 38
  and founding of Bluffton College, 183
  and fundamentalism, 252, 318
  Smith's membership with, 193–94,
    245, 356

Central Mennonite College, 83, 182, 188
Cheng, Eileen Ka-May, 105
Chicago, Illinois, 25, 30, 44, 53, 118,
  120, 122, 126, 129–30, 156, 342–43
  and Mennonite seminary, 276, 339–40
  and Mennonite union meeting, 183
Chicago Mennonite Mission, 58, 60, 67,
  72, 82, 93
Christian Evangel, 194, 206–7, 211, 233
Christian Exponent, 239, 247, 254, 263,
  269, 360
  and Bender, 258, 260
Christian Monitor, 151, 160, 162, 174,
  211, 217, 326
Christian Peace, 298
Citizens National Bank, 203–5, 278,
  291, 346
Civilian Public Service, 314, 317, 319,
  321–22, 337, 339, 342, 354
Clark, Norman, 50, 52
Coffman, John, 53–54
  and Byers, 56, 67–69
  death, 79
  and Elkhart Institute, 68
  and gender roles, 57–58
  and Hartzler, John E., 56, 72
  and Kauffman, 56–57
  and Mennonite progressivism, 149
  and Moody, Dwight, 168
  promoting missions, 60
  reinforces plain dress, 169
  as a revivalist, 54–55
  at Science Ridge, 55–56
  and Smith, Henry, 56, 69, 71, 80,
    150, 308, 325
  and Smith, John, 56–57, 82
  "Spirit of Progress" Address, 77–80,
    113, 136
  in Woodford County, 56–57
College Mennonite Church, Goshen,
  Indiana, 158–59
Coming of the Russian Mennonites, The,
  247–49, 270, 345
Conference on a Just and Durable Peace,
  319–20, 337–38
congregational polity in church governance, 76, 112, 145, 212, 222, 245,
  324

D

Defenseless Mennonites, 183, 253
Denck, Hans, 78
    and Baptist scholars, 133
    and Bender, 328
    and Horsch, 134, 136, 173, 275
    and Keller, 134
    Smith's inclusion of, 138, 141, 150, 199, 220, 250, 275, 331, 377n19
Detweiler, Irvin, 73, 98, 158, 287–88
Dienerversammlung (Amish ministers' meetings), 37–38, 50
dispensationalism, 167, 220
Dock, Christopher, 150, 162
Draper, Andrew, 84–85, 87
dress restrictions, 131, 151, 156, 198, 223, 282
    among Amish, 36, 47, 121
    and Coffman, 55
    and Laura Ioder Smith, 179–80, 194
    among MCs, 169–70, 176, 194, 223, 256, 258
Dulles, John Foster, 319, 337
Dunkards, 146, 185, 211
Dutch Mennonites, 112, 242, 301, 303–4, 208, 324
Dyck, Cornelius, 353

E

East White Oak Mennonite Church, Normal, Illinois, 193–94, 214, 277, 318, 399n20
Ebenezer Mennonite Church, Allen County, Ohio, 202, 252, 318
Eddy Seminars, 237–42, 296
Eddy, Sherwood, 66, 237–38, 240–41, 294, 296
Elkhart County, Indiana, 106, 159, 360
Elkhart, Indiana, 56, 61–62, 64, 97, 100, 163, 353
    and Bender, George, 255
    and Funk's *Herald of Truth*, 53–54
    Funk's library, 247
    and Horsch, 135
    Smith's residence in, 62, 70, 72, 80, 85

Elkhart Institute, 64, 77, 79–80, 100, 124
    founding of, 61–66
    becomes Goshen College, 97–98
    Smith on faculty, 69–71, 85, 90, 97
    Smith's departure, 75
    transformation, 68, 70
empiricism, 16, 103–4, 113, 164, 333, 335, 344, 357, 361. *See also* historical objectivity
Epp, Claas, 221, 353
Epp, Peter, 284
ethnicity, 147–48
    Mennonite, 14, 151, 222, 250, 281, 324, 329, 392n35
eugenics, 210
Eureka, Illinois, 45, 51, 290
evangelicalism, 52, 58, 67, 82, 87, 89, 179

F

Faith & Life Press, 23, 353
farm life, 28, 30, 32–34, 41–44, 47, 65
Federal Council of Churches, 89, 181, 187, 319
Findlay Dairy, 202, 253, 301n26
Findlay, Ohio, 202, 253, 312
First Mennonite Church, Berne, Indiana, 252, 273
First Mennonite Church, Bluffton, Ohio, 202, 205, 242, 276, 283, 318, 349, 398–99n20
First Mennonite Church, Halstead, Kansas, 249
First National Bank, 203–4, 348, 402n8
Flanagan (Illinois) Mennonite Church, 60, 109
Fox Farm, 203, 391n24
Fox, George, 114
Fretz, J. Winfield, 295, 316, 341–42, 357
Friedmann, Robert, 327, 344, 356, 361
    background, 331–32
    and Bender, 336
    debate with Smith, 331–35
    and Horsch, 135, 274
    and Mennonite Scholars Guild, 342
Friesen, Abraham, 134

frontier, 106, 226
  and Mennonites, 28, 30
  and Smith's writing, 115, 146, 222, 248
fundamentalism, 13, 17, 166–68, 170, 178, 258, 262, 265, 316, 318, 351
  and Bender, 258, 351
  GC, 252, 271–72, 276, 318
  and Horsch, 171–73
  in Illinois, 168
  MC, 168–70, 173–74, 252–53, 256–60, 270, 272, 306
  and Smith, 178, 275, 316, 318
Funk, John, 53–54, 61, 100
  and Elkhart Institute, 61, 97
  employs Coffman 54
  employs Steiner, 55
  and Horsch, 135, 171
  ordination of, 58
  and Smith, 110, 219
  Smith credits, 140, 309, 325

G

Gandhi, Mahatma, 295–96
gender roles, 57–58, 195, 342
General Conference Mennonite Church (GC), 13–14, 140, 186, 188, 198–99, 218, 223, 227, 230, 268, 300
  appreciation of Smith by, 240–41
  and Bender's Anabaptist Vision, 351–52
  colleges, 150, 181, 184
  congregations 112, 256, 346
  draft decisions, 316
  ecumenicity of, 186, 189–90, 282
  fundamentalism, 252, 271–72, 276, 318
  and the *Mennonite Encyclopedia*, 351
  and Mennonite union movement, 180–81, 354–55
  nonresistance during WWI, 212
  peace commitments, 316
  Peace Committee, 298, 306, 341
  publications, 112, 152, 180, 240, 275, 349
  Smith joins, 317–19

Smith's scholarship and, 141, 218–22, 243, 251, 264–65, 270, 326, 328, 331
Gingrich, Norman, 70
Gleijsteen, Jan, 303–4
Goshen College, 28, 100, 103, 106, 109, 140, 152, 156, 162–63, 181, 247, 286, 347
  birth, 96–97
  dress codes, 176, 179
  faculty, 294–95, 326–27, 330, 342, 348
  faculty departures from, 190, 193–95, 216, 255
  and fundamentalism, 175–78, 257–58, 266
  historical renaissance, 243, 257–59, 266–67, 269
  library historical collections, 306, 309–10, 331, 360
  perceived rigidity at, 175–78, 197
  progressivism, 255, 355
  salaries, 129, 155, 233
  Smith on faculty, 98–100, 124, 129–30, 139, 158
  Smith's departure, 183–85, 187, 194
  in Smith's scholarship, 150
  and Young People's Movement, 253–54
Goshen College Record, 100, 209
"Goshen group" on Bluffton faculty, 282–83, 287–89
Goshen, Indiana, 14, 156–57, 160–61, 177, 194, 202, 343, 360
"Goshen School" of Anabaptist historiography, 173, 327, 352, 413n48
Gospel Herald, 140, 151, 181, 210–11, 259, 269, 359
  and Kauffman as editor, 151, 163–64, 170, 172, 223, 380n12
Gospel Witness, 112, 137–38, 143, 163
Gottshall, William, 202, 252, 257, 262, 271
Grace Bible Institute, 318
Grace Mennonite Church, Pandora, Ohio, 198, 242
Great Depression, 203, 273, 291, 326

Grebel, Conrad, 133
  and Bender, 267
  Horsch on, 173, 261
  Smith's emphasis of, 78, 113, 133, 139, 141–42, 150, 219, 275
Gregg, Richard, 295–96
Gross, Leonard, 163, 166
Grubb, Nathaniel, 151–52
Grubb, Silas, 215

H

Halstead Seminary, 84, 150
Hanley, Edna, 281, 284–85
Hansen, Marcus, 249
Harper, William Rainey, 88–89, 91–92, 94–95
Harshbarger, Emmett, 294–95, 307, 355
Hartzler, John E., 56, 60, 175, 185, 360
  on American Seminar with Smith, 237–38
  attacked by Horsch, 263–64, 268
  and Coffman, 56–57, 72
  critiqued by Bender, 259, 329
  death, 350
  on Goshen's faculty, 72, 98
  at Hartford Seminary, 345
  leaves Goshen's presidency, 193, 256
  racism, 209
  Witmarsum Seminary president, 227, 257, 276
Hartzler, Jonas S. (J. S.), 139, 150, 151, 158
  and Elkhart Institute, 68–69
  Mennonite Church History, 109–10, 112–13, 136, 140, 149, 152, 223
Hartzler, Raymond L., 255, 280, 286, 318, 410n16
Heath, Richard, 132–33, 139
Heatwole, Lewis, 71
Hege, Christian, 241, 304
Herald of Truth, 50, 53–54, 135, 165
Hershberger, Guy F., 169, 295, 355, 357–58, 417n13
  and Smith, 326–27, 341–42
higher education, 43, 48, 56, 66, 84
  Mennonite, 68–69, 77–79, 101, 149–50, 154, 175, 182, 188, 196, 199

  Mennonite commitment to, 48, 56, 73, 78–79, 150
  Mennonite hostility toward, 16, 107, 116, 150, 175
  Smith and, 230, 246
Hirschler, Edmund, 247, 271
Hirschy, Noah, 83, 189, 246, 252
historical objectivity, 104–5, 335
  and Anabaptism, 132
  and Bender, 332, 348
  and Friedmann, 332
  in *The Mennonites of America*, 141
  relativist, 334–35, 344, 357
  and Smith, 103, 106, 139, 141, 151, 219, 245, 264, 344, 356, 361
  in *The Story of the Mennonites*, 329, 331
  at the University of Chicago, 103–4, 106
Hitler, Adolf, 305, 311–12, 317, 324
Hoffman, Melchior, 138, 141, 199, 219
Holdeman Mennonites, 144, 322
Horsch, John, 113, 139, 139, 176, 179, 272, 295, 362
  attacks perceived modernists, 262–70, 275
  background of, 134
  and Bender, 172, 258–60, 267–68, 276, 328, 331, 336, 352
  and *Christian Exponent*, 254
  death of, 327
  on Denck, 134, 136, 173, 275
  and Enss, 229
  fundamentalism of, 171–73, 252, 274
  and Gottshall, 257
  and Keller, 134–36, 171
  on the Mennonite union movement, 135, 181, 185, 265
  as self-confessed modernist, 172, 385n23
  and Smith, 103, 106, 139, 151, 173–75, 177, 219–22, 223, 261, 264–66, 268–70, 362, 377n19, 400–401n36, 411–12n32
  and Steiner, 171
Hostetler, Lester, 255
Hostetter, Douglas, 355

Houshower, Margaret Berky, 282–83, 403n11
Howe, Wilbur, 190, 282
Hubmeier, Balthazar, and Baptist scholars, 133
   Smith's inclusion of, 136, 138, 141, 150, 199, 220, 250, 275, 377n19
Hudson, Winthrop, 89
Huffman, Jasper, 190, 198, 204, 212, 216, 252, 348
Hut, Hans, 133, 138, 141, 219, 324, 328, 331

I

Illinois State Normal University, 63–66, 68–69, 85, 90, 125–26, 129
immigration, 80, 148, 308, 381n27
   from Alsace-Lorraine, 25–26, 50
   Mennonite, 25–26, 30, 121, 151
   in *The Coming of the Russian Mennonites*, 247–48
Indiana-Michigan Conference (MC), 256
Intercollegiate Peace Association, 99
Ioder, Almer, 195
Ioder, Clara ("Mace"), 179–80, 195
Ioder, Julius, 180
Ioder, Mary, 180, 195
Ioder, William, 31, 121–22, 201

J

Jameson, J. Franklin, 93, 101–3, 104, 106–7, 136
Jernegan, Marcus, 105–6
Jews, 24, 84, 282, 305
Joder, Joseph, 38, 149
Judson, Harry Pratt, 93–94, 103
Juhnke, James, 175, 198, 217, 231, 258

K

Kagawa, Toyohiko, 295
Kampen, John, 353
Kauffman, Daniel, 60, 142, 260, 306
   Bible Doctrines books, 164, 166
   and Coffman, 56–57, 308
   critiques Smith's history, 151–52, 261
   as editor of *Gospel Herald*, 164
   as editor of *Gospel Witness*, 138, 163
   on Elkhart Institute faculty, 70
   and Elkhart Publishing Co., 100
   and fundamentalism, 168, 170, 172, 253
   and higher education, 175–76
   and MC hierarchies, 112, 164
   Mennonite Church History, 109–10, 112–13, 136, 140, 149, 153, 223
   and Mennonite union movement, 181
   and the quickening, 58
   racism, 209
   relocates to Scottdale, 163, 171
   and Smith, 307–8
Kaufman, Edmund G., 14, 200, 294, 301, 317, 329, 342, 346, 355, 412n38
   advances Smith's historical reading, 351
   Bethel president, 294–95
   Bluffton dean, 273
   doctoral thesis, 274–75
   memories of Smith, 360
   and Mennonite Biblical Seminary, 339
   and *MQR*, 306
   noninterventionism in WWII, 408n6
   as Smith student, 198–99
Keim, Albert, 257–58, 262, 268, 327, 336, 340
Keller, Helen, 294
Keller, Ludwig, 134–36, 138, 142, 171–72
Klassen, John Peter, 290, 307
Klassen, Paul, 290
Kleine Gemeinde, 220
Kliewer, John, 182
Kohler, Walter, 132, 381n19
Krahn, Cornelius, 23, 341–42, 345, 348–49, 351–53
Kraus, C. Norman, 16–17, 164, 169
Krehbiel, Christian J., 338
Krehbiel, Henry J., 241
Krehbiel, Henry P., 108, 140, 185, 292
Kreider, Amos, 255, 277, 283
Kreider, Lois Sommer, 296
Kreider, Robert, 34, 112, 152, 247, 277, 282, 290, 304, 322, 348

recruited as Smith's successor, 339, 346
Kurtz, Jonathan, 161

L

Lake Geneva, Wisconsin, 66–67, 73, 86
Lake George, Michigan, 280, 287, 403n11
Lancaster, Pennsylvania, 26, 54, 97, 110, 144, 146, 295, 362
Langenwalter, Jacob, 190, 196, 198, 215, 228
Lantz, Lee, 168, 180
Lantz, Mabel, 348
Lantz, Russell, 226, 228, 397, 348
League of Nations, 237–40, 242, 312, 320
Lederach, John Paul, 355
Lend Lease, 313
Leyden, Jan van, 131–32, 142
Lima Democratic Women's Club, 300
Lima, Ohio, 202, 289, 300, 310, 347, 349, 355
  and WWI, 214
Lima Torch Club, 299, 312, 320
Lincoln, Abraham, 44, 82, 104, 208.
Loserth, Johann, 267, 269
Loucks, Aaron, 171

M

Machen, J. Gresham, 258, 261
Macintosh Supreme Court decision, 298–99, 301, 303, 311–12
Manz, Felix, 78, 112, 137, 141, 173
Marpeck, Pilgram, 267, 269, 270, 275, 324, 328
Marsden, George, 92, 95, 167
Martyrs Mirror, 100, 132, 139
Mast, Gerald, 336, 360
Matthews, Shailer, 89, 94, 161, 173
McKinley, William, 64
McLaughlin, Andrew C., 93, 104–7
McLean County, Illinois, 29
McMurry, Charles, 63
Meadows (Illinois) Mennonite Church, 109, 297, 310

Men and Religion Forward Movement, 160–61
Mennonite, The, 180, 211, 215, 240, 275, 316, 320, 357, 359
Mennonite acculturation, 13, 16, 26, 53, 58, 148, 163, 282, 363n1
  Smith's critique of, 16, 299, 357
Mennonite Biblical Seminary, 339–40, 354
  Smith advocacy for, 231, 299, 303, 308, 317, 326, 358
Mennonite Book Concern, 323
Mennonite Brethren Church, 13, 144, 183, 252, 325, 348, 353
Mennonite Brethren in Christ Church, 183, 326
Mennonite Central Committee, 304, 316, 321–22, 343, 345
Mennonite Church (MC), 13–14, 53, 55–56, 58, 140, 176, 180, 239, 276, 282, 417
  academic departures from, 189
  acculturation of, 58
  and Bender's Anabaptist Vision, 351
  boundary maintenance by, 75, 156
  congregations, 158, 163, 193–94, 211
  and dress codes, 176, 180
  fundamentalism, 168–70, 173–74, 252–53, 256–60, 270, 272, 306
  and education, 61, 68, 72
  historical scholarship of, 111, 136
  leadership of, 181, 295
  and Mennonite union movement, 181, 184, 212, 354
  merger with Amish Mennonites, 38
  missions, 209
  nonresistance during WWI, 212
  publications, 160, 163, 326
  Smith's decision to leave, 183–85, 187, 189
  Smith's scholarship and, 144–45, 150, 184, 219–20, 222–23, 267, 322, 325–28, 331, 353, 360
Mennonite Country Boy (Smith's autobiography), 23, 91, 101, 125, 251, 347
Mennonite Encyclopedia, 306, 322–43, 347–48, 351, 354

Mennonite General Conference, 164–66, 169, 170, 253
Mennonite Historical Society, 182, 259
Mennonite historiography, 107–9
Mennonite Immigration to Pennsylvania in the Eighteenth Century, The, 249–51
Mennonite Publishing House, 59, 140, 170–71
Mennonite Quarterly Review (MQR), 259, 327–28, 333, 336, 344, 358
    as counterpoint to *Christian Exponent*, 260
    founding of, 274
    and Smith, 306–7
Mennonite union movement, 180–85, 187
    and Bender, 269
    and Bluffton, 190, 257
    and Byers, 188
    and GCs, 180–81, 187, 354–55
    and Horsch, 135, 181, 185, 265
    and Kauffman, 181
    and MCs, 181, 184, 212, 354
    and Smith, 180, 183–85, 193, 199, 222, 229–32, 249, 266, 289, 354–56
Mennonite World Conference, 295, 301–4, 349
Mennonite Scholars Guild, 341–42
Mennonites in America pamphlet, 321–22
Mennonites, The: A Brief History, 218–24, 264
    and Anabaptism, 219–20
    and GCs, 222–23
    responses to, 223
    and Russian Mennonites, 220–22
Mennonites of America, The, 140–54, 173, 185, 360
    Anabaptism in, 141–43
    as dissertation, 140–41
    documentation in, 143–44
    inclusiveness of, 144
    and the Mennonite union movement, 154–55
    as a Mennonite usable past, 146–48
    narrative sweep of, 145–46
    as objective, 141
    as progressive, 148–49

    reception of, 151
    sales of, 152–53
Mennonitisches Lexikon, 241, 342
Merriam, Charles, 94–95, 159, 200, 371n43
Metamora Herald, 153, 238, 341
Metamora High School, 44, 47, 65, 74
Metamora, Illinois, 26, 31–32, 43–44, 63, 67–68, 82, 121, 169, 179, 233
Metamora Mennonite Church, 29, 36, 38, 56, 60, 214, 290
Metamora road, 31, 41, 42, 51, 116
Meulen, Jacob ter, 304, 308
Middle District Conference, 319, 337, 341
    Peace Committee, 319
Miller, James, 291–93
Miller, Orie, 255, 276, 295, 301–2
Miller, Susan Fisher, 35, 54
missions work, 53, 58, 98, 144, 160, 163–64, 221, 253, 324
    and YMCA, 66, 73, 197, 237
modernism, 88, 167, 169, 177, 357 400n34
    and Bender, 258
    and Bethel, 228
    and Bluffton, 252–53, 271–72, 276–77
    and Horsch, 172, 261–63, 266, 269
    and Smith, 263–66, 268, 357
Moody Bible Institute, 72, 88, 167–68, 227, 252, 277, 318
Moody, Dwight, 52–53, 66, 168, 321
Moon, M'Della, 190, 282
Morrison, Charles Clayton, 172, 237, 320
Mosemann, John, 295
Mosiman, Emilie, 190, 281–82, 286
Mosiman, Samuel, 182–83, 191, 193, 195, 198, 226, 246, 257, 270, 272, 350
    attacked as modernist, 263
    background of, 190
    and Bluffton faculty, 227, 285–87
    and Bluffton finances, 202–3, 279, 288
    death, 289
    and Mennonite union movement, 182–83, 189

and Smith, 185, 246, 280–81, 284–87
and WWI, 200, 212, 215–16, 252
Mumaw, Henry A., 61–62, 68, 97
Munsell, Leila, 73
Münster, 111, 142, 250, 324
Müntzer, Thomas, 133, 137, 142, 219, 261
Musselman Library, 273, 347–48
Muste, A. J., 315

N

Neff, Christian, 241, 302
New Deal, 279, 296, 312
Newman, Albert Henry, 132–33, 139
Newton, Kansas, 23.
Niebuhr, Reinhold, 237, 292, 313.
Nolt, Steven, 151
Normal, Illinois, 66, 193
North Newton, Kansas, 14, 343, 353
Novick, Peter, 103, 105, 264

O

Oak Grove Mennonite Church, 72
Oberholtzer, John, 111, 180
Ordnung, 36–37
Oyer, Daniel D., 60
Oyer, Noah, 255

P

Page, Kirby, 294, 296
Pannabecker, Sylvia, 285
Partridge Creek, Illinois, 26, 28, 32, 38, 118
Peace Oratorical Contest, 93
Peoria, Illinois, 26, 45, 98, 315
Pickett, Clarence, 293
postmodernism, 323, 335
Prairie Street Mennonite Church, 61, 68, 77, 97, 100, 162, 255
progressivism, 10, 49, 53, 67, 80, 96, 148, 160–61, 355
    in American higher education, 83–84
    Bender's historiography, 336
    Country Life Movement, 198
    at early Bluffton College, 187–88, 197, 253
    at early Goshen College, 72–73, 255
    at East White Oak Mennonite Church, 193
    ethnicity, 250, 324
    among GCs, 251
    and historiography, 106–7
    among MCs, 58, 60, 161, 309
    in Mennonite congregations, 227, 249, 256, 277
    in Mennonite higher education, 175
    among Mennonite intellectuals, 82–83, 156, 159, 168, 228–29, 253, 255
    and peace optimism, 217–18, 226–27
    racism, 207–9
    in Smith's scholarship, 112, 115, 147, 150–51, 156, 219, 221–24, 246, 249, 266, 270–71, 325, 351, 357
    at the University of Chicago, 91–92, 94–95
    and WWI, 211–12
    at Zion Mennonite Church, 194
Prohibition, 49–52, 58, 81–82, 159–60, 197, 199
Protestantism, 16, 53, 175, 236–37, 295, 312, 319
    racism and ethnocentrism, 208

Q

Quakers, 134, 254, 331
    in Smith's writing, 114, 116, 146, 218, 297, 302
Quandt, Jean, 81
quickening, the 53, 58, 63, 166, 209, 308
Quiring, Jacob, 222, 263, 268, 350

R

Ramseyer, Alice Ruth, 350
Ramseyer, Edna, 350
Ramseyer, Lloyd, 14, 306, 315, 339, 346, 348, 354
Rauschenbusch, Walter, 89, 161
Roanoke Mennonite Church, 31–32, 35–36, 38, 290
Robinson, James Harvey, 333
Rockefeller, John D., 80, 91–92, 160

Roosevelt, Franklin D., 278, 300, 312, 314, 408n6
Roosevelt, Theodore, 198, 209
Rosenberger, Arthur, 286, 288, 303, 306
Russia, 311, 339
Russian Mennonites, 187, 228, 262, 435, 365n15
   in Smith's writing, 144, 146, 220–22, 227, 230, 247–48, 321, 354

S

Sawatsky, Rodney, 262–63, 351–52, 360, 380n13
Sayre, John N., 315
Schertz, Ben, 45
Schirch, Lisa, 355
Schlabach, Theron, 53, 58, 163, 266, 335
Schleitheim Confession, 111, 137, 142
Schroeder, Peter, 252, 262, 271, 276, 301–2
Schultz, Jacob, 296, 315
Science Ridge Mennonite Church, Sterling, Illinois, 26, 55, 67, 128
Scofield, Cyrus, 167–68, 220
selective borrowing, 10, 57–58, 165–66, 205, 207, 270
Setran, David, 87, 89
Simons, Menno, 95, 198, 261, 303, 304
   in Smith's writing, 78, 133, 142, 150, 162, 250, 275, 320, 326
singing schools, 40
Smith, C. Henry
   adopts "C.," 75–76
   and All-Mennonite Conventions, 83, 198, 216, 218, 231, 251, 265, 292, 354
   and the "American Seminars," 237–42, 296
   Amish Mennonite heritage of, 72, 74, 128, 151, 156, 178, 189, 250, 283, 354, 356
   Amish (Old Order) in Smith's scholarship, 141, 144, 146, 149, 162, 247, 250
   and Anabaptist historiography, 132–32, 136–39, 141–42, 219–20, 324, 332–33, 361
   and Anabaptist individualism, 114–15, 150, 250, 263, 327, 331, 336, 353, 356
   ancestry, 25–31, 364–65n7
   antiracism, 305, 338
   as archetypal Mennonite historian, 14, 80, 144, 358–60
   autobiography of, 23–24, 91, 101, 125, 251, 347
   as banker, 15, 203–5, 223, 277–79, 308, 337, 348
   and Baptist historiography, 95–96, 114, 139, 146, 297, 302
   and Bender, Harold, 140, 144, 255, 260–61, 267–70, 306–7, 321–22, 325, 327–32, 344–45, 347, 349, 356, 361
   and Bender's Anabaptist Vision, 335–37, 351, 413n48
   and Bender's critique of *The Story of The Mennonites*, 327–32, 344, 356, 361, 413n48
   and Bethel College, 150, 200, 228–29, 246–47, 317, 346
   birth, 31
   and Bluffton bond crisis, 279–80, 285
   and Bluffton College, 197, 226, 245–46, 310, 315, 340, 346, 355
      arrival at, 187, 194, 245, 310
   and Bluffton faculty, 190–91, 196, 196, 216, 227, 263, 266, 280–89
   and Bluffton village, 191, 214, 223, 235, 290–91
   and Bluffton Village Council, 200
   book sales of, 152–53, 223, 323, 353–54
   busyness, 196, 225–26
   and Byers, Noah, 67, 70, 80, 84, 99, 135, 156, 166, 180, 195, 202–3, 264, 308, 340
   and Byers as Bluffton dean, 196–97, 215
   and Byers as Goshen president, 124, 129–30
   Byers as Smith's neighbor, 154, 191–92, 280, 415n67
   childhood and adolescence, 32–35, 39–48, 57, 60

church membership, 193–94, 277, 317–18, 356–57, 409–10n16
civil religion, 207–8
and Coffman, 56, 69, 71, 80, 150, 308, 325
and College Mennonite Church, 158
commitment to higher education, 116, 150
and the Conference on a Just and Durable Peace, 319–20, 337–38
and CPS, 37, 319, 337, 354
death and funeral, 349–50
decision to enter college teaching, 96
and Denck, Hans, 138, 141, 150, 199, 20, 250, 275, 331, 377n19
dissertation research, 109–10, 140–41
    and poor scholarly documentation, 143, 247, 249–51, 275, 323
early education, 40–45
and education: advocacy of, 9, 116, 154, 185–86, 221–22, 230, 232, 246, 297, 301, 311–12, 316
    hunger for, 23, 42, 48, 61–63
    and peace education, 292–93, 297, 308
    understanding of, 62–63, 75, 90, 184
at Elkhart Institute, 69–71, 75, 85, 90, 97
and eugenics, 109–10
final illness, 346–48
"Final Mennonite History" address, 343–44
financial investments, 201–3, 253
and First Mennonite Church, Bluffton, Ohio, 202, 205, 242, 276, 283, 318, 349
and Friedmann, Robert, 327, 331–35, 336, 344, 356, 361
and fundamentalism, 178, 275, 316, 318
and Funk, John, 110, 140, 219, 309, 325
and General Conference Mennonite Church, 141, 218–22, 240–41, 243, 251, 264–65, 270, 326, 328, 331
    Smith joins, 317–19

and Goshen College, 150, 152, 178, 187, 216, 255, 269, 309–10, 334, 344, 347
on Goshen faculty, 98–100, 103, 124, 129–131, 139, 155–56, 158, 162, 233, 355, 359
and "Goshen group" on Bluffton faculty, 282–83, 287–89
    Smith's departure from, 183–85, 187, 194
    in Smith's scholarship, 150
and Gottshall, William, 202, 253
and Grebel, Conrad, 78, 113, 133, 139, 141–42, 150, 219, 275
and Hartzler, J. E., 185, 227, 237–38, 259, 264, 268, 276, 329, 345, 360
and Hartzler, J. S., 109–10, 113, 136, 139, 150, 223
and Hartzler, R. L., 277, 280, 286, 318
and Hershberger, Guy, 326–27, 341–42
and higher education, 150, 175, 230, 246. *See also* Bluffton College, Elkhart Institute, Goshen College, ISNU, University of Illinois, University of Chicago
and historical objectivity, 103, 106, 139, 141, 151, 219, 245, 264, 344, 349, 356, 361
    "relativist objectivity," 332–335
    in *The Story of the Mennonites*, 329, 331. *See also* empiricism
historiographical debate with Bender and Friedmann, 327–337
and Horsch, John, 103, 106, 139, 151, 173–74, 177, 219, 245, 344, 356, 36, 223, 261, 264–66, 268–70, 397–8, 337n19, 400–1n36, 411–12n32
and Hubmaier, Balthasar, 136, 138, 141, 150, 199, 220, 250, 275, 377n19
and Hut, Hans, 133, 138, 141, 219, 324, 328, 331
infant son, 194–95, 389n11, 390n20
at ISNU, 63–66, 85, 90, 126, 129

and Jameson, Franklin, 101–2, 106, 136, 138
and Kauffman, Daniel, 151–52, 261, 307–8
and Kaufman, Edmund, 198, 273, 275, 294, 306, 317, 329, 346, 351, 360, 412n38
and Krahn, Cornelius, 23, 347–49, 353–53
and Kreider, Robert, 290, 304, 339, 346
at Lake George, 280–81
Lincoln, regard for, 44, 82
and *Macintosh* decision, 298–99, 301, 303, 311–12
and Matthews, Shailer, 161
and Men and Religion Forward Movement, 160–161
and Mennonite Biblical Seminary, 339–40
and Mennonite Church, 156, 178, 184, 189, 260, 266, 354
    and Smith's decision to leave, 183–85, 187, 189
    and Smith's scholarship, 144–45, 150, 184, 219–20, 222–23, 267, 322, 325–28, 331, 353, 360
Mennonite ecumenicity of, 14, 189
and *Mennonite Encyclopedia*, 342–43, 347–48, 354
and Mennonite ethnicity, 147–48, 151
and Mennonite individualism, 150, 184, 199, 232, 264, 325, 327, 332
and *Mennonite Quarterly Review*, 306–7
and Mennonite Scholars Guild, 341–42
and Mennonite union movement, 180, 183–85, 193, 199, 222, 229–32, 249, 266, 289, 354–56
at Mennonite World Conference, 301–4
"Mennonites in History" address, 112–16
and modernism, 263–66, 268, 357
and Mosiman, Samuel, 185, 246, 280–81, 284–87

and Müntzer, Thomas, 139, 142, 219–20, 261
narrative abilities, 145–46, 211, 221, 241, 248–50, 275, 296, 324, 328
peace, 9, 96
    in Smith's analysis of Anabaptism, 138, 142, 219, 275, 303
    in Smith's writing and speaking, 114–15, 160, 184, 222, 242–43, 292–93, 297–99, 301–3
    in WWII years, 308–9, 310–14, 316–17, 320–21
Peace Oratorical Contest, 93
pioneer motif in Smith's writing, 115, 184, 309, 321, 325
and progressivism, 112, 115, 147, 150–51, 156, 219, 221–24, 246, 249, 266, 270–71, 325, 351, 357
and Prohibition, 51, 159, 199
as public intellectual, 162, 205–7, 274, 193–94, 296–301, 310–14, 320, 338–39, 355–56
and Quakers, 114, 116, 146, 218, 297, 302
and Quiring, Jacob, 227, 268–69
racism of, 208–10, 392n36
and Ramseyer, Lloyd, 306–7, 339, 346, 348
regard for Franklin Roosevelt, 300, 312, 408n6
religious life, 36, 57, 60–61, 178–79, 356–57
residence in Elkhart, Indiana, 62, 70, 72, 80, 85
retirement, 339–41
as rural schoolteacher, 45–48, 117
and Russian Mennonites, 144, 146, 220–22, 227, 230, 247–48, 321, 354
seminary, Smith's advocacy of, 277, 299, 303, 309, 317, 326, 358
and Simons, Menno, 78, 133, 142, 150, 162, 250, 275, 320, 326
and Smith, Laura Ioder, 194–95, 277, 281, 285, 304–5, 340, 346–47
    and banking, 203
    courtship, 123–30, 141, 178
    marriage to, 128, 155

Index   449

travels with, 233–36, 271
and Smucker, Boyd, 72, 158, 202–3, 214, 280, 282
and Smucker, Donovan, 292, 319, 337
and Steiner, M. S., 60, 62, 119, 195, 355
student memories of, 226, 291–92, 340
and Swiss Brethren, 113, 153, 173–74, 199, 219–20, 324
and theological liberalism, 88, 90, 326
and Thierstein, Jacob, 179, 202, 223–24, 226, 228, 247, 323
as a travel writer, 233–35, 241–42, 271
travels, 15, 100, 225, 232–42, 247, 270–72, 296, 301–4
trip to Europe in 1924, 233–35
trip to Europe in 1926, 232–42
trip to Hawaii, 271–73
trip to Mexico, 270–71
as uncle, 289–90
at the University of Chicago, 91, 93–96, 101–2, 106–7, 117, 126, 140, 159, 161, 240
at the University of Illinois, 75–76, 80, 86, 103, 117
and a usable past, 101, 106, 113–16, 146–50, 156, 219, 221–22, 325, 345
wedding, 128
and Wilson, Woodrow, 200, 209, 216, 218, 236, 249
and WLOK radio, 311–14
and WWI, 210–11, 214–16
  impact on Smith's thought, 10, 213, 217–18, 357
and WWII, 310–16
  Smith's analysis of the postwar world, 338–39
and the YMCA, 65–67, 73, 86–88, 103, 130, 196, 216, 226, 236–37
and Yoder, Orie, 119–20, 126, 128, 130, 177
Smith, Catherine, 26, 28–29
Smith, Catherine (Katie), 31, 70
Smith, Christian, 26–29
Smith, Ellen (Ella), 31, 51, 346, 350

Smith, Emma, 31, 91, 109, 169, 179
Smith, John, 33, 42, 44, 69
  as Amish Mennonite leader, 38–39
  birth, childhood and courtship, 29–31
  and Coffman, 57
  death, 117–18
  factional independence, 100
  openness to innovations, 39–40
  ordained as minister, 35
  and Prohibition, 50
  remarriage, 116
  visits Bureau County, 121
  worries about Henry, 117
Smith, John J., 51
Smith, Joseph, 31, 39, 65, 72, 118
Smith, Laura Ioder, 23, 219, 233–34, 281, 283, 304, 315, 340
  background and childhood, 121–23
  and childbirth, 195, 389n11
  church membership, 277
  and Citizens National Bank, 203
  courtship of, 124–30, 141, 178
  death, 350
  depression, 195–96, 346, 389n13
  and domesticity, 122
  and dress codes, 121, 179–80, 194
  education of, 122
  financial independence, 201, 347
  marriage, 155
  meets Smith, 123–24
  moves to Bluffton, 191–92
  Smith's illness, 348
  travels of, 233–35, 238, 271–72
  wedding, 128, 155
Smith, Lydia Albrecht, 116
Smith, Magdalena Schertz, 29–31, 33, 36, 43, 65
Smith, Martha, 28–29, 31, 39, 61
Smith, Samuel, 71, 116–18, 240, 347
Smith, Tilman, 289–90
Smith, Willard, 28, 82, 127, 155, 202, 290, 396, 408n6
  as Goshen professor, 294
  on Illinois fundamentalism, 168
  on the Mennonite union movement, 180, 231
  at the University of Chicago, 105

Smucker, Boyd, 72, 83, 158, 195, 197, 214
  financial investor with Smith, 202, 390–91n24
  moves to Bluffton, 185, 190
  as Smith friend and neighbor, 193, 280–81
Smucker, Donovan, 282, 292, 319, 337
Smucker, Jesse, 255, 349
Smucker, Mary, 193, 214
Snell Hall, 103, 117–18, 130
Snyder, William T., 345
Social Gospel, 59, 87–88, 94–95, 160, 198, 237
Sommer, Isaac, 180–81
Sprunger, Keith, 103, 229, 294, 353
Stayer, James, 352, 416n4
Steiner, Menno Simon, 55–56, 140
  and Byers, 97–99, 176, 185
  and Coffman, 55
  death, 193
  Elkhart Institute, 68
  and gender roles, 57–58
  health problems, 79
  and Horsch, 171
  and Mennonite progressivism, 149, 164
  missions enthusiasm, 58, 67
  and Moody, Dwight, 168
  and the quickening, 55, 384n16
  and "the social question," 59–60
  and Smith family, 82
  and Smith, Henry, 60, 62, 119, 195, 355
Storch, Nicholas, 137, 142
Story of the Mennonites, The, 9, 336–37, 339, 348–49, 352–53
  and Anabaptism, 323
  as anti-Catholic, 323
  critiques of, 327–29
  organization of, 324
  as progressive, 324–26
  revisions of, 347–49, 352–53
  sales of, 326, 353–54
  similarities with previous histories, 324
Strong, Josiah, 59

Strubhar, Valentine, 149, 152
Sunday, Billy, 159
Sunday schools, 38–40, 53, 121, 149, 193
Stuckey Amish (Central [Illinois] Conference), 50, 56
Stuckey, Joseph, 38–39, 109, 149, 193
Swiss Brethren, and Bender 259–60, 268
  and Horsch, 173, 274
  and polygenesis debate, 352, 416n4
  and Smith, 113, 153, 173–74, 199, 219–20, 324

T

Tazewell County, Illinois, 29
theological liberalism, 88–89, 166, 170, 189, 252
Thierstein, Jacob, 179, 193, 223–24, 226, 229, 247, 323
  background of, 84
  on Bluffton faculty, 196, 198, 204, 215
  moves to Bethel, 227–28
  in Smith investing group, 202
Thutt, Benjamin, 284–85, 288
Tiskilwa, Illinois, 25, 121–22, 153, 179, 194
Tiskilwa Mennonite Church, 180
Toews, Paul, 168, 315, 326, 351, 358, 361
Trollinger, William, 167
Troyer, Amanda, 109–10
Troyer, Emmanuel, 149, 168, 193, 214, 276
Turner, Frederick Jackson, 106, 115, 146

U

Umble, John, 326, 342, 398–99n20
Ukraine, 115, 144, 163, 227–28, 248, 284
  increased Mennonite persecution in, 221, 324, 343
University of Chicago, 45, 91, 125, 160, 175–76, 189, 227, 274
  and Christian progressivism, 94

civil religion, 95
dedication to empiricism, 104–5
and historical theology, 88–89
history department, 104, 140
Smith graduate study at, 91, 93–96, 101–2, 106–7, 117, 126, 140, 159, 161, 240
University of Illinois, 75–76, 80, 84, 90, 103, 117

W

Wadsworth First Mennonite Church, 297, 319
Wadsworth Institute, 97, 150, 375n35
Waldenses, 78, 106, 113, 132, 134, 137, 306
Warkentin, Abraham, 339, 342
Weaver, Margaret, 296
Weaver, Richard, 292, 350, 360
Wedel, Cornelius H., 108
Wenger, John C., 327, 342–43
Western District Conference (Amish Mennonite), 37–39, 47, 50, 60, 121, 201
Western District Conference (GC), 229, 247, 249
Whitmer, Paul, 98, 117, 198, 203, 246, 267
    background of, 72
    and *Christian Exponent*, 254
    death, 350
    embraces progressivism, 83
    on Goshen faculty, 155, 158, 182, 185
    moves to Bluffton, 190–91, 216
    pastors at Zion, 193, 398–99n20
    and Witmarsum Seminary, 227
Whitmire, Willie, 41–42, 44
Willard, Frances, 52
Willow Springs Mennonite Church, 25
Wilson, Woodrow, 104, 211–12, 263
    Smith's regard for, 200, 209, 216, 218, 236, 249
Wisler Mennonites, 144
Witmarsum Seminary, 182–83, 190, 198, 226, 231, 276, 286–87, 339
    and Bender, 276
    and Hartzler, 209, 276

Witmarsum, The, 197, 215, 226
WLOK radio, 311–14
Women's Christian Temperance Union, 52, 160
Woodford County, Illinois, 29, 57, 117–18
World War I, 9, 107, 196, 200–201, 203, 210–12, 216, 227, 263, 256, 303
    impact on Smith's thought, 10, 213, 217–18, 357
    wartime persecutions of Mennonites, 211–15
World War II, 9, 24, 106, 152, 297, 308, 310, 337, 352, 357–58
    conscientious objection, 314, 315–16, 319
    Smith's analysis of the postwar world, 338–39
    Smith's analysis of the war's approach, 310–14
    Smith's curiosity about, 315–16

Y

Yarrington, Margaret, 122
Yoder, Harry, 292
Yoder, John Howard, 355
Yoder, Joseph W., 73
Yoder, Orie, 119–20, 123–24, 126, 128, 130, 177
Yoder, Paton, 36–37
Yoder, Sanford, 258, 342
Yost, Burton, 339
Young Men's and Young Women's Christian Association (YMCA/YWCA), 65, 84, 86–87, 103, 130, 160, 236, 294
    acceptance of theological liberalism, 81
    and Bible study, 66, 86–88
    at Bluffton College, 197, 226, 312
    at Elkhart Institute, 73
    founding of, 66–67, 87
    at Goshen College, 98
    and liberal Protestantism, 236–37
    and Smith, 65–67, 73, 86–88, 103, 130, 196, 216, 226, 236–37
    at University of Illinois, 86–88
    and WWI, 215–16

Young People's Conference, 253–57, 340
Young People's Paper, 59, 63, 355

Z

Zehr, Reuben, 277
Zion Mennonite Church, 55, 193–95, 398–99n20

Studies in Anabaptist and Mennonite History Series

Series editor Gerald J. Mast; with editors Geoffrey L. Dipple, Marlene G. Epp, Rachel Waltner Goossen, Leonard Gross, Thomas J. Meyers, Steven M. Nolt, John D. Roth, Theron F. Schlabach, and Astrid von Schlachta.

The Studies in Anabaptist and Mennonite History Series is sponsored by the Mennonite Historical Society. Beginning with volume 8, titles were published by Herald Press unless otherwise noted.

1. Harold S. Bender. *Two Centuries of American Mennonite Literature, 1727–1928.* 1929.
2. John Horsch. *The Hutterian Brethren, 1528–1931: A Story of Martyrdom and Loyalty.* 1931. Reprint, Macmillan Hutterite Colony, Cayley, Alberta, 1985.
3. Harry F. Weber. *Centennial History of the Mennonites in Illinois, 1829–1929.* 1931.
4. Sanford Calvin Yoder. *For Conscience' Sake: A Study of Mennonite Migrations Resulting from the World War.* 1940.
5. John S. Umble. *Ohio Mennonite Sunday Schools.* 1941.
6. Harold S. Bender. *Conrad Grebel, c. 1498–1526, Founder of the Swiss Brethren.* 1950.
7. Robert Friedmann. *Mennonite Piety Through the Centuries: Its Genius and Its Literature.* 1949.
8. Delbert L. Gratz. *Bernese Anabaptists and Their American Descendants.* 1953.
9. A. L. E. Verheyden. *Anabaptism in Flanders, 1530–1650: A Century of Struggle.* 1961.

10. J. C. Wenger. *The Mennonites in Indiana and Michigan.* 1961.
11. Rollin Stely Armour. *Anabaptist Baptism: A Representative Study.* 1966.
12. John B. Toews. *Lost Fatherland: The Story of Mennonite Emigration from Soviet Russia, 1921–1927.* 1967.
13. Grant M. Stoltzfus. *Mennonites of the Ohio and Eastern Conference, from the Colonial Period in Pennsylvania to 1968.* 1969.
14. John A. Lapp. *The Mennonite Church in India, 1897–1962.* 1972.
15. Robert Friedmann. *The Theology of Anabaptism: An Interpretation.* 1973.
16. Kenneth R. Davis. *Anabaptism and Asceticism: A Study in Intellectual Origins.* 1974.
17. Paul Erb. *South Central Frontiers: A History of the South Central Mennonite Conference.* 1974.
18. Fred R. Belk. *The Great Trek of the Russian Mennonites to Central Asia, 1880–1884.* 1976.
19. Werner O. Packull. *Mysticism and the Early South German-Austrian Anabaptist Movement, 1525–1531.* 1976.
20. Richard K. MacMaster, with Samuel L. Horst and Robert F. Ulle. *Conscience in Crisis: Mennonites and Other Peace Churches in America, 1739–1789.* 1979.
21. Theron F. Schlabach. *Gospel versus Gospel: Mission and the Mennonite Church, 1863–1944.* 1980.
22. Calvin Wall Redekop. *Strangers Become Neighbors: Mennonite and Indigenous Relations in the Paraguayan Chaco.* 1980.
23. Leonard Gross. *The Golden Years of the Hutterites: The Witness and Thought of the Communal Moravian Anabaptists during the Walpot Era, 1565–1578.* 1980. Rev. ed., Pandora Press Canada, 1998.
24. Willard H. Smith. *Mennonites in Illinois.* 1983.
25. Murray L. Wagner. *Petr Chelcický: A Radical Separatist in Hussite Bohemia.* 1983.

26. John L. Ruth. *Maintaining the Right Fellowship: A Narrative Account of Life in the Oldest Mennonite Community in North America.* 1984.
27. C. Arnold Snyder. *The Life and Thought of Michael Sattler.* 1984.
28. Beulah Stauffer Hostetler. *American Mennonites and Protestant Movements: A Community Paradigm.* 1987.
29. Daniel Liechty. *Andreas Fischer and the Sabbatarian Anabaptists: An Early Reformation Episode in East Central Europe.* 1988.
30. Hope Kauffman Lind. *Apart and Together: Mennonites in Oregon and Neighboring States, 1876–1976.* 1990.
31. Paton Yoder. *Tradition and Transition: Amish Mennonites and Old Order Amish, 1800–1900.* 1991.
32. James R. Coggins. *John Smyth's Congregation: English Separatism, Mennonite Influence, and the Elect Nation.* 1991.
33. John D. Rempel. *The Lord's Supper in Anabaptism: A Study in the Theology of Balthasar Hubmaier, Pilgram Marpeck, and Dirk Philips.* 1993.
34. Gerlof D. Homan. *American Mennonites and the Great War, 1914–1918.* 1994.
35. J. Denny Weaver. *Keeping Salvation Ethical: Mennonite and Amish Atonement Theology in the Late Nineteenth Century.* 1997.
36. Wes Harrison. *Andreas Ehrenpreis and Hutterite Faith and Practice.* 1997. Copublished with Pandora Press Canada.
37. John D. Thiesen. *Mennonite and Nazi? Attitudes among Mennonite Colonists in Latin America, 1933–1945.* 1999. Copublished with Pandora Press Canada.
38. Perry Bush. *Dancing with the Kobzar: Bluffton College and Mennonite Higher Education, 1899–1999.* 2000. Copublished with Pandora Press U.S. and Faith & Life Press.
39. John L. Ruth. *The Earth Is the Lord's: A Narrative History of the Lancaster Mennonite Conference.* 2001.

40. Melanie Springer Mock. *Writing Peace: The Unheard Voices of Great War Mennonite Objectors.* 2003. Copublished with Cascadia Publishing House.
41. Mary Jane Lederach Hershey. *This Teaching I Present: Fraktur from the Skippack and Salford Mennonite Meetinghouse Schools, 1747–1836.* 2003. Published by Good Books.
42. Edsel Burdge Jr. and Samuel L. Horst. *Building on the Gospel Foundation: The Mennonites of Franklin County, Pennsylvania, and Washington County, Maryland, 1730–1970.* 2004.
43. Ervin Beck. *MennoFolk: Mennonite and Amish Folk Traditions.* 2004.
44. Walter Klaassen and William Klassen. *Marpeck: A Life of Dissent and Conformity.* 2008.
45. Theron F. Schlabach. *War, Peace and Social Conscience: Guy F. Hershberger and Mennonite Ethics.* 2009.
46. Ervin R. Stutzman. *From Nonresistance to Justice: The Transformation of Mennonite Church Peace Rhetoric, 1908–2008.* 2011.
47. Nathan E. Yoder. *Together in the Work of the Lord: A History of the Conservative Mennonite Conference.* 2014.
48. Samuel J. Steiner. *In Search of Promised Lands: A Religious History of Mennonites in Ontario.* 2015.
49. Perry Bush. *Peace, Progress, and the Professor: The Mennonite History of C. Henry Smith.* 2015.

The Author

Perry Bush is professor of history at Bluffton University in Bluffton, Ohio. A native of Pasadena, California, Bush completed his BA at University of California–Berkeley and his MA and PhD in U.S. social history at Carnegie Mellon University in Pittsburgh. Bush's books include *Two Kingdoms, Two Loyalties: Mennonite Pacifism in Modern America* (Johns Hopkins University Press, 1998); *Dancing with the Kobzar: Bluffton College and Mennonite Higher Education* (Pandora Press, 2000); and *Rust Belt Resistance: How a Small Community Took on Big Oil and Won* (Kent State University Press, 2012). Bush's articles have appeared in *Sojourners, Peace and Change, Mennonite Quarterly Review*, the *Journal of Mennonite Studies*, and *Fides et Historia*. He resides in Bluffton, Ohio, and is a member of First Mennonite Church, Bluffton. Bush and his wife, Elysia Caldwell Bush, have three children.

www.ingramcontent.com/pod-product-compliance
Lightning Source LLC
Chambersburg PA
CBHW070746230426
43665CB00017B/2272